British Jacobin Politics, Desires, and Aftermaths

This book explores the hopes, desires, and imagined futures that characterized British radicalism in the 1790s, and the resurfacing of this sense of possibility in the following decades. The articulation of "Jacobin" sentiments reflected the emotional investments of men and women inspired by the French Revolution and committed to political transformation. The authors emphasize the performative aspects of political culture, and the spaces in which mobilization and expression occurred – including the club room, tavern, coffeehouse, street, outdoor meeting, theater, chapel, courtroom, prison, and convict ship. America, imagined as a site of republican citizenship, and New South Wales, experienced as a space of political exile, widened the scope of radical dreaming. Part 1 focuses on the political culture forged under the shifting influence of the French Revolution. Part 2 explores the afterlives of British Jacobinism in the year 1817, in early Chartist memorialization of the Scottish "martyrs" of 1794, and in the writings of E. P. Thompson. The relationship between popular radicals and the Romantics is a theme pursued in several chapters; a dialogue is sustained across the disciplinary boundaries of British history and literary studies. The volume captures the revolutionary decade's effervescent yearning, and its unruly persistence in later years.

James Epstein is Emeritus Distinguished Professor of History at Vanderbilt University, Tennessee.

David Karr is a Professor of History at Columbia College in Columbia, Missouri.

The Enlightenment World

Series Editor: *Michael T. Davis (Griffith University)*
Series Co-Editors: *Jack Fruchtman (Towson University), Kevin Gilmartin (Caltech), Jon Mee (University of York)*

For more information about this series, please visit: https://www.routledge.com/The-Enlightenment-World/book-series/ENW

British Jacobin Politics, Desires, and Aftermaths
Seditious Hearts

James Epstein and David Karr

 Routledge
Taylor & Francis Group

NEW YORK AND LONDON

First published 2021
by Routledge
52 Vanderbilt Avenue, New York, NY 10017

and by Routledge
2 Park Square, Milton Park, Abingdon, Oxon, OX14 4RN

Routledge is an imprint of the Taylor & Francis Group, an informa business

© 2021 Taylor & Francis

Library of Congress Cataloging-in-Publication Data
Names: Epstein, James, author. | Karr, David, 1963– author.
Title: British Jacobin politics, desires, and aftermaths : seditious
hearts / James Epstein and David Karr.
Description: First edition. | New York : Routledge Taylor &
Francis Group, 2021. |
Series: Enlightenment world ; no. 35 | Includes bibliographical
references and index.
Subjects: LCSH: Great Britain—Politics and
government—1789–1820. | Political culture—Great Britain—
History—18th century. | Political culture—Great Britain—
History—19th century. | Politics and literature—Great
Britain—History—18th century. | Politics and literature—
Great Britain—History—19th century. | Radicalism—Great
Britain—History—18th century. | Radicalism—Great Britain—
History—19th century. | France—History—Revolution,
1789–1799—Influence.
Classification: LCC DA520 .E67 2021 (print) | LCC DA520
(ebook) | DDC 941.07/3—dc23
LC record available at https://lccn.loc.gov/2020049565
LC ebook record available at https://lccn.loc.gov/2020049566

ISBN: 978-0-367-46444-8 (hbk)
ISBN: 978-1-003-02880-2 (ebk)

Typeset in Sabon
by codeMantra

For Sherry (again) and Tamara

Contents

Figures

Acknowledgments

This book has been a collaborative project, written over many years during which the authors have constantly exchanged ideas and research materials. The Introduction and Chapter 1 are co-written. Chapters 4–6 and 8 are the work of James Epstein; Chapters 2, 3, and 7 are the work of David Karr. As a joint enterprise, the goal has been something more than merely stringing together separate chapters by two authors. Readers can judge for themselves the success of this endeavor.

We have accumulated many debts to fellow scholars, particularly in the fields of British history and literary studies. We hope that these debts have been adequately reflected in the notes to this book. Rather than list all their names, and risk leaving anyone out, we have not repeated expressions of gratitude to those recognized in our previously published works on which we have drawn. We are grateful to the editors of publications where aspects of this book have appeared, including *Journal of British Studies*, *Journal of Modern History*, *Historical Research*, and the collection *Romantic Sociability: Social Networks and Literary Culture in Britain, 1770–1840*. We are most fortunate to have had the support of Michael T. Davis, editor of the *Enlightenment World* series, and the assistance of Jennifer Morrow and Max Novick at Routledge. An acknowledgment also goes to our mate Christopher Lamping, one of the last true Spenceans. In addition, James Epstein would like to thank Emma MacLeod, who read a draft of Chapter 5 and generously shared her knowledge on British views of America. And special thanks goes to Nick Rogers for reading and commenting on chapters, sharing notes and references, and for years of friendship. David Karr wishes to thank audiences at the Western Conference on British Studies, San Antonio, TX, 2018, for helpful comments on Chapter 2. Special appreciation goes to colleagues and friends at Columbia College, and especially to interlibrary loan wizard Peter Neely at the college's Stafford Library. For their encouragement and support, the book is dedicated to Sherry Baird and Dr. Tamara King.

Abbreviations

In notes and bibliography, the place of publication is London unless otherwise stated.

General
CUP	Cambridge University Press
LCS	London Corresponding Society
OUP	Oxford University Press
SCI	Society for Constitutional Information

Manuscript collections
BL, Add. MS.	British Library, London, Additional Manuscript
Bod. Lib., GD	Diary of William Godwin, Abinger-Shelley Papers, Bodleian Library, Oxford, http://godwindiary.bodleian.ox.ac.uk/index2.html

Public Record Office, The National Archives, London
C	Chancery papers
CO	Colonial Office papers
HO	Home Office papers
KB	King's Bench papers
PC	Privy Council papers
TS	Treasury Solicitor's papers

Newspapers and Periodicals
AGM	*Anti-Gallican Monitor*
AR	*Analytical Review*
BD	*Black Dwarf*
CWPR	*Cobbett's Weekly Political Register*
HRR	*Hone's Reformists' Register*
LR	*Left Review*
MC	*Morning Chronicle*
MPR	*Manchester Political Register*
MR	*Monthly Review*
NLR	*New Left Review*
NR	*New Reasoner*
PR	*Parliamentary Register*

QR	*Quarterly Review*
SWPR	*Sherwin's Weekly Political Register*
ULR	*Universities and Left Review*

Academic Journals

AHR	*American Historical Review*
ED	*Enlightenment and Dissent*
EHR	*English Historical Review*
HJ	*Historical Journal*
HWJ	*Historical Workshop Journal*
JBS	*Journal of British Studies*
JCHA	*Journal of the Canadian Historical Association/Revue de la Société Historique Canadienne*
JMH	*Journal of Modern History*
LH	*Literature and History*
P&P	*Past and Present*
SH	*Social History*
WC	*Wordsworth Circle*

Other Works

CLC	*Collected Letters of Samuel Taylor Coleridge*, ed. Earl Leslie Griggs, 6 vols. (Oxford: Clarendon Press, 1956–71)
CWC	*The Collected Works of Samuel Taylor Coleridge*, gen. ed. Kathleen Coburn (London: Routledge, and Princeton, NJ: Princeton University Press, 1969–)
CWH	*The Complete Works of William Hazlitt*, ed. P. P. Howe, 21 vols. (London: J. M. Dent and Sons, 1930–34)
HRA	*Historical Records of Australia*, 1st series
LCRS	*Life and Correspondence of Robert Southey*, ed. Charles Cuthbert Southey (New York: 1851)
LS	*The Letters of Percy Bysshe Shelley*, ed. F. E. Jones, 2 vols. (Oxford: OUP, 1964)
NLS	*New Letters of Robert Southey*, ed. Kenneth Curry. 2 vols. (New York: Columbia University Press, 1965)
ODNB	*Oxford Dictionary of National Biography* (Oxford: OUP, 2004), http://www.oxforddnb.com/subscribed/
PD	*Parliamentary Debates*, from the Year 1803 to the Present Time, 1st series (1803–)
PH	*Parliamentary or Constitutional History of England from the Earliest Period to the Year 1803*, ed. William Cobbett and J. Wright, 36 vols. (1806–13)
PP	*Parliamentary Papers*

SLPW   *Robert Southey: Later Poetic Works, 1811–1838*, gen.
              ed. Tim Fulford and Lynda Pratt, 4 vols. (London:
              Pickering & Chatto, 2012)
ST   *A Complete Collection of State Trials*, ed. T. B. and
              T. J. Howell, 36 vols. (1806–13)
Thale   Mary Thale, ed., *Selections from the Papers of the
              London Corresponding Society* (Cambridge: CUP,
              1983)

Introduction

In December 1794, speaking at the trial of John Thelwall for high treason, the crown prosecutor Serjeant James Adair told the court that the "secret purposes of men's hearts" were not to be judged by their professed beliefs, "not by the pretexts they held out to the ignorant and the unwary; but by their own acts coupled with their declarations."[1] Thelwall's trial was the third of the treason trials held that autumn, as the government of William Pitt sought to repress the movement for political reform. For government, the "Jacobin" heart, the deep intent of home-grown republicans, was not readily disclosed but insidiously disguised, thus requiring skillful interpretation and constructed meaning. Bringing enemies of established order to trial was one way to expose and to suppress treason and sedition.[2] Juries, as well as a wider public, were instructed in how to decipher the seditious motivations of British Jacobins: formal programs couched in terms of constitutional reform and committed to peaceable means were not as they seemed; professed beliefs were to be supplemented by other actions in order to derive true meaning.

Adair's proposition touches on one of the main themes of our study, which is to understand how to determine the desires of those committed to radical reform and inspired by events across the channel. How do we read the stirrings of the "Jacobin" heart? Sedition is a construct of the law. Seen from the other side of the law's force, the crime of sedition gestured toward transformation, sometimes carefully articulated, given shape in political programs, pamphlet literature, and well-monitored practice, but often seditious desire was inchoate, half-formed – uttered at raucous meetings, shouted across tavern tables, muttered in private conversations, chalked on walls. The chapters that make up this book are about cherished hopes, seditious designs, and imagined futures, about radical political culture during the 1790s, and its aftermath. The study concentrates on the public articulation of "Jacobin" sentiments, relating in turn to emotional investments, the desired object of men and women committed to political transformation. *Seditious Hearts* looks to capture the effervescent sense of possibility that characterized the decade, and its subsequent resurfacing.

In discussion of the oppositional political culture of 1790s, it is necessary to keep in mind the conditions affecting the costs to radicals of publication and speech: the inhibitions arising from the repression loosely associated with "Pitt's reign of Terror" or perhaps better termed the "Reign of Alarm," culminating in the "Two Acts" passed in late 1795, which effectively curtailed the public movement for reform, and capped off by the Unlawful Societies Act of 1799 banning the LCS and United Societies by name.[3] In its campaign against British Jacobinism, the government was able to enlist the support of a large loyalist public; unofficially sanctioned, loyalist violence was an aspect of the government's campaign of repression. Alarmed by the course of the French Revolution and fueled by patriotic fervor intensified by war and the threat of invasion, loyal subjects needed little convincing of the danger posed by those seeking to overthrow the monarchy and government, to subvert the nation's revered constitution, and to spread the contagion of social anarchy.[4] As John Barrell maintains, the repression and spirit of alarm created an "atmosphere of suspicion ... on both sides of the conflict," extending into the private sphere.[5] The paranoid fantasies of those in authority had real consequences for the opponents of government. There were certainly limits to the regime of repression; juries were sometimes rigged but the jury system remained, and government prosecutions often enough backfired with juries returning "not guilty" verdicts; habeas corpus was regularly suspended but not abolished.[6] Yet for democrats, there remained a troubling uncertainty about the danger to their safety and personal liberty.

While transparency may have been a cherished republican principle, the atmosphere of surveillance and suspicion dictated tactics of indirection, submerged meaning, and dissimulation, which is to acknowledge that Adair had a point: there might be more to the purposes of seditious hearts than what was registered in statements of their professed beliefs. For those tainted with the Jacobin label, caution was the order of the day; a measure of circumspection was required of radicals seeking safety from the force of loyalist intimidation and avoidance of the threat of government prosecution. As radical pressmen and publishers were acutely aware, publication carried risks, particularly publishing works by Thomas Paine. Loose talk in taverns, coffeehouses, meetings, and streets could result in trial and imprisonment. As the radical lawyer and Society for Constitutional Information (SCI) member Felix Vaughan observed, "We live in times, when word-catching and libel-catching seem to be the fashion of the day."[7] Risks were taken by the brave or foolish, and sometimes by unknowing subjects. There were, after all, cases of "the ignorant and the unwary," identified by Adair: ordinary people deceived by the designs of traitors. We find, for example, that in December 1792, William Carter was caught pasting up a seditious handbill at the corner of Crown Street in St. Giles. The London Corresponding

Society (LCS) had appointed Carter – an illiterate porter, watchman, and bill-sticker – to post the "Address of the London Corresponding Society, to the Other Societies of Great Britain, United for Obtaining a REFORM IN PARLIAMENT." Hauled before the sitting magistrates at Bow Street, Carter declared that he could not read and did not know the purport of the bills he was employed to paste; he was ordered to be held for trial. Tried at Clerkenwell sessions, Carter was sentenced to six months' imprisonment for promoting sedition, and was required to find sureties of £100 from himself and two sureties of £50 each (the LCS opened a subscription on his behalf). The attorney general Archibald Macdonald told the jury that they were punishing the offense not the offender, as "admonition to others, in order that no man should plead ignorance in the future"; he condemned the whole of the LCS address "under which ... were concealed rebellion and insurrection."[8]

The last decade of the eighteenth century witnessed an explosion in the production and circulation of printed works, and an expansion of print culture within the ranks of working men and women. The political culture of British Jacobinism was to a large extent a literate one, although a segment of society was unable to read, which is not to say that they were unconnected to the world of print as Carter's case illustrates. Radical pressmen supplied the reform movement with an extraordinarily diverse range of publications – including handbills, song sheets, mock playbills, caricatures, poetry, addresses to the public, cheap weekly journals, pamphlets, and books; as a runaway bestseller, Paine's *Rights of Man* was emblematic of a wider world of print and the democratic desire for political reading. One can readily agree with Jon Mee's view that "the medium of print and the associational world that surrounded it" constituted "a condition of possibility for a popular radical platform."[9] For a prominent strain of republicanism, a secularized faith was placed in the power of the printed word; it was enough merely for truths to be presented for reason to triumph over the fictions spun in the service of monarchical misrule. "Truth, wherever it can fully appear," wrote Paine, "is a thing so naturally familiar to the mind, that an acquaintance commences at first sight."[10] Moreover, much of that which was spoken was re-expressed in print: Thelwall, the period's most celebrated Jacobin orator, filled his journal *The Tribune* with the texts of his lectures. Trials were occasions of the spoken word, but all the major trials for sedition quickly found their way into print, and the trials themselves teemed with alleged seditious speech; the speeches of leaders were included in the proceedings of public meetings issued in pamphlet form. We are, of course, dependent on the printed word for access, however incomplete, to the spoken words and embodied actions of contemporaries.

That said, gestures mattered: a fraternal greeting to a fellow "citizen"; a shout-out in the street for "Paine and the Rights of Man"; a tavern refusal to toast "the King." No wonder that in their ascriptions of motivations and beliefs to reformers, loyalist commentators and agents of the state so often fixated on the gap between print and performance, looking to close the space between actions as discursively described and the elusive occurrence and intent of the acts themselves. Consider popular song. After the SCI anniversary dinner held on 2 May 1794 at the Crown and Anchor tavern, the Yorkshire MP and SCI member John Wharton's role as chair came under scrutiny. Examined by the Privy Council three weeks later, Wharton claimed that he assumed the role out of a mere constitutional "wish for a Reform" of Parliament.[11] At the treason trial of Thomas Hardy, secretary of the LCS, who attended the dinner, the prosecution read a long list of seditious toasts proposed at the dinner, starting with "THE RIGHTS OF MAN," and including such gems as "May Despotism be trodden under the Hoofs of the Swinish Multitude"; between the toasts a band played "popular tunes."[12] In decrying the government's failure to secure convictions in the treason trials, the anonymous author of *Treason Triumphant over Law and Constitution* set little store by Wharton's professed "wish" for constitutional reform, taking him to task for chairing "such a meeting, that breathed nothing but strong Jacobin principle" and pointing to the meeting's seditious theatricality: "Who countenanced *ca-ira*, in this loyal Reform meeting, to be struck up and continued during dinner? Who countenanced the *Marseilles* March?"[13] The performance conditions at the Crown and Anchor licensed the expression of "Jacobin principle"; exuberant singing was a truer sign of the meeting's intent than was the testimony of Wharton or other attendees, several of whom were soon to be arrested on charges of treason.

Performance is thus important to our understanding of British radical culture. In exploring connections among texts, actions, agency, and subjectivity, we have been influenced by scholars in various fields in the humanities and social sciences who have advanced the so-called performative turn.[14] As argued in Chapter 1, our use of the term "Jacobin" is linked to our approach to performance, including the performative aspect in shaping subjective identity. In choosing to invoke the term "Jacobin," which was the contemporary label given to popular radicals, we in no way seek to suggest a unified ideology; radicalism in the 1790s was characterized by a striking diversity of beliefs, including religious beliefs. Within the "fragmented ideology of reform," to borrow Mark Philp's phrase, we find strains of utopian expectation, entertaining the prospect that the world was newly open to being rethought, and remodeled.[15] British Jacobinism, as performed, involved creative experimentation in modes of political action and identification. Jacobinism emerged partly as a form of tactical identity, constructed at the intersection of conservative commentary, radical action, and state repression. Certainly, the term's ultimate referent – a segment of French revolutionaries – allowed British loyalists to paint all domestic reform efforts as disguised revolution. Sheffield's radical publisher Matthew Campbell Browne – a leading Sheffield SCI member, he was appointed as its delegate to the British Convention – noted the term's elasticity: "To extend the alarm, and give it as many ramifications as possible, was now the plan: the friends of reform were one and all denominated *republicans* and *levellers*; and these terms were *Frenchified* into *Jacobins*."[16] Yet the heightened meanings that loyalists and government prosecutors gave to Jacobinism made it available to British republicans as a vehicle for counter-theater. Restrictions on speech and action could be challenged through a form of subversive, serious play. Radicals thus inhabited, embodied, and performed Jacobinism in edgy confrontations with the state.

Writing to the poet Caroline Anne Bowles (who years later became his second wife), the poet laureate Robert Southey reflected on his Jacobin youth, noting that few of those who had not lived at the time "can conceive or comprehend what memory of the French Revolution was, nor what a visionary world seemed to open upon those who were just entering it. Old things seemed passing away, and nothing was dreamt of but the regeneration of the human race."[17] Southey's sentiments are echoed by William Wordsworth in *The Prelude*, and by many others commenting on the visionary world that appeared to open; testaments to the optimism and intense excitement ushered in by the French Revolution. It is a memory and set of feelings that we must try to recover in our attempt to suggest as best we can the motivations and affective desires of the subjects of this book, including "Jacobin" intellectuals and gentlemanly leaders such as Thelwall and the playwright Thomas Holcroft, as well as the artisans and tradesmen who filled the ranks of the popular societies. As historians of the emotions have shown, moving from the language of feeling to extrapolation about feelings themselves is a difficult undertaking, although it is reasonable to argue not only that the words and gestures used to express feelings, in some sense, signify emotions but that expressions of feeling, and community norms about how to feel, have an impact in shaping emotional responses.[18] We accept a certain provisionality as we try to get at that which is in excess of words: the desiring hearts and the dream of "the regeneration of the human race."

Overlapping "systems of feeling" coexisted among various emotional communities; we can, for example, regard members of the LCS sections as constituting such a community as distinct say from that of the intellectual coterie associated with William Godwin or those gathered around the dinner table of the radical publisher Joseph Johnson, although there were bridges between them.[19] Norms of behavior, and emotional expectations, were also dependent on sites of articulation, spaces for expression and performance – the iconic Crown and Anchor tavern is an example.[20] In the chapters that follow, the dynamics of radical politics are traced through a series of sites of articulation and feeling – the club room, lecture hall, mass outdoor meeting, theater, tavern, coffeehouse, street, chapel, courtroom, prison, convict ship – as well as the imagined space of America onto which both radicals and Romantics projected utopian designs and the experience of exile in the penal colony of New South Wales. Projections of radical desire during the 1790s were bound up in specific discursive motifs and ideological commitments. For example, Harriet Guest has explored the ways in which the language and codes of sensibility provided a context for literary women to imagine themselves politically within "the wider community of the nation"; Lynn Hunt and Margaret Jacobs have identified an "affective revolution," an experimental disposition to forming deep friendships between women and men within the circles of middle-class radicals, scientific investigators, rational Dissenters, and romantic poets.[21] Particularly suggestive for our purposes is Mee's careful consideration of radical "enthusiasm," as an ambivalently charged response to liberty in the age of revolution, variously associated with the discourse of rational Dissent, the appeal of millenarian prophecy, the rationalist abstractions of Godwin, the impassioned lecturing of Thelwall (as well as his speeches at the LCS's great outdoor meetings), and the culture of the LCS.[22] The guiding principles of Reason and the Enlightenment ideal were not necessarily incompatible with emotions but served as nourishing agents to natural sincerity and the benevolent heart.[23] If irrationality and "artificial feelings" were condemned, so was the lack of compassion for human suffering. What was often at issue were concerns about the excesses of emotional expression or sentiment and discernment of true or sincere feelings. While Mary Wollstonecraft took Edmund Burke to task for fostering "every emotion till the fumes ... dispel sober suggestions of reason," she also commented on his lack of feeling "for the silent majesty of misery," and asked, "is the humane heart satisfied with turning the poor over to *another* world" to receive its blessings?[24] By 1795, traveling for her *Letters Written during a Short Residence in Sweden, Norway, and Denmark* (1796), Wollstonecraft praised the "warm heart," based "on truth of sympathy," and "tenderness" derived from "a higher source; call it the imagination, genius, or what you will."[25] Navigating between the demands of reason and emotional sincerity was not without difficulty.

Part I of our study focuses on the political culture forged under the shifting influence of the French Revolution. Chapter 1, "Playing at Revolution," establishes many of the book's central themes, addressing the question of what the term "Jacobin" might have meant to those accused of harboring Jacobin beliefs. Once the French Revolution turned violence upon itself, particularly with the execution of leading Girondists with whom many British supporters of the Revolution identified, democratically inclined reformers were deeply conflicted about their attachment to the Revolution. Once the nation went to war with revolutionary France in February 1793 – the fears of war helped to fuel the French Terror and to encourage domestic repression – earlier confidence placed in feelings of cosmopolitan brotherhood and universal benevolence was called into question. This was the context in which the stigma of the Jacobin label gained force. There were, in fact, those who defended the Revolution, found mainly in the ranks of the LCS and other popular societies, as well as in a seditious plebeian underworld. As already noted, the chapter explores the role of performance: regarding the enactment of political desires as supplementary to formal statements of political beliefs, acts gesturing toward a horizon of possibility. The prohibitions that the government placed on the movement and the importance accorded to seditious posturing – to jokes, toasts, songs, satirical handbills, winks, and nods – encouraged Jacobin playfulness; as the authorities took play seriously, play became seriously charged. The chapter presents our argument for dropping the quotation marks around the Jacobin designation.[26]

Chapter 2, "Everyday Life and Everyday Sedition," considers the efforts of the organizers of the LCS and SCI to manage meeting spaces: the measures taken to create sites for well-ordered behavior, demarcated from the more raucous, everyday urban world, and resistant to seditious language and emotions. The goal was to establish self-regulated spaces for rational deliberation. Looking back from the security of old age and respectability, Francis Place, the major documentarian of the LCS, commented on the improvement in manners that had been achieved from the days of his youth, as the son of a publican and apprentice breeches-maker, noting that it was hard to comprehend "the grossness, the indecency, the positive nastiness, the drunkenness and lewdness which pervaded more or less every class of person in the Kingdom."[27] For artisans turned reformers, men like Place and the shoemaker Hardy, who also collected materials for a history of the LCS, their movement was characterized by the earnest desire to constitute "the people": forming an enlightened public organized for the pursuit of political reform, a transformation that required some distancing from the culture of the streets, low taverns, and brothels of the metropolis, from the vulgar habits pervading everyday life. The archives assembled by Place and Hardy, which have been extensively used by historians, reflect these commitments, although they leave traces of the overheated emotions and seditious politics which they sought to contain. Other sources – particularly the account of the former LCS member William H. Reid and the reports of government informers – perhaps bring us closer to the lived experience of metropolitan Jacobinism, to something rawer and more playfully subversive. In considering the relationship between ordinary life and radical organization, we find the theoretical concept of everyday life pioneered by Henri Lefebvre and Michel de Certeau most germane in its analysis of the non-formalized "tactics" of daily life, and for mapping the transgressive behavior that cropped up at popular meetings for political reform.

Chapter 3, "'Thoughts that Flash like Lightening,'" turns to the efforts of the political activist, novelist, and playwright Thomas Holcroft, to develop a "Jacobin" drama. A distrust of theater and theatricality based on rationalist norms was common among Holcroft and Godwin's circle of intellectual friends who associated theatrical performance with the mystifying artifice of monarchical rule. Holcroft elaborated principles of acting aimed to overcome such distrust, to stabilize meaning within theatrical performance, and to use the licensed theater to express sentiments of radical benevolence and sincerity. The government's traditional support for the didactic social purposes of theater only intensified as the French Revolution radicalized, and the war of ideas engulfed Britain; theaters were more closely policed and the content of plays more meticulously censored. Moreover, the conventions of sentimental drama in which Holcroft worked limited radical meanings. Despite these conditions of performance and reception, he seized on the opportunity to radicalize the genre of sentimental drama, allowing audiences to translate representations of family strife into wider social and political meanings. Holcroft appropriated contemporary physiological and psychological theory to produce what he considered to be a scientific method of acting which offered communicative ways for audiences to recognize emotional sincerity. Through a careful regulation of performance and gesture, Holcroft sought to open the theater to radical criticism of existing social institutions. The chapter explores these initiatives and their limitations. A reading of Holcroft's plays staged during his most active period of participation in radical politics – from 1792, when he joined the SCI, to 1795, in the aftermath of his indictment for high treason – illustrates the playwright's attempt to translate radical politics to the theater. *The Road to Ruin* (1792) and *The Deserted Daughter* (1795) expose the evils of a society in which the distribution of social power is based on aristocratic notions of luxury and display. Both plays also register deeper anxieties about the development of commercial society, revealing the commercialization of human bonds in a market culture. Holcroft pointed to a future characterized by a new transparency and sincerity in human relations. And yet, a fully realized "Jacobin" drama remained beyond the possibilities of the licensed stage in the 1790s.

While almost all the principal radical publishers of the day were prosecuted for seditious libel – in 1798 the government finally caught up with the cautious Joseph Johnson and Benjamin Flower, editor of the *Cambridge Intelligencer* – there were, in fact, more prosecutions brought for uttering seditious words than for setting them in type. The bold, often drunken carelessness of everyday life enacted in the tavern, coffeehouse, shop, and street was picked up on by vigilant loyalists, tavern owners, constables, and soldiers. The Scottish tourist Daniel Crichton, a journeyman tallow chandler, suitably in liquor, visited the Tower, and when shown the royal regalia, cried, "Damn the King! We have no king in Scotland, and we will soon have no King in England."[28] This outburst landed him a three-month prison sentence. Chapter 4, "Equality and No King," considers the more consequential case of the lawyer John Frost as a means to think about spaces of sociability – particularly the coffeehouse, classic site of the "bourgeois" public sphere – and the effects of surveillance and seditious expression. Like Holcroft, Frost was a leading member of the SCI, a friend of John Horne Tooke and Paine. As Frost was leaving London's Percy coffeehouse, his declaration in favor of "equality" and his elaboration that by "equality" he meant "no kings" caused a stir, forming the basis of the government's prosecution for seditious words. As the Sheffield republican Browne commented, authorities were wont to consider reformers to be republicans and levelers, terms that were in turn *"Frenchified* into *Jacobins."* But what did Frost mean in calling for "equality" and "no kings?" How were these terms to be understood and how were the norms of coffeehouse culture to be distinguished from the behavior of London's low alehouses and streets that bred seditious utterance? The equal footing of the coffeehouse as a space of free exchange among supposed equals would seem to mirror the desire for "equality" of condition; but despite the strenuous denials of radicals, the government and its supporters regarded "equality" as a barely concealed term for equalization of property. As for Jacobin inflections, Frost was responding to a direct challenge, being asked how things went in France where he had recently traveled with Paine who was fleeing from arrest. The chapter follows Frost on his second visit to Paris. Following his coffeehouse altercation, he returned to present the SCI's congratulatory address to the National Convention; he attended the trial of the king and joined the British expatriate community. Declared an outlaw, Frost chose, unlike Paine, to return to stand trial. His activities in Paris lent an unmistakable revolutionary complexion to the words "equality" and "no kings." Convicted for seditious speech, Frost was sentenced to a six-month term in Newgate prison, and an appointment to stand on the pillory at Charing Cross. As for the culture of sociability and its links to reform, the coffeehouse's decline during the 1790s paralleled the withdrawal of many middle-class reformers from radical politics.

There were plenty of convictions for seditious utterances performed in taverns and coffeehouses, but the prosecutions of the Rev. William Winterbotham were the only ones for speaking from the pulpit. On 5 November 1792 (the evening before Frost's visit to the Percy coffeehouse), Winterbotham delivered a sermon at How's Lane Baptist Chapel in Plymouth to commemorate the anniversary of the dual national deliverance of 1605 (the failed Gunpowder Plot) and 1688 (the landing of William of Orange). It was the wrong time, as Louis XVI was on trial before the National Convention, and wrong place, as Plymouth was a loyalist stronghold, to draw comparisons between England's Glorious Revolution and the liberties recently won by the French people. Sentenced to four years imprisonment for seditious words, Winterbotham entered Newgate's republic of letters, where he refashioned himself as a literary man.[29] The starting point for Chapter 5, "Writing America from Newgate Prison," is the four-volume *An Historical, Geographical, Commercial and Philosophical View of the American United States* (1795) that he compiled while serving time. The chapter brings together the practiced space of Newgate prison, as a site of literary production and radical sociability, and the imagined space of America. It was also at Newgate that Winterbotham and fellow radical pressmen crossed paths with the early Romantics, most notably Robert Southey who was looking for someone bold enough to publish his Jacobin verse drama *Wat Tyler*. Southey believed that he was bound for the American back-country along with Samuel Coleridge and a young group of literary friends to establish a utopian community founded on principles of benevolence and "equal government by all," or Pantisocracy. As confidence in the French Revolution was shaken, America came more clearly into view as representing republican hopes and an asylum for persecuted radicals and Dissenters. Winterbotham's *View of the American United States* forms a literary archive, an encyclopedic collection of excerpts from a large range of works; however, at its ideological core was a group of texts that were also important reading for Coleridge and Southey and for the romantic view of America: accounts authored by the Girondist leader Jacques-Pierre Brissot, who was executed in 1793; by the Manchester radical Thomas Cooper, who was to join Joseph Priestley's community in Pennsylvania; and by the American adventurer Gilbert Imlay, who became Wollstonecraft's lover. None of the chapter's principals made it to America, but the idealized vision of America's independent citizen-farmer continued to exert a powerful influence on the democratic imagination. The intersection between artisan radicals and the early Romantics is a theme carried over into Part II of our study.

Part II concerns the afterlives of British Jacobinism. Following the war, popular radicalism mobilized with renewed strength, more firmly rooted within the ranks of an emergent class of industrial workers and with a more pronounced emphasis on the language of constitutionalism and constitutional modes of agitation, most importantly mass-petitioning campaigns. Nonetheless, the charge of Jacobinism remained current, found particularly in tropes of recurrence or viewed as a political tendency with a submerged continuity. Fragments of Jacobinism returned to literary and political culture in unpredictable ways. Chapter 6, "1817: Return of the Suppressed," unfolds in four parts. In the government-sponsored press and reports of parliamentary committees of secrecy, the attack on the prince regent's carriage returning from the opening of parliament appeared to replay the infamous "popgun" plot and the mobbing of the king's coach in October 1795; the Spencean-inspired riots linked to the Spa Fields meeting of 2 December 1816 realized the danger previewed by the LCS at Copenhagen Fields; the "convention" of Hampden Club delegates meeting at the Crown and

Anchor to coincide with the presentation of reform petitions signed by over a million people actualized the treasonous plan of 1794 to convene a British Convention. The anachronistic parallels employed to justify the restoration of the regime of repression emphasized one key difference: postwar Jacobinism posed a greater threat than its original manifestation, having now taken greater hold within the lower ranks of society. From debates over the reinstitution of government repression, the chapter takes readers to the startling return of *Wat Tyler*. In 1795, Newgate's pressmen had decided not to risk government prosecution, but the manuscript survived in the possession of Winterbotham, and mysteriously made its way into the hands of publishers. For radical pressmen who pirated the drama, the indiscretion of Southey's Jacobin youth proved to be a bonanza. As Southey discerned, displaced from 1795 the expressed feelings of his youthful heart found a much larger readership: Jacobinism's recurrence posed a far greater danger than when, according to Southey, "republicanism was confined to a very small number of the educated classes," having now sunk into the rabble.[30] The episode occasioned a reexamination of the poet's Jacobin past; satirical attacks in the radical press reiterated charges of dissimulation and apostasy, charges most vociferously articulated by William Hazlitt.

In 1817, life seemed to imitate art. Plans to march to London to present petitions for economic relief and political reform to the prince regent took shape in Manchester's taverns and debating rooms. In the proposed confrontation between king and people, the peasants' revolt and their heroes were overt points of historical reference; arguably the suppressed parallel was to the "Marseillais" – the march of provincial soldiers to Paris to demand the dethroning of Louis XVI. The government's thwarting of the Blanketeers in mid-March, just before the Seditious Meetings Act went into effect, marked the moment when insurrectionary groups moved into the shadows, leading to the ill-fated Pentrich rising of June – instigated by "Oliver the spy." The government was finally able to bring traitors to the scaffold. Jeremiah Brandreth, William Ludlam, and Isaac Turner were executed at Derby on 7 November, the day after the death of Princess Charlotte, who was widely believed to embody hope for a renewed monarchy. The chapter concludes with a reading of Shelley's lament, *An Address to the People on the Death of Princess Charlotte*, in which the poet views the princess's death as an occasion for private rather than public mourning, directing attention to the deaths of the Pentrich rebels and the real tragedy worthy of national mourning: the death of Liberty. At the end of the year that saw the publication of the suppressed *Wat Tyler*, Shelley and his publisher suppressed publication of his *Address to the People*, a move emblematic of the predisposition of the younger generation of Romantics. It was left to the radical pressmen and journalists, who would have happily published Shelley's pamphlet had it fallen into their hands, to address the nation's misdirected feelings of sorrow, juxtaposing Charlotte's untimely death with the fate of poor laboring men entrapped by a corrupt government and branded as traitors.

Aftermaths of the 1790s also well up in Chapter 7, "'Embers of Expiring Sedition,'" as a later generation of British radicals sought to memorialize Maurice Margarot, who was one of the "Scottish Martyrs" transported for sedition in 1794 for his part in the British Convention at Edinburgh. Margarot, the first president of the LCS and one of its delegates at Edinburgh, became a vexed object of commemoration during the 1830s, when parliamentary radicals and the recently established London Working Men's Association launched a project to honor the political exiles of 1794 as heroic ancestors of the emergent Chartist movement. The project for a monument to the Martyrs would occur partly as a counterpoint to contemporary conservative, state-sanctioned collective memory, with many of London's public spaces having been transformed to represent the 1790s as a time of national triumph and of British power in the post-Napoleonic world. But as an object of an oppositional radical commemoration, Margarot exposed the limitations of collective memory in constructing a heritage of the 1790s. The experience of transportation and empire complicated remembrance and the stories told. The falling out between Margarot and Thomas Fyshe Palmer (Unitarian reformer and fellow Martyr), the accusations and counter-accusations over a putative plot to seize the transport ship, betrayals, and sexual rumors produced deep fissures compromising the symbolic value of the Scottish Martyrs. Moreover, Margarot's political actions in Australia, including conspiring with Irish revolutionaries transported in the wake of the 1798 rebellion, meant that any constitutionalist narrative would have to grapple with his connections to revolutionary activities in Britain and in its new prison colony. Margarot's experience also suggests how the very process of empire and exile, through the effects of travel on consciousness and subjectivity, might shape colonial expression of dissent. The secret journal that he kept during his exile reveals a projection of the unfinished desires of British Jacobinism onto empire. A generation later, Margarot's dreams and ambitions proved difficult to incorporate into a coherent drama of reform. In offering a counterpoint to conservative national memory, radical commemoration re-narrated the 1790s in restricted terms, expunging the more utopian and revolutionary longings of British Jacobinism.

In Chapter 8, "Among the Romantics," we return, like so many scholars have, to the work of Edward Thompson. The chapter stands as a coda to a book that retraces historical themes with which Thompson was concerned. Thompson was, of course, not only the most influential British historian of his generation but a socialist and peace activist. The chapter moves between his historical writing on popular radicalism, class, and romanticism and his own life as an activist, as interrelated aspects of his vision of a socialist future. In his writings on the 1790s, he addressed what he considered a major historical loss: the separation of the radical movement from the Romantics in mutual resistance to industrial capitalism and the values of what he termed, "the annunciation of Acquisitive Man." Britain's Jacobin decade ended in disappointed hopes for democratic reform. In his historical and political writing, Thompson discerned a recurrent pattern of political disenchantment and disavowal; he was sharply critical of intellectuals whom he felt had failed to come to an honest reckoning with their past commitments and altered perspectives. In both *The Making of the English Working Class* (1963) and his publications on the romantic movement of the 1790s, collected together and published posthumously in *The Romantics: England in the Age of Revolution* (1997), he addressed Wordsworth and Coleridge's progressive disenchantment with the cause of the French Revolution to the point at which disillusion turned to "default" or "apostasy": the charge of apostasy, as discussed in Chapter 6, was one voiced at the time and one that Thompson revived in his attack on former communists and socialists who moved into retreat and brandished confessions of disavowal. In his political writing, he constantly returned to the trajectory of the early Romantics in comparison to the trajectory of contemporary writers who shifted with the postwar political winds: the disenchantment of his own era appeared to parallel the failed aspirations of the age of revolution. In terms of literature, he was concerned with how disenchantment influenced the literary imagination. Thompson's reiterated critique of abstract theory as juxtaposed to the concept of experience also found a source of inspiration in Wordsworth's translation of lived experience into poetic language. And while he discerned common patterns of disenchantment, he retained his view of romanticism's powerful moral critique of capitalist values, and the literary and political capacities of utopian feelings. Thompson never completed his promised book on the early Romantics – although he published *Witness against the Beast: William Blake and the Moral Law* (1993) just before his death. In conclusion, some speculative musings are offered on what Thompson left unwritten, suggestions about what he might have added to an unfinished manuscript.

Notes

1 *State Trials for High Treason, Embellished with Portraits, Part Third, Containing the Trial of Mr. John Thelwall* (1795), 12.
2 The attorney general Sir John Scott stressed the importance of bringing the evidence presented at the treason trials before the country at large, so the public was "fully acquainted with the dangers" that were posed. John Scott (later Lord Eldon), *Lord Eldon's Anecdote Book*, ed. Anthony L. J. Lincoln and Robert Lindley McEwen (Stevens and Sons, 1960), 56.
3 For the term "reign of alarm," see Kenneth R. Johnston, *Unusual Suspects: Pitt's Reign of Alarm and the Lost Generation of the 1790s* (Oxford: OUP, 2013), xvii.

4 For the commitments required of both loyalists and radicals, see Mark Philp, "Disconcerting Ideas: Explaining Popular Radicalism and Popular Loyalism," in *Reforming Ideas in Britain: Politics and Languages in the Shadow of the French Revolution* (Cambridge: CUP, 2014), chapter 3.

5 John Barrell, *The Spirit of Despotism: Invasions of Privacy in the 1790s* (Oxford: OUP, 2006), 4, and introduction.

6 See Clive Emsley, "Repression, 'Terror' and the Rule of Law in England during the Decade of the French Revolution," *EHR* 100 (1985): 801–25. Emsley downplays the extent and impact of government repression.

7 *Trial of Thomas Briellat, for Seditious Words … 6 December 1793, Session House, Clerkenwell-Green* (1794), 33–34.

8 Thale, 32–34; TS 11/965/ 3501A, "Case of William Carter a Bill-Sticker"; *World*, 6 December 1792; *MC*, 8 January 1793. In calling for parliamentary reform, the address hailed the French Revolution, commenting that if in the course of struggle, "Cruelty and Revenge have arisen among a few in Paris, let us not attribute their acts to a whole nation."

9 Jon Mee, *Print, Publicity and Radicalism in the 1790s:* The Laurel of Liberty (Cambridge: CUP, 2016), 1, and introduction. See also Paul Keen, *The Crisis of Literature in the 1790s: Print Culture and the Public Sphere* (Cambridge: CUP, 1999), particularly chapter 3.

10 Thomas Paine, *Letter Addressed to the Addressers of the Late Proclamation* (1792), in *The Complete Works of Thomas Paine*, ed. Phillip S. Foner, 2 vols. (New York: Citadel Press), 2: 470. See also Oliva Smith, *The Politics of Language, 1791–1819* (Oxford: OUP, 1984).

11 PC 1/22/A, Examination of John Wharton MP before Privy Council, 24 May 1794, fol. 36a.

12 *ST*, vol. 25, "The Trial of Thomas Hardy for High Treason," cols. 571–72. For the importance of song to radical culture, see Michael T. Davis, "'An Evening of Pleasure rather than Business': Songs, Subversion and Radical Sub-Culture in the 1790s," *Journal for the Study of British Cultures* 12 (2005): 115–26.

13 *Treason Triumphant over Law and Constitution addressed to both Houses of Parliament* (1795), 22.

14 See, for example, the work of the feminist philosopher Judith Butler, *Gender Trouble: Feminism and the Subversion of Identity* (New York: Routledge, 1990), and *Excitable Speech: A Politics of the Performative* (New York: Routledge, 1997). In the field of anthropology, see Greg Dening, "Towards an Anthropology of Performance in Encounters in Place," in *Pacific History,* ed. Donald Rubenstein (Guam: University of Guam Press, 1992), 3–7, and *Performances* (Chicago, IL: University of Chicago Press, 1996).

15 Mark Philp, "The Fragmented Ideology of Reform," in *Reforming Ideas*, chapter 1, and "The Elusive Principle: Collective Self-Determination in the Late Eighteenth Century," in ibid., chapter 10.

16 Matthew Campbell Browne, *A Leaf Out of Burke's Book, being an Epistle to that Right Honourable Gentleman, in Reply to His Letter to a Noble Lord on the Subject of His Pension* (1796), 55. Browne edited the *Patriot* (1792–93) anonymously, and in December 1795, he presided over the last of the LCS's mass meetings held to protest the Two Acts.

17 Southey to Caroline Anne Bowles, 13 February 1824, in Edward Dowden, ed., *Correspondence of Robert Southey with Caroline Bowles* (Dublin, 1881), 52.

18 The scholarship on history of the emotions is large and expanding but see, in particular, William M. Reddy, *The Navigation of Feeling: A Framework for*

the History of the Emotions (Cambridge: CUP, 2001); Barbara H. Rosenwein, "Worrying about Emotions in History," *AHR* 107 (2002): 821–45, and "Problems and Methods in the History of the Emotions: Passions in Context," *International Journal of History and Theory of the Emotions* 1 (2010): 1–25; Sophia Rosenfeld, "Thinking about Feeling, 1789–1799," *French Historical Studies* 32 (2009): 697–706; Jan Plamper, *The History of the Emotions: An Introduction*, trans. Keith Tribe (Oxford: OUP, 2015). Reddy's concept of "emotives" is an extension of the concept of "performatives," seen as emotions enacted in speech and acting as agents.

19 Rosenwein, "Worrying about Emotions," at 842, and more generally for the concept of emotional communities. For Godwin's teas to which he invited LCS members, see Mee, *Print, Publicity, and Radicalism*, 43–45.

20 For the Crown and Anchor and radical political culture, see Christina Parolin, *Radical Spaces: Venues of Popular Politics in London, 1790 – c. 1845* (Canberra: Australian National University E Press, 2010), chapters 4 and 5.

21 Harriet Guest, *Unbounded Attachment: Sentiment and Politics in the Age of the French Revolution* (Oxford: OUP, 2013), 4; Lynn Hunt and Margaret Jacob, "The Affective Revolution in the 1790s," *Eighteenth-Century Studies* 34 (2001): 491–521. See also Rachael Hewitt, *A Revolution of Feeling: The Decade that Forged the Modern Mind* (Granta, 2017).

22 Jon Mee, *Romanticism, Enthusiasm and Regulation: Poetics and the Policing of Culture in the Romantic Period* (Oxford: OUP, 2003), chapter 2. See also Chris Jones, *Radical Sensibility: Literature and Ideas in the 1790s* (Routledge, 1993).

23 For the development of feelings of sympathy, the capacity to imaginatively identify with the suffering of others, and the role of the novel in fostering humane dispositions, see Lynn Hunt, *Inventing Human Rights, A History* (New York: Norton, 2007), chapter 2.

24 Mary Wollstonecraft, *Vindication of the Rights of Men*, 2nd ed. (1790), 6, 32, 150.

25 Mary Wollstonecraft and William Godwin, *A Short Residence in Sweden, Norway and Denmark and Memoirs of the Author of 'The Rights of Woman,'* ed. Richard Holmes (Harmondsworth: Penguin, 1987), letter 10, 128.

26 The term "radical" is used throughout the book, although until post-1815 the term "reformer" was the self-description most often used; "republican" signified opposition to monarchy; "democrat" was not commonly used in a positive sense.

27 British Library, Place Scrapbooks, set 36, "Libel, Sedition, Treason Prosecutions, 1792–94," introduction, dated August 1847; Francis Place, *The Autobiography of Francis Placed (1771–1854)*, ed. Mary Thale (Cambridge: CUP, 1972), 14.

28 In early 1793, Godwin took up the case in a series of letters to the *Morning Chronicle*. See Benjamin Pauley, "'Far from the Consummate Lawyer': William Godwin and the Treason Trials of the 1790s," in *Reactions to Revolutions: The 1790s and Their Aftermath*, ed. Ulrich Broich, et al. (Berlin: LIT Verlag, 2007), 203–30, at 206–07.

29 See Iain McCalman, "Newgate in Revolution: Radical Enthusiasm and Romantic Counterculture," *Eighteenth-Century Life* 22 (1998): 95–110.

30 Robert Southey, *A Letter to William Smith, Esq. M.P.* (1817), 7.

Part 1

Seditious Hearts

1790s

1 Playing at Revolution
British "Jacobin" Performance

The Argument

"Loudly as *Jacobin* is resounded through the land, yet none have condescended to explain its meaning: that must be gleaned from desultory harangues on its terrible nature, and effects." So wrote the abolitionist William Fox, in 1794, calling attention to how one of the most loaded terms in Britain's political vocabulary remained dangerously unfixed. According to Fox, "Jacobin" belonged to a "certain order of words" through which Britain's governing class resorted "to *artifice* to obtain or maintain dominion, no longer deeming it expedient to rely totally on *force*." "Jacobin" followed a tradition of "cant words" employed to sway subjects: "Puritan," "Papist," "Pretender," and more recently, "the dreaded words *Rights of Man*."[1] Certainly, it was the case that William Pitt, his government, and its loyal supporters used the word "Jacobin" promiscuously as part of their effort to influence the hearts and minds of British subjects. Lord Henry Cockburn, Scottish jurist, later recalled that for conservatives "everything alarming and hateful and every political objector was a Jacobin. No innovation, whether practical, or speculative, could escape from this fatal word."[2] More recently, historians have agreed that "Jacobin" was a term misascribed to British democrats of the 1790s, who were on balance attached to constitutionalist demands and peaceful modes of protest.[3] But what if we reverse field and ask what the political label might have meant to British democrats accused of embracing it? How attached was a section of British reformers to revolutionary principles associated with this highly contested label? Most crucially, how might such sentiments have been expressed and in what sense was it possible to assume or embody such a political allegiance? These are the questions that animate our discussion.

At the outset, it must be acknowledged that our argument is limited in important respects; it deals with public expression among popular radicals, primarily in London, during the early 1790s and, therefore, it does not consider the movements of United Englishmen, United Scotsmen, and United Irishmen; the naval mutinies of 1797 and the Irish rising of 1798; or the broader revolutionary underground.[4] We are concerned with the possibilities for public identification and articulation, not with the submerged, but very real, revolutionary network that developed after the so-called Two Acts of 1795. In addition, much of the material drawn on in this chapter – for example, the treason trials – is well known to scholars working on the political culture of British radicalism. In returning to these sources, however, we seek to shift interpretations beyond analysis of political ideas per se toward an appreciation of the role of performance in the production of political meaning, to examine the embodied practices of radicalism, its style and modes of theatricality, to which loyalists and conservatives so often turned in their portrayal of British "Jacobinism." At one level, this serves to synthesize interpretative trends. A number of scholars, particularly literary scholars and historians influenced by the "linguistic turn," have drawn attention to the importance of political theatricality and performance. Yet, this chapter gives the "performative turn" a sharper analytical edge with regard to British popular politics in the era of the French Revolution.[5]

First, it is now recognized that despite their often-voiced desire for political transparency, popular radicals never escaped the broader theatricality of Georgian political culture. However, radical theatricality has, at least implicitly, been considered as a relatively constant phenomenon, a reflection of the spectacle of Georgian society, or a tactical repository for publicizing dissent. In tracing the shifting construction of British Jacobinism during the early 1790s, we seek to make a stronger analytical point about the relationship among performance, agency, text, and meaning. Informed by the work of scholars who have theorized performance as an expressive mode and process of identification, this chapter explores this relationship as a political commitment specific to a moment in which possibilities opened up and were then largely closed down. Second, it seems difficult to avoid the long-standing historiographic question of how radical or revolutionary the British plebeian movement was in the wake of the French Revolution. In our view, the question is badly posed, particularly when framed as a stark dichotomy between constitutionalist and revolutionary agendas. Most significantly, responses to such questions have been limited by analyses that focus nearly exclusively on the reading of radical texts and that marginalize the place of performance in generating meanings during a period characterized by government surveillance and popular vigilantism. In stressing the importance of performance to the workings of political culture, it should be noted, as Roger Chartier writes, that access to "non-discursive practices is possible only by deciphering the texts that describe them."[6] In the 1790s, a large number of such descriptive texts reveal a sustained effort to read radicals' theatrical display as a manifestation of British Jacobinism, and to discern their true desires in terms of such actions.

This chapter argues three related propositions. First, it recognizes the deep intellectual, political, and emotional ambivalence that distinguished views of the French Revolution and Jacobin rule among British republicans. In turn, we are interested in how this ambivalence was translated into democratic discourse and practice. The second proposition argues that "Jacobinism" was a dialogic construction, produced at the intersections of loyalist, government, and radical exchange. Attention is here paid to confrontations between radical reformers and their opponents, and to how "Jacobin" meanings were created through such unequal exchanges. However, rather than emphasizing the purely negative or restrictive force of censorship in its various manifestations, we stress how these constraints reactivated meanings that they aimed to suppress. As Judith Butler demonstrates, state censorship inescapably activates the speech it seeks to constrain, becoming "caught in a circular, imaginary production of its own making."[7] This leads directly to our third proposition, from which the chapter takes its title. Namely, that the ambivalent and dialogic elements of British "Jacobin" identification were most powerfully expressed and inhabited at the level of serious play or counter-theater. "Playing at revolution," assuming the role of British Jacobin, was often produced as a response to restrictions on speech and action.

French Jacobinism

The question of what Jacobinism meant to contemporaries, particularly to British supporters of the French Revolution, is complicated for numerous reasons. First, we confront the difficulties associated with interpreting French Jacobinism and the fact that "Jacobin" as a designation in its native form was in constant motion. Indeed, movement was part of what French Jacobinism was about: the imperative need to move the Revolution forward, most intensely under the desperate pressures of war. Crucially important were the points at which various groups or leaders tried to arrest this movement. In a matter of months, men who had regarded each other as brothers – both Girondin "Jacobins" and "left Montagnard Jacobins" were originally club members – became mortal enemies.[8] By opposing the execution of Louis XVI, Thomas Paine, the only British member of the National Convention, moved across the line separating patriots from traitors to the Revolution. Shifts in alliance proved deadly; Paine barely escaped with his life. Jacobin rule itself lasted little over a year, and although French Jacobinism had an afterlife under the Directory, Jacobinism was indelibly associated with the centralized rule of Robespierre and the Terror.[9]

Ever since the 1790s, the question has loomed as to whether the turn to violence, to terror qua terror, was inherent to Jacobinism or the Revolution more generally.[10] Then, as now, it was not only conservatives who embraced the view that violence was inherent from the Revolution's outset. Mary Wollstonecraft, herself a witness to the Terror, never reads more like Edmund Burke than when reflecting on the Revolution, nor was she alone among reformers. Writing in 1795, she pronounced the French to be "the most unqualified of any people in Europe" to undertake the important task of revolution in the name of liberty. Unable to profit from "the wisdom of experience," the leaders of the Revolution moved too quickly; for, as she wrote, "Men are most easily led away by the ingenious arguments, that dwell on the equality of man."[11] An overreliance on abstract principles had led, as Burke charged, to violent anarchy and dictatorship pursued under the misconceived sign of equality. During the 1790s, "anti-theoretical rhetoric" became a central theme in defining British national identity: British experience stood opposed to French theory.[12]

French Jacobinism was itself composed from discordant ideological commitments: didacticism and terror enforced fraternity and republican virtue; rational transparency coexisted with the theatrics of revolution; the competing claims of individualism, social justice, and equality proved difficult to resolve; internationalism and nationalism vied for emotional support. Moreover, such commitments were framed by a historically transcendent worldview in constant confrontation with the necessities of the revolutionary moment and the realities of human frailty.[13] Clearly Jacobinism was not directly translatable to the political culture of British radicalism, due not least to the existence of representative institutions and the predominant discourse of constitutionalism.[14] It proved difficult for British radicals to succumb to the Revolution's "mythic present."[15] They often placed themselves within a rich domestic libertarian tradition, legitimating current demands by reference to a venerable past marked by popular resistance to tyranny. In turn, even in 1792 as the Revolution turned more threatening, British reformers might view French developments through the lens of English libertarianism. As for organizational practice, radicals often grafted gestures of "Jacobin" sociability onto preexisting vernacular modes. Anniversary dinners to commemorate 1688 at "Constitutional" or "Revolution" clubs became sites of "Jacobin" toasting and singing; commemorative medallions included French revolutionary icons; debating clubs entertained topics allowing sympathizers to hold forth on the virtues of France's revolution. "Jacobin" styles did not replace indigenous British radicalism but rather ultra-radicals adopted codes of speech and behavior associated with the Revolution alongside those of constitutionalism, inflecting British tradition with democratic possibilities previewed in France.

We can, in fact, cite British radicals who were sympathetic to the ideological inheritance of French Jacobinism. In 1838, the Chartist journalist and intellectual James Bronterre O'Brien published a carefully researched biography of Robespierre. As an advertisement for his book stated, instead of the image of a "'blood-thirsty Monster,'" the work proved Robespierre "was one of the most humane, virtuous, noble-minded, and enlightened Reformers that ever existed in the world."[16] And O'Brien's fellow Chartist leader G. J. Harney identified himself with Marat, adopting the pen-name of "L'Ami du Peuple."[17] However, such explicit identifications with Jacobinism were only possible at a distance of over a generation from the Revolution. During the 1790s, the immediacy of war (including the threat of invasion) and virtue's turn to terror, produced ambivalence on the left. By the Revolution's Year Two, Paine's claim of 1791 that "they order these things better in France" had become more difficult to sustain.

"Citizen" Thelwall

The career of John Thelwall proves instructive for thinking about the meanings of British Jacobinism. He represents a limit case, showing how far one could go in openly identifying with and giving formal expression to democratic ideals associated with the Revolution. Moreover, he combined this formal articulation of democratic belief with public identification with the Revolution that centered on his own theatricality and visibility. Orator, political writer, and poet, Thelwall was English Jacobinism's most articulate spokesperson. He commanded a sizable audience for his lectures and publications, and was largely responsible for popularizing Godwinian ideas of human benevolence and reason's capacity for remaking society.[18] Thelwall declared himself "a Republican and true Sans-Culotte," expressing support for "the Mountain" as the men best fitted to take the Revolution forward.[19] He was among the few "gentlemen" to join the London Corresponding Society and to lead the movement of artisan radicals. Tried and acquitted on charges of high treason in late 1794, he probably came as close as any major popular leader to being executed by Pitt's government. In attempting to place Thelwall along the spectrum of democratic politics, Gregory Claeys comments that despite the strong "Jacobin" element in his thought, particularly his desire for a measure of social equality, his attitude toward violence "perhaps" placed him, like Paine, with the Girondins. Without disagreeing with this judicious assessment, we prefer to stress the ambivalence within Thelwall's thought and sentiment, maintaining that the unresolved character of his political beliefs reveals something more generally about what the quotation marks around British "Jacobin" imply.[20] That said, it must also be remembered that Thelwall represented but one piece of what Mark Philp terms the "fragmented ideology" of British reform (Figure 1.1).

So what did Thelwall stand for? First, he was strongly committed to the ideals of cosmopolitanism, international fraternity, and universal benevolence. These were, of course, cherished Godwinian principles, but they were also associated with a broader strain of Anglo-American republicanism dating to the American Revolution in which local attachments

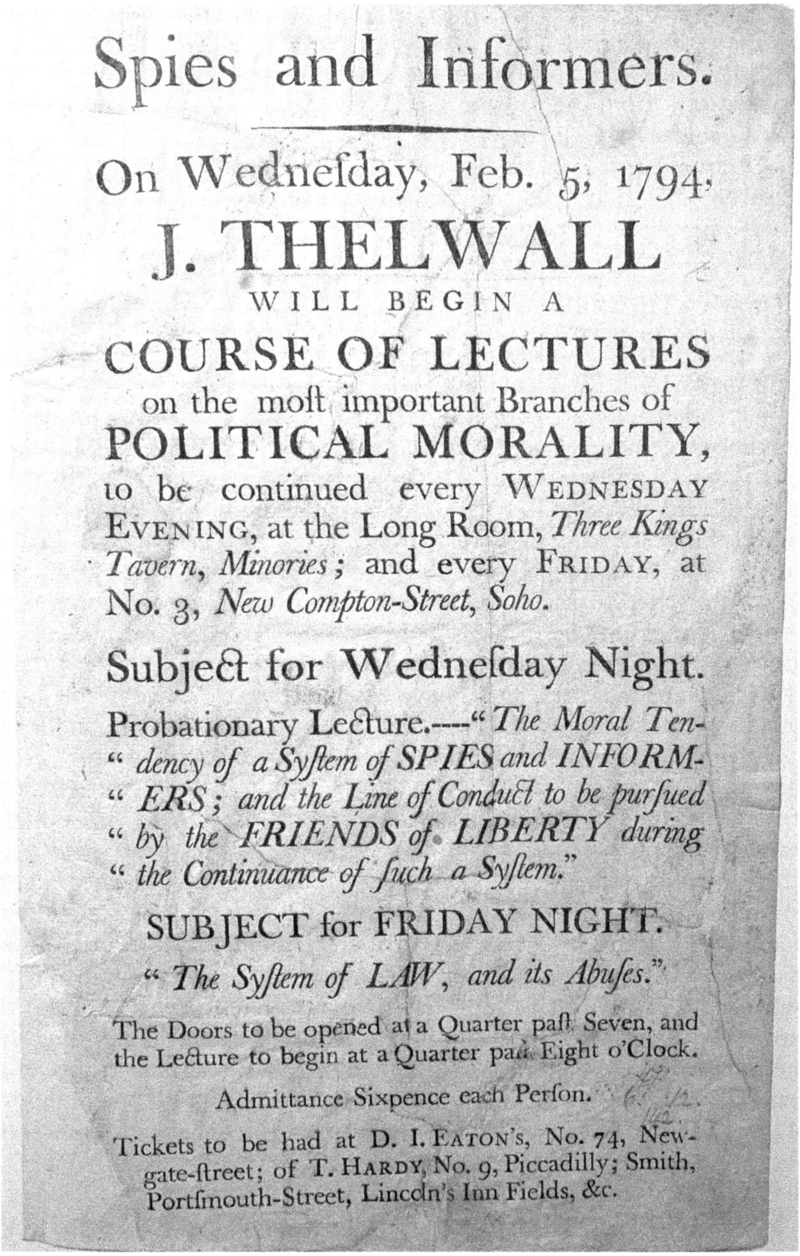

Spies and Informers.

On Wednesday, Feb. 5, 1794.

J. THELWALL

WILL BEGIN A

COURSE OF LECTURES

on the most important Branches of

POLITICAL MORALITY,

to be continued every WEDNESDAY EVENING, at the Long Room, *Three Kings Tavern, Minories;* and every FRIDAY, at No. 3, *New Compton-Street, Soho.*

Subject for Wednesday Night.

Probationary Lecture.----"*The Moral Ten-*
"*dency of a System of SPIES and INFORM-*
"*ERS; and the Line of Conduct to be pursued*
"*by the FRIENDS of LIBERTY during*
"*the Continuance of such a System.*"

SUBJECT for FRIDAY NIGHT.

"*The System of LAW, and its Abuses.*"

The Doors to be opened at a Quarter past Seven, and the Lecture to begin at a Quarter past Eight o'Clock.

Admittance Sixpence each Person.

Tickets to be had at D. I. EATON's, No. 74, New-gate-street; of T. HARDY, No. 9, Piccadilly; Smith, Portsmouth-Street, Lincoln's Inn Fields, &c.

Figure 1.1 John Thelwall, Spies and Informers. On Wednesday. Feb. 5, 1794, J. Thelwall will begin a course of lectures on the most important branches of political morality, etc., posting bill, 1794. Original source British Library. 648.c.26. Copyright © The British Library Board.

were displaced by an enlightenment cosmopolitanism, by the desire to be a citizen of the republic of humanity.[21] The French Revolution intensified this shift in meaning. To be a patriot in the narrow sense of mere love of one's own country possessed no claim to virtue; it was, according to Thelwall, a "contemptible and illiberal" feeling when compared to universal principles of reason, liberty, and human fellowship.[22] By 1793–94, however, it became difficult for British reformers to defend their support for universal liberty and humanity through reference to France.[23] Nonetheless, if radical constitutionalism tapped a wellspring of nationalist sentiment, Thelwall, who was not averse to praising Britain's libertarian heritage, refused to separate himself and the cause of British republicanism from the principles of the French Revolution, the Jacobin constitution of 1793, and the social radicalism of the Parisian sans-culottes.[24]

For Thelwall, and one may speculate for the large audiences who attended his lectures at the Beaufort Buildings off the Strand, the essence of the French Revolution was the reign of popular sovereignty, linked in turn to the role played by the sans-culottes. In a lecture comparing 1649 to 1789, he argued that in contrast to England's own experience, the French Revolution was based on principles rather than leaders: "it was not the revolution of Marat or Robespierre... but the revolution of the people. Their souls were altered, their habits were altered, their modes of thinking were altered, their capacities of acting were altered – there was a universal moral revolution throughout the country; and, whenever an universal moral revolution takes place, no power on earth... can prevent political revolution, also." "Universal moral revolution," a "revolution of the people," souls altered through revolutionary practice: Robespierre could not have put the Revolution's transcendence more eloquently. But Thelwall separated the principles of the Revolution from its violence, from the need to purify itself in its enemies' blood. "I glory in the principles of the French Revolution!," he boldly declared, "I exult in the triumphs of reason! I am an advocate for the rights of man!" It is important to recognize, in line with E. P. Thompson, the bravery of such a public statement in the year 1795. As for the Revolution's "excesses," Thelwall maintained that the Terror was not the consequence of new democratic doctrine but "of the old leaven of revenge, corruption and suspicion which was generated by the systematic cruelties of the old despotism."[25] More pointedly, he contrasted Pitt's "white" terror to that of the Jacobins: "Robespierre and his faction ravaged France, it is true, for the destruction of royalty. Pitt and his faction have depopulated Europe, and spread general famine through this quarter of the universe, for the annihilation of liberty." If Robespierre unjustly oppressed the rich to win popularity among the poor, Pitt oppressed the poor, through war and taxation, to win the support of the rich.[26]

The argument that a corrupt government oppressed the people by means of unjustified warfare and unfair taxation became a familiar theme of anti-war patriotism. However, Thelwall pressed his views on poverty, commercial society, and property well beyond this. He innovated with sophistication on natural-rights and natural-law theory, justifying a redistribution of property, including entitlements from the produce of commerce and manufacturing as well as agriculture.[27] A discussion of Thelwall's contribution to radical political economy is outside this chapter's scope. But it is worth noting that together with Paine's famous "social" chapter of *Rights of Man*, second part (1792), *Agrarian Justice* (1796), and the writings of the agrarian communitarian Thomas Spence, Thelwall expanded fundamentally the concept of citizenship to include social and economic rights. As developed in his writing, particularly in *Rights of Nature against the Usurpations of Establishments* (1796), the right to share in the increasing wealth of society was proportionate but not an entitlement to an equal share of society's wealth.[28] Not only did Thelwall insist that "equality of property" was "totally impossible in the present state of human intellect and industry," his theory provided no foundation for such a claim. Yet as he told his audience on the anniversary of his acquittal, "Woe to that country in which too much veneration is entertained for property... It is one thing to place a barrier round property; another to put property in the scale against the welfare, and independence of the people."[29]

"Equality" was, of course, among the Revolution's central ideals, dear to both Jacobins and sans-culottes, although they might mean different things by it.[30] A provisional understanding of British Jacobinism should include an appeal, however inchoate and ill-defined, to equality of condition and an expanded notion of democratic citizenship, encompassing social as well as political, religious, and civic rights – although it must also be noted that such "equality" rarely extended to women.[31] Despite their denials, republicans were unable to escape the charge that their real purpose was "leveling" all distinctions, including those of wealth. Natural-rights theory facilitated the slippage between political and social claims.[32] In his tract *The Commonwealth of Reason* (1795), the physician and LCS member William Hodgson registered equality's utopian potential. Hodgson offered a fully realized vision of society based on perfect equality among citizens, including a ban on all wealth accumulated by any means other than "personal industry, or equitable inheritance." His scheme provided for a minimum wage for all workers, linked to the price of wheat, a highly regulated market for necessities, "national manufactories" for the unemployed, abolition of the death penalty, compulsory secular education and the election of school teachers, and divorce by the consent of either party.[33] The following year, Hodgson proposed publishing a "treatise called the Female Citizen, or a historical enquiry into the rights of women."[34] Moreover, his commitment (shared by Thelwall as well as Thomas Hardy) to racial equality and the abolition of Caribbean slavery was apparent from the frontispiece to the *Commonwealth of Reason*, which pictures a black man classically dressed and a white man hand in hand. The figures hold aloft a cap of liberty along with a banner reading "Liberty Fraternity Equality," which proclaims, "Liberty is the Right and Happiness of all, for all by Nature are equal and free, and no one can without the utmost injustice become the Slave of his like."[35] As with Thelwall, Hodgson's commonwealth represented merely one version of British Jacobin thought, remarkable for its social reach and explicit formulation. Both his utopian pamphlet and proposed treatise on female citizenship were written from the confines of Newgate prison, where Hodgson was serving a two-year sentence for uttering seditious words, an episode to which we will return.

Impudent Bodies: Scottish Sedition Trials

Thus we can discern Jacobin strains in the writings of several intellectuals; such views could be publically articulated despite the nationalist pressures of war.[36] How many reformers may privately have held to such commitments is difficult to judge – bearing in mind that even private communications might be subject to government scrutiny.[37] John Binns, plumber and LCS leader, was later to reflect that while the LCS's "avowed" purpose was to reform parliament, "the wishes and hopes of many of its influential members carried them to the overthrow of the monarchy and the establishment of a Republic."[38] For Pitt's government and its loyal supporters, it was not merely, or even predominantly, that popular societies called openly for constitutional reform.[39] Rather, opponents maintained that at a deeper level, reformers' "secret" aims were modeled on Jacobin France. Moreover, this intent was disclosed not by their formal statements but through gestures and symbolic practices that, while seemingly unguarded, were in truth purposefully designed to seduce the unwary. Just after the government's roundup of leading radicals in May 1794, Edmund Burke, no stranger to dramatic performance, declared in the Commons that moderate demands cloaked dangerous designs: "This was parliamentary reform; and for this purpose, whole classes of the working people of the country were to be jacobinized!"[40] The problem for government was how to unveil to juries and the public at large the real goals of British Jacobinism. Over the winter of 1793 and through 1794, authorities came to represent a medley of gestures and symbolic actions as forming a distinct and coherent expression of widespread Jacobin allegiance. Accordingly, such gestures provided the key to reading and comprehending the true meaning of reformers' constitutional addresses, meetings, and conventions. In turn, plebeian radicals exploited the fears and ambiguities surrounding the government's interpretations of their actions in order to deepen the subversive tones of their own play; indeed, the government's own interpretative practice helped create the conditions for transgression and enactments of utopian desire. "Jacobinism" was produced in the dense interchange between plebeian radicals and government authority; Jacobin identities, as popularly understood, increasingly relied on performance and the theatrics of subversion.

Form, gesture, and style were crucial to the series of state prosecutions first staged at the court of High Judiciary at Edinburgh; the Scottish sedition trials were followed by the English treason trials.[41] The trials, along with the reports of the parliamentary committees of secrecy of 1794, need to be read together, as an unfolding text. In these proceedings, we see the government's developing interpretation of the intent of British reformers in terms of French republicanism. Although the LCS and SCI had been in formal contact with the French National Convention, it proved difficult to show that British reformers aimed at attacking the king or overthrowing the established government by force of arms, or that they were actively supported from France. This helps to explain the underlying logic of the government's construction of treason, where the issue of what "overt acts" constituted "compassing" and "imagining" the king's death loomed large.[42] Much turned on interpretation of the obscure words "compass" and "imagine" – usually glossed as "design" or "intend," and by the 1790s, already archaic as used in the fourteenth-century statute of treasons. Precisely because British revolutionaries disguised their real aims, "overt acts" had to be loosely constructed, the codes of treason had to be fleshed out for judge and jury. Both the particular legal requirements of the English statute on treason and the evolution of a performance-based understanding of Jacobinism ensured that the treason trials centered on the relationship among enactment, intent, and meaning. How, exactly, were meanings to be ascribed to acts; conversely when did words constitute acts; or when did acts signal the true meaning of words? The government attempted to convince juries that the embodiment of Jacobinism, its style and manner, was often more reliable than the written word for establishing intent, or that the meaning of formal statements could only be understood in terms of performance.

The trial of Maurice Margarot, the first president of the LCS and one of its delegates to the British Convention, held at Edinburgh in late 1793, provided the first opportunity for the government to fully describe British reformers in terms of the procedural structures of French Jacobinism. In January 1794, Margarot was tried at the High Court of Justiciary, charged with sedition for his part at the British Convention. He was among a group of British reformers associated with the Scottish convention schemes of 1793, all of whom were similarly charged. At these trials, the Scottish crime of sedition was interpreted as closely resembling that of treason; all those brought to trial were found guilty and sentenced to either seven or fourteen years' transportation. The sedition trials formed, in effect, the testing ground for the English treason trials of late 1794; constructive sedition paved the way for constructive treason. In both sets of trials, association with the British Convention was crucial to the prosecution's case, as representing a clear attempt to overawe and thus supplant the authority of parliament.[43] The Scottish trials reinforced the warning of loyalism: the secret design of popular reformers was violent revolution in imitation of Jacobin France, and this was disclosed not only, or even principally, in terms of the movement's formal political statements, but rather through mimetic gestures. Moreover, the higher standard of proof in trials for treason, requiring the demonstration of "overt acts," dictated that the English trials would again turn to the reading of performance. In all the trials associated with the British Convention, at both Edinburgh and London, indictments charged sedition based on the assembly's character: the style "The British Convention of the People," delegates addressing each other as "citizen," dividing into "sections," receiving reports from sections dated "Liberty Hall," "Liberty Stairs," "First year of the British Convention," and reports prefixed *vive la convention*" and ending "Ça Ira," granting honors of sitting, all this and more marked the Convention as an illegal body modeled on French revolutionary design, aiming to overthrow the British constitution.[44]

Looking back on the Scottish trials, Lord Cockburn noted the discrepancy between the vocabularies used to denigrate radicals and the actual import of their ideologies. From the safe distance of over half a century, he observed, "We had wonderfully few Jacobins; that is, persons who seriously wished to introduce a republic into this country, on the French precedent. There were plenty of people who were *called* Jacobins." Despite this admission, Cockburn mocked the manner in which so many British radicals embodied their political beliefs: "There was a short period... during which this imputation was provoked by a ridiculous aping of French forms and phraseology."[45] Thus Margarot marched to his trial attended by a procession headed by a twenty-foot tree of liberty in the shape of the letter M and carried on two poles by two former members of the Convention. The tree was demolished by a loyalist mob that also broke up the procession and dragged Margarot into court. Cockburn recalled Margarot in terms that registered James Gillray's satirical depictions of starving, frog-eating Parisian sans-culottes. In the dock, Margarot appeared "a dark little creature, dressed in black ... something like one's idea of a puny Frenchman, a most impudent and provoking body."[46]

Cockburn's reference to Margarot's "provoking body" was not singular in drawing attention to the Jacobin body. Thus the *Times* described Thomas Hardy, secretary of the LCS, at the time of his arrest on charges of high treason as "a tall thin man; much marked in the face with small pox; his manners low and vulgar; and in dress and habit quite a *Sans Culotte*."[47] These comments may serve to remind us that across the channel, where gestures of ordinary life took on extraordinary significance, signs of virtue were to be worn on the body of the citizen, inscribed in one's personal comportment and bearing.[48] British radicals followed suit. Joseph Gerrald, the LCS's other delegate to the Convention, appeared at the bar in Edinburgh in French revolutionary style, "with unpowdered hair, hanging loosely behind – his neck bare, and shirt with a large collar, doubled over."[49] As Hardy left Newgate each morning to be taken under guard to Old Bailey, he greeted his fellow prisoners as he passed their cells on the prison's State side: "Farewell, Citizens! death or liberty." *Vivre libre ou mourir* was the motto of the Jacobin society. But then, as Thelwall reminded his audience, this libertarian slogan, which had been chalked on the walls and gateways in Chelsea, was not exclusively French. "Citizens," he declared, "there was a time when Death or Liberty was the burthen of every Briton's song."[50]

While Cockburn viewed behavior such as Margarot's as "ridiculous aping," prosecutors at Edinburgh constructed the gestures and organizational forms displayed at the Convention as more indicative of the body's true purposes than its formal claims for constitutional reform. This is particularly clear at those moments when advocates or judges pulled together the disparate pieces of evidence into a closed whole.[51] In his concluding remarks for the prosecution, for example, Lord Advocate Eskgrove contrasted the explicitly moderate meanings of the words spoken at the British Convention with the implied sense as accented by French performance and organization. Eskgrove focused on the Convention itself, including the resolutions proclaiming its status as a permanent body (thus analogous to the French National Convention) and its right to resist being illegally broken up. Such structural elements offered the context for interpreting the "artful ambiguous terms" accompanying such resolutions.[52] In summing up the case against Margarot, Eskgrove also stressed the Convention's approval of universal manhood suffrage and annual parliaments. Radicals often traced these demands to the Duke of Richmond's reform agenda from a decade earlier in an effort to impart constitutional legitimacy to their own program. Eskgrove argued, however, that the associated meanings of such reforms became clearly seditious when placed within the context of the Convention's proceedings: "Still they run upon French expressions in every part of their minutes, in every speech in their Gazetteer, continuously recurring to French words, French terms, and French expressions."[53] Words, moderate and guarded, took on revolutionary meaning within a space governed by the style and specter of the real revolution in France.

Eskgrove's remarks pointed to one of the most pressing concerns of the government, which was to understand how to determine when words expressed became legally culpable as forms of action. For example, when in December the Convention had resolved to resist disbanding should parliament pass anti-convention legislation, did this mean that the Convention thereby had envisioned revolution? The resolution, according to Eskgrove, implied a contemplation of political violence, "that last and terrible decision, which comes to that in a neighbouring country, where blood and devastation are the certain consequences." The Convention was miming the Tennis Court Oath. Moreover, Gerrald's "ambiguous words" supporting the move revealed it as not simply a resolution of words but what Gerrald himself had called "a rule of action" – an awareness signaled by the "calm deliberative countenance of everyone present."[54] The resolution disclosed not merely the contemplation of violence but a determination on it – or did it? The problematic relationship between words and acts occupied a significant portion of this and other trials. Representing himself at trial, Margarot argued for a sharp distinction: "sedition must be some act; it cannot be a concealed operation of the mind, it must be an overt act." Yet he noted how the trial had turned on the reading of style: "there is that idea of our appearance being different from our real intention."[55] Eskgrove's strategy was effective, especially when combined with a hand-picked jury who returned a verdict of guilty.[56] As Margarot waited on board the prison hulk and then the *Surprize* transport ship during the spring of 1794, conservative and governmental commentators increasingly represented British radicalism as a thinly veiled, Jacobin conspiracy. However, the censorship of the state served not merely to restrict but to open a field of play, on which gestures that might otherwise be regarded as informal or insignificant assumed a dangerous edge. British Jacobin performance had been given a newly subversive valence by those who sought to repress its influence.

Conspiracy Unmasked

In May 1794, the government arrested thirty leading figures from five reform associations.[57] After collecting evidence – gleaned mainly from spies' reports and papers seized from the homes of those arrested – and interrogating prisoners, the government turned over the findings to a parliamentary committee in order to draft a report. The first and second reports of the parliamentary committees of secrecy, published in the summer of 1794, provided the most complete documentation of the government's case for the existence of a domestic conspiracy to overthrow the established constitution of the realm; it gave the road map for the English treason trials.[58] Again, the proceedings of the British Convention, plans to convene a further convention, communications with and praise for the French National Convention, the works of Paine, lists of toasts, and official addresses and resolutions from meetings and associations were reproduced. The reports wove a mass of disparate evidence into what was hoped to produce a coherent whole that any reasonable reader might grasp. This element of construction, which the government represented as natural inference, was not lost on commentators who defended the radical societies. Thus James Parkinson, radical surgeon and LCS member, maintained that "the connexion between the pretended conspiracies in London and in Edinburgh, is to be found not in the records of the popular Societies, but only in the registers of a Secret Committee."[59] As opposed to the candor and openness which radicals claimed for themselves and their societies, the government saw subterfuge. On the day the first report was released, Pitt argued in the parliamentary debate moving the suspension of habeas corpus that

> the House could not but remark upon the extraordinary manner in which those societies had varied their plans of operation; sometimes acting in audacious undisguised hostility, sometimes putting on the mask of attachment to the state and country; one day openly avowing their intentions, as if purposely to provoke the hand of justice; the next, putting on the mask of reform, and affecting the utmost zeal for the preservation of the constitution.[60]

Jacobinism was anything but transparent. Rather than revealing the "fragmented ideology" of reform, the different agendas, styles of agitation, and social composition of various associations (LCS, SCI, Friends of the People) paradoxically evidenced a unified conspiracy: "the result of deep design, matured, molded into shape, and fit for mischievous effect when opportunity arrived." In transforming this paradox into an obvious truth, radical performance played its role.

Of particular interest was the government's attempt to link the masked designs of British Jacobinism to the underworld of plebeian discontent. The committee of secrecy of the House of Commons reported that every possible artifice had been used to disseminate revolutionary principles – "to seduce and corrupt the thoughtless and uninformed" – taking the shape "even of play bills and songs, seditious toasts; and a studied selection of the tunes which have been in use in France since the revolution." The committee warned that this must be taken seriously: "The appearance of insignificance and levity, which belongs at first sight to this part of the system, is, in truth, only an additional proof of the art and industry with which it has been pursued."[61] In turn, we must take seriously the government's own paranoid style. The archive of state surveillance produced its own object, its own catalogue of misunderstanding. That such communicative modes must be understood as part of a "system" reflected authority's inability to comprehend the low culture of the street and tavern: the profane world of free and easies, raucous toasts and sing-songs, seditious riddles and blasphemous parody.[62] The danger they perceived, and here the government was surely right, was that "Jacobin" artisans and intellectuals might mediate between the literate culture of their own societies and the culture of this underworld; they might "seduce" the "thoughtless" by weaving subversive desire into the fabric of everyday life. During the crimp house riots of August 1794 (the most serious disorders since the Gordon riots), for example, authorities believed that the LCS was exploiting popular hostility to press gangs, spreading seditious propaganda on the streets and in the recruiting houses of the metropolis. Responding to this situation, Patrick Colquhoun, a Worship Street magistrate most active in providing information to the government, pressed the Home Office to detain ballad singers and hawkers for questioning, as "it is believed that they are made use of for the purpose of circulating Inflammatory and Seditious Writing."[63]

According to the reports of the committees of secrecy, Jacobin conspirators brought subversion from outside the locations of ordinary life. Rather than being part of the vernacular of everyday sociability and solidarity, radicalism mimed such practices: "The measures have been deliberately prepared, and every contrivance used to mix them (in the shape most likely to captivate attention) with the ordinary occupations or amusements of those on whom they were intended to operate."[64] According to William Hamilton Reid, "political missionaries" did not confine themselves to introducing "democratic songs" into benefit societies; "their business was to worm themselves into convivial societies of every kind." In his exposé of London's deist clubs, Reid, who was himself a knowing renegade from this culture, captured the texture of everyday irreverence.

> Next to songs, in which the clergy were a standing subject of abuse; in conjunction with pipes and tobacco, the tables of the club-rooms were frequently strewed with penny, two-penny, and three-penny publications, as it were so many swivels against established opinions while, to enable the members to furnish themselves with the heavy artillery of Voltaire, Godwin, &c. reading-clubs were formed. But still, so it happened, that those who despised the labour of reading, took their creeds from the extemporaneous effusions of others, whose talents were comparatively above their own.[65]

Reid's passage registers something else: the disdain that radicalism's intellectuals could express for those less serious than themselves and the distance separating them from this plebeian subculture. An uneasy tension existed between the LCS's formal emphasis on regulated behavior – including prohibitions on drinking, eating, smoking, speaking out of turn – and the less literate, unruly milieu of the taverns in which their sections usually met. The fervent desire for moral reform, educational improvement, and rational debate was often at odds with the norms of plebeian sociability (a theme take up in the next chapter).[66] Moreover, popular radicals often felt uncomfortable with their movement's own theatricality. Earnest artisans worried about pandering to popular irrationality and unrest; wary of appeals made to the senses rather than the mind, they were suspicious of rabble-rousing as opposed to deliberation. Radical claims to represent the people were founded on an appeal to rational transparency and modes of rational communication standing against the artifice of aristocratic spectacle and performance.

It was left to booksellers like Richard "Citizen" Lee and Thomas Spence, both LCS members, to tap the raw energies of the underworld of metropolitan discontent. Operating out of his British Tree of Liberty, which moved several times, Lee specialized in penny pamphlets and handbills, with titles such as *The Rights of Swine*, *License for the Guinea Pigs*, *The Death of Despotism and the Doom of Tyrants* (three poems published as a four-page handbill), and *The Happy Reign of George the Last, An Address to the Little Tradesmen, and Labouring Poor of England*.[67] In debates over the Two Acts in 1795 his republican tract *A Summary of the Duties [of] Citizenship*, and regicidal broadside *King Killing* – which concludes, "Let us destroy this huge Colossus, under which the tall aspiring head of liberty cannot pass!!!" – figured prominently.[68] Lee escaped to America.[69] Spence worked from his shop in Turnstile, Lincolns-Inn Fields, as a multimedia propagandist in the republican cause. Alive to the culture of the street and tavern, he turned revolutionary "bricoleur," re-mixing proverbs, millenarian prophecies, aphorisms, allegories, and songs in his pamphlets and cheap serial *Pig's Meat* (1793–95); he struck his own token coinage and chalked walls with republican slogans.[70] Spence was arrested on charges of treason in 1794, but was released following the acquittals of Hardy, John Horne Tooke, and Thelwall.

Playing at Revolution

It remains difficult to judge the success of radicalism's avant-garde in propagating their message farther down the social scale. Certainly, the government felt threatened by the prospect of such a conjuncture, but there were definite limits to radicalism's social reach and popular influence. During the early 1790s and the opening years of the war, the current of popular sentiment was predominately anti-French and anti-Jacobin.[71] We must credit the genuine appeal of popular loyalism and conservative patriotism – although mobilizing large-scale loyalist voluntary action raised its own dangers and called for careful handling.[72] But, as radicals understood, the heady mix of stout ale, bonfires, and licensed unruliness in the defense of British liberty, the constitution, church, and king attracted substantial numbers. Between late 1792 and early 1793, at the time of the trial and execution of Louis XVI, loyalists staged hundreds of effigy burnings of Thomas Paine in order to exhibit popular support and capture public space for loyalism.[73] Radicals faced harassment and intimidation not only from government and local authorities but from loyalists operating under semi-official sanction. At Sheffield, for example, the radical Henry Hill testified that loyalists threatened to pull down his house and burn it, "calling us Jacobines and Levellers, and calling the house Jacobine-hall, because the society [SCI] used sometimes to meet there."[74] In response to Jacobinism's submerged influence among the lower orders, the government extended its surveillance over unregulated spaces of everyday life. In addition to watchful government spies and constables, the royal proclamation of May 1792 invited private individuals to police spaces of urban sociability. Loyalist associations warned innkeepers and publicans that they could lose their licenses if they opened their rooms to seditious meetings. At Manchester, 186 innkeepers and alehouse-keepers signed a declaration banning "Jacobins" from their rooms; at Bath, 111 innkeepers and victualers did the same.[75] According to the LCS's missionary John Binns, the doors of Birmingham's loyalist taverns warned, "NO JACOBINS ADMITTED HERE."[76] Facing pressure from civil officials, proprietors of London's commercial debating societies banned political topics.[77] The taverns, coffeehouses, and debating societies of London, which earlier in the century Addison and Steele had regarded as spaces for engendering politeness and urban civility, became sites of seditious sociability and Jacobin performance.[78]

The stage was set for playing out (or overplaying) political pieces, for confrontations testing the courage of one's political convictions and for determining the limits of what could be expressed within public spaces. And while such incidents appear to arise from casual encounters, they were often highly stylized and calculated performances. The publicness of these encounters was crucial to both the government and to their radical opponents. Two well-studied examples (discussed more fully in Chapter 4) illustrate the hazards of Jacobin play.[79] On 6 November 1792, the attorney John Frost, who was a leading SCI member, dined at the Percy coffeehouse and tavern. When challenged by an acquaintance about the situation in France, from where he had recently returned, he loudly proclaimed his support for "equality" and "no king," refusing to back down when challenged. The encounter led Frost to trial at King's Bench, where he was convicted for words spoken, and to six months in Newgate prison. The following September, the LCS members Charles Pigott and William Hodgson went to the London Coffee House on Ludgate to read newspapers and engage in after-dinner conversation. Pigott was a notorious pamphleteer, dedicated to exposing the sexual misconduct of aristocrats.[80] As well as denouncing the king as a "German Hog Butcher," Hodgson boldly toasted "Equality" and the "French Republic." On being confronted by a group of loyalists, the men refused to drink to "The King," with Hodgson countering with a toast to "The French Republic, and May She Triumph Over All Her Enemies." On the basis of notes taken by informers, the republicans were arrested and driven to the New Compter, with Hodgson reportedly shouting from the coach window "Liberty!" "The French Republic!"[81] While a grand jury rejected the bill of indictment filed against Pigott, Hodgson was found guilty of seditious words, and followed Frost into Newgate prison for over two years.[82] These were "gentlemen" Jacobins, whose political opinions were well formulated and well known. Most anti-monarchical outbursts were less clearly staged and involved less prominent figures, but they often turned on similar challenges and resistance to loyalist coercion.[83]

Much could be said about what was going on in these and a host of similar confrontations that contributed to the mutual constitution of "Jacobinism," and formed an essential background to the treason trials. We might, for example, qualify idealized conceptions of the "public sphere" and the communicative conditions governing its classic sites that were hardly those of polite conversation and free exchange of ideas. We are here most interested in how republican sentiments were given public expression as performance. No doubt radicals such as Frost, Pigott, Hodgson, and others acted incautiously; at trial, they claimed to have been set up or to have been "in liquor." Still, it is difficult to escape the impression that radicals understood the risks they were taking and that their knowingness was matched by the excessiveness of their behavior; radicals did not merely play but overplayed their roles. Indeed, running a risk, playing on the edge, and perhaps getting away with it, these were part of the stakes of such unauthorized performance. It was this that endowed radicals' actions with the qualities of "deep" play.[84] By toasting and counter-toasting, exchanging words and slogans, in their refusals to back down, they were testing limits, exploring expressive boundaries, playing at the edge of the permissible – and perhaps suggesting other worlds, such as Hodgson's utopian commonwealth or Spence's "marine republic" of "Spensonia."[85] Here were cultural performances belonging to what Victor Turner has identified as the "subjunctive mood," conveying desires rather than actualities, hinting at "what might be."[86]

As the late Greg Dening observed, all societies mark out spaces "privileged for performance"; in the late eighteenth century, the trial, the gallows, and the theater were among those sites.[87] Courtrooms brought radicals into direct confrontation with the power and authority of the government and law. Trials possessed many of the attributes of theater: pomp and ritual spectacle, compelling stories, suspense and pathos, polished rhetoric and occasional humor. During the treason trials, the courtroom and gallery at Old Bailey were crowded, with spectators spilling out into the surrounding streets. Once more the government narrated the progress of British Jacobinism, in which the LCS – "formed on the principles of the Jacobin Club" and "spreading itself on the very model of those Societies in France" – figured at the center of an international conspiracy designed to bring "blood and desolation" to British shores.[88] The trials themselves restaged the performance of Jacobinism; this included radicalism's own appropriations of the theater. At Hardy's trial, the attorney general flourished a mock playbill that had captured the attention of the committee of secrecy. The broadside pasquinade advertised a new farce "called LA GUILLOTINE! or GEORGE'S HEAD IN THE BASKET!" to be performed at the "FEDERATION THEATRE IN EQUALITY SQUARE," on April fools' day, 4971, and featuring

> Dramatis Personae.
> Numpy the Third by Mr, GWELP,
> (Being the last time of his appearing in that character.)...
> Between Acts,
> A New Song, called "Twenty more, kill them!"
> By BOBADIL BRUNSWICK.
> Tight Rope Dancing from the Lamp-post,
> By Messrs CANTERBURY, YORK, DURHAM &c.
> In the course of the Evening, will be sung in full chorus,
> ÇA IRA,and
> BOB SHAVE GREAT GEORGE OUR ------!
> The whole to conclude with
> A GRAND DECAPITATION OF
> PLACEMEN, PENSIONERS, and GERMAN LEECHES.....
> *Vive la Liberté! Vive la République!*[89]

This playbill, which reappeared at Thelwall's trial, was introduced along with a spy's testimony about arming and magic lantern shows, with slides depicting scenes from the destruction of the Bastille.[90] The elusiveness of intent, however, behind such playful subversion rendered suspect the claim that "La Guillotine" was a text that offered clear access to the Jacobin mind or, at least, in terms of the overt acts required by the law of treason.

At Thelwall's trial, performance again figured prominently. John Taylor, journalist turned spy, testified about Thelwall's disruption of the theater. The theater was among the few socially heterogeneous spaces where reformers might stage confrontations with loyalists; moreover, the theaters at Covent Garden and Drury Lane were licensed by the government, giving an increased edge to any challenge to their authorized status. At his lecture on 31 January 1794, Thelwall told his audience that the next night Thomas Otway's *Venice Preserved* was opening at Covent Garden, passages of which he regarded as indicative of "true patriotism" and republican virtue. "He invited his friends, to meet him in the pit; he would have a book of the play in his hand, and if any of the passages were omitted, he would insist on their being recited. If it was performed as usual, they were to encore the favourite passages." In the event, Thelwall attended the theater with around twenty of his friends; according to Taylor, "[t]he piece was performed as usual, but their encores were not supported by the house."[91] Previous to Thelwall's intervention, Otway's play, which had originally been written to pay court to Charles II, was considered anything but subversive.[92] However, after one more night, the play was taken off. The LCS reprinted the lines that Thelwall had tried to encore as a cheap tract.[93] The significance of Thelwall's bit of counter-theater and his effort to steal Otway's play from the loyalist canon can only be understood when set against the enforced loyalism of the theater, where the audience had to stand and uncover their heads for the playing of "God Save the King," with military officers usually in attendance prepared to ensure compliance. Pigott's *Political Dictionary* thus defined "Theatre" as "the common sewer for the most beastly and most depraved sentiments of loyalty... It is in these places that a most impious, and blasphemous song is sung, during which time the obedient People are compelled, by force of arms, to stand up, uncovered, as if they were in church."[94] In 1792 the lord chamberlain warned Richard Sheridan, dramatist, theater manager, and Foxite Whig, to control the singing of the French revolutionary anthem "Ça Ira" in place of "God Save the King" at Drury Lane or his theater would be closed.[95]

As it happened, British radicalism's most sophisticated theoretician and celebrated orator was also its most theatrical or "enthusiastic." Thelwall was renowned for the theatricality of his lecturing style, for his use of "stage" effects to stir the passions of audiences.[96] According to John Gurney, one of Thelwall's lawyers who had heard him lecture, "he was a man liable in the warmth of speaking to be hurried away by his passion beyond the bounds of his cooler judgement."[97] The government compiled a catalogue of Thelwall's Jacobin posturing, much of which was presented at trial. His acting out of Jacobin allegiance was placed in evidence along with his avowal that he was a "true *Sans-Culotte*," his support of the Mountain as the best men to carry forward the Revolution, and his view that American liberty was burdened with "too great a reverence for property, too much religion and too much law."[98] Taylor testified that at a LCS meeting in February 1794, Thelwall had read aloud his own satire, "King Chaunticlere [sic]; or the Fate of Tyranny," which Thelwall had originally introduced the previous year at the Chapel Court debating society. Thelwall's barnyard fable was a sustained regicidal joke, in which farmer Thelwall was forced to behead the haughty game cock Chaunticlere for oppressing the "more industrious birds." The text had already formed the pretext for an earlier trial at which Daniel Isaac Eaton had been acquitted on charges of seditious libel.[99] Following Eaton's trial, Thelwall was reported to have toasted "God save the King – If God don't damn him, he will damn no man!" According to the government spy John Groves, after the LCS's great meeting at Chalk Farm on 14 April 1794, several LCS members retired to a tavern on Compton Street for dinner. Amidst "jokes about Sans Coulottes & [the] Swinish Multitude,"

Thelwall took up a pot of porter "and cut off the froth with a knife," and declared, "This is the Way I would serve kings." He then gave a toast to "The Lamp Iron at the End of Parliament Street."[100] Just before the government's round-up of "Jacobins" in May 1794, a spy reported on the SCI's anniversary dinner, held at the Crown and Anchor tavern, in the Strand, at which the 400 guests sang "Ça Ira" and the band played the "Carmagnole." Questioned by the Privy Council, the meeting's chairman John Wharton claimed that he disbanded the event after Thelwall jumped on a table and demanded the equalization of property.[101] The attorney general also presented to the jury a sheet of songs written by Thelwall that were sung at LCS meetings (songs had also been presented as evidence at Hardy's trial). The opening of "A Sheep Shearing Song" makes the government's point:

> But cease ye fleecing senators
> Your country to undo –
> Or know we British Sans Culottes
> Hereafter may fleece you,[102]

According to the crown prosecutor Serjeant James Adair the "secret purposes of men's hearts," were to be judged "[n]ot by the professions they made, not by the pretexts they held out to the ignorant and the unwary; but by their own acts coupled with their declarations."[103] Once again the jury was directed to disregard formal political statements or "considered speech" in favor of reading intent into "acts coupled with… declarations." Revolutionary songs and toasts, satirical allegory and after-dinner slogans, regicidal playbills and encoring theater performances, disclosed the secret purposes of the Jacobin heart. But however one interpreted the meaning of Thelwall's actions, the acts themselves were not very secret. The audience for his showmanship was composed of friends and fellow "Jacobins," but Thelwall performed openly at Covent Garden, the Beaufort lecture room, public houses, and dinners. Openness was critical to the contest over urban space and asserting freedom to express democratic sentiments within these spaces.

Of course, secrecy did pertain to certain acts, none more important than the acquisition of arms, which when linked to the summoning of conventions might well constitute an overt act of treason. As it turned out, this was something that the government was unable to prove to the satisfaction of juries. Just as the government maintained that irreverent play masked serious intent, radicals sought the legal shelter afforded by the ambiguities of performance, claiming that the government misread their actions. On occasion, radicals used public courtrooms to toy with established authority. At Hardy's trial, for example, the government labored to connect London's radical artisans to arming among members of the Sheffield SCI. Under examination, the Sheffield cutler William

Broomhead admitted that he and the radical carpenter Robert Moody had, indeed, been shown a small model for a night-cat (a four-pronged anti-cavalry weapon) at the shop of William Camage. While Broomhead claimed that the device was "only like the play thing of a child," presumably a jack, prosecution attorney William Garrow inquired, "What was the stated purpose of this play thing?" Broomhead merely responded that he recollected "no conversation upon that head," adding "but it was taken and thrown upon the floor." Garrow asked the witness if this act was not accompanied by any "description of the use it might be applied to, besides playing with it?" Broomhead demurred, "What might be said that night might not be serious." Having caught the witness in an apparent contradiction (having first testified that there had been no conversation about its purpose, he now claimed things might have been said), Garrow pressed him for the language that would disclose the real use of this "play thing." Broomhead repeatedly denied any speech regarding the cat being tossed to the floor, merely observing that those assembled responded by "laughing at it."[104] The model, the toss, the laughter itself remained subject to rival interpretations: what Broomhead claimed as harmless fun, Garrow figured as a small rehearsal for revolution. The testimony seemed to reveal a witness not merely involved in subversion but carrying subversion into the courtroom itself.

As highly public events, political trials reinforced popular understandings of Jacobinism as revolutionary in its intent, theatrical and playful in its expressive modes, and conspiratorial in its organization. Framed against the shifting Revolution in France, Jacobinism as produced in Britain by both the actions of radicals and the constraints imposed by government, became a template for subversion and serious play, performed in a dangerously parodic game with government.[105] The fluidity of roles, stances, and guises did not mean that radical identity was merely "up for grabs," endlessly and slyly assumable on the part of autonomous individuals. Rather, in an important sense, Jacobinism was citational, relying on an available set of representational images: the forthright cosmopolitan patriot, or the bloodthirsty, regicidal sans-culotte, for example. The development of British Jacobinism, as highlighted here – the forms dissent took – reflected both the individual agency of British republicans and the social construction of Jacobinism through a multitude of overlapping discourses. It was through social reiteration, appropriating vocabularies defining Jacobinism, that the subversive play of radicals might achieve its desired effect.[106]

The Closing of the "Jacobin Moment"

A month after the acquittals of Hardy, Horne Tooke, and Thelwall, as the House of Commons was consumed by debates over the meaning of the treason trials, the conservative John Bowles returned to the theatricality of British Jacobins, insisting that their performances offered true "windows into their minds." After rehearsing several of the instances cited in court, Bowles turned to the prisoners' behavior in court, as yet another sign of revolutionary desire. He reported:

> When one of [the prisoners] remarked, that the dagger-knives...were bread and cheese knives; the rest *smiled*. Although this is but a trivial circumstance, yet it is not difficult to develop from what emotion such smile [sic] of these reforming assassins proceeded.[107]

Bowles's mention of the cheeky Jacobin grins was anything but trivial; it went to the subtext of an ultra-radical culture, reveling in an elusive zone between stated claims and "true" intent and desire. In the space of the courtroom, according to Bowles, radicals had the audacity to gesture toward the secrets of a subaltern community even as they denied those very secrets. Yet three juries in succession had rejected the crown's argument that Jacobin style was sure evidence of interior disposition.

One year later, however, a conjuncture of events allowed Pitt's government to bring the curtain down on British Jacobin performance as an open mode of expression. On 29 October 1795, three days after the LCS staged a huge public meeting at Copenhagen Fields in Islington, and on the third day of a new run of *Venice Preserved*, a large crowd attacked George III on his way to open the new parliamentary session.[108] Pitt immediately brought forward the Seditious Meetings Bill, which severely restricted the availability of urban venues for political meetings.[109] Together with Lord Grenville's Treasonable Practices Bill, which effectively converted constructive treasons into substantive treason, making it easier to secure convictions, the government moved to shut down political dissent.[110] A full treatment of the reaction to the "Two Acts," which was national, sustained, and vehement, is outside the scope of our discussion. However, it is worth underscoring the reassertion of the linkage drawn between British Jacobinism and theater in the Commons' debates over the Seditious Meetings Bill – legislation which was crafted to contain performance-based dissent.[111]

The appropriation of the royal theater at Drury Lane for the radical cause formed a crucial background to these debates. In the days surrounding the assault on the king's carriage, Otway's play had again met with repeated interruptions by radicals. According to one observer, the purloined tragedy now constituted a political "Convention" in itself, which along with the attack on George III, "democrats call *well-timed*."[112] Supporters of the Seditious Meetings Bill portrayed the proposed legislation as an antidote to radical theatricality, singling out Thelwall's disturbing mixture of entertainment and politics, a blend suggestive of commercial theater.[113] John Anstruther, who had been a member of the prosecution team for Thelwall's trial, warned of the dangers of radical meetings, where "doctrines of holy insurrection and sovereignty were blended with amusement." Conservatives argued that audiences at radical lectures were subject to conditions of reception similar to those present at unregulated traditional theater. According to the MP George Hardinge, the bill remedied this by giving government the "power of access to the interior of the meeting; to the fountain-head of mischief in the oracles of sedition."[114] If radicalism was now dangerous theater, the Licensing Act of 1737, which structured the state's control of legitimate theater, provided legislative precedent for controlling the illegitimate theater of urban political sociability.[115] Thus Hardinge explicitly compared the Seditious Meetings Bill to the Licensing Act, demanding that parliament strike against "Mr. Thelwall's political theatre," and asking, "Are such theatres less prone to abuse [than official theater] for the purposes of sedition?"[116] Faced with the ambiguities of British Jacobin style, conservatives viewed plebeian political sociability as having all the dangerously liberating potentialities of the unregulated stage, including the imaginative power to summon subversive desire and turn it into action.

In late December 1795, the two bills received royal assent, and the conditions governing popular opposition to Pitt's government and expressions of support for democratic principles changed; despite attempts to maintain its public presence, the radical movement fragmented into quiescence, emigration, and the shadowy, revolutionary underground detailed by E. P. Thompson.[117] The "Jacobin moment," defined by possibilities for public identification with revolutionary principles associated with France, closed. One finds very occasional revivals of Jacobin ritual later during the war years, but they were distinguished by their rarity.[118] In conclusion, we should be clear about what we are arguing. First, we can discern a formally articulated strain of British Jacobinism which might include support for a democratic republic, a measure of social welfare reform or redistributive justice, and a defense of the French revolutionary principles of 1793, if not the violence of the Terror. And while Thelwall was hardly representative in terms of the coherence which he brought to such political expression, neither can he be considered as marginal to the radical movement. As he boldly explained in 1796,

> In this discussion I adopt the term *Jacobinism* without hesitation –
> 1. Because it is fixed upon us, as a stigma, by our enemies... –
> 2. Because, though, I abhor the sanguinary ferocity of the late Jacobins in France, yet their principles, generally speaking, are the most consonant with my ideas of reason, and the nature of man, of any that I have met with... I use the term Jacobinism simply to indicate *a large and comprehensive system of reform, not professing to be built upon the authorities and principles of the Gothic custumacy.*[119]

However, the purpose here has not been to correct the historical balance sheet by showing the existence of a significant faction of "real" or fully fledged British Jacobins. Rather, the goal has been to direct attention to something more ambiguous, something looser: a mood or temper inflecting political identification and allegiance. We have stressed the importance of communicative conditions governing all radical expression in the 1790s, particularly those imposed by government authority. Radical meanings cannot be understood independently from the terms restricting their articulation, including imperatives dictating strategies of indirection, the adaptation of language and behavior "on the margins of legal sanction."[120] In this sense, government prohibitions on expression were not wholly negative but productive of meaning. This did not mean, as the government claimed, that the constitutional rhetoric found in the manifestos of radical associations evidenced dissimulation or disguised conspiracy; on the contrary, such statements did, most certainly, represent the aims of radicalism. It was merely that constitutionalist-based reasoning and appeals for peaceful action did not exhaust the political desires of a moment that appeared to hold extraordinary democratic promise. The formal addresses, and the denials, of the LCS must be read against or along with more furtive gestures. At one level, adopting the Jacobin label was, as Thelwall indicated, to accept the stigma foisted on radicals by their enemies. But the restrictions placed on the movement and ideological ambiguities within democratic political culture more generally encouraged radicals to explore, to gesture toward Jacobin allegiance, to play outside the lines of safe formality. The government and loyalists' own assertion that these actions signaled serious intent, opening a window onto the Jacobin heart, made improvised performance all the more potent. In the play, we catch a glimpse at an unprescribed and unfinished script, desires displaced onto an ambiguous edge of becoming. Perhaps that is as close as we can come to grasping the meaning of British Jacobinism.

Acknowledgments

An earlier version of this chapter was published in James Epstein and David Karr, "Playing at Revolution: British 'Jacobin' Performance," *Journal of Modern History* 79 (September 2007): 495–530. ©2007 by The University of Chicago.

Notes

1 William Fox, *On Jacobinism* (1794), 4, 1–2.
2 Lord [Henry Thomas] Cockburn, *Memorials of His Time* (Edinburgh, 1856), 82.
3 A careful analysis is offered by John Dinwiddy, "Conceptions of Revolution in the English Radicalism of the 1790s," in *Radicalism and Reform in Britain, 1780–1850* (Hambledon Press, 1992), 169–94. See also, for example,

Albert Goodwin, *The Friends of Liberty: The English Democrat Movement in the Age of the French Revolution* (Cambridge, MA: Harvard University Press, 1979); H. T. Dickinson, *Liberty and Property: Political Ideology in Eighteenth-Century Britain* (Weidenfeld and Nicholson, 1977), 259–69; Mark Philp, "The Fragmented Ideology of Reform," and "English Republicanism in the 1790s," in *Reforming Ideas in Britain: Politics and Language in the Shadow of the French Revolution, 1789–1815* (Cambridge: CUP, 2014), 11–40, and 102–32; Richard Whatmore, "'A Gigantic Manliness': Paine's Republicanism in the 1790s," in *Economy, Polity, and Society: British Intellectual History 1750–1950*, ed. Stefan Collini, Richard Whatmore, and Brian Young (Cambridge: CUP, 2000), 135–57; Benjamin Weinstein, "Popular Constitutionalism and the London Corresponding Society," *Albion* 34 (2002): 35–57. Compare E. P. Thompson, *The Making of the English Working Class* (Gollancz, 1963), chapter 5; also Michael H. Scrivener, *Seditious Allegories: John Thelwall and Jacobin Writing* (University Park: Pennsylvania State University Press, 2001), chapter 1. Jonathan Clark claims that "Jacobinism" rather than "radicalism" was the "more obviously useful term to characterise the reforming doctrines of the 1790s," using the term without qualification throughout his work to refer to radical reformers and their political views. J. C. D. Clark, *English Society 1660–1832: Religion, Ideology and Politics during the Ancien Regime* (Cambridge: CUP, 2000), 8.

4 On this, see Roger Wells, *Insurrection: The British Experience, 1795–1803* (Gloucester: Alan Sutton, 1983), and "English Society and Revolutionary Politics in the 1790s: The Case for Insurrection," in *The French Revolution and British Popular Politics*, ed. Mark Philp (Cambridge: CUP, 1991), 188–226; Marianne Elliott, *Partners in Revolution: The United Irishmen and France* (New Haven, CT: Yale University Press, 1982); J. Ann Hone, *For the Cause of Truth: Radicalism in London, 1796–1821* (Oxford: OUP, 1982), chapter 2; Alan Booth, "The United Englishmen and Radical Politics in the Industrial North-West of England, 1795–1803," *International Review of Social History* 31 (1986): 271–97; Elaine W. McFarland, "Scottish Radicalism in the later Eighteenth Century: 'The Social Thistle and Shamrock,'" in *Eighteenth Century Scotland: New Perspectives*, ed. T. M. Devine and J. R. Young (East Linton: Tuckwell Press, 1999), 275–98.

5 For an assessment of the more general turn to performance in historical studies, see Peter Burke, "Performing History: The Importance of Occasions," *Rethinking History* 9 (2005): 35–52.

6 Roger Chartier, *On the Edge of the Cliff: History, Language, and Practices*, trans. Lydia G. Cochrane (Baltimore, MD: Johns Hopkins University Press, 1997), 59. Our approach shares much in common with that of Jon Mee, thinking of language "as embedded in social practice" and understanding the contests over these practices as essential to radical politics. Jon Mee, *Print, Publicity, and Popular Radicalism in the 1790s*: The Laurel of Liberty (Cambridge: CUP, 2016), 20.

7 Judith Butler, *Excitable Speech: A Politics of the Performative* (New York: Routledge, 1997), 131–33, and chapter 4 in general.

8 Patrice Higonnet, *Goodness Beyond Virtue: Jacobins during the French Revolution* (Cambridge, MA: Harvard University Press, 1995), 20, 36–44. See also Michael L. Kennedy, *The Jacobin Clubs in the French Revolution: The First Years* (Princeton, NJ: Princeton University Press, 1982), *The Jacobin Clubs in the French Revolution: The Middle Years* (Princeton, NJ: Princeton University Press, 1988), and *The Jacobin Clubs in the French Revolution: 1793–1795* (New York: Berghahn Books, 2000).

9 For Jacobinism under the Directory, see Isser Woloch, *Jacobin Legacy: The Democratic Movement under the Directory* (Princeton, NJ: Princeton University Press, 1970).

10 For a compelling treatment that captures "the moving reality" of the Revolution, and attempts to understand the emotion of fear and the contingencies that produced responses of revolutionary violence, see Timothy Tackett, *The Coming of the Terror in the French Revolution* (Cambridge, MA: Harvard University Press, 2015).

11 Mary Wollstonecraft, *An Historical and Moral View of the Origins and Progress of the French Revolution and the Effect It Has Produced in Europe* (New York: Scholars' Facsimiles and Reprints, 1975, first published 1795), 510–12, 467, 355. In fact, Wollstonecraft's view of the Revolution was both more complex and conflicted than this. For a careful interpretation, see Tom Furniss, "Mary Wollstonecraft's French Revolution," in *The Cambridge Companion to Mary Wollstonecraft*, ed. Claudia L. Johnson (Cambridge: CUP, 2002), 59–81, particularly.70–73.

12 David Simpson, *Romanticism, Nationalism, and the Revolt against Theory* (Chicago, IL: Chicago University Press, 1993), 4.

13 See Higonnet's analysis of Jacobin ideology and practice, in *Goodness Beyond Virtue*.

14 See Günther Lottes, "Radicalism, Revolution and Political Culture: An Anglo-French Comparison," in Philp, ed., *French Revolution and British Popular Politics*, 78–98; Philp, "English Republicanism."

15 Lynn Hunt, *Politics, Culture, and Class in the French Revolution* (Berkeley: University of California Press, 1984), 26–30.

16 J. B. O'Brien, *Life and Character of Maximilian Robespierre* (1838), and his earlier series of articles, "Real Character of Robespierre," *Poor Man's Guardian*, beginning 24 November 1832; Alfred Plummer, *Bronterre: A Political Biography of Bronterre O'Brien, 1804–1864* (Allen and Unwin, 1971), quotation at 68–69; Michael J. Turner, *Radicalism and Reputation: The Career of Bronterre O'Brien* (East Lansing: Michigan State University Press, 2017), 123–33. See also J. B. O'Brien, *Dissertation and Elegy on Maximilian Robespierre* (1859), in which Robespierre, St. Just, and Couthon are held up as the only worthy leaders of the Revolution.

17 A. R. Schoyen, *The Chartist Challenge: A Portrait of George Julian Harney* (Heinemann, 1958), 14, 161. On the anniversary of the French republic, Harney renounced the Girondists as constitutionalists, and praised Robespierre, St. Just, Marat, and Couthon as true revolutionaries. *Northern Star*, 27 September 1845.

18 Gregory Claeys, ed., *The Politics of English Jacobinism: Writings of John Thelwall* (University Park: Pennsylvania State University Press, 1995), xiii–lviii. The scholarship on Thelwall is large, but see in particular, E. P. Thompson, "Hunting the Jacobin Fox," in *The Romantics: England in a Revolutionary Age* (Woodbridge: Merlin Press, 1997), 156–217; Scrivener, *Seditious Allegories*; Andrew McCann, *Cultural Politics in the 1790s: Literature, Radicalism and the Public Sphere* (Houndmills: Palgrave Macmillan,1999), chapter 3; Steve Poole, ed., *John Thelwall: Radical Romantic and Acquitted Felon* (Pickering & Chatto, 2009); Mee, *Print, Publicity, and Popular Radicalism*, chapter 6.

19 TS 11/953, "Papers relating to the London Corresponding Society and Constitution Society," c. 1794, and TS 11/3506, Thelwall to [John] Allum, 13 February 1794, expressing his respect for Brissot, and his view that "the prevailing party are …… too little scrupulous of shedding blood, though of

this I am by no means as certain as some appear to be, and I make allowance for the situation in which the Despots of Europe have placed them."

20 Compare Michael Scrivener, "John Thelwall's Political Ambivalence: Reform and Revolution," in *Radicalism and Revolution in Britain, 1775–1848: Essays in Honour of Malcolm I. Thomis*, ed. Michael T. Davis (Houndmills: Palgrave Macmillan, 2000), 69–83.

21 Michael Scrivener, *The Cosmopolitan Ideal in the Age of Revolution and Reaction, 1776–1832* (Pickering & Chatto, 2007); Sophia Rosenthal, "Citizens of Nowhere in Particular: Cosmopolitanism, Writing, and Political Engagement in Eighteenth-Century Europe," *National Identities* 4 (2002): 25–43; Linda Colley, "Radical Patriotism in Eighteenth-Century England," in *Patriotism: The Making and Unmaking of British Identity*, vol. 1: *History and Politics*, ed. Raphael Samuel (Routledge, 1989), 169–87.

22 *Tribune*, 18 April 1795, 1: 132–33. See also [Richard Lee], *A Summary of the Duties of Citizenship, Written Expressly for Members of the London Corresponding Societies* (1795).

23 This is not to deny the strength of anti-war sentiment or the need to view patriotism as a highly variegated phenomenon. See J. E. Cookson, *The British Armed Nation, 1793–1815* (Oxford: OUP, 1997), 8–9.

24 Thelwall and his wife did name their two sons after the seventeenth-century martyrs, John Hampden and Algernon Sidney, both of whom were also heroes for French revolutionaries.

25 *Tribune*, 25 April 1795, 1:155–56. Significantly, he compared 1649, and not 1688, to 1789.

26 Ibid., 23 May 1795, 1: 241–42, 256–58. In this piece he also condemned Robespierre's lack of moderation and "tender sympathies," his gloomy fanaticism and "the monstrous vice of suspicion." In much the same spirit, defending the Revolution's glory, see LCS leader John Gale Jones, *Sketch of a Speech Delivered at the Westminster Forum…… on the Following Question: "Which have proved themselves the true friends of their King and country, those persons who have endeavoured to procure a constitutional reform in Parliament, or those who have opposed that measure as ill-timed and dangerous?"* (1795), 15–18.

27 Claeys, *Politics of English Jacobinism*, xxxv–lvi, and "Origins of the Rights of Labor: Republicanism, Commerce, and the Construction of Modern Social Theory in Britain, 1796–1805," *JMH* 66 (1994): 249–90; Iain Hampsher-Monk, "John Thelwall and the Eighteenth-Century Radical Response to Political Economy," *HJ* 34 (1991): 1–20; Robert Lamb, "Labour, Contingency, Utility: Thelwall's Theory of Property," in Poole, ed., *Thelwall*, 51–60.

28 John Thelwall, *The Rights of Nature Against the Usurpations of Establishments… … in Reply to the False Principles of Burke* (1796), Letter 1, p. 16.

29 *Tribune*, vol. 3, no. 46, 256, for a statement of the rights of "every man, and every woman, and every child" to comforts beyond the "necessaries of life."

30 On this point, see William Sewell, Jr., *Work and Revolution in France: The Language of Labor from the Old Regime to 1848* (Cambridge: CUP, 1980), 100–13; Gwyn A. Williams, *Artisans and Sans-Culottes: Popular Movements in France and Britain during the French Revolution* (Edward Arnold, 1968), 43–44. Neither Jacobins nor sans-culottes advocated equal distribution of property.

31 There were rare exceptions, most notably Thomas Spence who addressed himself to working women in his *The Rights of Infants; or, the imprescriptable Right of Mothers to such share of the Elements as is sufficient to enable them to suckle and bring up their Young* (1797).

32 See more generally, Gregory Claeys, "The French Revolution Debate and British Political Thought," *History and Political Thought* 11 (1990): 59–80. The LCS consistently denied the charge that their concept of "natural equality" extended to property.

33 William Hodgson, *The Commonwealth of Reason* (1795), 74–75, 78–80, 86–95, 99–100. The original translator of Baron d'Holbach's *System of Nature* into English, Hodgson was a leading infidel radical. See Stephen M. Lee, "William Hodgson," *ODNB*; Iain McCalman, *Radical Underworld: Prophets, Revolutionaries and Pornographers in London, 1793–1840* (Cambridge: CUP, 1988), 88, 158, 160, for his later political activity.

34 William Hodgson, *Proposals for publishing by subscription a treatise called the Female Citizen, or a historical enquiry into the rights of women* (1796). This treatise appears not to have been published.

35 For Thelwall's concept of racial equality, see Marcus Wood, *Slavery, Empathy, and Pornography* (Oxford: OUP, 2002), 169–80. For Hardy and his wife Lydia's friendship with Olaudah Equiano and commitment to the abolition of slavery, see Peter Linebaugh and Marcus Rediker, *The Many-Headed Hydra: Sailors, Slaves, Commoners, and the Hidden History of the Revolutionary Atlantic* (Boston, MA: Beacon Press, 2000), 334–41.

36 This group would also include Henry Redhead Yorke. See Amanda Goodrich, *Henry Redhead Yorke, Colonial Radical: Politics and Identity in the Atlantic World, 1772–1813* (Routledge, 2019), chapters 3–5.

37 Thus Thelwall recommended to his friend, "Seal your Letters with a Wafer, and then some good Wax over it." TS 11/951/3495, Thelwall to John Vellum [Allum], 10 March 1794. See more generally, John Barrell, *The Spirit of Despotism: Invasions of Privacy in the 1790s* (Oxford: OUP, 2006).

38 John Binns, *Recollections of the Life of John Binns* (Philadelphia, 1854), 45.

39 For a balanced discussion of Pitt and his government's motivations and policy, see Jennifer Mori, *William Pitt and the French Revolution, 1785–1795* (Edinburgh: Keele University Press, 1997), particularly chapter 8. See also Frank O'Gorman, "Pitt and the 'Tory' Reaction to the French Revolution and the French Wars, 1789–1815," in *Britain and the French Revolution, 1789–1815*, ed. H. T. Dickinson (New York: St. Martin's Press, 1989), 21–37, particularly 28–37.

40 *PH*, vol. 31 cols. 518–19, Commons, 16 May 1794. On Burke's theatrics, see Gillian Russell, "Burke's Dagger: Theatricality, Politics and Print Culture in the 1790s," *British Journal for Eighteenth-Century Studies* 20 (1997): 1–16. In *Letters on a Regicide Peace* (1796), Burke later claimed that out of a British "publick" or "people," whose number he put at 400,000, one-fifth were "Jacobins."

41 For an authoritative account, see John Barrell, *Imagining the King's Death: Figurative Treason, Fantasies of Regicide, 1793–1796* (Oxford: OUP, 2000). See also Alan Wharman, *The Treason Trials, 1794* (Leicester: Leicester University Press, 1992). For the Scottish trials, see Michael T. Davis, "Prosecution and Radical Discourses during the 1790s: The Case of the Scottish Sedition Trials," *International Journal of the Sociology of Law* 33 (2005): 148–58; and Emma Macleod, "The English and Scottish State Trials of the 1790s Compared," in *Political Trials in the Age of Revolutions: Britain and the North Atlantic, 1793–1848*, ed. Michael T. Davis, Emma Macleod, and Gordon Pentland (Cham: Palgrave Macmillan, 2019), 79–108.

42 According to the English statute of treasons, 25 Edward III (1351), the first of seven specified offences is "when a man doth compass or imagine the death of our lord the king." The meaning of these words and what constituted

what were termed "overt acts" drew plenty of contemporary commentary, most famously William Godwin's *Cursory Strictures on the Charge delivered by Lord Chief Justice Eyre* (1794). See also, for example, [Benjamin Hobhouse], *An Enquiry into What Constitutes the Crime of "Compassing and Imagining the King's Death," According to The Statute of Ed. 3* (Gloucester, 1795).

43 For accounts of the Scottish conventions, see Goodwin, *Friends of Liberty*, chapter 8; Henry W. Meikle, *Scotland and the French Revolution* (Glasgow: J. Maclehose and Son, 1912); Gordon Pentland, "Patriotism, Universalism and the Scottish Conventions, 1792–1794," *History* 89 (2004): 340–60.

44 The minutes of the British Convention are reprinted in *ST*, vol. 23, "Proceedings on the Trial of William Skirving," cols. 391–471. Extracts of the minutes are reprinted in *The Second Report of the Committee of Secrecy of the House of Commons ...... To Which are Added the First and Second Reports of the House of Lords* (1794), 100–11.

45 Cockburn, *Memorials of His Time*, 80. See also Gordon Pentland, "The French Revolution, Scottish Radicalism and the 'People Who were Called Jacobins,'" in *Reactions to Revolution: The 1790s and Their Aftermath*, ed. Ulrich Broich, et al. (Berlin: LIT Verlag, 2007), 85–108.

46 Lord [Henry Thomas] Cockburn, *An Examination of the Trials for Sedition ... in Scotland*, 2 vols. (Edinburgh, 1888), 1: 25. For general discussion of elite attitudes to the "impudence" of the lower orders, see Don Herzog, *Poisoning the Mind of the Lower Orders* (Princeton, NJ: Princeton University Press, 1998), 214–16, and chapter 5.

47 *The Times*, 13 May 1794, as quoted in David Vincent, *Testaments of Radicalism: Memoirs of Working Class Politicians 1790–1885* (Europa, 1977), 60, n.16.

48 On dress in the French Revolution, see Richard Wrigley, *The Politics of Appearances: Representations of Dress in the French Revolution* (Oxford: Berg, 2002); Lynn Hunt, "Freedom of Dress in the French Revolution," in *From the Royal to the Republican Body: Incorporating the Political in Seventeenth- and Eighteenth-Century France*, ed. Sara E. Melzer and Kathryn Norberg (Berkeley: University of California Press, 1998), 224–49.

49 Cockburn, *Trials for Sedition*, 43–44. For Gerrald's trial, see James Epstein, *In Practice: Studies in the Language and Culture of Popular Politics in Modern Britain* (Stanford, CA: Stanford University Press, 2003), chapter 3.

50 *Tribune*, vol. 3, no. 44, 212; ibid., vol. 2, no. 29, 302–03; Thomas Hardy, *Memoir of Thomas Hardy, Founder of, and Secretary to, the London Corresponding Society* (1832), reprinted in Vincent, *Testaments of Radicalism*, 71. In fact, the phrase has a deep history in the Anglo-American world. See Frederic M. Litto, "Addison's *Cato* in the Colonies," *William and Mary Quarterly* 23 (1966): 431–49.

51 As Alexander Welsh notes, the summary phase of trials offers the clearest instances where evidential claims are brought together into a coherent narrative whole. Alexander Welsh, *Strong Representations: Narrative and Circumstantial Evidence in England* (Baltimore, MD: Johns Hopkins University Press, 1992), chapter 1.

52 *The Trial of Maurice Margarot, delegate from London to the British Convention, before the High Court of Justiciary at Edinburgh, on the 13th and 14th of January 1794, for Sedition* (Edinburgh, 1794), 119–20, 123. In his tract *A Convention the Only Means of Saving Us from Ruin* (1794), Gerrald legitimated the British Convention on Anglo-Saxon precedent.

53 *Trial of Maurice Margarot*, 118.
54 Ibid., 123. For the Convention's struggle over how far to carry resistance should parliament pass anti-convention legislation, see Barrell, *Imagining the King's Death*, 153–57.
55 *Trial of Maurice Margarot*, 128–29.
56 For Margarot's subsequent history, see Michael Roe, "Maurice Margarot: A Radical in Two Hemispheres," *Bulletin of the Institute of Historical Research* 31 (1958): 68–78, and Chapter 7.
57 PC 1/21/A.35 (b), pt. 2, list dated 13 July 13, 1794; Barrell, *Imagining the King's Death,* 90–91.
58 The *First Report* was written upon review by the Secret Committee of the materials seized in the initial roundup of prisoners, and was presented to the Commons on 16 May. The *Second Report from the Committee of Secrecy appointed by the House of Commons* was produced on 6 June, after review of material collected after that period, and after initial interrogation of prisoners. *PH*, vol. 31, cols. 475–97, Commons, 688–879.
59 James Parkinson, *A Vindication of the London Corresponding Society* (1794), 9.
60 *PH*, vol. 31, col. 500, Commons, 16 May 1794. In the debate on the second report, Pitt argued, "Whatever shades or nice distinctions adopted by the different societies, there existed a systematic design" to subvert the constitution. *PH*, vol. 31, col. 914, Commons, 6 June 1795.
61 *Second Report of the Committee of Secrecy*, 26, 8.
62 See McCalman, *Radical Underworld*, and "Ultra-Radicalism and Convivial Debating-Clubs in London, 1795–1838," *EHR* 102 (1987): 309–33.
63 HO 42/33, Colquhoun to Portland, 21 August 21, 1794, fol. 160, cited in Mori, *William Pitt and the French Revolution*, 242–44; John Stevenson, "The London 'Crimp' Riots of 1794," *International Review of Social History* 16 (1971): 40–58.
64 *Second Report of the Committee of Secrecy*, 8.
65 William Hamilton Reid, *The Rise and Dissolution of Infidel Societies in this Metropolis* (1800), 20, 8. For Reid, see Iain McCalman, "The Infidel as Prophet: William Reid and Blakean Radicalism," in *Historicizing Blake*, ed. Steve Clark and David Worrall (Houndmills: Palgrave Macmillan, 1994), 24–42.
66 In their accounts of the LCS, Hardy and Francis Place placed particular emphasis on the society's rules and good order. See Chapter 2.
67 TS 11/837 (2832), crown brief, King vs. Lee, for copies of these and other of Lee's publications. On Lee, see Barrell, *Imagining the King's Death*, 608–22; Mee, *Print, Publicity, and Popular Radicalism*, chapter 5.
68 *History of the Two Acts* (1796), 204–07, 214, 231, 274–75. *The Duties of Citizenship* (1795) claimed to be written "expressly" for the LCS, a claim that the society denied.
69 For Lee's subsequent career as a radical publisher in Philadelphia, see Michael Durey, *Transatlantic Radicals and the Early American Republic* (Lawrence: University Press of Kansas, 1997).
70 See Marcus Wood, *Radical Satire and Print Culture, 1790–1822* (Oxford: OUP, 1994), chapter 2, and "Thomas Spence and Modes of Subversion," *ED* 10 (1991): 51–77; David Worrall, *Radical Culture: Discourse, Resistance and Surveillance* (Detroit, MI: Wayne State University Press, 1992), chapter 1. For the use of Lévi-Strauss's concept of "bricolage," see Jon Mee, *Dangerous Enthusiasm: William Blake and the Culture of Radicalism in the 1790s* (Oxford: OUP, 1992), 3–5.

71 John Dinwiddy, "England," in *Nationalism in the Age of the French Revolution*, ed. Otto Dann and John Dinwiddy (Hambledon, 1988), 53–70, 66–68; Thompson, *Making*, 78, 181–82, 603, for the later shift in popular sentiment.

72 Mark Philp, "Vulgar Conservatism," in *Reforming Ideas in Britain*; H. T. Dickinson, "Popular Conservatism and Militant Loyalism," in *Britain and the French Revolution*, 103–25; Michael Duffy, "Pitt and the Origins of the Loyalist Association Movement of 1792," *HJ* 39 (1996): 943–62; Austin Gee, *The British Volunteer Movement, 1794–1814* (Oxford: OUP, 2003). On popular monarchy, see Linda Colley, "The Apotheosis of George III: Loyalty, Royalty and the British Nation," *P&P* 102 (1984): 94–129.

73 Nicholas Rogers, "Burning Tom Paine: Loyalism and Counter-Revolution in Britain, 1792–1793," *Histoire Sociale/Social History* 32 (1999): 139–71; Frank O'Gorman, "The Paine Burnings of 1792–1793," *P&P* 193 (2006): 111–55.

74 *The Genuine Trial of Thomas Hardy for High Treason*, 2 vols. (1795), l: 426. See more generally, Alan Booth, "Popular Loyalism and Public Violence in the North-West of England, 1790–1800," *SH* 8 (1983): 295–313; Michael T. Davis, "The British Jacobins and the Unofficial Terror of Loyalism," in *Terror: From Tyrannicide to Terrorism*, ed. Brett Bowden and Michael T. Davis (Brisbane: University of Queensland Press, 2008), 92–113.

75 Archibald Prentice, *Historical Sketches and Personal Recollections of Manchester* (1851), 7–8; Thomas Walker, *A Review of Some of Events which have Occurred in Manchester* (1794), 41–44.

76 Binns, *Recollections*, 69–72.

77 Mary Thale, "London Debating Societies in the 1790s," *HJ* 32 (1989): 57–86.

78 See, for example, John Roach, *Roach's London Pocket Pilot* (1793), 51, where "the Union ...... should certainly change its name to the Jacobin, or Tom's [Paine's] Coffeehouse. The first waiter is an open mouthed republican ...... In short, it is a DEMOCRATIC DRAMA."

79 See Barrell, *Spirit of Despotism*, chapter 2; James Epstein, "'Equality and No King': Sociability and Sedition, the Case of John Frost," in *Romantic Sociability: Social Networks and Literary Culture in Britain, 1770–1840*, ed. Gillian Russell and Clara Tuite (Cambridge: CUP, 2002), 43–61.

80 For Pigott, see Nicholas Rogers, "Pigott's Private Eye: Radicalism and Sexual Scandal in Eighteenth-Century England," *JCHA* 4 (1993): 247–63; Mee, *Print, Publicity, and Popular Radicalism*, chapter 4.

81 *Oracle*, 3 October 1793, as quoted in Barrell, *Spirit of Despotism*, 88.

82 This brief account is based on Charles Pigott, *Persecution: The Case of Charles Pigott: Contained in the Defence He had Prepared and Would Have Delivered* (1793), and William Hodgson's preface to his *Commonwealth of Reason*, vii–xi. Unable to come up with the fine and sureties, Hodgson languished in Newgate beyond his two years, and was finally released in 1797 by means of a public subscription.

83 TS 11/- files are full of similar cases. For a good sampling, see Barrell, *Imagining the King's Death*, 100–3, 214–15.

84 See Greg Dening, *Mr. Bligh's Bad Language: Passion, Power and Theatre on the Bounty* (Cambridge: CUP, 1992), 79–80. The term "deep play" is borrowed from Clifford Geertz.

85 See Thomas Spence, *Marine Republic, or a Description of Spensonia* (1794).

86 Victor Turner, "Liminality and the Performative Genres," in *Rite, Drama, Festival, and Spectacle: Rehearsals toward a Theory of Cultural*

Performance, ed. John J. MacAloon (Philadelphia, PA: Institute for the Study of Human Issues, 1984), 19–41, 20–21.

87 Greg Dening, *Performances* (Chicago, IL: University of Chicago Press, 1996), 116–17.

88 *State Trials for High Treason, Embellished with Portraits, part third, containing the Trial of Mr. John Thelwall* (1795),13, Sergeant Adair's opening speech to the jury.

89 *The Trial of Thomas Hardy for High Treason ...... Taken in Short-hand by Joseph Gurney*, 4 vols. (1795), 2: 293–94. In fact, the handbill seems to have been suppressed so effectively that no known copies survive and the full contents are known only because of the trial transcripts. John Barrell, "'An Entire Change of Performances?' The Politicisation of Theatre and the Theatricalisation of Politics in the Mid 1790s," *Lumen* 17 (1998): 11–50, 18.

90 *Trial of Thomas Hardy*, 2: 300.

91 *Trial of Mr. John Thelwall*, 43, 35–36; TS 11/959/3505, "Report of evidence against Thelwall, Richter, Lovat [Lovett], Hardy," dated 3 May 1794, and spy's report on Thelwall's lecture. Thelwall was referring to the "liberty and revenge" dialogue between the conspirators Jaffeir and Pierre in Act II, scene 2.

92 For further appropriations of *Venice Preserved* and general discussion of the relationship between radical politics and theater, see John Barrell, "'An Entire Change of Performances?,'" and "Popular Political Culture in the Mid 1790s," *Anglistentag 1995 Greifswald: Proceedings*, ed. Jürgen Klein and Dirk Banderbeke (Tübingen: Max Niemeyer Verlag, 1996): 15–27; Jon Mee, "The Political Showman at Home: Reflections on Popular Radicalism and Print Culture in the 1790s," in Davis, ed., *Radicalism and Revolution*, 41–55.

93 TS 11/959/3505. The tract is also preserved in BL, Add. MS. 27828, fol. 3/4.

94 Charles Pigott, *A Political Dictionary: Explaining the True Meaning of Words* (1795), 148. On the military connection to the theater, see Gillian Russell, *The Theatres of War: Performance, Politics and Society, 1793–1815* (Oxford: OUP 1995), particularly chapter 5. For the possibility of staging "Jacobin" drama, see Chapter 3.

95 LC 7/74, "Letter to Richard Brinsley Sheridan from the Lord Chamberlain's Office," 30 March 1792.

96 See Jon Mee, *Romanticism, Enthusiasm, and Regulation: Poetics and the Policing of Culture in the Romantic Period* (Oxford: OUP, 2002), particularly chapter 2; Gillian Russell, "Spouters or Washerwomen: The Sociability of Romantic Lecturing," in Russell and Tuite, eds., *Romantic Sociability*, 123–44, 125–29; Thompson, *The Romantics*, 158–59. This was precisely what Godwin found objectionable about Thelwall's lecturing. However, as Mee argues, Thelwall was profoundly ambivalent about enthusiasm as a mode of producing sympathy.

97 *Trial of Mr. John Thelwall*, 32. Francis Place later noted that Thelwall's lectures contained "much bombast and loose declamation." BL, Add. MS. 27808, fol. 36.

98 *Trial of Mr. John Thelwall*, 21.

99 Ibid., 36; *Politics for the People*, vol. 1, 1793, no. 8, 102–07; TS 11/951, 3495, "King against Daniel Isaac Eaton;" *ST*, vol. 23, "Trial of Daniel Isaac Eaton," cols. 1013–54. See more generally, Michael T. Davis, "'Good for the Public Example': Daniel Isaac Eaton, Prosecution, Punishment and Recognition, 1793–1812," in *Radicalism and Revolution*, 110–32.

100 TS 11/3498, "Report, 14th April, Mr. Groves." Thelwall's exact words were variously reported. So, for example, TS 11/958/3503, the spy John Powell reported him as having said, "This is the way I would serve all tyrants."

101 TS 11/3498, Groves, "Report of the Anniversary Meeting of the Constitutional Society," 2 May 1794. A report of this dinner, including eighteen after-dinner toasts, was read out in court at Hardy's trial. *Trial of Thomas Hardy*, 2: 119–20.

102 *Tribune*, 1, 25 April 1795: 190–92, reprints in full this and the two other songs presented to the jury. See also Cecil Thelwall, *The Life of John Thelwall, By His Widow* (1837), 267–68. A song found at Hardy's house was produced at trial, which asked, "And shall a crown preserve the head/Of him who robs a nation?"

103 *Trial of Thelwall*, 12.

104 *Trial of Thomas Hardy*, 2: 179–81, and 272–73, for Moody's testimony.

105 On parody and performative reiteration, see Judith Butler, "For a Careful Reading," in *Feminist Contentions: A Philosophical Exchange*, ed. Seyla Benhabib, et al. (New York: Routledge, 1995), 119–43, and *Bodies that Matter: On the Discursive Limits of "Sex"* (New York: Routledge, 1993), 220; Vikki Bell, "Performativity and Belonging: An Introduction," special issue of *Theory, Culture and Society* 16 (2) (1999): 1–10.

106 As Butler writes, "Construction is not opposed to agency; it is the necessary *scene* of agency, the very terms in which agency is articulated and becomes culturally intelligible." Judith Butler, *Gender Trouble: Feminism and the Subversion of Identity* (New York: Routledge, 1990), 147. See also Terry Lovell, "Resisting with Authority: Historical Specificity, Agency and the Performative Self," *Theory, Culture and Society* 20 (2003): 1–17.

107 [John Bowles], *Treason Triumphant over Law and Constitution! Addressed to both Houses of Parliament* (1795), xi, 19. For Bowles, see Emma Vincent, "John Bowles and the Ideological War against Revolutionary France," *History* 78 (1993): 393–420.

108 *MC*, 30 October 1795. For a full account of the incident, see Steve Poole, *The Politics of Regicide in England, 1760–1850* (Manchester: Manchester University Press, 2000), 103–14.

109 For example, two magistrates had to approve the holding of a political lecture if admission was to be charged, and either one could shut down the meeting if he felt it was seditious or likely to become so. Once a meeting was shut down by a magistrate, any twelve or more persons who refused to disperse would be subject to capital punishment. See *History of the Two Acts*, 157–66.

110 For extended treatment of the Treasonable Practices Bill, see Barrell, *Imagining the King's Death*, 573–603.

111 For public reaction to the Two Acts, see Goodwin, *Friends of Liberty*, 388–98.

112 *A Narrative of the Insults Offered to the King, on his way to and from the House of Lords...... by an Eye-Witness* (London, 1795), 11; Barrell, *Imagining the King's Death*, 567–68. The play closed after only four nights.

113 Thus the solicitor general John Mitford, who had taken over the prosecution of Thelwall, claimed the bill would stop Thelwall's "private interests [as a lecturer] from prompting public grievances." *PH*, vol. 32, col. 306, Commons, 17 November 1795.

114 Ibid., cols. 326–27; col. 429, 3 December; and col. 407, 25 November, for John Grant's claim that if these lectures were permitted, "the English mind would undergo a complete and fatal change."

115 For Georgian notions of legitimate and illegitimate theater, and theater censorship and politics, see Jane Moody, *Illegitimate Theater in London, 1770–1840* (Cambridge: CUP, 2000); Leonard W. Connolly, *The Censorship of English Drama, 1737–1824* (San Marino, CA: Huntington Library,1976), chapter 4; George Taylor, *The French Revolution and the London Stage, 1789–1805* (Cambridge: CUP, 2000).

116 *PH*, vol. 32, col. 429, Commons, 3 December 1795.

117 Thompson, *Making*, 163–85.

118 Thus at the Nottingham election of 1802, it was reported that a naked "female representing the Goddess of Library" participated in a procession that also included the display of liberty trees, the tricolor, French national cockades, and the singing of "Millions be Free." [John Bowles], *Postscript to Thoughts on the Late General Election, As Demonstrative of the Progress of Jacobinism* (1803), 103, 109–10, 124, and *Thoughts on the Late General Election, as Demonstrative of the Progress of Jacobinism* (1802).

119 Thelwall, *Rights of Nature*, part 2, p. 32; Thompson, *The Romantics*, 185–86. Compare Richard Dinmore, junior, *An Exposition of the Principles of the English Jacobins* (Norwich, 1796). The Norwich radical was responding to loyalist misuse of the term "Jacobin." While Dinmore, who had decided to emigrate to America, denies the influence of French principles, he defends radicals calling each other "citizen," opposes monarchy and the connection between church and state, and in discussing "equality" maintains that radicals "consider that the laws ought to have a tendency to equalize property," adding that "this should simply be a tendency." The Stockport schoolmaster William Clegg, *Freedom Defended, or the Practice of Despotism Deposed* (Manchester, 1798), 11–12, declared he was proud to be an English "Jacobin."

120 Joseph Roach, *Cities of the Dead: Circum-Atlantic Performance* (New York: Columbia University Press, 1996), 56; Jon Mee, "'Examples of Safe Printing': Censorship and Popular Radical Literature in the 1790s," in *Literature and Censorship*, ed. Nigel Smith (D. S. Brewer, 1993), 81–95. See also Alan Liu, "Wordsworth and Subversion, 1793–1804: Trying Cultural Criticism," *Yale Journal of Criticism* 2 (1989): 55–100, for reflections on the relationship between subversion and containment, particularly the emphasis on what he terms, "a principle of action contained in politics-as regulated-activity."

2 Everyday Life and Everyday Sedition

Situating Radical Identities

In mid-April 1798, James Gillray produced a caricature of British radicals (Figure 2.1). *London Corresponding Society, Alarm'd* imagines an LCS meeting shortly after arrests of several United Irishmen and several of its own members. Gillray was at this time receiving a secret government pension – paid for by the group that funded *The Anti-Jacobin* – and had rushed the print into production. It was published on 20 April, only two days after the first wave of arrests that sent thirteen suspects into custody.[1] Between 19 and 22 April, an additional twenty-one suspects were taken in the largest single series of domestic political arrests since the arrests in May and June 1794 ahead of the treason trials that fall.

For the purposes of this chapter, the immediate political context of *London Corresponding Society, Alarm'd* is less important than the broader meanings about metropolitan radicalism that the print offered to the public who bought copies or who gazed at it in print-shop windows, taverns, and coffeehouses. Gillray's print offers viewers a vision of radicalism as a hell populated by subterranean satanic figures, representing them through the simian racial codes that often characterized contemporary English satirical images of the Irish and of African Blacks.[2] The crouched and lurking embodiment of sedition suggests radicals who act through enthusiastic mimesis, eager to "ape" the political ideas that emanate from John Horne Tooke and Thomas Paine, whose portraits honorably watch over the meeting-room table.[3] This was, of course, a constant theme in alarmist depictions of British Jacobins: once infected by radical propaganda, the popular ranks became bestial. For example, the "Eye-witness" to the attack on George III of 29 October 1795 described in a tract the dissatisfied crowd as "mean and dirty in their habits, with gloomy countenances, which threatened mischief," swarming out from London's ungoverned spaces like so many bugs.[4]

Gillray's representation of the LCS meeting room as one of those ungoverned sites contrasts to the orderly image of radical meetings presented by figures such as LCS founder Thomas Hardy and LCS member Francis Place. Gillray presents a scene of dirt and chaos, a close and crowded atmosphere. The minute book – one of the key rationalizing technologies that the LCS used to keep order – is present, but it has fallen

Figure 2.1 James Gillray, *London Corresponding Society, Alarm'd*, 1798.
© National Portrait Gallery, London.

to the filthy floor, and the tankard of Tom Treason ale looks soon to follow. Furniture is haphazard, clothing is tattered, and the entire room is awash in a muck-brown gloom. The imagined space is one of fevered unreason and disorder, worlds away from the project of rational deliberation envisioned in LCS self-representations.

This chapter explores the relationship between space and British radical identity through a twofold trajectory. First, it discusses the creation of radical meeting spaces as regulated sites where a transparent style of politics could flourish, uncorrupted by the theatricality of Georgian rule and insulated from the more vulgar and raw aspects of everyday metropolitan popular culture.[5] The second part of the chapter uses the theoretical concept of everyday life to interrogate these sites, suggesting that efforts to isolate radical politics from the everyday instead ensured that the LCS's meetings continually saw expressions of seditious desire. Rational-deliberative radicalism was but one of many stances radicals appropriated in a complex political culture where comportment and display of the self was deeply politicized. Histories of metropolitan British radicalism during the 1790 have emphasized the educative and constitutionalist aspect of the movement, especially during its more public period prior to the Treasonable Practices and Seditious Meeting Acts of late 1795. But that division between a public, constitutionalist LCS between 1792 and 1795, and a conspiratorial, subterranean society from 1795 until it was outlawed by name in 1799 may be overdrawn.[6] Even in meeting rooms designed to limit the vulgar culture of alehouse and street, and instead produce the deliberative practices of liberal democracy, radical politics was ironic, subversive, playful, joyful, millennial, and utopian. While on the whole, the radical movement of 1792–95 was constitutionalist and explicitly public in its efforts to effect reform ("the more public the better," wrote Hardy), seditious desire remained present as a feature of British Jacobinism, a presence that the turn to the everyday can illuminate.[7]

Constructing Radical Spaces

Conservative commentary such as Gillray's often portrayed radicalism as a kind of disordered performance. However, the meeting rooms of the LCS ideally formed sites where participants were their "natural," authentic selves, stripped of the social masking of status and wealth, so that pure logic could circulate freely. Thomas Hardy's notes for a history of the LCS, compiled in 1799, record this attempt to minimize the claims of social status inside its meeting rooms: "We were so scrupulous about the admission of any of those of the higher rank that when any of them offered to pay more than we usually demanded… we would not receive it… There was a uniform rule by which all Members were admitted high low rich and poor."[8] In Hardy's recollection, reformers were eager to construct a space where social status would not cloud the interrogation of political authority. Efforts to marginalize the role of status were joined by procedural apparatus such as detailed rules for decorum, strict procedures for debate, and the careful recording and double-checking of minutes, all of which sought to marginalize the power of less "rational" communicative modes and isolate radical politics from the everyday world of metropolitan popular culture. The construction of a radical politics of deliberative rationality required the policing of the cultural and physical borders of its spaces, so that LCS members would be seen as responsible persons who merited inclusion in the political nation. As Günther Lottes has noted, rules for political decorum sought to turn meeting spaces into sober "political classrooms."[9]

Yet the origins of the LCS were firmly located in the realm of urban work-life and sociability.[10] Writing of how he came to organize the society, Hardy noted that he and several others met at a public house, "as was customary for tradesmen to do" at the end of the workday.[11] Hardy's account here registers the repetitive and cyclical nature that theorists of everyday life have noted: "cyclical time underlies all quotidian and cosmic duration," writes Henri Lefebvre.[12] Modern everyday life incorporates the rhythms of work but is also characterized by small evasive modes of resistance to the productivist world.[13] Hardy recalls the rituals of sociability and solidarity that he and colleagues share during leisure time, and notes that their primary topic of conversation was in "condoling with each other about the miserable and wretched state the people were reduced to." These moments of everyday resistance were key for the origin of the LCS. Hardy writes that the group watched "astonished" when he explained a table depicting "the short state of representation" that John Cartwright had published a decade earlier in the pamphlet *Give Us Our Rights*.[14] After that epiphany, Hardy writes, they agreed to form a political society dedicated to parliamentary reform, and elected Hardy treasurer and secretary.[15]

The LCS grew rapidly during the spring of 1792. By May, it had adopted its distinctive divisional structure, having formed nine divisions, each one sending a delegate to a central, General Committee meeting on Thursday nights. Expansion made issues of decorum critical; the increasing presence of spies and agent provocateurs required new measures. Context is important. In May 1792, the crown issued the royal proclamation against seditious publications that reformers had "industriously dispersed" among the popular classes in order to create "tumult and disorder." The crown urged magistrates to step up their efforts to locate the authors, printers, and others who circulated the material, and to submit reports to the government on all others whom they suspected were assisting distribution of seditious literature.[16] Such measures affected the self-policing of radical meetings, as the LCS began to enforce a stricter separation of meeting spaces from the disorder of popular sociability:

> About this time we began to be a little more particular about the admission of people into the room where the divisions of the society met on account of several improper persons intruding and intriguing to get into the room as members and afterwards endeavouring to disturb the harmony of the Society by their noisy and virulent

> declamations designing thereby to through [sic] them into confu-
> sion and anarchy that they might become an easy prey to their evil
> designs.[17]

Some sense of the effect these policies had upon admission practices is
borne out by reports from spies seeking to infiltrate the LCS. The spy
John Groves, for example, successfully joined division two in February
1794, but noted in his report to the government that it had been difficult.
After taking maneuvers that were "too circuitous to be communicated
by Letter," Groves noted that for all his caution, had he "pressed it, or
seemed anxious I should most likely have been disappointed."[18]

As Hardy's notes indicate, the LCS leadership defined proper decorum
contextually, against the intrusion of other modes and manifestations
of popular politics. Moreover, the notes were written at the end of the
1790s, a context that significantly informs his differentiation of legitimate and illegitimate attendees. Hardy wrote his history of the LCS
after the narrative had become established that it was spies, not regular
LCS members, who were responsible for instances of sedition and treasonable utterances at LCS meetings. In the treason trials of 1794, the
defense case made by the barristers Thomas Erskine and Vicary Gibbs
relied heavily on the disruptive presence of spies at radical meetings. In
Hardy's account, too, illegitimate sedition is a product of outside provocateurs. Hardy's narrative, written shortly after the LCS had been outlawed by name in 1799, registers the construction of radicalism made for
the jury and the wider public in the treason trials.

But Hardy's convoluted description also betrays the sheer difficulty of
separating everyday "noisy" behavior from the rarified spaces of rational
radicalism. As Hardy's "theirs," "thems," and "theys" (in the passage
quoted above) rebound against one another, we might begin to glimpse
the dense weave of everyday theatrics and seditious desire in radical
culture. Consider an example from the spring of 1794. According to
the physician and LCS member James Parkinson, when the spy Edward
Gosling joined the society, he "sought to recommend himself to the division by the most excessive violence of language; but soon curbed in this
proceeding, he adopted more artful methods." Unable to convince the
division as a body to agree to his plans, Gosling befriended a member
who already had a pike and began making "artful and guarded proposals for establishing a club, the members of which should be furnished
with pikes like his, and learn military exercise." Parkinson wrote that
several members objected to the plan but that Gosling rebutted them by
claiming that having a pike in one's house and learning military exercise
were legal. Gosling "by these artifices gained the attachment of two or
three zealots."[19] Parkinson, like Hardy, represented sedition as alien to
the society proper; manifestations of extralegal arming only came from
outside the society.

The LCS responded to what Hardy characterized as the intrusion of seditious outsiders by being more restrictive about admittance.

> In each of the divisions it was agreed to appoint a Chairman every meeting night, by acclamation or a Show of hands–on the next meeting night the Chairman was to descend to become door keeper in rotation. It was not deemed any degradation to the man who filled that high and elevated Station of <u>president</u>, to stoop to take upon him the <u>lowest office</u> in Society, <u>door-keeper</u>, when it was for the express purpose of promoting, and securing happiness, order, and Tranquility in the Society.[20]

Alongside Hardy's emphasis on the egalitarian sharing of committee duties, his remembrance here also shows a careful attention to policing the boundaries of division meetings, again separating the vulnerable spaces of the society's deliberative democracy from the outside world of "confusion and anarchy." But it is worth noting that if Parkinson's account of Gosling's provocations is accurate, the spy *did* gain recruits from among "authentic" members. In the treason trials, Erskine explicitly depicted such activities as drilling as mere ludic fantasy, having no real intention at all.[21] Erskine's comments certainly reflect the discursive conditions of their expression. In the courtroom, defining what was play and what was real held fatal consequences. But Parkinson's comments also register the element of transgression and enactment in radical identity. If participation in the ongoing formal work of LCS meetings – the democratic debate and educative processes of its internal processes – offered "jam today" along with the possibility of "jam tomorrow" in the form of parliamentary reform, its margins also offered the enactment of revolutionary desire, the *frisson* of going beyond constitutional limits.[22]

The suspension of social status, the use of gatekeepers to limit the presence of spies, and the technology of the minute book for orderly record-keeping were meant to train LCS members in democratic practices while restraining the possibility of disorder and sedition. Long after the demise of the LCS, Francis Place began assembling notes for a history of the radical movement of the 1790s in which he offers a detailed description of the room in the Beaufort Buildings where the LCS General Committee met during 1794 and 1795.

> The Committee held its sittings in a large room, in Beaufort Buildings in the Strand, under which in another large room Mr. Thelwall delivered political Lectures. The committee room was fitted up with benches and desks in the manner of a school room, the president's chair was at one end of the room and was a sort of pulpit raised about 3 feet from the floor.[23]

Place's attention to space asks us to defamiliarize the familiar, for his detailed description of the setting does more than simply describe a room. It is, after all, not self-evident why a description of furniture and distribution of space should inform this section of Place's history. The description marks off this space as a zone of educative politics, driven by the authority of the meeting's chairperson. The desire to represent the meeting room as a space of order and sober rationality is reflected in the streamlined placement of attendees in this remembered room.[24] "A sort of pulpit" registers the sense of hierarchy that such order requires. But Place's notes also belie the notion that this pure zone could ever be fully achieved. In his narrative, the space of rational politics is intimately linked with his own self-representation as one of the few LCS leaders who could actually wield the force of personality needed to tame popular disorder.

> As it was found that I as Chairman kept good order and dispensed the business in less time than most of the other members who presided, I was frequently voted into the chair. The duty of chairman was arduous, frequently very difficult, it required quickness to perceive and resolution to decide, combined with conduct which while it was preemptory and inflexible was not calculated to give much offense.[25]

Place's comparison of his own leadership to that of others suggests that radical audiences did not necessarily adopt the deference the furniture encouraged: "among so many persons, of various dispositions no small portion of whom were eager to make speeches, and impatient of control the office of Chairman was not an ordinary one."[26] Respectable radicalism could shade into its other and chairs had to limit transgressive behavior.

"The Nation at Large": LCS Field Meetings

The most ambitious radical efforts to claim public space were the mass meetings that the LCS held during the second half of 1795. On four occasions, between June and December, the society convened large outdoor meetings to express popular support for political reform and latterly to demonstrate opposition to the Treasonable Practices and Seditious Meetings Bills. Estimates of attendance across the events total between 85,000 and 350,000.[27] Taken together we get a sense of the radical desire to refound the nation on principles of democratic reason. To appreciate the sheer ambition behind the effort to constitute a public, to produce an embodiment of the people, we must understand the difficulties in controlling a large number of people in open urban space; unlike LCS meeting or lecture rooms, there was very little or no barrier to attendance and few means for maintaining order or ensuring proper behavior. At what point might such an amorphous assembly turn into a riotous mob? This was a concern not only for magistrates and the government but for the organizers of and speakers at these meetings. It was important to exemplify good order and norms of rational deliberation and to draw the contrast between their own proceedings and the drunken violence of loyalist mobs and liberally bribed election crowds.[28]

In the later eighteenth century, London's open spaces remained available as sites of everyday ludic behavior and also had a historical association with crowd action. From Lamb's Conduit Fields, Finsbury Fields, and the fields around Copenhagen House on the northern outskirts of the city, to Tothill Fields south of Westminster, to Stepney Field in east London, to St. George's Fields in Southwark, London's open spaces provided important recreational and political resources for urban dwellers.[29] In addition to hosting a well-known tea house, Copenhagen Fields offered visitors the opportunity to play at skittles and Dutch pins and view blood sports such as boxing, dog-fights, and bear-baiting.[30] As late as 1793, Tothill Fields held a bear-garden, and bull-baiting was on display there through the 1820s.[31] Open spaces also provided a resource for the poor. After the terrible Ratcliff fire in July 1794, dozens of tents were set up in Stepney Field for poor East End Londoners displaced by the destruction of housing.[32] Homeless Londoners also set up squatter settlements on Hampstead Heath, using its common land for peat, turf, and grazing, and seeking in time to become copyholders.[33] Finally, open spaces also offered resources for street politics; here, urban geography meant that some held particular status as sites of crowd action. After the completion of Westminster Bridge in 1750, for example, St. George's Fields became a regular site of urban protest, for the bridge offered a clear route to Parliament and St. James Palace.[34] Masses of striking sailors assembled on St. George's Fields on 7 May 1768. Three days later, it was the site of the "Wilkesite massacre," when troops opened fire on crowds protesting John Wilkes's imprisonment for libel. A decade later, the site was a starting point for the anti-Catholic Gordon Riots. On 2 June 1780, around 50,000 members of the Protestant Association gathered there, parading around the field holding aloft flags and playing festive music, before moving west across the bridge toward Parliament.[35] The scale and scope of the ensuing riots distanced middling-class radicals from the urban crowd, and for authorities, drew new attention to patrolling London's spaces, and to restricting sites for radical activity.[36]

By the later eighteenth century, London's fields were under greater governmental pressure as landowners and authorities restricted the radical uses of city space through legislation and development projects.[37] Lightly policed urban fields licensed the political imagination, and could be something like what Michel Foucault termed "heterotopias" – places where rules were altered, and transformation hovered in possibility.

Such sites sat in contradiction to emerging concepts of the governed city and the governed individual.[38] The LCS's own use of London's open spaces registered not only the surviving availability of fields as spatial resources but also the risks inherent in appearing to mobilize the crowd. By the time of the great mass meetings of summer and fall 1795, the society had already encountered government hostility to outdoor meetings. In October 1793, the LCS had organized its first open-air gathering at Spitalfields, in a field loaned by the pump-maker and LCS member Thomas Briellat. While such a venue offered the possibility of direct engagement with the public, the LCS was also to some degree compelled to seek an open-air site.[39] Since the formation of John Reeves's loyalist Crown and Anchor Association in November 1792, LCS divisions had increasingly been denied access to taverns and coffeehouses for meetings, as magistrates threatened publicans with the loss of licenses.[40] That same month, Justice William Ashhurst's charge to the grand jury for Middlesex urged greater surveillance of radical activity and on 1 December, a new royal proclamation activated militia forces against radical activity from abroad. As publicans withdrew support during 1793, LCS divisions increasingly resorted to meeting in private houses large enough for the purpose. The brief turn to the open-air meeting in October 1793 demonstrated that authorities would act against outdoor meetings. The meeting's purpose was to elect delegates for the upcoming convention in Edinburgh. In selecting Joseph Gerrald and Maurice Margarot as delegates, the LCS would openly demonstrate to the public the society's democratic practices. The meeting was announced in newspapers, and government responded. An elaborate security plan was enacted by the stipendiary magistrate Patrick Colquhoun, who assembled around one hundred constables as security forces – "totally out of view [emphasis in original] of any person" at the meeting – and appointed another dozen Spitalfields weavers as constables who could merge into the crowd and provide nearby magistrates with running reports on the meeting.[41] Security was tight. Although the meeting itself passed peacefully, in its aftermath, Colquhoun retaliated. Briellat was discreetly arrested after the meeting ended and was quickly charged with having uttered seditious words while at a public house eleven months earlier. At his trial, prosecutors referenced the Gordon riots as a caution against open-air political meetings, and repeatedly used Briellat's provision of a meeting space for the LCS as evidence that his words were sincerely meant. Whereas the defense claimed Briellat's seditious words were not his at all, but merely taken from a decades-old book of prophecy that the pump-maker had brought to the pub, prosecutors framed Briellat's willingness to offer spatial resources to the LCS as an overt act demonstrating his seditious heart.[42] Seditious space closely followed seditious space, a point not lost on the LCS. John Martin, a prominent LCS member and attorney who advised Briellat, later stated that Briellat would not have been arrested had he not allowed the society to use his field for the meeting. Several other members felt the same.[43]

The four open-air LCS meetings held during the late summer and fall of 1795 thus occurred against a backdrop of increasing governmental surveillance and control of urban space – factors that added transgressive intensity to radical claims to space. The 29 June meeting, for example, was originally to be held on the bowling green owned by the Gun Tavern, Lambeth Road, but evidently magistrates pressured the publican to refuse the green as a site.[44] The LCS then shifted to an enclosed field near the bowling green. While urban fields offered a space in which resource-poor Londoners might exercise a degree of what William Sewell terms "spatial agency," that agency had to be exercised cautiously.[45] Given the risks, it is hardly surprising, then, that these meetings created controversy within the radical movement, as they were inevitably theatrical events dependent upon high emotion and prone to demagoguery. Speakers tread a rhetorical tightrope, repeatedly emphasizing the need for good order and peaceable behavior but also continually seeking to activate the crowd's emotions. John Thelwall's remarks at the 26 October meeting swing from one pole to the other:

> Let it not, however, be supposed that while I wish to recommend to you a scrupulous respect for peace and order, that I wish to repress the generous ardor and enthusiasm in behalf of liberty, with which I know your bosoms are at this time burning. No, Citizens, I would increase that enthusiasm, I would disseminate that ardour…live free or die![46]

Four days after the 12 November meeting, William Godwin began writing *Considerations on Lord Grenville's and Mr. Pitt's Bills*, in which he admonished Thelwall for his willingness to stir the passions of the crowd, and perhaps become, in Jon Mee's memorable phrase, "an errant magician's nephew, who could not direct the spells he was raising."[47] At the meeting itself, several rostra had been set up to facilitate the semblance of deliberation, but it remained doubtful whether such events could meet the demands of deliberative-rationality.

Sympathetic accounts of the mass meetings held at St. George's Fields in June 1795, and at Copenhagen Fields in October and again in November 1795, illustrate the pains taken to represent outdoor meetings as sober assemblies of the respectable nation, providing a manifestation of rational public opinion. Since the acquittals in the treason trials of fall 1794, membership in the LCS had increased considerably, reaching a high point by summer of perhaps three thousand.[48] During late spring, leadership began to plan for a public meeting to be held in June, in order to "shew the nation at large" that the LCS remained a vigorous advocate of thorough political reform.[49] Yet within the LCS, support for the event was not unanimous. Some members argued that mass meetings would give government the pretext to continue the suspension of habeas corpus, and likely damage the society's public image.[50] Direct engagement with the nation risked the growth achieved since the acquittals of a half-year earlier. Moreover, sections of the public were already restive. The planning for 29 June occurred amidst widespread unrest over war-driven taxation, and bread riots and emergency food provision across the south.[51] Internal LCS discussions thus emphasized the "necessity of rendering the meeting as respectable as possible."[52]

At the meeting itself, John Gale Jones began his remarks as chair by noting the respectable decorum of the outsized gathering of some 50,000 persons, and urged a rejection of all "tumult and violence."[53] Positive accounts afterward also stressed the orderliness of the crowd. Dispatches to provincial newspapers, for example, noted the event was "conducted in the most tranquil manner" – a depiction echoed by the LCS in its summary of 1795, claiming that "never was so vast an assemblage conducted in so orderly and peaceable a manner."[54] Similarly, the LCS account of the 26 October meeting at Copenhagen Fields prefaced its description of the events with statements about the precautions that the organization had taken to ensure decorum. Noting suspicions that hired agent provocateurs would likely be present, the LCS had displayed "several thousand" advertisements along principal routes to Copenhagen House, each requesting "orderly and peaceable behavior."[55] Thelwall's address to the crowd also emphasized the need to avoid "tumults and disturbances" excited by spies and government agents, and the meeting ended, according to the LCS account, in the "utmost harmony" and good order.[56] Thelwall would also speak at the 12 November meeting, again at Copenhagen Fields, and the LCS meeting held at Marylebone Fields on 7 December – though at the latter he appeared ill and spoke only briefly.[57] The printer Richard Lee's account of the 12 November meeting immediately pointed to the "decency, gravity, and decorum" of the vast crowd, writing in wonder at the "mental energies" shown by "thousands of free-born Britons."[58] The closing lines of the LCS's declaration of its principles – published as loyalists inside and outside of parliament were blaming the mass meetings for the attack on George III's carriage on 29 October – repeatedly merge the LCS into the nation at large.[59]

Yet a key concern for radicals was that the very nature of public meetings made them far more open to unwanted disorder and intrusion than were more controlled spaces. This helps explain the repeated exhortations to the crowd to behave peacefully and the careful attention to language in addresses to be read. Moreover, the LCS tried to enforce a 6d. admission charge to the 29 June meeting.[60] Nonetheless, incendiaries seem to have been present. The militia officer John Lewis de Koven alerted the Alien Office in mid-November that the Copenhagen Fields meeting had been attended by "one of the most dangerous foreigners in

London," a son of the Baron de Bérenger, but now known as "Random," and a seditious habitué of coffeehouses and taverns frequented by democratic Europeans. When, at Brunswick Coffeehouse in Golden Square, de Koven had interrupted one of Random's insults to the government, where the German exclaimed, "I wish there would be a revolution, I should have my hand in it!" [61]

De Koven's letter calls attention to the manner by which loyalist representations of the mass meetings of fall 1794 gave them an entirely different color. For example, in the immediate aftermath of the attack on George III's carriage, notables in town after town issued declarations of loyalty to the sovereign, typically making a strong link between the public meetings and mob violence. The address from Durham, for example, blamed the attack on "discontented factious Inflammatists" similar to those causing "Anarchy, Distress, and Ruin" in France.[62] The LCS was not an organic voice of the rational public but was instead a French import. From Hampshire, Gosport subjects congratulated the king on escaping a "desperate Banditti of Assassins" inspired by "Tumultuous and seditious meetings."[63] Durham and Gosport were of course far from London and it is highly unlikely that loyalists in either town had been present for any of the LCS meetings in the fall of 1795 – but their association of mass meetings with disorderly sedition is a common theme in such addresses.

Pamphleteers like the "Eyewitness," who wrote the *Narrative of the Insults Offered to the King* on 29 October, likewise represented LCS field meetings as sites of disordered unreason.[64] The seditious energies unleashed at Copenhagen Fields spilled over into the attack on George III. The pamphlet offers a panoramic view of the loyalist imagination, moving from images of the Mountain in Paris as a kind of eighteenth-century Comintern with "emissaries in every capital"; to British radicals' careful selection of an appropriate pool from which to recruit followers, "a set of persons who may be said to hang loose upon Society"; to its centerpiece discussion of the "thirst for blood and plunder" encouraged by the speakers at the 26 October meeting. Altogether, the process produced

> the concatenation which linked together by some who assumed the character of orators, extended the chain of sedition through the land…. These were the worthies who held their public lectures and disputations, these private conclaves, these field meetings, and who were the instigators and actors of the insults which have been offered to the sacred person of his Majesty.[65]

Since the acquittals in the treason trials, the LCS had "carried on its machinations with more energy, and perhaps less secrecy, than before." The author represents the Copenhagen Fields meeting as a wellspring of regicidal, ungovernable forces, where "all the strength of democracy was drawn out" from the meeting, and then redeployed on the morning of the attack on the sovereign.[66]

To be sure, loyalist addresses written from faraway towns and alarmist pamphlets conflating mass meetings with assassination do not demonstrate that LCS field meetings were chaotic and riotous assemblies of the mob. Yet for all their exaggeration, such representations present a side of the field meetings that LCS-authored depictions rigorously deny. Here, as elsewhere, the appeal to reason and order could not fully exclude the seditious desire that was also part of British Jacobinism. If alarmist representations of radical meetings signal a less decorous set of events than those presented by the LCS, it owes less to revolutionary intent than to the imbrication of field meetings within the broader urban fabric of London. Like other spaces inhabited by British Jacobins, the enclosure beside the bowling green at St. George's Fields and the fields around Copenhagen House were also part of urban everyday life.

The Sedition of the Everyday

This chapter has argued that British radicals represented the origins and practices of the reform movement as being driven by the pure logic of rational-deliberative practice. Memoirs from key figures like Hardy and Place represented the movement as constitutionalist democracy-in-training, for members at meeting rooms and for the wider public assembled in London's fields. They represented instances of extralegal sedition and revolutionary desire as intrusions by outsiders rather than common at the margins of radical culture. The LCS General Committee journal and minutes would also seem to indicate that the society was successful in its efforts to rein in undisciplined enthusiasm. On one level, such documentation no doubt reflected awareness that just as the radical societies' public speech and official publications were subject to surveillance and possible prosecution, their more private records could also be seized – as of course they were. The formal practices and apparatus of record-keeping excluded the preservation of unguarded expression. In their regular, routine recording of correspondence from provincial societies, discussion of proclamations, and other society work, such records present a ghostly and partial after-image of LCS meetings – shorn of their emotional content, and absent of unacceptable behavior.[67]

Sources more open to the everyday, however, complicate the dichotomy. For example, consider William Reid's *Rise and Dissolution of the Infidel Societies in this Metropolis* (1800), one of the rare exposés informed by a deep sense of authentic context derived from its author's own position embedded within radical culture. A member of the LCS from 1793, Reid was arrested in 1798 in a raid by magistrates on a debating club.[68] Certainly part of what attracted Reid to convivial debating culture in the mid-1790s was its prolix energy, as club sedition infected popular culture more broadly. Attendees hurried from venue to venue – from division-rooms, to debating clubs, to fields, to benefit societies – seeking to make converts through street-level proselytizing.[69] Reid's account asks readers to close the distance between reform politics in LCS meeting rooms and reading clubs, and the prosaic world of London's teeming streets. Other sources, too, indicate that LCS meetings were characterized by a wide range of political styles and identities, from the deliberative sobriety encouraged by rules for debate, to seriously playful sedition explored in Chapter 1, to intimations of insurrection.

Here, the theoretical concept of everyday life helps to explain why despite careful self-policing, radical meetings so often resembled the rougher "free and easies" of metropolitan popular culture. To be sure, as a coherent category of analysis, "everyday life" is elusive. Its practices, "tactics" in Michel de Certeau's usage, cannot be apprehended as a totality but rather lie "scattered in the totality of social life."[70] Yet despite their widely diverse theoretical stances, scholars of everyday life have been concerned with a number of related themes central for understanding radical culture in the 1790s: the place of emotions, embodied experience, practical knowledge, and the role of lived time and space.[71] Thus, theorists of everyday life emphasize the unofficial, non-formalized aspects of social interaction, such as routines of work-life, informal conversation, and sociability. This, of course, creates some difficulties for recovery. For the historian, everyday tactics of the past typically only generate evidence for their historicity through the effects they have on some more formal practice – a consideration that helps explain why evidence for seditious politics at LCS meetings appears more often in governmental records than in texts produced by radicals themselves.[72] Such sources show that the boundaries between the sites of rational radical politics and the everyday often proved to be fluid. Spaces that were constructed discursively were also created and inhabited through practice; radical spaces, like other aspects of culture, were not fully separate from other social spaces but were instead "loosely bounded."[73] In his discussion of social space, Lefebvre notes, "Visible boundaries, such as walls or enclosures in general, give rise... to an appearance of separation between spaces where in fact what exists is an ambiguous continuity."[74] Moreover, in creating rules for decorum and in the minuting of acceptable discussion, the LCS leadership opened up a field of play for its members, a space for license, for challenges to restrictions on behavior. Seeking to isolate their practices from rougher, "irrational" elements of vulgar popular culture, the LCS endowed such behavior with greater transgressive appeal. The result was what we might call everyday sedition.[75] Widening the lens momentarily to examine the everyday world of street and work-life clarifies what was at stake in the self-policing of LCS meeting spaces. Two examples of informal, quotidian sedition help to underscore why LCS leaders were concerned about what might break out in their own ranks if political discussion were not separated from vernacular popular culture.

In mid-June 1794, a London coal merchant named George Perry warned government officials about a carpenter in Shoreditch named William Thompson, who was using workplace contacts to "sow the seeds of Sedition amongst his fellow workmen." Thompson's work was flourishing (he had taken a "Great number of Houses to finish") and Perry wrote that this gave the seditious carpenter wide exposure to others, which Thompson used to continually lure fellow workmen to join popular political clubs.[76] Perry had heard Thompson making a number of incendiary comments: "you have no more Right to a King here than they have in France," and "Damn me I hope they will soon Cut King George's Head off for he Deserves it as bad as the King of France Did." Moreover, the republican carpenter seemed to suggest it was not just talk. Alluding presumably to the LCS and SCI prisoners arrested the previous month, Thompson claimed that his club was going to mount a rescue, then rise up and "their Heads would be Suspended that suspended the Habeas Corpus Act."[77] For our purpose, the importance of Perry's account lies in its weaving of Thompson's everyday work-life – the commonplace, cyclical world of daily labor – into popular and organized politics. There is no separation between work and insurrectionary direct action, no divide between popular clubbing and street-level sedition. Radical identity and work-life are seamlessly integrated.[78] In constructing sites of sociability, political clubs and trade societies often shared the same spaces; spaces of everyday work-life and political clubbing were not distinct from one another.[79]

As Perry's alarmed letter indicates, perhaps the most worrisome aspect of the blending of radical politics into everyday life was that it easily shaded into riot and violence. In the loyalist imagination, popular political clubs were often blamed. An example from Chelsea at the end of 1792 usefully illustrates what we refer to as "everyday sedition." In mid-December, residents there were in a state of unease; rumors swirled of a riot planned for 19 December and a handbill warning residents had been posted in Chelsea, Kensington, and Knightsbridge.[80] William Bulkeley, an officer from the Chelsea Royal Hospital, wrote to the Home Office alarmed by a report that a "large mob was collected in Sloane Square" – though dozens of constables had been posted and no crowd actually seems to have materialized.[81] But a brawl between a group of republican roughs and several hospital pensioners demonstrates how connections between rough radicalism and political clubbing were often associated in the minds of loyalists, and showed the danger of radical affiliation mixed with everyday alehouse sociability.

Around 9:00 pm on Wednesday, 19 December (the same evening as the feared riot), a whitesmith named John Martin and several friends came singing through the hospital grounds. To the pensioner Joseph Webb, the singing at first sounded like "God Save the King," but he quickly learned that the men had altered lines, and "God Damn the King" was the verse of choice, followed by shouts of "Tom Paine for Ever Liberty and Equality." Webb, dressed in his regimentals, quickly became a target of abuse; as they passed by him, one of the men named George Sutter challenged Webb, saying "I am a real Tom Paine man." Webb began to remonstrate with the men for displaying such disloyalty – on the hospital grounds no less – and Sutter responded with "You are a Soldier Built Bugger," and, worse, with his fists. Sutter's friends joined in. Webb cried "murder!," and other pensioners came to assist the old man. The seditious language escalated. Martin's friend Edward Jones punched Webb, yelling "Damn the King"; Robert Holmes damned the king as well, piling in on Webb, shouting "Tom Paine for Ever, Liberty and Equality"; Martin removed his coat, damning the king as well, and adding "I am Tom Paine's Man." Martin then offered to fight "any Bugger that would take the King's part." The fracas has the atmosphere of drunkenness; at one point, Jones offered Webb two pence if he would "damn the King."[82]

The fight ended with the arrest of Martin and several others – later including Sutter.[83] Of particular interest, however, is the manner by which this expression of alcohol-fueled political violence was linked with metropolitan radical politics. Evidence collected for Martin's case included a printed card inviting guests to a meeting of the Arthurian Society held at the Star and Garter, Sloane Square, with "Yours, & c. George Sutter, President" at the bottom. Prosecutors evidently regarded the card as an invitation to the political riot planned for that evening.[84] Martin and the others arrested were suspected of belonging to the club as well. Moreover, Bulkeley's letter to the Home Office closed with an appended note, explicitly stating that the "abandoned and hardened knot of villains" who called themselves the Arthurian Society was in "regular correspondence with similar Clubs in Town."[85]

It is not unreasonable that officers like Bulkeley might fear that radical clubs were mixing it up with troops. At this very time, the spy George Lynam was alerting government authorities that LCS interaction with military personnel was on the increase. On 11 December, he reported that a shoemaker named Davis, a member of LCS division twenty-three, claimed to have "made a Convert" of several soldiers at the Tower, and in the meantime, during December and January, the General Committee had requested delegates to take the sense of their divisions on whether soldiers should be admitted and on what terms.[86] (The General Committee withdrew a proposal for the "gratuitous admission" of soldiers in mid-January 1793.[87]) The point is not that there was some connection between Martin and Sutter's republican brawling and LCS activity in the military but rather that loyalists could easily infer such a connection.[88]

Here we also see outlines of the increasingly unrespectable, libertine masculinity that LCS meeting regulations sought to repress.[89] Space, too, was a factor: Chelsea Hospital was a politicized site deeply associated with loyalism and royal magnanimity toward aging and infirm soldiers.[90] To damn the king and praise Tom Paine there served to heighten emotions. The magnified transgression licensed Webb to censure Sutter, Martin, and the others. For the group of republican toughs, damning George III and beating up pensioners on hospital grounds deepened the seditious play.

Reports of instances such as these lie scattered among Home Office files.[91] They call attention to the weaving of radical affiliation into everyday life, manifested in ordinary ways such as through relationships with friends and work colleagues, or through the casual violence ingrained in tavern and alehouse culture.[92] Authorities often connected everyday sedition to radical-political clubs, as did some participants. Such cases suggest that being a British "Jacobin" was sometimes less a matter of formal participation in club meetings, and instead more densely woven into the quotidian world of popular culture. Whereas Chapter 1 explored British Jacobinism as a dialogic construction at the intersection of radicalism and government repression, here we can also understand it as the outcome of a different dialogue: that between the self-imposed restrictions on behavior adopted by LCS leadership, and the incessant, lived space and time of everyday life.

Everyday Sedition and the LCS

In 1795, the relationship between reform meetings and popular disturbances was carefully explored in an essay that appeared in *The Cabinet*, a Norwich journal produced by a group of young radical intellectuals. "Of Popular Societies" addresses the political clubs' need for meeting spaces at a time when many societies found themselves being shut out of taverns as landlords came under pressure from local magistrates.[93] The essay carries an anti-theatrical tone. The author conceded that clubs that "formed, not for a distinct object, but aiming at public favour, by pompous festivals, and the fascinating language of liberty" were a menace to the true project of constitutional reform. But responsible clubs needed access to private spaces in order to remain separate from "unlicensed and uncontrolled congregation." The spatial norms of taverns and other sociable sites policed behavior, and while the popular societies continued to exist, it would be wise to allow them access to the restraining effects of regulated urban spaces. "It is not in taverns but in crouds [sic] that disorder originates," wrote the author, and "Quiet must be promoted by insulating discontent."[94] Tavern speechifying kept popular politics within bounds.

Perhaps. Yet if we return to the spaces of LCS meetings themselves, we can now see the repeated instances of violent or insurrectionary expression in the reports of spies not as signs of conspiracy among LCS malcontents hoping to foment a rising from the margins but as a result of the tension between formal, organized politics and the informal world of the everyday. Consider the description of a typical meeting offered by the watchman Joseph Goulding. Goulding was arrested in November 1793 after a fellow watchman reported him for using seditious language and reading anti-government pieces from the *Morning Chronicle* to his fellow watchmen. In his interview, he told the magistrate William Wickham that he had been a member of LCS division twenty-five for about three months prior to his arrest, and described the tumult of a typical meeting: "almost everybody Speaks, and there is always a very great noise, till the Delegate gets up – People generally grow very outrageous and won't wait, then the Delegate gets up and trys [sic] to soften them."[95] Goulding's information points to a category of analysis that is useful for exploring the spaces of radicalism in the 1790s. Having noted the role of physical boundaries in marking off the zones of rational politics, Goulding's description also highlights the role of time in creating space. "Till the delegate gets up," Goulding wrote. "Soften them" and the meeting can turn to real business. As Doreen Massey has noted, social space is, equally, social time. Practices that move between spatial zones necessarily move across significant temporal boundaries as well.[96] In Goulding's remark, "People generally grow very outrageous," we see a degree of resistance to the disciplining of time, manifested at the blurred outlines of temporal borders.

By disciplining everyday practices, LCS rules for procedure and comportment helped produce the sedition they sought to proscribe; at times of heightened pressure, seditious desire threatened to overtake regulated order. Thus tensions in meetings during spring 1794 – before and after the mass arrests of mid-May – reached critical levels; violent imaginings surface and resurface in spy reports, as ostensibly sociable radical gatherings could quickly turn in more seditious directions. For example, on Friday, 2 May the Society for Constitutional Information held an anniversary dinner in the elegant Great Assembly Room at the Crown and Anchor tavern on Arundel Street – a space by then already associated in the broader public sphere with political reform. Three years earlier, the Crown and Anchor had been the site of an anniversary celebration of the fall of the Bastille. Since then, the tavern had become an over-coded sign in print-culture depictions of reform and radical politics.[97] Space inflected meaning as attendees gathered. Among those present at the SCI dinner were some thirty to forty LCS members, several of whom had been given free tickets. For LCS and SCI members the day was significant since that very morning, the *Surprize* transport carrying Thomas Muir, Thomas Fyshe Palmer, William Skirving, and Maurice Margarot had begun its long and soon notorious voyage to New South Wales – a journey that would trouble later efforts by radicals to commemorate the movement of the 1790s, as we discuss in Chapter 7. The report of Groves, who was in attendance, reveals how seditious desire could overtake sociable gatherings mixing formal politics and everyday play. The informer's account begins by noting the unexpected respectability of the SCI:

> I must say my surprise at the decent and respectable appearance of the persons assembled together.
>   I had judged, but I found myself wrong in my judgment, comparatively, i.e. of one society by the other; and, as the great majority of the L.C.S'y. consisted of a set of ragamuffins, that the Society for Constitutional Information, were composed of an equal description of people, but as it is my duty to report Truth, I must say, I was greatly deceived.[98]

Despite the "decent and respectable" appearance, the room was filled with conversation about recent French military successes. Soon, the convivial atmosphere and the excitation of such news began to work upon the attendees, some 400 in number: "at the same time that this news spread an universal satisfaction – I also heard the words ça-ira repeated."[99] Copies of songs, such as "The Free Constitution," were distributed shortly thereafter. As the dinner room was opened and attendees took their places at table, "Ça Ira" was again called for and this time a full band joined in. The song met with "the most loud applause" and was "vociferously encored." Next, the "Carmagnol… was played & encored with every token of the warmest approbation." Then the military march, the "Marseilles" – a song that "electrified the whole company – & bravo, encore, huzzaing & clapping of hands, even during dinner, made up the choruses."[100] In usual fashion, the dinner was concluded with a series of toasts, such as "To the Free Constitution!" – practices that allowed radicals to make claims on emblematic categories that were often enunciated by conservatives.[101] The spy's initial impressions of respectability were undermined, as the dinner escalated into a more confrontational and finally violent tone: in the heated atmosphere of spring 1794, violent imaginings and seditious longing challenged expectations about comportment. After Horne Tooke gave a series of toasts lambasting parliament, and drunkenly leading the crowd in singing an inversion of "God Save the King" ("See George the good swine, / Roll round his stupid eyes"), he left the chair. "There was a noise & confusion throughout the room," wrote Groves. [102] When questioned later in May by the Privy Council, the meeting's chairperson John Wharton claimed that he had broken up the meeting when Thelwall jumped up onto a table and demanded the equalization of property.[103] As the meeting ended, the adrenaline unleashed by so much sociable sedition continued to energize the attendees. Groves wrote that "several of the members of the L. C. Society came to me & begged me to go with them to Thelwall's

Lecture, as they expected a riot."[104] In this spy's account, the rapid shift from respectability to sedition to chaos and implied (and hoped-for?) violence proved that the SCI was as treasonable and dangerous as the LCS: "I drew the inference, that altho' the London Corresponding Society might differ from the Society for Constitutional Information in point of cloaths & conditions in life, yet that the same sentiments governed the two societies."[105]

The chaotic SCI anniversary dinner of 2 May 1794 features in histories of the radical movement, but during this intense period, tensions between deliberate politics and everyday sedition also roiled formal LCS meetings. After the arrest of Hardy, Thelwall, and six others, spy reports indicate a heightened level of violent language within LCS division meetings. For example, George Saunders informed the government that a meeting of division thirteen opened with one member standing up to let others know that William Pitt would be crossing Putney Bridge at noon the following day on his way to Parliament. "No explanation was made," and immediately a clap on the table halted discussion ("some said it was improper to discuss such a matter"), but the inference seemed clear to Saunders that an invitation was made to assassinate the prime minister. He reported several other comments suggesting or celebrating anti-government violence during the tumultuous meeting; the norms of deliberative politics seemed incapable of containing a desire, evidently felt by several members, to move beyond constitutional action.[106]

LCS meeting rooms were venues of everyday life, where seditious pamphlets and subversive songs circulated. Meeting rooms were filled with singing and other modes of incorporating and expressing political identities. Temporal descriptions that marked off radical meetings sought to reject these practices, but that was a formality resisted by everyday ludic behavior.[107] So much so, William Reid complained, that far from insulating subversion as had been claimed by the author of "Of Popular Societies," radical meeting rooms served as staging grounds for the expansion of sedition.

> the introduction of democratic songs was another part of the duty of the political missionaries; but their elects were not confined to Benefit Clubs, their business as to worm themselves into communal societies of every kind; where, though scuffles have frequently ensued, these delegates have succeeded in erecting a party or an interest, which otherwise would not have had an existence.[108]

Reid's commentary must of course be taken for what it is: a propagandist work that belongs to the old genre of secret history. He wrote it after the naval mutinies and invasion scares of 1797–98, events that the government and many of its supporters viewed as connecting radicalism with damage to the nation's defense capabilities. In Reid's account, reformers sang out against clerics in the smoky meeting rooms; these spaces of sedition "were frequently strewed with penny, two-penny, and three penny publications." At such sites, "extemporaneous harangue… had an effect not easily ignored." [109] Reid's "bottom-up" description of radical conviviality contrasts with Place's prescriptive narrative. But there is plenty of evidence to suggest that, with respect to practices at radical meetings, his account is at least as accurate as those offered by Place and Hardy.

Reid presented radical culture as dynamic, blending into other urban associational spaces, and mixing democratic processes and playful sedition. This sense is reinforced by a spy's report that introduces another manifestation of the everyday: casual print satire. British Jacobins occasionally enlivened gatherings through the sharing of self-created republican art and anti-government caricature. For example, on their way to a meeting of division six on 19 May 1794, the spy William Metcalfe reported that he and the engraver William Worship stopped by Daniel Isaac Eaton's bookshop in Newgate Street, because Worship had completed a drawing to accompany a new edition of the periodical *Politics for the People*. The drawing was an illustration of the fable of Chaunticlere, which Thelwall had reworked as a satire culminating in the execution of "King Chaunticlere," understood by the government to represent George III. Eaton was tried for and acquitted of charges of seditious libel for having published the regicidal satire. Metcalfe noted the general interest in the drawing by those at the shop; one person suggested the rooster should have been drawn without a head, or perhaps with a fool's cap on. Chaunticlere's beheading was running joke among Jacobins.

From Eaton's shop in Newgate Street, Metcalfe and Worship made their way to the Parrot near the Old Bailey for the division meeting, but after the meeting the seditious sociability carried over into the street. As Metcalfe, Worship, and Joseph Burks headed home, they soon encountered a musical party playing "God Save the King." A contest for aural dominance of London's streets now erupted, for the radicals intervened by calling out "God Save the Rights of the People," and "God save the rights of Man."[110] Formal LCS meetings were inescapably bound up in a complex urban spatial dynamic, as attendees moved through different "before- and - after" temporal sites. Radical affiliation shaded into everyday sociability, whether through challenging loyalist celebrations of monarchy, or gathering with others in the radical community to laugh at republican cartoons like Chaunticlere.[111]

Radical art also brings into view the visual world of everyday sedition. The more public, published political images that circulated, and which have been well studied, are here less relevant than art produced in ad hoc form by radicals themselves.[112] On 19 May 1794, for example, a drawing of a liberty tree, made up of a pike surmounted by the liberty cap, was slipped under the door at the Guildhall in Kingston-upon-Hull.

Distressed local authorities offered a £100 reward for information concerning the "inflammable and treasonable" image.[113] A similar drawing also appears in the Treasury Solicitor's papers, as part of evidence collected by government in the aftermath of the first wave of arrests in mid-May 1794 (Figure 2.2). While the second image may simply have been copied from the Home Office correspondence and then inserted in crown documentation of radical activity, there is an intriguing second possibility. Groves noted discussion of designs for new LCS membership cards at a meeting of the LCS Committee of Emergency. In the days following the arrests of Hardy, Thelwall, Tooke, and several other members of the LCS and SCI, the spy's reports suggest that LCS meetings were often agitated. With Hardy's arrest, current membership tickets were now in government hands and John Pearce, the assistant secretary of the LCS, worried that this might result in a flood of new spies. Worship agreed to design a new card without charge and discussion followed on what sort of images might be appropriate. [114] The highly charged atmosphere of May 1794 may help explain the nature of Worship's design, if indeed this was his.

As a condensed set of revolutionary icons – the pike, the French revolutionary cockade, the assassin's dagger, the reference to the slavery of subjects (quite literally) under the British crown, and the caption's

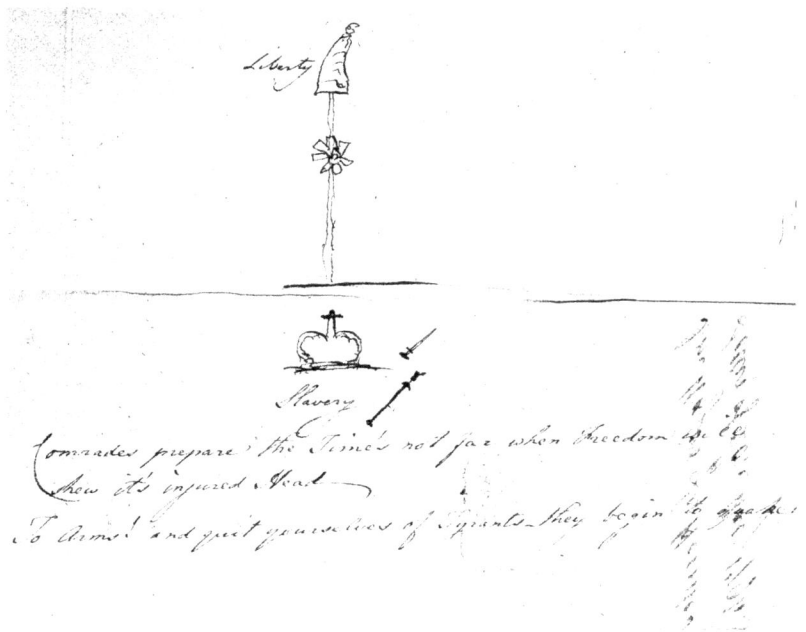

Figure 2.2 "Comrades, Prepare...," TS 11/957/3510 [1794] © The National Archives.

invocation of the anthem *La Marseillaise* – the iconography suggested for the ticket had excited strong feelings. During the emergency meeting of 22 May, as suggestions for the new cards were first discussed, the printer Edward Hodgson had spoken against incorporating a liberty cap or other perceived "French" iconography: "French Insignias and devices had prevailed too much already & had done the Society no Service." But Worship –again, *if* the image is his – appears to have been allowed relatively free rein.[115] The result is powerful: the liberty cap rests on the bastion of the people's resistance, the Jacobin pike.[116] Scattered around the crown are the defeated accoutrements of tyrannical power, the scepter and, in a reversal of anti-radical propaganda, a dagger. So too, the distance between the lowly crown and the triumphant cap inverts the usual iconography of ancien-régime secular authority. Hodgson's resistance to "French" imagery thus might well stem not only from the way the image could be read by authorities but also for the way it allowed revolutionary imagining among fellow radicals. The text that was to have accompanied the image – "To Arms! and quit yourselves of Tyrants" – certainly allowed for such a reading.

In the midst of the arrests, LCS members such as Hodgson became wary of revolutionary semiotics. The meanings of other radical ephemera were more ambiguous. Consider "To Hell by Hanover" (Figure 2.3).[117] The ominous question at its center, "Who Knows How Soon?," seems to have interested Pitt's ministry. During Horne Tooke's trial for high treason, the prosecution questioned witnesses about the drawing, but no person admitted to having ever seen it.[118] The cartoon is subversively playful. As the caption states, poor George III has been endured long enough, and "canst not" be mended. So John Bull (British popular opinion awakened at last) drives the Hanoverians to hell, as the caption imagines the destruction of the king's body: "burn him devil burn him." Yet it is unclear just who the final targets of this satire are. One horned Jacobin fiend reaches to snatch the ass's crown, but the other sings the title of the French revolutionary song "Ca Ira, Ca Ira, Ca Ira," and is seemingly – madly – unable to get past the refrain. The image offers an ambivalence that suggests a teasing self-mockery; less a vision of radical intent, than a knowing iteration of alarmist fantasies. As a surviving fragment of British Jacobin visual culture, it testifies to a rich world of affiliation and seditious laughter. Here, everyday life tells a "bigger story from a smaller one."[119]

Conclusion: Everyday Life and Radical Identity

Between 1793 and 1796, visitors to the radical printer James Ridgway's bookshop in Marylebone could purchase a *Patriot's Calendar*. This striking assemblage contained the French revolutionary calendar, Fabre d'Eglantine's essay on the significance of the new calendar, and the words and music to a collection of French revolutionary and British radical songs.

Figure 2.3 "To Hell by Hanover," TS/11/957 [1794?] © The National Archives.

Also included was a British almanac: readers could thereby locate domestic events against the revolutionary reconfiguration of time.[120] Placing British Jacobinism within everyday life allows us to better understand the cultural politics that produced an artifact like the *Patriot's Calendar*, as something like a pocket guide to British Jacobinism. What songs to sing, what days to mark with a greeting to one's fellow *citoyen*, what toasts to declare – such repertoires of identity connected the formal and regulated practices of LCS meetings with the everyday world of metropolitan popular culture. This chapter has sought to examine the connection, exploring the margins of Corresponding Society's more formal practices, and understanding those margins as themselves meaningful in terms of lived space and time, and embodied practice. The array of unofficial radical practices reflects that encounter of the necessarily regulated spaces of formal radical practice with the prolix world of everyday life. They remind us that British radicalism was not simply an ideology –whether coherent or fragmented – but also a cluster of identities that were used and creatively reused, in the policed meeting rooms of taverns and ale houses, and in the looser, desirous world of London's fields and streets.[121]

Theorists of everyday life have often been accused of valorizing what is in effect no more than the banal politics of gesture, detached from any effort at broader social transformation. As Lefebvre wrote, "any transgression which ceases to be an act and becomes a state is in fact no more than a flight (needless to say, a flight backwards)."[122] And yet, much of the radical movement of the 1790s took the form of struggle over symbol, ranging from contestations over political vocabulary in satires like Charles Pigott's *Political Dictionary Explaining the True Meaning of Words*, to caricatures visible to the public in print shops scattered across the capital, to interventions staged at theaters to secure alternative meanings in ostensibly loyalist drama. The 1790s were a moment of extraordinarily deep and sustained interrogation of the relationship between power and representation. In this sense, the furtive, sometimes intentional and sometimes spontaneous irruptions of sedition or utopian desire, suggest a half-articulated contest over what radical politics would be, as embodied in day-to-day practice and as represented in historical memory.

Notes

1 Ian Haywood, *Romanticism and Caricature* (Cambridge: CUP, 2013), 60; Marilyn Butler, *Romantics, Rebels, and Reactionaries* (Oxford: OUP, 1981), 53.
2 John Brewer, *The Common People and Politics, 1750–1790s* (Cambridge: Chadwyck-Healey, 1986), 232–33. Saree Makdisi uses Gillray's print to suggest a parallel tendency to exoticize and demean plebeian Britons in ways similar to colonial representations of Indian criminality. Saree Makdisi, *Making England Western: Occidentalism, Race & Imperial Culture* (Chicago, IL: University of Chicago Press, 2014), 30–32. On the conflation of Irish and black representational codes, see Marcus Wood, *Blind Memory: Visual Representations of Slavery in England, 1780 – 1865* (Routledge, 2000), 165–68. For a contemporary literary evocation, see Timothy Thurm, Esq. (pseud.), *The Monkeys in Red Caps, an Old Story; Newly Inscribed to the Club of Jacobins* (1797).
3 E. H. Gombrich, "The Cartoonist's Armoury," in *Meditations on a Hobby Horse and other Essays on the Theory of Art* (Phaidon, 1963), 127–42, at 128, 138–39.
4 *A Narrative of the Insults Offered to the King on his Way to and from the House of Lords* (1795), 13–14. On London's late eighteenth-century ungoverned spaces, see Makdisi, *Making England Western*, 47–49.
5 Michael T. Davis rightfully notes that such self-representations acted to provide structure for meetings but also to explicitly counter loyalist accusations of disorder and incivility. See Michael T. Davis, "'The Mob Club?' The London Corresponding Society and the Politics of Civility in the 1790s," in *Unrespectable Radicals: Popular Politics in the Age of Reform*, ed. Michael T. Davis and Paul Pickering (Aldershot: Ashgate, 2008), 21–40.
6 Steve Poole notes the absence among many radicals of a clear contemporary distinction between insurrection and constitutionalism, since as he puts it, the "latter was often cited in justification of the former." Steve Poole, "The Politics of Protest Heritage, 1790–1850," in *Remembering Protest in Britain since 1500: Memory, Materiality and the Landscape*, ed. Carl J. Griffin and Briony McDonagh (Cham: Palgrave Macmillan, 2018), 187–213, at 189.
7 BL, Add. MS. 27817, Thomas Hardy, "Introductory Letter to a Friend," 1799, fol. 62.
8 BL, Add. MS. 27814, Thomas Hardy, "A History of the Origin and Progress of the London Corresponding Society," 1799, fol. 23.

9 Günther Lottes, "Radicalism, Revolution and Political Culture: An Anglo-French Comparison," in *The French Revolution and British Popular Politics*, ed. Mark Philp (Cambridge: CUP, 1991), 78–98, at 95.

10 E. P. Thompson took Hardy's later account of the origin of the LCS as self-evident: Hardy's role as primary founder was unquestioned. E. P. Thompson, *The Making of the English Working Class* (Gollancz, 1963), 17–18. Mary Thale's investigation complicated this reading by noting discrepancies between Hardy's later account (from 1799), and earlier remarks made during his trial about being introduced to the society by an unnamed person. Thale, xvi–xxii. More recently, Jenny Graham has argued that SCI figures such as Horne Tooke may well have had a primary role in creating and encouraging the LCS. Jenny Graham, *The Nation, the Law and the King: Reform Politics in England, 1789–1799*, 2 vols. (Lanham, MD: University Press of America, 2000), 1: 276–78.

11 Thomas Hardy, *Memoirs of Thomas Hardy, Written by Himself* (1832), 16. Hardy began assembling notes for the history of the LCS in 1799. See BL, Add. MS. 27817, Hardy, "Introductory Letter to a Friend," 1799, fol. 7.

12 Henri Lefebvre, *Everyday Life in the Modern World*, trans. Sacha Rabinovitch (New York: Harper and Row, 1971), 6. For German labor historians related explorations of the everyday lives of German workers, see Geoff Eley, "Labor History, Social History, *Alltagsgeschichte*: Experience, Culture, and the Politics of the Everyday – A New Direction for German Social History?," *JMH* 61 (1989): 297–343; Paul Steege, Andrew Stuart Bergerson, Maureen Healy, and Pamela E. Swett, "The History of Everyday Life: A Second Chapter," *JMH* 80 (2008): 358–78.

13 Michael E. Gardiner, *Critiques of Everyday Life* (Routledge, 2000), 87.

14 BL, Add. MS. 27814, Hardy, "Origin and Progress of the LCS," 1799, fol. 7.

15 BL, Add. MS. 27817, Hardy, "Introductory Letter to a Friend," 1799, fol. 7.

16 *PH*, vol. 39, cols. 1476–77, Commons, 25 May 1792.

17 BL, Add. MS. 27814, Hardy, "Origin and Progress of the LCS," 1799, fol. 18.

18 TS 11/954/3498, report from Groves, 13 February 1794, in Thale, 113.

19 James Parkinson, *A Vindication of the London Corresponding Society* (1794), 8–9.

20 BL, Add. MS. 27814, Hardy, "Origin and Progress of the LCS," 1799, fol. 18.

21 *State Trials for High Treason, Embellished with Portraits. Part Third, Containing the Trial of Mr. John Thelwall, Reported by a Student in the Temple* (1795), 60.

22 For the attractiveness of the LCS's participatory processes, see John Barrell, *The Spirit of Despotism: Invasions of Privacy in the 1790s* (Oxford: OUP, 2006), 57.

23 BL, Add. MS. 27808, "Notes respecting the London Corresponding Society," fol. 28.

24 For a sensitive evocation of the democratic space of the Beaufort Buildings, see Judith Thompson, "From Forum to Repository: A Case Study in Romantic Cultural Geography," *European Romantic Review* 15 (2004): 177–91.

25 BL, Add. MS. 27808, "Notes respecting the London Corresponding Society," fol. 29.

26 Ibid.

27 Michael T. Davis, ed., *London Corresponding Society, 1792–1799*, 6 vols. (Pickering & Chatto, 2002), 2: 29, 51, 65, 83.

28 For constant links made by loyalists and conservatives between radicalism and the "noisy," ungovernable "mob," see Michael T. Davis, "The Noise and

Emotions of Political Trials in Britain during the 1790s," in *Political Trials in an Age of Revolutions: Britain and the North Atlantic, 1793–1848,* ed. Michael T. Davis, Emma Macleod, and Gordon Pentland (Cham: Palgrave Macmillan, 2019), 137–61.

29 For the importance of such space to popular mobilization, see Katrina Navickas, "Moors, Fields, and Popular Protest in South Lancashire and the West Riding of Yorkshire, 1800–1848," *Northern History* 46 (March 2009): 93–111; William H. Sewell, Jr., "Space in Contentious Politics," in *Silence and Voice in the Study of Contentious Politics,* ed. Ronald R. Aminzade, et al. (Cambridge: CUP, 2001), 51–88; Anthony Taylor, "'Commons-Stealers,' 'Land-Grabbers' and 'Jerry-Builders': Space, Popular Radicalism and the Politics of Public Access in London, 1848–1880," *International Review of Social History* 40 (1995): 383–407.

30 Edward Warford, *Old and New London: The City Ancient and Modern,* 6 vols. (1881), 2: 275–76.

31 Ibid., 4: 14–26.

32 *Gentleman's Magazine,* vol. 74 (1794), 668–69; David Hughson, *London: Being an Accurate History and Description of the British Metropolis and its Neighborhood to Thirty Miles Extent, by an Actual Perambulation* (1808), 443–45.

33 Elizabeth McKellar, "Peripheral Visions: Alternative Aspects and Rural Presences in Mid-Eighteenth-Century London," in *The Metropolis and its Image: Constructing Identities for London, c.1750–1950,* ed. Dana Arnold (Oxford: Blackwell, 1999), 29–47, at 40–41.

34 Robert Shoemaker, *The London Mob: Violence and Disorder in Eighteenth-Century England* (Hambledon, 2004), 19.

35 On the sailor's strike, see Nicholas Rogers, *Crowds, Culture, and Politics in Georgian Britain* (Oxford: OUP, 1998), 102–03. See also Adrian Randall, *Riotous Assemblies: Popular Protest in Hanoverian England* (Oxford: OUP, 2006), 133–37. For the Gordon Riots, see Rogers, *Crowds, Culture, and Politics,* 152–75; Shoemaker, *London Mob,* 117–18; Ian Haywood and John Seed, eds., *The Gordon Riots: Politics, Culture and Insurrection in Late Eighteenth-Century Britain* (Cambridge: CUP, 2012).

36 Nicholas Rogers, "Crowds and Political Festival in Georgian England," in *The Politics of the Excluded, c.1500–1850,* ed. Tim Harris (New York: Palgrave Macmillan, 2001), 233–64, at 250–51; Rogers, *Crowds, Culture, and Politics,* 171–72.

37 See Miles Ogborn, *Spaces of Modernity: London's Geographies, 1680–1780* (New York: Guilford Press, 1998), 75–115; Peter Borsay, "Culture, Status, and the English Landscape," *History* 67 (1982): 1–12; Joanna Innes, "Managing the Metropolis: London's Social Problems and their Control, c.1660–1830," in *Two Capitals: London and Dublin, 1500–1840,* ed. Peter Clark and Raymond Gillespie (Oxford: OUP, 2001), 53–80; Barrell, *Spirit of Despotism,* 48. Moorfields, a site of Gordon rioting in 1780, is an example of this process, having been under increasing development since the previous decade. See Henry Lawrence, *City Trees: A Historical Geography from the Renaissance through the Nineteenth Century* (Charlottesville: University of Virginia Press, 2006), 148–49.

38 Michel Foucault, "Of Other Spaces: Utopias and Heterotopias," *Diacritics* 16 (Spring 1986): 22–27. See also Navickas, "Moors, Fields, and Popular Protest," 109–10; idem, *Protest and the Politics of Space and Place, 1789–1848* (Manchester: Manchester University Press, 2016), 236–47; Patrick Joyce, *The Rule of Freedom: Liberalism and the Modern City* (Verso, 2003), 221–23.

39 Hardy later noted that the Spitalfields meeting attracted curious onlookers merely by being held so publically: "God bless them says some of the women and poor working people—success to them said others." BL, Add. MS. 27814, fol. 57, in Thale, 87.

40 Ibid., fols. 39–43, 48, in Thale, 30–31.

41 HO 42/26, Colquhoun to Evan Nepean, 25 October 1793, fols. 806–07.

42 *The Trial of Thomas Briellat for Seditious Words before Mr. Mainwaring, at the Sessions-House, Clerkenwell-Green, December 6, 1793, taken in Shorthand by Mr. Ramsay* (1794), 8, 14–15, 20, 22–23, 40.

43 BL, Add MS. 27812, Minutes: LCS General Committee, 21 September 1796, fols. 225–67, in Thale, 366–69.

44 Thale, 252.

45 Sewell, "Space in Contentious Politics," 54–56.

46 *Proceedings of a General Meeting of the London Corresponding Society, Held on Monday October the 26th, 1795, in a Field Adjacent to Copenhagen House, in the County of Middlesex* (1795), 15.

47 *Considerations* would be published on 21 November. See Bod. Lib., GD, entries for 16–21 November 1795, accessed 10 February 2020. Jon Mee, *Print, Publicity, and Radicalism in the 1790s:* The Laurel of Liberty (Cambridge: CUP, 2016), 184.

48 Thale, xxiii–xxiv. See also John Barrell, *Imagining the King's Death: Figurative Treason, Fantasies of Regicide, 1793–1796* (Oxford: OUP, 2000), 551–54; Mee, *Print, Publicity, and Radicalism*, 107–08.

49 *The Correspondence of the London Corresponding Society, Revised and Corrected* (1795), 3, in Davis, ed., *London Corresponding Society*, 2: 111.

50 Ibid.

51 See Roger Wells, *Wretched Faces: Famine in Wartime England, 1793–1801* (Gloucester: Alan Sutton, 1988), chapters 3 and 7.

52 Davis, *Correspondence of the London Corresponding Society*, 2: 111.

53 *Narrative of the Proceedings at a General Meeting of the London Corresponding Society* (1795), 1–2. For the size of the gathering, see Thale, 252, n29.

54 *Kentish Weekly Post*, 30 June 1795; Davis, *Correspondence of the London Corresponding Society*, 2: 111.

55 *Proceedings of a General Meeting of the London Corresponding Society, Held on Monday October the 26th, 1795, in a Field Adjacent to Copenhagen House, in the County of Middlesex* (1795), 2.

56 Ibid., 14.

57 *London Corresponding Society, Meeting at Mary-Le-Bone Fields*, in Davis, ed., *London Corresponding Society*, 2: 58.

58 *Account of the Proceedings of a Meeting of the People in a Field near Copenhagen House, Thursday, Nov. 12* (1795), 3.

59 *To the Parliament and the People of Great Britain. An Explicit Declaration of the Principles and Views of the London Corresponding Society* (1795).

60 Albert Goodwin, *The Friends of Liberty: The English Democratic Movement in the Age of the French Revolution* (Cambridge, MA: Harvard University Press, 1979), 373.

61 HO 42/36, John Lewis de Koven to John Carter, 25 November 1795, fol. 286. The German revolutionary would later be known as Charles Random de Barenger, a swindler and confidence man at the center of the 1814 Stock Exchange fraud. See Ian Klaus, *Forging Capitalism: Rogues, Swindlers, Frauds, and the Rise of Modern Finance* (New Haven, CT: Yale University Press, 2014), 27–61.

62 HO 42/36, "Address of the Gentlemen, Freeholders, Freemen, and Inhabitants of the City of Durham," 14 November 1795, fol. 245.

63 HO 42/36, "Address of inhabitants of the borough of Gosport and parish of Alverstoke," 16 November 1795, fol. 249.

64 For suggested identification of John Reeves as the author of the *Narrative*, see Barrell, *Spirit of Despotism*, 68.

65 *Narrative of the Insults Offered to the King*, 9, 12.

66 Ibid., 11.

67 On minutes as a form that tends to marginalize unofficial behavior, see Courtney Bender, "Bakhtinian Perspectives on 'Everyday Life' Sociology," *Bakhtin and the Human Sciences: No Last Words*, ed. Michael Mayerfeld Bell and Michael Gardiner (Sage, 1998), 181–95, at 189.

68 Reid wrote the pamphlet as a bargaining chip against prosecution; the preface gives his authority as witness: "the Author of this undertaking, having been involved in the dangerous delusion he now explodes, may reasonably be admitted a competent witness of the events he describes." William Reid, *Rise and Dissolution of the Infidel Societies in this Metropolis Rise and Dissolution* (1800), iv. For an excellent discussion of Reid and his work, see Iain McCalman, "The Infidel as Prophet: William Reid and Blakean Radicalism," *Historicizing Blake*, ed. Steve Clark and David Worrall (Palgrave Macmillan, 1994), 24–42.

69 Reid, *Rise and Dissolution,* 18–21. On street-level radical proselytization, see HO 42/31, letter from James Bennett, 5 June 1794, fols. 15–17, complaining about a LCS pamphlet "being put into my hand this Morning between 1 and 2 O'Clock." The society's account of Hardy's arrest had been published and freely distributed after 22 May 1794. See TS 11/956/3501, report from Metcalfe: Committee of Emergency, 22 May 1794, in Thale, 171. Or consider HO42/31, George Rose to Home Office, 17 June 1794, fol. 189, where the collar-maker James Becket illuminated his window in Putney with a "wretched transparent painting" of a liberty tree in "open defiance" of the local churchwarden's orders. A crowd of supporters gathered outside for much of the night.

70 Juan Manuel de Queiroz, "The Sociology of Everyday Life as a Perspective," *Current Sociology* 37 (Spring, 1989): 31–39, at 34. For his distinction between strategies and tactics, see Michel de Certeau, *The Practice of Everday Life*, trans. Steven Rendall (Berkeley: University of California Press, 1988), 34–39.

71 Gardiner, *Critiques*, 3. See also Steege et al., "History of Everyday Life."

72 Gardiner, *Critiques*, 34–35.

73 William H. Sewell, Jr., "The Concept of Culture(s)," in *Beyond the Cultural Turn: New Directions in the Study of Society and Culture*, ed. Victorian E. Bonnell and Lynn Hunt (Berkeley: University of California Press, 1999), 35–61, at 54.

74 Henri Lefebvre, *The Production of Space*, trans. Donald Nicholson-Smith (London: Blackwell, 1991), 87.

75 See Gardiner, *Critiques*, 16–17, quoting Laurie Langbauer, "Cultural Studies and the Politics of the Everyday," *Diacritics* 22 (1992): 47–65, at 51, noting the everyday "marks the site not only where people are determined in ways they cannot see, but where they project and imagine utopically how to think outside and elude what determines thought and imagination."

76 HO 42/31/88, George Perry to William Pitt, 17 June 1794, fols. 200–01.

77 Ibid.

78 Although Perry does not identify Thompson's club as a division of the LCS, John Barrell's mapping of LCS meeting places indicates that divisions met in

several close-by sites between 1792 and 1795. Barrell, *Spirit of Despotism*, 50–51, 53. Interestingly, a little over a year later, one "Joseph Thompson" appears in LCS General Committee minutes as one of twenty-three men wishing to establish a LCS division to meet at the Fountain public house on Virginia Row in Shoreditch. BL, Add. MS. 27813, Minutes, LCS General Committee, 27 August 1795, fols. 113v-21, in Thale, 291. Ian Newman has mapped out and offered some history of the Fountain and many other LCS meeting sites. See his fine website "London Corresponding Society Meeting Places: Exploring the 1790s Alehouse," accessed 1 August 2018, http://www.1790salehouse.com/search/label/Fountain.

79 Thus Colquhoun stressed the responsibly of landlords to prohibit seditious political clubs and raucous trade societies alike. Patrick Colquhoun, *Facts Relative to Public Houses in the City of London and Its Environs* (1794), 35–37.

80 TS 11/1118/5748, crown brief, "The Case of John Martin," February 1793.

81 HO 42/23, letter from William Bulkeley, 22 December 1792, fol. 486B-486C. It was a busy week for Bulkeley, who on 19 December, the very night of the brawl at Chelsea Hospital, had written to Henry Dundas with information of another man who had damned the king. According to Bulkeley, Thomas Welford, a 72-year-old invalid pensioner at the hospital, was drinking at a tavern in Jews Row the previous Monday, when one of his companions offered a toast to the king, Welford had loudly replied "Damn the King I have lost more than I have got by him." Welford was reported but not charged after Bulkeley spoke to his good character. HO 42/23, Bulkeley to Dundas, 19 December 1792, fols. 430B–C.

82 TS 11/1118/5748, crown brief, "The Case of John Martin," February 1793.

83 Martin, Sutter, Jones, and Holmes seem to have been fined and bound for recognizance at the February 1793 Middlesex Sessions. See *London Lives,* Middlesex Sessions: Justices Working Documents, February 1793 (LMSMPS508810028-30), www.londonlives.org, version 2.0, accessed 26 August 2018.

84 TS 11/1118/5748, deposition of Joseph Webb, February 1793.

85 HO 42/23, William Bulkeley to David Puttee, 22 December 1795, fols. 486B-486C.

86 TS 11/959/3505, report from Lynam, LCS division twenty-three, 11 December 1792, in Thale, 34; TS 11/954/3498, report from Lynam, LCS General Committee, 27 December 1792, in Thale, 36.

87 BL, Add. MS. 27812, Journal: LCS General Committee, 17 January 1793, fols. 30v–1v, in Thale, 43.

88 By mid-May 1794, the spy William Metcalfe was reporting that some members of the LCS Committee of Emergence, formed after the arrest of Hardy, Thelwall, and others, believed that regular soldiers were "3 to 1" in favor of the LCS's program. See TS 11/956/3501, report from Metcalfe, Committee of Emergency, 22 May 1794, in Thale, 172. See also Barrell, *Imagining the King's Death*, 212.

89 See Anna Clark, *The Struggle for the Breeches: Gender and the Making of the British Working Class* (Berkeley: University of California Press, 1995), 153–57. Yet women also formed part of everyday anti-monarchism. In January 1793, for example, James Saunders warned magistrates about a Mrs. Redan in Haymarket, whose husband had left the country "for being a strong Democrat." Saunders claimed that despite her husband's absence, Mrs. Redan continued to organize plans to facilitate a successful French invasion. HO 42/28, 23 January 1793, fol. 108.

90 See Caroline Louise Nielsen, "The Chelsea Out-Pensioners: Image and Reality in Eighteenth-Century and Early Nineteenth-Century Social Care" (PhD thesis, Newcastle University, 2014), 219–24. See also Nielsen, "Continuing to Serve: Representations of the Elderly Veteran Soldier in the late Eighteenth and early Nineteenth Centuries," in *Men after War*, ed. Stephen McVeigh and Nicola Cooper (Routledge, 2013), 18–35.

91 See, for example, HO 42/27, letter from William Jones, 9 November 1793, fols. 81–82, reporting that during the attack at the Sir John Falstaff public house in Thames Street, a group of king-damning "vile republicans" led by an Indiaman commander named Faro assaulted a retired military office, William Jones, and his friend, Captain Donald Cameron. The republicans were brought before the magistrate James Sanderson, but by then had bribed the landlord to hush up evidence supporting a charge of seditious words.

92 While Robert Shoemaker finds that public violence declined across all classes during the late eighteenth and early nineteenth centuries, Anna Clark notes the continued importance among some urban artisans of a code of masculinity informed by ribald libertinism and continued readiness to violence until after 1815. See Robert Shoemaker, "Male Honour and the Decline of Public Violence in Eighteenth-Century London," *SH* 26 (2001): 190–208; Anna Clark, *Struggle*, chapter. 8.

93 "Of Popular Societies," *The Cabinet,* 3 vols. (Norwich, 1795), 2: 234–6. See also Penelope J. Corfield and Chris Evans, eds., *Youth and Revolution in the 1790s: Letters of William Pattison, Thomas Amyot and Henry Crabb Robinson* (Stroud: Alan Sutton, 1996), 187. Corfield and Evans were unable to determine the essay's author. On the LCS's harried efforts to secure meeting spaces, see Barrell, *Invasions of Privacy*, 51–52; and more broadly, see Katrina Navickas, *Protest and the Politics of Space and Place* (Manchester: Manchester University Press, 2016), 23–50.

94 "Of Popular Societies," 236.

95 TS 11/965/3509, "Voluntary Examination of Joseph Goulding of the Parish of St. Mary White-Chapel," 18 May 1794. Wickham was the JP who employed Gosling to infiltrate LCS meetings starting in April 1794. Thale, 135, n92.

96 Doreen Massey, "Politics and Space/Time," in *Place and the Politics of Identity*, ed. Michael Keith and Steve Pile (Routledge, 1993), 141–61, at 156, 59. See also Veena Das, "Violence and the Work of Time," in *Signifying Identities: Anthropological Perspectives on Boundaries and Contested Values*, ed. Anthony P. Cohen (Routledge, 2000), 159–73.

97 On the Crown and Anchor tavern as a visual icon, see Christina Parolin, *Radical Spaces: Venues of Popular Politics in London, 1790–c.1845* (Canberra: Australian National University E Press, 2020), 105–15.

98 TS 11/954/3498, "Report on the Anniversary Meeting of the Constitutional Society at the Crown & Anchor, Friday 2 May, 1794," fol. 2.

99 Ibid.

100 Ibid.

101 See James Epstein, *Radical Expression: Political Language, Ritual, and Symbol in England, 1790–1850* (Oxford: OUP, 1994), chapter 5.

102 TS 11/954, report on the SCI anniversary meeting, 2 May 1794.

103 TS 11/955/3500. See also Christina Bewley and David Bewley, *Gentleman Radical: A Life of John Horne Tooke, 1736–1812* (I. B. Taurus, 1998), 149.

104 TS 11/955/3500.

105 Ibid.

106 TS 11/963/3509, oral report of George Saunders: LCS division thirteen, 19 May 1794, fols. 158–8v, in Thale, 171.

107 For the presence of songs and singing at LCS meetings and Place's refusal to acknowledge their importance, see Mee, *Print, Publicity, and Radicalism,* 82–83. See, more generally, Ian Newman, "Civilizing Taste: 'Sandman Joe,' the Bawdy Ballad, and Metropolitan Improvement," *Eighteenth-Century Studies* 48 (2015): 437–56.

108 Reid, *Rise and Dissolution,* 20.

109 Ibid., 14.

110 TS 11/956/3501, report from Metcalfe: LCS division six, 19 May 1794, in Thale, 168–69. The drawing later reappeared on the reverse side of the celebratory token Thomas Spence produced in 1795 commemorating Eaton's acquittal the previous year.

111 Steege, et al., "History of Everyday Life," 365.

112 See Marcus Wood, *Radical Satire and Print Culture* (Oxford: OUP, 1994); Vic Gatrell, *City of Laughter: Sex and Satire in Eighteenth-Century London* (New York: Walker and Co., 2006), 483–529.

113 HO 42/30, fols. 137–39, Mayor John Wray to Henry Dundas, 20 May 1794.

114 TS 11/965/3510a, report from Groves: Committee of Emergency, 22 May 1794, in Thale, 174. In the end, Worship produced a different design for the new tickets, featuring Britannia with a liberty cap on one side, and a dove on the other. See TS 11/956/3501, report from Metcalfe: LCS General Committee, 12 June 1794, in Thale, 182.

115 TS 11/965/3510a.

116 For the pike's symbolic importance within British radicalism, see Barrell, *Imagining the King's Death,* 227–30.

117 TS 11/957 (undated, but before John Horne Tooke's trial which began 17 November 1794).

118 *ST,* vol. 25, "Trial of John Horne Tooke," col. 425.

119 The phrase belongs to Steege, et al., "History of Everyday Life," 375.

120 *The Patriot's Calendar, for the Year 1794, containing the Usual English Almanack, the Decree of the French National Convention for the Alteration of the Style* (1794).

121 Compare de Certeau's comments about the North African living in Paris, who "insinuates *into* the system imposed upon him." Certeau, *Practice of Everyday Life,* 30.

122 Henri Lefebvre, *The Survival of Capitalism: Reproduction of Relations of Production,* trans. F. Bryant (New York: Allison and Busby, 1976), quoted in Gardiner, *Critiques,* at 9.

3 "Thoughts That Flash Like Lightning"

Thomas Holcroft and Radical Theater

Reviewing George Watson's loyalist historical drama *England Preserved* (1795), the popular dramatist, novelist, and translator Thomas Holcroft lamented the use of the stage to reinforce militarism and anti-French bigotry. The play, he wrote, taught

> that a man, who is ready to plunge his sword into the hearts of all who shall differ from him in action or opinion, is a hero; and particularly that France breeds such a pestiferous swarm of wretches, that to sweep them from the face of the earth would be the summit of virtue.[1]

England Preserved had used events during the Hundred Years War – duplicitous statesmen making secret alliances with France – to comment on contemporary treason and sedition. It was a charged moment for topicality. The play debuted at the Theatre Royal, Covent Garden in February 1795, two months after the treason trials had ended with John Thelwall's acquittal. In his critique, Holcroft noted that while Watson's play portrayed "hatred, revenge, and a thirst for blood" as social goods, this was not a product of the author's ill intent but rather a matter of error. Watson was simply one of many who had imbibed those "lawful prejudices" that produced the chauvinism and violence that had now claimed "many hundreds of thousands" of victims. Theater was complicit in making war.

In contrast, Holcroft saw theater as an instrument of radical reform; his efforts to create a "Jacobin" theater guide this chapter. Self-educated son of a failed shoemaker, then stable boy, then traveling actor, he made his way into London's literary world during the 1770s and 1780s. By the early 1790s, he was in his mid-forties and was a well-established author, closely associated with William Godwin and part of an influential circle of Jacobin intellectuals. However, unlike Godwin, or many of the romantic poets who were influenced by Godwin's ideas, Holcroft was a leading member of the SCI, whose political activism caught the attention of Pitt's government, leading to charges of high treason and imprisonment during the fall of 1794. He thus wrote his review of *England Preserv'd* having already been publically labeled as an "acquitted felon" – technically speaking, Holcroft was discharged rather than acquitted on charges of high treason – by Secretary at War William Windham in the House of Commons immediately after the acquittals.[2]

As a "Jacobin" dramatist, Holcroft sought to harness the liberating nature of performance; theater could speak and signify what he called "moral and political truths" that would educate subjects into citizens.[3] At the center of such truths lay universal benevolence – a conception of social relations based upon sincerity, sentiment, and sympathy inherited from earlier eighteenth-century commentators, together with a revolutionary-era emphasis upon egalitarian reason that would extend benevolence across society as a whole, stripping away the social artifices and prejudices so injurious to humanity. This conception deeply informs Holcroft's novels; *Anna St. Ives* (1792) is often credited with establishing the Jacobin novel as a genre.[4] But in seeking to appeal to the theater audience's own reason and sympathetic emotion, the central question was whether such a conception of social relations could actually be represented on stage. Could the sincere radical heart be portrayed in performance? Could the commitment to British Jacobinism be part of the public identity of the Georgian stage, or was "Jacobin" theater an impossibility, a horizon too far, a desire for something not yet possible in the social world?

As a social, cultural, and political space, Covent Garden theater was well suited for the production of loyalist drama such as Watson's but the conditions of communicative possibility for republican representations were highly restricted. Together with the Royal Theatre, Drury Lane, Covent Garden was the only theater in London holding a royal patent allowing the performance of spoken drama, and its content was subject to strict pre-production censorship by the lord chamberlain's office. Even as a more anarchic and subversive "illegitimate" theatrical culture had begun to develop away from the two patent theaters (as shown brilliantly by the late Jane Moody), spoken drama in London generally was politically loyalist, ideologically conservative, and emotionally xenophobic.[5] Through its invocations of domesticity, sentiment and patriarchy, the antirevolutionary drama of the 1790s formed a potent ideological response to revolutionaries and sympathizers at home.[6] It provided a hegemonic, ordered world to viewers, ensuring their complicity in the production of conservative ideology.[7]

Yet not entirely. As Roger Chartier notes, "no work has any meaning outside of the varied forms that offer it for decipherment."[8] The meanings of a work performed at the theater, especially when performed under the control of a state censor, are produced through a complex negotiation among playwright, manager, actors, audiences, and the state. Moreover, the space of the theater itself informs meaning.[9] Despite the enforced loyalism surrounding performances at the patent theaters, audiences in late-Georgian London were highly skilled at appropriating a theatrical grammar by which to demand their perceived rights as English subjects.[10] Such strategies revealed the potency of theatrical representation in a society where, as Gillian Russell notes, "performance, display and spectatorship were essential components of the social mechanism."[11] As official space tied to the crown and state, the patent theaters had to be controlled. Despite the segregation of audiences through private boxes, gallery, and pit, the crowd remained socially mixed, and so was always present as a potential threat to order and authority.

During the 1790s, London's theaters saw repeated "disruptions" that gave dramatic texts and performances new, radical meanings, despite the strict control of drama's explicit content by the lord chamberlain's office. At the Haymarket theater in 1792, audiences challenged the traditional singing of "God Save the King" by singing the French revolutionary anthem "Ça Ira" instead. To the Pitt ministry, such refashionings were a threat. The lord chamberlain's office vowed to close down the theater at Haymarket if Richard Brinsley Sheridan continued to allow the seditious singing.[12] As discussed in Chapter 1, John Thelwall roused the crowd at Covent Garden theater in January 1794 to cheer the "true patriotism" he detected in Thomas Otway's *Venice Preserv'd* so that he might "feel the sense of the audience."[13] Thelwall's intervention formed part of the character evidence brought against him at his trial for high treason later that year.[14] As these counter-performances show, British radicals saw that meaning was something that was produced through performance and reception: supposedly hegemonic displays were open to alternative readings. [15] Arguably, the state inadvertently assisted this production of meaning, just as government efforts to repress radical speech and action instead created a field of play, endowing republican dissent with greater transgressive force. A similar dynamic affected the space of the theater and contributed to the openness of performance: state censorship produced audiences more willing to read political meanings into the drama. For example, the evening after Thelwall's acquittal for high treason, a Drury Lane production of Mary Robinson's satirical farce *Nobody* saw rioting when audience members protested revisions that emphasized a loyalist theme by replacing its civilian hero with a soldier. The ministerial-funded *Sun* blamed the rioting that resulted on "that spirit of Equality which certain persons so seditiously inculcate."[16] Both political authorities and political radicals saw the theater as a space in which texts and performance could be appropriated and moved to new ends.

This chapter first discusses Covent Garden theater as a space informed by cultural and political practices that, though dominated by conservative and loyalist drama, nonetheless remained a potential site during the 1790s for representing socially and politically radical ideas. To be sure, radical theater faced far greater restrictions then did radical literature.

Jacobin publications were subject to prosecution for seditious libel, but in contrast to the pre-publication regulation of plays through the lord chamberlain's office, censorship of texts followed the act of publication, and charges were subject to the uncertainties of trial by jury. Moreover, theatrical performance was also restricted by the conventions of sentimental comedy. Yet despite such limitations, these conventions gave British audiences an interpretive scheme that allowed them to translate representations of family strife into wider social and political meanings.[17]

The second part of the chapter examines Holcroft's science of acting, as constituted through his autodidactic reading of Enlightenment texts on cognition, physiology, and acting. Focusing on the physicality of performance, the space where the actor's body signed the meanings of the play, his conception of acting sought to generate specific affective reactions in the audience. This approach would stabilize meanings that too often seemed to slip out of control, opening space for meanings that offered a radical critique of existing social institutions, thus enlisting theater to work toward cultural and social reform.

The chapter concludes by examining two texts in terms of their embodiment on stage: Holcroft's *The Road to Ruin* (1792) and, more briefly, *The Deserted Daughter* (1795). The point here is not that Holcroft's practice inscribed a fixed meaning on the plays' actions. Rather, the chapter argues that these strategies made radical meanings available to the various audiences who attended the plays. Meaning did not rest upon a simple correspondence between the events of the play's text and the world outside of the theater. Rather, meaning lay in the sets of relationships supplied by the characters, and the ways in which the different audiences who attended performances of the plays could comprehend and order those arrangements, and relate them to the structures that underlay social relations in the larger world.[18] Both plays explored the impact of luxury and commerce upon human social structures – a key concern of radicalism in the 1790s.[19] At Covent Garden theater, Holcroft transformed long-popular conventions of sentimental comedy into socially revolutionary signs, seeking to produce the sincere Jacobin heart on stage.

"Such Irresistible Force"

From its emergence in the first half of the eighteenth century, sentimental comedy – a genre exploring the bonds and relationships of domestic life – was a genre of social reform. Theater had long been seen as a powerful institution for forming, maintaining, and (according to some commentators) destroying the social order.[20] With the expansion of networks of sociability in the late seventeenth and early eighteenth centuries, manners, politeness, and theatricality became objects of increased cultural commentary.[21] In his essay written in 1710 upon the death of the noted actor Thomas Betterton, for example, Richard Steele celebrated the theater's role in "forming a free-born people."[22] Still reflecting on the phenomenon of theater a month after Betterton's funeral, Steele – whose *The Conscious Lovers* (1722) is often cited as establishing the sentimental genre – noted the social role of play-going, foregrounding as he did so the larger spectacle of mutual appreciation and apprehension among the audience:

> So many persons of different ranks and conditions are placed there in their most pleasing aspects....and the musical airs which are played to us put the whole company into a participation of the same pleasure, and by consequence, for that time, equal in humour, in fortune, and in quality.[23]

Few venues in London concentrated together a greater social range of subjects than the great patent theaters. For Steele, the mass of humanity at the theater worked to govern the otherwise centrifugal force of social difference. Plays, Steele suggested, should turn from the "history of princes and princesses," whose catastrophes "pass through our imaginations as incidents in which our fortunes are too humble to be concerned," toward "such adventures as befal persons not exalted above the common level."[24] Steele's colleague Joseph Addison thus advocated that playwrights make the stage "contribute to the advancement of morality, and to the reformation of the age."[25] The relationships and crises explored in sentimental drama – being closer to the experiences of the majority of the theater audience – would more deeply impress the minds of the audience and therefore reinforce the civilizing influence of polite sociability. Steele and Addison's insistence on the reciprocal influence of stage and social life registered larger concerns of social theorists about the power of the emotions and the role of imaginative impression in forming and maintaining the foundations of a society.[26] As the dramatist George Lillo wrote in the preface to *The London Merchant* (1731), sentimental comedy would carry "conviction to the mind with such irresistible force as to engage all the faculties and powers of the soul in the cause of virtue."[27] Social theorists thus invested the familial relationships explored in sentimental drama with great importance: the representation of such relationships on stage both reflected and informed that wider social world – which itself then constantly circulated back into the space of the theater.

This economy of the passions influenced continental theorists as well and directly influenced Thomas Holcroft's own dramaturgy. In the prefatory essay to his *Le fils naturel* (1757), Denis Diderot called for a greater use of scenic accuracy and pantomimic effects on the stage, giving detailed instructions in the play for pose and gesture. Such physical signs not only aided spoken dialogue, he suggested, but could even replace it.[28] The dramatist (and later member of the revolutionary Convention) Louis-Sébastien Mercier, who became friends with Holcroft during the latter's first trip to Paris in 1783, further democratized Diderot's sentimental drama to embrace a radicalized vision of drama as political intervention.[29] Holcroft returned to Paris the following year: having heard about the phenomenal success of Beaumarchais's *The Marriage of Figaro*, he was determined to adapt it for the English stage.[30] With the help of the poet Nicholas de Bonneville – who was to become a leading revolutionary and close friend of Thomas Paine – Holcroft succeeded in copying Beaumarchais's tale of aristocratic intrusion into the virtuous domestic sphere. He presented the adaptation, *The Follies of a Day*, in late 1784, with Holcroft himself taking the part of Figaro for its debut.[31] It was his greatest success until *The Road to Ruin* in 1792. By the 1790s, sentimental comedy had for decades been an important component in the staged drama of British urban life. Its conventions had become part of social and political commentary in France as well. Holcroft himself was in the thick of the dense cultural and literary exchange between London and Paris.[32] He was also beginning to write drama of his own: *Duplicity* had appeared at Covent Garden in 1781; *Seduction* in 1787.

During the 1790s, with revolution across the channel, and significant political ferment at home, John Larpent, the licenser of plays, saw the power of the genre as potentially dangerous.[33] Thus even a moderately satirical play such as Lady Eglantine Wallace's *The Whim* (1795) was banned by Larpent for its unfavorable representation of the aristocracy.[34] Usually, however, the censor had no need for such action: an unspoken agreement by managers and playwrights kept explicitly radical politics out of view. Even so friendly a figure to reform as Richard Sheridan, Foxite Whig and owner of the theater at Drury Lane, shied away from using the theater to score political points. In December 1795, during the height of debate in Parliament on the Treason and Sedition Bills, he praised the radical societies such as the LCS and the SCI, arguing that their "great meetings were a source of the virtues of the people, and a security for the preservation of the national character." Yet he "deemed a theatre no fit place for politics, nor would he think much of the principles or tastes of the man who should wish to introduce them into stage representation."[35] Sheridan's depiction of the unmediated authenticity and political discipline of the mass meeting contrasted sharply with the more threatening representation of political reform – always liable to slip out of control – at the theater. His caution, however, was hardly needed. Far from manifesting revolutionary sentiments, playwrights in the 1790s bombarded the London stage with representations of low foreigners, English martial prowess, and works seeking to counteract revolutionary history by dramatizing it along conservative narrative lines.[36]

"Thoughts that Flash like Lightning"

Theater and theatricality were complex signifiers in British Jacobin critiques of the Georgian social and political order, usually deployed metaphorically to register the inauthenticity and corruption of existing institutions. For example, at one point in the *Enquiry Concerning Political Justice* (1793), William Godwin, Holcroft's closest friend, considers the place of the stage in his imagined, benevolent world, and asks,

> Shall we have theatrical exhibitions? This seems to me to include an absurd and vicious cooperation. It may be doubted whether any men will hereafter come forward in any mode to repeat words and ideas not their own?… We yield supinely to the superior merit of our predecessors, because we are accustomed to indulge the inactivity of our own faculties. All formal repetition of other men's ideas seems to be a scheme for imprisoning for so long the operations of our own mind.[37]

Godwin himself was no stranger to theater, writing several plays himself and, as David O'Shaughnessy notes, attended the theater almost 2,000 times during his life.[38] But historians have rightly taken his missive as representing a larger radical project about moving social and political relationships from behind the mystifying draperies of tradition and convention into a perfectly rational and transparent representational economy. British radicals cast their debate in a language that insistently returned to themes of theatricality and authenticity: semiotic reform would address social and political ills. Paine, for example, responded to Edmund Burke's *Reflections on the Revolution in France* by pointing out its staged quality: "I cannot consider Mr. Burke's book in scarcely any other light than a dramatic performance; and he must, I think, have considered it in the same light himself."[39] Casting the Revolution as drama, Burke revealed performance's ability to shape and deform truth.[40] Burke's elaborate sorrow for the sufferings of Marie Antoinette, Paine argued, disguised a more complicated reality: "It is one of the arts of the drama to do so. If the crimes of men were exhibited with their sufferings, the stage effect would sometimes be lost, and the audience would be inclined to approve where it was intended they should commiserate."[41] Mary Wollstonecraft connected Burke's staginess to elite self-fashioning: his sentimental exclamations – emotion deserted by reason – would be "retail[ed] in theatrical attitudes" throughout "the fashionable world."[42] In similar fashion, other radicals depicted monarchical ritual as mystifying corruption. In his *A Political Dictionary* (1795), Charles Pigott defined "Pageant" as a

> spectacle, by the lure of which a minister may draw money for himself and his friends, by amusing the public mind; … and whilst

the People of England suffer their privileges to be restrained, their rights pillaged, and immunities plundered, the same pageants will be erected, and the same spectacles displayed.[43]

A major thrust of radicalism in the 1790s, then, involved a reforming impulse to move from theatricality to authenticity, from corrupted mediation to pure transparency.[44] The varied answers to the problem of representation – from new political arrangements demanded by radical societies, to new gender codes argued for by writers such as Wollstonecraft, to new language schemes envisioned by linguists as dissimilar as John Horne Tooke and Thomas Spence – demonstrate radical culture's insistent emphasis on representational clarity.[45] Their work represents a British Jacobin social imaginary that would offer new forms of egalitarian sociability and intellectual exchange.[46]

Holcroft shared in this painstaking attention to the problem of meaning and representation. Consider his extended review of the Scottish philosopher Dugald Stewart's *Elements of the Philosophy of the Human Mind* (1792), where he castigated the "loose and inaccurate manner in which the terms employed to explain the phenomena of mind have been used." This call for clearer prose was not simply the cry of a disgruntled critic. Holcroft focused on Stewart's division of consciousness into a reflective self, distinct from its sensory input, and countered that the mind's "whole knowledge consists of individual facts, occurring in succession."[47] Holcroft's critique reflected his own appropriations of Enlightenment theories concerning cognition and language, in particular the French materialists Etienne Bonnot de Condillac and Claude-Adrien Helvétius. Condillac, writing on the origin of language, moved away from Locke's ambiguous suggestion that language had originated in sensation and reflection, and instead argued that primitive signs – gestures and *cris naturel* – had allowed idea-formation through sensation alone. Primordial signs allowed ideas to be connected because such gestures were themselves spontaneous and universal. Thus the accretion of knowledge through association was a primarily sensational process.[48] Helvétius moved even farther in this direction, arguing that feelings, moral and abstract qualities, were themselves the product purely of physical sensation.[49] Thus Holcroft insisted that the two "facts" that Stewart had put forward in his examination of psychology – the existence of sensation and the existence of one's own self – were "in reality but one fact." "Where," Holcroft asked, "is the difference between *remembering* that he felt a sensation, and *conceiving* that he feels it again?...What is reflection, what is experience, but sensation?...Is there to man any other actual existence than that of sensation?"[50] For Holcroft, as for Condillac and Helvétius, signs had their origins in sensory data and hence were universal in their meaning. The errors of humankind in its long, bloody history were due in part to the corruptions that had moved language away from its original transparency. Precision in language, especially when writing of the operations of the mind, was of absolute importance. In Stewart's case, Holcroft maintained, his opacity of language led him to introduce mysterious and "occult" metaphysical causes as explanations of mental phenomena. As Holcroft's response to Stewart indicates, British radicals' understandings of contemporary science significantly informed their commitment to transparency.[51] This commitment influenced not only Holcroft's literary practice but also the signs he put on stage. When Holcroft wrote that the literary arts had "the power to impress imitation in an irresistible manner," that through "the power of playing on the mind, interesting the affections," art had the power to "teach moral and political truths," he was using a scientific vocabulary.[52] For Holcroft, in order for theater to teach, communicative transparency was of paramount importance. It was needed not only in language but in bodily representation, gesture, and performance.[53]

By the 1790s, an ample body of scientific literature proclaimed the universality and purity of gestural communication. With the mechanization of medical physiology, as seen for example in George Cheyne's *The English Malady* (1733), and the popularization of materialist philosophy from the mid-eighteenth century onward, theories on acting underwent significant changes.[54] John Hill wrote at mid-century on the sympathy between player and audience: "we swelled and trembled as he did; like strings which are so perfectly concordant, that one being struck, the other answers, tho' distant."[55] Hill's description of the theater experience in turn reflected broader theories about the nervous system.[56] David Hartley, for example, described the expression and transmission of the passions among humans as the result of associations that played upon the vibratory qualities of the nerves.[57] Thus, as theorists of acting reminded their readers, players tapped into a reservoir of extraordinary power.[58]

Holcroft marveled at this phenomenon: "the sympathy between minds is wonderful, but we don't try to estimate it; one man laughing shall make a whole audience laugh."[59] Late in his career, in an essay on "The Art of Acting," Holcroft extended this understanding of the space between player and audience, writing that the player must have a "magnetic power of mind," a power that gave action an immediacy so strong "that words, after they are spoken, seem only to elucidate what appeared before."[60] Indeed, the player, he wrote, should work to "embue his soul with recollections never to be erased," and note

> all the wild starts of passion, to which the character to be represented is subject...and at that happy instant when he conceives them in their fullest force; should study all the various ways in which they show themselves ...their marks, prognostics, and appearance.[61]

Perfect gesture rendered meaning purely visible.[62]

The categorization and cataloguing of bodily signs in physiological treatises reveal the nearly universal belief that bodily language could be transparently performed and read. From John Bulwer's *Chirologia: Or the Natural Language of the Hand and Chironomia: Or the Art of Manual Rhetoric* (1644) through Johann Lavater's *Essays on Physiognomy* (1775–78), and indeed on into the early nineteenth century with Gilbert Austin's *Chironomia; or a Treatise on Rhetorical Delivery* (1806), gestural transparency was a constant trope in literature about communication and acting.[63] Time and again theorists charted the physical signs of gesture's universal language. In *Chironomia* for example, Austin caged the human body in a spherical grid, where gesture could be accurately and mathematically positioned (Figure 3.1). He followed this with plate

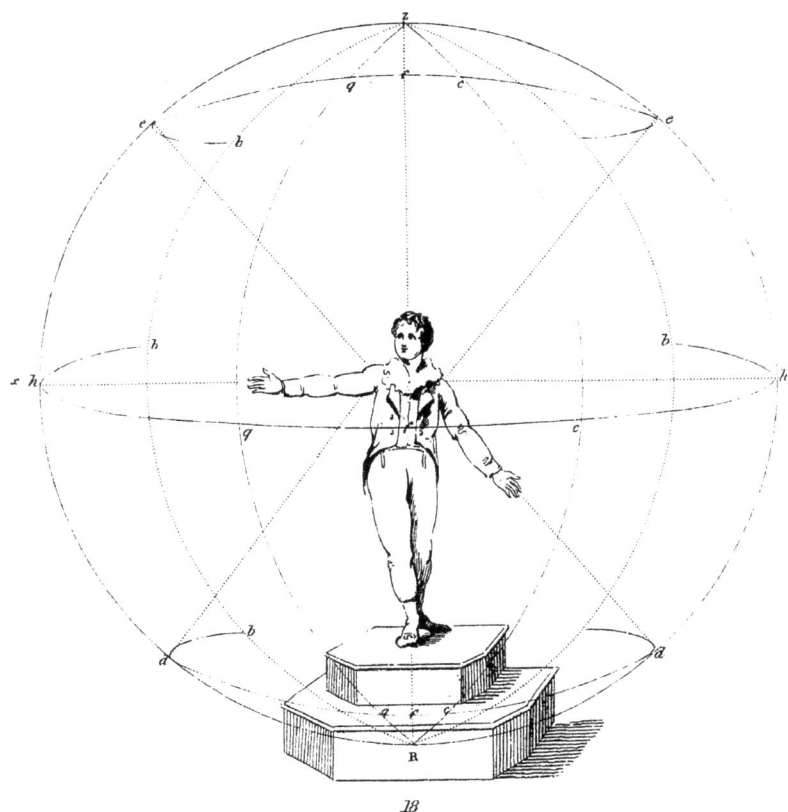

Figure 3.1 Gilbert Austin, *Chironomia; or, A Treatise on Rhetorical Delivery* (London, 1806; reprint, Carbondale; Southern Illinois University Press, 1966, ed. Mary Margaret Robb and Lester Thonssen), plate 2.

after plate of precise direction for the fully governed sign. For example in Fig. 3.2, "Aversion" first directed the subject's attention toward the object; then "suddenly the eyes are withdrawn, the head is averted, the feet retire, and the arms are projected out extended against the object." "Horror," however, "remains petrified."[64] These geometric, notational systems depended on the cultural power of the idea that gesture was, at heart, a universal and transparent language.[65] As Hill bluntly put it, gestures "are not arbitrary, or what the player pleases; they are dictated by nature; they are common to all mankind, and therefore all men understand them."[66]

Thus theater worked because between actor and audience there lay a space in which gesture invisibly traveled, a space filled with the acoustic vibrations of sensation. How else to explain the remarkable guide to performance that Holcroft offered in his short-lived periodical, *The Theatrical Recorder*, which gave gestural, emotional code for line after line of *Hamlet*? A brief sample of his text illustrates this point.

> *Deep but*
>   *articulate grief. Hamlet*: Oh, that this too *too* solid flesh would melt, *Thaw*, and *resolve* itself into a *dew*!
>   *Solemn alarm.* Or that the *Everlasting* had not fix'd
>   *Dissatisfaction,*
>   *but dignified* His *cannon* against *self-slaughter*! O God! O God!

Hamlet's mind, Holcroft wrote, was a perfect example of heroic genius: he had "exquisite sensibility, a judgment scarcely able to err, and boundless comprehension."[67] In Holcroft's rendering of the soliloquy, frozen

Figure 3.2 Gilbert Austin, *Chironomia; or, A Treatise on Rhetorical Delivery* (London, 1806; reprint, Carbondale; Southern Illinois University Press, 1966, ed. Mary Margaret Robb and Lester Thonssen), plate 10.

moment succeeds moment, each one a condensed and heightened tableau of thoughts that "flash like lightning."[68] And so each line is rendered utterly transparent – by language, but more so by gestural shorthand: "(Abhorrence) Fie on't! O fie! 'tis an unweeded garden,/ (Contempt) That grows to seed; things rank, and gross in nature,/ (Painful recollection) Possess it merely. That it should come to this!"[69] As Holcroft discusses the scene where Hamlet speaks to the ghost of his father, he makes clear this link between gestured emotion and the audience's own affective response. If all goes as directed, the scene "will again rekindle all the feelings of the audience."[70] Through gesture, both actor and audience create the Danish prince: "If memory fails but for a moment," Holcroft wrote,

> if the associations, or ideas, which the words are intended to convey, do not precede the words, if they are not marked by a sudden change of look and demeanor, or if, in either associations or words, the memory be at any loss, again Hamlet *is no longer before us.*[71]

Indeed, the difficulty of playing Hamlet, Holcroft wrote, consisted primarily in the display of these physical signs: "the coloring, and the display of the passion which tortures his mind ...all the forms and tints to which this passion gives birth."[72] Given the shared physiology of player and audience, however, the proper representation of those signs could efface the gap between textual intention and audience reception. Meaning could be wholly, perfectly performed. For British radicals, such a program could enlighten those trapped in a social order whose power seemed to rely precisely on the intentional, theatrical, and spectacular abuse of signs.[73]

Given this search for a rational system of signification – emotion understood through reason – it is not surprising that Holcroft found Johann Lavater's science of physiognomy appealing. Lavater's work merged a mystical Christology with a scientific program that gave a visible, readable image to the invisible world of human intentions and motivations.[74] Holcroft's translation of Lavater's *Essays on Physiognomy* appeared in England in 1789, a decade after its publication in Europe.[75] Although Henry Hunter's translation, priced at £5.5, had begun to appear a year earlier, Holcroft's cheaper edition, at 30 shillings, sought a wider audience and was to become the most popular of the contemporary English translations.[76] Other members of Holcroft's circle contributed to the physiognomic epistemology. Mary Wollstonecraft began an abridgment of Lavater's *Essays* in 1788; the novelist Mary Hays emphasized the physiognomical gaze in her fiction, as did William Godwin; William Blake and Henry Fuseli each contributed engravings to translations of the *Essays*.[77] By the 1790s, at least a dozen translations of the *Essays* were in circulation in England, not to mention the French and German editions also available.[78] Physiognomic language rapidly suffused print culture. Poetry, medical guides, travel accounts, and conduct books all registered Lavater's influence.[79]

Yet while Lavater's own work was deeply informed by Christian theology, Holcroft sought to produce a more universal program of secularized benevolence, joining bodily transparency to social and political practice.[80] Holcroft's move in democratizing Lavater's *Essays* was not lost on contemporary reviewers. *The Analytical Review*, for example, argued that Holcroft's translation radically simplified a practice that was dependent upon a certain level of taste and sensibility. In making Lavater so easily accessible, Holcroft had perverted its true nature.[81] Holcroft responded to such claims by emphasizing the importance of the doctrine for recognizing sincerity in social life, and he continued to defend physiognomics during the 1790s.[82] British Jacobin attraction to Lavater's science illustrates a profound collective desire to understand the visible signs of natural sincerity. Opposed to a regime that depended upon theatrical display and spectatorship, they sought to establish one of openness – of plain language and legible bodies. This effort can be illustrated through a brief consideration of two of Holcroft's most critical plays: *The Road to Ruin* and *The Deserted Daughter*.

"The Tradesman's Bow"

The Road to Ruin was first performed on 16 February 1792, at Covent Garden Theater. It was an immense success, being played night after night for the remainder of the 1791/92 season, and it was brought back by Thomas Harris, the manager of Covent Garden, for the opening of the 1792/93 season. *The Deserted Daughter* was less successful. It debuted at Covent Garden on 2 May 1795, and ran through twelve performances during the rest of that season.[83] Both plays critique a society where the distribution of social power is based on aristocratic notions of luxury and display. The plays also register deeper anxieties over the direction of commerce in society, a fundamental concern of members of Holcroft and Godwin's circle – especially during the growing poverty and dearth of the mid-1790s.[84] Both plays explore the corrosion of human bonds in a market culture driven by emulation and pursuit of aristocratic luxury. Finally, both plays gesture toward an imagined future characterized by a new transparency in human relationships and in social organization. By looking across the channel to the ongoing Revolution in France, *The Road to Ruin* realizes this future. By invoking the science of Lavaterian physiognomics, *The Deserted Daughter*, achieves that imaginary future at a time when any positive mention of the Revolution was prohibited both by the censor and by theater managers who hoped to avoid trouble. At each moment where the contradiction between human morality and a degraded market culture is represented most acutely, Holcroft turns to the physicality of gesture to make the dislocation fully apparent.

The Road to Ruin opens with the elder Dornton, a prominent banker in London, discovering that his son Harry has once again stayed late at the horse races in Newmarket, engaging in the "deep play" (as it was known) of high-stakes betting.[85] When a newspaper report appears noting that "the junior partner of a great banking house" has just lost £10,000 at the races, the news of the loss threatens a run on Dornton's banking firm. At this point, the elder Dornton seems on the verge of losing his mind. The exchange between Dornton and his servant, Mr. Smith, as Dornton struggles to reconcile his identity as a banker and his identity as a father, renders this instability through gesture.

DORNTON: [*Passionately*] … Though you should hereafter see him begging, starving in the streets, not so much as the loan or the gift of a single guinea!

MR. SMITH: I shall be careful to observe your orders, Sir.

DORNTON: Sir! [*Terror*] Why, would you see him starve? Would you see him starve and not lend him a guinea? Would you, Sir? Would you?[86]

Recall Holcroft's vision of acting as demonstrated in *The Theatrical Recorder*. Ideally, each of these intense transitions would have been accompanied in representation by a certain mapped gesture, a universal code that would reinforce the player's intended meaning by awakening in the spectator's mind some remembrance of the represented emotional state. The scene continues with Dornton swinging wildly from "terror" to "amazement and compassion," "horror," and tearful resignation as Dornton expresses his simultaneous revulsion and dismay that a father could disinherit a son, and his resolve to do precisely that, in obedience to the dictates of the capital-exchange market.[87]

The Road to Ruin's popularity was surely derived in part from its topical focus on the social problems associated with gaming. Condemnations of gambling were voiced across the political spectrum throughout the eighteenth century, but the revolutionary context of 1790s gave particular impetus to both radical critiques such as Holcroft's and loyalist critiques.[88] Moreover, the play's debut occurred in the midst of a new round of state-level attention to the problem. At the beginning of February, the magistrate William Ashhurst's recent charge to the King's Bench grand jury had been published in the *Evening Mail* and then in *The Times*; in it, Ashhurst called for the jury to shut down gaming houses throughout London. The charge initiated a new wave of state-led efforts to crack down on urban gaming.[89] Moreover, only a few days after the *Road to Ruin*'s 16 February debut, Londoners were starkly reminded of gaming's deleterious social effects. On Wednesday, 22 February, an army colonel "of large property" lost his entire fortune at a faro house managed by a female hostess. Suspecting he had been swindled, he retrieved a pistol from downstairs, and tried to shoot the female cheat. When the gun misfired, the desperate officer then turned it on himself, only to suffer a second misfire. He was then secured by those at the house. The *Ipswich Journal* made explicit the connection between Holcroft's play and the hapless colonel's ruin, publishing a brief notice of *Road to Ruin*'s debut immediately above its account of the near-murder/near-suicide.[90]

These conjunctions allow us to place the initial staging of *Road to Ruin* into a deeper context. Consider the elder Dornton's wild oscillation of emotion. Gillian Russell notes that eighteenth-century critics often gendered gambling as feminine – a coquette who destroyed man's Enlightened reason, and subjected him instead to the "mad joy" of success, or the "bottom of despair by misfortune, always in extreams, always in a storm."[91] While commentators argued that it was the addicted gamester who would suffer such feminization, Dornton's frantic state of mind suggests that his son's excesses bring in their train an unmanning of the father, too. Here, gaming renders impossible the achievement of the model of masculinity advocated in much of Holcroft's other work – the ideal sympathetic incorporation of passion and reason embodied in republican manhood.[92]

Moreover, we must also consider Dornton's economic place in society as a banker, for it is suggestive that Holcroft chose to make a banking family the center of action for this play addressing the problem of gambling. Eighteenth-century commentators often described a range of activities commonly associated with urban sociable commerce in terms of gaming; investing in life insurance, pooling of capital in business ventures, and banking itself were among the polite and commercial ventures that nonetheless at times of crisis became signs of speculative excess.[93] *Road to Ruin* registers such concerns once the news of Harry's losses begins to circulate among those who have extended credit to the firm.[94] Merchants immediately invade Dornton's house to present their bills, as they experience the risk of commercial credit.[95] Awaiting Dornton, they attempt to read the status of the bank from the news they have heard: "I don't like all this! What does it mean?" Discussing the implications of the news, they then engage in a chatty unveiling of the duplicity and theater involved in commerce: "He has been a good customer – None of your punctual paymasters, that look over their accounts." One trader wonders if Dornton is trying to trick them in order to inspect the accuracy of their charges. Another justifies the rupture between exchange value and profit by noting that tradesmen must ratchet up the latter in order to "live in style": "Can't have less than fifty per cent. for retail credit trade!"[96] Only by marking up goods and bills can tradesmen, another argues, display the required social identity necessary to attract equally status-conscious customers. Yet this hard-headed, if dissimula-tive, conversation among the tradesmen is interrupted when Dornton reappears to answer their claims. When he asks why they have come, the tradesmen instantly shift from being assertive and relatively transpar-ent proponents of market ideology to the other face of market culture, that of cringing servility: "First trader: Happy to serve you, sir./ Second trader: We shall be glad of your custom, sir./ Omnes: All! All!"[97]

Both Holcroft and Godwin deplored the theatrical deception involved in commercial exchange and its broader effects on social life. In his trea-tise on acting, Holcroft required that the actor playing a merchant should be "always ready with the tradesman's bow, not only at meeting and parting but whenever it can be intruded… his eye, attitudes and slightest actions …all anxiously intent on and subservient to that eager desire of gain." It was a performative role engraved on the trader's very being, since such habits were "inevitably fostered by barter and sale."[98] The interiority of commerce's effects – its destruction of an authentic self and its damage to sincerity in human relations – was produced on the body as a visual sign.[99] Godwin wrote in similar terms of the "servile and con-temptible arts which we see so frequently played off by the tradesman." The trader exhibits a "bended body"; his predacious accommodation plays upon the passions through a sexualized and gendered performance: "He exhibits all the arts of the female coquette; not that he wishes his fair visitor to fall in love with his person, but that he might take off his goods."[100] And while the merchant's self-representation was the "oppro-brium of a rational nature," nevertheless market society granted traders a "large discretionary power" in adjusting the prices of goods.[101] Such a system, driven by aristocratic demand and corrupted through the grasp-ing servility of traders, caused widespread suffering. Holcroft's public letter to William Windham MP (after Holcroft's "acquittal" for high treason) highlighted the connection between luxury and poverty: "Who impose the taxes? – the rich, whose luxury devours what the labours of the poor produce. – On what do the rich feed? – On the product of the poor's misery."[102] Both Holcroft and Godwin held significant concerns about commerce because of its contributions to social inequity.

The above scene from *Road to Ruin* highlights the complex theater of self-representation produced in exchange relationships. Each trader seeks to maximize gain through "adjusting" bills, and inflating price. Yet through their performance of deference, each seeks to retain enough reputational credit to remain a player in the market. The staging of this process at Covent Garden, however, undermined the coherence of market culture's set of conventions, highlighting its performative as-pect by revealing a careful construction of a strategic "self" deployed for gain.[103] A commercial culture driven by emulation of aristocratic luxury dissolved the boundaries between human relationships and commodity-exchange relationships.

Key elements of emergent British feminism also find expression in the play. Indeed, the play's debut occurred at a key moment for discussion of women in society. Mary Wollstonecraft's *A Vindication of the Rights of Woman* had been published by the liberal bookseller Joseph Johnson the month before the play's first performance. Her call for women's rational education centered on the exercise of sincere emotion grounded in true reason so that women could escape the artificial "regal homage" that in reality kept them in subjection: "Let the honest heart show itself, and *reason* teaches passion to submit to necessity."[104] *Road to Ruin* highlights this contrast between socially constructed female artifice and natural sincerity. When Harry repents of his gaming habit, he resolves to save the bank by marrying a wealthy widow, Mrs. Warren. Unknown to Harry, Warren has only a tenuous hold on her wealth: her late husband's will is missing, and so its absence hovers over the play's action. When a messenger bearing the newly found will arrives from France, he mistakenly gives the will to a dishonest servant of Dornton's, Mr. Silky. Silky, knowing Mrs. Warren to be morally corrupt, contacts the gamester Goldfinch, informing him that he has a deed in his possession that puts the widow's fortune in his power. For a cut of the fortune, he continues, Silky will put the deed in Goldfinch's hands, depriving the rightful inheritors, Mr. Warren's natural son Milford and daughter Sophia, of their patrimony.

These machinations are intimately tied to the systemic corruption of the larger social and political order, including the construction of femininity. The bank's solvency depends on the marriage fortunes of a habitual gambler; Harry speculates on his fortunes with the widow in the same way he has done at the Newmarket races. His rival, the would-be blackmailer Goldfinch, carries the comparison further by constantly referring to Warren – and to women in general – as commodities to be bought, groomed, and displayed. For example, he complains while waiting for her, "A hundred to eighty I'd sup up a string of twenty horse in less time than she takes to dress her fetlocks, plait her mane, trim her ears, and buckle on her body clothes!"[105] In contrast, Sophia (who manifests a true republican sincerity) ironically comments on her own bodily subjugation:

JENNY: And now your mamma has sent for you up to town to finish your edication. [sic]
SOPHIA: Yes, she began it the first day. There was the stay-maker sent for, to screw up my shapes; the shoe-maker, to cripple my feet; the hair-dresser, to burn my hair; the jeweller, to bore my ears; and the dentist, to file my teeth.[106]

Female education consists of accretion after accretion of artificial bodily signs, and turns women into objects for acquisition, luxury goods. Wollstonecraft considered it a form of servitude: "genteel women are, literally speaking, slaves to their bodies, and glory in their subjection."[107] Holcroft too noted that this construction of femininity prevented women from acquiring that "courageous spirit of inquiry, which should lead the mind from truth to truth," toward intellectual equality with men.[108] In *The Road to Ruin* and other works, Holcroft portrayed social relations as produced by commerce, against those which would blossom in an unfolding, revolutionary era of universal benevolence. His aim was not lost on viewers: the conservative writer Thomas Green wrote in his diary upon seeing *The Deserted Daughter*,

> Dec. 17, 1796... H[olcoft] is very busy at his purpose: his aim, to those who are conversant with the tenets of his sect, is sufficiently manifest; but he manages and conceals it with a discretion not very consistent, surely, with his principles.[109]

The universal language of gesture expressed specific emotions, and ideally would produce corresponding emotions in the spectator. The science of acting made available radical meanings that could not be expressed at the theater in more explicit ways. *The Road to Ruin* castigated the affective masks and performances that social actors assumed in pursuit of wealth, luxury goods, status, and patriarchal power.

Finally, during its first six weeks of performance, Holcroft gave *The Road to Ruin*'s audience at Covent Garden an additional filter through which to read the play, offering a concrete vision of a wholly different political order that was arising across the channel. He did this through the ambivalent, amphibious space of the prologue. As Greg Dening has noted, prologues mark an important transition between the audience's varied experiences of everyday life and the communal experience of the drama, facilitating the suspension of disbelief that enabled the audience to identify with the drama's characters.[110] The prologue enticed audiences to imagine that the represented could be the real. By liberating the imagination, prologues seduced the spectator into becoming, as the French bishop Jacques-Bénigne Bossuet wrote, "a secret player" in the represented action.[111] The prologue speaker, neither actor nor watcher, but rather some being in-between, encouraged audiences to see that meaning was made through representation and reception. Like the soliloquy speaker, the speaker of the prologue dangerously marked the power of performance for constructing meaning and reality, freeing the audience to create their own meanings.[112]

In his prologue to *The Road to Ruin*, Holcroft uses the liminality of the prologue to help encode the play itself.

> Oh sirs! The prompter has mislaid the prologue, and we are all a mort.
>   I suppose our friends above yonder will soon be making pretty sport!

>   For pity's sake, suffer us to go on without it – Good, dear sirs, do!
>   'Twas most abominably dull – Zounds! There stands the writer.
> Well! It's very true.
>   One of our te tum ti heroes was to have spoken it, who measure
> out nonsense by the yard;
>   And our chief hope was you'd make too much noise for it to be
> heard.[113]

The "substitute" prologue multiplies the frames of representation and signification, producing Holcroft himself as a character and playfully undermining his authority as the omnipotent creator of the fictional play-world shortly to be entered. (Such a self-deprecatory move may have played a part in getting the prologue past John Larpent, the inspector of plays.) Like many eighteenth-century prologues, Holcroft's also invokes the theater audience – "our friends above yonder." Betsy Bolton has noted that eighteenth-century theater audiences could be exceptionally large, sweeping in significant portions of the urban population during consecutive performances. By 1792, Covent Garden theater could seat more than 2,000 spectators, and would be enlarged slightly for the start of the fall 1792 season (which as noted earlier, opened with *Road to Ruin*).[114] Prologues that addressed the crowd, Bolton argues, imaginatively constructed the nation in its component parts, and invited audiences to imagine themselves as that nation.[115] In Holcroft's prologue, that imagined nation is asked to consider revolutionary culture, for we are then told that the fugitive prologue would have lauded the events across the channel in unrepentant terms:

>   The author had mounted on the stilts of oratory and elocution:
>   Not but he had a smart touch or two, about Poland, France, and
> the – the revolution;
>   Telling us that Frenchman, and Polishman, and every man is our
> brother:
>   And that all men, ay, even poor negro men, have a right to be free;
> one as well as another!
>   Freedom at length, said he, like a torrent is spreading and swelling,
>   To sweep away pride and reach the most miserable dwelling:
>   To ease, happiness, art, science, wit, and genius to give birth;
>   Ay, to fertilize a world, and renovate old earth![116]

Both prologues, the performed one and the absent one, explicitly invoke the French Revolution as heralding a utopian era of fraternity and peace. But the substitute prologue performs the invisible prologue's unmediated praise of revolution with a hesitant stutter ("the—the revolution"), registering the transgression involved in a positive reference to French events. Moreover, the missing prologue signaled the association of democratic principles to the problem of slavery; universal benevolence demanded humanitarian redress. At a crucial instant for the viewer's entrance into the fictional world of the play and his or her understanding of the drama about to be performed, Holcroft emphasizes the connection among representation, imagination, and the production of meaning in creating new social worlds and relationships. The play itself portrays the fragmentation of those authentic bonds of benevolence and fraternity in the old world of display, luxury, and greed, and the recovery of such bonds in the new world of transparency, social virtue, and candor, precisely the bonds invoked in the fugitive, "authentic" prologue. In short, Holcroft's prologue is a playfully serious instance of paratextual "overcoding."[117] Though the prologue is ostensibly outside the action of the play, it nonetheless offers a framing device for the audiences' reception of that performance, allowing a viewing of the play "as if" the fugitive prologue had been the real one. In *The Road to Ruin*, aristocratic luxury and the commercialization of human bonds are compared with an imaginary future in the play-world, and with a real present in France.

Indeed, given that this prologue was no longer performed after 29 March 1792, it is tempting to speculate that this intertextuality between prologue and play had become quite apparent.[118] The immediate political context is significant; that spring witnessed the rapid growth of the LCS. During January 1792, Thomas Hardy had formed the LCS; by March it was in communication with reform societies in Manchester and Sheffield. In February, Paine's *Rights of Man, Part II* was published. From early March, the SCI had become a principal conduit for communications between British radicals and their French correspondents.[119] With the escalation of radical activity in London during the spring of 1792, perhaps a play that allowed more incendiary readings than its "text" might indicate had become too dangerous to leave unamended. The playfully subversive prologue was dropped.

"What should I fear?"

From 1792, Holcroft took an active part in metropolitan radicalism. During the three-year interval between the staging of *The Road to Ruin* and *The Deserted Daughter* (first performed on 5 May 1795), he became increasingly well-known not simply as a playwright but as a "moral mastiff," "fixed on rank," with "democratic sentiments."[120] He joined the SCI on 5 October 1792; two weeks later he was made a member of the committee to confer with delegates of the LCS over a proposed address to the French National Convention.[121] Shortly after that, Holcroft was appointed to the Committee of Correspondence to represent the SCI to other reform societies in England, and over the course of the next eighteen months, he took part in numerous committees, including that formed in early April 1794 to discuss with the LCS the structure of the proposed British Convention.[122] In May, the Pitt ministry's "Jacobin round-up" imprisoned the leaders of the LCS and SCI upon charges of high treason. Holcroft was not among those arrested in May, but in October, he learned that his name was included in the true bill found by the Middlesex grand jury. At that point he dramatically surrendered himself and was taken to Newgate to await trial.[123] After Hardy and Horne Tooke's acquittals, the government dropped its case against Holcroft, and he was discharged on 1 December 1794, just prior to the start of Thelwall's trial.

After the ordeal of arrest and imprisonment, the year 1795 marked Holcroft's return to theater with *The Deserted Daughter*, which reiterates many of the key themes of *The Road to Ruin*. While for the purposes of this chapter there is no need to give an extended reading of the entire play here, it is worth considering one additional device through which Holcroft offered audiences heightened meanings. The central character of the play, Mordent, is a moody and pessimistic misanthrope – an aging rake. He has abandoned Joanna, his daughter from a previous clandestine marriage, in order to keep his current wife ignorant of that marriage. As the action of the play opens, he has not seen Joanna for some twenty years, but attempts to provide for her by having a servant, Item, find Joanna employment. Item tells Mordent that he has found Joanna employment as a seamstress; in reality Item sells Joanna into the custody of Mrs. Enfield, a brothel-keeper.[124] As Joanna talks with her new employer, in a scene full of veilings and misrecognitions of character and motive, Holcroft provides a device by which the audience might better read the scene:

MRS. ENFIELD: ... You say you can draw?
JOANNA: It has been my delight. I have studied the human countenance, have read Lavater.
MRS. ENFIELD: Anan! Will you copy the engraving I shewed you? –
JOANNA: What, the portrait of that strange – ?[125]

Unbeknownst to Joanna, it is an engraving of her father. Joanna, so attuned to the signifying power of countenance, reads Mordent's portrait; he is "a wicked man," with a "wild eye." Mordent's visible interiority causes Joanna to reconsider her hostess as well: "Looking at such a face, who can fail? (*Examining Mrs. Enfield*) You are a worthy lady; a kind lady; your actions bespeak it: and yet – Don't be angry – there is something about your features – that I don't like!"[126] Thus Holcroft sets up two worlds: an immediate one, beset by the corrosive influence of corrupted signs – painted faces, elaborate dress and manners – and one where outward representation makes interior motive readable. All of this is happening in a brothel, a space in which the larger corruption of human relationships in market culture is condensed and emphatically realized. Female bodies there are commodified in a pure exchange system, yet one that throws back at the world that world's obsessions with dissimulative signs of prestige, luxury, and painted-on politeness. As the play continues, Holcroft constantly juxtaposes the present world of misapprehensions and duplicity, and the "as if" world of transparent relationships and unmediated meanings.[127] Later, Mordent arrives at Enfield's (she has sent him an "invitation to a new sample of beauty"), and even as the threat of unintended incest hangs over the scene, Joanna demolishes it by reading Mordent's face, dissecting his history of abuse toward women.

JOANNA. Either it indicates falsely or you have flattered, promised, deceived, and betrayed.
MOR. (Aside) Astonishing! – Who?
JOANNA. More poor girls than one![128]

Just as radicals sought to replace the polite draperies of political structures with a representational system that would correspond more transparently to what they regarded as natural law, so too did Holcroft hope to enlist Lavater's system of ultimate signs to redress the fictions told by social convention. For Holcroft, this was not a silent world of mystical immediacy but rather a secularized, rational means toward heightened awareness, a shield against social dissimulation:

MOR. (Aside) Is this real? – You judge and speak freely, madam. I applaud your sincerity.
JOANNA. What should I fear? Beside, you have not the features of revenge.[129]

Besides allowing Joanna to discern the "real" Mordent beneath the incrustations of his social corruption, physiognomy also legitimizes her ability to "speak" as a morally and socially equal woman: "What should I fear?"[130] During the autumn previous to the staging of *The Deserted Daughter*, even as he found himself under the lens of the parliamentary committee investigating radical political societies, Holcroft had shown a similar concern over the social construction of femininity. In a review of *Dramas for the Use for Young Ladies* (1792), he decried the "precise and chilling confines of the governess's decorum," where "shoulder straps, back-boards, and neck-setting," literally buttressed an educational regimen of "French, music and drawing." For Holcroft, such bodily rigidity produced an equally rigid mind, for such a system, inculcating "as large a dose of mawkish sentiment as the tutoress knows how to administer," formed women who were destined to live an apolitical – and hence, in the discourse of civic virtue, reactionary – life of "inanity or dissipation."[131]

Here we see the greater social and political implications of Holcroft's invocation of Lavater. Through physiognomy, truth could circulate through a universal system of meaning, one untouchable by social reference. The true self could be discerned; springs of action understood. Hence Joanna's certitude in her rhetorical question: "What should I fear?" Though one may still remain in a world limited by social convention and governed by spectacular display, physiognomics, whispering "to the heart when it is necessary to speak, when to be silent; when to forewarn, when to excite; when to console, and when to reprehend" provides a parallel world of moral guidance in which to move.[132]

Conclusion: Glimpses of a Jacobin Dreamworld

Struggles over what could be presented at the state-associated patent theaters, were not "isolated debates about the eccentricities of dramatic licensing. Rather, they are concerned with such vexed and controversial questions as the political control and consumption of culture in a democratic age."[133] Much of the emphasis in Holcroft's drama centers on ways to uncover and make known the sincere heart, the true self, of universal benevolence. The theme reverses claims by loyalist commentators that British Jacobin constitutionalism was but a mask hiding their true intentions; that British Jacobinism itself was a disguise, secret revolution masquerading as public reform. In contrast, Holcroft's plays sought to stage the imagined world of republican social relations in crystalline clarity, aided by science rather than depicted through alarmism and "lawful prejudices." The work displayed a British Jacobin social imaginary where society was cleansed of the aristocratic detritus of artificial signs. In order to offer his critique in the theater, Holcroft had to temporarily abandon the Godwinian tenets of transparency and the power of undiluted truth and instead turn to the looser conditions of performance. Yet, despite such dissimulation, this vision of a social world informed by candor, rational debate, and egalitarianism was not merely a utopian dream. As Mark Philp notes, the nature of the Godwinian circle – with its members' constant exchange of ideological, moral, and material support – afforded British radicals a sense that such a world was indeed reachable.[134]

Yet in some ways, Holcroft's practice did mark a failure. Like many other intellectuals and artists of the 1790s, he was a casualty of government efforts to restrict radicals' access to the public.[135] Upon Holcroft's release from Newgate, he increasingly found his work stigmatized by the identity he had received as an "acquitted felon," and despite turning to anonymous publication, his popularity as a playwright sank.[136] After selling off his library in 1799, he left Britain for Hamburg and then Paris, where his reputation was further damaged when *The Times* labeled him a spy for the French government.[137] His letters to Godwin from this period are filled with anxious queries about the availability of work, and the difficulties of selling himself to publishers suspicious of his name. They carry telling refrains such as "you understand that I wish my name not to be known," or "Pray, do not communicate my literary projects, especially theatrical, to any human being."[138] Like Godwin's own fictional character Caleb Williams, who is pursued relentlessly by his master and forced to publish his literary works secretly, Holcroft was reduced to anonymity. His experience – this cultural eradication – reveals the limitations for reform during a period of profound governmental caution and reaction, and reveals the power of a conservative backlash against a cultural avant-garde. From a perspective that judges success based on institutional change, then his career was a failure. Yet we can conclude another way.

Surely, the Godwin circle's desire to ratchet down and fix meaning, and create a cultural and social world of non-exploitative and non-dissimulative signs, was naïve. After the mid-1790s, with the passage of bills that further limited popular political speech and action, with the continuance of the war despite widespread dearth at home, a belief in the irrepressible victory of rational discussion over error became harder to sustain. Many other radicals – contemporary ones such as Thomas Spence, Daniel Isaac Eaton, and Citizen Richard Lee, or later ones such as T. J. Wooler and William Hone – instead found the multivalent play of satire more effective at tearing aside the curtains of elite governance.[139] But just as surely, the Godwinians' ability to create and sustain for a number of years a community that was centered precisely around their philosophical tenets – during a period when such practices were denigrated and reviled by a substantial portion of their larger social world – is a hopeful indication of the capacity of human communities to resist the hegemonic power of the state and the market.[140] This creative sociability was not merely reactive and sheltering.[141] Few persons within the Godwin circle of radical intellectuals were as committed as Holcroft was to reaching a public, whether through literary efforts such as novels, and endless reviewing, or through his own dramatic self-representation when denied the opportunity to address the jury upon his release in December 1794, and his quick publishing afterward of his intended address.[142] Theater, too, offered possibilities; for one, it provided a broader audience than did his Jacobin novels. Holcroft's career speaks to a deep hunger for a kind of civic publicity that perhaps only live performance could offer. Yet in the communicative conditions of the 1790s, radical theater was in the end an impossibility. The structural limitations of pre-performance censorship, managerial risk-aversion, popular taste, and the limits of sentimental comedy as a genre – all disallowed a comprehensive British Jacobin drama. While Holcroft managed to produce representational fictions that allowed radical meanings to break through the stage's regular fare of British martial prowess and cultural complacency, these efforts remained glimpses – "thoughts that flash like lightning" – rather than fully realized fictive worlds. The science of acting could pull back the draperies of social convention, but could only gesture toward the British Jacobin dreamworld of universal benevolence.

Acknowledgments

An earlier version of this chapter was published in David Karr, "'Thoughts that Flash like Lightening': Thomas Holcroft, Radical Theater, and the Production of Meaning in 1790s London," *Journal of British Studies* 40 (July 2001): 324–56. © The North American Conference on British Studies, 2001. Reproduced with permission of Cambridge University Press.

Notes

1 *MR*, 16, September 1795: 98. On *England Preserved*, see Terence Allan Hoagland, "Romantic Drama and Historical Hermeneutics," in *British Romantic Drama: Historical and Critical Essays*, ed. Terence Allen Hoagwood and Daniel P. Watkins (Vancouver, BC: Fairleigh Dickinson University Press, 1998), 22–55, at 30–31.

2 For the "acquitted felons" remark, see *PH*, vol. 31, col. 1027, Commons, 30 December 1794.

3 Holcroft, review of Robert Bage's *Man as He Is*, in *MR*, 10, March 1795: 297.

4 Since this chapter was first published as an article in *Journal of British Studies*, Holcroft's work has received considerable attention. See, for example, Miriam L. Wallace and A. A. Markley, eds., *Re-viewing Thomas Holcroft, 1745–1809* (Aldershot: Ashgate, 2012); Amy Garnai, "'A Lock Upon my Lips': The Melodrama of Silencing and Censorship in Thomas Holcroft's *Knave, or Not?*," *Eighteenth-Century Studies* 43 (2010): 473–84; Miriam L. Wallace, "Discovering the Political Traveler in Wollstonecraft's *Letters* (1796) and Holcroft's *Travels (1804)*," *Journeys* 12 (2011): 1–21; Eliza O'Brien, "'The Greatest Appearance of Truth': Telling Tales with Thomas Holcroft," *Eighteenth-Century Fiction* 28 (2016): 501–26; Diane Long Hoeveler, *Gothic Riffs: Secularizing the Uncanny in the European Imaginary, 1780–1820* (Columbus: Ohio State University Press, 2010), chapter 4; Jeffrey N. Cox, "Holcroft's Parisian Expedition," in *Romanticism in the Shadow of War: Literary Culture in the Napoleonic War Years* (Cambridge: CUP, 2014), 25–58.

5 See Theodore Grieder, "Annotated Checklist of the British Drama, 1789–99," *Restoration and 18th Century Theatre Research* 4 (1965): 21–47; and Leonard Conolly, *The Censorship of English Drama* (San Marino, CA: The Huntington Library, 1976), chapter 4. On illegitimate theater, see Jane Moody, *Illegitimate Theater in London, 1770–1840* (Cambridge: CUP, 2000). For the effects of the formal and energetic mechanism of the Licensing Act upon the patent theaters, see David Worrall, *The Politics of Romantics Theatricality, 1787–1832* (Houndmills: Palgrave Macmillan, 2007), chapters 1 and 7.

6 Jeffrey N. Cox, "Ideology and Genre in the British Antirevolutionary Drama of the 1790s," *English Literary History* 58 (1991): 579–610, at 588. See also Terence M. Freeman, *Dramatic Representations of British Soldiers and Sailors*

on the London Stage, 1660–1800: Britons Strike Home (Lewiston, NY: Edwin Mellen, 1995). More generally, see Kathleen Wilson "Pacific Modernity: Theater, Englishness, and the Arts of Discovery," in *The Age of Cultural Revolutions*, ed. Colin Jones and Dror Wahrman (Berkeley: University of California Press, 2002), 62–93, and her *The Island Race: Englishness, Empire, and Gender in the Eighteenth Century* (Routledge, 2003). David Worrall notes that drama at the patent theaters was able to respond obliquely to contemporary political events. Worrall, *Politics of Romantics Theatricality*, 48–67. See also Daniel O'Quinn, "Bread: The Eruption and Interruption of Politics in Elizabeth Inchbald's *Every One Has His Fault*," *European Romantic Review* 18 (2007): 149–57; and Amy Garnai, "Radicalism, Caution, and Censorship in Elizabeth Inchbald's *Every One Has His Fault*," *Studies in English Literature 1500–1900* 47 (2007): 703–22. For the representation of revolutionary events at the minor theaters, see Gillian Russell, *The Theatres of War: Performance, Politics and Society, 1793–1815* (Oxford: OUP, 1995), 66–74.

7 Paula S. Backscheider, *Spectacular Politics: Theatrical Power and Mass Culture in Early Modern England* (Baltimore, MD: Johns Hopkins University Press 1993), 233, and more generally, chapters 5 and 6.

8 Roger Chartier, *Forms and Meanings: Texts, Performances and Audiences from Codex to Computer* (University Park: University of Pennsylvania Press, 1995), 46.

9 Marvin Carlson, *Places of Performance: The Semiotics of Theatre Architecture* (Ithaca, NY: Cornell University Press, 1989), 11; Joseph Roach, *Cities of the Dead: Circum-Atlantic Performance* (New York: Columbia University Press, 1996), 28, 88–90; Jim Davis, "Spectatorship," in *The Cambridge Companion to British Theatre, 1730–1830*, ed. Jane Moody and Daniel O'Quinn (Cambridge: CUP, 2007), 57–70; Betsy Bolton, "Theorizing Audience and Spectatorial Agency," *The Oxford Handbook of Georgian Theater*, ed. Julia Swindells and David Francis Taylor (Oxford: OUP, 2014), 31–52; Susan Bennett, *Theatre Audiences: A Theory of Production and Reception*, 2nd ed. (Routledge, 1997), 125–39; Erika Fischer-Lichte, *The Shadow and the Gaze of Theatre: A European Perspective* (Iowa City: University of Iowa Press, 1997), 319–37. See also Bruce Kapferer, "Performance and the Structuring of Meaning and Experience," in *The Anthropology of Experience*, ed. Victor Turner and Edward M. Bruner (Urbana: University of Illinois Press, 1986), 188–203.

10 Marc Baer, *Theatre and Disorder in Late Georgian London* (Oxford: OUP, 1992), chapter 4. On theater audiences and riot more broadly, see Heather McPherson, "Theatrical Riots and Cultural Politics in Eighteenth-Century London," *Eighteenth Century: Theory and Interpretation* 43 (2003): 236–52.

11 Russell, *The Theatres of War*, 17.

12 At this time, Sheridan's company was performing out of the King's Theatre at Haymarket while his regular theater at Drury Lane, was being rebuilt. The Haymarket was allowed to stage spoken drama during the summer off-season. See LC 7/ 74, "Agreement between Wm. Taylor Esq. And R.B. Sheridan," 12 August 1791. For the lord chamberlain's warning see LC 7/74, "Letter to Richard Brinsley Sheridan," 30 March 1792.

13 See above Chapter 1, 37–38, 41–42.

14 *State Trials for High Treason. Embellished with Portraits. Part Third. Containing the Trial of Mr. John Thelwall, Reported by a Student in the Temple* (1795), 35–6.

15 Marco De Marinis, "The Dramaturgy of the Spectator," *The Drama Review* 31 (1986): 100–14, at 103.

16 *Sun*, December 8, 1794.

17 John Loftis, "Political and Social Thought in the Drama," in *The London Theatre World, 1660–1800*, ed. Robert D. Hume (Carbondale: Southern Illinois University Press, 1980), 253–85, at 278–85; Scott Bryson, *The Chastised Stage: Bourgeois Drama and the Exercise of Power* (Stanford, CA: Anma Libri, 1991), chapter 2; Lisa A. Freeman, "The Social Life of Eighteenth-Century Comedy," in Moody and O'Quinn, eds., *Cambridge Companion*, 73–86; Frank Ellis, *Sentimental Comedy: Theory and Practice* (Cambridge: CUP, 1991).

18 Chartier, *Forms and Meanings*, 49.

19 See Iain Hampsher-Monk, "John Thelwall and the Eighteenth-Century Radical Response to Political Economy," *HJ* 34 (1991): 1–20; Gregory Claeys, "The Origins of the Rights of Labor: Republicanism, Commerce, and the Construction of Modern Social Theory in Britain, 1796–1805," *JMH* 66 (1994): 249–90.

20 See the classic work by Jonas Barish, *The Antitheatrical Prejudice* (Berkeley: University of California Press, 1981).

21 Roy Porter, "The Enlightenment in England," in *The Enlightenment in National Context*, ed. Roy Porter and Mikuláš Tiech (Cambridge: CUP, 1981), 1–18, at 11–12; John O'Brian, *Harlequin Britain: Pantomime and Entertainment, 1690–1760* (Baltimore, MD: Johns Hopkins University Press, 2004), 99–102.

22 *Tatler*, no. 167 (4 May 1710).

23 Ibid., 183 (8 June 1710).

24 Ibid., 172 (16 May 1710).

25 *Spectator*, no. 370 (5 May 1712). See also No. 446 (1 August 1712).

26 David Marshall, "Adam Smith and the Theatricality of Moral Sentiments," *Critical Inquiry* 10 (1984): 592–613, and *The Figure of Theater: Shaftesbury, Defoe, Adam Smith, and George Eliot* (New York: Columbia University Press, 1986), 171–74; G. J. Barker-Benfield, *The Culture of Sensibility: Sex and Society in Eighteenth-Century Britain* (Chicago, IL: University of Chicago Press, 1992), 62–5, 67–98, 132–48.

27 George Lillo, *The London Merchant; or, the History of George Barnwell* (1731), Dedication.

28 An example: "Constance, un coude appuyé sur la table, et la tête penchée sur une de ses mains, demeure dans cette situation pensive." ["Constance, with an elbow on the table and her head resting on one hand, remains in this thoughtful pose."] Denis Diderot, *Le Fils Naturel,* Act 1, scene 4, in Diderot, *Oeuvres Completes*, ed. J. Assézat, 20 vols. (Paris: Garnier Freres, 1875), 7: 26.

29 See L. S. Mercier, *Du théatre, ou novel essai sur l'art dramatique* (Paris, 1773), chapter 10; Roman Graf, "Voicing Limits: Rereading the Dramatic Theories of J. M. R. Lenz and L. S. Mercier," (PhD. diss., University of North Carolina at Chapel Hill, 1992), 93–5, 114–19, 136–37; Sophia Rosenfeld, *A Revolution in Language: The Problem of Signs in Late Eighteenth-Century France* (Stanford, CA: Stanford University Press, 2001), chapter 2. In 1799, Holcroft would marry Mercier's daughter Louisa.

30 Thomas Holcroft, *The Life of Thomas Holcroft, Written by Himself, Continued . . . by William Hazlitt,* ed. Elbridge Colby, 2 vols. (New York: Benjamin Blom, 1968, first published 1852), 1: 256–73. Beaumarchais' piece was written in 1778; it was suppressed for six years, and then allowed to be performed in 1784.

31 Ibid., 1: 272–74.

32 Besides helping Holcroft pirate *Figaro*, Bonneville acted as a literary scout in Paris after Holcroft returned to London, sending Holcroft notices of

marketable and "curious" works. See Gregory Maertz, "The Transmission of German Literature and Dissenting Voices in British Culture: Thomas Holcroft and the Godwin Circle," in *1650–1850: Ideas, Aesthetics, and Inquiries in the Early-Modern Era*, ed. Kevin L. Cope and Laura Morrow (New York: AMS Press, 1997), 271–300; Elbridge Colby, *A Bibliography of Thomas Holcroft* (New York: New York Public Library, 1922), 11–12; Miriam L. Wallace, "Holcroft's Translations of the 1780s and Isabelle de Montolieu's *Caroline de Lichtfield*," in Wallace and Markley, eds., *Re-Viewing Thomas Holcroft*, 51–68.

33 The Licensing Act clarified the role of the royal theaters at Covent Garden and at Drury Lane by reinforcing their monopoly on the production of plays. It stipulated that a copy of any play to be produced must be given to the lord chamberlain at least fourteen days in advance of first night. If the lord chamberlain found any parts of the play objectionable, and wished to prohibit their performance, he would communicate these objections to the playhouse manager, who would lose £50 – and worse, his license – if he allowed the play to go forward uncorrected. To further streamline the process, in 1738, the offices of examiner and deputy examiner were created to handle the actual inflow of plays. See Conolly, *Censorship of English Drama*, 13–17 and chapter 4. See also Worrall, *Theatric Revolution*, chapter 4.

34 Conolly, *Censorship of English Drama*, 102–3.

35 *PR*, vol. 43, col. 548, 550, 10 December 1795.

36 Cox, "Ideology and Genre," 580–87. See also Grieder, "Annotated Checklist," 21–47.

37 *Enquiry Concerning Political Justice*, in *Political and Philosophical Writings of William Godwin*, ed. Mark Philp, 7 vols. (Pickering & Chatto, 1993, first published 1793), 3: 452.

38 Randall A. Sessler "Print Takes the Stage: The 'Great Engine' of Literature, 'Invidious Practices,' and British Romantic Theatre," *Nineteenth-Century Contexts* 32 (2017): 105–16; and David O'Shaughnessy, *William Godwin and the Theatre* (Pickering & Chatto, 2010).

39 Thomas Paine, *The Rights of Man* (Harmondsworth: Penguin, 1984, first published 1791), 59.

40 For a more sustained analysis of Paine's use of theatrical metaphors, see James T. Boulton, *The Language of Politics in the Age of Wilkes and Burke* (Routledge and K. Paul, 1963), 144–47.

41 Paine, *Rights of Man*, 31.

42 Mary Wollstonecraft, *A Vindication of the Rights of Men*, ed. Sylvana Tomaselli (Cambridge: CUP, 1995, first published 1790), 6. See also Chris Jones, *Radical Sensibility: Literature and Ideas in the 1790s* (Routledge, 1993), chapter 3.

43 Charles Pigott, *A Political Dictionary: Explaining the True Meaning of Words* (1795), 111. See also *A Political Dictionary for Guinea-less Pigs* (1795). Thomas Spence apparently began work on a dictionary during the middle of the decade. See BL, Add. MS. 27808, William Hone to Francis Place, 23 September 1830, fol. 314. See also Nicholas Rogers, "Pigott's Private Eye: Radicalism and Sexual Scandal in Eighteenth-Century England," *JCHA*, new series, 4 (1993): 247–63.

44 That those on the other side of the ideological fence were theatrical rather than rational actors was a charge made by all sides in the pamphlet wars of the 1790s. See Russell, *Theatres of War*, 23–4, 85–6, and "Burke's Dagger: Theatricality, Politics and Print Culture in the 1790s," *British Journal for Eighteenth-Century Studies* 20 (1997): 1–16. See also Tom Furniss,

Edmund Burke's Aesthetic Ideology: Language, Gender and Political Economy in Revolution (Cambridge: CUP, 1993), 257; Don Herzog, *Poisoning the Minds of the Lower Orders* (Princeton NJ: Princeton University Press, 1998), chapter 4.

45 Olivia Smith, *The Politics of Language, 1789–1815* (Oxford: OUP, 1984), 21, 43, 50; Russell, *Theatres of War*, 23–25; James Epstein, *Radical Expression: Political Language, Ritual and Symbol in England, 1790–1850* (Oxford: OUP, 1994), chapter 3; Philip Harling, "Leigh Hunt's *Examiner* and the Language of Patriotism," *EHR* 111 (1996): 1159–81; John M. Turner, "Burke, Paine, and the Nature of Language," *Yearbook of English Studies* 19 (1989): 36–53, at 51; John Barrell, "Imagining the King's Death: The Arrest of Richard Brothers," *HWJ* 37 (1994): 1–32, at 1–2.

46 Jon Mee's evocation of radical culture as informed by a belief in a kind of "print magic" is relevant here, but can be extended to non-discursive communication more broadly. Jon Mee, *Print, Publicity, and Radicalism in the 1790s:* The Laurel of Liberty (Cambridge: CUP, 2016), 34–42. See Rosenfeld, *A Revolution in Language*, Chapter 4, for the fullest exploration of French revolutionary struggles over the politics of signs.

47 *MR*, 10, February 1793: 208–9. Holcroft would later repeat this refrain in his essay on acting in "The Art of Acting," *Theatrical Recorder* 1 (February 1805), 134.

48 See Hans Arsleff, *The Study of Language in England, 1780–1860* (Princeton, NJ: Princeton University Press, 1967), 17–20; Stephen K. Land, *From Sign to Propositions: The Concept of Form in Eighteenth-Century Semantic Theory* (Longman, 1974), 87–92; Rosenfeld, *A Revolution in Language*, chapter 1.

49 John C. O'Neale, *The Authority of Experience: Sensationist Theory in the French Enlightenment* (University Park: Pennsylvania State University Press, 1996), 83–90. Like many in the Godwin circle, Holcroft was familiar with the work of both Helvétius and Condillac; the 1806 sale catalogue of his library listed works by each. See "A Catalogue of the Library of Books, of Mr. Thomas Holcroft, To be Sold at Auction by King & Lochee, 13 Jan. & 4 Following days, 1807" (1806), Houghton Library, Harvard University.

50 *MR*, 10, February 1793 and April 1793: 210, 367.

51 For Thelwall's commitment to cognitive materialism, see Yasmin Solomonescu, *John Thelwall and the Materialism Imagination* (Houndmills: Palgrave Macmillan, 2014).

52 *MR*, 10, March 1793: 297.

53 For broader view of the cultural significance of physiology and visuality in the epistemological changes of the eighteenth century, see Barbara Maria Stafford, *Body Criticism: Imaging the Unseen in Enlightenment Art and Medicine* (Cambridge: Massachusetts Institute of Technology Press, 1991), 47–49.

54 See Joseph Roach, *The Players Passion: Studies in the Science of Acting* (Ann Arbor: University of Michigan Press, 1985), chapter 2; Fischer-Lichte, *Shadow and the Gaze of Theatre*, 31–34, 39; O'Brien, "Greatest Appearance of Truth."

55 John Hill, *The Actor: Or a Treatise on the Art of Playing* (1755). See also G.S. Rousseau, "John Hill: Universal Genius *Manqué*: Remarks on His Life and Times, with a Checklist of His Works," in *The Renaissance Man in the Eighteenth Century*, ed. J.A. Leo Lemay and G. S. Rousseau (Los Angeles, CA: Clark Memorial Library, 1978), 49–95.

56 As David Hume wrote, the nature of the passions resembled "a string-instrument, where after each stroke the vibrations still retain some sound,

which gradually and insensibly decays." David Hume, "Of the Passions," *Treatise on Human Nature* (1739), 440–41, as quoted in Roach, *Player's Passion*, 105.

57 See Hartley's 11th position, which asserted, "Any Vibrations, A, B, C, &c. by being associated together a sufficient Number of Times, get such a Power over a, b, c, &c. the corresponding miniature Vibrations, that any of the Vibrations A, when impressed alone, shall be able to excite b, c, &c. the Miniatures of the rest." See David Hartley, *Observations on Man, His Frame, His Duties and His Expectations* (1749), 67. See also Richard C. Allen, *David Hartley on Human Nature* (Albany: State University of New York Press, 1999), 182–85; and Roach, *Player's Passion*, 107. For the vibratory nerve paradigm more generally, see Barker-Benfield, *Culture of Sensibility*, chapter 1. Hartley's theories were popular in radical Dissenting culture in the late eighteenth century. Joseph Priestley, Richard Price, and William Godwin found his doctrines useful in explaining necessitarian philosophy. See Allen, *David Hartley*, 192, 376–88.

58 Roach, *Player's Passion*, 25.

59 Holcroft, *Life of Thomas Holcroft*, 1:xiv.

60 Holcroft, "The Art of Acting," 64.

61 Ibid., 136.

62 Bolton notes that theater audiences of the 1790s made for some of the largest public gatherings legally allowed by the state. Bolton, "Theorizing Audiences," 32. For the greater focus on gesture due to audience size, see Frederick Burwick "Georgian Theories of the Actor," in Swindells and Taylor, eds., *Oxford Handbook of The Georgian Theatre*, 177–96, at 183; and O'Brian, *Harlequin Britain*, 63–70.

63 In addition to Roach, *Player's Passion*, see Jan Bremmer and Herman Roodenburg, eds., *A Cultural History of Gesture* (Ithaca, NY: Cornell University Press, 1991); Dene Barnett, "The Performance Practice of Acting: The Eighteenth Century. Part II: The Hands," *Theatre Research International* 3 (1977): 1–19; James R. Knowlson, "The Idea of Gesture as a Universal Language in the XVIIth and XVIIIth Centuries," *Journal of the History of Ideas* 26 (1965): 495–508.

64 Ibid., 487–88.

65 Roach, *Player's Passion*, 76.

66 Hill, *The Actor*, 232.

67 *Theatrical Recorder* 2 (July 1805), 44.

68 Ibid., 45.

69 Ibid., 139–40.

70 Ibid., 192.

71 Ibid., 45. Emphasis in the original.

72 Ibid.

73 See William Fox, *On Jacobinism* (1794), 1–2. Consider Charles Pigott's arresting definition of "Throne" in *A Political Dictionary* (1795), 172:

> A sumptuous, richly furnished and elevated seat . . . . A man, fantastically drest out in ermine, velvet, gold and silver spangles, squirrel and rabbit skins. Thus tricked out, like the wooden god of Otaheite. . . it is no wonder that men should be so deluded, as to think him more than mortal, when it requires so little of imagination to metamorphose him at once into an object of worship. Under this impression, when they approach the throne, they are struck with awe and dismay, and address this bundle of fine clothes with bended knee and humble voice, as if they were attempting to appease an irritated Deity. . . . And yet if you ask one

of these despicable wretches, after having gone through this pantomimic
scene, whether he is a lunatic? 'No,' he will tell you, 'I'm a loyal man.'
Pitiful, sorry wretch!

74 Stafford, *Body Criticism*, 1.
75 Johann Caspar Lavater, *Physionomische Fragmente, zur Beförderung der
Menschenkenntniss und Menschenliebe* (Leipzig, 1775–78).
76 John Graham, "Lavater's *Physiognomy* in England," *Journal of the History of Ideas* 22 (1961): 561–72.
77 Scott J. Juengel, "Godwin, Lavater, and the Pleasures of Surface," *Studies
in Romanticism* 35 (1996): 73–97, at 74. More generally, see idem, "About
Face: Physiognomics, Revolution, and the Radical Act of Looking," (Ph.D.
diss., University of Iowa, 1997). See also Lucy Hartley, *Physiognomy and
the Means of Expression in Nineteenth-Century Culture* (Cambridge: CUP,
2001); Sharonna Pearl, *About Faces: Physiognomy in Nineteenth-Century
Britain* (Cambridge: CUP, 2010).
78 For a useful summary of the publishing history of the *Essays* during the
1790s, see Graham, "Lavater's *Physiognomy* in England," and "Lavater's
Physiognomy in England: A Checklist," *Papers of the American Bibliographic Society* 55 (1961): 297–308.
79 See, for example, William Sotheby, *Poems: Consisting of a Tour through
Parts of North and South Wales, ... and an Epistle to a Friend on Physiognomy* (1790); George Woodward, *Eccentric Excursions: Or, Literary and
Pictorial Sketches of Countenance, Character and Country* (1798); Johann
Musus, *Physiognomical Travels, Preceded by a Physiognomical Journal*
(1800); *The Ladies Physiognomical Mirror, or Lovers Portraits* (1798).
80 For different orientation that Holcroft brought to the *Essays*, see Joan
Stemmler, "The Physiognomical Portraits of Johann Caspar Lavater," *Art
Bulletin* 75 (1993): 151–68, at 152–53. Diane Long Hoeveler charts how
illustrations of Holcroft's *Tale of Mystery* (1802), often cited as the first
British melodrama, registered the influence and popularity of Lavater's
theories. Diane Long Hoeveler, "Illustrating Thomas Holcroft's *A Tale of
Mystery* as Physiognomical Tableaux Vivant," in Wallace and Markley,
eds., *Re-Viewing Thomas Holcroft*, 103–17.
81 *AR*, 5, December 1789: cols. 459–62; *AR*, 6, April 1790: cols. 426–31,
471–72.
82 For Holcroft's letter in response, see *AR*, 6, January 1790: cols. 110–2.
For his critique of Edmund Morris's *False Colours* (a farce that ridiculed
physiognomics), see *MR*, 11, August 1793: 410.
83 It was performed an additional five times in the 1795/96 season. See Charles
Beecher Hogan, ed., *The London Stage, 1660–1800: Pt 5: 1776–1800*, 3
vols. (Carbondale: Southern Illinois University Press, 1969), 3: 1681, 1751.
84 Claeys, "Origins of the Rights of Labor," 256–57.
85 Thomas Kavanaugh, *Enlightenment and the Shadows of Chance: The
Novel and the Culture of Gambling in Eighteenth-Century France*
(Baltimore, MD: Johns Hopkins University Press, 1993), 38–46; Marilyn
Morris, "Princely Debt, Public Credit, and Commercial Values in Late
Georgian Britain," *JBS* 43 (2004): 339–65; A. A. Markley, "Aristocrats
Behaving Badly: Gambling and Dueling in the 1790s Novel of Reform,"
European Romantic Review 17: 161–68.
86 Thomas Holcroft, *The Road to Ruin* (1792), 2–3.
87 Ibid., 3.
88 See Donna Andrew, *Aristocratic Vice: The Attack on Duelling, Suicide,
Adultery, and Gambling in Eighteenth-Century England* (New Haven,

CT: Yale University Press, 2013), chapter 5; Gillian Russell, "'Faro's Daughters': Female Gamesters, Politics, and the Discourse of Finance in 1790s Britain," *Eighteenth-Century Studies* 33 (2000): 481–504.

89 Andrew, *Aristocratic Vice*, 128–29.

90 "Friday's Post," *Ipswich Journal*, 25 February 1792, 2, British Library, British Newspaper Archive, accessed 29 March 2020, https://www.british newspaperarchive.co.uk/viewer/BL/0000071/17920225/002/0002.

91 Russell, "Faro's Daughters," 485, quoting Charles Cotton, *The Compleat Gamester* (1674), 1–2; Andrew, *Aristocratic Vice*, 647–53.

92 Miriam L. Wallace, *Revolutionary Subjects: In the English "Jacobin" Novel, 1790–1805* (Lewisburg, PA: Bucknell University Press, 2009), 29–30 and chapter 3. For an examination of the contradictions in this model, see Hilary N. Fezzey, "Examining Jacobin Sexual Politics in *Anna St. Ives*," in Wallace and Markley, eds., *Re-Viewing Thomas Holcroft*, 133–45.

93 For the use of Peter de Bolla's exploration of the "discourse of debt" to interrogate banking as sober gambling, gendered as male, see Russell, "Faro's Daughters," 497–98. See also Peter de Bolla, *The Discourse of the Sublime: History, Aesthetics, and the Subject* (Oxford: Basil Blackwell, 1989), 103–40. As Ian Klaus notes, anti-City rhetoric was part of a broader concern and recognition that modern capitalism *was* partly driven by speculative excess, "deep play," and fraud. Ian Klaus, *Forging Capitalism: Rogues, Swindlers, Frauds, and the Rise of Modern Finance* (New Haven, CT: Yale University Press, 2014), chapters 1 and 2.

94 The evils of gaming were not a new theme for Holcroft. In the later 1750s, he had been a stable boy at Newmarket, and devotes the last self-authored chapter of his *Memoirs* to his experiences there, focusing to a large extent on his own efforts at betting. One of his earliest plays, *Duplicity* (1781), features both a wealthy gambler who fixates ruinously on his losses, and a character named Scrip, who speculates on the London Exchange. For Holcroft's portrayal of gaming, see A. A. Markley, "Transforming Experience into Reform in Holcroft's *Memoirs*," in Wallace and Markley, eds., *Re-Viewing Thomas Holcroft*, 181–95.

95 On common concerns about private credit in an economy dominated by paper instruments and public reputation, see Donna T. Andrew and Randall McGowen, *The Perreaus and Mrs. Rudd: Forgery and Betrayal in Eighteenth-Century London* (Berkeley: University of California Press, 2001), chapter 6.

96 Holcroft, *Road to Ruin*, 54.

97 Ibid., 55.

98 Holcroft, "The Art of Acting," 66.

99 For the distinction between identicality – "highlighting whatever a person has in common with others" – to a modern "regime of selfhood" emphasizing personal uniqueness, see Dror Wahrman, *The Making of the Modern Self: Identity and Culture in Eighteenth-Century England* (New Haven, CT: Yale University Press, 2004), 276, and more generally, chapter 7.

100 William Godwin, "Essay V: Of Trades and Professions," in Philp, general editor, *Political and Philosophical Writings of Godwin*, Pamela Clemit, ed., vol. 5, *Educational and Literary Writings*, 174.

101 Ibid. John Barrell notes that as persons without gentility, but nonetheless obligated to wear hair powder to flatter their customers, small tradesmen were perhaps the largest group affected by Pitt's hair-powder tax in 1795. John Barrell, *The Spirit of Despotism: Invasions of Privacy in the 1790s* (Oxford: OUP, 2006), 157–59.

102 Holcroft, *Letter to the Right Honorable William Windham, On the Intemperance and Dangerous Tendency of His Pubic Conduct*, 2nd ed. (1795), 47.

103 For the marked concerns over personal theatricality and authenticity in an expanding market culture, see Jean-Christophe Agnew, *Worlds Apart: The Market and the Theater in Anglo-American Thought, 1550–1750* (Cambridge: CUP, 1986).

104 Mary Wollstonecraft, *A Vindication of the Rights of Woman*, ed. Miriam Brody (Harmondsworth: Penguin, 1992, first published 1792), 115. On Wollstonecraft's conception of sensibility tempered by reason, see among others, G. J. Barker-Benfield, *Culture of Sensibility*, chapter 7. Godwin first met Wollstonecraft at a dinner at Joseph Johnson's on 13 November 1791; he had supper with Holcroft that evening. Bod. Lib., GD, 13 November 1791, accessed 6 August 2018, http://godwindiary.bodleian.ox.ac.uk.

105 Holcroft, *Road to Ruin*, 28.

106 Ibid., 18.

107 Wollstonecraft, *Vindication of the Rights of Woman*, 130.

108 Holcroft, *MR*, 15, September 1794: 107–08. For the possibility that an unsigned letter from January 1796, proposing marriage to Wollstonecraft, may be from Holcroft, see Gary K., *Revolutionary Feminism: The Mind and Career of Mary Wollstonecraft* (New York: St. Martin's Press, 1992), 196. On Holcroft and femininity, see Nancy Johnson, *The English Jacobin Novel on Rights, Property and the Law: Critiquing the Contract* (New York: Palgrave Macmillan, 2004); Katherine Binhammer, "The Political Novel and the Seduction Plot: Thomas Holcroft's *Anna St. Ives*," *Eighteenth-Century Fiction* 11 (1999), 205–22; Fezzey, "Examining Jacobin Sexual Politics."

109 Thomas Green, *Extracts from the Diary of a Lover of Literature* (Ipswich: John Raw, 1810), 19.

110 Greg Dening, *Performances* (Chicago, IL: University of Chicago Press, 1996), 111.

111 Jacques-Bénigne Bossuet, *Maxims et réflexions sur le comédie* (Paris, 1694), 178–79, quoted in Barish, *Antitheatrical Prejudice*, 202.

112 Dening, *Performances*, 111–12; Peter Stallybrass and Allon White, *The Politics and Poetics of Transgression* (Ithaca, NY: Cornell University Press, 1986), 80–99. The prologue speaker's liminal position vis-a-vis the play-world and the world outside helps explain the scrutiny given the speaker/actor of the prologue by anti-theatrical critics. See Barish, *Antitheatrical Prejudice*, 334; Agnew, *Worlds Apart*, 106, 109–11; Mary Knapp, *Prologues and Epilogues of the Eighteenth Century* (New Haven, CT: Yale University Press, 1961), 23–29, 108; Hogan, *London Stage, Pt. 5*, 1: ixxiv–lxxv; Dror Wahrman, "Percy's Prologue: From Gender Play to Gender Panic in Eighteenth-Century England," *P&P* 159 (1998): 113–60.

113 Holcroft, *Road to Ruin*, ii.

114 Greater London Council, *Survey of London, vol. 35: The Theatre Royal, Drury Lane, and the Royal Opera House, Covent Garden* (Athlone Press, 1970), 90–91.

115 See Bolton, "Theorizing Audiences," 36–37.

116 Holcroft, *Road to Ruin*, ii.

117 Bennett, *Theatre Audiences*, 113–14.

118 See Hogan, *London Stage, Pt. 5*, 3: 1443.

119 Albert Goodwin, *The Friends of Liberty: The English Democratic Movement in the Age of the French Revolution* (Cambridge, MA: Harvard University Press, 1979), 193–94; 198; 216.

120 *St. James Chronicle*, 4 February 1794, and see also 8 October 1794.
121 TS 11/ 962/3508, SCI minute-book, 18 October 1792.
122 Ibid., 4 April 1794.
123 See Holcroft, *Life of Holcroft*, 2: 46–49, for his surrender to the magistrate at the Clerkenwell Sessions House. See also Goodwin, *Friends of Liberty*, 216–17; 239–67.
124 In addition to the many instances in the play where Enfield's house is represented as scandalous ("detestable," a place of "bad company," etc.), the Scottish servant Donald refers to Mrs. Enfield as an *elritch limmer* – in Scots slang, a hideous prostitute. See Scottish Language Dictionaries, *Dictionary of the Scots Language/Dictionar o the Scots Leid*, https://dsl. ac.uk/,hog accessed July 25 2019. Enfield's house is located in Dover Street, one of the most notorious areas of late eighteenth-century Southwark.
125 Thomas Holcroft, *The Deserted Daughter* (1795), 17.
126 Ibid., 18.
127 Diane Long Hoeveler interprets *The Deserted Daughter* as the play whose tensions begin to shift towards the heightened Manichean world of melodrama. As a genre, sentimental comedy was nearing exhaustion under the pressures of revolutionary culture and state repression. Diane Long Hoeveler, "The Temple of Morality: Thomas Holcroft and the Swerve of Melodrama," *European Romantic Review 14* (2003): 49–63. See also Garnai, "A Lock Upon my Lips," 478–79.
128 *The Deserted Daughter*, 49.
129 Ibid., 50.
130 Nora Nachumi suggest that the science of gesture offered female novelists space in which to describe male and female sensibility as essentially equivalent, and thereby sidestep a logocentric theory of communication that had privileged male sensibility. Nora Nachumi, "'Those Simple Signs': The Performance of Emotion in Elizabeth Inchbald's *A Simple Story*," *Eighteenth-Century Fiction* 11 (1999): 317–38.
131 *MR*, 15, September 1794: 107–8.
132 Lavater, *Essays on Physiognomy*, 80.
133 Moody, *Illegitimate Theatre in London*, 4.
134 Philp, *Godwin's Political Justice*, 169–73, 214–20, 229.
135 Kenneth R. Johnston rightfully includes Holcroft among the those harassed and damaged by the Pitt ministry during the 1790s. Kenneth R. Johnston, *Unusual Suspects: Pitt's Reign of Alarm and the Lost Generation of the 1790s* (Oxford: OUP, 2013); see especially 162–63.
136 Amy Garnai persuasively argues that Holcroft's *Knave or Not* (1798) reflects this awareness of the limitations of unmediated truth as a solution to social problems. Garnai, "A Lock Upon My Lips," 482.
137 See *The Times* 26 January 1800. For the impact on Holcroft's life abroad, see his letter to Godwin, 17 February 1802, Bod. Lib., Abinger Shelly Papers, MS. Dep. c. 511.
138 Holcroft to Godwin, 29 April 1800; Holcroft to Godwin, 13 May 1800, Bod. Lib., Abinger Shelly Papers, MS. Dep. c. 511.
139 See Worrall, *Radical Culture*, 17–34; Jon Klancher, *The Making of English Reading Audiences, 1790–1832* (Madison: University of Wisconsin Press, 1987), 113–19; James Epstein, *In Practice: Studies in the Language and Culture of Popular Politics in Modern Britain* (Stanford, CA: Stanford University Press, 2003), 89–90, 97–105; John Barrell, "'An Entire Change of Performances?': The Politicization of Theatre and the Theatricalisation of Politics in the mid 1790s," *Lumen* 17 (1998): 11–50.

140 Philp, *Godwin's Political Justice*, 173.
141 Jon Mee notes that during the mid-1790s, Godwin was meeting with LCS members as a group. Mee, *Print, Publicity, and Radicalism*, 43–44.
142 Thomas Holcroft, *A Narrative of the Facts, Relating to a Prosecution for High Treason: Including the Address to the Jury, which the Court Refused to Hear* (1795).

4 "Equality and No King"
Sociability and Sedition

On the evening of 6 November 1792, John Frost dined at the tavern above the Percy coffeehouse in Marylebone.[1] Given that this was the evening after politically charged celebrations of the anniversary of the "Glorious" Revolution, feelings may have still been running high.[2] A few months earlier, Frost had accompanied his friend Thomas Paine in his escape to France to avoid arrest. On the night in question, as he left the building through the coffeehouse, Matthew Yateman, an apothecary who knew Frost as a commissioner of the watch and lightening of streets, engaged him in conversation about the situation in France from where Frost had recently returned. According to Frost's version of events, Yateman set out to entrap him, asking "Well, Mr. Equality, [when] did you arrive? I suppose you are for equality and no kings." Whatever Yateman's exact words, Frost proclaimed for all to hear, "I am for equality; I can see no reason why man should not be on an equal footing with another; it is every man's birthright." He defended this proposition when challenged by various persons, adding when pressed that by "equality" he meant "no kings." Asked specifically if he meant no king "in this country," he responded, "Yes, no king, the constitution of this country is a bad one." It was this encounter that took Frost from a site of sociability, dining, and conversation to King's Bench and eventually to Newgate prison – sites of law, justice, majesty, and punishment.[3] Frost's case provides a point of departure for thinking about the nexus among sites of sociability, politics, and law, and the behavior and language appropriate to each. His case also marks the historical moment at which the boundaries between sociability and sedition, polite conversation and political commitment became extremely difficult to negotiate, particularly for a certain brand of gentleman radical.

Coffeehouse Sociability under Pressure

The tavern and the coffeehouse are, of course, classic sites of the "bourgeois" public sphere, places for the reading of newspapers, conversing among friends and other informed citizens, sometimes hosting formal debating clubs, a space of conviviality where ideas circulate freely among supposed equals.[4] It was here that Britain's other political nation gathered to form and to express "public opinion" on the events of the day; it was here that private individuals traded information and formed commercial and social bonds.[5] Indeed, before leaving the Percy, Frost had been deep in conversation about questions of agricultural improvement. This was predominately, if not exclusively, male space; it was space marked off, at least ideally, not only from the controls of royal government but also from the street, the fair, and the low tavern culture of the metropolis.[6] In certain respects, therefore, the belief in some form of "equality" would seem appropriate to coffeehouse culture, and the demand for "no king" would seem to affirm the status of the public sphere itself, a zone removed from royal authority.

Yet, the consideration of the public sphere and the norms of sociability cannot be separated so neatly from other spaces and sites of discourse and power. Thus, Frost's claim to equality and no king raised the issue, on the one hand, of disconnecting this space from norms of social hierarchy, which in the last instance resided in the figure of the king and, on the other hand, threatened to connect the coffeehouse to the street and the alehouse culture of artisans and the laboring poor. The classic manifestation of the coffeehouse as a site of bourgeois sociability continued to be founded on a double denial of, or separation from, both aristocratic and plebeian culture. The Percy was a well-known coffeehouse and tavern located in a socially exclusive part of town, at Rathbone Place, off Oxford Street, where a generation earlier James Boswell had dined with literary friends.[7] The distinction still maintained in residual form at the Percy between its upstairs tavern and lower-floor coffeehouse had, in fact, broken down earlier in the century: coffeehouses often served good food and wine, distinguishing features of the gentlemen's tavern. The equal footing of the Percy was that between gentlemen of a certain social standing.

The hallmark of such discursive space was its consensual character, embodying common standards of taste and conduct that were first and most famously articulated by Joseph Addison and Richard Steele in their *Tatler* and *Spectator* essays. The suspension of social status, if not political difference, at such sites of sociability was predicated on shared standards of the sayable, on norms of politeness, good behavior, restrained conversation, and good writing. The blending of "grace, and gravitas, urbanity and morality, correction and consolidation" was, as Terry Eagleton writes, directly linked to a "polite" reading public and the growing legitimacy of essay-writing, to the republic of *belles lettres*.[8] In addition, it was thought that the coffeehouse might play a moral role equivalent to that played by the "polis" in ancient Athens and Rome, functioning as a breeding ground for citizens and civic virtue – or "virtue" reconstituted in terms of manners and politeness. The coffeehouse was a self-regulating republic of urban civility.[9] However, this civility was always subject to a series of tensions between the permissive pleasures of heavy drinking and good order, between accessibility to customers of various social backgrounds and distinctions based on the appearance of good taste and manners, between free conversation and the hazardous subjects of politics and religion.

By the late eighteenth century, the ideals of civility associated with the coffeehouse had become at best tenuous. While taverns and coffeehouses had from the late seventeenth century been contentious political sites, in the wake of the American and French Revolutions consensual norms of "bourgeois" conduct, of politeness and sociability, could not withstand the disruption of revolutionary politics. Taverns and coffeehouses were hardly safe havens for those committed to the politics of the French Revolution. If, as Jürgen Habermas proposes, the rationality of the public sphere was in the first instance the product of private subjectivity originating in the conjugal family (later extended into the market), by 1792 the capacity for private individuals to exchange views with a measure of security was in jeopardy. Suspicion was the order of the day. The watchfulness of government spies, and more significantly that of private individuals responding to the royal proclamation of May 1792 against sedition, now policed the space of the tavern and coffeehouse – their rooms, boxes, and tables.[10] Taverns and alehouses were subject to the control of licensing by local magistrates, and many proprietors were, in fact, pressured to ban supporters of Paine from their premises.[11] Moreover, the "publicness" of the coffeehouse and tavern was not of a piece: Frost had been dining in a "private" box of the tavern before entering the more public space of the coffeehouse below. John Binns, who himself faced trial on charges of sedition, recalled that John Thelwall never felt comfortable even in "private" conversation:

> If he went into an oyster house, or an *à-la-mode* beef-shop, he would conceit that one-half of the boxes in the room had government spies in them, whose especial business was to watch and report, as far as possible, all he said and all he did.[12]

In light of his own trial for high treason, Thelwall's paranoia was understandable, and as the case of Charles Pigott and William Hodgson illustrates, it was not entirely misplaced. Both men were leading LCS members. Pigott was a prominent radical author of gentry background who specialized in scurrilous exposés of the sexual morals of the aristocracy; Hodgson was a physician.[13] Nearly a year after Frost's encounter, the two men dined "convivially together" and read newspapers at the London coffeehouse on Ludgate Hill. Hodgson spoke freely of the "bad private character" of the Duke of York, commander-in-chief of the British forces, commenting that he "respected no man however exalted by rank, unless dignified by virtue." Less decorously, he called the Elector of

Hanover (i.e. George III) and Landgrave of Hesse Cassell "German Hog Butchers," and toasted "Equality" and the "French Republic." While in private conversation – conversing with an "openness and freedom" natural to their surroundings – the two men attracted a crowd of loyalists who "laid siege" to their table, one of whom ordered a glass of punch and repeatedly proposed, "The King! The King! The King!," Pigott and Hodgson refused to drink, but Hodgson countered with a toast to "The French Republic, and May She Triumph Over All Her Enemies." At this point the proprietor, who was a member of John Reeves' Association for Preserving Liberty and Property against Republicans and Levellers, locked the door to the coffeehouse and sent for a constable. On the basis of notes taken by informers, the two republicans were arrested and eventually brought to trial. According to Pigott's account, at the New Compter, they were told that they were arrested because "we were TOM PAINE'S Men, and rebels; and he [the jailer] had been told we were GENTLEMEN, but it was a lie, we were d__d BLACKGUARD RASCALS." Stripped of the social garb of being "gentlemen," and unable to meet the exorbitantly high bail set at £500 each, the two men remained in prison for over three weeks before being brought to trial.[14]

When the two men were brought before a grand jury, the legal case turned, according to Pigott, on whether words "passing between two friends in a public coffeehouse, at a table where they were sitted [*sic*] by themselves" could be the subject of an indictment; did freeborn Englishmen have a right as to their own thoughts and private words? "Till now," declared Pigott, "it had been supposed, that the table or box in a coffee room was as sacred and inviolable as a private room, nay, even as our house." There was, however, a paradox to Pigott's argument since he maintained not merely that he and Hodgson were in "private" conversation but that the "publicness" of the coffeehouse and freedom and loudness with which they spoke – including toasting "the French Republic'" – demonstrated that they were not engaged in seditious activity. Rather than conspiring sedition – sedition being characterized by "silence and concealment," shunning "the light" – they appeared and spoke together openly at one of the most frequented coffeehouses in the city of London. It was precisely the "publicness" of their "private" conversation that guaranteed the good intent of their actions and words; they had not sought the protections of secrecy.[15] As it turned out, the grand jury rejected the indictment brought against Pigott, while Hodgson was tried and convicted for seditious words and sentenced to two years' imprisonment, fined £200, and required to find sureties for his good behavior in the amount of £400. From Newgate, where he languished beyond his sentence due to inability to pay the fine, Hodgson reiterated his sentiments in print:

> I am neither ashamed of the language I held, nor do I feel the slightest contrition for having used it; I here, in the face of the whole

world, avow my opinion to be, that a REPUBLIC is the best suited
to the happiness of the French people.[16]

This could, of course, be construed as a confirmation of Jacobin belief,
although Hodgson avoided proposing republicanism as universally desirable or as best suited to the happiness of the British people.

Frost's situation was, of course, not strictly analogous to that of Pigott and Hodgson (a point Pigott made) in that he had been challenged
to state his views "publicly" and had voluntarily obliged. On the other
hand, like the two men, Frost had almost certainly been set up by
vigilant subjects who knew him for his radical sympathies. A site of
sociability had been transformed into "AN INQUISITION," according to Pigott. Furthermore, after refusing to back down, one witness
related that Frost was fortunate not to be kicked out of the coffeehouse
into the street where he would be unprotected by the protocols of coffeehouse culture. Frost responded by asking whether his opponents
"doubted his courage." The incident, as reported, tested not merely
Frost's republicanism but his commitment to a code of male honor.
Such situations had to be carefully negotiated if one were successfully
to maintain face without leading to serious altercation or prosecution.
For instance, in the heated conditions following the Priestley Riots of
July 1791 – an organized loyalist response to an occasion of radical
dining and sociability to celebrate Bastille Day – Samuel Parr, "the
Whig Dr. Johnson," was compelled to toast church and king while
dining out in the vicinity of Birmingham. He boldly added his own
gloss: "Church and King – Once it was the toast of Jacobites; now it
is the toast of incendiaries. It means church without the gospel – and
king above the law."[17] In 1796, Binns (an Irishman working in London as a plumber) and John Gale Jones were delegated by the LCS to
travel to Birmingham to consult with local activists and agitate for
reform.[18] Binns courageously paid a visit to the "Church and King"
tavern where the Priestley Riots were believed to have been planned;
the panel of plate glass on the entranced displayed in "large polished
gilt letters, the words, "NO JACOBINS ADMITTED HERE." Entering loyalist territory, Binns was apparently recognized as an LCS delegate, and in an attempt to smoke him out, he was greeted by the toast
"Church and King," followed by "Damn all Jacobins." After Binns
refused to drink the second toast, customers shouted for him to be
thrown out of the tavern. According to Binns, he then defended his
political principles in a conciliatory speech; he was allowed to finish
his drink and retire at his own discretion.[19] A victory of sorts. Binns
was subsequently prosecuted (and acquitted) on charges of seditious
speech, for addressing a meeting of Birmingham's United Corresponding Society at the Swan public house, met for what the prosecution
claimed as the "PRETENDED purpose of reform."[20]

The tavern and coffeehouse were arenas for testing the courage of men's political convictions; male honor was thus bound with politics and sociability. The challenges and counter-challenges to drink particular toasts or to stand to one's words and allegiances were in certain important respects analogous to the code of the duel. Standing to one's word had been crucial to an earlier regime of truth based on the presumed reliability of a gentleman's speech – gentlemen being independent and thus honest.[21] The code of the duel was, however, also linked to upper-class bouts of massive drinking and rowdiness, and increasingly was seen as an atavistic expression of aristocratic manliness in a commercial age.[22] As sites of sociability, commerce, and conversation, coffeehouses were subject to persuasive conditions that in practice fell short of Enlightenment notions of truthful discourse or for that matter norms of "bourgeois" propriety. They represented an ideal of rational sociability while at the same time housing emotions and behavior that might undermine that ideal.

Conversation, Association, and Revolution

Despite the less-than-ideal realization of the norms of rational sociability, it is nonetheless important to recognize that Enlightenment-based concepts of conversation, free discussion, and "truth" were crucial to a distinct strain of British radicalism deeply influenced by the overlapping traditions of radical Dissent and eighteenth-century rationalism. In William Godwin's *Caleb Williams* (1794), the aristocratic Falkland's major character flaw is his overriding, and ultimately self-destructive, regard for his honor and reputation over truth and benevolent understanding. Written in the shadow of the government's campaign against the likes of Frost, the novel is itself a commentary on the conditions governing rational persuasion and truthful representation.[23] In Godwin's *Enquiry Concerning Political Justice* (first published in early 1793), the section on the "utility of social communication" provides a model of Habermas's "ideal speech situation" – what Godwin calls "candid and unreserved conversation." "Let us suppose," writes Godwin, unimpaired conversation between two sensitive truth-seekers, "desirous extensively to communicate the truths with which they are acquainted," and distinguished by "mildness of their temper, and a spirit of comprehensive benevolence." Unlike the "cold" encounter with the printed page, vigorous private conversation provides a variety of views, stimulating "freedom and elasticity of disquisition."[24] Godwin's model is based on controlled conditions of free discussion among intellectual equals.

Moreover, for followers of Paine and Godwin, rational communication, whether through discussion or reading, stood in striking opposition to aristocratic and royal spectacle, and the appeal to the senses or emotions. Royal pomp, splendor, and ornamental display were calculated "to bring over to its party our eyes and our ears." Godwin argued, as did Paine, that kings set out with "every artifice that may dazzle our sense, and mislead our judgement."[25] Despite radicals' own extensive use of ritual and symbolic expression, there was a lingering suspicion that such gestures pandered to popular irrationality, appealing to the senses rather than the mind. Similarly, public oratory, particularly rabble-rousing, was suspect since it did not allow for deliberation.[26] Radicals often contrasted the decorum of their own proceedings, discussed in Chapter 2, to the drunken spectacle of loyalist mobs burning Paine in effigy or to the disorder of heavy-drinking and liberally bribed election crowds.

As Mark Philp comments, "sociability is the basic fabric of late eighteenth-century intellectual life." Godwin and his friends "lived in a round of debate and discussion, in clubs, associations, debating societies, salons, taverns, coffee houses, bookshops, publishing houses and in the street."[27] This was the social and intellectual milieu that nurtured radical ideas extolling the value of conversation and sociability, the power of reason and opinion; this was also the social world in which Frost moved. He was a close friend of John Horne Tooke, whose house at Wimbledon was a center of continuous dining, drinking, conversation, and conviviality. Leading figures of London's radical intelligentsia, generally drawn from the middling social ranks, gathered at Tooke's table – including Paine, Thelwall, Godwin, the playwright Thomas Holcroft, the publisher Joseph Johnson (whose own dinners featured many of the same people), the poet Robert Merry, the engraver William Sharp, the sculptor Thomas Banks, Archibald Hamilton Rowan of the United Irishmen, the radical lawyer Felix Vaughan, and the republican scientist Thomas Cooper, among others.[28] Conversation could be contentious, and not necessarily constrained. Frost related to Thelwall that at one of his dinners, Tooke expressed the view that cutting off the head of a king every fifty or one hundred years was a good thing, much to the annoyance of Paine who responded, "Ah, Tooke! You are a true royalist! You love blood."[29]

In contrast to rational conversation, Godwin was wary of political associations. Subject to conditions of partisanship, enforced programs, harangues of demagogues, and a tendency to disorder, they were unsuited to achieving political reform through the discovery of truth. Frost was, however, an activist; as a leading member of the SCI, his reform credentials dated back to the famous Thatched House program of 1782.[30] His attendance and active participation in the affairs of the SCI in the years 1791–1793 can be followed in the society's carefully maintained minute book, which the government confiscated.[31] As a prominent lawyer who had been educated at Winchester School, he assisted Tooke in coordinating communication among provincial associations of artisans and tradesmen, offering editorial advice in the drawing up of their constitutions and rules. Thomas Hardy, the founder and first secretary of the LCS, consulted Tooke and Frost when he established the society.[32]

In the early 1790s, radicals were organized across a spectrum of socially differentiated (and exclusively male) associations, each offering their own brand of sociability: ranging from the aristocratic Foxite Whigs of the Friends of the People, to the largely middle-class members of the revived SCI, to the shoemakers and tailors who joined the LCS with its policy of "members unlimited" (although even the LCS's weekly membership fee of one penny excluded the lower ranks of London's laboring poor.) The boundaries separating members of these political groups were not fixed; moreover, places like Daniel Isaac Eaton's bookstore and his journal, *Politics for the People*, provided fluid sites of social and literary contact between polite and plebeian culture.[33] Nonetheless, the social distinctions separating democrats in the 1790s were quite real, as were the differences separating varying sites and styles of sociability. The raucous "free and easies" held at alehouses frequented by ultra-radical artisans constituted a masculine world of plebeian sociability quite distinct from that of the dinner parties of Tooke or Johnson (at whose table Godwin first met Mary Wollstonecraft).[34] The SCI's annual subscription of one guinea ensured a "polite" membership. In May 1794, at the dinner held at the Crown and Anchor tavern to celebrate the fourteenth anniversary of the SCI, free tickets were distributed to some LCS members unable to afford the price of seven shillings and six pence, several of whom were reported to have behaved "improperly."[35] Despite increased cooperation between the two societies, Frost was among the few gentlemen, along with Tooke, Thelwall, and Joseph Gerrald, to directly associate themselves with the LCS.[36] A week after Frost's encounter at the Percy coffeehouse, a spy reported that at an LCS division meeting held at the Green Dragon in Golden Square, Soho, attended by more than 200 people, Frost "made a long inflammatory speech, which he concluded by recommending to the members to deffend [sic] their opinions with their lives and property," adding "this man seem'd very popular." He also noted that Frost was "almost the only decent Man I have seen at any of their [LCS] Divisions."[37] Frost was a bridging figure, and was for that reason particularly vulnerable; he was a gentleman out of place.

The same spy who reported on the meeting at the Green Dragon, Captain George Monro, was soon to follow Frost to Paris: Frost's second revolutionary excursion.[38] Earlier, in September, Frost had traveled with Paine to Paris. The *World* reported, "Tom Paine is OFF" from Dover, accompanied "by his *San Culotte* Secretary, John Frost," also acting in the role of interpreter since Paine knew little French.[39] Hardly a sans-culotte, Frost was a British Jacobin, a republican inspired by the quickening pace of events in France. In a letter to Tooke, he described Paine's reception at Calais where a young woman presented Paine with the national cockade; Paine was soon elected Calais's representative to the National Convention. From Paris, Frost observed that the "treachery of Louis [XVI]

is so great, that the indignation of the people cannot be wondered at."[40]
The two men arrived at Paris a fortnight after the "September Mas-
sacres" (2–6 September) in which crowds broke into the city's prisons
and systematically executed over a thousand "counter-revolutionaries."
The first republic was established on 22 September, two days after their
arrival. Frost witnessed the Revolution firsthand, as monarchy was abolished and the initial terror sought vengeance against recalcitrant aristocrats and clergy. He was there as the revolutionary army turned back the
Prussian advance at the Battle of Valmy, and for the opening sessions of
the National Convention.[41] Returning to London around mid-October,
Frost resumed his political activities; he was appointed to SCI committees to confer with delegates of the LCS and to correspond with the
Sheffield SCI.[42] His experience in France gives context to the declaration
"equality and no king."

Three days after having dined at the Percy, Frost and the American
revolutionary Joel Barlow were delegated by the SCI to present a fraternal address to the National Convention. Addressing the Convention as
"Servants of a Sovereign People, and Benefactors of Mankind," the SCI
pronounced in poet Barlow's florid style that

> the lustre of the American Republic, like an effulgent Morning,
> arose with increasing vigour, but still too distant to enlighten our
> hemisphere, till the splendour of the French Revolution burst forth
> upon the nations in the full fervor of a meridian Sun.

Philosophical principles had been transformed into practical results.[43]
On 28 November, the SCI's delegates were admitted to the Convention
where Barlow, his French being better than Frost's, introduced their address. Looking into Britain's revolutionary future, Barlow opined,

> After the example given by France, Revolutions will become easy:
> Reason is about to make rapid progress, and it would not be ex-
> traordinary, if in much less space of time than can be imagined,
> the French should send Addresses of congratulations to a National
> Convention of England.

The address also announced that as a "patriotic gift to the Soldiers of
Liberty," the SCI would send one thousand pairs of shoes a week for six
weeks to be transported to Calais. The Convention voted Frost and Barlow "the honors of the session," ordering their address to be printed and
distributed throughout France's eighty-three departments and to the gen-
erals in the field, as well as translated into other European languages.[44]
The SCI's address was one among many sent by the popular societies
expressing solidarity with the newly established republic; formal gestures that embodied the utopian expectations and internationalism of

late 1792.[45] The addresses were subsequently reprinted in the reports of the parliamentary committee of secrecy, and cited at the 1794 treason trials as evidence of revolutionary designs in coordination with Jacobin France.[46]

In December 1792, responding to Charles James Fox's proposal for the king to send an ambassador to France, Burke delivered a two-hour speech in which he declared sarcastically that it was absurd to send an ambassador to negotiate with the French republic when England was already represented by the likes of Barlow and Frost. He singled out Frost as "notorious ... his character was well known to both sides of the House," and "gentleman of the Treasury had particular reason for knowing it."[47] At this point Frost was a hunted man. The *London Gazette*, the government's official journal, had just announced that the commissioners of the treasury were offering a reward of £100 for anyone apprehending or aiding in the apprehension of Frost, "late of Westminster," who had been indicted on charges of sedition in King's Bench and who "now absconds from justice."[48] Burke, having declared that "Kings were anointed with oil – the new sovereignty of the people with blood," argued that war with France was necessary and just in order to safeguard "the liberties of England, and the interests of Europe, and the happiness of mankind."[49] Pitt prepared the nation for war.[50]

Burke also drew parliament's attention to an address of the "English, Scotch, and Irish resident and domiciled in Paris" presented at the same session of the National Convention as the SCI address. "The residents expressed their hope that the victorious troops of liberty will lay down their arms only when there are no more tyrants and slaves. Of all these pretended governments, works of the fraud of priests and coalesced tyrants, there will soon remain only a shameful memory." They were in no doubt that "the great majority of our countrymen if public opinion were consulted, as it ought to be, in a national convention" shared their own desire to see a close union between the French republic and their respective nations in order to ensure "the enjoyment of the rights of man and establish on the firmest basis universal peace" throughout Europe. The address of these British expatriates originated at a dinner meeting held at White's Hotel, or the *Hotel Angleterre*, on 18 November to celebrate France's "brilliant success at arms," and was signed by fifty members of the committee appointed for its composition, including Frost.[51] The celebration itself featured a series of militant, ultra-radical toasts: hailing the French republic and its armies, the National Convention and "the coming Convention of England and Ireland," "the abolition of hereditary titles throughout the world" (proposed by Lord Edward Fitzgerald and Sir Robert Smith, former MP), to the women of Great Britain, "particularly those who have distinguished themselves by their writing in favour the French revolution, Mrs. [Charlotte] Smith, and Miss H. M. Williams," and to the women of France, "especially those who have had the courage to take up arms to defend the cause of liberty, *citoyennes* Fernig, Anselm, &c." Two bands played the "Marseillaise," "Ça Ira," and the "Carmagnole," and the toast to "The Republic of Men" was accompanied by "an English song to the air of the 'Marseillaise,' written by an English lady" (probably Helen Maria Williams).[52] Paris offered British Jacobins the space to openly celebrate the French Revolution's triumphs in the terms of the Revolution itself. It was, however, an expressive freedom that proved short-lived.

White's Hotel, at 8 Passage des Petits-Pères (not far from the Palais Royal), and the adjoining Hôtel des Etats-Unis, catered to British and American visitors. Frost initially took up residence at White's (Barlow was living permanently in Paris with his wife Ruth), and immediately became an active member of the community of radical expatriates. Around this time, the British Club, or Society of the Friends of the Rights of Man, was officially established. Meetings were held on Thursdays and Sundays at White's (named for its owner, the wine-merchant Christopher White). Here was another associational network composed predominately of members of the lettered middle class; a site of sociability dedicated to the free exchange of ideas among equals of a certain social standing, to the success of the French Revolution, and the universal expansion of republicanism. Members addressed each other as *citoyen*. The club was described by Monro as a "party of conspirators," whose views went far beyond the reform of parliament: "they extend their damnable ideas to the tottal [sic] subversion of Royalty, and the entire overthrown of the British Constitution on which they mean to form a Republic." They were in league with French revolutionaries now in power who would gladly assist them "in their diabolical schemes."[53] Many of the club's eighty to hundred members were SCI members, associating in Paris with the Cercle Social, Cordeliers Club, and Jacobin Club.[54] Their political sympathies and personal friendships linked them to Jacques-Pierre Brissot's circle and the Girondins. As an itinerant group of British and American radicals, the club included among its members the following people: Paine, Barlow, Frost, and Merry; the Scottish journalist and poet John Oswald who contributed to the Cercle Social's publications, and who was to die commanding a battalion of Parisian pikemen; the journalist Sampson Perry who as editor of *The Argus* was convicted *in absentia* of seditious libel; the radical printer John Hurford Stone and his brother Robert Stone, a coal merchant who was acquitted of high treason in 1796; the SCI member Dr. Robert Maxwell who facilitated efforts of English radicals to supply money and arms to France; and the writer and fiery orator Henry Redhead Yorke who was convicted of seditious conspiracy in 1795.[55] There was a strong Irish contingent that included the brothers John and Henry Sheares, and "Citizen" Edward Fitzgerald, all three of whom died in the cause of the 1798 Irish rebellion; as well as William Duckett, Edward Ferris, and Nicholas Madgett, part of an underground mission to coordinate intelligence between the United Irishmen and France and foster plans for a French invasion of Ireland.[56] As their dinner toasts indicate, club members honored British feminist writers such as Williams and Smith, both of whom attended the dinner (Wollstonecraft arrived in Paris the following month), along with paying tribute to French women revolutionaries such as the pistol-packing Théroigne de Méricourt.[57] Advanced ideas of women's rights were current, with the Cercle Social urging the vote for women, the availability of divorce, and the abolition of male primogeniture.[58] Williams's Sunday evening salon in the Rue de Bac facilitated the polite exchange of ideas among a mixed company of Girondists and foreign republicans.[59]

Frost was moving in a world of cosmopolitan republicanism committed to universal principles of liberty and inspired by the examples of the French and American Revolutions, a world tinged with conspiratorial tones. But the space of direct revolutionary encounter was closing down, whereas England held its own risks. Monro reported that Frost showed himself "a good deal alarmed at his situation," with an award offered for his apprehension. His correspondence was being opened by British government officials, and his funds may have been running low.[60] Frost had left England before an indictment was brought against him, and in a letter to Pitt, copied and published in the *Morning Chronicle*, he denied that he had gone to France to avoid prosecution, promising to return to face trial armed with a bundle of letters written to him by Pitt in the early 1780s favoring parliamentary reform.[61] The letter was dated 19 December, "1st Year of the Republic." According to the *World*, a paper that kept its satiric eye on the expatriate, Frost "clatters about the streets in a pair of French wooden *shoes* – John would gladly return to England, but he is afraid of being provided a *wooden cravat*, legally called the *Pillory*."[62] Along with other club members, Frost attended the trial of the king. By this time there was growing discord within the British Club. On 11 January 1793, Frost opposed a proposal from Paine and Merry to present another address to the National Convention, encouraging the French to invade England in the cause of bringing liberty to British shores.[63] His enthusiasm for the Revolution may have waned in the wake of the king's execution ten days later – "no king" may not have encompassed the spilling of royal blood. Perhaps like many other British republicans, he was torn between his cosmopolitan allegiance and feelings for his country. By the spring, the British Club had disbanded; with the Jacobin seizure of power in June, Robespierre's call for the expulsion of foreign nationals, and the arrest decree of October, British expatriates faced the prospect of imprisonment and the possibility of the guillotine.[64] The National Convention, seen as the embodiment of the popular will, less abstractly was subject to armed intervention from the Parisian sections. For many British middle-class reformers, the onset of terror reinforced the concern that Godwin expressed that popular mobilization might unleash uncontrolled violence and destroy rational debate. Barlow's confident forecast of Reason's "rapid progress" seemed less certain.

From King's Bench to Newgate Prison

Returning from France, Frost arrived in London on 9 February 1793; several days later he voluntarily surrendered himself and was granted bail. Having previously refused to retract his statement for equality and no king, Frost's case was settled not in the street or by a duel, but in a court of law. The conditions of discursive exchange and symbolic power were now constructed quite differently; the space of the coffeehouse was reiterated within the determinate place of the trial and the law, its language and protocols. In contrast to the relatively "open" or fluid space of the coffeehouse or tavern – a freewheeling zone of political, cultural, and commercial interchange – the court was hierarchically ordered. Certain speakers, judges and lawyers, spoke with the law's authority.[65] Space was demarcated; bodies were placed in their assigned places: the bench, the bar, the jury box, and public gallery. Wigged and sumptuously robed judges, barristers, and costumed court officials were distinguished from the defendant, jurors, and spectators in their ordinary clothes, organized as part of the law's ensemble of visual effects aimed at inspiring terror and awe.[66] Thus the courtroom was predicated on the norms of stability. As officially sanctioned discursive space, it was constructed ideally as anything but an occasion for free speech among equals.

It is important to recognize, however, that such pretentions to stability were not realized in practice, any more than were the contrasting pretensions of the coffeehouse; they constituted an ideal or a limit rather than a reality. The law's ambition to completely fill or produce its own social reality was constantly challenged and occasionally undone by its own contradictions, particularly the gap between law and its own legitimating rhetoric of justice.[67] Moreover, counter-notions of British citizenship were partly founded on the participatory experience of what Margaret Somers terms the "national legal sphere."[68] Courtrooms were often sites of disorder and subversion. In fact, the potential for delinquency, for making a stand against government injustice, was enhanced by the law's very own ambitions and measures to command space, bodies, and speech. Unlike other European countries, in England the courtroom was a public space; there was a popular audience for key trials. Not only were trial texts published but courtrooms were open to the public at large – on occasion tickets were even sold. Attending court could be a form of sociability or leisure entertainment. The central courts of King's Bench, Common Pleas, and Chancery were located in the open interior of Westminster Hall, where there was constant noise and milling about of strollers, booksellers, witnesses, jurymen, and others.[69]

Like the coffeehouse, the courtroom was gendered space, all those who spoke were men, although public galleries were open to women. As a young woman, Amelia Alderson, subsequently Opie, was a frequenter of the assize court at Norwich, her hometown, "delighting in the excitement of trials there." As a visitor to London, she attended the treason trial of John Horne Tooke, sending home full accounts of the proceedings to her radical father.[70]

In May 1793 the press reported that Westminster Hall "was prodigiously crowded" for Frost's trial.[71] The government in the person of the attorney general Sir John Scott (the future Lord Eldon) took over what had been initiated as a private prosecution. Frost was tried before a special jury, which meant, in effect, that it was packed. Despite being a lawyer, he "spoke" only by proxy, through his attorney Thomas Erskine. For radicals facing trial, the decision whether to represent themselves or to engage counsel was often a tough one. Radicals were generally suspicious of lawyers and the language of the law. Pigott, for example, roundly denounced the "chicanery" of lawyers and the law; although ignorant of the law, "and wholly unpractised in the meretricious arts of elocution, thank Heaven! I am full acquainted with *equity and right*."[72] Pigott's popular *Political Dictionary* defines "barrister" as "loquacity, impudence, presumption, vanity, consequence, sophistry, inconsistency, and self-interest. Erskine, Garrow."[73] The technical language and practice of the law were seen as contrary to the communication of truth, the antithesis to the truth-bearing properties of unrestricted conversation among equals. To be represented by counsel was, at least for the moment, to be reduced to silence. Radicals sometimes resorted to publishing the defenses that they "would have" given: the social world of the text substituting for that of the courtroom.

It was Erskine who read to the court Pitt's correspondence with Frost from 1782 in which the future prime minister had stated his support for the Thatched House resolutions for parliamentary reform. And it was Erskine who devised a defense that turned on a somewhat cowardly dodge, one that did not work. Erskine, the most accomplished trial lawyer of the day and who was to successfully lead the defense team in the 1794 treason trials, endeavored to show that Frost had been "in liquor"; he had spoken "in the heat and levity of wine." As Erskine told Frost's story, the company of diners "did not retire till the bottle had made many merry circles; and it appears ... that Mr. Frost, *to say the least*, had drunk very freely." In his drunken state, Frost was entrapped. Erskine asked the jury to consider whether "an English gentleman in future [must] fill his wine by measure," lest he risk having his character "blasted" and his person carried off to prison. "Does any man," asked Erskine, "put such constraint upon himself in the most private moment of his life, that he would be contented to have his loosest and lightest words recorded" and presented against him in court? If such an invasion of privacy and polite sociability were to be so allowed, "scarcely a dinner would end without a duel and an indictment." While presenting an eloquent plea for rights of free speech and private conscience, Erskine, at least implicitly, defended the manly pleasures of heavy drinking. Privacy was defined in homosocial terms; the rights of masculinity were asserted rather than the rights of man. Erskine also opened the possibility that Frost had not been himself and thus not meant what he had said – equality and no king were reduced to the "loosest and lightest words." Indeed, the trial text includes a long extract from Locke's *Essay Concerning Human Understanding*, discussing whether since punishment is annexed to personality, and personality to consciousness, drunkenness should excuse a criminal act.[74] Leaving aside the legal and philosophical niceties of the case, Erskine had found a way for Frost to retract or excuse his statement favoring equality. Moreover, rather than sociability leading to rational, free exchange, and therefore a version of "truth," due to his dining and wining Frost had spoken without proper regard for himself and others. The court had called the equality and sociability of the coffeehouse to account.

The narrative logic of Frost's story was transformed by the space of the trial and by Erskine's defense – a defense which the *Monthly Review* and *Critical Review*, literary journals sympathetic to reform, found to be among "his most eloquent," "able and ingenious."[75] Ingenious it may have been but whether in the coffeehouse or at trial, the question occurred: did Frost express the sincere sentiments of the Jacobin heart? After some time, the jury returned a verdict of guilty. On pronouncing the judgment of the court, Justice William Ashhurst chastised the defendant, whose words "argue a malignity of the heart," adding that having lately returned from France one might have expected Frost to have been convinced "of the superior advantages to be derived from a free constitution."[76] Not surprisingly, Joseph Johnson's *Analytical Review* drew a contrary conclusion, asking readers to reflect "on beholding a miscreant race of informers starting up ... who entrap, ensnare, and betray their fellow citizens."[77] Frost was sentenced to six months in Newgate prison, struck from the court rolls, and was also condemned to stand in the pillory at Charing Cross for one hour. Henry Redhead Yorke, having recently returned from Paris, framed his Paineite tract *These are the Times that Try Men's Souls!* as a letter to "John Frost Prisoner at Newgate." He assured Frost that the case was now before "the most solemn tribunal upon the earth:" "the judgment of an enlightenment public" would deliver a final "verdict of truth."[78] To this end, the radical publishers James Ridgway and Henry Symonds brought out a popular edition of Frost's trial.[79]

Ridgway and Symonds were themselves among the group of radical pressmen lodged at the time in Newgate, and were business partners of their follow prisoner Rev. William Winterbotham, the subject of the following chapter. Newgate was itself an extraordinary site of radical sociability and literary production, its own enlightened sphere of civility, hosting a constant stream of visitors.[80] There was a remarkable degree of free exchange and comfort, available for a price. Soon after Frost joined this community, Godwin and Holcroft (imprisoned the following year on treason charges) visited him, dining in the company of Joseph Gerrald (waiting to be transported to New South Wales) and Pigott.[81] Although Newgate may have allowed for an ideal staging of radicalism's "public sphere" and its principles, the prevailing atmosphere of sociability was never free of fears of illness and death. Frost wrote the press to disabuse the public about health conditions at Newgate. Lord George Gordon had recently died of "a putrid fever," which it was believed that he had caught from his fellow prisoner Thomas Lloyd. Lloyd, an American citizen, was convicted for a conspiracy to escape from the Fleet prison, where he was confined as a debtor, and for posting a seditious bill reading: "This house to let, and peaceable possession to be given by the present tenants, on or before the 1st of January, 1793, being the commencement of liberty in Great Britain."[82] A nice bit of Jacobin play, for which he was sentenced to three years in Newgate. Frost reported, "notwithstanding every precaution of bark and other remedies, my medical friends are daily fearful of finding me attacked by some disease." Together with Lloyd, Ridgway, and Symonds, he signed a certificate verifying that jail-fever had spread throughout the prison.[83]

At the conclusion of his sentence, Frost was condemned to stand in the pillory; street spectacle was to speak over and against the discourse of the coffeehouse. He was, however, excused this final indignity due to ill heath, although handbills circulated throughout London announcing that "Living or Dead," Frost would be condemned to stand on the pillory for "supporting the Rights of the People."[84] An immense crowd had gathered at Charing Cross to support the prisoner, threatening to demolish the pillory. The following day the ailing Frost was released from Newgate wrapped in blankets, put into a coach, and taken to the house of a local magistrate to enter into sureties. He was accompanied from prison by Tooke, Thelwall, and William Sharp. The *Morning Chronicle* reported that "As soon as he was at liberty the multitude" took the horses from his carriage and drew him along the streets, stopping at "every marked place, particularly St. James's Palace, Carlton House, Charing Cross [where the pillory was set up] ... to shout and express their joy." The crowd responded to those in power, countering the ritual of public shame with a carnivalesque remapping of urban, royal space; the radical crowd extended the call for "equality" from the confines of the coffeehouse to the more leveling zone of the street. Outside Frost's house at Spring Gardens, Thelwall addressed the crowd, entreating them to separate peaceably.[85] Twenty years later, as if to add retrospective commentary on the interactions between royal power and the private citizen, government authority and the public sphere, the prince regent, acting in the name of the king, granted Frost a free pardon.[86]

The Coffeehouse in Retreat

Certain points can be grasped from this account of Frost's case. We might chart, for instance, a discursive and spatial trajectory. As Frost moved successively from dining at Marylebone, to White's Hotel, to trial at Westminster, to imprisonment at Newgate, and back into the streets of the fashionable West End, we can see precisely how meaning is dependent on spatial circuits, and on the balance between power and delinquency governing different sites; a spatial economy becomes evident. The tavern, coffeehouse, courtroom, prison, pillory, and street are not merely backgrounds to the production of meaning, passive contexts within which utterance takes place. Rather, as Lynda Nead comments, social space is part of the "active ordering and organizing" of subjective identities, social relations, and meanings.[87] In order to understand Frost's case, we must know something about how the sites of assembly through which his story circulates came into being. "Patterns of discourse are regulated through the forms of corporate assembly in which they are produced," write Peter Stallybrass and Allon White. And they continue,

> the formulation of new kinds of speech can be traced through the emergence of new public sites of discourse and the transformation of old ones. Each "site of assembly" constitutes a nucleus of material and cultural conditions which regulate what may and may not be said, who may speak, how people may communicate and what importance must be given to what is said ... in large part, the history of political struggle has been the history of the attempts made to control significant sites of assembly and spaces of discourse.[88]

In large part the history of early nineteenth-century popular radicalism can, indeed, be written as a contest to gain access to, and to appropriate, sites of assembly and expression to produce, at least potentially, a "plebeian counter-public sphere."[89]

However, to understand political struggles for control of such sites and the meanings attached to these struggles, we must also consider the relationship between sites of assembly and the historical transformations in these sites. The sociability of the coffeehouse or tavern was never independent of other sites of assembly or the controls of government and law. As we have noted, the polite culture of the coffeehouse was organized in contradistinction to both aristocratic and vulgar forms of conviviality. The norms and spaces of bourgeois sociability were situated within a shifting field of social, political, and discursive forces. In addition, the relationship between reading and sites of assembly was hierarchically governed. Certain kinds of text were closely connected to particular spaces: the handbill joins the street; the quarterly journal lodges in the coffeehouse and gentleman's private library; Jacobin journals – Eaton's *Politics for the People* and Thomas Spence's *Pig's Meat* – are read aloud in low taverns and alehouses, the haunts of radical artisans and the laboring poor.[90] As for Frost's trial, it was the medium of print that freed the event from a particular moment and place, making its eventual way from Ridgway and Symonds's pamphlet edition into the collection of *State Trials*.

By the early 1790s, the culture of the coffeehouse and tavern had come under intensified political pressure. For Burke, the French Revolution represented a bout of insane linguistic and ideological disorder – "the political nonsense of ... licentious and giddy coffee-houses" underdoing the silent "work of ages."[91] The babble of coffeehouse conversation symbolized the broader danger to the state and its silent design, whereas for Paine the coffeehouse offered a truthful indication of the state of public opinion; here one could read the mind of the nation. Refusing to return from Paris to stand trial for publishing the second part of his *Rights of Man*, Paine wrote to Sir Archibald Macdonald, the attorney general, so that his opinions would not be misrepresented. In his letter, he taunted the attorney general with being unable to get convictions without the aid of packed juries; he appealed to the opinion of the coffeehouse in direct opposition to the law and jury. "I have gone into coffeehouses and places where I was unknown, on purpose to learn the currency of opinion, and I never yet saw any company of twelve men that condemned the book [*Rights of Man*]; and this I think is a fair way of collecting the natural currency of opinion." The attorney general responded by asking the special jury of "merchants" to decide "whether the sense of this nation is to be had in some pot-houses and coffee-houses."[92] Despite Erskine's best efforts, the jury returned its verdict on the sense of the "nation," finding Paine guilty of seditious libel.

The sociability of the coffeehouse could no longer be secured against sedition. Indeed, in 1790 the *Bee*, an Edinburgh journal, proposed that the gentleman's journal might displace the coffeehouse altogether; the "society of the text" might permit a retreat from sociability to domesticity.

> A man, after the fatigues of the day are over, may thus sit down in his elbow chair, and together with his wife and family, be introduced, as it were, into a spacious coffee-house, which is frequented by men of all nations.[93]

Polite society's retreat from the coffeehouse and tavern to the home, from masculine carousing to the domestic safety of wife and family, was indicative of the times.[94] And if wealthy men often paid mere lip-service to idealized notions of the home and family, the nineteenth-century gentleman's club offered a surrogate "family," a home away from home. If sociability is among the key terms for understanding the social and literary world of the eighteenth century, respectability is among the key terms for understanding the nineteenth century: the shift is an important one.

As for Frost, after his release from Newgate, he remained under government suspicion. On 15 May 1794, he and Tooke went to the house of Thelwall, who had been arrested two days earlier, to see Mrs. Thelwall – although according to the industrious spy John Groves, the two men were not admitted to the meeting of the Emergency Committee of the LCS being held there since they were not LCS members.[95] Tooke was arrested the following day. At the end of May 1794, following the government's round-up of the main LCS and SCI leaders, Frost was brought before Privy Council for intense questioning. He was told that he was not being sought as a witness but for treasonable practices connected to the activities of the SCI: this was an opportunity to remove suspicions. Henry Dundas, secretary of state, and a group of aristocrats questioned him about entries in the SCI minute book linking him to various resolutions, including the resolution thanking Paine for the second part of *Rights of Man*; they pressed him on his mission to Paris with Barlow, his personal association with Paine, and connections to the LCS, Margarot, and the British Convention at Edinburgh. He had not been active at SCI meetings since his release from prison. However, privy councilors confirmed his presence at the SCI dinner of 2 May 1794 to which LCS members were invited; he had "heard the Toasts and the Music" – inserted in the records is the toast, "The Armies contending for Liberty – May the Abettors of the War be its victims."[96] In the event, Frost was not arrested for treason; although reformers no more active in the movement than himself – such as Thomas Holcroft, the Rev. Jerimiah Joyce, and Augustus Bonney, an attorney who had succeeded to Frost's practice – were less fortunate. In November, Frost attended Tooke's trial at the Old Bailey. Throughout the proceedings, the prosecution brought up Frost's role as a leading figure in the SCI in association with Tooke, particularly his presentation of the SCI address to the National Convention.[97]

In conclusion, we can return to Frost's statement, his declaration for equality and no king. The 1790s witnessed a crisis in representation, including a contest over how and where meanings were legitimately to be articulated.[98] As the National Convention abolished monarchy, tried and executed Louis XVI, the declaration for "equality and no king" became supercharged. One only needed to look across the channel, where the sans-culotte leader François Hanriot (the son of a peasant from the outskirts of Paris) told a meeting of his section: "The rich have made the laws for long enough. Now it's the time for the poor to make them, so that equality will reign between rich and poor."[99] The month follow-ing the incident at the Percy coffeehouse, the Manchester SCI insisted that "equality" meant equality of rights not property or wealth. They blamed loyalists for propagating a "perversion in terms," warning that by the continual repetition that "equality" referred to property, "the informed, or as they are now arrogantly styled, the SWINNISH MUL-TITUDE" might attempt to enforce "so dangerous a doctrine."[100] But by late 1792, just as it became increasingly difficult to protect the term "equality" from being perversely understood, it was impossible to seal off the coffeehouse from the street and plebeian tavern or host polite debating clubs and lectures without raising the specter of democracy and alarming those in authority.[101]

And what about the phrase "no king?" Frost's utterance was easily confused with that of the less celebrated, but perhaps no less inebriated, Edward Swift (a "clothesman"). Swift was convicted at Berkshire sum-mer assizes in 1794 for having declaimed

> Damn the King and Queen, they ought to be put to death the same as the king and queen of France were ... Damnation, blast the King, I would as soon shoot the King as a mad dog. I will go down to Birmingham and bring up a set of rioters and make Windsor worse than ever France was.[102]

How was Frost's proposition to be distinguished from regicidal handbills circulating in metropolitan streets, such as the mock theater-advisement, presented in evidence at Thomas Hardy's trial for high treason, announc-ing the performance for the benefit of John Bull at the "FEDERATION THEATRE IN EQUALITY SQUARE" of the farce "LA GUILLOTINE OF GEORGE'S HEAD IN A BASKET!?"[103] Or more furtively, it was reported that at taverns in Bethnal Green and Spitalfields where repub-licans gathered, "the word is No King – if this is not acquiesced in, the word is Out, and the stranger is obliged to leave the House."[104] Frost's declaration of anti-monarchial sentiment was readily associated with the "everyday sedition" of plebeian Jacobins.

As middle-class reformers retreated from the political fray (not Frost as it happens), they retreated from both the language of "equality" and the spaces that had bred and sustained such language. [105] Crucial dis-tinctions could no longer be maintained: the space and language of po-lite sociability and reform sentiment had to be more clearly demarcated from the raucous, dangerous places and tones of plebeian culture. Social and political ambiguities became less ambiguous. It was, as Jon Klancher argues, in the 1790s that alehouses displaced coffeehouses as centers of "insurgent public discourse."[106] While the odd *declassé* gentleman drifted into the underworld of low alehouses and taverns, debating clubs and blasphemous sing-songs, this masculine world of anti-authoritarian conviviality belonged to artisans and small tradesmen.[107] The appeal to "equality and no king" – as well as those supporting such views – was banished from polite society and had found its proper nineteenth-century home.

Acknowledgments

A shorter version of this chapter was published as James Epstein, "'Equality and No King': Sociability and Sedition: the Case of John Frost" in Gillian Russell and Clara Tuite, eds., *Romantic Sociability: Social Networks and Literary Culture in Britain, 1770–1840* (Cambridge: CUP, 2002). © Cambridge University Press 2002. Reproduced with permission of the Licensor through PLSclear.

Notes

1 For a superb discussion of Frost's case and coffeehouse culture in the 1790s, see John Barrell, *The Spirit of Despotism: Invasions of Privacy in the 1790s* (Oxford: OUP, 2006), chapter 2. For discussion of the broad range of sites and practices of eighteenth-century sociability, see Gillian Russell and Clara Tuite, eds., *Romantic Sociability: Social Networks and Literary Culture in Britain, 1770–1840* (Cambridge: CUP, 2002); Kevin Gilmartin, ed., *Sociable Places: Locating Culture in Romantic-Period Britain* (Cambridge: CUP, 2017).

2 On political controversy over these commemorations and their associated meanings, see Kathleen Wilson, "Inventing Revolution: 1688 and Eighteenth-Century Popular Politics," *JBS* 28 (1989): 349–86.

3 *ST*, vol. 22, "Proceedings against John Frost for Seditious Words," cols. 471–522.

4 Jürgen Habermas, *The Structural Transformation of the Public Sphere: An Inquiry into a Category of Bourgeois Society*, trans. Thomas Burger (Cambridge: Massachusetts Institute of Technology Press, 1989), particularly 34–67. See also Richard Sennett, *The Fall of Public Man: On the Social Psychology of Capitalism* (New York: Vintage Books, 1978), 80–83; Brian Cowan, *The Social Life of Coffee: The Emergence of the British Coffeehouse* (New Haven, CT: Yale University Press, 2005); John Brewer, "Commercialization and Politics," in *The Birth of a Consumer Society: The Commercialization of Eighteenth-Century England*, ed. Neil McKendrick, John Brewer, and J. H. Plumb (Hutchinson, 1982), 197–262; Kathleen Wilson, *Sense of the People: Politics, Culture and Imperialism in England, 1715–1785* (Cambridge: CUP, 1995), chapter 1; Steve Pincus, "'Coffee Politicians Does Create': Coffeehouses and Restoration Political Culture," *JMH* 67 (1995): 807–34; Mary Thale, "London Debating Societies in the 1790s," *HJ* 32 (1989): 57–86.

5 For a discussion of "public opinion," see Dror Wahrman, "Public Opinion, Violence and the Limits of Constitutional Politics," in *Re-reading the Constitution: New Narratives in the Political History of England's Long Nineteenth Century*, ed. James Vernon (Cambridge: CUP, 1996), 83–122.

6 Cowan, *Social Life of Coffee*, 242–54; Wilson, *Sense of the People*, 47–54; Donna T. Andrews, "Popular Culture and Public Debate: London 1780," *HJ* 39 (1996): 405–23.

7 Bryant Lillywhite, *London Coffee Houses* (Allen & Unwin, 1963), 445–46. For the hierarchy of inn, tavern, and alehouse, see Peter Clark, *The English Alehouse: A Social History, 1200–1800* (Longman, 1983), 6–14,

8 Terry Eagleton, *The Function of Criticism: From* The Spectator *to Post-Structuralism* (Verso, 1984), chapter 1, quotation at 24. See also Roy Porter, "Enlightenment in England," in *The Enlightenment in National Context*, ed. Roy Porter and Mikuláš Teich (Cambridge: CUP, 1981), 8–18. Compare Jon P. Klancher, *The Making of English Reading Audiences, 1790–1830* (Madison: University of Wisconsin Press, 1987), chapter 1.

9 Nicholas Phillipson, "The Scottish Enlightenment," in Porter and Teich, eds., *Enlightenment*, 19–40, 26–30; J. G. A. Pocock, "Virtues, Rights, and Manners: A Model for Historians of Political Thought," in *Virtue, Commerce, and History: Essays in Political Thought and History* (Cambridge: CUP, 1985), 37–50; David S. Shields, *Civil Tongues and Polite Letters in British America* (Chapel Hill: University of North Carolina Press, 1997), chapters 2 and 3.

10 Barrell, *Spirit of Despotism*, introduction. Paid government informers were fairly light on the ground until late 1793, when the administration increased its determination to break up the popular societies. See Michael Durey, *William Wickham, Master Spy: The Secret War against the French Revolution* (Pickering & Chatto, 2009), 39–41.

11 Habermas, *Public Sphere*, 51; Nicholas Rogers, *Crowds, Culture, and Politics in Georgian Britain* (Oxford: OUP, 1998), 195–210; Alan Booth, "Provincial Loyalism and Public Violence in the North-West of England, 1790–1800," *SH* 8 (1983): 295–313; Michael T. Davis, "The British Jacobins and the Unofficial Terror of Loyalism," in *Terror: From Tyrannicide to Terrorism*, ed. Brett Bowden and Michael T. Davis (Brisbane: University of Queensland Press, 2008), 92–113. For prosecutions, see Clive Emsley, "An Aspect of Pitt's 'Terror': Prosecutions for Sedition during the 1790s," *SH* 6 (1981): 155–84, and "Repression, 'Terror' and the Rule of Law during the Decade of the French Revolution," *EHR* 100 (1985): 801–25. Compare Steve Poole, "Pitt's Terror Reconsidered: Jacobinism and the Law in Two South-Western Counties, 1791–1803," *Southern History* 17 (1995): 63–87.

12 John Binns, *Recollections of the Life of John Binns* (Philadelphia, 1854), 44.

13 See Nicholas Rogers, "Pigott's Private Eye: Radicalism and Sexual Scandal in Eighteenth-Century England," *JCHA*, new series, 4 (1993): 247–63; Jon Mee, "Libertines and Radicals in the 1790s: The Strange Case of Charles Pigott I, in *Libertine Enlightenment: Sex, Liberty and License in the Eighteenth Century*, ed. Peter Cryle and Lisa O'Connell (Houndmills: Palgrave, 2004), 183–203, and "'A Bold and Outspoken Man': The Strange Case of Charles Pigott II," in *Cultures of Whiggism: New Essays on English Literature and Culture in the Long Eighteenth Century*, ed. David Womersley (Newark: University of Delaware Press, 2005), 330–50.

14 The following account is based on Charles Pigott, *Persecution. The Case of Charles Pigott: Contained in the Defence He had Prepared and Would Have Delivered* (1793), and William Hodgson's preface to his *Commonwealth of Reason* (1795).

15 On the relationship between "private" and "public" spheres as not in strict opposition, see Dena Goodman, "Public Sphere and Private Life: Towards a Synthesis of Current Historiographical Approaches to the Old Regime," *History and Theory* 31 (1992): 1–20; John Brewer, "This, That and the Other: Public, Social and Private in the Seventeenth and Eighteenth Centuries, in *Shifting Boundaries: Transformations of the Languages of Public*

and Private in the Eighteenth Century, ed. Dario Castiglione and Lesley Sharpe (Exeter: University of Exeter Press, 1995), 1–21.

16 William Hodgson, *The Case of William Hodgson, Now Confined in Newgate* (1796), 9. He was released after the fine was paid by public subscription.

17 William Field, *Memoirs of the Life, Writings, and Opinions of the Rev. Samuel Parr, LL.D*, 2 vols. (1828), 1: 309. For the riots, see R. B. Rose, "The Priestly Riots of 1791," *P&P* 18 (1960): 68–88.

18 Thale, 349–51.

19 Binns, *Recollections*, 69–72.

20 *The Trial of John Binns, Deputy of the London Corresponding Society, for Sedition* (1797), 13. For the government's case, see TS 11/959/3505, "Seditious papers found in Binns's box." Jones, who was also arrested, was later convicted of seditious speech but never sentenced.

21 Steven Shapin, *A Social History of the Truth: Civility and Science in Seventeenth-Century England* (Chicago, IL: University of Chicago Press, 1994), particularly chapter 3.

22 See Charles Moore, *A Full Inquiry into the Subject of Suicide. To which are added ... Two Treatises on Duelling and Gaming*, 2 vols. (1790), vol. 2; Donna Andrew, "The Code of Honour and Its Critics: The Opposition to Duelling in England, 1700–1850," *SH* 39 (1980): 409–34; Jon Elster, *Alchemies of the Mind: Rationality and the Emotions* (Cambridge: CUP, 1999), 203–38.

23 Kristen Leaver, "Pursuing Conversations: *Caleb Williams* and the Romantic Constitution of the Reader," *Studies in Romanticism* 33 (1994): 589–610, argues that Godwin uses the novel form as a means of "private conversation" between text and reader. See, more generally, Jon Mee, *Conversable Worlds: Literature, Contention, and Community 1762 to 1830* (Oxford: OUP, 2011), particularly chapter 3.

24 William Godwin, *Enquiry Concerning Political Justice and Its Influence on Modern Morals and Happiness*, ed. Isaac Kramnick (Harmondsworth: Penguin, 1976, based on 3rd ed. 1798), 289–90.

25 Ibid., 441. For Paine, see James Epstein, *Radical Expression: Political Language, Ritual, and Symbol in England, 1790–1850* (New York: OUP, 1994), 111–12.

26 Nicholas Rogers, *Crowds, Culture, and Politics in Georgian Britain* (Oxford: OUP, 1998), 211. Thus at the outdoor meeting at Copenhagen Fields in 1795, several rostra were set up, so that there might be deliberations. See *Account of the Proceedings of a Meeting of the London Corresponding Society, Held in a Field near Copenhagen House, Thursday, Nov. 12* (1795), and Chapter 2 above.

27 Mark Philip, *Godwin's Political Justice* (Duckworth, 1986), 127.

28 Christina and David Bewley, *Gentleman Radical: A Life of John Horne Tooke, 1736–1812* (I. B. Tauris, 1998), 85.

29 [Cecil Thelwall], *The Life of John Thelwall, by his Widow* (1837), 242–43.

30 Michael T. Davis, "John Frost," *ODNB*; *ST*, vol. 22, "Proceedings against Frost," cols. 492–94.

31 TS 11/962/3508, SCI Minute Book, vol. 2 (1791–94).

32 J. Ann Hone, *For the Cause of Truth: Radicalism in London, 1796–1821*(Oxford: OUP, 1982), 15; Bewley, *Gentleman Radical*, 105.

33 The point is made forcefully by Michael T. Davis, "'That Odious Class of Men Called Democrats': Daniel Isaac Eaton and the Romantics 1794–95," *History* 84 (1999): 74–92, and 75–78, for Eaton's shop in Newgate Street.

34 For a superb discussion of this milieu, see Iain McCalman, "Ultra-Radicalism and Convivial Debating-Clubs in London. 1795–1838," *EHR*

102 (1987): 309–33. See also Peter Denney, "Clamouring for Liberty: Alehouse Noise and the Political Shoemaker," *Eighteenth-Century Life* 41 (2017): 105–21.

35 See Chapter 2 for a discussion of this meeting. See also Bewley, *Gentleman Radical*, 147.

36 In June the SCI resolved to admit to associate membership six LCS members to be nominated by the LCS. Hardy attends meetings starting in July. TS 11/962/3508, SCI Minute Book, fol. 86.

37 TS 11/959/3505 (2), report of George Munro (also spelled Monro), 15 November 1792. Questioned later before the Privy Council, Frost stated that he was not a member of the LCS but remembered attending a LCS meeting along with the radical lawyer, and SCI member, Felix Vaughan.

38 For Barlow, see Richard Buel, Jr., *Joel Barlow: American Citizen in a Revolutionary World* (Baltimore, MD: Johns Hopkins University Press, 2011), chapter 8. Barlow, who was living in Paris, had just published his *Letter to the National Convention of France, on the Defects of the Constitution of 1791* (1792).

39 *World*, 18 September 1792. The loyalist journal mocked Frost's own limited knowledge of French, and maintained a steady barrage of mockery aimed at the two men and their activities in Paris.

40 TS 11/951/3495, "J. F." to Tooke, 20 September 1792; John Keane, *Tom Paine: A Political Life* (New York: Grove Press, 1995), 349–51.

41 For the crisis of September 1792, see Timothy Tackett, *The Coming of the Terror in the French Revolution* (Cambridge, MA: Harvard University Press, 2015), chapter 8.

42 TS 11/962/3508, SCI Minute Book, fols. 112, 114.

43 Ibid., fols. 116–17; *MC*, 16 November 1792. Frost attended the society's meeting on 16 November, after which he and Barlow departed for Paris.

44 *Gazette Nationale, ou Le Moniteur Universal*, 29 November 1792, 1415; *A Collection of Addresses Transmitted by Certain English Clubs and Societies to the National Convention of France* (1793), 24–25; *Procès-verbal de la Convention Nationale*, 28 November, 381, quoted in Albert Goodwin, *The Friends of Liberty: The English Democratic Movement in the Age of the French Revolution* (Cambridge, MA: Harvard University Press), 254–55.

45 Goodwin, *Friends of Liberty*, 244–62. The LCS declared its wish to see *"A Triple Alliance, not of Crown Heads, but of the People, of America, France, and Britain will give Liberty in Europe, and Peace in the World."*

46 *The First and Second Reports, from the Committee of Secrecy* (1795?), 104–05; *ST*, vol. 24,"Trial of Thomas Hardy," cols. 526–30, and vol. 25, "Trial of John Horne Tooke," cols. 43–49, the solicitor general Sir John Mitford read the addresses in his opening statement; John Barrell, *Imagining the King's Death: Figurative Treason, Fantasies of Regicide, 1793–1796* (Oxford: OUP, 2000), 196–97, and chapter 6 for the work of the secret committees.

47 *PH*, vol. 30, cols. 53–55, Commons, 13 December 1792; *World*, 15 December 1792. Britain had withdrawn its embassy to France.

48 *London Gazette*, 11–15 December 1793, 933.

49 *PH*, vol. 30, cols.110–11,115, Commons, 15 December 1792; *MC*, 17 December 1792.

50 On the government's thinking and response to domestic radicalism, and the threat of insurrection, and shifting stance toward revolutionary France, see Jennifer Mori, "Responses to Revolution: The November Crisis of 1792," *Historical Research* 69 (1996): 284–305.

51 J. G. Alger, "The British Colony in Paris," *EHR* 13 (1898): 672–94, 62–74. The text provided by Alger is based on the original address in the *Archives Nationales*, Paris, which includes the signatures of the committee. Frost was not at the dinner, having yet to arrive in Paris, but signed the address that was dated 24 November.

52 J. G. Alger, *Paris in 1789–1794: Farewell Letters of Victims of the Guillotine* (George Allen, 1902), 325–26; David V. Erdman, *Commerce Des Lumières: John Oswald and the British in Paris, 1790–1793* (Columbia: University of Missouri Press, 1986), 230–31; Goodwin, *Friends of Liberty*, 249–50. Félicité and Théophile Fernig were young women who dressed as men and helped defend their village of Mortagne-du-Nord against Austrian troops. The sister of General Anselme led a troop of volunteers and national guards against invading forces on the Alpine border.

53 TS 11/959/3505 (2), Monro, "Notes on English Democrats in Paris 1792," 6 December 1792; Monro to Grenville, 17 December 1792, in Oscar Browning, ed., *The Dispatches of Earl Gower, English Ambassador at Paris, from June 1790 to August 1792* (Cambridge: CUP, 1885), 260.

54 Erdman, *Commerce Des Lumières*, chapter 8; Rachel Rogers, "Vectors of Revolution: The British Radical Community in Early Republican Paris, 1792–1794" (PhD. thesis, Université Toulouse le Mirail, 2013), 11–15, and chapter 2.

55 For an excellent account of Yorke's time in Paris, as well as for the politics of the British Club, see Amanda Goodrich, *Henry Redhead Yorke, Colonial Radical: Politics and Identity in the Atlantic World, 1772–1813* (Routledge, 2019), chapter 3.

56 For the United Irish mission, see Marianne Elliott, *Partners in Revolution: The United Irishmen and France* (New Haven, CT: Yale University Press, 1982), 58–60. Rev. Robert Jackson, another club member, was also involved as an agent of the United Irishman. The Irish nationalist Robert May O'Reilly was the club secretary. It is possible that a separate Irish club was formed. Rogers, "Vectors of Revolution," 66. See also idem, "The Society of the Friends of the Rights of Man, 1792–94: British and Irish Radical Conjunctions in Republican Paris, *La Révolution française* 11 (2016), https://journals.openedition.org/lrf/1629; Mathieu Ferradou, "Historique d'un 'festin patriotique' à l' hôtel white (18 novembre 1792): les irlandais patriotes à paris, 1789–1795," *Annales Historiques de la Révolution française*, December 2015, no. 4: 123–43.

57 Erdman, *Commerce Des Lumières*, Appendix E, 305, for a list of those who attended the dinner. Yorke left a vivid account of visiting Théroigne, who he claims rejected a marriage proposal from John Sheares. Henry Redhead Yorke, *Letters from France: Describing the Manners and Customs of Its Inhabitants … Interspersed with Interesting Anecdotes of Celebrated Public Characters*, 2 vols. (1814, first published 1804), 1: 140–42.

58 Peter McPhee, *Liberty or Death: The French Revolution* (New Haven, CT: Yale University Press, 2016), 111. See also Gary Kates, *The Cercle Social, the Girondins, and the French Revolution* (Princeton, NJ: University of Princeton Press, 1985).

59 For an account of the soirees held by Williams, "the priestess of the Revolution," see Yorke, *Letters from France* 2: 389–90. Rumors were rife about her relationship with John Hurford Stone, whose wife divorced him in 1794. See Deborah, F. Kennedy, "Helen Maria Williams," *ODNB*.

60 Monro to Grenville, 17 December 1792, and 31 December, in Browning, *Dispatches of Earl Gower*, 260, 268–69; Rogers, "Vectors of Revolution," 189–91, 333.

61 *MC*, 1 January 1793; Barrell, *Spirit of Despotism*, 78–79. Barrell suggests that the government may have hesitated to move ahead with the trial since Pitt did not want his earlier relationship with Frost exposed.

62 *World*, 7 January 1793. Frost's wife Eliza wrote a letter to the press, stating that Frost intended to return and had enough funds to pay his various creditors. *World*, 10 January 1793.

63 Alger, "British Colony," 675–76; Erdman, *Commerce Des Lumières*, 242–43; Goodrich *Yorke*, 86–87. A second address was presented to the Convention the day after the king's execution.

64 For French policy toward foreigners under the Convention and during the Terror, see Michael Rapport, *Nationality and Citizenship in Revolutionary France, 1789–1799* (Oxford: OUP, 2000), chapters 3 & 4.

65 As Pierre Bourdieu comments, "Legal Discourse is creative speech which brings into existence that which it utters." Pierre Bourdieu, *Language and Symbolic Power*, trans. Gino Raymond and Matthew Adamson (Cambridge, MA: Harvard University Press, 1991), 42.

66 The courtroom thus conforms to De Certeau's concept of a "place." Michel De Certeau, *Practice of Everyday Life*, trans. Steven Rendall (Berkeley: University of California Press, 1984). For the effects of majesty, terror, and awe, see Douglas Hay, "Property, Authority and the Criminal Law," in *Albion's Fatal Tree: Crime and Society in Eighteenth-Century England*, ed. Douglas Hay, et al. (New York: Pantheon, 1975), 17–63.

67 On this point, one that is contested, see Jacques Derrida, "Force of Law: The 'Mystical Foundation of Authority,'" *Cardoza Law Review* 11 (1990): 921–1039; Drucillia Cornell, "The Violence of the Masquerade: Law Dressed up as Justice," *Cardoza Law Review* 11 (1990): 1047–70. Compare Stanley Fish, *Doing What Comes Naturally: Change, Rhetoric, and the Practice of Theory in Literature and Legal Studies* (Durham, NC: Duke University Press, 1989), particularly, 503–24.

68 Margaret R. Somers, "Citizenship and the Place of the Public Sphere: Law, Community, and Political Culture in Transition to Democracy," *American Sociology Review* 58 (1993): 587–620, 596–97, and "Rights, Rationality, and Membership: Rethinking the Making and Meaning of Citizenship," *Law and Social Inquiry* 19 (1994): 63–112.

69 See James Oldham, *The Mansfield Manuscripts and the Growth of English Law in the Eighteenth Century* (Chapel Hill: University of North Carolina Press, 1992), 2 vols., 1: 119–21.

70 Cecilia Lucy Brightwell, *Memoir of Amelia Opie* (1855), 9–10. See also Amanda Vickery, *The Gentleman's Daughter: Women's Lives in Georgian England* (New Haven, CT: Yale University Press, 1998), 236–38.

71 *MC*, 28 May 1793; *Evening Mail*, 29 May 1793.

72 Pigott, *Persecution*, 1–2. Pigott's tract purported to be the defense that he would have given. Representation by counsel in criminal cases was a fairly recent development. See J. M. Beattie, "Scales of Justice: Defence Counsel and English Criminal Trial in the Eighteenth and Nineteenth Century," *Law and History Review* 9 (1991): 221–67.

73 Charles Pigott, *A Political Dictionary Explaining the True Meaning of Words* (1795), 6. In a similar vein, see *Advice to a Certain Lord High Chancellor, Twelve Judges, 600 Barristers, 700 English and 800 Irish Students of Law, 30,000 Attorneys!* (1791).

74 *ST*, vol. 22, "Proceedings against Frost," cols. 499–52, 520–21. See, more generally, Dana Rabin, "Drunkenness and Responsibility for Crime in the Eighteenth Century," *JBS* 44 (2005): 457–77.

75 *MR*, October 1794, vol. 15: 200–01; *Critical Review*, January 1795, vol. 13: 107.
76 *ST*, vol. 22, "Proceedings against Frost," cols. 519–22.
77 *AR*, 19, August 1794: col. 407.
78 Henry Redhead Yorke, *These are the Times that Try Men's Souls! A Letter to John Frost a Prisoner in Newgate* (1793), 3.
79 *The Trial of John Frost for Seditious Words in Hilary Term 1793* (1793). The text published in *State Trials* is based on this pamphlet, which sold for 1s/6d.
80 See Iain McCalman, "Newgate in Revolution: Radical Enthusiasm and Counterculture," *Eighteenth-Century Life* 22 (1998): 95–110; editors, "'Patriots in Prison': Newgate Radicalism in the Age of Revolution," in *Newgate in Revolution: An Anthology of Radical Prison Literature in the Age of Revolution*, ed. Michael T. Davis, Iain McCalman, and Christina Parolin (Continuum, 2005), ix–xxv.
81 Bod. Lib., GD, 7 August 1793. Godwin and Holcroft returned the next month to visit Frost. Pigott was a visitor in August 1793, but soon found himself in Newgate, where he was held for five weeks before the grand jury dismissed his case.
82 *World*, 21 November 1792; *The Trial of P. W. Duffin, and Thomas Lloyd ... for a Libel in the Fleet Prison* (1793).
83 *Cambridge Intelligencer*, 9 November 1793; *Gazetteer and New Daily Advertiser*, 16 November 1793.
84 Scrapbook of Political Broadsides, British Library (pressmark 648.c. 26), handbills, fol. 29.
85 *MC*, 20 December 1793; *Public Advertiser*, 19 December 1793; *Annual Register for 1793*, vol. 35 (1821 ed.), 59; BL, Add. MS. 27817, obituary, "Death of the Oldest Reformer in England;" Bewley, *Gentleman Radical*, 134. The decision to forego having Frost stand in the pillory may have been influenced by the size and disposition of the crowd.
86 *ST*, vol. 22, "Proceedings against Frost," col. 522. A motion to return him to the court rolls of King's Bench was denied.
87 Lynda Nead, "Mapping the Self: Gender, Space, and Modernity in Mid-Victorian London," in *Rewriting the Self: Histories from the Renaissance to the Present*, ed. Roy Porter (Routledge, 1997), 167–85, at 167. For the classic theoretical formulation, see Henri Lefebvre, *The Production of Space*, trans. Donald Nicholson-Smith (Oxford: Blackwell, 1991).
88 Peter Stallybrass and Allon White, *The Politics and Poetics of Transgression* (Ithaca, NY: Cornell University Press, 1986), 80.
89 For two excellent studies that fully illustrate this point, see Christina Parolin, *Radical Spaces: Venues of Popular Politics in London* (Canberra: Australian National University E Press, 2010); and Katrina Navickas, *Protest and the Politics of Space and Place, 1789–1848* (Manchester: Manchester University Press, 2016). On the concept of counter-public sphere, see Kevin Gilmartin, *Print Politics: The Press and Radical Opposition in Early Nineteenth-Century England* (Cambridge: CUP, 1996), 4–6, 30–31; Craig Calhoun, *The Roots of Radicalism: Tradition, the Public Sphere, and Early Nineteenth-Century Social Movements* (Chicago, IL: University of Chicago Press, 2012), chapters 4 and 5; Geoff Ely, "Nations, Publics, and Political Cultures: Placing Habermas in the Nineteenth Century," in *Habermas and the Public Sphere*, ed. Craig Calhoun (Cambridge: Massachusetts Institute of Technology Press, 1992), 289–339.
90 See Klancher, *Reading Audiences*, chapter 1; James Raven, "New Reading Histories, Print Culture and the Identification of Change: The Case of Eighteenth-Century England," *SH* 23 (1998): 268–87, 281–85.

91 Edmund Burke, *Reflections on the Revolution in France*, ed. Conor Cruise O'Brien (Harmondsworth: Penguin, 1969, first published 1790), 160.

92 *The Genuine Trial of Thomas Paine, for a Libel, Contained in the Second Part of Rights of Man* (1793), 36. Erskine argued, without success, against allowing Paine's letter to be read to the jury.

93 *Bee*, vol. 1 (1790–91), 14, quoted in Klancher, *Reading Audiences*, 23–24.

94 On this point, see Leonore Davidoff and Catherine Hall, *Family Fortunes: Men and Women of the English Middle Class, 1780–1850* (Chicago, IL: University of Chicago Press, 1987), particularly part 1.

95 TS 11/965/3510A, report from John Groves, 15 May 1794, in Thale, 164–65.

96 PC 2/140, 31 May 1794, fols. 278–82. Frost was brought back in early June for a shorter bout of questioning.

97 *ST*, vol. 25, "Trial of Tooke," col. 520, the attorney general Sir John Scott directly asked why Frost had not been called on to explain his mission to France on behalf of the SCI.

98 See Barrell, *Imagining the King's Death*, 1–46.

99 Quoted in Tackett, *Coming of the Terror*, 252.

100 *Manchester Herald*, 8 December 1792, and reprinted as a handbill, copy to be found in TS 11/3505/2. Compare *Equality, as Consistent with the British Constitution, In a Dialogue between a Master-Manufacturer and one of his Workmen* (1792), published by the Hackney Association for the Preservation of Peace, Liberty, and Property. There is a large sermon literature on the evils of the demand for equality. For the debate over "equality," see Gregory Claeys, ed., *Political Writings of the 1790s*, 8 vols. (William Pickering, 1995), 1, xxx–xliii.

101 For the self-censorship of debating clubs, see Mary Thale, "London Debating Societies in the 1790s," *HJ* 32 (1989): 57–86, 64–66.

102 TS 11/944/3433, "King v. Edward Swift." For a sensitive discussion of radical-reform attitudes and ideas concerning monarchy, see Marilyn Morris, *The British Monarchy and the French Revolution* (New Haven, CT: Yale University Press, 1998).

103 *ST*, vol. 24, "Trial of Hardy," 682–83.

104 TS 11/959/3505 (pack 2), report of meetings of the "People's Friends."

105 For Frost's later political career, see Hone, *Cause of Truth*, 134, 141. He worked with Horne Tooke as an agent and legal adviser for Sir Francis Burdett's Middlesex election campaigns in 1802 and 1804, after which he seems to have retired from politics.

106 Klancher, *Reading Audiences*, 26–27.

107 For the longer term growth of "two autonomous spheres," see Peter Borsay, "'All the Town's a Stage:'" Urban Ritual and Ceremony, 1660–1800," in *The Transformation of Provincial Towns, 1600–1800*, ed. Peter Clark (Hutchinson, 1984), 228–58.

5   Writing America from Newgate Prison, 1795

In late 1794, a four-page prospectus was circulated for a forthcoming publication. Boldly headed, "**AMERICA**," it announced a comprehensive work to be completed in thirty-three numbers, the first to be published on 31 January 1795, and to be continued weekly at the price of one-shilling each. The set was to be "uniformly and elegantly printed on fine Wove Demy Paper," making four octavo volumes; bound volumes were also to be made available in various qualities of binding. This "VIEW OF THE PRESENT SITUATION of the **UNITED STATES OF AMERICA**" encompassed "their Extent, Civil Division, Chief Towns, Climates, Curiosities, Soils, Mountains, Lakes, Bays, Rivers, Springs, and Islands, Natural History, Productions, Populations, Character, Government, Constitutions of different States, Courts of Justice, Religion, Literature, Agriculture, and History." In addition, it promised "*a copious and interesting*" account of the "late war" and detailed descriptions of the "WESTERN TERRITORY, particularly of KENTUCKY." A long list of subjects (motives for emigration, what persons were likely to succeed in America, choice of residence, land prices, methods of clearing land, crop rotations, etc.) provided information for those considering emigration. The first volume featured a general account of Columbus's "discovery" of America, together with general descriptions of the entire continent and the manners and customs of the numerous Indian tribes. The work was to contain a whole sheet plan of the recently designed city of Washington, the nation's future capital, and every number was to be accompanied by a large sheet map; the various maps, charts, and plans "engraved in the most elegant manner" formed a complete American atlas, along with portraits of famous Americans such as Benjamin Franklin, George Washington, and William Penn. Plates "descriptive of the NATURAL HISTORY OF AMERICA" representing "all the most remarkable *Quadrupeds, Birds, &c. &c.* peculiar to the American continent," too numerous to list, were included. The "Editor" had distilled this vast store of knowledge from at least one hundred volumes that would collectively cost the reader at least forty to fifty pounds. The editor's aim was "to strip this voluminous mass" of its miscellaneous and uninteresting parts, "and to form one complete History of America, at a moderate price."[1]

This was a strong sales pitch reflecting the experienced hands behind the publication: the London booksellers and printers, James Ridgway of York Street and Henry D. Symonds of Paternoster Row, along with Daniel Holt, former publisher of the *Newark Herald*. The prospectus neglected to mention that the work, *An Historical, Geographical, Commercial, and Philosophical View of the American United States,* was a product of Newgate prison, where these pressmen were serving time on seditious-libel convictions for printing and selling copies of the second part of Thomas Paine's *Rights of Man*, Paine's *Letter Addressed to the Addressers*, and Charles Pigott's *The Jockey Club*.[2] The "editor," Rev. William Winterbotham, was new to the world of radical publishing, having been convicted of preaching sedition at How's Lane Baptist Church in Plymouth. His history of America has until recently been ignored by scholars.[3]

For students of romanticism, Winterbotham receives mention in the story of how Robert Southey's dramatic poem *Wat Tyler*, written in 1794, found its way into print in 1817, when it mysteriously fell into the hands of radical publishers to become the era's most successfully pirated literary text. At the same time that Winterbotham was putting together his *View of the American United States*, Southey turned to Newgate's radical pressmen to find a publisher for his poem. Newgate prison was a place where Jacobin intellectuals crossed paths with the less fortunate victims of state repression; there they encountered the world of seditious literary production. More indirectly, the early Romantics and artisan radicals shared visions of America as a desired space of republican-democratic fulfillment. When Southey encountered Winterbotham and Newgate's Jacobin pressmen, he fully believed he was destined to start a new life in America. Winterbotham's compendium offers one point of entry to the textual resources that supported views of the transatlantic republic as a space of possibility. The romantic poets' project to found a utopian community on the banks of the Susquehanna provides another such entry point. In charting their overlapping beliefs, projected futures, desires, and disappointments, this chapter seeks to draw out connections, among radical craftsmen, the early Romantics, middle-class intellectuals, and rational Dissenters; between the world of print culture and political activism; between Newgate as a practiced site and America as an imagined space. The chapter is less about coalescence than paths crossed, openings, and crossed purposes; about personal, spatial, and textual entanglements; and the operation of America in the political imagination.

A Newgate Production

Something needs to be said about the editor of *View of the American United States*, and the circumstances that landed him in prison.[4]

On Monday evening, 5 November 1792, Winterbotham preached a sermon at How's Lane Baptist Chapel in Plymouth to commemorate the dual national deliverance from the Gunpowder Plot of 1605 and of the Glorious Revolution of 1688. He preached a second sermon on 18 November entitled "The Dawning Day." What brought Winterbotham to the pulpit, and eventually to face trial at Exeter assizes in summer 1793 can be quickly sketched. Trained as a silversmith and largely self-educated, he emerged from the milieu of artisan London. He supported the cause of the American colonists, and as a militant Protestant (at this time, he was an Anglican) and member of the Protestant Association he took part in the anti-Catholic campaign of 1780. Having fallen into dissolute habits, not uncommon among London's skilled workers, he failed to establish himself in the West End's silver-buckle trade. In 1786, however, he underwent a life-changing conversion. On accompanying his brother to a non-conformist meeting house, Winterbotham was moved by the simplicity of the service, sincerity of the worshipers, and the language of the preacher. Out of an intense struggle with his own spirituality and sense of sinfulness, Winterbotham was reborn as a Calvinistic Methodist; without formal training he moved from lay preaching into the regular ministry, although in 1789 he rejected the doctrine of infant baptism. The same year he was recommended to Rev. Philip Gibbs to fill the position of assistant minister at Plymouth's Baptist church. His youthful energy and powerful preaching style proved popular, attracting new members to the congregation.[5]

On 5 November 1792, Winterbotham addressed a gathering of between two and three hundred women and men. The commemoration of the 1688 Revolution appeared uneasily on the ritual calendars of both loyalists and reformers. In testing the political waters, Winterbotham took advantage of the authorized celebration of Britain's deliverance from papal despotism and the restoration of political liberty. The Book of Common Prayer gave the form of service to commemorate the national holiday in which clergymen were instructed to read one of the homilies on obedience and against rebellion and to preach to these texts. While the prosecution at Winterbotham's trial argued the impropriety of preaching politics to a congregation "of low ignorant people," in fact the purpose of celebrating the nation's dual deliverance was deeply political.[6] The decision to bring prosecutions against the preacher for seditious words was not necessarily based on what was said, but on the "low" audience to whom the sermons were addressed, as well as when they were delivered. As E. P. Thompson notes, of the Old Dissenting sects the Baptists remained "most plebeian in their following."[7] Winterbotham appears to have said little beyond what Richard Price had asserted three years earlier in his *Discourse on the Love of our Country*. By November 1792, for Winterbotham to have discussed the legitimacy upon which British monarchy derived its authority and to express approval, however qualified, of the French Revolution – France was now a republic and the king was soon to face trial before the National Convention – drew the attention of loyalists and the administration.[8] The government charged, among other things, that Winterbotham approved of the French Revolution which had opened the eyes of the English people to the "necessity for a similar Revolution" in Britain. In separate trials Winterbotham was convicted for both sermons and sentenced to a total of four years in Clerkenwell prison, fined £200, and compelled to find sureties of £900. At his sentencing before King's Bench, Justice William Ashhurst expressed the hope that the French Revolution would open Winterbotham's eyes, "and be a scourge to those who wish to introduce Anarchy and Confusion."[9] The convictions and harsh sentencing had a chilling effect among rational Dissenters, contributing to a general retreat from politics. For Joseph Priestley, Winterbotham's case was crucial to his decision to leave for America, signaling "that no man who is obnoxious, however innocent, is safe."[10]

In thinking about the circumstances surrounding the production of Winterbotham's four volumes on America, as well as his connection to Southey's *Wat Tyler*, Newgate prison comes into view as a key site of exchange between the world of Jacobin politics and the republic of letters. After several months in Clerkenwell's new prison, suffering from poor health and declining spirits, Winterbotham was permitted to transfer to Newgate, with the consent of the attorney general John Scott.[11] Moving into Newgate's "state-side," he occupied a room in a suite of apartments with Ridgway, Symonds, and Holt with whom he shared a servant chosen from the female prisoners at a total weekly cost of eight shillings. Winterbotham was a poor man and his legal costs were heavy, as was the expense of Newgate's purchasable freedoms. Various friends of liberty came to his assistance, particularly better-off Unitarians, along with members of his church in Plymouth.[12] Priestley appealed to fellow Dissenters to make Winterbotham's confinement "as easy as possible"; he visited him in prison before leaving for America and informed his publisher Joseph Johnson to supply the prisoner with any of his own works upon request.[13] Priestley's close colleague and friend, Theophilus Lindsey, visited Winterbotham regularly, helping to coordinate financial support. Near the end of his confinement, we find the Liverpool Unitarian minister, William Shepherd, writing his wife to say that Winterbotham appeared in good spirits, adding, "When I took leave I put my annual subscription of two guineas into his hand, which I trust will be my last payment."[14] Such visits and contributions were regarded as obligations paid by an embattled community to brethren who had suffered in the cause of religious and political freedom. Despite theological differences between Winterbotham, as an orthodox Dissenter, and Unitarians who came to his aid, they shared a strong commitment to the unfettered exercise of individual conscience,

freedom of worship and expression, and an agenda of progressive political reform.[15]

In a sense, Newgate served as Winterbotham's America, a space for new
beginnings. He turned to publishing as a means of occupation and financial support, joining Ridgway, Symonds, and Holt in a loose publishing
consortium. He reinvented himself as a "literary man." Through the act
of publication and his association with seditious booksellers, the Baptist
preacher moved closer to the culture and organized sphere of Jacobin politics.[16] From prison he published versions of his two sermons, *The Commemoration of National Deliverances, and The Dawning Day* (1794), and
an annotated account of his two trials. The following year, he published his
View of the American United States, along with editing the two-volume *An
Historical, Geographical and Philosophical View of the Chinese Empire*,
linked to Lord Macartney's failed embassy to open China to British trade.
He also edited a two-volume *Selection of Poems Sacred and Moral*, bearing the strong flavor of rational Dissent in the poetry he chose to reprint.[17]

Silenced in court, where his attorney Vicary Gibbs spoke on his behalf,
the publication of his sermons and trials allowed Winterbotham to comment on these proceedings and amplify meanings. The trials, printed by
Ridgway and Symonds and priced at two shillings, went through four
editions in 1794.[18] Winterbotham's lengthy notes to the trials, running
in small print at the bottom of the pages, provide a supplementary text
in which Burke is lambasted, Blackstone quoted on the constitution,
prosecution testimony challenged, and the prosecuting attorney, Sergeant Rooke, taken to task. Winterbotham was thus able to expand on
his politics and religious belief and to display his hard-earned learning.
He countered Rooke's assertion that the pulpit was not the place to discuss politics with a disquisition on biblical prophecy:

> the *whole of the prophetic part of Scriptures...* is connected not only
> with Governments that have been, but with all that now are, or that
> will be on earth... the study of SCRIPTURE PROPHECY is a duty
> *incumbent* on a Christian minister.

The prosecution's attack on the social status of ordinary Baptists –
variously described as "low," "ignorant," "vulgar," "deluded" – rankled,
especially for a self-educated man proud of his learning and spiritual
quest. Winterbotham shot back that though they were Dissenters, and if
it would give Rooke and Burke a measure of satisfaction,

> they have no objection to admit that they are part of what the latter
> *so politely dignifies* with the title of the SWINISH MULTITUDE –
> yet they contend that *their situations...* are such as to render the
> PRINCIPLES of the Revolution, and the TERMS on which his
> Majesty holds his Crown, objects of vast importance to them.[19]

Glossing his expressed views on the French Revolution, Winterbotham asked those persons "whose tender minds are harassed with the ideas of republican ferocity" to consider the full history of the barbarities under the former monarchical government. Despite the scenes of violence that had "tarnished" the Revolution, he could not bring himself "to be an enemy of what I consider as a praise worthy attempt of a great nation, to recover that Liberty, which is their *inherent* right, and which despotism had deprived them of." To which he added that his sentiments on the change in French government, and "on the awful consequences that have followed, must remain, *at present*, within my heart."[20] The Jacobin heart remained undisclosed.

In some respects, the commentary in the published versions of his sermons and trials reinforced the government's charge that Winterbotham's real sentiments favored the "rights of man" and the principles of the French Revolution. The experience of government prosecution and exposure to Newgate's Jacobins deepened his radicalism and encouraged more unvarnished expression of his views. In a reported conversation involving Winterbotham; Thomas Briellat, a Shoreditch pump-maker and LCS member; and Daniel Jones, a whitesmith and LCS member who came to visit Briellat (serving a one-year sentence for seditious words), we catch the tones of a raw, profane, and decidedly masculine Jacobinism. Amid plans for the procurement of daggers, it was said that it had been determined "to put an end to Mr Pitt & all the leading men on that side." That while "the *Boys*" of the royal family "must shift for themselves," it was decided no harm would come to the girls, although Winterbotham jested that they might remedy the condition by which the princesses "are denied the first Rights of Nature." The repartee constituted a throwback to the plebeian sociability of Winterbotham's unreformed youth, and mimicked the torrent of abuse that had landed Briellat in prison – "Reformation cannot be effected without a Revolution;" "We have no occasion for kings;" "There never will be good times until all kings are abolished from the face of this earth."[21] More soberly, and speaking presumably from the heart, Winterbotham added his opinion that "the people had began at the wrong end – that violent & *noisy* people wod. do no good but great harm to the cause – & that cool determined *acting* Men were the Men that were wanted, & that it was his Advice for the people to begin afresh."[22]

As a place of incarceration, Newgate constituted its own space of possibility, defined as standing apart and yet curiously central to politics and letters. Pressmen continued to operate with little restraint; prisoners and their visitors socialized with remarkable freedom, with the state-side opened from eight in the morning to nine at night. Iain McCalman has ably described the social world of Newgate as a "site of Jacobin civility," a "salon of radical philosophes."[23] Richard Brothers, millenarian preacher and self-styled "nephew of God," wrote to inform

Winterbotham, "you are the person who is appointed to shew me all manner of civilities in doing which you will render Yourself acceptable to the sight of God... you will therefore prepare your room for the reception of the Prophet."[24] The Jacobin propagandist and sometime Newgate resident Thomas Spence listed a token coin with a view of Newgate in 1794, reading on the reverse, "Payable at the Residence of Messers Simmonds [sic], Winterbotham, Ridgeway, and Holt."[25] Their "residence" saw a constant flow of visitors, some of them seeking a publisher; the sociability of Ridgway's bookseller's shop in Marylebone was transferred to his rooms in Newgate.[26] William Godwin, the polite Jacobins' philosopher of the day, was a regular Newgate visitor, socializing with Winterbotham on several occasions when he also came to see Joseph Gerrald and Maurice Margarot, LCS leaders elevated to the status of patriot martyrs.[27] The Welsh poet Edward Williams became a friend. On a visit to see Winterbotham, Williams signed his name in the visitors' book with a flourish – "The Bard of Liberty." On this next visit, Iolo Morganwg, to use his bardic name, was refused entry by the jailer John Kirby, prompting the bard to compose his "Newgate Stanzas": "'twas to scorn a Tyrant's claim, / Wrote Bard of Liberty my name, / And Terror seized all!" Williams, whose papers were seized by the government in 1794, resolved to emigrate to America to find safety and to pursue the descendants of the Welsh Indians whose arrival in America, according to the Madoc legend, had pre-dated Columbus by hundreds of years.[28]

Like many friends of liberty, Winterbotham considered joining the exodus to America.[29] The circuits connecting Newgate to America were long-standing. Before American independence the hulks carried convicts across the Atlantic; in early 1794 the Scottish martyrs – Gerrald, Margarot, Thomas Muir, William Skirving, and the Unitarian minister Thomas Fyshe Palmer – waited to be transported to Botany Bay. Voluntary exile to America was on the rise, particularly among radical Dissenters. A steady stream of Dissenters paid their respects to Newgate friends. In February 1794, Elizabeth Pattisson wrote to her stepson, William Pattisson, with news that their relative, John Towill Rutt, a prominent Unitarian and member of the Society for Constitutional Information, had gone to see Muir, remarking "in the same honourable mansion, he met Mr Frend, Mr Hall of Cambridge [,] Wakefield, Margarott, Skrving [sic] &c fine Newgate Birds he says. And I would ask what Palace can shew a more respectable party." Her letter moves directly from Newgate to the subject of those seeking refuge in America:

> While some are forced from England, others are voluntarily quitting it to seek in America, that security and peace, there is so little probability of enjoying in England. Those who have settled their affairs and are ready to set off, appear to me almost objects of envy.[30]

She expressed the solidarity found among radical Dissenters as well as their vulnerability at the moment when many of their number contemplated withdrawing from political engagement or removing themselves to the United States.[31] John Thelwall thought at least 80,000 had emigrated to America in the summer of 1794 alone.[32] *The Times* complained, "The Jacobin Prints dwell almost daily on the emigrations from this country to America," fostering the false impression that "they will find more real liberty in that Republic than they do under our limited Monarchy."[33] For many readers of the "Jacobin" press, liberty's utopian promise was projected onto America. In a poem published in Benjamin Flower's *Cambridge Intelligencer*, entitled "The Prospect of Emigration," Rutt imagined an escape from "Europe's servile coast" to "beyond the western wave," where he sees God's children "In friendship join, on Nature's equal plan, / To virtue's true nobility aspire, / and boast alike the *Dignity of Man*."[34]

It remains unclear whether Rutt met Winterbotham at Newgate, although both he and the Pattissons are found among the subscribers to his *View of the American United States*. The full list of subscribers running to over 600 names reveals the closely knit web of rational Dissent. It was a veritable roll-call of prominent Dissenters and middle-class radical reformers, including the poet Anna Laetitia Barbauld's husband, Rev. Rochemont Barbauld, and her brother, John Aikin (physician and literary figure), Thomas Belsham (Unitarian minister and Lindsey's biographer), Thomas Cooper (founder member of the Manchester Constitution Society, Unitarian, and writer on America), George Dyer (Unitarian poet associated with Coleridge and Southey's "Pantisocracy"), Benjamin Flower (Cambridge publisher later imprisoned in Newgate), William Hodgson (physician imprisoned for seditious words and author of *The Commonwealth of Reason*), Andrew Kippis (prominent Unitarian minister and man of letters), Jeremiah Joyce (Unitarian minister and former Newgate resident), James Mackintosh (Scottish philosopher and author of *Vindiciae Gallicae*), Earl "Citizen" Stanhope (radical Whig and Joyce's patron), Gilbert Wakefield (biblical scholar convicted in 1798 for seditious libel), Thomas Walker (former president of the Manchester Constitution Society, tried and acquitted on charges of seditious libel), and Rev. David Williams (political-religious theorist and founder of the Literary Fund).[35]

By the time that Winterbotham organized his encyclopedic view of America, a reordering had taken place among British republicans, whereby America rather than France served more readily as the model of a functioning democratic republic. As Mark Philp has stressed, in the second part of Paine's *Rights of Man* (1792), the republican center of gravity shifted to America, as the exemplar of popular sovereignty, representative democracy, constitution-making, and egalitarian society.[36] The American Revolution allowed the idea of democratic government to be reconceived; no longer restricted to classical city-states, America testified to the possibility of a modern republic based on representative democracy and successfully functioning on a large scale. Thus Paine proclaimed, "What Athens was in miniature, America will be in magnitude."[37] The meaning of republicanism, at least for radicals, became unequivocally distinct from forms of mixed government and social hierarchy.[38] Republicanism took on a social dimension, as American prosperity was linked to democratic governance. Gerrald, who had practiced law in Pennsylvania where he met Paine, told readers,

> In America, that country which God and man have concurred to render the blissful habitation of abundance and of peace, the poor are not broken down by taxes to support the expensive trappings of royalty, or to pamper the luxury of an indolent nobility. No lordly peer tramples down the corn of the husbandman, no proud prelate wrings from him the tythe of his industry... Plenty is the lot of all, superfluity of none.[39]

In a sense, such views revived an earlier veneration for America's revolutionary future. The "visionary expectations" of Richard Price echoed Paine in greeting "a revolution... which begins a new aera in the history of mankind," a millenarian framing that no doubt appealed to Winterbotham.[40] In his visionary poem *America* (1793), Blake picked up the millenarian fervor rekindled by the French Revolution, as he imagined the American Revolution in apocalyptic fury sweeping citizens into resistance to British authority.[41] And despite the "excesses" of Year One, and the deism of the leaders of the Convention, the French Revolution could be viewed as pointing to the prophetic fulfillment announced by its American counterpart.[42] In Winterbotham's view, France had attempted "what has so successfully been adopted in America, but whether she will succeed or not is still in the womb of province."[43] For many British radicals, however, the turn to America represented at least a partial turn away from the French Revolution, although support remained for the Revolution's spirit of popular sovereignty and the destruction of aristocratic privilege. The violent course of the Revolution reinforced loyalist images of British reformers as disguised agents of regicide and French-style anarchy. Loyalist vigilance, along with government prosecutions, increased the cost of openly supporting the French Revolution.[44]

The "Preface" to Winterbotham's *View of the American United States* reflected the reorientation of British republicanism. According to the author, America's discovery "gave rise to a revolution in the commerce and in the power of nations, as well as in the manners, industry and government of almost the whole world." In Europe,

> every thing has been changed in consequence of its commerce and connection with the American continent; but the changes which

took place prior to the late revolution... only served to increase the misery of mankind, adding to the power of despotism, and rivetting farther the shackles of oppression.

The late revolution transformed America's influence on Europe:

the glorious struggle... did much to raise mankind from the state of abject slavery and degradation, to which despotism, aided by superstition had sunk them: from that period the rights of man began to be understood, and the principles of civil and religious liberty have been canvassed with freedom before unknown, and their influence has extended itself from the palace to the cottage.

In a reversal of world order, America stands as the exemplar for Europe. Not only does the American Revolution bid fair ultimately "to occasion the emancipation of other European colonies on the continent, but to accomplish a complete revolution in all the old governments of Europe." Europe has already "witnessed a perjured despot expiating his crimes on the scaffold, at the command of people roused to a sense of injuries and rights, by men who had assisted in establishing the liberties of America." The French Revolution's "glory" has been "tarnished, but not destroyed." Once peace has come to Europe, other nations will be able to assess without prejudice not only their own situation but France's achievement in constituting "an energetic government, founded on the will of the people," administered without aristocratic corruption and expense. In the meantime, the United States prospers to "a degree hitherto unparalleled in the history of nations." America beckons to merchants and manufacturers, artisans and industrious laborers. And soon, predicts Winterbotham, "the man of science, as well as the contemplative and experimental philosopher" will find "the shores of Columbia equally propitious to their wishes."[45]

The preface is among the few places where the author provides his own sustained commentary. *View of the American United States* is a composite work, constructed of extracts from the publications of other authors, the most important of which are acknowledged in the preface, but otherwise extensively borrowed material is usually reproduced without attribution. The list of acknowledged authors includes "Abbé Raynal, Franklin, Robertson, Clavigero, Jefferson, Belknap, Adams, Catesby, Buffon, Gordon, Ramsey, Bartram, Cox, Rush, Mitchel, Cutler, Imlay, Filson, Barlow, Brissot, Morse, Edwards... together with the transactions of the English and American philosophical societies, American Museum, &c."[46] Volume one opens with the "discovery," drawn almost exclusively from William Robertson's classic *History of America* (1777). Robertson's work formed part of the eighteenth-century debate over commercial civilization and modern progress through the expansion of global trade. Columbus appears as an active man of genius, an enterprising and enlightened individual, struggling heroically against adversity and corrupt European court culture.[47] The first volume provides ethnographic descriptions of Native Americans, a timeline of settlement, an account of the major geological formations, climate, soils, population statistics, a section on the American "character and manners," discussions of agricultural and commercial progress, and a summary of the nation's religious dominations. Conjectural debate over Nature's status in the new world challenged Rousseau and Chateaubriand's ideas about the superiority of natural man and America as a second Eden. Winterbotham extracted the opinions of de Pauw, Raynal, and Buffon about the degeneration of species, including humans, under America's natural conditions. Against these thinkers' unjust speculations, he reprinted Jefferson's detailed, scientific repudiation and confident prediction that the young United States, already boasting the likes of Washington, Franklin, and David Rittenhouse, will match the artistic, philosophical, and scientific attainments of Europe.[48] Winterbotham's first volume concludes with an extensive "History of the Rise, Progress, and Establishment of the United States," featuring an extensive account of the revolutionary war lifted from David Ramsey's history of the Revolution.[49] The founding documents of the republic, including the Declaration of Independence, Articles of Confederation, and Constitution, are reproduced along with a history of the federal union. In this era of constitution writing, radicals showed intense interest in the new constitutions of America, including state constitutions, many of which Winterbotham reprinted. Volume two and half of volume three give lengthy descriptions of the natural, material, and cultural conditions of life in each state and region.

Perhaps we can imagine Winterbotham in Newgate poring over volumes lent to him by friends and fellow pressmen, copying out or marking passages for reprinting, taking an autodidact's pleasure in absorbing the wealth of literary learning. The frontispiece author's portrait presents an image of the respectable literary man (Figure 5.1). In its notice of *View of the American United States*, the *Monthly Review* compared Winterbotham's situation to that of Raleigh:

> The public is certainly much indebted to Mr. Winterbotham for having, in the tedious hours of imprisonment, laudably exerted himself in compiling this work. Like Raleigh, who produced his valuable history of the *old world* while he was confined *as a state prisoner* in the Tower of London, this historian of the *new world* writes in a similarly unfortunate situation.[50]

Winterbotham may have turned to the American citizen Thomas Lloyd, who was sent from the Fleet prison (where he was being held for debt) to Newgate after his conviction for seditious libel.[51] Lloyd's *Congressional*

Record (1789–90) provided the fullest account of the proceedings of the first federal congress. On each 4th of July, Lloyd, who had fought in the Revolutionary War, marked his prison diary, "declaration of American independence."[52] No doubt Ridgway, who was a major publisher of books on America, played a role in helping Winterbotham to construct his volumes. Winterbotham refers to having undertaken the project "at the instigation of some particular friends." We know that Ridgway encouraged Winterbotham to add a final volume on European colonial settlements in North and South America and the Caribbean.[53]

As for the pirating of literary works, the pirating of American publications was common enough among London publishers.[54] In Winterbotham's case, this was a selling point. The prospectus informs potential buyers that everything that is "valuable" in Jedidiah Morse's *American Geography*, the quarto edition priced at £1. 5s., "is comprised in about eight numbers of the present Work."[55] As author or editor, Winterbotham was responsible for the selection, compression, and summarization of published texts, occasionally adding linking sentences or slight alterations to wording. This sort of literary operation was not all that unusual. Travel books often recycled and absorbed previously published materials. Anthologies, abridgements, and adaptations were a means by which texts and knowledge were diffused more widely to the reading public. In producing his large-scale compendium and lowering the price for readers, Winterbotham democratized access to knowledge about America. Arguably, what distinguishes Winterbotham's project is less its borrowed quality than its scale and ambition; four volumes running to over 2,000 pages, along with a full complement of zoological illustrations and statistical tables, encompassing the fields of history, exploration, conjectural theory, politics, government, economics, religion, geography, cartography, and natural history. The work reflects an Enlightenment desire for universal knowledge. Unsurprisingly, given its sheer size and eclecticism, the work falls short of producing a fully consistent perspective, while it acquires interest as a literary archive, one that had to be constructed. Winterbotham's selection and ordering of texts constitute a form of authorship (Figure 5.2).

Questions about circulation, readership, and reception are often difficult to answer, but in the case of Winterbotham's history we have considerable evidence of its publication history and readership. The serial publication in weekly numbers was designed to increase sales. The London edition of 1795 was accompanied by *The American Atlas*, which included nine large maps of sections of America engraved by John Russell. In 1799, Ridgway and Symonds brought out a new and enlarged edition, featuring a portrait of the author.[56] Winterbotham's work quickly made its way across the Atlantic, with editions published in New York and Philadelphia. This led Morse to successfully sue the book's New York publisher John Reid for plagiarism, with Alexander Hamilton acting as legal counsel for Morse. We have no information about the size of

Figure 5.1 "Wm. Winterbotham," portrait, frontispiece, William Winterbotham, *An Historical, Geographical, Commercial, and Philosophical View of the American United States, etc.*, 2nd edition, volume 4, 1799, engraved by John Scoles. Print Collection, The New York Public Library.

print-runs in London, but in the case Morse brought against Reid, we learn that by 1798, 1,700 copies of an American print-run of 3,000 had been sold.[57] By the standards of the day, this made the work a best-seller.[58] As for its readership, in describing the republicanism of members of the London Corresponding Society, Francis Place commented, "This [republicanism] they were taught by the writings of Thomas Paine, and confirmed in them by Mr. Winterbotham's history of the United States, a work which was published in numbers, and generally read by members."[59] Paine himself recommended "Mr. Winterbotham's valuable History of America" to readers.[60] The list of subscribers includes a division of the LCS, and along with the worthies of the reform movement and rational Dissent, together with the crowd of lawyers and esquires, we find among those identifying their occupations a sprinkling of shopkeepers

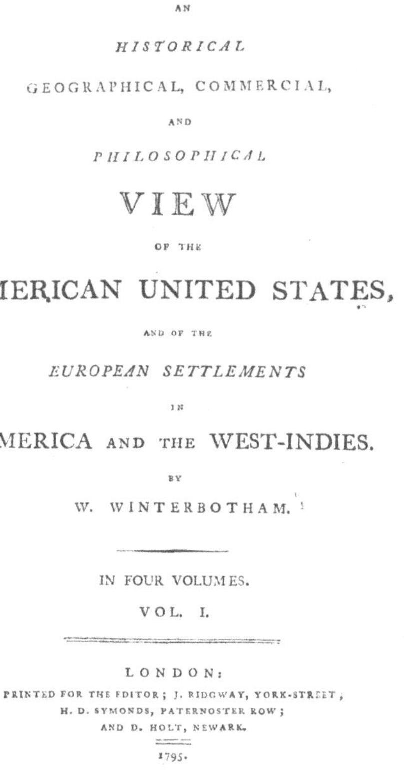

AN

HISTORICAL

GEOGRAPHICAL, COMMERCIAL,

AND

PHILOSOPHICAL

VIEW

OF THE

AMERICAN UNITED STATES,

AND OF THE

EUROPEAN SETTLEMENTS

IN

AMERICA AND THE WEST-INDIES.

BY

W. WINTERBOTHAM.

IN FOUR VOLUMES.

VOL. I.

LONDON:

PRINTED FOR THE EDITOR; J. RIDGWAY, YORK-STREET,
H. D. SYMONDS, PATERNOSTER ROW;
AND D. HOLT, NEWARK.

1795.

Figure 5.2 Title page, *An Historical, Geographical [,] Commercial, and Philosophical View of the American United States...* by W. Winterbotham, volume 1, 1795. Courtesy of HathiTrust. https://hdl.handle.net/2027/aeu. ark:/13960/t1ng5g79z

and artisans – printer, cabinet-maker, joiner, carpenter, bookseller, engraver, ironmonger, coach-maker, watchmaker, and schoolmaster. Among the subscribers, the former Newgate prisoner, Briellat, is found, now living in Kentucky.[61] The readership appears to have reached deep into the ranks of republicans. Interestingly, Southey had a copy of the 1795 edition in four bound volumes in his library.[62]

Romantic America

We do not know when the romantic poet acquired Winterbotham's history; we do know that Southey encountered Winterbotham in his attempt to find a publisher for *Wat Tyler* – another Newgate story. The desire to establish a utopian community in America and the composition of Southey's verse-drama flowed from the same moment and political commitments. Winterbotham and Southey's versions of how the manuscript of *Wat Tyler* fell into Winterbotham's hands differ, but a brief summary of the probable circumstances will suffice.[63]

Robert Lovell, fellow poet, pantisocrat, and Southey's future brother-in-law, was initially charged with placing the manuscript with Ridgway. In a courting letter written in January 1795 to his future wife, Edith Fricker, Southey reported on his own visit to Newgate to see Gerrald and to consult with Ridgway. A deal was struck: "I am to send them more sedition to make a 2 shilling pamphlet. They [Ridgway and Symonds] will print it immediately, give me 12 copies and allow me a sum proportionate to the sale if it sells well." To which he added, "All the risk is their own."[64] At the same time that Southey was hawking his work to Newgate's pressmen, he and his new friend Samuel Coleridge were frantically trying to raise enough money to purchase land in America. According to Winterbotham, on what was presumably a subsequent visit, Southey arrived in the company of Daniel Isaac Eaton, who had been recently released from Newgate after his acquittal on charges of seditious libel. On parting, Southey gifted the manuscript of *Wat Tyler* to Winterbotham, commenting, "You may do as you like with it, probably I shall never see you again unless you cross the Atlantic." That evening Winterbotham and Holt read the manuscript and decided against publication on the grounds that "the visionary schemes of equality... and the levelling doctrines... were more calculated to serve the cause of Faction than to promote the happiness of mankind."[65] More likely, the pressmen were disinclined to assume the legal risks involved in publishing more sedition. Eaton, among the most audacious Jacobin publishers, retained an interest in the work, with a view to publish it as a serial in his journal *Politics for the People*.[66] Southey claimed never to have known Eaton, although the previous spring, in a letter to Lovell, he included a long poem, "To the Exiled Patriots," which he intended to send to Eaton for publication. He suggested to Lovell that he too might want to contribute to the journal, "we may raise the reputation of Hog Wash."[67]

Whatever exactly went down at Newgate in 1795, Winterbotham held onto the manuscript of *Wat Tyler*. As it happened, Eaton was the only one of the party to make it to America, slipping out of England in early 1797, with a conviction for seditious libel and the threat of further government prosecutions hanging over his head. Winterbotham did not publish *Wat Tyler*, but he included Southey's ode to "Romance" in his collection of sacred and moral poems, with its tribute to Rousseau, "Fain would the grateful Muse, to thee Rousseau,/Pour forth the energic thanks of gratitude."[68] Rousseau's views on nature, moral virtue, and cottage-life exerted a major influence on the poets' "visionary schemes of equality" imagined for an agrarian community set in America. In addition, it is worth noting that George Dyer's "Address to the Deity" opens the first volume of Winterbotham's collection: "Greatest of Beings, source of life, / Sov'reign of air, and earth, and sea, / All nature feels thy pow'r, and all / A silent homage pay to thee!" In his *Dissertation on Benevolence* (1795), Dyer drew attention to Winterbotham's plight, and touted his history of America, being presently published in weekly numbers.[69] Dyer (himself a subscriber to Winterbotham's volumes), was keen to sign up for America, "enraptured," according to Coleridge, by "our System."[70]

The story of Pantisocracy is well enough known.[71] Plans to form a small community of equals emerged during the summer of 1794 from discussions between Coleridge and Southey who had only recently met, and among their Oxbridge circle of friends. "Pantisocracy" was Coleridge's coinage for the scheme to found a small community based on "equal government by all" and the abolition of private property, or "aspheterization." The scheme assumed great urgency, reflected in the exchange of letters, publication of poetry, lecture tours, recruitment, research on land prices, and a series of engagements to the dazzling Fricker sisters – Lovell was married to Mary, Southey was to marry Edith, Coleridge was to marry Sara, and George Burnett unsuccessfully proposed to Martha.[72] The community was to be composed of twelve well-educated young men and their wives, bound by friendship and a shared commitment to moral virtue and benevolence. The philosophy of Pantisocracy drew its ideas from Godwin, Rousseau, Priestley, Locke, Hartley (associationism), Harrington (republicanism), Moses Lowman (on Hebraic law), and various writers on America. Pantisocracy was among several contemporary schemes for establishing utopian communities across the Atlantic, including Iolo Morganwg and the group of Welsh radicals planning to form an egalitarian Welsh-speaking community in the back parts of America. At the same time that he was lecturing in Bristol to raise money for the Pantisocracy, Southey started composing his massive epic of American discovery, *Madoc* (1805), which was influenced by Iolo's researches,[73] In September 1794, Southey wrote to his brother about Coleridge's visit to Bristol, "we preached Pantisocracy and Aspheterism every where," and explained these are "two new words, the first signifying the equal government of all – and the other – the generalization of individual property, words well understood now in the city of Bristol."[74] Joseph Cottle, the Unitarian publisher soon to publish Southey's *Joan of Arc*, remembered a recruiting visit in late 1794 from the enthusiastic Lovell (a Quaker) with the news that he and his wife Mary were about to set sail for America, describing the "Social Colony" to be founded on the banks of the Susquehanna, where "he felt quite assured that he and his friends would be able to realize a state of society free from the evils and turmoils that then agitated the world, and to present an example of the eminence to which men might arrive under the unrestrained influence of sound principles."[75] There was little doubt that by the following year, they would be settled in America. It is easy to dismiss the scheme as the sort of fantasy that undergraduates dream up in their college rooms, and on long cross-country walks. Coleridge encouraged such a view in later years when he distanced himself from his Jacobin past, character-izing "the experiment in human Perfectability," as being "as harmless as it was extravagant."[76] The biographer of his Somerset friend Thomas Poole gets closer to the mark in her assessment:

> Nothing is easier now, than to see that the entire plan was the base-less fabric of a vision; but it was different then, to those eager young hearts spell-bound by Coleridge's eloquence, and to Coleridge him-self, fairly intoxicated with hope, and full of faith in the impossible.[77]

Indeed, "it was different then," the line separating the impossible from the possible was less clear, and demarcating idle thoughts from sedition was anything but straightforward. Taking Pantisocracy seriously re-quires an appreciation of its historical context rather than jumping for-ward to the nineteenth century and removing the romantic Imagination from history and politics.[78] If we return to the conditions of 1794–95, a more complicated story emerges, one that can be linked to Winterboth-am's history and to a set of key texts that informed the projects of both the poets and the Newgate editor.

We can agree that Pantisocracy represented a retreat but it was also subversive in its imaginative power, and its attack on property relations and the corruptions of commercial society. It represented a regrouping of ideological resources, the product of an extraordinary moment when the realm of the possible had opened wide its doors, but just at the point at which those doors were closing. For the early romantic poets, for Wordsworth as well as the pantisocrats, their political ideals no longer aligned with prevailing social and political realities. The French Revo-lution had lost its innocence. With the execution of the Girondist leader Jacques-Pierre Brissot, Southey wrote to his friend Grosvenor Bedford, "Oppression is triumphant every where." America beckoned as an asy-lum from European corruption.

> I should be pleased to reside in a country where men's abilities insure respect, where society was upon a proper footing, and man consid-ered more valuable than money; and where I could till the earth, and provide by honest industry the meat which my wife would dress with pleasing care.[79]

This was before he met Coleridge. Several months earlier, with war rag-ing against France, Poole felt "weary of thinking of politicks... America seems the only asylum of peace and liberty – the only place where the dearest feelings of man are not insulted." Even were France to prevail militarily and the Revolution saved, "the vice deeply rooted in France, will prevent it ever being what America is. England is a declining country, and now too guiltily leagued with despots."[80] Pantisocracy took shaped in tandem with the poets' complex response to the French Revolution's changing prospects. In August 1794, Coleridge and Southey dashed off their verse-drama *The Fall of Robespierre*, ambivalent about the death of "the tyrant guardian of the country's freedom."[81] Against this background America shone brightly, conjuring a sort of magic in the romantic imagination.

The poets' optimistic musings come through in their correspondence and poetry. In a letter written at the close of 1793, Southey invited Grosvenor Bedford to share his fantasy:

> Now, if you are in the mood for a reverie, fancy only me in America; imagine my ground uncultivated since the creation and see me wielding the axe, now to cut down the tree, and now the snakes that nestled in it. Then see me grubbing up the roots, and building a nice, snug little dairy with them: three rooms in my cottage, and my only companion some poor negro whom I have bought on purpose to emancipate. After a hard day's toil see me asleep upon the rushes... Do not imagine I shall leave rhyming or philosophizing; so then your friend will realize the romance of Cowley, and even outdo the seclusion of Rousseau; till at last comes an ill-looking Indian with a tomahawk, and scalps me.[82]

Much could be said about this passage, about images of the new world intersecting with a young man's subjective exploration of self. Southey projects himself at the moment of "discovery," encountering a new Eden for his cultivation. The Edenic image of America fused the secular with religious or spiritual impulses, as the offhand humor, the emancipated companion and "ill-looking Indian," betrayed deeper anxieties about America's natural innocence. It remained for Southey to join with Coleridge and convert his solitary reverie into a communal vision.

Just as Southey fancied himself in America, Coleridge followed his "Visionary Soul" to dwell in seclusion, "Wisely forgetful" of the burdens of the past and the evils of Europe.

> ... O'er the Ocean swell
> Sublime of Hope I seek the cottag'd Dell,
> Where Virtue calm with careless step may stray,
> And dancing to the moonlight Roundelay
> The Wizard Passions weave an holy Spell.

The sonnet, "Pantisocracy," appears in a letter to Southey, dated 18 September 1794.[83] In an earlier letter, Coleridge hoped that Southey admired the word "aspheterized." "We really *wanted* such a word – instead of travelling along the circuitous, dusty, beaten high road of Diction you thus cut across the soft, green pathless Field of Novelty."[84] As America opened a pathless space for renewal, the field of language opened itself to new words – indeed, required new figural expressions. And as the image of the secluded cottager gave way to a communal ethos, Pantisocracy desired to foster virtuous feelings among its group of friends. The scheme was intended to demonstrate the possibilities of benevolence based on a select group. Coleridge maintained that the "ardour of private Attachments makes Philanthropy a necessary *habit* of the Soul," feelings of benevolence were developed and sustained through concrete processes of life.[85] "In the book of Pantisocracy," Coleridge expressed his hope to "have comprised all that is good in Godwin," while acknowledging that Southey thought more highly of *Political Justice* than he did. For the pantisocrats, as for Godwin, sincerity and truth were key terms; men's hearts must be ever attentive to the imperatives of justice: "It is not enough that we have once swallowed it – The *Heart* should have *fed* upon the *truth*." But according to Coleridge, "The leading idea of Pantisocracy is to make men *necessarily* virtuous by removing all Motives to Evil – all temptations."[86] Hartley's name, and his materialist psychology, were thus writ large in the unwritten book of Pantisocracy.[87]

Private property was the prime motive of evil. In his "Lectures on Revealed Religion," delivered at Bristol in May 1795, Coleridge alluded with admiration to Jewish agrarian law, "The Law of the Jubilee," the equal distribution and periodic redistribution of land, although he believed that the abolition of all individual property was "perhaps the only infallible Preventative against accumulation." In a passage combining Lowman's scholarship on the Hebrew constitution with Godwin's ideas on property, Coleridge declared there to be "nothing more pernicious" than the notion of the right to absolute ownership of the land: "The Land is no one's – the Produce belongs equally to all, who contribute their due proportion of Labour."[88] Coleridge's views on property bear comparison to those of Spence, the agrarian socialist and popular Jacobin propagandist. While there is no evidence to suggest any direct contact or influence between the two men, they drew on some of the same sources, notably Harringtonian republicanism, the example of the early Hebrew republic and the Levitical law of the Jubilee – with perhaps faint echoes, in Spence's case, of the Digger leader, Gerrard Winstanley.[89] Both appealed to anti-commercialism and to a millennialist sensibility. In Spence's pantisocratic allegory, a group of maritime republicans bound in brotherly love and dissatisfied with the government of their country, set sail for America, where they expect to find government more agreeable "to their notions of equality and equity." Blown off course, they arrive

Crusoe-like on an uninhabited island with rich soil and mild climate, where they adapt their maritime constitution of equal shares to the island named for their wrecked ship, "Spensonia." As the island republic prospers and expands, a small-scale communal, parish government is established. Unlike the young intellectuals enthused by the Pantisocracy, Spence's writings in the 1790s emerged from the artisan milieu of radical London. The parable of Spensonia was published in Spence's one-penny, weekly journal *Pig's Meat*.[90] Moreover, by 1795 Spence's utopian thought-experiment was now combined with his endorsement of the need for physical revolution to end aristocratic oppression, reclaim the land, and establish the real or "whole" rights of British men and women.[91]

The pantisocrats were not revolutionaries, but their embryonic theory of property was subversive, founded on an unmistakable doctrine of leveling. Central to their doctrine was the simplicity of manners associated with a republican critique of wealth and luxury. As the French revolutionaries abandoned powdered wigs, knee breeches, silver-buckled shoes, and silk vests, they set a standard for republican style. As early as 1789, Brissot identified "simplicity of style" as "a characteristic of the free man."[92] A stern sense of republican virtue was common among democrats on both sides of the Atlantic, an ethic that also corresponded to an austere moral code found among British Dissenters. The republican ethos had a long history, but the American revolutionaries enshrined the image of modern republican citizenship as embodied in a simple life of self-sufficiency.

Accounts by Brissot, Gilbert Imlay, and Thomas Cooper appeared in rapid succession between 1791 and 1794; together they defined the republican ideal of America for British democrats and reformers, and were eagerly read by the pantisocrats. In 1791, Brissot published his three-volume *Nouveau Voyage dans les État-Unis*. Paine's publisher J. S. Jordon quickly brought out an abridged translation by Joel Barlow, the American revolutionary and author of *Vision of Columbus* (1787) and *Advice to the Privileged Orders* (1792). Barlow insisted on the direct relevance of the American experience: the natural principles exercised in the United States, where "the science of liberty is universally understood," stood as an example for Europe.[93] According to Brissot, it was no longer necessary to learn from America how to acquire their liberty, the French must learn from America the secret of how to preserve it: "This secret lies mainly in the moral principles and practices of the nation... Moral principles are simply the application of reason to human action." The attempt to distinguish between public and private morals was a false one, "he who is without private virtue can never truly possess public morality."[94] In his address to the people at Bristol, dated February 1795, Coleridge quoted a passage from Brissot's preface:

> The simplicity of wants and of pleasures may be taken as the criterion of Patriotism. Would you prove to me your Patriotism? Let me

penetrate into the interior of your House... I walk upon the richest Carpets – the most costly Wines, the most exquisite Dishes, cover your table – a crowd of Servants surround it – you treat them with haughtiness; – No! you are not a Patriot.[95]

In the series of letters to a friend that compose the account of his American travels, Brissot embraced the enduring image of the independent citizen-farmer to which St. John de Crèvecoeur gave classical expression in his *Letters from an American Farmer* (1782).[96] Here European luxury and decadence, hierarchy and oppression, are dispelled through regeneration in the new world governed by natural abundance, simplicity of manners, social equality, and individual liberty. The figure of the citizen-farmer occurs prominently throughout Winterbotham's history. The idea of the producer reaping the full fruits of his labor was attractive to both the poets and to the craftsmen seeking independence from various forms of economic exploitation. It was linked in turn to discussions of necessary labor and to broader critiques of aristocratic luxury and the artificial wants produced within a consumer-based society. Coleridge stressed the practicality of their communal scheme, fixing March 1795 for their date of departure, with the intention of spending the winter toning bodies used to "the habits of sedentary study," and learning "the theory and practice of agriculture and carpentry."[97] Coleridge and Southey convinced themselves of the charms of farm labor. They believed that they could support themselves and their families by working daily for only three hours, a projection they found in their reading.[98] In the fertile Ohio Valley, Brissot reported that once new settlers had cleared their land and built their first cabins, the land was so rich that "A Man living in these areas still surrounded by wilderness works scarcely two hours a day... and spends almost all his time loafing, hunting, or drinking. The women spin and make clothes for their husbands and children."[99] Female partners were consigned to much the same duties in the patriarchal Pantisocracy, raising children and maintaining the home. Southey estimated a mere two hours of daily work should suffice where all members were equally engaged in the common cultivation of the soil, citing Adam Smith's calculations of the labor time required to provide the necessary comforts of life. Their Georgic ideal of redemptive labor allowed for social and literary pursuits. "When Coleridge and I are sawing down a tree," Southey imagined, "we shall discuss metaphysics; criticise poetry when hunting a buffalo, and writing sonnets whilst following the plough."[100]

In October 1794, having assumed responsibility for researching land prices, Coleridge asked Southey's opinion on the prices provided in Cooper's recently published *Some Information Respecting America*. The pantisocrats were now attracted to the settlement Cooper established in conjuncture with the Priestleys near Northumberland along the Susquehanna River and to the idea of having Priestley and a community of

like-minded Dissenters for neighbors. The list of land purchases registered in Harrisburg's land office under tract names such as "Liberty,"
"Independence," "Friendship," "Equality," "Eden," and "Utopia" captures their hopes and commitments.[101] The pantisocrats shared in the
spirit of anti-commercial agrarianism. As a manufacturer himself (a
calico printer), Cooper lamented a system where "a large portion of the
people [must be] converted into mere machines... that the surplus value
of their labour of 12 or 14 hours a day, may go into the pockets and
supply the luxuries of rich, commercial, and manufacturing capitalists."
He reconfirmed the view of agricultural America as the home of pros-
perous men and women, the site of productive labor that offered the
opportunity for the economic, moral, and intellectual development of
ordinary people, believing as he did that "even manhood was not intended for incessant labour."[102] Cooper's critique must have appealed to
those readers undergoing the effects of industrial capitalism's emerging
work discipline.

Significantly, Cooper's path to America ran through France. On an
extended business trip to Paris in spring 1792, he and his associate James
Watt, Jr. (son of the famous inventor and friend of Wordsworth) made
fraternal contact with the revolutionary societies on behalf of the Manchester Constitutional Society, among the first societies to bring the reform politics of rational Dissent together with popular radicalism. They
befriended Brissot and were introduced at the Jacobin club by Robespierre. They took part in a great civic festival, the first fête orchestrated
by Jacques-Louis David (the "pageant-master" of the Revolution), with
Watt carrying a British flag and Cooper a bust of Algernon Sydney.[103] In
the commons, Burke called Cooper and Watt out for having presented a
fraternal address to the Jacobins, for having embraced Robespierre and
"kissed the bloody cheek of Marat."[104] In his trenchant reply to Burke,
Cooper defended the exchange of political knowledge among patriotic
societies, attacked hereditary distinctions as "directly opposed to Nature," and dismissed Burke as having spent the last two years writing
"discourses of political Mysticism." Yet at the same time that he defended the French revolutionaries, Cooper pointed to the United States
as "the most flourishing nation on the face of the Globe," whose constitutions showed that where the whole people are governors they pursue
the welfare of all; the experiment of representative government having
been in existence for nearly twenty years, "with success fully equal
to the most sanguine expectations of her best wishers," he concluded,
"therefore, we tread on better than speculative ground."[105]

By early 1793, government repression closed in on Manchester's radical community. Served with ex-officio informations, the publishers of
the radical *Manchester Herald*, Matthew Falkner and Samuel Birch, left
for America, and were soon followed by a group of plebeian radicals, escaping arrest for sedition. In late summer, Cooper and two of Priestley's

sons sailed for America to explore the prospects for emigration. Cooper's book was based on these travels. He returned in time to assist in securing the acquittal of his friend, Thomas Walker, tried along with nine others on charges of conspiracy to overthrow the constitution.[106] As attacks mounted domestically on radicals and rational Dissenters, and as the cheeks and hands of the French revolutionaries grew bloodier, America grew in the esteem of men like Cooper and Priestley.[107]

At Newgate, Winterbotham was reacting to the same situation. According to the preface to his *View of the American United States*, "one object has been constantly kept in view, namely, to afford the emigrator to America a summary of general information that may in some measure serve as a directory to him in the choice of a residence."[108] In volume three, he developed the case for America as opposed to Europe; he rhapsodized, "The government of America is making rapid strides towards perfection, it being contrary to all the old governments, [it is] in the hands of the people... Their laws and government have for their basis the imprescriptible rights of man." Religious freedom prevailed, "the unnatural alliance of church and state is broken," "the monster is dethroned." Republican virtue was secured by an equality of condition among farmer-citizens.[109] Winterbotham consulted the same authorities as the pantisocrats, citing Brissot and extracting large sections from Cooper. Cooper had, in turn, appended Benjamin Franklin's *Information to Those Who Would Remove to America* (first published 1782), a text from which Winterbotham heavily excerpted and which Ridgway and Eaton republished as a six-penny pamphlet. In a section quoted by Winterbotham, Franklin presents America as a society with "few people so miserably poor as in Europe, there are also very few that in Europe would be called rich. It is rather a general happy mediocrity that prevails... most people cultivate their own land, or follow some handicraft or merchandise." Men and women are respected for what they can do. "The husbandman is in honour there, and even the mechanic, because their employments are useful."[110] Those wishing to purchase land needed a moderate amount of capital, but the cheapness of land and high wages meant that hard-working artisans could save enough to purchase homesteads. The themes struck – America as a land without real poverty, where equality of condition, sturdy independence, and a respect for hard work and ingenuity prevail – are recurrent in the literature, although a certain tension exists between the value placed on useful labor and the natural abundance that renders men free of such burdens.

The most successful account of America as an ideological space for republican virtue was that of Imlay, an American adventurer and writer recently moved to London. The title page of his *A Topological Description of the Western Territory of America*, first published in 1792, describes the author as "A Captain in the American Army during the War,

and a Commissioner for laying out Lands in the Back Settlements."
The enlarged second edition, published the following year, appended
John Filson's *The Discovery, Settlement, and Present State of Kentucky*
(1784), along with "The Adventures of Daniel Boone," "The Minutes
of the Piankasahw Council," "An Account of the Indian Nations," and
Jefferson's 1791 report as secretary of state on the public lands available
in the western territories. Together with Filson, Imlay was responsible
for putting Kentucky firmly "on the map as the utopian idea-image of
an alternative society."[111] Winterbotham followed Imlay in directing
emigrants to Kentucky, the newest state to join the union.[112] Written in
the form of letters received by the editor from a friend, *A Topological
Description* purports to give an eyewitness account from a man who
has lived for more than twenty-five years "in the back parts of America... accustomed to that simplicity of manners natural to a people in a
state of innocence," and reflecting on the differences between American
and European society, morals, and manners.[113] Interlaced with practical
guidance, the Ohio Valley's back-country is portrayed as the space for
fashioning the independent democratic self. In a passage reproduced by
Winterbotham, Imlay expressed the sense of sheer wonderment evoked
by America's natural beauty, its pristine harmony and God-given innocence at the moment of its creation. Having followed the river from
Pittsburgh into Kentucky, Imlay describes the scene above the Ohio, like
Moses's first view of the Promised Land.

> Every thing here assumes a dignity and splendour I have never seen
> in any other part of the world... Here an eternal verdure reigns...
> The sweet songsters of the forest appear to feel the influence of this
> genial clime, and, in more soft and modulated tones, warble their
> tender notes in unison with love and nature. Every things here gives
> delight, and in the mild effulgence which beams around us, we feel
> a glow of gratitude for that elevation our all-bountiful Creator has
> bestowed upon us. Far from being disgusted with man for his tur-
> pitude or depravity, we feel that dignity nature bestowed upon us
> at the creation; but which has been contaminated by the base alloy
> of meanness, the concomitant of European education, and what is
> more lamentable is, that it is the consequence of your laws and your
> governments.[114]

In his insightful analysis, Wil Verhoeven observes that here Imlay not
only drew a "moral watershed" between America and Europe but created "a fundamental schism between the Atlantic states and the trans-
montane regions in the West," projecting an agrarian, "physiocratic
utopia" in the West.[115]

The pantisocrats' initial inclination to move to Kentucky was influenced by Imlay's romantic America combined with his detailed

information about material conditions of life.[116] Cooper and Imlay's books became rival texts in the revolution debate in Britain and in debate over republican settlement in America. The *British Critic* thought of the two men as "two rival auctioneers, or rather two show-men, stationed for the allurement of incautious passengers" to Kentucky and Pennsylvania, respectively. Indeed, Cooper and Imlay were interested parties seeking to turn a profit on land sales.[117] Free enterprise was seen as an element of revolutionary freedom. Barlow and Brissot had earlier invested in complex land deals in America, including the ill-fated Scioto Company that sold land to unwary French emigrants.[118] In truth, America was taking rapid strides as a commercial society, and while the back-country was represented as a space of independence and individual freedom, it was hardly free from financial speculation and sharp dealing. There was a conservative counter-narrative that portrayed America not only as unfit for refined living but as a land of grasping, money-hungry people. An anonymous pamphlet entitled *Look Before You Leap* sought to counter false descriptions "so luxuriantly picturesque of American scenery, and the exaggerated encomiums upon the state of American society," and to expose land agents "hovering like birds of prey" to exploit credulous British settlers. The author invited readers to compare a series of letters purported to come from disappointed immigrants, including those from a former LCS member, with the accounts "given by Franklin, Morse, Jefferson, Brissot, Winterbotham, and... the puffs of the Agents for the sale of American lands" – noting that Winterbotham "was never out of this kingdom in his life."[119] But it was not just conservatives who thought Americans too enamored of wealth and property. In a confidential letter to a friend, Thelwall complained that Americans "have too much veneration for property – too much religion – and too much law."[120] Mary Wollstonecraft, who became Imlay's lover in Paris in spring 1793, came to bitterly resent the whirl of business interests that consumed her American partner's life and commercial dealings that corrupted natural sentiments. Her own dream of finding domestic happiness and a life of simplicity farming in America came to nothing as her relationship with Imlay unraveled. In her *Letters Written during a Short Residence in Sweden, Norway, and Denmark* (1796), she re-channeled her Rousseauian desires in her descriptions of the landscape and sturdy farmers of Norway.[121]

As Coleridge gathered information on land prices in autumn 1794, he lodged at the "Salutation and Cat" coffeehouse at 17 Newgate Street, where he drank "Porter & Punch round a good fire" with an old school friend who had lived for five years in the United States. Now working as a land agent, he advised Coleridge that it would be cheaper to purchase land after their arrival in the United States, calculating that "two thousand pounds will do." He thought that twelve men could "easily" clear three hundred acres in four or five months, and recommended the Susquehanna for "its excessive Beauty and, its security from hostile Indians."[122] A few months later, perhaps on his mission to place *Wat Tyler*, Lovell discussed the Pantisocracy with Thomas Holcroft, who was being held at Newgate on treason charges. In turn, Southey reported to his brother that Gerrald, Holcroft, and Godwin, "the three first men in England, perhaps in the world – highly approve our plan."[123] There is no evidence that Coleridge sought advice from any of the patriots housed in the prison at the western end of Newgate Street, or dropped in at Eaton's shop at number 75, where democrats quietly gathered on evenings to discuss politics. But he resided in close proximity to various haunts of plebeian radicalism. The Salutation and Cat, described by Coleridge as "an Ale-house by courtesy called 'a Coffee House,'" was connected by an open yard at the back to the Crown tavern, where division twelve of the LCS had met until magistrates threatened to withdraw the owner's license.[124] As he was discussing poetry in the evenings with his friend Charles Lamb, perhaps Coleridge also crossed paths with members of London's popular societies, exchanging words about the freedom to be found across the Atlantic.[125]

In December 1794, Lovell wrote to Holcroft, congratulating him on his release from prison, and soliciting the playwright and Godwin's thoughts about "our projected plan of establishing a genuine system of property." They sought the approbation of two men from whom "our minds have been illuminated, we wish our actions to be guided by the same superior abilities." A new possibility had emerged with a friend's suggestion that "the plan is practicable in some of the uncultivated parts of Wales." As Lovell explained, America presented many advantages, not least "the easy rate at which land can be purchased," but he emphasized, "Principle not plan, is our object." He remembered that Holcroft had expressed the desire that they might form such a society without leaving Britain. Wales would be cheaper, perhaps less dangerous, "and at the same time be more agreeable to our private inclination; but the probability of being obnoxious to Government, and subject to tythes, are in our opinion serious objections."[126] Coleridge dismissed the notion of Pantisocracy outside of America, as "nonsense."[127] The practical objections raised by Lovell were real, a colony of Jacobin levelers in Wales would certainly have drawn the unwelcome attention of authorities. Yet one feels that Coleridge's objection was not merely a practical one but reflected the romantic ideal of America, an emotional investment in something beyond what could be dreamed in Wales.

Nonetheless, Lovell's mention of "private inclinations" to remain in Britain signaled that their plans had run into trouble. They had been unable to raise the requisite funds, and Southey's aunt Elizabeth Tyler, displeased by his plans to emigrate and even more displeased by his intention to marry the lowly Edith Fricker, booted him out of her house and disinherited him.[128] Moreover, Coleridge chaffed at Southey's suggestion that they bring servants to help with the hard labor as compromising their principles of full equality.[129] In part the decision to shift their plans from Kentucky to Pennsylvania was taken in order to avoid contact with the institution of slavery. But there was a shortage of men willing to work for wages in the back-country, and despite the advice of Coleridge's friend, clearing land was back-breaking work. Southey's earlier premonition about his poor Negro companion, and his subsequent scalping, point to the suppressed colonial terms underpinning projections of Rousseauian innocence onto the American frontier. The women also posed a problem. Despite Coleridge's admiration for Wollstonecraft's writings, he questioned whether the women possessed the required "generous enthusiasm for Benevolence," and whether "in the present state of their minds" mothers might not "tinge the Mind of the Infants with prejudications." Southey's insistence that each man be accompanied by a spouse, and differences over the "regulations" pertaining to females and the terms of marriage, pointed to a conflicted patriarchy.[130] The pantisocrats ultimately could not help but reinscribe the hierarchies of their own condition of privilege as colonizing European men.

By the anticipated spring date of departure, the scheme for America had fallen apart in the face of practical obstacles and perhaps a failure of collective will.[131] Arguably, the significance of the plan relates less to the internal contradictions leading to its collapse than to the dream itself and what it reveals about how America figured in the Jacobin imagination. While the utopian scheme could never have been realized as in the book of Pantisocracy, a compromised version could have been achieved, although confronted with American realities the result would have likely contributed to the experience of political disenchantment. The image of America as a space free from European despotism primed for the full development of the republican male-self required key elisions and deferrals, evasions recurrent in such idealized constructions; it was an image more easily sustained at a distance.

Empire of Liberty and Modern Development

The 1790s were a crucial decade in determining the meaning of American democracy and the direction of the country's development as a modern nation. The politics of Winterbotham's history are republican and generally democratic; in terms of America's political landscape, the work can be said to reflect a Jeffersonian outlook, although it is unclear the degree to which Winterbotham or most British radicals followed the intricacies of day-to-day politics in the United States. *View of the American United States* exudes an optimistic view of America as a land of liberty, although given the way in which volumes were constructed, contradictions remain, reflecting the differing perspectives of the authors consulted, but which in turn point to unresolved questions about American development.

While avoiding direct reference to Paine, Winterbotham followed his lead on the subject of constitution-making; America's constitutions represented an unparalleled historical achievement, worthy of "the respect of every friend of freedom and happiness of mankind." Winterbotham viewed with pleasure the pervasive sentiment "that the supreme power resides in the people; and that they never can part with it. It may be called the *Panacea* in politics." He offers a thoughtful discussion of the 1787 constitution, critical of specific parts (for example, disapproving of the fact that Senate members are not directly elected by the people) but certain that any defects will in time be corrected. The carefully drawn line between the powers of the federal government and individual states secured "the harmony of their union, while the powers of both DE-RIVED BY REPRESENTATION FROM THE PEOPLE, must effectively prevent any disagreement or discontent from taking place. – Thus a principle of democracy being carried into every part of the constitution, and representation, and direct taxation, going hand in hand, the prosperity of the country and the stability of its government, will keep pace with each other." America, as a democratic republic, thus achieved a true balance of constitutional authority residing ultimately in the sovereignty of the people.[132]

Yet, alert readers of the constitutional documents reproduced by Winterbotham could determine for themselves the limitations placed on democratic representation. Positive usage of the word "democracy" was more widespread in American discourse than in Britain, but the real question concerned precisely how much equality and popular rule were desirable.[133] Just as Winterbotham was gathering sources for his history, America witnessed intensified partisan conflict, with the mushrooming of popular Democratic societies pressing a Paineite agenda and with government suppression of rebellion in western Pennsylvania. By 1799, when the second edition of his work came out, the Federalist-dominated Congress had passed the Alien and Sedition Acts, aimed at suppressing radical or "Jacobin" opinion. Exiled former LCS members reinforced by United Irishmen played leading roles in this democratic challenge.[134] Having escaped prosecution in Britain, in 1800 Cooper was convicted in Philadelphia of seditious libel for his attack on President John Adams.[135] Democracy in America was an unfinished project, one that faced strong opposing forces.

The relative equality of condition to be found in America was clearly of crucial importance to Winterbotham and his readers. Yet, the growth of commercial prosperity raised concerns about widening disparities in wealth and status. Economic development encroached on a national republican ideal based on the moral virtue of the simple life.[136] A key question on both sides of the Atlantic was how, or if, equality of condition was compatible with the growth of commerce and manufacture. Gareth Stedman Jones has argued that the 1790s constituted a lost moment when the prospect of an end to poverty together with achieving a rough equality among a democratic citizenry appeared as a possibility.[137] Paine and Thelwall, Britain's two leading popular radical theorists, favored in varying degree a modified commercial society that combined abolition of hereditary privilege along with support for free trade and individual enterprise, the rights of the poor to a portion of society's wealth, a labor theory of value, limited rights to property (particularly in land), and a measure of wealth redistribution. Writing in early 1795, Thelwall pressed the need "to abolish luxury: and every man may do much towards this reformation... persuade mankind to discard those tinsel ornaments and ridiculous superfluities which enfeeble our minds." While recommending a personal reformation in manners, he urged readers to consider the "real utility of commerce," whereby the exchange of surplus resources among nations served to prevent needless scarcity; he contrasted the "real advantages of commerce" to the present commercial system that merely swelled "the opulence of a few individuals."[138] Thelwall struck an uneasy balance between stoic republican virtue and a cautious acceptance of modern commercial society. In contrast to utopian idealism based on agrarian primitivism, writers such as Thelwall and Paine (giving their own twist to Adam Smith) moved toward what might be termed a "pragmatic utopianism," a sophisticated plan to reap the benefits of commercial prosperity without generating poverty, severe inequality, or the corruption of human affection.[139] For Paine, certainly, America offered a better opportunity than Europe for realizing such a state of prosperity and equality.

Volume one of *View of the American United States* provides a full account of America's commercial progress, extracted principally from Morse's *American Geography*. British protectionism is condemned and paeans offered to the principles of international free trade – Winterbotham published his work just as the controversial Jay Treaty between Britain and America was being signed.[140] Moreover, the author added a lengthy section on manufacturing extracted almost verbatim and without attribution from Alexander Hamilton's *Report on Manufactures*, originally submitted to Congress at the end of 1791.[141] While Hamilton conceded the importance of agriculture as the main source of national wealth, he countered the physiocratic belief in agriculture as the only true source of wealth. He proposed the development of manufacture, foreseeing increased prosperity based on a diversified economy that would put America on equal terms with Europe; to this end, he suggested the provision of government bounties to encourage industry. The prospect of good profits would attract foreign capital and higher wages would increase the immigration of skilled European artisans. As in his political thinking, Hamilton was drawn to Britain as a model for America's economic future. He extolled the potential derived from the division of labor, extensive use of machinery, and expanded employment of women and children for which he cited the example of Britain's cotton factories.[142] He proposed introducing a labor regime that writers like Cooper condemned and against which America's back-country was seen as a safeguard.

Winterbotham made no attempt to reconcile Hamilton's program for manufacture with the predominant image of America's future cast as a democratic republic founded on small agricultural proprietorship. His volumes reveal few signs of the brewing political conflict between American Federalists and Jeffersonians. Moreover, according to Joyce Appleby, Jefferson's vision of America should be understood not as backward-looking, but rather as a progressive, commercially orientated society of agricultural producers – an alternate version of capitalist growth.[143] For Winterbotham and his readers, certainly for the sort of LCS members to whom Place referred, one senses deeper feelings, more radical, or even utopian, associated with American democracy and the archetype of the republican farmer. As Cooper stressed, the word "farmer" meant something different in America than in England: the American farmer was not the tenant of some lord, paying rent, tithes, and high taxes – "an inferior rank in life" – but was himself "a land owner... equal in rank to any other rank in the state."[144] The anxiety about whether such independence could be sustained within a burgeoning capitalist nation was allayed by the vast uncultivated lands available for settlement. The Jeffersonian ideal was by definition expansionist.[145] In countering Hamilton's views on manufacturing, Cooper observed that unlike France, where land was bound to become scarce, "America... has land which will be unoccupied for ages."[146] Eaton's *Politics for the People* carried an address to Priestley, "on his quitting England for America," from the Society of United Irishmen of Dublin. The United Irishmen accompany the exiled philosopher in their imagination:

> Again do we participate in your feelings, on first beholding nature in the noblest scenes and grandest features; on finding men busied in rendering himself worthy of nature, but more than all, on contemplating with philosophic preference, the coming period when the St. Lawrence and Mississippi shall stretch forth their arms to embrace the continent in a great circle of internal navigation; when the Pacific Ocean shall pour into the Atlantic; when *man* will become more precious than *fine gold*, and when his ambition shall be to *subdue the elements*, not to *subjugate his fellow creatures*.[147]

Such iterations of America's manifest continental destiny, with humankind subduing nature, glossed over the question of whether Native Americans counted as "fellow creatures" not to be subjugated or removed.

In the literature on settlement cited by Winterbotham, the presence of Native Americans registers as a danger but not as an ultimate impediment to unlimited expansion, and hardly a whisper is heard about what rights Indians may have to their own land. Winterbotham treats the subject of American Indians in his first volume, discussed as part of Enlightenment debates about hierarchies of humankind.[148] Well-worn passages from Raynal, Robertson, Clavigero, Jefferson, and Franklin are pressed into service. In many respects, Indians receive favorable treatment. They are presented as locked in the "savage" stage of development, sharing a rough equality due to a lack of riches or luxury; they display a passion for liberty, extraordinary courage, hospitality, and natural eloquence. Indians possess an admirable primitive dignity, signaling virtues lost in the progress of human civilization and commercial society. The figure of the noble savage was, however, undercut by lurid descriptions of torture and the barbarities of warfare, a counter-image of "hell-hounds" that emerged with force following the Seven Years' War. The rival images remained in unresolved tension.[149] Winterbotham's selections discussing Native Americans were no doubt interesting as ethnography, but such speculative philosophizing ignored the violence on the ground. The Indian presence hardly troubles the descriptions of present conditions or the prospects for settlement. Readers are assured that "slight skirmishes with the Indians have been magnified to the most tremendous battles" by opponents of emigration.[150] Yet despite Imlay's efforts to downplay the threat of Indian attack in Kentucky, Southey's joke about being scalped was not without substance. Nothing is said about the federal government's campaign of "pacification" as a cause of increased confidence for settlement in the Ohio Valley. By 1795, ingrained racial hatred of Indians and a genocidal impulse common among western settlers became the basis of a new national covenant of imperial expansion. The question of whether Indians could be brought within the civilizing compass of the nation had largely been resolved.[151] The romantic Indian, a symbol of natural liberty and simple manners, was imaginatively divorced from brutal reality.

What then about slavery in America? Winterbotham was an abolitionist who had preached the dawning of "the day of universal Liberty" as extending to enslaved people. In the fourth volume of his *View*, which covered European settlements in the Americas and the West Indies, he excerpted a substantial proportion from William Roscoe's anonymously authored *An Inquiry into the Causes of the Insurrection of the Negroes in the Island of St. Domingo* (1792), to which he added his own view that the French government would ultimately succeed in "extending peace and liberty" to all inhabitants of this and other islands under their dominion. Winterbotham expressed his hope that France's "godlike plan" to abolish slavery would soon be imitated by those European governments lacking "sufficient virtue to set the example."[152] As for the pantisocrats, in his "Lecture on the Slave-Trade" delivered at Bristol in June 1795, Coleridge chastised his audience for their addiction to artificial wants supplied by slave labor, eating food "polluted with the blood of [God's] own innocent Children." Africans, "who were situated beyond the contagion of European vice," offered a pantisocratic counter-model, as they peacefully cultivated their fertile fields "in common and reap the crop as the common property of all."[153] Southey, in turn, penned his popular "Poems on the Slave-Trade," in which he decried "the cold-hearted Commerce" and provocatively raised the prospect of slave rebellion: "Did the bold Slave rear at last the Sword, / of Vengeance?" – a question to which revolutions in Saint-Domingue and Guadeloupe lent substance.[154] In his *Letters on the Slave Trade*, published in 1787, Cooper had denounced slavery as "the most diabolical exertion of political tyranny, which the annals of oppression can exhibit an instance of." With early news from Saint-Domingue of slave insurrection, Cooper thought that "their brethren" in other islands "may be influenced by their example, and that the infamous trade... may terminate in the expulsion of the West Indian Planters."[155]

Yet the vehement denunciations of the British trade and slavery in the West Indies were not matched by fundamental concerns about American slavery. The republican writers who advanced the agrarian idyll situated in America's back-country were ardent opponents of slavery; the republican farmer possessed a direct relationship with the land he and his family farmed. But the dream of a democratic social order, of human freedom based on farming and prosperity supplied by nature's abundance, sidestepped the issue of American slavery, projecting an uncomplicated vision of America's development as a nation on the right side of history.[156] Brissot organized the first meeting of France's antislavery society of *Les Amis des Noirs*, but in his writings about America he stressed the progress that had been made toward ending slavery, expressing his belief that in the near future Congress would overcome the self-interested opposition of the southern states and humanity would prevail.[157] It was the case that the Northwest Ordinance of 1787 banned slavery in the northwest territory; the first Slave Trade Act of 1794 limited American involvement in the international trade; and by the end of the eighteenth century every northern state had legislated some form of emancipation.[158] However, even before the onset of the cotton revolution, expectations of an early end to slavery were arguably misplaced, a way to avoid confronting America's dark side.

Winterbotham followed suit in terms of his complacency about slavery's future in the United States. "As the people of England have opposed the system of negroe slavery," he assumed that most emigrants would settle outside the country "that supports this humiliating distinction between man and man." He included some anodyne observations about the superiority of free wage-labor and the bad effects that slavery had on the industry, manners, and morals of whites, drawing on Jefferson's *Notes on the State of Virginia* (1785).[159] He did not cite Jefferson's speculations on biological difference and naturally inferior capacities of Africans; nor did he include Imlay's attack on Jefferson's "disgraceful prejudices." As opposed to Jefferson's proposals to expatriate or to establish a separate colony for emancipated slaves, Imlay favored incorporating freed people within the republic as useful citizens.[160] Winterbotham assumed the gradual abolition of American slavery. By sliding past American's most glaring contradictions, *View of the American United States* sustained a narrative of human progress, portraying a thriving modern republic based on democratic citizenship, religious freedom, and egalitarianism.

Moving On

> Not in Utopia – subterraneous fields,
> Or some secreted island, heaven knows where! –
> But in the very world which is the world
> Of all of us...
>
> (*Prelude*, 1805, bk. 11, 723–26) [161]

Such was Wordsworth's memory of how it felt to be alive during the early years of the French Revolution. By 1795, as this enthusiasm dimmed, America offered itself to the British democratic imagination as less thrilling in its immediacy, but appealing to a sense of promise that existed "in the very world" found across the Atlantic. America's historical fate has been to fall short of that promise, to disappoint such hopes, but in the 1790s Jacobin hearts still turned to the new world for inspiration.

Winterbotham and the pantisocrats moved on. By 1796, Southey was in Portugal with his uncle. The pantisocratic impulse was vicariously transferred to his massive epic *Madoc*.[162] By early 1797, Coleridge had established his young family at Stowey in the Quantocks, where he was soon joined by the Wordsworths. As late as 1801, having moved to the Lake District, Coleridge expressed a longing to escape to America in order to avoid the sight of destitute beggars "with their half-famished children" wandering the countryside.[163] Dyer remained in contact with Priestley who happily reported from Pennsylvania in autumn 1796:

> Here we have no poor, we never see a beggar, nor is there any family in want. We have no church establishment, and hardly any taxes... The press is perfectly free, and I hope we shall always keep out of war. I don't think there ever was any country in the world in a state of such rapid improvement as this at present.[164]

Poor Lovell died earlier the same year of a fever. Coleridge was at his bedside trying to offer Christian consolation to his atheist brother-in-law.[165] None of the original pantisocrats made it to America.

Over the course of his sentence, Winterbotham seems to have moderated his views. He regained his faith "in the gospel revelation on the best rational grounds," according to Lindsey, who thought Newgate had served as "a school of moral discipline."[166] Priestley was pleased to learn of Winterbotham's improved spiritual condition; he asked to be remembered to him, adding, "I admire his industry & spirit... He would be very useful here. Men's minds change with circumstances."[167] Winterbotham was released from Newgate on 27 November 1797. The same day he and his "sweetheart" Mary Brend were married by the Newgate chaplain at the church opposite the jail. Mary had regularly visited William during his long imprisonment. At the invitation of Lord Stanhope, the couple spent the first days of their honeymoon at Chevening House in Kent. Winterbotham returned to Plymouth where he resumed his duties at How's Lane Church; in 1801, he was ordained as minister, succeeding Rev. Gibson as the congregation's pastor. He seems to have lost some of his earlier vitality, and despite the support of local Baptists, hostilities in the town led him to move in 1804 to become minister of the Baptist church at Shortwood, Gloucestershire, settling in the Nailsworth Valley, and later moving to the nearby village of Newmarket. He sought a quieter life, while remaining a proponent of religious and civil liberty and an ardent abolitionist. [168]

Nothing suggests that Winterbotham maintained a connection to his former Newgate publishing partners. Yet in 1817, the manuscript of *Wat Tyler* made its way into print. In the third act, John Ball answers his accuser:

> If it be guilt,
> To preach what you are pleased to call strange notions,
> That all mankind as brethren must be equal;
> That privileged orders of society
> Are evil and oppressive; that the right
> Of property is a juggle to deceive
> The Poor that you oppress; I plead me guilty.
> (*Wat Tyler*, Act III, 193–99)[169]

Winterbotham had been convicted for preaching "strange notions" that were less revolutionary than those of Ball. And while Winterbotham's America stood for principles subversive to Britain's government, his *magnum opus* was safe from government prosecution. It is, however, worth reflecting that had Newgate's pressmen published *Wat Tyler* in 1795, and had they failed to successfully shield the author's identity, Southey might have found himself sharing rooms with Winterbotham and company, and wishing he had made it to America.

Notes

1 "**AMERICA**. To be completed in thirty-three numbers" (nd., [1794]), 1–4. An earlier version of the prospectus announced thirty numbers to be published on 28 June.

2 TS11/41/151 (5), crown brief Ridgway prosecution; Daniel Holt, *A Vindication of the Conduct and Principles of the Printer of the Newark Herald* (Newark, 1794); Ralph A. Manogue, "The Plight of James Ridgway, London Bookseller and Publisher, and the Newgate Radicals, 1792–1797," *WC* 27 (1996): 158–66.

3 See Wil Verhoeven, *Americomania and the French Revolution Debate in Britain, 1789–1802* (Cambridge: CUP, 2013), chapter 6; Emma Macleod, "British Radical Attitudes towards the United States of America in the 1790s: The Case of William Winterbotham," in *Liberty, Property and Popular Politics England and Scotland, 1688–1815: Essays in Honour of H. T. Dickinson*, ed. Gordon Pentland and Michael T. Davis (Edinburgh: Edinburgh University Press, 2016), 149–62, and "Civil Liberties and Baptists: William Winterbotham of Plymouth in Prison and Thinking of America," *Baptist Quarterly* 44 (2011): 196–222.

4 The following two paragraphs draw on James Epstein, "Sermons of Sedition: The Trials of William Winterbotham," in *Political Trials in an Age of Revolutions: Britain and the North Atlantic, 1793–1818*, ed. Michael T. Davis, Emma Macleod, and Gordon Pentland (Cham: Palgrave Macmillan, 2019), 109–35.

5 William Howard Winterbotham, *The Rev. William Winterbotham, A Sketch* (1893),1–20; W. J., "Memoirs of the Rev. William Winterbotham," *New Baptist Miscellany* 4 (January, 1830): 1–5; Henry M. Nicholson, *Authentic Records Relating to the Christian Church Now Meeting in George Street and Mutley Chapels, Plymouth. 1640 to 1870* (1870), 82–83. See also Michael Durey, "William Winterbotham's 'Trumpet of Sedition': Religious Dissent and Political Radicalism in the 1790s," *Journal of Religious History* 19 (1995): 141–57. As a Particular Baptist, Winterbotham retained a Calvinist view of salvation.

6 *The Trial[s] of Wm. Winterbotham … for Seditious Words* (1794), 67–68. See Robert Hole, *Pulpits, Politics and Public Order in England, 1760–1832* (Cambridge: CUP, 1989), chapter 1, and "English Sermons and Tracts as Media of Debate on the French Revolution, 1789–99," in *The French Revolution and British Popular Politics*, ed. Mark Philp (Cambridge: CUP, 1991), 18–37.

7 E. P. Thompson, *The Making of the English Working Class* (Gollancz, 1963), 31. The development of the government's case can be traced in TS 11/954 and TS 11/458 (1524), crown brief.

8 William Winterbotham, *The Commemoration of National Deliverance, and the Dawning Day: Two Sermons … Preached at How's Lane Chapel, Plymouth* (1794). Winterbotham claimed to have provided verbatim texts, although there was controversy over the exact words spoken.

9 *Trials of Winterbotham*, 2; *ST*, vol. 22, "Proceedings … against William Winterbotham for Seditious Words," cols. 906–08; *True Briton*, 28 November 1793.

10 Thomas Belsham, *Memoirs of the Late Theophilius Lindsey, M. A.* (1812), 275–77; Joseph Priestley to John Wilkinson, 9 January 1794, as quoted in Jenny Graham, "A Hitherto Unpublished Letter of Joseph Priestley," *ED* 14 (1995): 88–104, at 92. In fact, Winterbotham's sermons were the only ones to be prosecuted.

11 At Clerkenwell Winterbotham was denied separation from felons and regular exercise due to the governor's extortionate fees.
12 Winterbotham, *Sketch*, 36–41; W. J. "Memoirs," *New Baptist Miscellany* 4 (March, 1830): 89–90; Thomas Belsham, *Memoirs of the Late Reverend Theophilus Lindsey, M. A.* (1812), 273–75. Mrs. Rayner, a wealthy member of Lindsey's Unitarian congregation, contributed an annual £50 during Winterbotham's imprisonment. His legal costs totaled £337.
13 Joseph Priestley, *Memoirs of Dr. Joseph Priestley to the Year 1795* (Northumberland, PA, 1806), 159–61.
14 [H. Ridyard], *A Selection from the Early Letters of the Late Rev. William Shepherd, LL. D.* (Liverpool, 1855), letter dated 2 July 1797, 64.
15 See John Seed, "'A Set of Men Powerful Enough in Many Things:' Rational Dissent and Political Opposition in England, 1770–1790," in *Enlightenment and Religion: Rational Dissent in Eighteenth-Century Britain*, ed. Knud Haakonssen (Cambridge: CUP, 1996), 14–66; Mark Philp, "Rational Religion and Political Radicalism," *ED* 4 (1985): 35–46; Stuart Andrews, *Unitarian Radicalism: Political Rhetoric, 1770–1814* (Houndmills: Palgrave Macmillan, 2003).
16 For the importance of the act of publishing to radical political identity, see Jon Mee, *Print, Publicity and Radicalism in the 1790s:* The Laurel of Liberty (Cambridge: CUP, 2016), 21–24.
17 The volumes include, for example, a good helping of Anna Laetitia Barbauld's poems, and those of other Unitarians such as George Dyer and William Edwards, as well as poems of Gilbert Wakefield and Robert Merry.
18 As well as Ridgway and Symonds's three editions, *The Evidence, Cross-Examinations, Arguments of Counsel … on the Two Trials of Wm. Winterbotham* (Exeter, 1794) sold for 6d. D. I. Eaton commended "the *very valuable Notes*" as well as the full trials to his readers, and published an extract from the notes in his journal *Politics for the People*, 1, pt. 2, no.1 (February 1794):14–16, and 2, no. 28 (February 1795): 433–36.
19 *Trials of Winterbotham*, 67–69. Hailing the "the dawn of liberty opening" in France, Winterbotham's second sermon had a decidedly millenarian tinge. For the porous boundary between "respectable" millenarian preaching and the prophetic impulse of autodidactic intellectuals, see Iain McCalman, "New Jerusalems: Prophecy, Dissent and Radical Culture in England, 1786–1830," in Haakonssen, ed., *Enlightenment and Religion*, 312–35.
20 Winterbotham, *Sermons*, 9–10, 34.
21 *The Trial of Thomas Briellat, for Seditious Words … December 6, 1793, Session-House, Clerkenwell Green* (1794), 2–4. The defense disputed the words that were spoken. For the popular view that Briellat's real offense was for having allowed his field to be used by the LCS for an outdoor meeting, see Chapter 2.
22 TS 11/954 (3498), report of John Groves, 13 February 1794, in Thale, 113. Jones, a relative of Briellat, reported the conversation to Groves not knowing he was speaking with a government spy. Jones was himself mistakenly accused of being a spy due to the violent resolutions he proposed at LCS meetings.
23 Iain McCalman, "Newgate in Revolution: Radical Enthusiasm and Romantic Counter-Culture," *Eighteenth-Century Life* 22 (1998): 95–110, at 95–99. See also editors, "Patriots in Prison," in *Newgate in Revolution: An Anthology of Radical Prison Literature in the Age of Revolution*, ed. Michael T. Davis, Iain McCalman, and Christina Parolin (Continuum, 2005), ix–xxv; Christina Parolin, *Radical Spaces: Venues of Popular Politics in*

London, 1790 – c. 1845 (Canberra: Australian University E Press, 2010), chapter 1.

24 PC 1/28/A62, Brothers to Winterbotham, 5 March 1795. For Brothers, see John Barrell, *Imagining the King's Death: Figurative Treason, Fantasies of Regicide, 1793–1796* (Oxford: OUP, 2000), chapter 15. In the event, Brothers was not sent to Newgate, as Privy Council concluded that he was probably a lunatic rather than a traitor.

25 *The Coin Collector's Companion. Being a Descriptive Alphabetical List of the Modern Provincial, Political, and other Copper Coins … Printed for T. Spence, Dealer in Coins* (1795), 35.

26 Interestingly, John Thelwall turned to Eaton, Ridgway, and Symonds to publish his *Poems Written in Close Confinement* (1795). See Jon Mee, "The Dungeon and the Cell: The Prison Verse of Coleridge and Thelwall," in *John Thelwall: Radical Romantic and Acquitted Felon*, ed. Steve Poole (Pickering & Chatto, 2009), 107–16.

27 Godwin visited Winterbotham and Joseph Gerrald on 28 March and 7 April 1794, Bod. Lib., GD.

28 Elizabeth Edwards, *English-Language Poetry from Wales, 1789–1806* (Cardiff: University of Wales Press, 2013), 145; Damian Walford Davies, *Presences that Disturb: Models of Romantic Identity in the Literature and Culture of the 1790s* (Cardiff: University of Wales Press, 2002), chapter 4; Gwyn A. Williams, *Madoc: The Making of a Myth* (Eyre Methuen, 1979), particularly chapters 5–9. Williams's poem, "On Religion," is the final selection in William Winterbotham, ed., *Selection of Poems Sacred and Moral*, 2 vols. (1796–97), 2: 172–76.

29 W. J., "Memoirs," *New Baptist Miscellany* 4 (March 1830): 91.

30 Penelope Corfield and Chris Evans, eds., *Youth and Revolution in the 1790s: Letters of William Pattisson, Thomas Amyot and Henry Crabb Robinson* (Stroud: Allen Sutton, 1996), 51–53, and editors' introductions. William Pattison was one of the young intellectuals associated with Norwich's ambitious journal *The Cabinet*. Several days before his Newgate visit, Rutt had dined on the hulk with Palmer. Rev. Robert Hall, William Frend (expelled from Cambridge in 1793), and Gilbert Wakefield were connected to Cambridge's coterie of radical Dissenters.

31 In March 1794, Lindsey reported, "Five vessels, to my knowledge, have been filled up with different parties of our countrymen … these all flee the country as in Laudian times." Quoted in John Seed, "Jeremiah Joyce, Unitarianism and the Radical Intelligentsia in the 1790s," *Transactions of the Unitarian Historical Society* 17 (1981): 97–108, at 103.

32 *Tribune*, "On the means of Redressing the Calamities of Nations," 1, no. 1 (14 March 1795): 3–4.

33 *The Times*, 29 August 1794, quoted in Mark Philp, "Representing America: Paine and the New Democracy," in *The American Experiment and the Idea of Democracy in British Culture, 1776–1914*, ed. Ella Dzelzainis and Ruth Livesey (Farnham: Ashgate, 2013), 15–29, at 23.

34 *Cambridge Intelligencer*, 21 December 1793, reprinted in *Politics for the People*, 2, no. 26 (1795): 415–16. See John Barrell, "Rus in Urbe," in *Romanticism and Popular Culture in Britain and Ireland*, ed. Philip Connell and Nigel Leask (Cambridge: CUP, 2009), 109–27, at 115–17, on "pastoral utopia."

35 Library copies, and therefore digital reproductions, of the first edition often do not contain the list of subscribers that appears after the author's preface. The same list is found at the end of volume 4 of the second edition, William

Winterbotham, *An Historical, Geographical, Commercial, and Philosophical View of the American United States, and of the European Settlements in America and the West-Indies* (1799).

36 Mark Philp, "The Role of America in the 'Debate on France' 1791–5: Thomas Paine's Insertion," *Utilitas* 5 (1993): 221–37. See also Emma Macleod, *British Visions of America, 1775–1820* (Pickering & Chatto, 2013), chapter 6.

37 Thomas Paine, *Rights of Man* (Harmondsworth: Penguin, 1984, first published 1791–92), part 2, 180.

38 See Arthur Sheps, "The American Revolution and the Transformation of English Radicalism," *Historical Reflections/Réflexions Historiques* 2 (1975): 3–28.

39 Joseph Gerrald, *A Convention, the Only Means of Saving Us from Ruin* (1793), 73.

40 Richard Price, "Observations on the Importance of the American Revolution" (1785), in *Political Writings*, ed. D. O. Thomas (Cambridge: CUP, 1991), 117, 151.

41 See Jon Mee, *Dangerous Enthusiasm: William Blake and the Culture of Radicalism in the 1790s* (Oxford: OUP, 1992), chapter 1.

42 For a discussion of Priestley and the French Revolution's millenarian significance, see Clarke Garrett, *Respectable Folly: Millenarians and the French Revolution in France and England* (Baltimore, MD: Johns Hopkins University Press, 1975), 126–43.

43 *Trials of Winterbotham*, 80.

44 Mark Philp, *Reforming Ideas in Britain: Politics and Language in the Shadow of the French Revolution, 1789–1815* (Cambridge: CUP, 2014), 94–95.

45 William Winterbotham, An *Historical, Geographical, Commercial, and Philosophical View of the American United States, and of the European Settlements in America and the West-Indies*, 4 vols. (1795), 1, iii–v. Subsequent references are to this edition.

46 Ibid., vii. In places, he leans heavily on the *Encyclopedia Britannica*, which extracts from many of the same sources as he does. My thanks to Danielle Beaujon for her assistance in tracking down excerpted sources in Winterbotham's work.

47 See David Armitage, "The New World and British Historical Thought: From Richard Hakluyt to William Robertson," in *America in European Consciousness, 1793–1750*, ed. Karen Ordahl Kupperman (Chapel Hill: University of North Carolina Press, 1995), 52–75. See also Fiona Robertson, "British Romantic Columbiads," *Symbiosis: A Journal of Anglo-American Literary Relations* 2 (1998): 1–23. *Critical Review*, 15, September 1795: 87, notes the eloquence of the section on "discovery," adding anyone familiar with Robertson's work will recognize the portrayal of Columbus.

48 Winterbotham, *View of the American United States*, 1: 204–06. See Durand Echeverria, *Mirage in the West: A History of the French Image of American Society* (Princeton, NJ: Princeton University Press, 1957), chapters 1–2; Pamela Regis, *Describing Early America: Bartram, Jefferson, Crèvecoeur, and the Rhetoric of Natural History* (DeKalb: Northern Illinois University Press, 1992), chapter 3.

49 Winterbotham also published Ramsey's *An Oration Delivered on the Anniversary of the American Independence, July 4, 1794 … to the Inhabitants of South Carolina* (1795).

50 *MR*, 18, December 1795: 471–72.

51 *The Trial of P. W. Duffin, and Thomas Lloyd ... For a Libel in the Fleet Prison* (1793). See Chapter 4.

52 "The Diary of Thomas Lloyd kept in Newgate prison, 1794–96," in Davis, McCalman, and Parolin, eds., *Newgate in Revolution*, 95, 108; Marion Tinling, "Thomas Lloyd's Reports of the First Federal Congress," *William and Mary Quarterly* 18 (1961): 519–45. Lloyd became known as the "father" of American shorthand reporting.

53 Ralph A. Manogue, "James Ridgway and America," *Early American Literature* 31 (1996): 264–88; Winterbotham, *View of the American United States*, 1: v.

54 Macleod, "Case of Winterbotham," 151–52; Colin Bonwick, *English Radicals and the American Revolution* (Chapel Hill: University of North Carolina Press, 1977), 221–22. It is worth noting that after 1774, English copyright restrictions were temporarily relaxed.

55 "**AMERICA**," prospectus, 4.

56 Verhoeven, *Americomania*, 209–10.

57 Report of the case in the federal circuit court of New York, April 4, 1798, in *Collections of the Massachusetts Historical Society* 5 (1798):123; Alexander Hamilton to Jedidiah Morse [4 January 1796], *The Papers of Alexander Hamilton*, vol. 20, ed. Harold C. Syrett (New York: Columbia University Press, 1974), 11–13. Jeremy Belknap put out a notice to booksellers in December 1796, cautioning them that his "literary property" had been "invaded" by the American reprinting of Winterbotham's work. Morse, who acknowledged his own free use of "the words as well as the ideas of writers" without attribution, was himself accused of plagiarism.

58 See Richard B. Sher, *The Enlightenment and the Book: Scottish Authors and Their Publishers in Eighteenth-Century Britain, Ireland, and America* (Chicago, IL: University of Chicago Press, 2006), 86–87, on print runs.

59 BL, Add. MS. 27808, fol. 113. Place was himself collecting materials for a history of America, see Add. MS. 27857–58.

60 Thomas Paine, *Letter to George Washington, on the Subject of the Late Treaty* (1797), 37.

61 Not much is known about Briellat's subsequent life in America, but see Michael Durey, *Transatlantic Radicals and the Early American Republic* (Lawrence: University of Kansas Press, 1997), 38–39.

62 *Catalogue of the Valuable Library of the late Robert Southey, Esq., LL.D, Poet Laureate ... Which Will be Sold by Auction ... by Messrs. S. Leigh Sotheby & Co.* (1848), 152.

63 For the publication history of *Wat Tyler*, see the editors' account in *SLPW*, vol. 3, *Poems from the Laureate Period, 1813–1823*, ed. Lynda Pratt et al., 441–60. See also *LCRS*, 346–51; Jean Raimond, "Southey's Early Writings and Revolution," *Yearbook of English Studies* 19 (1989): 181–95; F. T. Hoadley, "The Controversy over Southey's *Wat Tyler*," *Studies in Philology* 38 (1941): 81–96; R. A. Manogue, "Southey and Winterbotham: New Light on an Old Quarrel," *Journal of the Charles Lamb Society*, new series, 38 (1982): 105–14.

64 Southey's affidavit, C31/372 Pt.2, reprinted in Pratt et al., eds., *SLPW*, 3: 511–12; Southey to Edith Fricker, [January 12, 1795], *NLS* 1: 91.

65 Winterbotham's affidavit, C31/372 Pt. 2, reprinted in Pratt et al., eds., *SLPW*, 3: 513–15; Winterbotham, *Winterbotham Sketch*, 50–53.

66 Michael T. Davis, "'That Odious Class of Men Called Democrats': Daniel Isaac Eaton and the Romantics 1794–1795," *History* 84 (1999): 74–92, and "'Good for the Public Example': Daniel Isaac Eaton, Prosecution,

Punishment and Recognition," in *Radicalism and Revolution in Britain, 1775–1848* (Houndmills: Palgrave Macmillan, 2000), 110–32.

67 Southey to Lovell, 5–6 April 1794, in *The Collected Letters of Robert Southey*, ed. Lynda Pratt, no. 85, https://www.rc.umd.edu/editions/southey_letters. *Hogwash* was the journal's original title. The poem appeared in S. T. Coleridge, *A Moral and Political Lecture* (Bristol, 1795). Southey may have published two poems in *Politics for the People* under the initials "W. T.," which he sometimes used to identify himself as a descendant of Wat Tyler. Davis, "'That Odious Class of Men,'" 83.

68 Originally published in *Poems: Containing the Retrospect, Odes, Elegies, Sonnets, &c. By Robert Lovell and Robert Southey* (1795), 17–27.

69 George Dyer, *A Dissertation on the Theory and Practice of Benevolence* (1795), 87. For Dyer, see Nicholas Roe, *The Politics of Nature: William Wordsworth and Some Contemporaries*, 2nd ed. (Houndmills: Palgrave Macmillan, 2002), chapter 1.

70 Coleridge to Southey, 1 September 1794, in *CLC*, 1: 98. Coleridge reports that Dyer's close friend Priestley is sure to join them.

71 The scholarship is extensive, but see J. R. MacGillivray, "The Pantisocracy Scheme and Its Immediate Background," in *Studies in English* (Toronto: University of Toronto, 1931), 131–69; Sister Eugenia, "Coleridge's Scheme of Pantisocracy and American Travel Accounts," *PMLA* 45 (1930): 1069–84; W. A. Speck, *Robert Southey: Entire Man of Letters* (New Haven, CT: Yale University Press, 2006), chapter 3.

72 See Kathleen Jones, *A Passionate Sisterhood: The Sisters, Wives and Daughters of the Lake Poets* (Constable, 1998), particularly chapters 1 & 2; M. Ray Adams, *Studies in the Literary Backgrounds of English Radicalism: With Special Reference to the French Revolution* (Lancaster, PA: Franklin and Marshall College, 1947), chapter 5, on Lovell and Burnett.

73 For the work's shifting valence from its "Jacobinical" origins in 1794, see Nigel Leask, "Southey's *Madoc*: Reimagining the Conquest of America," in *Robert Southey and the Contexts of English Romanticism*, ed. Lynda Pratt (Aldershot: Ashgate, 2006), 133–50.

74 Southey to Thomas Southey, 7 September 1794, in *NLS*, 1: 74–75.

75 Joseph Cottle, *Reminiscences of Samuel Taylor Coleridge and Robert Southey*, 2nd ed. (1848), 2–4.

76 *The Friend*, no. 10, 26 October 1809, in *CWC*, vol. 4, pt. 2, *The Friend*, ed. Barbara E. Rooke (1969), 146.

77 Mrs. [Margaret] Henry Sandford, *Thomas Poole and His Friends*, 2 vols. (1888), 1: 99.

78 My argument follows that of Nigel Leask, *The Politics of Imagination in Coleridge's Critical Thought* (Houndmills: Palgrave Macmillan, 1988), particularly chapters 1–3, and "Pantisocracy and the Politics of the 'Preface' to *Lyrical Ballads*," in *Reflections of Revolution: Images of Romanticism*, ed. Alison Yarrington and Kelvin Everest (Routledge, 1993), 39–58. See also Kenneth R. Johnston, "The Political Science of Life: From American Pantisocracy to British Romanticism," in *Samuel Taylor Coleridge and the Sciences of Life*, ed. Nicholas Roe (Oxford: OUP, 2001), 47–68.

79 Southey to Grosvenor Bedford, 11 November, and Southey to Horace Bedford, 13 November 1793, in *LCRS*, 67–68.

80 Sandford, *Poole*, 1: 77–78.

81 Mark Storey, *Robert Southey: A Life* (Oxford: OUP, 1997), 59–63. Flower published the work as a one-shilling pamphlet.

82 Southey to Grosvenor Bedford, 14 December 1793, in *LCRS*, 68. For a discussion of the course of Southey's ideas on Pantisocracy, see Roe, *Politics of Nature*, chapter 2.

83 Coleridge to Southey, 18 September, 1794, in *CLC*, 1: 104. These lines were incorporated in "Monody on the Death of Chatterton," first published in 1796.
84 Coleridge to Southey, 6 July 1794, in *CLC*, 1: 84. For a suggestive discussion, see Colin Jager, "A Poetics of Dissent: Or, Pantisocracy in America," *Theory & Event* 10 (2007): 1–25.
85 Coleridge to Southey, 13 July 1794, in *CLC*, 1: 86. This points to what Coleridge found wanting in Godwin's abstract concept of benevolence.
86 Coleridge to Southey, 21 October 1794, in *CLC*, 1: 114–15.
87 Coleridge to Southey, 11 December 1794, in *CLC*: 137, declaring himself "a compleat Necessitarian – and understand the subject as well almost as Hartley himself."
88 Samuel Taylor Coleridge, "Lectures on Revealed Religion," in *CWC*, vol. 1, *Lectures 1795: On Politics and Religion*, ed. Lewis Patton and Peter Mann (1970), 119, 124–28.
89 Peter J. Kitson, "'Our Prophetic Harrington': Coleridge, Pantisocracy, and Puritan Utopia," *WC* 24 (1993): 97–102; Malcolm Chase, "From Millennium to Anniversary: The Concept of the Jubilee in Late Eighteenth- and Nineteenth-Century England," *P&P* 129 (1990): 132–47, and *The People's Farm: English Radical Agrarianism, 1775–1840* (Oxford: OUP, 1988), chapters 1–2; Greg Claeys, "Four Roads from 'Genesis': Spence, Paine and Rights to Property," in *Thomas Spence: The Poor Man's Revolutionary*, ed. Alastair Bonnett and Keith Armstrong (Breviary Stuff, 2014), 27–34.
90 Thomas Spence, "The Maritime Republic" and "A Further Account of Spensonia," *Pig's Meat*, 2 (1795): 68–72, 205–18, reprinted in H. T. Dickinson, ed., *The Political Works of Thomas Spence* (Newcastle: Avero, 1982), 25–33. For Spence's involvement with the popular societies, see Jon Mee, "Thomas Spence and the London Corresponding Society, 1792–1795," in Bonnett and Armstrong, eds., Poor *Man's Revolutionary*, 53–64.
91 Thomas Spence, *The End of Oppression* (1795), in Dickinson, ed., *Political Works of Spence*, 34–37.
92 Timothy Tackett, *The Coming of the Terror in the French Revolution* (Cambridge, MA: Harvard University Press, 2015), 246.
93 Joel Barlow, *Advice to the Privileged Orders in the Several States of Europe*, 2nd ed. (1792), 19, 30.
94 J. P. Brissot de Warville, *New Travels in the United States of America, 1788*, ed. and intro. Durand Echeverria, trans. Mara Soceanu Vamos and Echeverria (Cambridge, MA: Harvard University Press, 1964), 3–4. Barlow's edition of *New Travels in the United States of America, Performed in 1788 ... Translated from the French* (1792), constitutes about 55% of the original and suffers in translation.
95 Samuel Taylor Coleridge, *Conciones ad Populum or Addresses to the People* (1795), in Patton and Mann, eds., *CWC*, 1: 47. In her review of Brissot's *Nouveau Voyage*, Wollstonecraft praises the author's pure moral principles "and most expansive humanity," while questioning his overly sympathetic portrait of America. *AR*, 11, September 1791: 37–43.
96 For Crèvecoeur and the "agrarian myth," see Manuela Albertone, *National Identity and the Agrarian Republic: The Transatlantic Commerce of Ideas Between America and France (1750–1830)* (Farnham: Ashgate, 2014), chapter 1.
97 Coleridge to Charles Heath, 29 August 1794, in *CLC*, 1: 96–97.
98 Information about Coleridge and Southey's reading at this time can be gleaned from their correspondence, lecture manuscripts, and publications, as well as from their library borrowing, for which see George Whalley, "The Bristol Library Borrowings of Southey and Coleridge, 1793–8," *The Library* 4 (1949): 114–31.

99 Brissot, *New Travels*, 214–15.
100 Southey to Horace Bedford, 22 August 1794, in *NLS*, 1: 70–72; Sandford, *Thomas Poole*, 1: 97–98; Samuel Taylor Coleridge, "Lectures on Revealed Religion," in Patton and Mann, eds., *CWC*, 1: 223. Coleridge also draws on Smith's estimate. The vision of human fulfillment through undivided labor prefigures the famous passage from Marx and Engels's *German Ideology* (1845–46), hunting, fishing, rearing cattle, criticizing, "without ever becoming hunter, fisherman, shepherd or critic."
101 See "List of Land Purchases," in Mary Cathryne Park, "Joseph Priestley and the Problem of Pantisocracy," *Proceedings of the Delaware County Institute of Science* 11 (1947): 1–60, at 52–57. American founders are well represented, including plots named for Washington, Jefferson, Franklin, Madison, Hamilton, and Jay – Brissot represents the sole French patriot.
102 Thomas Cooper, *Some Information Respecting America* (1794), 78–79, and *Political Essays*, 2nd ed. (Philadelphia, 1800), at 83, declaring that any country where "unremitting labour is necessary to the comfortable subsistence of any class of the community ... there is despotism in it."
103 David V. Erdman, *Commerce Des Lumières: John Oswald and the British in Paris, 1790–1793* (Columbia: University of Missouri Press, 1986), 150–55; Albert Goodwin, *The Friends of Liberty: The English Democratic Movement in the Age of the French Revolution* (Cambridge, MA: Harvard University Press, 1979), 201–03; *Société des Amis de la Constitution, séante aux Jacobins à Paris. Discours MM. Cooper et Watt, députés de Société Constitutionelle de Manchester* (Paris, 1792); *Manchester Herald*, 28 April and 5 May 1792, for Cooper's account of "the first festival, truly civic, that Europe has seen."
104 *PH*, 30, col. 552, Commons, 30 April 1792.
105 Thomas Cooper, *A Reply to Mr. Burke's Invective against Mr. Cooper and Mr. Watt*, 2nd ed. (1792), 9, 21, 26–29.
106 Dumas Malone, *The Public Life of Thomas Cooper, 1783–1839* (New Haven, CT: Yale University Press, 1926), 59–79; Frida Knight, *The Strange Case of Thomas Walker: Ten Years in the Life of a Manchester Radical* (Lawrence and Wishart, 1958), chapters 11–15; Durey, *Transatlantic Radicals*, 31–36; Jenny Graham, *Revolutionary in Exile: The Emigration of Joseph Priestley to America, 1794–1804* (Philadelphia: University of Pennsylvania Press, 1995), 21–41. Walker was acquitted largely due to the perjury of the main witness.
107 Cooper, *Some Information*, 75–76. Cooper expressed his disgust for the "ferocious injustice" presently practiced, "the compleat and absolute despotism" established over "the words, actions, and writings" of French citizens.
108 Winterbotham, *View of the American United States*, 1: v.
109 Ibid., 3: 281–86.
110 Benjamin Franklin, *Information to Those Who Would Remove to America* (1794), 5, 8. The title page states, "Sold by" M. Gurney, J. Johnson, Eaton, R. H. Westley, and Ridgway, with no further publishing information. Winterbotham, *View of the American United States*, 3: 297–98, quotes this section from Franklin, more or less verbatim.
111 Verhoeven, *Americomania*, 187, and see, more generally, chapter 3 for his superb discussion of Cooper and Imlay's books. In 1793, John Stockdale, Ridgway's brother-in-law, published a free-standing edition of Filson's book.
112 The long section on Kentucky, Winterbotham, *View of the American United States*, 3: 125–91, is largely derived from Imlay. In his detailed

discussion, *Americomania*, chapter 6, Verhoeven argues that Winterbotham, perhaps inadvertently, functions like a land agent touting parcels of land – including the plans of three townships in Kentucky that were not yet built, and never did come about.

113 Gilbert Imlay, *A Topographical Description of the Western Territory of North America* (1792), iv.

114 Ibid., 40; Winterbotham, *View of the American United States*, 3: 161–62.

115 Wil Verhoeven, *Gilbert Imlay: Citizen of the World* (Pickering & Chatto, 2008), 101–03.

116 Stuart Andrews, "Fellow Pantisocrats: Brissot, Cooper and Imlay," *Symbiosis: A Journal of Anglo-American Literary Relations* 1 (1997): 35–47. Lovell borrowed Imlay's book in July 1794. Whalley, "Bristol Library Borrowings," 127.

117 *British Critic*, 5, January 1795: 27; Verhoeven, *Imlay*, chapters 1–4. When he arrived in England in 1787, Imlay left behind litigious creditors from his failed business dealings, although it is unclear if he still owned land in America in 1792.

118 Eloise Ellery, *Brissot de Warville: A Study in the History of the French Revolution* (New York: Houghton Mifflin, 1915), 85–90; Richard Buel, Jr., *Joel Barlow: American Citizen in a Revolutionary World* (Baltimore, MD: Johns Hopkins University Press, 2011), chapters 6–7.

119 *Look Before You Leap: Or, a Few Hints to Such Artizans, Mechanics, Labourers, Farmers, and Husbandmen, As Are Desirous of Emigrating to America* (1796), iv–v, xiv, 72–78, letters 7 and 8.

120 *State Trials for High Treason ... Part Third. Containing the Trial of John Thelwall* (1794), 31; John Thelwall, *The Natural and Constitutional Right of Britons to Annual Parliaments, Universal Suffrage, and the Freedom of Popular Associations* (1795), 82–83, glossing his words, and explaining by "veneration of property," he implied "looking up to *affluence* as an honourable distinction," instead of esteeming talents and virtues of mankind.

121 Verhoeven, *Imlay*, chapter 9; Andrew Cayton, *Love in the Time of Revolution: Transatlantic Literary Radicalism and Historical Change* (Chapel Hill: University of North Carolina Press, 2013), chapters 2–4; Jon Mee, "Morals, Manners, and Liberty: British Radicals and Perceptions of American in the 1790s." in Dzelzainis and Livesey, eds., *America Experiment*, 31–41, at 36–38, noting the attendant ambivalence about such views of simple living. Imlay headed to Paris just as war broke out between Britain and France, with a letter of recommendation from Cooper to Brissot.

122 Coleridge to Southey, 1 September 1794, in *CLC*, 1: 99; *LCRS*, 74.

123 Southey to Thomas Southey, 12 November 1794, in *NLS*, 1: 86.

124 TS 11/958/3503, reports of Lynam, 21 February 1793 and 12 November 1793, noting that division twelve was now meeting at Spence's Holborn shop, in Thale, 52, 92. For the Crown, see http://www.1790salehouse.com/2011/08/crownnewgatestreet.html.

125 Charles Lamb to Coleridge, 8–10 June 1796, in *The Letters of Charles and Mary Lamb*, ed. Edwin W. Marrs, Jr., 3 vols. (Ithaca, NY: Cornell University Press, 1975), 1:18, remembering "the little smoky room" where they had conversed.

126 Lovell to Holcroft, 11 December 1794, in Thomas Holcroft, *Memoirs of the Late Thomas Holcroft* (1816), 311–15. According to Coleridge, who took an instant dislike to Holcroft, Lovell had misrepresented their system, and Holcroft "*opposes* it violently." Coleridge to Southey, 17 December 1794, in *CLC*, 1: 138–39.

127 Coleridge to Southey, [9 December 1794], in *CLC*, 1:132; Southey to Thomas Southey, 3 January 1795 and Southey to Edith Fricker, [12 January 1795], expressing disappointment that Coleridge still objected to Wales, in *NLS*, 1: 90–91.

128 Southey, *LCRS*, 75–76; Storey, *Southey*, 63–66. Neither Edith nor Southey's mother were keen to leave Britain.

129 Coleridge to Southey, 21 October 1794, Coleridge to Southey, [c. 23 October 1794], and Coleridge to Southey, [3 November 1794], in *CLC*, 1: 113–14, 119–20, 121–22.

130 Coleridge to Southey, [c. 23 October, 1794], *CLC*, 1: 119; James C. McKusick, "'Wisely Forgetful': Coleridge and the Politics of Pantisocracy," in *Romanticism and Colonialism: Writing and Empire, 1780–1830*, ed. Tim Fulford and Peter J. Kitson (Cambridge: CUP, 1998), 107–28, particularly 122–28.

131 By March, Coleridge wished they "could form a Pantisocracy in England." Coleridge to Dyer, [late February 1795] and Coleridge to Dyer, 10 March 1795, in *CLC*, 1: 151, 155.

132 Winterbotham, *View of the American United States*, 1: 230–35, quotations at 232, 235, 224–26, for specific reservations about the federal constitution; Macleod, "Case of Winterbotham," 153–55; Paine, *Rights of Man*, part 2, chapter 4, "Of Constitutions." Significantly, Paine focuses on Pennsylvania's constitution.

133 Seth Cotlar, "Languages of Democracy in America from the Revolution to the Election of 1800," in *Re-Imagining Democracy in the Age of Revolutions: America, France, Britain, Ireland 1750–1850*, ed. Joanna Innes and Mark Philp (Cambridge: CUP, 2013), 101–13; Mark Philp, "Talking about Democracy: Britain in the 1790s," in Innes and Philp, eds., *Re-Imagining Democracy*, 3–27; Armin Mattes, "Paine, Jefferson, and the Modern Ideas of Democracy and the Nation," in *Paine and Jefferson in the Age of Revolutions*, ed. Simon P. Newman and Peter S. Onuf (Charlottesville: University of Virginia Press, 2013), 95–117.

134 Seth Cotlar, *Tom Paine's America: The Rise and Fall of Transatlantic Radicalism in the Early Republic* (Charlottesville: University of Virginia Press, 2011), chapter 5; Richard J. Twomey, "Jacobins and Jeffersonians: Anglo-American Radical Ideology, 1790–1810," in *The Origins of Anglo-American Radicalism*, ed. Margaret Jacob and James Jacob (Allen & Unwin, 1984), 284–99.

135 Joanne B. Freeman, "Explaining the Unexplainable: The Cultural Context of the Sedition Act," in *The Democratic Experiment: New Directions in American Political History*, ed. Meg Jacobs, William J. Novak, and Julian Zelizer (Princeton, NJ: Princeton University Press, 2003), 30–49; Malone, *Life of Thomas Cooper*, chapter 4.

136 See T. H. Breen, "'Baubles of Britain': The American and Consumer Revolutions of the Eighteenth Century," *P&P* 119 (1988): 73–104, and *The Marketplace of Revolution: How Consumer Politics Shaped American Independence* (Oxford: OUP, 2004).

137 Gareth Stedman Jones, *An End to Poverty? A Historical Debate* (Profile Books, 2004). Compare Emma Rothschild, *Economic Sentiments: Adam Smith, Condorcet, and the Enlightenment* (Cambridge, MA: Harvard University Press, 2001), 48–49, and chapter 2.

138 *Tribune*, 1, no. 1 (1795): 13. For Thelwall's views on commerce, see Gregory Claeys, ed., *The Politics of English Jacobinism: Writings of John Thelwall* (University Park: Pennsylvania State University Press, 1995), xl–lv;

Iain Hampsher-Monk, "John Thewall and the Eighteenth-Century Radical Response to Political Economy," *HJ* 34 (1991): 1–20; Robert Lamb, "Labour, Contingency, Utility: Thelwall's Theory of Property," in Poole, ed., *Thelwall*, 51–60. For Paine views, see Gregory Claeys, *Thomas Paine: Social and Political Thought* (Boston, MA: Unwin Hyman, 1989), particularly 96–101, 198–203.

139 Thanks to Sandra den Otter for permission to borrow her phrase "pragmatic utopianism" from her unpublished paper delivered at a roundtable on the works of Gareth Stedman Jones, North American Conference on British Studies, Dallas, November 2017. Adam Smith believed that the unlimited availability of uncultivated land, combined with the lack of a feudal past, made America the model of natural progress. Donald Winch, *Riches and Poverty: An Intellectual History of Political Economy in Britain, 1750–1834* (Cambridge: CUP, 1996), 149–56.

140 Winterbotham, *View of the American United States*, 1: 283–93.

141 Ibid., 1: 293–363. Winterbotham probably picked up on a note to Hamilton's report in Stockdale's new edition of Morse's book. Jedidiah Morse, *The American Geography: Or a View of the Present Situation of the United States of America* (1794), 211.

142 Winterbotham, *View of the American United States*, 1: 303–07.

143 Joyce Appleby, *Capitalism and a New Social Order: The Republican Vision of the 1790s* (New York: Columbia University Press, 1984), and *Liberalism and Republicanism in the Historical Imagination* (Cambridge, MA: Harvard University Press, 1993), chapter 10.

144 Cooper, *Some Information*, 73.

145 See Peter S. Onuf, *Jefferson's Empire: The Language of American Nationhood* (Charlottesville: University of Virginia Press, 2000).

146 Cooper, *Some Information*, 79. Elsewhere, in a passage not included by Winterbotham, Cooper warns that few parts of Kentucky are "perfectly safe from the incursions of Indians." *Some Information*, 24.

147 *Politics for the People*, 2, no. 2 (1794): 24–28, 25.

148 Winterbotham, *View of the American United States*, 1: 88–124, section on "Aborigenes." For Enlightenment debate, see P. J. Marshall and Glyndwr Williams, *The Great Map of Mankind: Perceptions of New Worlds in the Age of the Enlightenment* (Cambridge, MA: Harvard University Press, 1982), chapter 7; Troy O. Bickham, *Savages within the Empire: Representations of American Indians in Eighteenth-Century Britain* (Oxford: OUP, 2005), chapter 5.

149 Tim Fulfold, *Romantic Indians: Native Americans, British Literature, and Transatlantic Culture, 1756–1830* (Oxford: OUP, 2006), chapters 2–3; Fred Anderson, *Crucible of War: The Seven Years' War and the Fate of Empire in British North America, 1754–1766* (New York: Vintage, 2000), 102–04.

150 Winterbotham, *View of the American United States*, 3: 295.

151 Patrick Griffin, *American Leviathan: Empire, Nation, and Revolutionary Frontier* (New York: Hill and Wang, 2007).

152 Winterbotham, *View of the American United States*, 4: 321–26, quotation at 326. For British abolitionist attitudes to the Haitian Revolution, see David Geggus, "British Opinion and the Emergence of Haiti, 1791–1805," in *Slavery and British Society, 1776–1846*, ed. James Walvin (Baton Rouge: Louisiana State University Press, 1982), 23–49.

153 Samuel Taylor Coleridge, "Lecture on the Slave Trade," in Patton and Mann, eds, *CWC*, 1: 248, 240.

154 Robert Southey, *Poems* (Bristol, 1797), Sonnet 1, 32 and Sonnet 5, 37. See also Carol Bolton, *Writing the Empire: Robert Southey and Romantic Colonialism* (Pickering & Chatto, 2007), 23–42; Peter J. Kitson, "Fictions of Slave Resistance and Revolt: Robert Southey's *Poems on the Slave Trade* (1797) and Charlotte Smith's 'The Story of Henrietta' (1800)," in *Race, Romanticism, and the Atlantic*, ed. Paul Youngquist (Farnham: Ashgate, 2013), 107–23, particularly 108–19.

155 Thomas Cooper, *Letters on the Slave Trade* (Manchester, 1787), 4, and *Considerations on the Slave Trade; and the Consumption of West Indian Produce* (1791), 16. In 1819, Cooper moved to South Carolina, where he became president of South Carolina College; here he became a defender of southern slavery, while remaining a critic of the labor regime of northern factories.

156 Appleby, *Capitalism*, 102.

157 Brissot, *New Travels*, 224–25.

158 Jonathan Israel, *The Expanding Blaze: How the American Revolution Ignited the World, 1775–1848* (Princeton, NJ: Princeton University Press, 2017), chapter 6, stressing the gradual and limited progress towards full emancipation.

159 Winterbotham, *View of the American United States*, 3: 306, 310; 1: 206–08.

160 For his handling the question of slavery, see Imlay, *Topographical Description*, 185–202.

161 William Wordsworth, *The Prelude: The Four Texts (1798, 1799, 1805, 1850)*, ed. Jonathan Wordsworth (Penguin, 1999), 442.

162 Storey, *Southey*, 80–85; Bolton, *Writing the Empire*, 76–80.

163 Sandford, *Thomas Poole*, 2: 40.

164 Priestley to Dyer, 4 October 1794, in *Theological and Miscellaneous Writings of Joseph Priestley, LLD, FRS, etc.*, ed. J. T. Rutt, 25 vols. (1817–31), 1, pt. 2: 356.

165 Richard Holmes, *Coleridge: Early Visions, 1772–1804* (New York: Pantheon, 1989), 116.

166 Lindsey to John Rowe, 10 June and 23 December 1796, in *The Letters of Theophilus Lindsey (1723–1808)*, ed. G. M. Ditchfield, 2 vols. (Woodbridge: Boydell Press, 2012), 2: 389, 414–15. Winterbotham named one of his four children Lindsey.

167 Priestley to Lindsey, 1 August 1796, in Rutt, ed., *Writings of Joseph Priestley*, 1, pt. 2: 350.

168 Winterbotham, *Sketch*, 42–45.

169 Robert Southey, *Wat Tyler. A Dramatic Poem*, in Pratt et al., eds., *SLPW*, 3: 503.

Part 2

Aftermaths and Recurrence

6 1817
Return of the Suppressed

Trajectories of Recurrence

> It is a matter of history, that whilst the laurels were yet cool in the brows of our victorious soldiers... the elements of convulsion were at work amongst the masses of our labouring population; and that a series of disturbances commenced with the introduction of the Corn Bill in 1815, and continued, with short intervals, until the close of the year 1816.

This is how Samuel Bamford, the weaver-poet of Middleton, opens the second chapter of *Passages in the Life of a Radical* (1844). More than two decades of war ended with the demobilization of thousands of soldiers and sailors returning to find unemployment in their villages and towns. The summer rains of 1816 delivered the century's worst harvest. The political mobilization of 1816, the national petition campaign orchestrated by the veteran Major John Cartwright and the recently established Hampden clubs harnessed the demand for the relief of economic distress to the political demand for popular representation. William Cobbett launched a mass-circulation edition of his *Political Register*, the "two-penny trash," that spread radicalism's message widely throughout the country. At the end of 1816, "Orator" Henry Hunt took the same message to the mass platform at meetings in London's Spa Fields. From this point, according to Bamford, working people "became deliberate and systematic in their proceedings."[1]

Popular radicalism returned after the war with increased strength, more clearly working-class in its social composition, its center of gravity shifting from London to the manufacturing districts of the North and Midlands. As E. P. Thompson points out, the democratic movement was not extinguished with the breaking up of the corresponding societies at the end of the 1790s but lost coherence, as the twin forces of government repression and patriotism fueled by national defense militated against manifestations of Jacobinism or Paineite expression. "Radicalism" superseded "Jacobinism" as a broader movement less precise in its ideological underpinnings.[2] It must again be stressed that the political demands and formal public statements of the popular societies of the 1790s were made almost exclusively in constitutionalist language and their commitments were largely to peaceful agitation and open organization. Moreover, despite the pronouncements of government reports and crown prosecutors, such language and commitments were not simply signs of dissimulation, attempts to disguise the real motivations of British Jacobinism aiming at French-style revolution. However, as the first part of this study argues, there was a complex interplay between appeals to popular constitutionalism as the basis for reform and Paineite republicanism, inspired in part by the example of the French and American Revolutions.

Postwar radicalism was, as Thompson perceived, less "Jacobin" in its commitments and expressive modes; the movement emerged more strongly tied to the language and agitational repertoire of popular constitutionalism.[3] The French Revolution had lost much of its appeal as a reliable point of democratic reference. Yet, as a tainted label, "Jacobin" resisted its own demise. Not only did old "Jacks" provide a source of continuity with the republican movement, the London Spenceans, self-proclaimed followers of the agrarian socialist Thomas Spence, who had died in 1814, included a small party of revolutionaries for whom the ancient constitution held no charm. In the industrial districts, working-class radicals tested the boundaries of constitutionalist mobilization, moving to the brink of insurrectionary confrontation. Significantly, 1817 saw the return of Paine's works into print, replenishing the supply of editions still in circulation. In London, a few veterans of the 1790s, such as John Gales Jones, had struggled to keep alive the ideas of Paine.[4] However in early 1817, the popular radical press, largely silenced during the wars, flourished as William Hone, T. J. Wooler, and W. T. Sherwin brought out new weekly journals, stepping in to fill the gap left when Cobbett fled to America following the suspension of habeas corpus.[5] After the first five issues, Sherwin changed the title of his journal from the *Republican* to *Sherwin's Weekly Political Register*. Persuaded that such a change would bring a wider readership, he explained, "there are many, who agree with the principle, but who actually are afraid of the paper, bearing such a name, being found in their possession."[6] Sherwin's title changed, but the journal's republican politics remained constant. In June, juries acquitted Wooler's *Black Dwarf* of seditious libel, and at the end of the year, London juries confirmed their support for liberty of the press, acquitting Hone in three trials brought for seditious and blasphemous libel. As Sherwin's partner Richard Carlile reflected, "In this year [1817] in London, the Press was free. The Political works of Thomas Paine, were publicly published and unopposed by the Government, though they had previously so often been prosecuted."[7]

This chapter considers the ways in which the politics of the 1790s returned in the year 1817, as a displaced term of reference. On the one

hand, suppressed Jacobin modes recurred in altered circumstances opening possibilities for ultra-radicals. On the other hand, the government
was able to exploit the threat of Jacobinism's return to justify enact-
ing measures to curtail popular political mobilization. The chapter is
organized around four moments or themes. The first section concerns
the early months of 1817 as the reform movement's mass petitioning
campaign reached its climax with the meeting of Hampden and Union
society delegates in London and the opening of parliament. The attack
on the prince regent's coach returning from the opening of parliament
provided the occasion for alarm, just as the attack on the royal coach in
October 1795 had prompted Pitt's government to quickly bring in the
Two Acts. Ministers schooled under Pitt reintroduced in peacetime earlier measures of repression. The government of Lord Liverpool and the
ministerial press stressed the parallels between postwar radicalism and
the 1790s, casting Jacobinism as a recurrent danger that required vigilance and firm handling. As in the 1790s, reciprocity existed between
the efforts of authorities to identify the revolutionary motives of radical
reform and the corresponding actions popular radicals adopted in pursuit of democratic change.

In 1817, it was not only Paine's writings that reappeared, as the poet
laureate's long-lost verse drama *Wat Tyler* mysteriously found its way
into print. The second section explores the return of Robert Southey's
work, a skewed (in part comical) recurrence of Jacobinism. Southey and
Coleridge had long since repudiated their youthful republicanism, having joined Wordsworth in support of the campaign against subversion.[8]
However, the publication of *Wat Tyler* occasioned a public reckoning
with the romantic poets' youthful dreams and disappointments, and
their repudiation of Jacobin pasts. In turn, radicals appropriated Southey's work and claimed the history of the Peasants' Revolt for their own.

From the controversy over Southey's drama, the chapter moves to
plans to march thousands of Lancashire weavers with blankets strapped
to their backs to London in order to present petitions to the prince regent. The Blanketeers' march would seem to be an instance of life following art, a re-staging of Tyler's march on London to demand bread
and freedom cast in terms of the anachronistic myth of king and people.
Local authorities assisted by the military had little trouble dispersing
the march and arresting hundreds of would-be petitioners. Yet the idea
of marching on London to overthrow the government took hold among
hard-core militants, culminating in the ill-fated Pentrich rising of June.
On 7 November, Jeremiah Brandreth, William Turner, and Isaac Ludlam were executed as traitors. The day before the executions at Derby,
Princess Charlotte had died in delivering a stillborn son. The deaths of
the Pentrich rebels and Princess Charlotte prompted widespread commentary, including P. B. Shelley's *Address to the People on the Death
of Princess Charlotte*, about meanings associated with royalty and high

treason, rituals of mourning for the young princess and the rituals of the scaffold, the plight of ordinary working people and fate of British constitutional liberty. The final section considers the conjunction of the royal death and the execution of traitors, reading Shelley's lament in the context of the reactions of popular radicals.

Pop-Gun, Again

The Manchester Political Register, another newly launched radical journal, gave a summary of the prince regent's speech in the House of Lords to open parliament, and featured a short notice of the attack on the royal carriage, reporting two bullets "are also said to have shot through the glass... We should not be surprised if some wicked Jacobin insinuated that it is all a pop gun plot."[9] The original "Pop-Gun Plot" was allegedly hatched in autumn of 1794, a plan linked to various LCS members to assassinate the king by shooting a poisoned arrow through an air gun, and for which Robert Crossfield (who later became president of the LCS) was tried and acquitted on treason charges.[10] The *Manchester Political Register* followed the notice of the attack with brief accounts of the daily sessions of the "Deputy Meeting" held between 22 and 27 January at London's Crown and Anchor tavern in the Strand and the King's Arms in Palace Yard. Significantly, the journal did not refer to the meeting as a "convention" or the deputies as "delegates," mindful of the law and the sedition trials that followed the "British Convention of Delegates" of 1793.[11] The meeting brought together 70 Hampden Club and Union Society deputies representing over 150 communities, and bearing petitions signed by half a million people. At the first session, resolutions in favor of universal male suffrage and annual parliaments were carried over a resolution introduced by Cobbett limiting the suffrage to householders.[12] Sir Francis Burdett, who did not attend the meeting and who favored the more limited suffrage proposal, subsequently agreed to move a reform bill. On having adjourned their proceedings in London, Hampden delegates and their communities waited with a sense of anticipation to see how parliament would deal with the demand for reform. Coinciding with the state opening of parliament on January 28, a large reform meeting assembled at Palace Yard, from which Hunt and around twenty Hampden delegates carried rolled parchment petitions to the nearby house of the radical MP Lord Thomas Cochrane, who agreed to present their petitions. A counter-procession to that of royalty proceeded from Palace Yard to Westminster, with Cochrane carried aloft in an armchair, bearing Hunt's Bristol petition and a bundle of sticks symbolizing the united people, a stick for each county, as well as appropriating the republican image of Roman fasces denoting magisterial authority.[13] Throughout the opening weeks of the new session, hundreds of petitions flooded parliament.

The next two months witnessed a highly compressed chronology of events, culminating with the implementation of government repression in the face of large-scale radical mobilization around which a drama of recurrence unfolded, starting with the air gun and the threat to the regent's life. On his way to the Lords to deliver his opening address, the state carriage drawn by eight cream-colored horses ornamented with light blue ribbons, passed along a route heavily lined with spectators who greeted the regent with a mixture of applause and disapprobation. On the return of the regent's entourage, the crowd, which had grown in size, greeted the procession with sustained taunts, hisses, and groans, along with shouts of "pull him out, pull him out," "there goes the old [bugger]," "seize him, seize him"; insults were directed at the Horse Guards with shouts of "Piccadilly butchers! Knock them down!"[14] To cries of "throw, throw," mud, gravel, and stones were hurled at the regent's carriage. Threatening action increased on the entrance to the Mall, and as the procession moved through Spring Garden toward Carlton house, a projectile passed through the window of the royal carriage, which perhaps had already been partially shattered by one or more stones. With their swords drawn, the Life Guards dispersed the crowd without major incident. Lord Sidmouth, the home secretary, announced news of the attack to the Lords, at which point discussion of the prince regent's address was adjourned. Lord James Murray, lord-in-waiting, who was riding with the regent, returned to give parliament an eye-witness account, stating he was in no doubt that two bullets, along with a volley of stones, broke the carriage window. On questioning, Lord Murray surmised that since there was no smoke, rather than pistol shots the bullets were probably shot from an air gun or pistol, perhaps from the trees.[15]

No bullets were found. But the unfortunate Thomas Scott was seized by an off-duty officer who saw him throw gravel and hit one of the Life Guards with an umbrella. On being examined at Bow Street, Scott admitted only that he had shouted "shame, shame" at a horse soldier who was striking a woman. Reported to be respectably dressed, Scott did not fit the role of a would-be regicide. The government was unable to link him to the radical societies, although they obtained information that Scott had once apprenticed for the same Soho jeweler as the pop-gun conspirator, Paul Lemaitre (a watch-case maker and LCS leader). Under examination for high treason, the presiding magistrates could find no clear proof that Scott threw a stone at the carriage or that he was in the vanguard of the attack. Scott was eventually admitted to bail to face misdemeanor charges.[16] The idea that someone had shot at the royal person with an air gun lost credibility. The government would have to wait to bring true insurgents to trial on charges of high treason.

In its detailed report of the attack, the *Courier*, the chief treasury journal, commented that it was "impossible not to recollect" what had happened on 29 October 1795, when George III's coach was mobbed on his way to the opening of parliament. The paper predicted that few readers would "not be struck by the coincidence," particularly after reading the account of the earlier attack from the *Annual Register* for 1796, which the paper conveniently reprinted. *The Times* reprinted the same description, under the headline "THE TRAITOROUS ATTEMPT IN 1795."[17] 1795 offered the template for 1817; once again, the attack on the royal person provided the ministers with the pretext for repression. In his opening address to parliament, the regent had anticipated the need for implementing measures to counteract "the most dangerous innovations" intended to undermine the people's confidence in the wisdom of parliament and "to shake the security of the constitution." On 3 February, the regent gave orders for papers to be laid before parliament pertaining to the practices of meetings and associations in London and other parts of the country.[18] In coordination with government moves to quell sedition, the ministerial press advocated the need to reintroduce earlier measures to maintain order and protect the royal person. The *Courier* reviewed the two key, earlier moments of alarm. In contrast to the situation in May 1794, when Pitt introduced the suspension of habeas corpus to foil plans for a second British Convention, now "the system of appointing Delegates to a Convention has been acted upon." As for the second point of alarm, the *Courier* quoted from the government proclamation of 4 November 1795, linking the LCS's Copenhagen Fields meeting to acts endangering the king. According to the *Courier,* "every word" of the proclamation, which had led directly to Lord Grenville's introduction of the Treasonable Practices Bill and Pitt's introduction of the Seditious Meetings Bill, "might be applied to the present period."[19] In his *Reformists' Register*, Hone contested the *Courier's* characterization of the Hampden delegates, as well as rejecting the general comparison of the present-day reform movement to the Jacobins of 1794–95. "Where is the analogy between the present circumstances and those of 1795," asked Hone, "except, indeed in the throwing of stones at the royal carriage... He would be a bold man who should say, that no person was HIRED to throw the stone, for the purpose of giving effect to *certain measures*."[20] Once again, the government involved itself in a regicidal fantasy of its own contrivance.

The attack became a joke. More or less immediately, Hone published his parody, *The Bullet Te Deum; with the Canticle of the Stone,* mocking the government and its hireling press: "We praise thee O Stone: we acknowledge thee to be a Bullet.... The Savior of an expiring Ministry." The prayer concludes,

> Vouchsafe, O Bullet: to keep us this year without Reform.
> O Bullet, have mercy upon us: have mercy upon us.
> O Bullet, keep Reform afar from us; as our trust is in thee.
> O Bullet, in thee have we trusted: let the Reformists for ever be confounded.

Quickly pirated by a host of radical pressmen, *Te Deum* was the fourth in a series of five parodies, based on the liturgical forms from the *Book of Common Prayer*, three of which were prosecuted in the trials of December from which Hone emerged victorious.[21]

From bullets and stones, Wooler took up the joke of the potatoes. John Wells, a yeoman of the guards, who was examined at Bow Street, could not identify Scott but did reveal that potatoes as well as stones had been thrown. Hicks, one of the two examining magistrates, took this as a serious threat: "The potatoes speak for themselves; they must have been brought for the purpose of being thrown at the carriage, and prove a predetermination to the commission of treasonable acts."[22] In the *Black Dwarf*, Wooler pursued the matter, reporting the full proceedings, "High Treason: Examination of the Treasonable Potatoes." The potatoes were quite unable to explain what they were doing "outside the kitchen or the market place."

> When questioned, the poor potatoes *said nothing*. They had not even an excuse to offer... The worthy Magistrate then proceeded to substantiate the charge. — '*The Potatoes*,' my lords and gentlemen, '*speak for themselves!*' I do not mean that they express themselves in the common form of language. But there is my lords and gentleman, as *we* all *know*, *a dumb sort of eloquence* that speaks louder than words, and silences the most noisy advocates... Their language is a silent confession of their evil intentions, which as I said before is palpable from the very presence of the potatoes at such a place.[23]

As Marcus Wood comments, Wooler's spoof was "everything that the state hoped radical satire could not be – bold, sophisticated, jubilant... able to attack state appropriation of the law through parody of legal language." Wood shows, moreover, that the array of publications that Daniel Isaac Eaton and Spence put out in the 1790s provided a set of models for the later period of radicalism.[24] The week before the first Spa Fields meeting in November 1816, the *Courier* complained that cheap tracts were being widely circulated in the same mode and to the same end as twenty years ago when a bookseller in Newgate street published small tracts of sedition under the title "Pig's Meat for the Swinish Multitude," ominously warning, "cheap tracts are the *instruments* to be used *at present* for the overthrow of the Government."[25]

The "dumb eloquence" of the potatoes, the language that confessed evil intent, was given full expression in the mass of petitions laid before parliament. The Hampden petitioners appealed on the basis of Cartwright's researches to the "true principles of the English constitution" and an inclusive notion of "the people."[26] At issue was the meaning of the constitution. The majority of members of parliament were not persuaded by the constitutional language and modes of radical reformers.

The constitutional right to petition for the redress of grievances was sacred, but the language of address was called into question. On the day after the attack on the regent, Cochrane followed his presentation of Hunt's Bristol petition bearing nearly 16,000 signatures, by reading a petition from Quick in the parish of Saddleworth, Yorkshire, which asserted that "taxation without representation is slavery"; pointing to the excessive taxation caused by the late war and "the harvest of those who live by corruption… in whose mad and wicked counsels it had its origins"; attacking parliament for having usurped the people's right to representation and produced conditions that could no longer be endured "without being unceasingly resisted by all possible means warranted by the constitution;" and demanding representation "co-extensive with taxation," equal distribution of seats, and annual parliaments. Such language was deemed by its members as insulting to the dignity of the Commons, denying the body's legitimacy and authority to legislate. According to George Canning, for the petitioners "to assert, that the constitution had been subverted, this was no longer the language of petition; it was a direct incitement to rebellion." In response to the refusal to receive the petition, Cochrane complained that given the abuses that had crept into the constitution it was not appropriate to "cavil about the mere form or construction of words, but to receive the petitions of the people"; he feared the consequence of insulting the people. Later in February, Henry Brougham maintained that the people were "deluded" about the ancient constitution; they were being told falsehoods, fed nonsense about having had a "free and perfect" constitution 1200 years ago, a constitution about which almost nothing was known.[27] The language and constitutional reasoning of radicals were subject to dismissal. On 3 March, Burdett presented over 500 petitions signed by nearly one million people, the vast majority of which were deemed unacceptable, either because they were printed or because they were identical to petitions deemed to be insulting. Only thirteen petitions were found unexceptionable.[28]

On 19 February, the reading of the reports of the committee of secrecy coincided with the first reading of the bill to suspend habeas corpus presented by Sidmouth, soon followed by Lord Castlereagh's reintroduction of the Seditious Meetings Prevention Act. The provisions of the 1795 Treasonable Practices Act were extended to protect the prince regent and the 1797 Incitement to Mutiny Act against the seduction of soldiers from their duty was made permanent. The full apparatus of repression was completed with Sidmouth's "Circular Letter" of 27 March drawing magistrates' attention to their power to arrest persons suspected of disseminating seditious or blasphemous libels. In debates over the suspension of habeas corpus, passed on 3 March, and the Seditious Meetings Act (with clauses added, including one outlawing the Spencean societies), finally renewed on 29 March, lines were drawn as to whether the present crisis constituted a repetition of the Jacobin alarm of 1794–95.

The reformers Burdett, Cochrane, and Sir Samuel Romilly, joined by various liberal Whigs such as Brougham and Henry Grey Bennet, and reinforced in the Lords by Whig stalwarts such as Lord Holland and Earl Grey, rejected such comparisons. For the government, Sidmouth and Castlereagh pressed the issue. Castlereagh acknowledged that unlike the earlier period the treasonable disposition of the nation was now largely restricted to the lower orders, the revolutionary spirit "gradually descending from those higher and better informed, in which it formerly betrayed itself, to those lower in which it was now principally to be found" – which was not to deny that some men of talent and "station" were not aiding and abetting plebeian conspirators. Speaking in the Lords, Sidmouth stressed that the emergency measures of 1795 and 1799 had the salutary effect of shutting down the activities of the LCS and Societies for Constitution Information. Liverpool noted that there "was a double engine at work," one aimed to overthrow the constitution and the other "calculated to produce a complete convulsion in the elements which composed the system of social life." The danger in 1794 was great, but the present situation featured more desperate and malignant characters, conspirators who had learned the lesson of the earlier period and proceeded with greater caution and secrecy.[29] In countering Lord Thomas Erskine's objections to the Seditious Meetings Act, the Marquis of Buckingham put it quite explicitly,

> when he saw the same combinations as in 1794 – when he saw the same means wielded by the same hands, when he saw the same instruments at work – when he saw the same principles promulgated, the same doctrines advocated with undiminished energy – when he saw the same system of conduct begun, the same rallying signs used, the same banners of rebellion displayed... when he saw religion as openly scoffed at as it was in 1794... he could not disguise from himself that the evil was the same then as now.[30]

Liverpool's allusion to the "double engine" of sedition was the key note struck, as the designs of a small group of Spencean revolutionaries in London were conflated with the large national petitioning campaign for economic relief and the recovery of constitutional rights. The government's rhetorical strategy was to place the Spenceans at the center of a conspiratorial network, aiming at a republican revolution and the abolition of private property. The narrative had been tried before to good effect. In 1817, the Spa Fields meetings stood in for the meetings of 1795 at Copenhagen Fields and Jew's Harp, the last times that London radicals had held mass outdoor demonstrations. Hunt stepped into the role of John Thelwall, portrayed as the Jacobin demagogue making a vulgar appeal to an unruly populace.[31] The difference was that the Spenceans conspired to hijack the meeting in order to stage a *coup d'état* hoping that violent action would spark a spontaneous rising among workers and soldiers.[32] The badly planned events emanating from the second Spa Fields meeting of 2 December 1816 brought the Jacobin conspiracy into the light of day. Even before this, the ministers were looking for an opportunity to suppress the activities of popular radicalism. The government-sponsored press prepared the way, collapsing the distinction between reform and revolution: "As the word 'Equality' was the howl of the Demagogues of France, so is 'Reform' the popular catchword of our Modern Patriots."[33] The committee of secrecy provided the government's narrative, revealing revolutionary plans to overthrow the government and the established constitution – unlike the reports of 1794, however, those of 1817 did not include the underlying documentation contained in the infamous "green bags," so as to protect their sources, most notably John Castle and a host of government informers.[34] The reports traced a general conspiracy dating from the insurrectionary riots of 2 December through to the Hampden "convention" and other delegate bodies, extending to the industrial districts of England and Scotland.

As heirs to Spence and his utopian scheme of parish-based land redistribution, the Society of Spencean Philanthropists operated within London's tavern culture, organizing around convivial "free and easies," meeting for informal debate and scurrilous sing-songs. Thomas Evans (secretary of the LCS in 1797–98) and his son represented themselves as true custodians of Spencean doctrine and were interested primarily in educational propaganda. The "revolutionary party," headed by the gentlemanly Arthur Thistlewood, "Dr." James Watson Sr., James Watson Jr., and the shoemaker Thomas Preston, were more directly the successors of the extreme Jacobins and underground tradition represented by Colonel Edward Marcus Despard.[35] The Spa Fields meeting was called by a nominal committee headed by John Dyall (a Spitalfields weaver who had been an active LCS member), as chairman, and Preston, as secretary. Having recruited Hunt as the main speaker at the first meeting of 15 November, the orator disappointed Spencean plans to use the meeting as a springboard for insurrection. Although Hunt managed to control the meeting, which passed a series of resolutions and a properly worded memorial addressed to the regent, young Watson succeeded in moving an amendment for the meeting to reconvene on 2 December to receive the regent's response to their request for relief.[36] Before Hunt's arrival at the second meeting, the Spenceans set up a cart at Pie-House corner, from which the two Watsons harangued crowds returning from the execution of four criminals at Old Bailey. At the climax of his address, young Watson asked the crowd if they would follow him, and seizing the larger of two tricolor flags, he jumped among the throng. Several hundred followed Watson, his father, and the shoemaker John Hooper through the streets of Smithfield, where Watson accidently shot a customer in the groin while raiding a gunsmith's shop. Small crowds rampaged through the Minories breaking into gun shops and seizing weapons. "Head General" Thistlewood was left stranded at the Tower, where the soldiers declined to join the revolution. No doubt the taking of the Tower was intended as the equivalent to the storming of the Bastille. One of the flags displayed at Spa Fields proclaimed, "The Brave Soldiers are our Brothers; Treat them Kindly."[37] A substantial number of soldiers and sailors were at Spa Fields, but the expectation that the army was on the verge of mutiny was ill-founded. It took the authorities until nightfall to restore order in all parts of the city.[38]

The meeting itself was large and peaceful; around twenty to thirty thousand people assembled at Spa Fields where stalls were set up to sell fruit and gingerbread. The reports of the committee of secrecy focused not on the good order or formalities of the meeting but on the preparations for insurrection and the symbolism of the occasion: "the intended Insurrection assumed the symbols of the French Revolution; a Committee of public Safety was agreed upon... A tricolor Flag and Cockades were actually prepared." "The three-coloured flag of Rebellion was openly spread in the streets of London," crowed the *Anti-Cobbett, or Patriotic Register*, "the same flag that carried bloodshed and devastation, for so many years, throughout France".[39] At the elder Watson's trial for high treason, at issue was whether the large flag bearing the Spencean inscription (Figure 6.1) was actually "the" tricolor, the symbol of the French Revolution.[40]

In fact the flag, which had been made by Thistlewood's wife, Susan, was what Thistlewood described as "the real tri-colored Green, Red and White," representing the republican union of Ireland, Scotland, and England. There was a strong Irish dimension to the attempted rising, including the presence of the United Irish envoy William McCabe, who had slipped over from Paris. The leaders wore cockades in their hats and distributed tricolor ribbons. The production of flags and cockades was taken most seriously, viewed as emblems of republican allegiance possessing a talismanic capacity of "arousing" the crowd.[41] It was reported that the hoisting of the cap of liberty at the first Spa Fields meeting had been hailed with shouts and "rapturous applause."[42] The committee of secrecy also drew attention to Spencean songs "of a seditious and treasonable nature." Republican favorites, such as "Ça Ira," were sung, along with the comically regicidal "Pig of Pall Mall," which the Spencean songster Thomas Porter, a stone-cutter by trade, directed at the

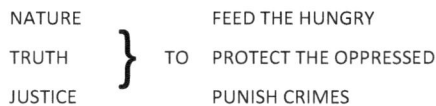

Figure 6.1 Inscription on Spencean flag carried at Spa Fields Meeting, 2 December 1816.

corpulent prince regent. "This Pig so sweet, so full of Meat, / He's one I wish to kill. / I'll fowls resign on thee to dine, / Sweet Pig of fine Pall Mall."[43]

The regent was a target of popular ridicule and hatred. Having been denied an audience with the regent to present their memorial, on 2 December Hunt derided the regent's response to their request for relief, a donation of £4,000 to the Spitalfields Soup Committee drawn not from his own purse but from the Droits of Admiralty intended for demobilized seamen as their right to prize money. Earlier in the day, Dr. Watson asked the crowd whether they would suffer themselves "to be treated with contempt":

> Are we to go on from time to time, from month to month, from year to year, crying to the Father of the People, as he is called, in vain for redress? [*No, No!*]... What! Will men with the minds and hearts of Englishmen continue... to be starved. [*No, No!*] How then are we to be restored our rights? Not by petitions, for our petitions are not heard. [*Bravo!*]... Have we not been in a state of bondage longer than the Israelites: they were in bondage but four hundred years, but we have been longer. Ever since the Norman Conquest, Kings have been admitted by you to do as they like... but this must last no longer! [*Cries, of "No, No!" and loud shouts*]

His son likewise condemned the indifference shown by the so-called Father of the People. "Yet there is no *luxury* that he spares himself"; he donates funds "which do not touch his own pocket. He robs you of millions, and then gives you part of the spoil. [*Applause!*]"[44]

The attack on the regent's carriage was to demonstrate that the royal person stood in danger of physical as well as verbal attack. For the government, Spa Fields was the prelude to the attempt to assassinate the regent. The legal case for high treason was predicated on a desire to either kill or to depose the king and to bring down his government. The reports of the committee of secrecy previewed the mass of evidence brought forward at the elder Watson's trial in King's Bench, opening on 9 June, the same date as the Pentrich rising. Again, credence was given to fanciful plans to attack army barracks at night and seize artillery, fire bridges, and take the Bank and Tower. Much was made of the purchase of 250 pike heads, as well as Watson's purported invention of an anti-cavalry device with four wheels and many knives or scythes; the display of symbols of the French Revolution; plans to appoint a committee of safety; and the speeches of Watson and his son aimed at the regent. Watson was charged with four counts, two under the act of Edward III and two under the Treasonable Practices Act. As at the treason trials of 1794, the legal definition of high treason needed to be glossed, with the difference that the Treasonable Practices Act, now extended to the regent, sought to resolve the ambiguities of "constructive treason," whereby conspiracies against the "state" were conflated with "imagining" the death of the king.[45] Sir Samuel Shepherd, the attorney general, explained to the jury that there was no substantive difference between the charges brought under the statute of Edward III, for "compassing and imagining the death of the king" and "levying war," and those brought under the act of 1795, for "compassing and imagining to depose the king" and "conspiring to levy war, for the purpose of compelling the king to change his measures." In his very lengthy summation, Lord Chief Justice Ellenborough directed the jury's attention away from the charges brought under the medieval statute, placing emphasis on overt acts indicating an intent to depose the king or to levy war to force him to change measures. After a week-long trial, it took the jury composed mainly of small tradesmen an hour and a half to come to the verdict of "not guilty."[46] The following day the attorney general presented no evidence against Thistlewood, Preston, and Hooper and the men were summarily acquitted – Watson's son had managed to escape arrest and flee to America. Presenting Castle as the crown's star witness, a man who was a spy and *agent provocateur*, as well as a perjurer and a pimp, undermined the government's case. Relying on the evidence of their chief informer was a mistake not to be repeated at the trials of the Pentrich rebels.

"JURY. ACQUITTAL OF WATSON," read a huge poster, listing all the jurors' names, addresses, occupations, and across the bottom, "Deserve the Thanks of the Country." As in 1794, a London jury had come through, performing their duty as citizens. Preston recorded that Watson was acquitted "amidst the acclamations of tens of thousands, in whose bosoms burned the hallowed fires of freedom." "After all the preparations, the pomp, the pride, and folly, the industry and the contrivances... it appears that the Minsters have not been able to find a Jury that would answer their design in suffering Watson to be hanged," wrote Sherwin. During the trial, crowds had greeted the prisoners on their arrival at Westminster Hall and on their way back to the Tower with "loud huzzas."[47] Yet despite the popular rejoicing and the public dinner held at the Crown and Anchor to celebrate the acquittals, the Spenceans were left an isolated band of Jacobin conspirators. Place's later dismissal of them as "few men, contemptible in number," "next to nobody and nothing," smacks of partisanship, but his judgment that the ministers "purposely and dishonestly mixed" them together with the legal reform movement seems right.[48] In insisting at the third Spa Fields meeting, 10 February 1817, that their sole intention was to petition for parliamentary reform, Hunt was careful to dissociate the radical movement from Spencean doctrines.[49] As the government no doubt realized, the greater threat came from the industrial districts, and from working-class radicals mixing constitutionalist modes with deeper desires and possibilities, a reworked "Jacobinism."

Wat Tyler's Return

> A friend of mine here had been designated by the Treasury Journals
> as a second Wat Tyler – no bad title; for be it recollected that Wat
> Tyler rose for the purpose of putting down an oppressive tax, and
> would have succeeded, had he not been basely murdered by William
> Walworth then Lord May of London; but we have no basket-work
> Lord Mayor now; and if he was surrounded by thousands of his
> fellow-countrymen, as I am, he need fear no Lord Mayor whatever
> [*Huzzas!*][50]

Speaking at Spa Fields, young Watson thus claimed Wat Tyler for the
Jacobin cause. Moreover, as Iain McCalman comments, despite the
French revolutionary trappings, Spa Fields more closely resembled "a
plebeian rising like that of Masaniello or Wat Tyler."[51] A spy's report of
a later Spencean meeting held on 23 March 1817 at the Mulberry Tree
tavern, Moorfields, recorded that various journals, including *Cobbett's
Political Register* and *Black Dwarf*, were read aloud, along with a letter
from the "executor of Tom Payne" (presumably Thomas Addis Emmet,
the Irish revolutionary living in American exile), "and a part of the poem
of Wat Tyler."[52] By March 1817, Southey's drama was well on its way to
becoming a radical bestseller.

On 12 February, the *Morning Chronicle* carried an advertisement for *Wat Tyler: A Dramatic Poem*, to be published by the firm
of Sherwood, Neeley, and Jones, for 3s/6d. Although no author was
given, two mock quotations with Southey's name – "And I was once
like this.../.......... Twenty years,/Have brought strong alterations!
Southey" – identified the poet. William St Clair, historian of the reading nation, regards *Wat Tyler*'s publication as "the most decisive single event in shaping the reading of the romantic period."[53] Although
Sherwood, Neeley, and Jones ceased publication when Southey sought
an injunction for breach of copyright, radical pressmen had no such
qualms. Southey's failure to establish his legal ownership of the text,
left *Wat Tyler* to be freely and safely pirated.[54] Hone, Carlile, Sherwin, John Bailey, and John Fairburn produced cheap editions. Sherwin
published the entire work in the final issue of the *Republican,* which
he reprinted in a poorly produced, sixteen-page edition selling for 3d.,
soon reduced to 2d. (Figure 6.2). Immediate sales were believed to
reach around 60,000 copies, twice the number of Walter Scott's most
popular works.[55] Along with cheap editions, radical journals liberally
excerpted *Wat Tyler. The Black Dwarf* published lengthy extracts,
along with Wooler's scathing commentary on Southey.[56] "Every political reader read it," recalled Carlile, observing that the publication
of *Wat Tyler* prepared the way for the reception of Paine's republished
works.[57] It also opened the way for radicals to pirate works by Shelley

SHERWIN'S EDITION.—*Price Three Pence.*

WAT TYLER,

A Dramatic Poem,

BY ROBERT SOUTHEY, POET LAUREATE.

THE history of Wat Tyler has always held a distinguished place in the English records; and though some men affect to disapprove of his conduct, all men have concurred in admiring his courage. The Nation, even at that distant period, had begun to rise above the barbarous state into which the conquest, by William the Norman, had plunged it, and to shew strong signs of returning life. Such is the effect which society works upon a people—such the consequence which the human mind will produce upon itself, when left to pursue its natural course without interruption.

The wars between the English and the French Governments, which took place in those days, were like all others, ruinous and expensive. To defray the costs of these, a tax of three groats was ordered to be paid by every man and woman above the age of fifteen years: this unheard of imposition had too much in it of the nature of conquest, and savoured too strongly of the nature of despotism, to be willingly submitted to. It gave rise to a discussion, amongst the people, about the right of the govern[ment] it to adopt such a measure,

and the result of that discussion, was resistance. Their motto was:

When Adam delv'd, and Eve span, Who was then a gentleman?

" The first disorder (says Hume,) was raised by a blacksmith, in a village of Essex. The tax-gatherers came to this man's shop while he was at work; and they demanded payment for his daughter, whom he asserted to be below the age assigned by the statute. One of these fellows offered to produce a very indecent proof to the contrary, and at the same time laid hold of the maid, which the father resenting, immediately knocked out the ruffian's brains with his hammer. The by-standers applauded the action, and exclaimed that it was full time for the people to take vengeance on their Tyrants, and to vindicate their native liberty. They immediately flew to arms; the whole neighbourhood joined in the sedition; the flame spread in an instant over that county, and many others, before the government had the least warning of the danger."

The populace, amounting to one hundred thousand men, assembled on Blackheath, under their leaders,

Printed by W. T. Sherwin, Fleet Street, London.

Figure 6.2 Wat Tyler, A Dramatic Poem, By Robert Southey, Poet Laureate, W. T. Sherwin's edition, 1817. Original source British Library. 11642.c.56. Copyright © The British Library Board.

and Byron, dropping prices and vastly enhancing the poets' popularity with readers.[58]

There was something uncanny about the return of Wat Tyler. Watson's embrace of the rebel leader preceded the publication or any public knowledge of the poem. At Spa Fields, he was responding to attacks aimed at Spencean leaders published in journals loyal to the government. For example, in the *Anti-Gallican Monitor*, Lewis Goldsmith published a parody of "*The HUMBLE PETITION of the SOVEREIGN PEOPLE, assembled at the Spa-Fields, to his Royal Highness the PRINCE REGENT*," stating,

We, the Representatives of the British nation, having as usual a prison before our eyes, considering that we made a contract with

your progenitors... the Lord knows when; and moreover considering... we all lived in equality, eating our acorns and drinking our
creuww [i.e. cheap wine] in comfort, and being real *sans-culottes*,
must humbly beg your Royal Highness will restore that blessed state
of things.[59]

The petition was signed by various mock citizens and citizenesses, including Captain Macheath, Jenny Diver and Sisters, Jack Cade, and Wat
Tyler Jr. Twenty-five years earlier, Paine had responded to anti-Jacobin
jibes by appropriating Tyler's memory. In the second part of *Rights of
Man*, Paine added a lengthy footnote to his discussion of the dramatic
escalation of taxes over the last three hundred years, remarking on the
frequent mention of Wat Tyler in "several of the court newspapers."
"That his memory should be traduced by court sycophants... is not to
be wondered at. He was, however, the means of checking the rage and
injustice of taxation in his time, and the nation owed much to his valor."
Paine gave a short history of how Richard II's poll tax had led to Tyler slaying a tax gather who "began an indecent examination" of his
daughter to determine her age.[60] No doubt the twenty-year-old Southey,
who fancied a family connection to Wat Tyler, took inspiration from
Paine's treatment. In a letter to his brother, Southey reports on Hardy's
acquittal, plans for Pantisocracy, and his current work on "a tragedy on
my Uncle Wat Tyler," noting "Our toast to day was: May there never be
wanting a Wat Tyler whilst there is a Tax-gather."[61]

In fact, however, neither Jacobins nor radicals prior to 1817 were apt
to honor Tyler, John Ball, Jack Straw, or the fifteenth-century rebel,
Jack Cade – figures who fell outside the Whig-libertarian pantheon of
political martyrs and the prevailing myth of British constitutional liberty secured by seventeenth-century struggle. In popular literature and
historical accounts, the Peasants' Revolt represented a breaking loose of
the forces of misrule among the "rude" commoners, stirred by the fa-
natical preacher Ball, and led by Tyler and Straw, that embodied the sort
of violence and demands for the equal redistribution of property that
radicals were intent on denying. At the Beaufort lecture room, Thelwall
made glancing reference to "that great and glorious character... so wick-
edly blasphemed by courtly historians," for "though an ignorant man
(one of swinish multitude!)," Wat Tyler "had an honourable mind that
disdained every subterfuge." But Thelwall went on to argue that these
early insurgents were not members of corresponding societies, they never
attended meetings to discuss political principles or heard lectures at the
Beaufort buildings; the disposition "to tumult and violence" was linked
historically to primitivism and ignorance. His purpose was to dissociate
present-day radicals from the violence that loyalists charged them with
having instigated.[62] Thus, in his *Appeal from the New Whigs to the
Old Whigs*, published in August 1791, Burke drew an analogy between

the anarchy of 1381 and that unleashed in 1789, quoting the "maxim" offered by "Abbé John Ball" to the ignorant multitude, "When Adam delved and Eve span,/Who was then the gentleman?," as "fully equal to all the modern dissertations on equality of mankind," with the advantage "that it is in rhyme."[63] In summer 1791, Wat Tyler and his crew became something of a running joke in the loyalist press, which produced mock reports of dinners to celebrate the anniversary of the French Revolution. The new rules for the Revolution Dinner included, "Whatever Nobleman may chuse to dine with us, to be Mr. Stanhope, Mr. Cade, Mr. Tyler, or whatever his proper appellation may be – without reference to his rank." Not only are all titles to be abolished but all property of those at the dinner is to be divided equally. The report in the *Evening Mail* placed "Mr. Leveller" in the chair, with "Mr. Equality" giving the first speech. Mr. Wat Tyler moves that an order should be sent to the Crown and Anchor revoking the former order directing "that knives and forks should be chained to the table on the 14th instant, as, according to the last advices from France, freemen have the right to take away whatever they please from their fellow-creatures."[64] The jokes ran along with reports of the Priestley Riots in Birmingham, and loyalist mob violence.

Southey certainly turned rhyme to advantage. It is important to recognize in appropriating Wat Tyler's story, he wrote against popular literary and conservative political representations of the Peasants' Revolt while exploiting the chap-book mode of dramatic dialogue.[65] *Wat Tyler* was intended as a piece of cheap sedition; as such, one can understand why scholars of romanticism dismiss the work on aesthetic grounds. At the same time, one can understand why radical artisans and journalists loved the work. Southey said what they could not say, at least not without risking prosecution, and he said it in popular verse that fit the oral culture of the street and tavern. Written in the immediate aftermath of Thomas Hardy's acquittal, Southey gave imaginative expression to the regicidal fantasy that Pitt's government took as manifesting the "real" treason of British Jacobins, erasing the distinction between imaginative play and purposeful intent. Like many supporters of the French Revolution, Southey was morally ambivalent about the turn to insurrectionary violence, an ambivalence discernible in his drama.[66]

Displaced from the political context of 1794–95, the publication of *Wat Tyler* mediated between the two moments of Jacobin alarm, refracted through the distorting lens of its author's reputation and charges of apostasy.[67] It remains unclear how the manuscript came into the possession of Sherwood, Neeley, and Jones; although the firm was the business successor of Henry Symonds, the associate of James Ridgway approached by Southey in 1795 (see above Chapter 5), Sherwood maintained that the manuscript was not found among Symonds's papers. William Winterbotham surmised that someone must have secretly made a copy of the manuscript which he still had in his possession.[68] However the manuscript resurfaced, the timing of its publication was calculated to embarrass Southey and to counter justifications for emergency measures to suppress popular disaffection. The day before the publication of *Wat Tyler*, the *Quarterly Review* published Southey's alarmist attack on the reform movement, warning that as "Marat and Herbert followed in the train of Voltaire and Rousseau," Leigh Hunt's *Examiner* "does but blow the trumpet to usher in Mr. Orator Hunt in his tandem, with the tri-color flag before him," and in the orator's wake marches young Watson and the Spenceans. And while Spence himself may have been "poor and despised, but not despicable," for he was at least sincere and stoical, the government of the day would have done better to transport him from England, for "The harvest is now beginning to appear."[69] In a private memorandum to the prime minister, Southey questioned whether it would be possible to stave off revolution "till the moral and physical condition of the populace shall be so far improved that they will cease to desire one, feeling that they have more to lose than to gain." To this end, the government must "stop the seditious press" by whatever means; if juries "give their verdicts in the very face of facts," he urged using "that vigour beyond the law," including making transportation the punishment for seditious libel.[70] Little wonder that Southey was excoriated in the radical and reform press.

Hone was quick to strike in the *Reformists' Register* of 22 February, with notice of "A curious little Dramatic poem, entitled 'WAT TYLER,'" attributed to

> no less a person than the Poet Laureate, one MR. ROBERT SOUTHEY, a gentleman of credit and renown, and until he became Poet Laureate, a Poet. The present poem appears to have been written many years ago when Mr. Southey had not merely reforming opinions but very wild notions indeed. In consideration of a courtly pension, he now regularly inflames his verse, in praise of official persons and business ... Poor Southey! a pensioned Laureate! compelled to sing like a blind linnet by a sly pinch, with every now and then a volume of his old verse flying into his face, and putting him out![71]

On 9 March, the *Examiner* published an article by William Hazlitt, part of a sustained series in which Hazlitt charged Southey with apostasy. Contrasting the politics of *Wat Tyler* with the reactionary *Quarterly Review* article on parliamentary reform, Hazlitt declared,

> The author of *Wat Tyler* was an Ultra-Jacobin; the author of Parliamentary Reform is an Ultra-royalist; the one was a frantic demagogue; the other is a servile court-tool... the one did not stop short of general anarchy; the other goes the whole length of despotism; the

one vilified kings, priests, and nobles; the other vilifies the people...
the one admired the preaching of John Ball; the other recommends
the Suspension of Habeas Corpus and the putting down of the *Examiner* by the sword, the dagger, or the thumb-screw, – for the pen,
Mr. Southey tells us, is not sufficient.[72]

During ongoing debate over the Seditious Meetings Bill, William Smith,
reform member for Norwich, raised the publication of a piece of sedition
dating from the earlier period of alarm. Taking his cue from Hazlitt,
Smith read a passage from the *Quarterly Review* article followed by an
extract from *Wat Tyler*. According to Smith, the poem was "the most
seditious book ever written"; compared to the Spencean plan, the poem
made no attempt at argument but rather "appealed to the passions, and
in a style which the author, he supposed, at the time, conceived to be
eloquent. Why, then, had not those who thought it necessary to suspend
the Habeas Corpus act taken notice of this poem?" Without naming
Southey, Smith explained that he understood that a man might sincerely
change his political opinions, "when that change was unattended by any
personal advantage... But what he most detested... was the settled, determined malignity of a renegado."[73]

The charge stung. Coleridge responded in a series of articles for the
Courier. He asked whether Southey should then "use sweet words to
Jacobins, because he, a youth of nineteen, was deluded by such writings
as those of Thomas Paine into Jacobinism?" Coleridge dismissed the
drama "as an admirable burlesque" on the demagogues of the day, af-
fording "just such amusement in respect to politics as Tom Thumb does
in respect to tragedy." The "silly," "school-boy dialogue" turned to "political poison" when circulated "among the ignorant, distressed, of the
lower class."[74] The poet laureate's seditious piece of juvenilia was read
in taprooms like the Mulberry Tree in Moorfields, circulated among ragged artisans who were not laughing at the bad verse and wicked dialogue
of medieval rebels. As with Southey's proposal to shut down the popular
press by any means, the controversy over the publication of *Wat Tyler*
put the constitution of a legitimate reading public into sharp relief.[75] In
this regard, it is worth noting that Wordsworth's acceptance of the office
of distributor of stamps for Westmorland in 1813 (the year Southey became poet laureate) made the lake-poet the direct beneficiary of a state
agency set to restrict the reading public.[76] It was in the context of the
Wat Tyler controversy, that *Biographia Literaria* was published; in his
"literary life," Coleridge did not repent or excuse the politics of his own
youth but claimed to always have been an enemy of Jacobinism.[77]

Coleridge's defense of Southey brought Hazlitt's rebuke, "the author of *Cociones ad Populem*, and the author of THE *Wat Tyler*, are
sworn brothers in the same cause of righteous apostasy."[78] The *Morning
Chronicle* picked up on Coleridge's reference to Southey as "the stripling

bard," reminding readers that while Coleridge and Wordsworth "were also obnoxious Jacobin poets," in 1797–98 Southey was the main target of ridicule in the *Anti-Jacobin*. The article provided examples taken from later poems to demonstrate Southey's continued "Jacobinal" opinions, including his inscription for a national monument to honor the regicide Henry Marten, and proposal for a column to be erected at Smithfield to mark where Wat Tyler was killed.[79] In turn, Hone reprinted "The Stripling Bard" as part of the preface to his edition of *Wat Tyler*, and Fairburn included the *Morning Chronicle's* article as well as Hazlett's initial attack on Southey. However we distinguish between the "bourgeois" public sphere and an alternative or radical counter-public, we should recognize that literary boundaries were porous. As Kevin Gilmartin shows, while writing for "polite" journals, Hazlitt was capable of incorporating elements drawn from "vernacular radical journalism," an ability well demonstrated by his highly charged engagement in the controversy over Southey's "apostasy."[80] Conversely, popular radical journalists such as Hone (an admirer and friend of Hazlitt's) and Wooler looked beyond the literary restrictions of a purely vernacular style, often making demands that no doubt taxed ordinary readers.[81]

In his published response to Smith, Southey denied that *Wat Tyler* was a "seditious performance," arguing that it places words in the mouths of historical characters as "correct statement of their real principles," and not as the views of the author. The work constituted the "verses of a boy," mere "school-boy exercises" written when "my heart was full of poetry and romance," believing that the inequalities of rank "were light evil compared to the inequalities of property." With these "feelings," rooted "in the heart and not in the understandings," he had written *Wat Tyler*.[82] Again, the issue of the sincere heart was a matter of importance. In his court affidavit, Winterbotham related that Southey had professed no intention of making a profit from his work, telling him that "it was the offering of his heart to the cause of Freedom."[83] The offering of the Jacobin heart was now displaced, recurring as an anachronism. If the reintroduction of the repressive measures of the 1790s were justified by parallels drawn between the two periods of alarm, the deeper logic of conservatism was that 1817 was not the same as 1794 or 1795 but constituted a more dangerous conjuncture as Jacobinism had sunk deeper, lower in the social register. Thus Southey noted that *Wat Tyler* was written "when republicanism was confined to a very small number of the educated classes." He wrote to Liverpool more vividly, "The spirit of Jacobinism which influenced men in my sphere of life four and twenty years ago... has disappeared from that class and sunk into the rabble, who would have torn me to pieces for holding those opinions then, and would tear me to pieces for renouncing them now."[84] Echoing Southey's claims, Goldsmith observed that if during his younger days as a republican his principles had been mistaken, "I erred in common with great names, and found myself surrounded by respectable men." In 1795, he had attended the LCS meeting at Copenhagen Fields. Two decades later, he attended the second Spa Fields meeting, which he reported as wearing the appearance of "misery" and class war; "it was vermin, rags, and idleness [the meeting was held on Saint's Monday], about to declare war against whole clothes and industry." He asked a crowd member whether Hunt had spoken, "upon which an ill-looking fellow, a sturdy *san-culotte*" eying the well-dressed journalist with suspicion exclaimed, "I am a Jacobin, and I glory in it," and proceeded to tell Goldsmith, "we don't want any fine-coated gentlemen here."[85]

For reasons both humanitarian and prophylactic, Southey expressed a sincere interest in the "improvement of mankind" – including the relief of the poor, reform of prisons, and the advance of national education.[86] He had involuntarily gifted his text to an enlarged and radicalized reading public among whom there was little support for paternalistic solutions to economic distress and none for his entrenched defense of the unreformed constitution. Ironically, the readership for his drama was much larger than if it had been published in 1795, and carried little risk to publishers and booksellers. Whether read aloud in low taverns or excerpted in radical journals, the set speeches abound in seditious sentiment. Wooler sardonically hailed the revelation that the poet laureate is "a *friend of liberty… a jacobin*, a *leveller*, and a *republican!*" Take Ball's full speech from act two that Smith read to the Commons and the *Black Dwarf* excerpted:

> My brethren, these are truths, and weighty ones:
> Ye are all equal: nature made ye so,
> Equality is your birth-right; – when I gaze
> On the proud palace, and behold one man
> In the blood-purpled robes of royalty,
> Feasting at ease, and lording over millions;
> Then I turn to the hut of poverty,
> And see the wretched labourer, worn with toil,
> Divide his scanty morsel with his infants;
> I sicken, and indignant at the sight,
> "Blush for the patience of humanity."
>
> [Act 2, 101–112][87]

A flag carried at Spa Fields bore the inscription "Nature To Feed the Hungry." As if to underscore the message, the *Black Dwarf* quotes Tyler's closing speech to act one.

> Think of the insults, wrongs, and contumelies,
> Ye bear from your proud lords – that your hard toil
> Manures their fertile fields – you plow the earth,
> You sow the corn, you reap the ripen'd harvest, –

> They riot on the produce! That, like beasts,
> They sell you with the land – claim all fruits
> Which the kindly earth produces as their own.
>
> [Act 1, 246–52][88]

The blacksmith concludes by exhorting the crowd to feel their collective strength in order to force "these destructive tyrants" to "shrink before your vengeance." To which Wooler adds, "Almost the very words of *Watson in the Wagon*; and certainly the very ideas better spoken."[89] Southey's fusing of Paine's attack on monarchy with Godwin's utopian views on property, and Tyler's summons to rise up against tyranny, played well among the revolutionaries of 1817.

The attack on literary and political apostasy was part of the ongoing radical critique of "Old Corruption," viewed as a primary manifestation of elite rule. Southey numbered among the pensioners of the state, listed in the 1817 edition of the *Red Book,* the predecessor to John Wade's *Black Book* (1820), which commented on his entry, "Author of *Wat Tyler*, and many other works – *crazy, loyal,* and *jacobinal.* Poor Apostate Southey! what a miserable termination of his career! When he could barter principle, consistency, and independence for a paltry £300."[90] In his role as courtier commissioned to offer effusions of loyalty and praise for royalty, Southey was an easy target of ridicule. Shortly before the publication of *Wat Tyler*, Hone's two-penny parody of *The Sinecurist's Creed* appeared. Hone brings the romantic poets before the ministerial trinity of "Old Bags" (Lord Eldon), "Derry Down Triangle" (Castlereagh), and "the Doctor" (Sidmouth):

> and the Laureate in token of joy, shall mournfully chaunt the most doleful Lay in his Works. And they that have said Aye!, Aye! shall go into Place everlasting; and they that have said No! shall go into everlasting Minorities. And COLERIDGE shall have a Jew's Harp, and a Rabbinical Talmud, and a Roman Missal: and WORDSWORTH shall have a Psalter, and a Primer, and a Reading Easy: and unto SOUTHEY's Sack-but shall be duly added: and with Harp, Sack-but, and Psaltery, they shall make merry, and discover themselves before Derry Down Triangle, and HUM his most gracious master, whose Kingdom shall have no end.[91]

It is worth noting that Hone brings the romantic poets before "Derry Down Triangle," an allusion to Castlereagh's alleged role in the torture of United Irishmen in 1798. Hone added a note to explain the meaning of the wooden frame used in the torture of Irish rebels, "*Triangle*, s. a *thing* having three *sides*; the meanest and most tinkling of all musical *instruments*; machinery used in military *torture.* Dictionary." In parliament, old charges were raised against Castlereagh, with Burdett warning that they were being asked to follow "the same bloody track which the noble lord marked out in Ireland."[92] The image of "Bloody Castlereagh" embodied the coercive violence at the disposal of the corrupt state.[93]

In its first issue (November 1797), the *Anti-Jacobin* had detailed the attributes of the Jacobin poet, maintaining that "The Poet of other times has been an enthusiast in the love of his native soil. The *Jacobin* Poet rejects all restriction in his feelings. *His* love is enlarged and expanded so as to comprehend all human kind."[94] In fact, Southey had looked to the past to find a cast of national heroes to which the "Exiled Patriots" of 1794 could be added, although he never composed an epic of the nation set in England.[95] According to Sherwin, "The History of Wat Tyler has always held a distinguished place in English records."[96] In fact, it was with the belated publication of Southey's drama that Tyler truly entered the historical pantheon of radicalism, with his name toasted at dinners and Southey's text kept in print, although the linkage of Wat Tyler's memory to the 1790s, much less to the events of 1817, became increasingly tenuous.[97]

To London to see the Prince Regent

> Found the Road all the Way to Manchester full of People & the Public Houses crowded with company chiefly from the Country. There was a Group of two or three hundred in one House all Delegates or Leaders from the Country. When the Mail Coach drove up they ran towards the Bridgewater from all sides. Josiah Booth addressed the Guard & asked him what News from London. The Guard ordered him to stand off, & told him if he did not he would blow his brains out… Finding the Guard so resolute the Crowd retired. The People all the Way upon the Road & in the neighbourhood adjoining it, were up all Night in a state of the most anxious Suspense. In the Course of the Day it had been reported that the Tower in London was taken by the Rioters. Pretty general Credit was given to this Report.

This report comes from an informer on the road from Oldham to Manchester. Word had reached the district that the Spa Fields insurgents had attacked the Bank and taken the Tower. It was said that a pound note was not worth two pence anymore, and instructions circulated to arm to support London comrades in the event they met with success.[98] In the industrial districts, where the groundwork was laid for a mass movement, leaders were in contact with London's revolutionary party, with delegates from the Oldham district reportedly in attendance at the second Spa Fields meeting.[99] According to Bamford, it was in London that plans for the Blanketeers' march, and the revolutionary schemes that followed, were hatched. During the evenings of late January 1817, various northern delegates attending the Hampden Club "convention," including William Benbow, a Manchester shoemaker, and Joseph Mitchell, Liverpool draper and pamphlet seller, conversed over glasses of porter and long pipes with "the Watsons, Prestons, and Hoopers" at the Cock in Grafton Street, one of the Spenceans' regular meeting places. To this company, Hunt added the name of the London shoemaker Charles Pendrill, who had been arrested in connection with the United movement of 1798 and subsequently linked to the Despard conspiracy of 1802.[100] Thomas Bacon, Derbyshire framework-knitter, veteran Jacobin, and a key figure in the plans that led to the Pentrich rising, represented the East Midlands at the Hampden convention and was present for discussions at the Cock.[101]

Whatever the exact substance of discussion among the provincial delegates and London Spenceans, the revolutionary initiative moved north. Throughout the country, meetings were scheduled for 10 February to coincide with the third Spa Fields meeting, to consider how the reform petitions had been received.[102] Public meetings in Lancashire went off peacefully, under the watchful eye of local authorities. The *Manchester Political Register* complained of the efforts made to prevent the people from meeting. At Manchester "tyrannic" masters forbid workers from attending the meeting on pain of dismissal. Some factories "were converted into Bastiles," with workers locked inside for most of the day.[103] While monitoring the reception of their petitions and waiting for Burdett to present a reform bill, radicals grew increasingly frustrated with the tactic of petitioning parliament. They were also aware that the opportunity for open mobilization was closing down with the imminent suspension of habeas corpus. The idea of marching *en masse* to London was likely mooted in London and set in motion at private meetings of provincial delegates. In fact, the idea had been floated earlier. In late December 1816, the Oldham magistrate William Chippendale reported that Lancashire leaders were being advised by Cartwright of a plan for a simultaneous march of petitioners to London, a proposal "to bring a tenth part of a Mass of People to the Metropolis whose minds he has for years been labouring to influence... the old Major is evidently aiming at Rebellion." Chippendale thought that parliament's rejection of their petitions would bring "the crisis for the full and final Development of their ultimate views," and that until then their actions "will be trimmed in such a way as to sail upon the utmost verge of the constitution without transgressing its bounds."[104] The concern for strictly constitutional modes was characteristic of Cartwright's leadership, but not with a view to open rebellion. What the alarmist magistrate correctly perceived was the capacity for militants to play dangerously on the edge of constitutional agitation. He also understood that having "given up every expectation of bringing over the middling and upper classes," radicals directed their efforts at influencing "the minds and... the passions of the Working Class, who they now urge to trust to their own exertions without looking for aid to those above them."[105] From the loyalist side, as Katrina Navickas observes, there was a continuity constructed "from the Church-and-King organisations and principles of the 1790s to the new Pitt clubs, defence associations, and loyalist addresses," local agents prepared to reinforce the government's repressive measures.[106]

The plan to present petitions to the regent in person upped the constitutional ante. The scheme called for thousands of men, with blankets strapped to their backs for rough sleeping, to march from Manchester; gathering numbers and collecting small donations as they moved through the Midlands, the petitioners would present an irresistible force. Care was taken to conform to the letter of the law, specifically the 1661 Act against Tumultuous Petitioning. Marchers were to form themselves into groups of ten, each group with a leader who had tied to his wrist a petition signed by twenty people.[107] The act prohibited more than twenty persons to sign a petition aimed at altering "matters established by the law in church or state," unless first ordered by at least three magistrates or the majority of the grand jury of the county; furthermore, no petition could be presented by more than ten persons.[108] From the perspective of ultra-radicals, the petitioning plan combined "all the advantages of legality with all the opportunities to develop into something else."[109] Cartwright's motto of "hold fast by the laws" was a flexible creed. Ironically, a law intended to restrict the right to petition was exploited for mass mobilization aimed at coercing the crown to meet radical demands.

Formally, the plan centered on an engagement with the monarch, in the person of the prince regent. At the first Spa Fields meeting, Hunt had scotched the Spenceans' proposal to march to Carlton House to enforce an audience with the regent. Just as at the Spa Fields meetings, Lancashire's radical leaders recast the well-worn trope of the king as father of his people. Playing on a standard myth in which the king is portrayed as misled by wicked ministers who shield him from the people, radicals sought to "undeceive" the monarch; once informed of his children's real plight, the king is called to heal his people's suffering and restore justice to the land. In his *Address to the People*, which he circulated in October 1816 on his tour of south Lancashire, Mitchell recommended reformers to address the crown rather than a corrupt parliament. The rambling text features a reverential address to the regent: "We approach the throne in this once happy land, with the *mingled* feelings of banished children." The address warns of injuries inflicted by evil ministers of the sort "who betrayed the unfortunate Charles; who deceived the besotted James, and perplexed the bewildered Louis; and, at the expence of the peace of your family and the risk of the state... this monster corruption, in some fit of hunger, may turn its foul breath to the sacred edifice you adorn, and at one gripe, crush and crumble that heavenly fabric amidst the anarchy and confusion of an unfortunate people."[110] The overwrought image of the "heavenly fabric" of the monarchical state brought low by its own creatures is followed by a

litany of liberties guaranteed in medieval and seventeenth-century constitutional documents. Mitchell, the constitutionalist, was subsequently
drawn into plans for a general rising until his arrest in May 1817.

The actual petitions carried by marchers complain that repeated appeals to the crown and parliament for redress of grievances had not
received the attention merited by their importance, as now "when the
waste of war is over, our sufferings are become both more general and
deeper than ever." They expressed the conviction that had the House of
Commons been "wholly and annually appointed by the People at large,
this War, and the Taxation, resulting therefrom, would long ago have received sufficient check." Moreover, the law designed to raise the price of
grain would not have been enacted. The petitions protest the use of the
law of libel to suppress truths beneficial to humankind and the suspension of habeas corpus to imprison people without proof. They "humbly
but fervently pray" for the instant dismissal of all ministers responsible
for devising "such cruel, such unjust measures," and the appointment of
declared friends of parliamentary reform and "a general and very considerable retrenchment in every department of national expenditure."
The appeal concludes, "Our lives are in your hands – our happiness in
a great measure depends on you" to adopt measures calculated to offer
relief, "you may then safely rely on our support and gratitude, without
this, we can neither support you nor ourselves."[111]

The Blanketeers' petition blended the formal language of supplica-
tion with an allegiance contingent on the relief of economic distress
and fundamental political change. More generally, the rhetoric of Lancashire radicals oscillated between mock deference to monarchy and an
overt challenge to its authority. Unlike his father, George III, who had
managed to restore the aura of kingship as an embodiment of the nation and a model of probity, the regent was a gluttonous figure of royal
excess, accruing massive debts paid for by his poor subjects.[112] The
appeal to his royal highness for retrenchment in wasteful state expenditure was a calculated contradiction. The petitioners and their leaders
appealed to an idealized image of what constitutional kingship should
be, and thereby made a claim on monarchy. Moreover, beneath the
constitutional surface, ran strongly anti-monarchial currents. The raw
language is recorded not in published works or official programs but in
the reports of informers and magistrates archived in Home Office files
(often in multiple copies), some of which was reinscribed in reports of
the parliamentary committees of secrecy. These soundings have all the
problems associated with their sources; informers looked to impress
their paymasters and authorities looked for evidence to bring prosecutions. There is no "authentic" voice of the Blanketeer movement available to historians. But in the archived reports of their meetings in the
months preceding 10 March, we can gauge something of the ideological temper, catch a sense of the motivations and rhetoric associated

with the plan to march to London either to entreat or confront the royal person.

In debate over the report of the Commons secret committee, of which he was a member, William Elliot observed that in the neighborhood of Manchester, there was a society of "the lowest of the people meeting for the discussion of the foundation of government and society, the extent of obedience due the civil power, and meeting the most delicate questions on resistance or submission."[113] Indeed, working people were discussing fundamental questions. In December 1816, the Manchester Constitutional Society opened a meeting room at New Islington, Ancoats. A range of garrets formerly used separately as picking rooms of a cotton factory (known as Bibby's rooms) was combined to make a long meeting hall, fifty by nine yards, large enough to accommodate a thousand persons. "There was a Table by way of Hustings and a Bench as a seat on which People got up to speak."[114] On the very day that Elliot spoke in the Commons, it was reported that radicals debated the question, "Suppose a Number of Men was cast upon a Desolate Island, What kind of Governt. [sic] would they Adopt?" Joseph Johnson, a brushmaker and key local activist, held up republican America as an example for Britons.[115] Earlier, in December 1816, at the Lord Wellington, the question "Ought Religion to be inimical to Parliamentary Reform?" was debated. John Johnston, a Manchester tailor, who was one of the four missionaries just appointed to promote the Lancashire petitioning campaign, observed that various sects had forbidden hearers from attending reform meetings. After denouncing the established church as "the greatest Enemy of Reform," John Bagguley, an eighteen-year-old Manchester turner and filer (a branch of machine making), endeavored to show that god never intended for there to be kings, although he was at a loss for a term to give a king, "Robber" was shouted from the audience, to which the speaker readily agreed.[116] The same month, radicals meeting in Salford debated "whether the Jacobin or the Loyalist commonly called was the best friend to his country," deciding by a large majority that the Jacobin was the true patriot.[117] On the evening of 3 February, with Benbow in the chair, the Manchester society debated the question whether "Englishmen answered the end of their creation?" Samuel Drummond, a twenty-four-year-old reed-maker, asked

> what business a man had with £39,000 per annum, & another with £38,000, and another with two million who had lost his senses if he ever had any – another fat man with [£]1,500,000… what right have they with this money – whilst those whom they have robbed are starving for want.[118]

Bagguley and Drummond were the most vocal advocates of the proposed march to London.

The movement's spokesmen appealed to the history of English constitutional struggle. According to Bagguley, although their meetings might soon be shut down, "the law says that [if] the King did not give an Answer to the Petition within the space of 40 Days. He was liable to be seiz'd & all his family and confined in prison till he gave an Answer" – a point of "law" that he supported by reference to Magna Carta. As a Manchester magistrate informed Sidmouth, "Baguley [sic] is well versed in the history of his country, & has the consummate art to invest & torture it to his own purpose."[119] At meetings at New Islington, Johnston warned that if the prince regent "will not harken to our Petition, but we will punish him by taking off his head as was formerly by Charles 1st;" Benbow announced his willingness to die in the sacred cause of liberty, informing his audience of their statutory right to arm, "although he would not say what to do with their arms." A week before the scheduled march, Benbow reminded a packed room that "a blacksmith in the reign of Richard 2nd went to London with 20,000 men and got their Liberties which remained till they were destroyed by Tyranny."[120] The precedent of 1381 was telling. Winterbotham later claimed that 40,000 copies of the 2d. edition of *Wat Tyler* were sold in the manufacturing districts; however, the cheap editions published by radical pressmen did not appear until after 10 March.[121] Still, the controversy over Southey's drama was current, and Tyler's confrontation with the king offered a convenient point of historical reference as radical speakers summoned condensed images of civil war: the armed barons confronting King John at Runnymede, the Peasants' Revolt against unjust taxes, and the awful act of tyrannicide. Left unspoken was the parallel to the citizen soldiers of Marseilles who marched to Paris in summer 1792 to save the Revolution.[122] In private conversation, responding to an informer's question about how they would manage once their petition was rejected, Bagguley reportedly replied, "three fourths of us are already organis'd for we have been the Militia in volunteer Corps & the regular Army."[123]

Despite what went unsaid, tinges of Jacobinism emerged at the edges of constitutional protest. In January, several thousand people attended an outdoor meeting held at Oldham, where a band arrived playing the tune "The Way to London," as a send-off for the Hampden delegates. Chippendale complained that "all loyal tunes were cautiously avoided," adding that the people frequently called for "Ca ira," "Millions be Free," and "March on, March on, by which they meant the Marseillaise Hymn, of which they have all got a Translation."[124] At the same meeting at which Benbow summoned Wat Tyler, Bagguley declared, "I am a <u>Republican</u>, a leveller, and will never give it up till we have established a Republican government." At this point, other speakers tried unsuccessfully to check the young firebrand. George Bradbury, a Manchester stone-cutter, spoke of the achievement of the French Revolution in the same breath as he described how King John was compelled to sign Magna Carta on one knee.[125] While the younger radicals took the lead, Mitchell reported that "old Friends of the Corresponding Societies" provided advice and support but were keeping themselves "in the background till affairs were in a state of forwardness."[126] Some veterans stepped forward from the outset of the renewed movement. John Knight of Oldham assumed a prominent role in 1816–17, and on to Peterloo. Having been arrested in 1795, Knight was tried in 1812 as one of the thirty-eight radicals charged with administering unlawful oaths during the Luddite agitation.[127] John Haigh, an Oldham silk weaver, was identified as "a disseminator of Sedition from the very commencement of the French Revolution." He was also among those who were acquitted in 1812; in 1817 he was a delegate to the London deputies meeting. Henry Rose had been active in Scottish Jacobinism and served as one of the Glasgow delegates to the second Scottish Convention of 1793. Having moved to Stockport, he was a regular speaker at local meetings leading up to the anticipated march.[128] Seventy-three-year-old William Ogden, a Manchester letter-press printer, was a veteran publicist responsible for printing copies of the Blanketeer petition. John Kay, small cotton manufacturer from Royston, a town "notorious for disaffection since the commencement of the French Revolution," was described as "a man of considerable knowledge, acquired by self-instruction, an Infidel in Religion, – being a Devotee of Paine's *Age of Reason.*"[129]

On the morning of 10 March, between ten and twenty thousand persons assembled in St. Peter's Fields, Manchester, to send off the marchers. Drummond addressed the gathering, declaring "it is not riot and disturbance we want, it is bread we want and we will apply to our noble Prince as a child would to its Father for bread." Bagguley turned to history, declaring that

> never was such a thing done before... In the reign of Richard II [,] about 40,000 men want to London to demand their rights of the King... But they only came a little way from London, they did not go from Manchester.

Bagguley instructed the marchers to form themselves in tens, with their lead man in front and two rows of five. Money was collected in hats to support the marchers, "copper was poured out of the hats into pocket handkerchiefs." The authorities were well prepared; General Sir John Byng, commander of the northern district, in consultation with local magistrates, had no intention of allowing the Blanketeers to gather strength as their leaders intended.[130] The meeting was dispersed; Drummond and Bagguley were taken into custody, and sent along with Ogden and Johnston in chains to London (other leaders had gone into hiding). Six to seven hundred marchers were pursued by dragoon guards, yeomanry, and special constables; some were arrested before they reached

Stockport; many made it to Macclesfield and Leek; a group of bedraggled men were apprehended at Ashbourne in the Derbyshire Dales.[131]

In all, 247 men were arrested, most of whom were discharged rather than brought to trial.[132] On addressing fifty-three prisoners at Salford's New Bailey courthouse, the stipendiary magistrate W. D. Evans gave a stern lecture on constitutional law, stressing that their leaders' allusion to the rebellion of 1381 as a precedent for their own actions made the marchers liable to charges of high treason. As for their formal compliance with the 1661 statute, it was

> perfectly ridiculous to suppose that the law would suffer itself to be so trifled with, as to permit its provisions to be evaded by such a contrivance, where, in fact, a large body of several thousand persons intended to advance to the presence of the exalted person now invested with the powers of government, in regular array.

Four persons, who persisted in asserting the legality of their conduct, were committed to Lancaster, "to await such prosecution as it may be there thought proper to instigate against them," along with several others, including the Manchester weaver Matthew Lythgoe, who had provided himself with a knife "not calculated for ordinary purposes." The bulk of the prisoners were discharged on the provision that they expressed contrition for their conduct, and gave assurance that they had been misled by others.[133] At the very least, local magistrates wanted to see before them chastened subjects willing to show due humility to the law's authority. The lists of the arrested men show a preponderance of weavers, most of whom were young men, including a good number in their teens. While spinners were not prominent among those arrested, unlike weavers they were mostly in work; moreover, spinners helped to provide financial support for the journey.[134] Unsurprisingly, the depositions of those who were arrested downplay political motivations, stressing their poverty and innocent intent. Not untypical was Benjamin Broadbent, a young weaver from the village of Hurst Cross near Ashton-under-Lyne, who stated that he "came along with others to petition the Prince – to make a better living... I am a poor weaver... They informed me I should have a little better living."[135]

The government was keen to bring charges of high treason against the main Lancashire leaders, on the grounds that the Blanketeers' intention was to overawe the regent and compel him to change measures of government. Writing to Sidmouth, the Duke of Northumberland thought that the intended march from Manchester to London "must too forcibly have reminded your Lordship of the march of the Marseillois to Paris, at the commencement of the French Revolution, not to have convinced your Lordship that the copy must have been at least recommended by some persons deeply concerned in the original."[136] Petitioning had been

Jacobinized. Of this, Sidmouth may well have been convinced, but could a jury be convinced enough to send these men to the gallows? In the aftermath of the abortive march and the initial arrests, open meetings were no longer possible; radical delegates now met in secret. As Bamford relates, "The proscriptions, imprisonments, trials, and banishments of 1792, were brought to our recollection by the similarity of our situation to those of the sufferers of that period." Bamford was arrested at Middleton on 29 March, the day after the arrest of delegates at a late-night "private meeting" at Ardwick Bridge.[137] Plans were floated for a coordinated attack on the barracks, the New Bailey prison, the police offices, houses of the borough-reeve and constables, and banks: a Manchester version of the Spencean strategy, with Manchester providing the signal for a general rising.[138] While the "Ardwick conspiracy" did not pose a serious threat, it provided authorities with the opportunity to make further arrests. Many of the leading figures of Lancashire radicalism were brought before Privy Council to be examined on suspicion of high treason.[139] The government chose, however, to hold the prisoners rather than bring them to trial. Once again, secret committees reported and habeas corpus was suspended until March 1818. Forty-four radical leaders and printers were imprisoned for up to a year on warrants charging high treason issued by the home secretary.[140]

On the night of 8–9 June, the framework-knitter Jeremiah Brandreth led a band of lightly armed, Derbyshire workers to join their Nottingham confederates, thinking they were part of a widespread rising of men carrying pikes rather than petitions to overthrow the government. The Pentrich men were caught up in the machinations of government ministers, and betrayed by Oliver "the spy" (W. J. Richards) acting as an agent provocateur.[141] The networks exploited by Oliver were established as the opportunity for open agitation closed. Mitchell was implicated in the scheme, and despite accusations of having acted as a government agent, he was an innocent participant deceived by Oliver.[142] As Thompson writes, from this point in 1817 "until Chartist times, the central working-class tradition was that which exploited every means of agitation and protest short of active insurrectionary preparation."[143] Radicalism's recurrent dilemma turned on the question of what could be done once peaceful means for democratic change were exhausted.

The Blanketeers failed, and no doubt their failure was predictable. Mitchell later asked whether there was "anything more truly great in the annals of history," anything to compare with thousands of men "poor in circumstances, but rich in mind," with the purpose of peaceably marching to Carlton House to "ask modestly to tender their complaints themselves."[144] Mitchell was typically melodramatic and at least partially disingenuous. The movement was distinguished by its lack of men of substance at its head; it was a movement directed by working people. But it was also distinguished less by its legality and modest representation to the monarch as a paternalist benefactor than by its creative play with an idealized version of monarchy that translated into confrontational force. In both the myth of king-and-people and the crime of high treason, the king's person operates as its central term. The Blanketeers skillfully played on this centrality as a projection of revolutionary desire.

Shelley's Lament

At Derby's county jail, on the morning of 7 November, Brandreth along with William Turner, a stonemason and ex-solider, and Isaac Ludlam, the elder, part owner of a stone quarry and known locally as a Methodist preacher, prepared themselves for a traitor's death. A troop of dragoons was kept at a distance, as the civil power was thought sufficient to maintain order. "The drop was enclosed by special constables, and in the rear of these the javelin men, on horseback, took their station." Unable to sleep the night before, Ludlam and Turner prayed and early in the morning sang a psalm. Brandreth wrote a letter to his wife. Late morning the men were conducted to the prison chapel by the chaplain George Pickering, who had prayed with the men in their cells. The other Pentrich prisoners, those spared from the death sentence, attended the service, although only the condemned men took the sacrament. The under-sheriff arrived at the chapel around noon to demand the prisoners to be delivered to the scaffold. The smith attended in order to "knock off" the prisoners' irons, replacing them with irons with locks, which could be more easily removed "when the last struggle should be over." Brandreth came into the prison yard first to be drawn on a hurdle before felons and debtors, followed by Turner and Ludlam. The scaffold, which was set up in front of the jail, on Nun's Green, was equipped with a block, two sacks of sawdust to absorb the blood, two gleaming axes, two sharp knives with black handles, and a basket for the heads. Three coffins chalked with the men's respective names were placed at the back. The men were placed in a row at the foot of the ladder leading to the scaffold. The executioner and his assistant climbed up the ladder followed by the chaplain and Brandreth. The arrangements were designed "with as much expedition as possible, after they had once been exposed to the gaze of the multitude"; the nooses were ready, and the ends of the ropes tied to a suspending beam, so that once "the sufferers were led forth, nothing might remain to be done but pass the rope over the head of the man for whom it was destined, to pull down the caps, and let the drop fall." On mounting the scaffold, Brandreth exclaimed, "God be with you all and Lord Castlereagh" – although many spectators claimed that he said, "God bless you all, BUT Lord Castlereagh." Once the rope was adjusted and the knot placed behind Brandreth's left ear, Turner was brought up. On reaching the platform, Turner called out, "This is all Oliver and the government, the Lord have mercy on my soul."

At which point, the chaplain interposed himself between the condemned men and the crowd, there were to be no gallows speeches. As the halter was placed around his neck, Ludlam prayed to the Lord for forgiveness of his sins, and continued, "Bless the King of this nation... bless all the people, high and low, rich and poor, bond and free." The chaplain recited a prayer, and the men joined him in reciting the Lord's Prayer. The executioner put the caps on the men's heads and pulled them over their faces, and with Ludlam still in the midst of prayer, "the bolt was drawn, and they were launched into eternity." Brandreth and Turner seem to have died at once, while Ludlam "repeatedly convulsed after he had been thrown off." Despite the plans for efficiency, the bodies were allowed to hang for more than half an hour, before they were taken down and hoisted up to the scaffold. The crowd groaned as the masked executioner made a bad job of chopping at Brandreth's head. His assistant completed the task by cutting through the sinews with a knife.

> The blood flowed copiously, the head fell in the basket, and the hangman seizing it by the hair, held up the ghastly countenance of the Nottingham Captain, with the left side of the face and beard, besmeared with blood, forming a horrible spectacle for the view of the multitude. He proceeded with it to the left, to the right, and to the front of the scaffold, bearing the trunkless ball in his hand, and exclaiming at each place, 'BEHOLD THE HEAD OF THE TRAITOR BRANDRETH!' The head was then carefully deposited in the coffin, which immediately afterwards received the body.

The same procedure followed with the bodies and heads of Turner and Ludlam. The entire theater of execution finished in an hour. Some hisses and groans, and sounds of horror were heard. The crowd of over six thousand peaceably dispersed from the front of the prison, though panic ensued with the mistaken word that the dragoons were poised to attack[145] (Figure 6.3).

All in all, the spectacle of the old-style execution for high treason had gone well. Reports commented on Brandreth's stoic composure, and resolute silence, his own form of resistance. He knew what to expect, having been present at Despard's execution. The risk of serious disorder had been averted. Injured sovereignty was imaginatively restored in the scaffold's sheer measure of excess, exhibited on the desecrated bodies of the condemned.[146] Treason was the ultimate crime against the royal person and the state, requiring the maximum reactivation of power. It was this reactivation that ministers sought, and which had eluded them – Watson's acquittal having been followed by the acquittals of the Folley Hall insurgents at York and the acquittal of Andrew McKinlay at Edinburgh of the capital crime of administering unlawful oaths connected to an

Figure 6.3 Execution of Jeremiah Brandreth a Traitor, 1821 Anonymous.
© picturethepast.org.uk, Derbyshire Records Office, DRBY007175.

alleged conspiracy in the West of Scotland.[147] The executions at Derby thus satisfied the desired taste for traitors' blood.

As for justice, the trials at Derby the previous month had been as carefully stage-managed as were the executions. In light of the failures to this point, the government was determined to win convictions for high treason and demonstrate the awful consequences of rebellion.[148] A special commission with four judges was instigated. Thirty-five men were charged with high treason; jury lists were vetted; the prosecution employed ten lawyers, with the accused being represented by John Cross and Thomas Denman. Expressive of the local atmosphere, "Hang All Jacobins" was chalked on the walls of All Saint's Church. Most crucially, the prosecution went to great lengths to prevent Oliver's name and role as instigator from being introduced in court. Whether the defense lawyers acted on sound legal reasoning, as Denman later argued, or connived in this silence, as some radicals charged, remains debatable.[149] The exposure in the *Leeds Mercury* of Oliver's part as agent provocateur had already helped to secure the acquittals at York. The bill of indictment charged the men with levying "insurrection [,] rebellion [,] and war" against the king, without "having the fear of God in their hearts... but being moved and seduced by the instigation of the devil as false traitors."[150] Brandreth's case was a lost cause, since he had killed a man. Once he had been convicted, the defense pleaded that the other rebels had been moved and seduced by the charismatic Nottingham Captain, whom Denman likened to the character of Conrad in Byron's *Corsair*:

> What is that spell that thus his lawless train
> Confess and envy, yet oppose in vain ...
> There breathe but few, whose aspect could defy
> The full encounter of his searching eye; [...]
> There was a laughing devil in his sneer,
> That roused emotions both of rage and fear.[151]

At the end of ten days of trials, Brandreth, Turner, Ludlam, and George Weightman (a sawyer) were sentenced to be drawn on a hurdle, hanged to death, and their heads severed from their bodies – the prince regent, acting on behalf of the king, "having graciously remitted the remainder of their sentence," that is, the quartering of their bodies. An agreement was made not to bring the remaining men to trial on the condition that they plead guilty. Weightman's sentence was respited, and he joined ten others who "received his majesty's pardon" to be transported for life; three prisoners were transported for fourteen years; and six were sentenced to various terms in prison.[152] Justice was thus tempered by the king's mercy, the discretionary side to the monarch's full exercise of power.

Another death, recorded by the noted diarist Henry Crabb Robinson: "The death of the Princess Charlotte has excited more general sorrow than I ever witnessed raised by the death of a royal personage." On 19 November, he observed, "This being the day of the funeral of the Princess Charlotte, all the shops were shut, and the churches everywhere filled with auditors."[153] The borders of newspapers were outlined in black; detailed diagrams of the order of the funeral procession to Windsor were published. Provincial newspapers carried the deputy marshal's command for general mourning, along with advertisements for proper funeral attire. A flood of sermon literature came out; assemblies, theater performances, balls, and public dinners were cancelled or postponed; throughout the nation, local ceremonies of mourning were planned; and the muffled peals of church bells were heard daily. On the evening of 18 November, spectators and carriages lined the road from Claremont in Surrey to Windsor as the vast funeral procession, headed by thirty horsemen, three abreast, in full mourning, arrived in the early hours of the morning.[154] "A valuable Correspondent," most probably Coleridge, penned an obituary for the *Courier*. Death was a particular sorrow when the victim was in the prime of life,

> but we are most inconsolable, when to youth, are united virtue, rank, and station, which make the loss a general calamity. – Such is the condition of England! All those fond anticipations which pointed to her offspring as the future glory and security of the realm, are for ever destroyed.[155]

Byron paid sentimental tribute to the princess, "Those who weep not for kings shall weep for thee/... in dust/ The fair-haired Daughter of the Isles is laid/ The love of millions!"[156]

Here was an image of the nation coming together in sorrow for the death of the presumptive heir to the throne and her stillborn son. As Linda Colley comments, Princess Charlotte had become "a focus of sentimental attachment, particularly among women." The "posthumous cult of Charlotte," built around her "sex, youth, virtue, imminent maternity and tragic demise," embodied the lost hope of "an embattled dynasty."[157] "The love of millions" shown to Princess Charlotte contrasted to the reception that her royal father had received at the beginning of the year on his return from opening parliament. The regent allowed his estranged wife, Caroline, only limited access to their daughter. The extent to which Charlotte embraced the radical politics of her mother's circle (including Byron) is unclear; her husband Prince Leopold of Saxe-Coburg, whom she married in 1816, was known to have liberal political views.[158] Henry Hunt's assessment no doubt reflected the view of many radicals:

> The whole nation appeared to mourn her loss, much more, I believe, in consequence of her having always espoused the cause of her unhappy and persecuted mother, than from any conviction or well-grounded hope that any public good would ever be derived from her being our future Queen.[159]

The part of counter-monarch in the figure of a woman was to be fully realized in 1820 with the mass agitation in favor of Queen Caroline.

On 6 November, dining at Godwin's, Crabb Robinson first met Shelley. The young poet "was very abusive towards Southey" for having "sold himself to the court." He spoke somewhat less bitterly of Wordsworth.[160] Earlier in the year, the poet had published *A Proposal for Putting Reform to the Vote throughout the Kingdom* under the pseudonym "The Hermit of Marlow." The pamphlet caught the attention of Southey, who grouped it with the report of the committee of secrecy in his *Quarterly Review* article, "Rise and Progress of Popular Disaffection." Southey took the occasion for a veiled attack on Shelley, chiding "literary adventurers" who "commit moral suicide" by pandering to "the lowest vices or worst passions of man's corrupted nature."[161] Southey did not deal with the substance of Shelley's proposal, which was intended as a moderate intervention in debates among reformers and radicals. Shelley acknowledged the abstract right to universal male suffrage but favored a franchise based on direct taxation.[162] With the exception of Southey's attack, and two puffs in his friend Leigh Hunt's *Examiner*, his pamphlet went largely unnoticed.[163] At the same dinner, Shelley heard of the sudden death of Princess Charlotte. He had closely followed the trial of the Pentrich leaders in the radical press, particularly in the *Examiner*, which also carried a report of the executions.[164] Writing with speed and energy, Shelley produced his finest political pamphlet, commenting on the conjunction of the death of the princess and the execution of working-class traitors.[165]

Shelley's opening to *An Address to the People on the Death of Princess Charlotte* is stark.

> The Princess Charlotte is dead... It is a dreadful thing to know that she is a putrid corpse, who but a few days ago was full of life and hope, a woman young, innocent, and beautiful, snatched from the bosom of domestic peace, and leaving that single vacancy which none can die and leave not.

The leveling tone is continued in the next paragraph, in which the princess's death is compared with "the death of thousands" of women in childbirth, who leave grieving husbands and motherless children deep in sorrow and "legible despair." "Do not their hearts beat in their bosoms, and the tears gush from their eyes? Are they not human flesh and blood?" Yet none but their immediate families weep for them or mark the lost hope and joy of a newborn child – "none when their coffins are carried to the grave (if indeed the parish furnishes a coffin for all) turn aside and moralize upon the sadness they have left behind."[166] In rendering the royal death as ordinary, while eliciting sympathy for the misery of "the poorest poor," Shelley asks readers to consider the circumstances that merit true feelings of grief, and the proportionality of such feelings. The pamphlet engages the empathy of readers, placing faith in the human capacity to identify with the suffering of others. Shelley's romantic sensibility here reflects the influence of Rousseau's ideas of natural feeling and sincerity.

In her superb reading, Esther Schor examines the classically trained poet's address as rooted in the rhetorical tradition of the classical funeral oration. Shelley's appeal to pathos turns on the distinction between private and public mourning.[167] "The Athenians did well to celebrate, with public mourning, the death of those who had guided the republic with their valour and their understanding, or illustrated it with their genius." The power of such ritual mourning is to bind the community together. Thus should England have marked Milton's death and the French nation mourned the deaths of Rousseau and Voltaire. Significantly, Shelley returns to the 1790s and to what he referred to elsewhere as "the master theme of the epoch in which we live– the French Revolution."[168] The title page of Shelley's address carries the epigraph "WE PITY THE PLUMAGE, BUT FORGET THE DYING BIRD," Paine's famous riposte to Burke's apostrophe to Marie Antoinette and regret for the end of "the age of chivalry." In similar fashion, Mary Wollstonecraft, whose daughter Shelley had married at the end of 1816, condemned Burke's "notions of gothic beauty," taking him to task for reserving his tears "for the downfall of queens... whilst the distress of many industrious mothers, whose *helpmates* have been torn from them, and the hungry cry of helpless babes, were vulgar sorrows that could not move your commiseration, though they might extort an alms."[169] In his discussion of deaths worthy of public mourning, Shelley cites the death of innocent victims of state tyranny

> which make all good men mourn in their hearts... Thus, if Horne Tooke and Hardy had been convicted of high treason, it had been good that there had been not only the sorrow and indignation which would have filled all hearts, but the external symbols of grief. When the French Republic was extinguished, the world ought to have mourned.[170]

For Shelley, it was the ideal of the Revolution that was to be mourned, an ideal that remained worth cherishing even in its defeated form.[171]

In contrast to the public love due to objects of universal human feeling, Charlotte's death was an occasion best left to private mourning. To this assessment, however, Shelley adds a paragraph spiked with republican venom, worthy of Paine. Charlotte may have been "the last and the best hope of her race," but "the accident of her birth neither made her life more virtuous nor her death more worthy of grief." Born into royalty, her superficial education had rendered her incapable of undertaking large measures of public service. "She had accomplished nothing, and aspired to nothing, and could understand nothing respecting those great political questions which involve the happiness of those over whom she was destined to rule." No fault of her own, for "Such is the misery, such the impotence of royalty. – Princes are prevented from the cradle from becoming any thing which may deserve that greatest of all rewards next to good conscience, public admiration and regret."[172] Shelley uses the death of Charlotte for a general attack on royalty and aristocratic privilege to which he links an economic critique. "Kings and their ministers have in every age been distinguished from other men by a thirst for expenditure and bloodshed." This thirst reached its peak in "the war against the republic of France," generating an enormous public debt responsible for producing "an unequal distribution of the means of living" and creating "a double aristocracy," so that twice as many people live "in luxury and idleness, on the produce of the industrious and the poor." Exhibiting his antipathy for the bourgeoisie, Shelley contrasts the "pride and honour" of the old aristocracy to the new aristocracy of finance, "petty piddling slaves," having enriched themselves "by gambling in the funds, or by subserviency to government." It is the laborer who now must work sixteen hours a day to make what they had previously earned in eight hours to support this system of luxury and disproportionate inequality that erodes the fabric of society and leads to anarchy.[173] Shelley's analysis of the effects of the public debt and attack on the *nouveaux riche* shares much in common with Cobbett's famous address "To the Journeymen and Labourers" (2 November 1816).[174]

For Shelley, the execution of Brandreth, Ludlam, and Turner "is an event of quite a different character from the death of Princess of Charlotte." It is the different character of these deaths on which Shelley elaborates, viewing the executions as emblematic of the real national tragedy. The address hinges on this juxtaposition. As a matter of private mourning, these men also had "domestic affections, and were remarkable for the exercise of private virtues." Although they were of "low station," they too had families who loved them. Shelley evokes the terror of the scaffold, imagining the agony of the men's families sitting in solitude as the howling of the crowd "told them that the head so dear to them was severed from the body!" and the "groans and hootings which told them that the mangled and distorted head was then lifted in the air." This was more than an occasion for private grief. The events that led these men to the scaffold "are a public calamity." The disaffection in the manufacturing districts was a consequence of "that system of double aristocracy." The workers, "'the helots' of our luxury, are left by this system famished," deprived of "the leisure or opportunity for such instruction as might counteract those habits of turbulence and dissipation, produced by the precariousness and insecurity of poverty." These conditions open the way "for any adventurer... to incite a few ignorant men to acts of illegal violence," "innocent and unsuspecting rustics" deceived by agents of despotic government. Shelley observes, "We feel for Brandreth the less," for he killed a man, but records in mitigation his reported words, "that 'OLIVER *brought me to this*' – that, *'but for* OLIVER, *he would not have been there.'*"[175] The government is indicted for instigating the conspiracy. Shelley strikes his sole false note by mistaking Brandreth and his comrades for merely ignorant dupes. They were, in fact, men of standing in their communities, committed to principles of political and economic justice for which they were prepared to risk their lives.

Shelley concludes with a brilliant peroration in which the dead princess is transformed into the figure of Liberty, a spirit or vision that replaces a corpse. "A beautiful Princess is dead; – she who should have been the Queen of her beloved nation… but she was young, and in the flower of youth the despoiler came. LIBERTY is dead." The shift is abrupt, moving to the final funeral procession and universal grieving, and then to enchantment as the phantom spirit of Liberty is resurrected amidst the broken symbols of monarchy – the republican ideal restored to life.

> Slave! I charge thee disturb not the depth and solemnity of our grief by any meaner sorrow. If One has died who was like her that should have ruled over this land, like Liberty, young, innocent, and lovely, know that the power through which that one perished was God, and that it was a private grief. But *man* has murdered Liberty… Let us follow the corpse of British Liberty slowly and reverentially to its tomb: and if some glorious Phantom should appear, and make its throne of broken swords and sceptres and royal crowns tramped in the dust, let us say that the Spirit of Liberty has arisen from its grave and left all that was gross and mortal there, and kneel down and worship it as our Queen.[176]

Shelley's pamphlet was the most sustained and eloquent radical-republican response to the death of the princess and the executions at Derby. Unfortunately, the work was voluntarily suppressed, although the details of its suppression remain unclear. There is no record of how many copies were printed or if there were plans for wider distribution. No copies of the original edition survive. The work did not fall into the willing hands of radical pirates; when it was eventually published the tract had lost its political currency.[177] In 1817, Shelley already feared a criminal information might be filed against *Queen Mab*; printed in 1813, his most subversive work was limited to private circulation.[178] As with his reform proposal, his *Address to the People* was authored by "The Hermit of Marlow," thin protection against government prosecution. At the end of the year, Charles Ollier published his long poem *Laon and Cythna: Or, the Revolution of the Golden City: A Vision of the Nineteenth Century*, only to immediately withdraw it on hearing of protests from customers; he insisted that Shelley revise the work, retitled *The Revolt of Islam*, with slight tempering of the poem's revolutionary values of republicanism, atheism, and free love.[179] As Shelley reflected, "All reformers have been compelled to practise this misrepresentation of their own true feelings and opinions."[180] Marilyn Butler observes that after 1817 the style of liberal poetry was effected not only by the censorship imposed by cautious publishers but by "a kind of self-censorship." Despite his radical politics, heterodoxy religious views, and sympathy for the Pentrich victims, Shelley felt an ambivalence toward popular disaffection and the mass mobilization of 1817.[181] The spirit of "Jacobinism" had, as Southey maintained, disappeared not only from the ranks of the propertied classes but from the circle of liberal intellectuals; the radical cause of liberty was championed by a new breed of writers and journals responsible for creating an expanded readership, an alternative public sphere. These were "the people" Shelley may have wished to address; they were certainly the readers among whom his pamphlet would have registered an enthusiastic response.[182] A brief survey of the popular radical journals' handling of the themes of high treason, monarchy, and public grief illustrates this point. Shelley's failure to connect with this audience in 1817 illustrates what was lost in romanticism's separation from an active engagement with popular radicalism.

On the trials at Derby, Wooler commented,

> these mock-important trials have now terminated, and all the parade and expense with which they have been attended, are appreciated in their true light. The people, who must furnish the funds for the one, have not been deceived by the other... The *'treasonable projects'* had alarmed no one, and the prosecutions for treason were only regarded as ridiculously claiming protection of the state when it had been in no possible danger.

The prisoners had committed "many foolish and many villainous actions," but these actions were "committed under the seduction of spies." As for the executions, he expressed his astonishment that the sentences were carried out "at a moment which the executioners of that sentence are eager to designate as one of the greatest national calamity."

> That the death of the Princess Charlotte should have been immediately followed by such a scene of blood as that exhibited upon the scaffold at Derby, is as shocking to the understanding, as it is abhorrent to the feelings. Was the vulture of law so eager for the banquet of mangled carcases, that it could not fast through the solemnity of those funeral preparations, which we are told will inhume *all the virtues* of humanity, and all the hopes of England.

The incongruity and inhumanity are illustrated by a lengthy description of the executions, "the sanguinary spectacle which the government had got up for the amusement and edification of the people." To this Wooler adds a note, quoting Paine's comments on the punishment of hanging, drawing, and quartering:

> The effects of those cruel spectacles exhibited to the populace, is to destroy tenderness, or excite revenge; and by the base and false idea of governing men by terror, instead of reason, they become precedents.[183]

It was thus from the barbarity of the ancien régime that the Parisian crowd learned to carry aloft heads stuck on pikes. Whether or not Shelley read the *Black Dwarf*, intertextual affinities are discernible, including the return to Paine at the moment when his works were returning to print.[184]

Under the headline, "DEATH OF THE PRINCESS CHARLOTTE, AND THE EXECUTIONS AT DERBY," *Sherwin's Political Register* commented: "The public mind has been led from the contemplation of the infamous proceedings at Derby, by an event which is likely to render the 'throne of these realms,' a subject of serious discussion, if not of dispute." The death of Charlotte, "which some have been warm enough to lament as a National misfortune," had already given rise to speculation about the line of royal succession. The predicament of the nation, or more accurately that of the court, was understandable, "for if the Crown should be vacant for a short time, it is possible that the People might discover the practicability of managing their concerns *without* a King." Sherwin makes the mock recommendation that ministers might turn to a passage in the first part of Paine's *Rights of Man* (which the journal was serializing) for the proposal that a French nobleman made to Benjamin Franklin, offering to move to America as king and touting his Norman lineage. Paine's point was to illustrate the arbitrary origins of the claims of hereditary succession. According to Sherwin, the situation was enough "to explain to the world the nature of monarchy,"

> and to exhibit in its most glaring characters, the absurdity of hereditary successions. It shews the childishness of a Nation pinning its affairs upon the sleeve of any individual, who is liable to be snatched off at a moment's notice, and the Government to be thereby... turned upside down. What an unsound, ridiculous frame of Government the English system must be while the death of a *girl of twenty-one* has the powerful effect of deranging its affairs, and of placing the future Government at the disposal of a set of the most treacherous and contemptible men in the whole country!

To which Sherwin adds a note that no disrespect is meant to the memory of the princess, "whose character, as far as I have been able to learn, was truly admirable. What an unpardonable libel is that stainless character upon the blood of royalty!" On the quick succession of the Derby executions by the death of Princess Charlotte, Sherwin ventured, "Some will say that one of those events was intended by providence as a punishment to the party which was meditating vengeance on the other." History would record,

> as a most singular event, that the hope of the Brunswick family was cut down by the scythe of death, when the supporters of that family were preparing to take the lives of those poor mechanics who had been seduced by Government agents, into a commission of an act which in the language of perverted law, is called High Treason.[185]

Unlike Wooler, who aligned himself with Cartwright's constitutionalism, Sherwin was a full-throated Paineite republican. The Spenceans, who were avid readers of Sherwin's journal, dispensed with the slight care Sherwin took to cover his republican tracks. At the Knave of Clubs, Preston was reported to declare, "it was a happy [thing] that the young one was Dead the other day for it would save them [£]30,000 and would be no matter how soon some more of them were dead." This followed his complaint that it cost £400,000 to keep "a madman" when £400 would do.[186]

From America, Cobbett published a letter to Hunt in his *Political Register*, in which he promised to open a fund in the United States for the relief of Brandreth's wife, Ann, and the families of the other victims, to which he committed twenty guineas. Hunt had attended the entire proceedings at Derby. Cobbett reprinted the heart-wrenching final correspondence between Brandreth and his wife. While stating that he could countenance nothing that threatened the life or "lawful authority" of the king – "I detest traitors" – he adds somewhat ambiguously, "as we do not call Russell and Sidney traitors, so am I at liberty to judge, whether I am to consider Brandreth and his associates in that light." He closes by noting that concern for Charlotte's death is properly restricted to the event's political consequences: "We can not have any personal feelings upon the occasion. It is a young wife dead in child-birth; and this happens in many parts, of every great country, every twenty-four hours."[187] Like Shelley, Cobbett reduced the royal death to the experience of ordinary life. The radical journalists similarly maintained that to embrace Charlotte's death as a "national calamity" or "national misfortune" was to mistake the true national crisis and natural objects of communal sorrow, to "pity the plumage, but forget the dying bird." Here was a concerted effort to undermine the popular appeal of monarchy as a symbol of national unity and well-being.

It is a historical irony that in the same year that *Wat Tyler* became a publishing sensation, Shelley's *Address* was withheld from the public. In 1795, Newgate's pressmen balked at publishing Southey's drama; in 1817, Shelley chose not to turn to the next generation of radical printers who might have hazarded putting his pamphlet into circulation. The year ended with Hone's stunning courtroom performances and series of acquittals. Shelley contributed five guineas to the subscription opened to help Hone sustain the disabling costs of his legal battle.[188] In March 1818, Shelley left for Italy, never to return to Britain. The suspension of habeas corpus expired the same month and the Seditious Meetings Prevention Act expired in July, allowing for the national mass platform campaign that culminated on "the never to be forgotten," 16 August 1819 at St. Peter's Field. From self-imposed exile, Shelley wrote his great poem "The Mask of Anarchy" to commemorate the Manchester massacre. The poem was sent to Leigh Hunt who decided against publishing it in the *Examiner*, waiting until 1832 to issue it as a pamphlet.[189] In the wake of William Clarke's pirating of *Queen Mab* in 1821, editions of Shelly's poem proliferated. Carlile, who spent most of the decade in prison, alone brought out four separate editions of *Queen Mab*, as well as pirating Byron's *Cain* and *The Vision of Judgement* (Byron's parodic attack on "the author of 'Wat Tyler'"). These were decisive works for the infidel-republicans who throughout the 1820s read and sold Carlile's *Republican*.[190] The pirating of *Wat Tyler* anticipated the enormous popularity and sales of Bryon and Shelley's poetry. Among the following generation of working-class radicals, "The Mask of Anarchy" and *Queen Mab* became the poems most frequently reprinted and excerpted in the poetry columns of Chartist journals. Chartist poets regarded Shelley and Bryon as their models and forbears in democratic verse.[191]

The trajectories of these later literary and political appropriations form another chapter in the complicated history of radical recovery and transmutation. This chapter has sought to elucidate the ways in which Jacobinism returned to political and literary culture in 1817, as its terms were reanimated in the context of popular radicalism's resurgence and government efforts to maintain established authority. During the immediate postwar years, there was a continued ambiguity to popular radicalism, a persistently "fragmented" ideology. If its dominant mode was that of popular constitution, Jacobin inflections remained current. The "heroic age" of postwar radicalism closed with the passage of the Six Acts (December 1819), which codified and expanded the repression legislation of 1795 and 1817, and with the desperate Cato Street conspiracy and the risings in Yorkshire in the early spring of 1820 as its concluding act. The Chartist movement (1838–c.1850), which marked the next phase of mass mobilization, was not without its insurrectionary moments, but as the next chapter shows, the Jacobin heritage of the 1790s was problematically situated as a focal point of remembrance.

Notes

1 Samuel Bamford, *Passages in the Life of a Radical* (Oxford: OUP, 1984, first published 1844), 13. For the food riots and machine-breaking of 1815–1816, see John Bohstedt, *The Politics of Provision: Food Riots, Moral Economy, and Market Transition in England, c. 1550–1850* (Farnham: Ashgate, 2010), 246–49. For the revival of Lancashire radicalism during the last years of the war, see Katrina Navickas, *Loyalism and Radicalism in Lancashire, 1798–1815* (Oxford: OUP, 2009), 230–48; Rachel Eckersley, "The Drum Major of Sedition: the Political Life and Careers of John Cartwright (1740–1824)" (Ph.D. thesis, Manchester University, 1999), chapter 6.

2 E. P. Thompson, *The Making of the English Working Class* (Gollancz, 1963), 450, 466. The most common term for the popular movement for democratic change in the immediate postwar years was "radical reformer," with "radical" only beginning to be used on its own. See Joanna Innes, "'Reform' in English Public Life: the Fortunes of a Word," in *Rethinking the Reform Age: Britain 1780–1850*, ed. Arthur Burns and Joanna Innes (Oxford: OUP, 2003), 71–97, at 92.

3 See Jonathan Fulcher, "The English People and Their Constitution after Waterloo: Parliamentary Reform, 1815–1817," in *Re-Reading the Constitution: New Narratives in the Political History of England's Long Nineteenth Century*, ed. James Vernon (Cambridge: CUP, 1996), 52–82.

4 Iorwerth Prothero, *Artisans and Politics in Early Nineteenth-Century London: John Gast and His Times* (Baton Rouge: Louisiana State University Press, 1979), 84.

5 William Wickwar, *The Struggle for the Freedom of the Press, 1819–1832* (Allen and Unwin, 1928), 52–59.

6 *Republican*, 29 March 1817, 80. The first issue, 1 March 1817, consists of a lengthy essay cautiously defining republican government as based on representative democracy.

7 *Republican*, 30 May 1823, 675–76; *Isis*, 7 July 1832, 342–43. Sherwin and Carlile brought out cheap editions of Paine's political works, which Carlile collected into a two-volume edition of complete political writings. *SWPR* serialized *Commonsense,* starting 6 September, and *Rights of Man*, starting 4 October. According to Carlile, Paine's works had become "so nearly extinct as to be found nowhere for sale, but in a clandestine manner." *The Following Works are to be Had of R. Carlile,* handbill (c. 1818), 3, copy in HO 42/202.

8 See Kevin Gilmartin, *Writing against Revolution: Literary Conservatism in Britain, 1790–1832* (Cambridge: CUP, 2007), chapter 5.

9 *MPR*, 1 February 1817, 72–73. The journal ran for only eight numbers from 4 January to 1 March, ceasing publication with the suspension of habeas corpus.

10 For a full account, see John Barrell, *Imagining the King's Death: Figurative Treason, Fantasies of Regicide, 1793–1796* (Oxford: OUP, 2000), chapter 14; Clive Emsley, "The Pop-Gun Plot, 1794," in *Radicalism and Revolution in Britain, 1775–1848: Essays in Honour of Malcolm I. Thomis*, ed. Michael T. Davis (Houndmills: Palgrave Macmillan, 2000), 56–68.

11 For the concept of the convention as anti-parliament, see T. M. Parssinen, "Association, Convention and Anti-Parliament in British Politics, 1771–1848," *EHR* 88 (1973): 504–33.

12 *MPR*, 1 February 1817, 73–76. See also Bamford, *Passages*, 19–22; Henry Hunt, *Memoirs of Henry Hunt, Esq., Written by Himself in His Majesty's Jail at Ilchester*, 3 vols. (1820–22), 3: 411–23; Christiana Parolin, *Radical*

Spaces: Venues of Popular Politics in London, 1790–c. 1845 (Canberra: Australian University E Press, 2010), chapter 5.

13 Hunt, *Memoirs* 3: 424–29; *Courier*, 29 January 1817; John Belchem, '*Orator' Hunt, Henry Hunt and English Working-Class Radicalism* (Oxford: OUP, 1985), 66–67. Thanks to Nick Rogers for pointing out the connection to the Roman republic.

14 "Piccadilly butchers" was the satiric name awarded to the Life Guards for their violent handling of the crowd in 1810 on the arrest of Burdett at his house in Piccadilly.

15 *Courier*, 29–30 January 1817; *The Times*, 29–30 January 1817; *PD*, vol. 35, cols. 32–37, Commons, 28 January 1817.

16 *Courier*, 30 January 1817, 1,3,5 February; *The Times* 30 January 1817, 3 and 6 February; HO 42/159, Capt. Fairman to Sir Henry Torrens, 3 February, fols. 115–16; Steve Poole, *The Politics of Regicide in England, 1760–1850* (Manchester: Manchester University Press, 2000), 145–47.

17 *Courier*, 29 January 1817; *The Times*, 30 January 1817; *The Annual Register for the Year 1796* (1796), 6–7.

18 *PD*, vol. 35, cols. 8–9, Commons, 28 January 1817, and vol. 35, col. 173, Lords, 3 February 1817.

19 *Courier*, 4 February 1817. The *Courier* was the most liberally funded and widely circulated treasury journal. See James J. Sack, *From Jacobite to Conservative: Reaction and Orthodoxy in Britain, c. 1760–1832* (Cambridge: CUP, 1993), 15–24.

20 *HRR*, 8 February 1817, cols. 49–56.

21 Reprinted in David A. Kent and D. R. Ewen, eds., *Regency Radical: Selected Writings of William Hone* (Detroit, MI: Wayne State University Press, 2003), 38–41; Kyle Grimes, "Spreading the Radical Word: The Circulation of William Hone's 1817 Liturgical Parodies," in Davis, ed., *Radicalism and Revolution*, 143–56. For the order of publication of the parodies, see Ann Bowden, "William Hone's Political Journalism, 1815–1821," 2 vols. (Ph.D. diss., University of Texas, 1975), 1:103. For Hone's radical career, dating back to the late 1790s, see J. Ann Hone, "William Hone (1780–1842), Publisher, and Bookseller: An Approach to Early 19th Century London Radicalism," *HJ* 16 (1974): 55–70. The government considered prosecuting *Te Deum*. TS 24/3 (160).

22 *The Times*, 6 February 1817.

23 *BD*, 19 February 1817, cols. 59–62.

24 Marcus Wood, *Radical Satire and Print Culture, 1790–1822* (Oxford: OUP, 1994), 1–2, 67. In response to a request for information about Spence, Hone detailed the works of Spence he still had in his possession, noting that he had little personal contact with Spence, "but I was a frequent observer of him, on account of his fearless thinking & printing." BL, Add. MS., 27808, William Hone to Francis Place, 23 September 1830, fol. 314, reprinted in Kent and Ewen, eds., *Regency Radical*, 366–67.

25 *Courier*, 7 November 1816; *MP*, 8 November 1817.

26 Fulcher, "English People and Their Constitution," 60–72.

27 *PD*, vol. 35, cols. 78–83, 85 (Canning), 91–92, Commons, 29 January 1817, and cols. 365–68, Commons, 14 February 1817. In spring 1793, parliament had also rejected reform petitions from radical societies on the grounds of their inappropriate language.

28 Ibid., cols. 859–63, Commons, 3 March 1817, and cols. 991–1004, 12 March 1817; N. C. Miller, "John Cartwright and Radical Parliamentary Reform, 1808–1819," *EHR* 83 (1968): 705–28, at 720–24; John Cannon,

Parliamentary Reform, 1640–1832 (Cambridge: CUP, 1974), 170. Cartwright pioneered the printed petition, believing them to be legal and superior to written ones. *HRR*, March 29, col. 311, claimed a total of 1.2 million signatures; estimates reached as high as 1.5 million.

29 *PD*, vol. 35, cols. 590–92 (Castlereagh), Commons, 24 February 1817, and cols. 556–58 (Sidmouth), 572–73 (Liverpool), Lords, 24 February 1817.

30 Ibid., cols. 1258–59, Lords, 25 March 1817.

31 See Ian Haywood, *Romanticism and Caricature* (Cambridge: CUP, 2013), 151–54, for recycling of anti-Jacobin tropes of the speakers.

32 HO 40/8/1, "B" [John Shegog], report of conversations with Thistlewood, Preston, et al., 19–27 September 1816, fols. 31–42.

33 *Gentleman's Magazine*, 86, 2 (1816): iii; *Reform, the Watch-word for Revolution by a Civilian of Oriel Coll. Oxford* (Chelmsford, 1816).

34 *PD*, 35, cols. 438–47, "Report of the Secret Committee of the House of Commons," Commons, 19 February 1817, and cols. 411–20, "Report of the Secret Committee of the House of Lords," Lords, 18 February.

35 Iain McCalman, *Radical Underworld: Prophets, Revolutionaries and Pornographers in London, 1795–1840* (Cambridge: CUP, 1988), particularly chapters 1, 5 and 6; David Worrall, *Radical Culture: Discourse, Resistance and Surveillance, 1790–1820* (Detroit, MI: Wayne State University Press, 1992), chapters 3–4; T. M. Parssinen, "The Revolutionary Party in London, 1816–20," *Bulletin of the Institute of Historical Research* 45 (1972): 266–82; Thompson, *Making*, 613–16. For Despard, see Peter Linebaugh, *Red Round Globe Hot Burning: A Tale at the Crossroads of Commons and Closure, of Love and Terror, of Race and Class, and of Kate and Ned Despard* (Oakland: University of California Press, 2019).

36 *Fairburn's Account of the Meeting in Spa-Fields*, November 15, 1816; *The Times*, 16 November 1817; *Examiner*, 17 November 1816, 730–32; Hunt, *Memoirs*, 3: 334–43; BL, Add. MS. 27809, fols. 22–25, for Place's account; Belchem, *'Orator' Hunt*, 58–70, for all three Spa Fields meetings.

37 Preston related that if the soldiers came out, they would cheer them and win them over. HO 40/3 (pt. 3), T. Thomas to N. Conant, c. 27 November 1816, fols. 5–6. Thistlewood had been heavily treating soldiers at garrison public houses.

38 This account is based on William Hone, *The Meeting in Spa Fields. Hone's Authentic and Correct Account of All the Proceedings on Monday December 2nd: With Resolutions and Petition of Nov. 15 1816* (1816); idem, *The Riots in London. Hone's Full Account of the Events in the Metropolis, on Monday 2 Dec. 1816* (1816); Hunt, *Memoirs*, 3: 366–72; HO 40/3 (pt. 3), fols. 28–33; J. Ann Hone, *For the Cause of Truth: Radicalism in London, 1796–1821* (Oxford: OUP, 1982), 261–65.

39 *Report from the Committee of Secrecy*, PP, 1817, iv, 5; *Anti-Cobbett, or the Weekly Patriotic Register*, 15 February 1817, col. 10. The Committee of Public Safety, which was to sit until a national convention could be convened, was to include the reform leaders Burdett, Cochrane, Cartwright, and Hunt; former LCS leaders Hardy and Gale Jones; the United Irishman Roger O'Connor; along with Spenceans Evans, Thistlewood, the Watsons, and Edward Blanford.

40 *ST*, vol. 32, "Proceedings in the Case of James Watson, the Elder," cols. 106, 124–25.

41 TS 11/197/859, Crown case, Thistlewood, et al.; HO 40/3 (pt. 3), notice of the "Tri- Coloured Committee," fols. 36–38; McCalman, *Radical Underworld*, 23–24,110. Preston's daughters assisted in sewing cockades and

ribbons. The title of Watson's short-lived journal *Shamrock, Thistle and Rose* (1818) represented the same notion of a tricolored British republic.

42 *AGM*, 17 November 1816, 4842; *Sun*, 16 November 1816.

43 *Committee of Secrecy*, *PP*, 1817, iv, 3; HO 42/158, report of Mulberry Tree meeting,16 January 1817; TS 11/197/859, report of John Williamson, 30 September 1817, Waterman Arms; McCalman, *Radical Underworld*, 118–19; Worrall, *Radical Culture*, 92–95; Paul Pickering, "'Confound Their Politics': The Political Uses of 'God Save the King-Queen,'" in *Cheap Print and Popular Song in the Nineteenth Century: A Cultural History of the Songster*, ed. Paul Watt, Derek B. Scott, and Patrick Spedding (Cambridge: CUP, 2017), 112–37, 125–26.

44 Hunt, *Memoirs*, 3: 357–62; Hone, *Riots*. More directly, according to a spy's report of a Spencean debating club, one member declared "that reform was of no use whilst the Family of George Gulph of Hanover was at St. James." HO 40/3 (pt. 3), James Munro to N. Conant, February 1817, fol. 42.

45 Barrell, *Imagining the King's Death*, chapter 16; Michael Lobban, "Treason, Sedition and the Radical Movement in the Age of Revolution," *Liverpool Law Review* 22 (2000): 205–34, at 225. The Treasonable Practices Act was claimed to be declaratory but was not in fact used during the 1790s. In 1803 Despard was charged under the Treasonable Practices Act, along with the acts of 1796 and 1797 against the seduction of soldiers and against taking unlawful oaths.

46 *ST*, vol. 32, "Proceedings Watson," cols. 26–30, 579–82, 672–74.

47 BL, Place Scrapbooks, set 39, vol. 1, fols. 121, and 124, for report of public dinner; Thomas Preston, *The Life and Opinions of Thomas Preston, Patriot and Shoemaker* (1817), 35; *SWPR*, 21 June 1817, 192; *MC*, 12, 14, 17 June 1817, reporting that with the acquittal, "the venerable roof of Westminster-Hall vibrated to the thundering cheers of thousands."

48 BL, Add. MS. 27809, fols. 67–68, 100.

49 William Hone, *Full Report of the Third Spa-Fields Meeting; With the Previous Arrests* (1817), col. 13. This was two days after the arrests of Watson, the two Evans, Preston, and others.

50 Hone, *Riots in London*; HO 40/3 (pt. 3), "Narrative of the Proceedings at the Spa Fields Meeting on 2 Dec. 1816," fol. 28.

51 McCalman, *Radical Underworld*, 109.

52 HO 42/162, fols. 280–81. The old "Jack" John Baxter (silversmith) was present.

53 William St Clair, *The Reading Nation in the Romantic Period* (Cambridge: CUP, 2004), 316.

54 A good deal of misunderstanding, including on Southey's part, has surrounded Lord Eldon's refusal to issue an injunction. While Eldon might have ruled that Southey's work was unprotected due to its seditious nature, he ruled that Southey must first show that the work was his own property, a matter which was not established. For a lucid discussion, see Lynda Pratt, et al., eds., *SLPW*, 3: 442–48.

55 St Clair, *Reading Nation*, 316–18; *LCRS*, 350; *Republican*, 29 March 1817. A WorldCat search turns up at least ten editions published in 1817, including Fordyce's Newcastle edition. Most of these editions were priced at one shilling.

56 *BD*, 26 March 1817, cols. 139–44.

57 *Isis*, 7 July 1832, 343. According to Carlile, his decision to become a bookseller was due to his experience hawking *Wat Tyler: Republican*, 3 November 1826, 524. Linton later claimed that Carlile had sold 25,000 copies of

his pirated edition. W. J. Linton, *James Watson: A Memoir* (New Haven CT, 1879), 11.

58 St Clair, *Reading Nation*, 318–27; Joss Marsh, *Word Crimes: Blasphemy, Culture, and Literature in Nineteenth-Century England* (Chicago, IL: University of Chicago Press, 1998), 99–104.

59 *AGM*, 1 December 1816, 4852. The *Sun* maintained a barrage of mockery, aimed particularly at Dyall, Preston, and Hunt. For Goldsmith, his anti-Napoleonism and liberal government subsidies, see Stuart Semmel, *Napoleon and the British* (New Haven, CT: Yale University Press, 2004), chapter 4.

60 Thomas Paine, *Rights of Man* (Harmondsworth: Penguin, 1985, first published 1791–92), 231. In fact, Paine drew on histories that confused Wat Tyler with John Tyler who killed the tax-collector with a hammer. See Lister M. Matheson,"The Peasants' Revolt through Five Centuries of Rumor and Reporting: Richard Fox, John Stow, and Their Successors," *Studies in Philology* 95 (1998): 121–51, 138–39.

61 Robert Southey to Thomas Southey, 6 November [1794], *NLS*, 1: 85–86.

62 Report on the State of Popular Opinion," *Tribune*, 2, no. 28, 18 September 1795: 281–95, at 294; "A Warning Voice to the Violent of All Parties," *Tribune* 3, no. 47 (6 November 1795): 263–77, at 271–72. See also Steve Poole "'Not Precedents to be Followed but Examples to be Weighed': John Thelwall and the Jacobin Sense of the Past," in *John Thelwall: Radical Romantic and Acquitted Felon* (Pickering & Chatto, 2009), 161–73.

63 Edmund Burke, *An Appeal from the New Whigs to the Old Whigs ... Relative to the Reflections on the Revolution in France* (1791), 132–33.

64 *World*, 24 June 1791; *Evening Mail*, 13 July 1791. Many thanks to Nick Rogers for sharing his list of references to the Peasants' Revolt from 1791. Richard Dent's 1791 caricature, *Revolution Anniversary or Patriotic Incantations*, portrays posters of Wat Tyler and Jack Cade on the walls of the Crown and Anchor, celebrating the French Revolution.

65 See, for example, John Cleveland, *The Idol of Clownes, or, Insurrection of Wat the Tyler, with his Priests Baal and Straw* (1654); *Wat Tyler and Jack Straw; or, the Mob Reformers. A Dramatic Entertainment as Performed ... in Bartholomew Fair* (1730); *The History of Wat Tyler, and Jack Straw* (1730?, reprinted many times, including 1790?). Richard Cumberland, *The Armorer*, a comic opera about Tyler, was produced at Covent Garden in April 1793. *A Catalogue of the Larpent Plays in the Huntington Library*, compiled by Dougald MacMillan (San Marino, CA: Huntington Library, 1939), 162.

66 See Ian Haywood, "'The Renovating Fury': Southey, Republicanism and Sensationalism," *Romanticism on the Net* (November 2003/February 2004): 32–33.

67 For a summary of the controversy, see Frank T. Hoadley, "The Controversy over Southey's *Wat Tyler*," *Studies in Philology* 38 (1941): 81–96. For an analysis of how the controversy affected the character of the poet and romantic notions of self-hood, see Kim Wheatley, *Romantic Feuds: Transcending the "Age of Personality"* (Farnham: Ashgate, 2013), chapter 1.

68 Pratt, et al., eds., *SLPW,* 3: 445–48, and 507–15, for legal documents pertaining to the case; William Howard Winterbotham, *The Rev. William Winterbotham. A Sketch* (1893), 52–53.

69 *QR*, 16, 31 (October 1816): 225–78, at 248, 267–68, 275; Geoffrey Carnall, *Robert Southey and His Age: The Development of a Conservative Mind* (Oxford: OUP, 1960), 162. The article was unsigned but the author was obvious.

70 Southey to Liverpool, 19 March 1817, in C. D. Yonge, *The Life and Admin-istration of Robert Banks, Second Earl of Liverpool*, 3 vols. (1868), 2: 298–99; Ian Packer, "Robert Southey, Politics, and the Year 1817," *Romanticism on the Net* (2017): 68–69, noting the full letter was sent through Canning, and can be found among the Canning papers in the BL.

71 *HRR*, 22 February 1817, cols. 157–58.

72 William Hazlitt, "Wat Tyler; A Dramatic Poem; The Quarterly Review: Ar-ticle, 'On Parliamentary Reform,'" *Examiner*, 9 March 1817, in *CWH*, 7: 168–76, 170.

73 *PD*, vol. 35, cols. 1088–92, Commons, 14 March 1817. For an earlier attack from Brougham, see *PD*, vol. 35, col. 626, Commons, 24 February 1817. On the general charge of apostasy, see Charles Mahoney, *Romantics and Rene-gades: The Poetics of Political Reaction* (Houndmills: Palgrave Macmillan, 2003), chapter 1.

74 *Courier*, 17 March 1817, in Samuel Taylor Coleridge, *Essays in Our Time*, *CWC*, ed. David V. Erdman, 3, pt. 2: 449–54, at 451, 453–4.

75 For Southey and Coleridge's attempt to define an appropriate readership for their own work, see Kevin Gilmartin, "The 'sinking down' of Jacobinism and the Rise of the Counter-Revolutionary Man of Letters," in *Romanti-cism and Popular Culture in Britain and Ireland*, ed. Philip Connell and Nigel Leask (Cambridge: CUP, 2009), 128–47.

76 St Clair, *Reading Nation*, 310–11; Stephen Gill, *Wordsworth: A Life* (Ox-ford: OUP, 1990), 295–97.

77 Samuel Taylor Coleridge, *Biographia Literaria* (1817), in *Samuel Taylor Coleridge: The Major Works*, ed. H. J. Jackson (Oxford: OUP, 2000), chap-ter 10.

78 William Hazlett, "Mr. Coleridge and Mr. Southey,"*Examiner*, 6 April 1817, in *CWH*, 19: 196–98, at 197. For Hazlitt and Coleridge's literary encounter over *Wat Tyler*, see Robert Keith Lapp, *Contest for Cultural Authority: Ha-zlitt, Coleridge, and the Distresses of the Regency* (Detroit, MI: Wayne State University Press, 1999), chapter 5.

79 *MC*, 22 March 1817. Duncan Wu challenges David Erdman's ascription of this unsigned article to Hazlitt, in Duncan Wu, ed., *New Writings of Wil-liam Hazlitt*, 2 vols. (Oxford: OUP, 2007), 2: 474–76. For Southey's 1798 inscription for Tyler, see Kenneth Curry, ed., *The Contributions of Rob-ert Southey to the* Morning Post (Tuscaloosa: University of Alabama Press, 1984), 31–32.

80 Kevin Gilmartin, *William Hazlitt: Political Essayist* (Oxford: OUP, 2015), chapter 1. See also Philip Harling, "William Hazlitt and Radical Journal-ism," *Romanticism* 3 (1997): 53–65.

81 Craig Calhoun, *The Roots of Radicalism: Tradition, the Public Sphere, and Early Nineteenth-Century Social Movements* (Chicago, IL: University of Chicago Press, 2012), chapter 5, with Michael McQuarrie. See also Paul Magnuson, *Reading Public Romanticism* (Princeton, NJ: Princeton Univer-sity Press, 1998), chapter 1; Kevin Gilmartin, *Print Politics: The Press and Radical Opposition in Early Nineteenth-Century England* (Cambridge: CUP, 1996), introduction, and 30–31.

82 Robert Southey, *A Letter to William Smith, Esq. M.P.* (1817), 6–7, 13–14.

83 C 31/372 Pt. 2.

84 Southey, *Letter to Smith*, 7; Southey to Liverpool, 19 March 1817, in Yonge, *Life and Administration of Robert Banks*, 2: 298–99. Southey made the same point in a letter to the *Courier*, 17 March, in Southey, *LCRS*, 350–51.

85 *AGM*, 8 December 1816, 4861–62.

86 Southey, *Letter to Smith*, 27, 31–42. See more generally, David Eastwood, "Robert Southey and the Intellectual Origins of Romantic Conservatism," *EHR*, 104 (1989): 308–31; Philip Harling, "Robert Southey and the Language of Social Discipline," *Albion*, 30 (1999): 630–55; David Craig, *Robert Southey and Romantic Apostasy: Political Argument in Britain, 1780–1840* (Woodbridge: Royal Historical Society, Boydell Press, 2007).

87 Robert Southey, *Wat Tyler: A Drama*, in Pratt, et al., eds, *SLPW*, 3: 485. The final line is a quotation from James Mackintosh's *Vindiciae Gallicae*.

88 Ibid., 480.

89 *BD*, 26 March 1817, cols. 139–41. On Spencean appropriation of *Wat Tyler*, see David Worrall, "Agrarians against the Picturesque: Ultra-Radicalism and the Revolutionary Politics of the Land," in *The Politics of the Picturesque: Literature, Landscape, and Aesthetics since 1770*, ed. Stephen Copley and Peter Garside (Cambridge: CUP, 1994), 240–60; on radical journalists' excerpting *Wat Tyler*, see Casie LeGette, *Remaking Romanticism: The Radical Politics of the Excerpt* (Cham: Palgrave Macmillan, 2017), 68–84.

90 *The Extraordinary Red Book … by a Commoner*, 2nd ed. (1817, published by John Fairburn), 150; [John Wade], *The Black Book; or, Corruption Unmasked!* (1820), 78. For Wade and the radical critique of state corruption, see Philip Harling, *The Waning of 'Old Corruption': The Politics of Economical Reform in Britain, 1779–1846* (Oxford: OUP, 1996), 139–50.

91 William Hone, *The Sinecurist's Creed, or Belief* (1817), 7.

92 *PD*, vol. 35, col. 612, Commons, 24 February 1817, and cols. 714–18, Commons, 26 February, for Henry Gray Bennet's attack and Castlereagh's vehement objection. *HRR*, 19 July 1817, returned to the subject of "Torture in Ireland – and Lord Castlereagh."

93 For a provocative discussion of "Bloody Castlereagh," see Clara Tuite, *Lord Byron and Scandalous Celebrity* (Cambridge: CUP, 2014), chapter 5,

94 "Introduction to the Poetry of the *Anti-Jacobin*," *Anti-Jacobin; or, Weekly Examiner*, 1, 1, 20 November 1797: 31–34, 33. See more generally, Stuart Andrews, *The British Periodical Press and the French Revolution, 1789–99* (Houndmills: Palgrave, 2000), chapter 7, on "Jacobin Poetry."

95 See Lynda Pratt, "Patriot Politics and the Romantic National Epic: Placing and Displacing Southey's *Joan of Arc*," in *Placing and Displacing Romanticism*, ed. Peter J. Kitson (Aldershot: Ashgate, 2001), 88–105. Southey's "To the Exiled Patriots," his tribute the Scottish martyrs, was published in 1795; Wooler reprinted it in the *BD*, 13 March 1822, 372–73.

96 Southey, *Wat Tyler* (Sherwin's edition), 1.

97 However, see the report of London Chartists celebrating the founding of the French republic of 1792, *Northern Star*, 27 September, 1845, 5, at which Wat Tyler led off an omnibus toast that included the memories of Hampden, Sidney, Pym, and Elliott, as well as Milton, Byron, and Shelley.

98 HO 40/4/1 (pt. 2), report of agent no. 2 [James Rose], enclosed in William Chippendale to General Sir John Byng, Oldham, 5 December 1816, fols. 42–46; Byng to John Beckett, Oldham, 7 December 1816, fols. 21–23.

99 H. W. Davis, "Lancashire Reformers, 1816–1817," *Bulletin of the John Rylands Library* 10 (1926): 47–79. It was rumored that the younger Watson was in the Manchester district in December 1816, which is possible given that he escaped arrest, and sailed from Liverpool to America.

100 Bamford, *Passages*, 25–26, 29–30; Hunt, *Memoirs*, 3: 423. For Pendrill's links to Despard and the United Britons, see Roger Wells, *Insurrection: The British Experience, 1795–1803* (Gloucester: Allan Sutton, 1986),

205–07, 243–45. Bamford also records breakfasting with the elder Watson and Preston.

101 For Bacon, see Thompson, *Making*, 653–56. Pendrill was also involved in the plans that developed in the spring.

102 Hone, *Report of the Third Spa-Fields Meeting*.

103 *MPR*, 15 February 1817, 109–12; HO 42/159, James Green to Sidmouth, 10 February 1817, Manchester meeting; John Lloyd to Beckett, 10 February, Stockport meeting; Green to Sidmouth, 10 February, Oldham meeting; HO 40/10, Chippendale to Sidmouth, 10 February, Oldham.

104 HO 42/158, Chippendale to Matthew Fletcher (Bolton J. P.), 29 December 1816.

105 HO 40/4/1 (pt. 2), Chippendale to Home Office, 2 December 1816, fol. 41; Robert Poole, *Peterloo: The English Uprising* (Oxford: OUP, 2019), 115–16, and chapter 6 more generally.

106 Katrina Navickas, *Protest and the Politics of Space and Place, 1789–1818* (Manchester: Manchester University Press, 2016), 69–70.

107 HO 40/5/4A, examination of John Livesey, 11 March 1817, fols. 57–58, for Bagguley's careful instructions.

108 *The Statutes at Large*, vol. 3 (1770), 2 Car. II. *cap.* 5, 208–09. In 1795 the meaning and scope of the act were matters of debate as a precedent for the Seditious Meetings Bill. *History of the Two Acts*, (1796), 260.

109 R. J. White, *Waterloo to Peterloo* (Harmondsworth: Penguin, 1968), 164, and see chapter 13 more generally.

110 Joseph Mitchell, *An Address to the People* (Liverpool, 1816), 3, copy in HO 42/153, enclosed in Chippendale to Beckett, 7 October 1816, fols. 374–82. In early November, Mitchell visited Cartwright in London, and met with Cobbett who made him an agent for the *Political Register*.

111 HO 42/162, fol. 408. The petition's concluding line was cited in the *Second Report from the Committee of Secrecy*, Commons, 20 June 1817, *Parliamentary Papers*, 1817, iv.

112 See Linda Colley, "The Apotheosis of George III: Loyalty, Royalty and the British Nation 1760–1820," *P&P* 102 (1986): 94–129.

113 *PD*, vol. 35, col. 615. Commons, 24 February 1817.

114 HO 40/4/1 (pt. 2), 28 January 1817, fol. 108; HO 40/10, 3 March 1817, report no. 28, fol. 142, this is part of a series of numbered reports from two informers, Michael Hall (no. 1) and James Rose (no. 2), who monitored the New Islington room meetings; HO 40/5/4A, examination of Livesey, 11 March 1817, fol. 54; HO 40/9, digest of evidence against Lancashire reformers, fol. 54. See also Jacqueline Riding, *Peterloo: The Story of the Manchester Massacre* (Head of Zeus Ltd., 2018), chapter 5.

115 HO 40/10, 24 February 1817, fols. 134–35, report no. 22.

116 HO 40/4/2 (pt. 2), report of 17 December 1816, fols. 101–02; HO 40/10, report no. 4, 17 December 1816, fol. 117; HO 40/5/4B, information of William Axson, enclosed in William Hay to Sidmouth, 4 April 1817, fol. 28. For Bagguley's occupation, see HO 40/162, Hay to Beckett, 23 March 1817.

117 HO 40/10, 31 December 1816, informer's report, fol. 121. The same question was debated for two weeks at New Islington.

118 HO 40/4 (Supplementary Papers), informer's report, 3 February 1817, reprinted in Davis, "Lancashire Reformers," 74. See also HO 42/159, report of Peter Campbell, 4 February 1817; HO 40/5/5, information of P.C., 3 February 1817, fols. 34–36.

119 HO 40/10, 27 January 1817, report no. 13, fol. 126; HO 42/159, C. W. Ethelston to Sidmouth, 5 February 1817. Bagguley was referring to cap. 61

of Magna Carta to which he gave a radical (mis-) reading. For cap. 61, see J. C. Holt, *Magna Carta* (Cambridge: CUP, 1965), 238–39.

120 HO 40/9, Digest of evidence against Lancashire reformers, fols. 458, 461; HO 40/5/4A, deposition of John Livesey, 4 March 1817, fol. 12. There were reports of pikes being secretly stored.

121 Winterbotham, *Sketch*, 54.

122 See Robert Poole, "French Revolution or Peasants' Revolt? Petitioners and Rebels in England from the Blanketeers to the Chartists," *Labour History Review* 74 (2009): 6–26.

123 HO 42/158, fols. 55–56, "Information of Peter Campbell," enclosed in Ethelston to Sidmouth, 16 January 1817. Bagguley went on to describe their access to arms. For military service and radical mobilization, see Gordon Pentland, "Militarization and Collective Action in Great Britain, 1815–20," in *Crowd Actions in Britain and France from the Middle Ages to the Modern World*, ed. Michael T. Davis (Houndmills: Palgrave Macmillan, 2015), 179–92.

124 HO 40/4/1 (pt. 2), Chippendale to Sidmouth, 4 January 1817, fols.72–77. The band refused the magistrate's offer of five shillings to play "God Save the King."

125 HO 40/5/4A, deposition of Livesey, 4 March 1817, fol. 13; HO 40/5/4B, report of A. B., 5 March 1817, fol. 48.

126 HO 42/163, information of P.C., before Ethelson, 15 January 1817.

127 Katrina Navickas, "John Knight," *ODNB*. For Knight's wife Elizabeth and the gender dynamics between imprisoned radicals and their wives and families, see Katrina Navickas, "'A Reformer's Wife ought to be an Heroine': Imprisoned under the Suspension of Habeas Corpus Act," *History*, (2016): 246–64. Knight was imprisoned in 1817 and was back in prison in 1819 for his part at Peterloo.

128 According to Lloyd, Rose "confesses to have been president of the Convention of Jacobins in the time of Muir," HO 42/158, Lloyd to Beckett, 2 January 1817. See Henry W. Meikle, *Scotland and the French Revolution* (Glasgow: J. Maclehose and Son 1912), 274; Robert Glen, *Urban Workers in the Early Industrial Revolution*, (Croom Helm, 1984), 212, and chapter 9 more generally for the movement in Stockport.

129 HO 42/158, "Characters of certain Deputies," report of XY to Joseph Warren, 23 January 1817, forwarded to John Hiley Addington, fols. 115–16; Bamford, *Passages*, 14–15.

130 For preparations and communications between the Home Office and Lancashire magistrates, see Nathan Ashley Bend, "The Home Office and Public Disturbance, c.1800–1832" (Ph.D. thesis, University of Hertfordshire, 2018), 166–70.

131 HO 40/5/4A, William Hay to Sidmouth, 10 March 1817, fols. 41–43, and report of 10 March meeting, fols. 43–46; HO 40/10, Rob Baker to Beckett, 10 March 1817, fols. 102–03, and 11 March, fols. 104–06; HO 42/162, Lloyd to Beckett, 11 March 1817; HO 42/161, William Greaves (Staffordshire J. P.) to Sidmouth, 12 March 1817; TS 11/347 (1077), including "The Meeting at Peters Church;" *Manchester Gazette,* 15 March 1817, estimated 40,000 were present. The leaders were alert to the need for each marcher to carry sufficient funds to avoid charges against begging and vagrancy.

132 HO 42/172, fols. 251–61, for lists of all those arrested giving age, occupation, and residence; TS 11/347 (1077), statement of Ethelston, sets the number at 267; HO 42/175, for information on how those arrested were disposed of.

133 W. D. Evans, *Address of W. D. Evans, at the New Bayley Court House, Salford, On Discharging Prisoners* (Manchester, 1817), 4–6; TS 11/347 (1077), Evans to Sidmouth, 17 March 1817. True bills were found against those bound over, based on laws against vagrancy and against tumultuous assembly. TS 11/347 (1077), "King v William Strandring, and eight others." However, when brought to trial at Lancashire Assizes, it was decided not to proceed further; the jury was instructed to issue not-guilty verdicts. See *BD*, 10 September 1817, cols. 520–21, for Wooler's scathing ridicule of the authorities' false benevolence, for "the PROSECUTOR DARE NOT PROCEED," for fear of the jury acquitting the Blanketeers.

134 Spinners were reported to have contributed £ 20 from the box of their sick club, as well as subscribing five shillings each. HO 40/10, Baker to Beckett, 9 March 1817, fols. 106–07; HO 40/5/4A, deposition of Livesey, 8 March 1817. For a summary breakdown of the ages, occupations, and districts of the marchers, see Poole, *Peterloo*, 130–31.

135 HO 44/3/188, for the statements of twenty-two men, including Broadbent.

136 Northumberland to Sidmouth, 21 March 1817, in George Pellew, *The Life and Correspondence of the Right Hon. Henry Addington, First Viscount Sidmouth*, (1847), 3 vols., 3: 178.

137 Bamford, *Passages*, 39–40, 64–69; idem, *An Account of the Arrest and Imprisonment of Samuel Bamford, Middleton, on Suspicion of High Treason* (Manchester, 1817); *Second Report from the Committee of Secrecy*, Commons, 20 June 1817, *PP*, 1817, iv.

138 Davis, "Lancashire Reformers," 60–64; Poole, *Peterloo*, 133–51. While there were clearly links between the movement leading up to 10 March and its conspiratorial aftermath, the emphasis of leaders such as Bagguley was on open agitation. Bagguley reportedly thought Watson to be "a fool," for his "precipitate measures" that "injured the scheme of the Hampden Clubs." HO 42/163, information of P. C., 15 January 1817.

139 HO 40/5/7, rough minute book, including notes of Sidmouth's examinations of prisoners and records of warrants issued.

140 HO 42/172, fols. 333–34, List of prisoners held on warrants of high treason; Navickas, "'A Reformer's Wife,'" 246. Most of the prisoners were from Lancashire, along with several from Nottingham, South Yorkshire and the West Riding, as well as Evans Sr. and his son. See also HO 40/9, Digest of evidence to be brought against Lancashire prisoners.

141 Thompson, *Making*, 649–69; J. L. and Barbara Hammond, *The Skilled Labourer* (Longmans, 1920), chapter 12; John Stevens, *England's Last Revolution: Pentrich 1817* (Buxton: Moorland Publishing, 1977). For the role of radical Nottingham and links to the Luddite movement, see R. A. Gaunt, "The Pentrich Rebellion: A Nottingham Affair?," *Midland History* 43 (2018): 208–28.

142 For Mitchell's account, see *Blanketteer*, 23 October and 6 November 1819; for Oliver's narrative, see HO 40/9. On Mitchell's innocence, see Robert Poole, "The Risings of 1817," Luddite Memorial lecture, Huddersfield Local History Society, 21 April 2016, https://www.huddersfieldhistory.org.uk/events/ludditelecture/

143 Thompson, *Making*, 670.

144 *Blanketteer*, 30 October 1819, 19–20.

145 *Report of the Whole of the Proceedings … including the Trials of Jeremiah Brandreth … William Turner, Isaac Ludlam, the Elder, and George Weightman, for High Treason: with the Speeches of the Counsel, and Other Interesting Particulars* (Nottingham, 1817), 130–37; HO 42/171,

Jeffrey Lockett to Addington, 7 November 1817, fols. 159–64; V. A. C. Gatrell, *The Hanging Tree: Execution and the English People, 1770–1868* (Oxford: OUP, 1996), chapter 11.

146 See Michel Foucault, *Discipline and Punish: The Birth of the Prison*, trans. Alan Sheridan (New York: Vintage, 1979), 48–49.

147 See Alan Brooke and Lesley Kipling, *Liberty or Death: Radicals, Republicans and Luddites, 1793–1823*, 2nd ed. (Huddersfield: Huddersfield Local History Society, 2012), 73–89; *ST*, 33, cols. 275–628, "Proceedings against Andrew M'Kinlay"; Gordon Pentland, *The Spirit of Union: Popular Politics in Scotland, 1815–1820* (Pickering & Chatto, 2011), 39–44.

148 See Pellew, *Life and Correspondence of Addington*, 3: 182–83, 200–01.

149 Hammonds, *Skilled Labourer*, 366–69; Thompson, *Making*, 663–65.

150 *ST*, vol. 32, "Trial of Jeremiah Brandreth," cols. 759–60.

151 Ibid.,"Trial of Isaac Ludlam, the Elder," cols. 1229–30. The lines are quoted from Canto 1, stanzas 8–9.

152 Ibid., "Trial of George Weightman," col. 1394. Twelve of the younger prisoners were set free. Thomas Bacon, who was deeply involved with Oliver, was allowed to tender a guilty plea and was transported for life, thus ensuring he would not bring up Oliver's name in court.

153 Thomas Sadler, ed., *Diary, Reminiscences, and Correspondence of Henry Crabb Robinson*, 2 vols. (Boston, 1871), 1: 370–71.

154 Charles Howard Ford, "Political and Religious Responses to Royal Ritual: The Funeral of Princess Charlotte in 1817" (master's thesis, Vanderbilt University, 1988), 13–16, 19–23; Robert Huish, *Memoirs of the Late Royal Highness Charlotte Augusta, Princess of Wales* (1818), 571–85. See more generally, Stephen C. Behrendt, *Royal Mourning and Regency Culture: Elegies and Memorials of Princess Charlotte* (Houndmills: Macmillan, 1997).

155 *Courier*, 7 November 1817, in Coleridge, *Essays in Our Time*, CWC, ed. Erdman, 3, pt. 2: 478–79.

156 Lord Byron, *Childe Harold's Pilgrimage*, Canto IV (1818), in *Lord Byron, The Major Works*, ed. Jerome J. McGann (Oxford: OUP, 2000), 196–97.

157 Linda Colley, *Britons: Forging the Nation, 1707–1837* (New Haven, CT: Yale University Press, 1992), 269, 220–1.

158 Dorothy Thompson, *Queen Victoria: Gender and Power* (Virago, 1990), 6–7; Christopher Hibbert, *George IV: Regent and King, 1811–1830* (Allen Lane, 1973), chapter 4.

159 Hunt, *Memoirs*, 3: 507.

160 Sadler, *Reminiscences of Crabb Robinson*, 1: 369.

161 *QR*, January 1817, 16, 32: 511–52, 538–39. The article was published in April, and Shelley's pamphlet in March. For a convincing case made for Southey knowing that Shelley was the author, see Kenneth Neill Cameron, "Shelley vs. Southey: New Light on an Old Quarrel," *PMLA* 57 (1942): 489–512. At the end of 1816, Shelley's wife Harriet, whom he had left for Mary Wollstonecraft Godwin, committed suicide, presumably prompting the reference to "moral suicide." Southey may also have seen a copy of *Queen Mab*.

162 Percy Bysshe Shelley, *A Proposal for Putting Reform to the Vote throughout the Kingdom*, in *The Prose Works of Percy Bysshe Shelley, Volume 1*, ed. E. B. Murray (Oxford: OUP, 1993), 169–76. For the list of those to whom Shelley wished to send copies of the proposal, see Shelley to Charles Ollier, February 1817, *LS*, 1: 532–34. The list includes Cobbett and Place along with various liberal Whigs and gentleman reformers such as Burdett, Cochrane, and Cartwright.

163 Kenneth Neill Cameron, *Shelley: The Golden Years* (Cambridge, MA: Harvard University Press, 1974), 122–25.

164 *Examiner*, 9 November 1817, 716–17, report of the executions from which Shelley quotes.

165 The essay was finished in two days, between 10 and 12 November. Paula R. Feldman and Diana Scott-Kilvert, eds., *The Journals of Mary Shelley, 1814–1844*, 2 vols. (Oxford: OUP, 1987), 1 (1814–22): 183–84. For the best account of Shelley's life and politics in 1816–17, see Richard Holmes, *Shelley: The Pursuit* (New York: New York Review of Books, 1994), chapters 14–15.

166 Percy Bysshe Shelley, *An Address to the People on the Death of Princess Charlotte*, in Murray, ed., *Prose Works*, 231–32.

167 Esther Schor, *Bearing the Dead: The British Culture of Mourning from the Enlightenment to Victoria* (Princeton, NJ: Princeton University Press, 1994), 200–07. Compare Stephen C. Behrendt, *Shelley and His Audiences* (Lincoln: University of Nebraska Press, 1989), 33–38.

168 Shelley to Byron, 8 September 1816, *LS*, 1: 504.

169 Mary Wollstonecraft, *A Vindication of the Rights of Men*, ed. Sylvana Tomaselli (Cambridge: CUP, 1995, first published 1790), 8, 14 (discussing penal laws). Shelley had recently reread Paine's *Rights of Man* and Godwin's *Political Justice*, and was well acquainted with Wollstonecraft's writing. For a list of Shelley's reading, see Feldman and Scott-Kilvert, eds., *Journals of Mary Shelley*, 1: 102.

170 Shelley, *Address to the People*, 232.

171 Shelley describes the Revolution in *Laon and Cythna* in relation to "the *beau ideal* ... of the French Revolution." Shelley to [A Publisher], 13 October 1817, *LS*, 1: 563–64. For Shelley's idealization of the Revolution, see David Duff, *Romance and Revolution: Shelley and the Politics of a Genre* (Cambridge: CUP, 1994), 158–61,

172 Shelley, *Address to the People*, 233.

173 Ibid., 235.

174 For Cobbett's influence on Shelley's economic and political views, see P. M. S. Dawson, *The Unacknowledged Legislator: Shelley and Politics* (Oxford: OUP, 1980), 49–51; Michael Henry Scrivener, *Radical Shelley: The Philosophical Anarchism and Utopian Thought of Percy Bysshe Shelley* (Princeton, NJ: Princeton University Press, 1982), 112, 131, 136. No doubt Shelley's own aristocratic background influenced his attitude to the "new" aristocracy.

175 Shelley, *Address to the People*, in Murray, ed., *Prose Works*, 236–38.

176 Ibid., 238–39. For a fine reading of the final section, see Michael O'Neill, "'Pictures' and 'Signs': Creative Thinking in Shelley's Prose, 1816–21," in *Thinking through Style: Non-Fiction Prose of the Long Nineteenth Century*, ed. Michael D. Hurley and Marcus Waithe (Oxford: OUP, 2018), 70–86, 73–75.

177 On 12 November, Shelley rushed the pamphlet to Charles Ollier to be printed, and Mary Shelley records reading it three days later. Shelley to Ollier, 12 November 1817, *LS*, 1: 566; Feldman and Scott-Kilvert, eds., *Journals of Mary Shelley*,1: 184; Holmes, *Shelley*, 388. When it was reprinted in 1843, the publisher claimed that only twenty copies had been printed, but it is possible that the "facsimile" reprint was taken from a manuscript copy.

178 Shelley to Byron, 23 April 1817, *LS*, 1: 539; Holmes, *Shelley*, 356–57, 369. Shelley feared that a prosecution of *Queen Mab* might arise from the custody suit over his children in Chancery.

179 Shelley to Ollier, 11 December 1817, Shelley to Ollier, 16 December 1817, and Shelley to Thomas Moore, 16 December 1817, *LS*, 1: 578–83; Behrendt, *Shelley and His Audiences*, 24–28; Holmes, *Shelley*, 389–402.

180 Percy Bysshe Shelley, "An Essay on Christianity" (1816–17), in *Shelley's Prose in the Bodleian Manuscripts*, ed. A. H. Koszul (Frowde, 1910), 38.

181 Marilyn Butler, *Romantics and Rebels: English Literature and Its Background, 1760–1830* (Oxford: OUP, 1981), 146. See also P. M. S. Dawson, "Shelley and Class," in *The New Shelley: Later Twentieth-Century Views*, ed. G. Kim Blank (New York: St. Martin's Press, 1991), 34–41.

182 See Martin Priestman, "A Place to Stand: Questions of Address in Shelley's Political Pamphlets," in *The Unfamiliar Shelley*, ed. Alan M. Weinberg and Timothy Webb (Farnham: Ashgate, 2009), 221–38, at 233–38; William Keach, "The Political Poet," in *Cambridge Companion to Shelley*, ed. Timothy Morton (Cambridge: CUP, 2006), 123–42, at 130–32.

183 *BD*, 12 November 1817, cols. 687–90; Paine, *Rights of Man*, 57–58. Despite the verdicts at Derby, Wooler maintained his faith in the institution of the English jury. *BD*, 29 October 1817, cols. 655–63, and 19 November 1817, col. 706.

184 See Behrendt, *Royal Mourning*, 20–22; Scrivener, *Radical Shelley*, 137–38. Shelley's address bears comparison to Hunt's "Death of the Princess Charlotte, and … Lamentable Punishments at Derby," *Examiner*, 16 November 1817, 721–23.

185 *SWPR*, 15 November 1817, 33–39. Sherwin opened volume two of his journal with an attack on "The Blessings of Hereditary Succession," *SWPR*, 4 October 1817, 1–2.

186 TS 11/197/859, report of John Williamson, 10 November 1817.

187 *CWPR*, 25 April 1818, cols. 475–505, 500–02, 505; Belchem, *'Orator' Hunt*, 75–76. For Hunt's account of events, and his attack on Thomas Cleary and Burdett for failing to rally support for the Derbyshire men, see Henry Hunt, *The Green Bag Plot* (1819).

188 Shelley to Robert Waithman, 4 January 1818, *LS*, 1: 591–92.

189 Nicolas Roe, *Fiery Heart: The First Life of Leigh Hunt* (New York: Random House, 2005), 323–24.

190 Holmes, *Shelley*, 208–10; McCalman, *Radical Underworld*, 155; William St Clair, *The Godwins and the Shelleys: The Biography of a Family* (Faber and Faber, 1989), appendix 3, "Shelley and the pirates." Between 1822 and 1841, there were at least twenty-six pirated editions of *Queen Mab*. Neil Fraistat, "Illegitimate Shelley: Radical Piracy and the Textual Edition as Performance," *PMLA* 109 (1994): 409–23, 412; St Clair, *Reading Nation*, appendix 11, 68–82.

191 Anne Janowitz, *Lyric and Labour in the Romantic Tradition* (Cambridge: CUP, 1998), 149–51; Mike Sanders, *The Poetry of Chartism: Aesthetics, Politics, History* (Cambridge: CUP, 2009), chapter 3. According to Engels, Shelley ("the genius, the prophet") and Byron found most of their readers among the working class. Friedrich Engels, *The Condition of the Working Class in England*, ed. Victor Kiernan (Penguin, 1987, first published 1845), 245.

7 "The Embers of Expiring Sedition"

Maurice Margarot, the Scottish Martyrs Monument, and Radical Memory across the South Pacific

Recovery

In 2002, a headstone commemorating a once-notorious British couple resurfaced in London. Excavations for the new London terminus of the Channel Tunnel Rail Link had disturbed the St. Pancras burial grounds, requiring the assistance of exhumation and archeological teams. It was the second time that railway projects had disrupted the grounds. During the expansion of the Midland Railway in the 1860s, the architect and later novelist Thomas Hardy was hired to oversee the removal and reburial of thousands of the St. Pancras dead. This caused a public outcry and Hardy later expressed his own sense of sardonic pity in the poem "The Levelled Churchyard."[1] Now, in 2002, human remains were once more to be exhumed and relocated. Teams recovered a number of displaced headstones as well, among them one honoring Maurice Margarot and his wife Elizabeth.[2] As the first president of the LCS, Margarot had been a leading figure in British radical circles during the 1790s, and was one of five political prisoners transported to Australia in 1794 for sedition. The five were immediately seen by fellow activists as heroic sufferers for the cause, in time becoming known as the "Scottish Martyrs to liberty." Of the five, Margarot and his wife were the only ones who returned to Britain, landing in 1810.

Maurice Margarot's burial at St. Pancras in 1815, after the ill health and poverty of his last several years, was a quiet occasion: only eleven people attended his funeral.[3] When his wife Elizabeth died in 1841, her body joined his in the grounds and the headstone dedicated to them was placed there after her death (Figure 7.1). Following the disruption to the southern portion of the grounds in the 1860s and 1870s, theirs and others' burial markers ("this jumbled patch of wretched memorial stones," in Hardy's words) would be used in later dry-stone construction of a southern wall for St. Pancras Park. As generations of Londoners strolled through the grounds, these hidden memorials would remain there until the railways returned in 2002.

The recovery of the Margarots' memorial calls attention to the construction of radical memory after the 1790s and the headstone itself

Figure 7.1 The burial ground at Old St. Pancras Churchyard, London, 1876. The Margarots' marker is at middle distance. It has a rounded top and is leaning precariously to the right. Photograph © Parish of Old St. Pancras Church.

registers memory's contested terrain. The Maurice Margarot produced by it bore only passing resemblance to the British republican who was its object – a figure who continually participated in the subversive, desirous, and seditious political culture that has animated this book. Rather, the headstone's engraved text produces Maurice Margarot as an activist whose behavior was "able, legal, and upright" throughout, acting with "conscious rectitude and unsullied honour" – omitting mention that the Margarots' house in Australia was a center of conspiratorial sedition at the time of Irish convict uprisings in 1800 and 1804, and was at times full of excited conjecture about the possibility of revolution back in Britain. The marker erases controversies about Margarot voiced by British radicals as well, stating that he returned to Britain "injured in health, ruined in fortune, yet still esteemed and revered by his enlightened fellow-citizens." As this chapter will show, his reputation was rather more complex. Likewise, Elizabeth Margarot is engendered as an apolitical partner who during their exile "solaced him with the tenderest affection … characterized by every female virtue."[4] A couple who were under constant surveillance and policing by the British state between 1793 and 1815 are safely redrawn into a narrative of polite domesticity and constitutional progress.

The Margarots' case is not unique. Radical efforts at establishing continuity across the divide of the Napoleonic Wars involved a welter of memorial practices: narrative histories, built-form monuments, and ritual celebrations such as funerals or anniversary dinners marking political trials of the 1790s.[5] Radical culture itself was never monolithic. On occasion, later radical memorialists told stories that registered the fuller spectrum of behavior animating British republicanism. Celebration of insurrectionist heroes such as the United Irishman Robert Emmet, for example, pointed toward a different way of remembering the struggles of the 1790s.[6] Commemoration of British radicalism developed within a complex landscape of ideological conflict, but by the 1830s the dominant narrative of the radical past had marginalized its more conspiratorial desires and practices.[7] By exploring Maurice Margarot as a troubled object of radical commemoration, this chapter offers a microhistory through which to examine the limits of collective memory in the aftermath of the 1790s.

In doing so, the chapter advances two central propositions. First, constructions of a radical heritage during the later 1830s provided an alternative to contemporary conservative, state-sanctioned collective memory. In the decade preceding the project to commemorate the Scottish Martyrs, many of London's public spaces had been ideologically transformed to represent the 1790s as a time of loyalist triumph over French revolutionary conspiracy and of British power in the post-Napoleonic world.[8] All through the nineteenth century, ceremonial spaces in London were reconfigured to befit its status as "the heart of the empire."[9] By the later 1800s, Londoners inhabited a world of material and discursive reminders of Britain's global reach: consumer goods, advertisements, rational recreational practices, and the built-form of the capital itself manifested an imperial identity.[10] This process began early in the nineteenth century. Nelson's Column was, of course, modeled on Trajan's Column at Rome, a marker that registered the period of the Roman Empire's greatest extent.[11] By contrast, radical memorialists explicitly juxtaposed the Martyrs project against the ongoing conservative appropriations of urban space. The radical commemorative practices discussed in this chapter may then stand as an early instance whereby British reformers sought to counter an emerging loyalist reconfiguration of London's symbolic spaces, one that in time produced the later nineteenth-century metropolis as empire's heart.

The chapter's second proposition argues that in offering that alternative history, radical commemoration nonetheless represented the 1790s in a highly restricted way, marginalizing its more utopian, ludic, and subversive aspects, and re-presenting the movement as unproblematically constitutionalist. As argued in Chapter 1, while reformers certainly made constitutionalist demands for British rights, many also simultaneously engaged in "French" republican gestures, embracing a politics of symbolic expression that both parodied loyalists' imagined construction of revolutionary sedition, and expressed, however provisionally, utopian desires for a world of cosmopolitan Jacobinism. Revolutionary expression and constitutional claims were not necessarily competing styles but often defined poles of a tactical continuum that gave radical sedition its challenging edge and subversive attraction.[12] The case of the Martyrs monument, however, reveals how efforts in the late 1830s to forge a reform alliance of moderate and radical supporters of the People's Charter created pressures to represent the radical past as purely constitutionalist. This misremembering circumscribed the movement's heritage and marginalized the place of "deep play" in radical political culture. Margarot, in particular, posed challenges to the construction of a coherent radical heritage. Central to the radical movement's public, his alleged behavior on board the transport ship *Surprize* threatened the symbolic unanimity of the transported Martyrs. Moreover, Margarot's activities in Australia gestured toward an underground revolutionary current informing British republicanism.

The Martyrs' Australian experiences also remind us that radical commemoration occurred within the context of empire, and so this chapter also seeks to contribute to an ongoing, broader discussion about the place of empire within early nineteenth-century popular radicalism. Commemorating the transportees of 1794 helped widen the boundaries of radical culture to include colleagues in the British South Pacific: the viability of the Martyrs monument as a *lieu de mémoire* depended upon recognition that in an important sense, radicalism was trans-imperial.[13] But this sense of a trans-Pacific radical culture was only unevenly produced. In contrast to high political culture's consistent invocation of imperial themes, empire occupied popular radical discourse inconsistently, as different reform topics selectively encouraged discussion that was wider than affairs "at home."[14] Along with other imperial topics that impinged upon domestic reform agendas – such as British "Jacobin" critiques of slavery during the 1790s or the upheaval of the 1798 Irish Rebellion – transportation invariably drew attention within radicalism to the darker side of empire.[15] The case of Maurice Margarot – as seen in his criticisms against colonial misrule made in a secret journal he kept while in Australia, and in public letters sent "home" to the Colonial Office and to fellow radicals – demonstrates that reforms of domestic and imperial political abuses were not seen as wholly separate agendas.[16]

The Convict Ship: "Intimacy Begets Words–"

The St. Pancras burial ground was a principal site for the burial of French revolutionary refugees, so it was ironic that Margarot was buried there.[17] But from his first appearance in the archives of state surveillance, Margarot's character presented puzzles. A loyalist spy report of early 1793 hints at the confusion over his identity: "Margarot is, I believe, an American, seemingly without any visible means of support, is the Chairman of an infernal club of Chimney Sweeps, Car-men, etc."[18] We still know few details of Margarot's life before 1790. He was born in Exeter in 1745 of mixed English–French parents. His father was a wine merchant operating between France, Portugal, and the West Indies, and published a cosmopolitan account of his travels.[19] The younger Margarot also traveled widely: baptized in Portugal at the British Factory Chaplaincy in 1749, he later attended the University of Geneva.[20] Moreover, the Margarots were a political family. During the Wilkesite agitation, their London home was a center of radical activity. In the 1780s, the younger Margarot began managing his father's interests in France, and was in Paris from 1789 through early 1792. Returning to London, he immediately became a central figure in the LCS (that "infernal club") during its earliest phase. He wrote its first public address, and in September 1792, Margarot helped present the LCS's formal congratulations to the newly established French Republic at the National Convention in Paris. The following year he carried out a great deal of its secretarial work during preparations for the British Convention at Edinburgh in November. Upon serving as one of the two LCS delegates to the Convention, in December 1793 Margarot was arrested and charged with sedition, together with his co-delegate Joseph Gerrald, and William Skirving, the Convention's secretary.[21] In 1794, along with the radical barrister Thomas Muir and reforming Unitarian minister Thomas Fyshe Palmer, they would become political exiles in Australia, where Margarot remained until 1810.

Radicals in Britain immediately valorized the Martyrs as a corporate symbol of the Pitt government's repression of popular rights. In March 1794, for example, the Sheffield Constitutional Society printed a public address to the prisoners that protested the "tyrannical decree" of transportation and promised that the society would keep the prisoners' fate visible in the public mind.[22] But as 1794 ended, supporters of the reform movement had to grapple with the mysterious events that happened on the *Surprize* transport as it carried Margarot, Muir, Palmer, and Skirving to Australia between April and October 1794, when the discovery of an alleged mutiny plot caused the republican brotherhood to fragment amidst mutual acrimony.

Surviving accounts of the discovery of the plot disagree on the level of its support among the crew, as well as the identities of its ringleaders.[23] The following narrative offers a sense of what we can say happened, keeping in mind the ambiguities of this set of events and nonevents. For radicals in Britain who interpreted the mutiny, its most salient feature seemed to be its maddening lack of resolvability. Many years later, when Chartist-era memorialists sought to use the political transportees as mythic ancestors to their own program, they had to grapple with the mutiny, either by writing some of its participants out of the radical progressive narrative or by constructing some version of events that would bear the weight of conflicting and overlapping claims about a plan to take over the *Surprize* and murder its captain, Patrick Campbell.

On 31 May 1794, as the *Surprize* neared Rio de Janeiro, Campbell announced to the passengers and crew that he had discovered a plot. He was to have been killed and the ship was to have been commandeered to either France or the United States.[24] The scope of the conspiracy widened, as Campbell began to question passengers, some of whom began to implicate Palmer and Skirving.[25] Skirving had bribed guards with wine; Palmer had given convicts and soldiers money as well as "Spirits, Tea and Sugar."[26] They turned their mess table into a center of revolutionary sentiment, filled with toasts such as "Damnation to the King, his Family and all Crowned Heads!"[27] International politics figured into the plot as well. According to one convict, Palmer and Skirving had claimed that the French National Convention, who had "a great regard" for the Martyrs, would welcome the mutinied ship into protection.[28] Given this evidence, Campbell locked the two in the brig, where they would stay for the next several weeks.

This state of unease continued until the *Surprize* reached Port Jackson in Australia on 25 October. Unlike Skirving and Palmer, however, Margarot and Muir were spared any discipline, and seemed to have remained on good terms with the captain. Campbell had already written from Rio de Janeiro that "Muir and Margarot conducted themselves with every degree of propriety, and offered their assistance to protect the Ship, with Readiness and Willingness."[29] The fact that Muir, and Margarot especially, had escaped punishment while Palmer and Skirving had not, upset the social dynamics of the Martyrs from the moment they arrived in Australia. There, Margarot was ostracized by Palmer and Skirving. Meanwhile, Palmer penned an account of the voyage (published in Britain in 1797) in which Margarot is continually represented as a close confidant and advisor to Campbell, helping the captain to keep close watch over Skirving and Palmer. Nowhere in the account does Palmer supply Margarot with a motive and all evidence of Margarot's advisory role to Campbell is presented through third-party accounts.[30] The narrative presents readers with a murky conspiracy-without-cause. What had happened to the heroic band of British reformers?

Several factors help explain why the group fragmented into mutual suspicion. A growing hostility between Palmer and Margarot was key. The animosities between them reflected different political and religious backgrounds, as well as jealousies on Margarot's part over Palmer's greater economic resources, partly created by the latter's place within a dense network of Unitarian supporters. Some of these tensions had emerged even before the *Surprize* had weighed anchor in April, but the ship itself likely exacerbated them, for the unique nature of the transport ship required constant negotiations over the authority of the ship's captain, the Martyrs' identities as political prisoners, and the very real differences among the group of Martyrs themselves. Before exploring what kind of radicals Palmer and Margarot were, then, we must move into the politics of space onboard the *Surprize* itself.

Transport ships were extraordinarily dense spatial sites, where the contradictions of cultural, social, and political power were made real and material.[31] As in other sailing vessels attached to the state, the spaces of the transport ship were highly public: privacy was reserved for those who had privileged position, yet the notion of a purely personal space created unsettling ambiguities over the reach and scope of the captain's authority.[32] Additionally, the nature of transport ships' main criminal "cargo" meant that rules governing use of space were particularly rigid. Finally, transport ships brought together in close and continual proximity a wide range of social classes, from sons of the gentry sent to learn shipcraft and command (often under masters of ostensibly lower social status), to sometimes middling-class free settlers, to the roughest of convicted felons. Space onboard the *Surprize* thus mattered for both practical and cultural reasons. Where one slept, walked, ate, and in what company, deeply affected perception of self and other.

Moreover, at 400 tons the *Surprize* was a small ship for the long voyage to Australia. In even moderate conditions, its decks were perpetually swept by breaking waves, which meant that convicts had to remain imprisoned below for long periods of time.[33] During rough weather on the *Surprize*'s first run to Australia in 1790, the ship's captain wrote that the convicts were "considerably above their waists in water" and crew members were also "nearly up to their middles."[34] Filled with eighty-two convicts (fifty-nine women, twenty-three men), a dozen free settlers and their children, between thirty and forty crew members, and twenty-one soldiers of the New South Wales Corps, the *Surprize* was a crowded vessel.[35] Space was in short supply.

The weeks prior to the *Surprize*'s departure in April 1794 had been filled with the anxious efforts of passengers to secure spaces and goods. Palmer and Muir were originally supposed to have sailed on a different ship, the *HMS Canada*, and had paid £50 apiece for private cabins on that ship in order that they might travel in "the characters of gentlemen," a phrase that registers the relationship among space, performance, and identity. When the *Canada* was found to be too rotten to sail, Palmer and Muir were transferred to the *Surprize*. After first being assigned shared quarters with soldiers, they quickly found that they were to be given regular convict quarters instead. This prompted a flurry of lobbying to Campbell, and after some time they were allowed cabins on the soldiers' deck level.[36]

For his part, Margarot had arranged for his wife Elizabeth to travel with him as a free settler. Here again, public and private spaces blurred together, inflecting the desire for accommodations with prickly political overtones. When Elizabeth was finally awarded a cabin next to that of some of the ship's officers, they promptly complained to Campbell that her seditious husband would share it with her: "having the liberty of comeing into the Cabbin will create a particular intimacy, & intimacy begets words –," the dash signaling that words might lead to more dangerous events.[37] When Elizabeth was moved to a different cabin housing wives of other free settlers and officers, the incoming New South Wales civil service superintendent William Baker complained about the new arrangement; he didn't like having to pass by the prisoner's wife in order to get to his own wife's bed.[38] These claims and counter-claims regarding private space in turn forced Campbell into an exasperating series of exchanges with superiors.[39]

Space as a commodity became almost palpable in its desirability; its denial or misappropriation was jealously resented, and this wore away at the perceived unanimity of the Scottish Martyrs. When Campbell combined the officers' mess and the cabin passengers' mess in order to save money, Palmer was soon dismissed from the mess table – possibly in deference to the complaints of officers and voluntary settlers. Palmer was now ordered to dine with Skirving and the Margarots in steerage. Palmer seems to have paid acute attention to status. He resented his demotion and soon formed his own table with his companion James Ellis, Skirving, and the family of John Boston, a Birmingham surgeon and radical who had sailed with Palmer as a volunteer settler.[40] As noted above, their politically blasphemous table-talk would figure in the accusations against Palmer and Skirving.

The *Surprize*'s spatial dynamics also affected sexualities in ways that may have exacerbated the split between Palmer and Margarot. Palmer's *Narrative* continually portrayed the *Surprize*'s women convicts as rough and publically sexual beings. Thus when Palmer's companion James Ellis was denied a cabin, Palmer complained that Ellis was to be housed alongside the common convict quarters, given "a cot in the most flagitious brothel in the universe."[41] There was more to Palmer's aversion than the discomfort of a minister faced with the rough crowd, for sexuality onboard the *Surprize* was in fact a public matter – highly gendered and sometimes violent. As in many other early convict ships, spaces for male and female prisoners were typically not formally separated but instead were combined into a single large area; on the *Surprize*, it measured around 75 feet by 35 feet. It was not until after 1817 that the hold area of convict transports would allow a more rigorous separation of female and male prisoners.[42] Moreover, like many early transport shipmasters, Campbell allowed a relatively open sexual circulation between the crew and female convicts. Crew members' potential abusiveness in these liaisons forced many female convicts into a strategy of becoming the acknowledged partner of a particular crew member. "Coupling," as it was sometimes known, was thus a survival tactic that traded sex for a measure of security; women prisoners displayed sexual alliances as markers of protection.[43] Palmer himself, sent to dine in steerage after the discovery of the alleged plot, was separated from the convicts by only a wooden screen; he recalled their spaces as "that infernal brothel," filled with women, "perpetually drunk, and perpetually engaged in clamours, brawls and fighting."[44] At other times, he and Skirving expressed horror as women were flogged or beaten.[45] Palmer's reaction to the convict women is similar to that found in many other polite transportation narratives; it registers the sexualization of disorder and violence as the boundary between the polite and the rough was compressed to almost nothing, a thin pane of wood. That unease, and the half-enunciated links made among public sexuality, gender, and class is a common theme in polite male transportation narratives.[46] Finally, there may have been other sexual tensions here as well. Palmer, a lifelong bachelor, had paid passage for his former servant and companion Ellis. On the passage down to Rio de Janeiro, Campbell implied that Palmer was homosexual; rumors swirled that Palmer and Ellis were romantic partners. Two decades later, Francis Place obtained an anonymous letter hinting that Palmer had made advances to Margarot during the voyage, and Margarot's rejections of these "unnatural propensities!!!" had factored into their deteriorating relationship.[47]

It seems clear that the *Surprize* became a socially pressurized vessel, reflecting the frustrations, desires, and fears of its prisoners as they faced an unknown future. With regard to Margarot and Palmer, their very different pasts also informed the nature of their growing distrust. Their social and cultural backgrounds, divergent political ideologies, and religious beliefs may have produced a growing mutual distrust in the weeks prior to the ship's voyage, and Palmer's position within a developing but already dense network of Unitarians ensured that his framing of the mutiny, particularly as presented in his *Narrative of the Sufferings of T.F. Palmer and W. Skirving* (1797), would dominate radical discourse about the Scottish Martyrs for the next two generations.

By the time of his trial upon charges of sedition in September 1793, Palmer was an important figure in the Unitarian circle surrounding Joseph Priestley and Priestley's successor as the movement's leader, Theophilus Lindsey. Palmer came from a fairly wealthy family and had been educated at Eton before taking degrees in Divinity at Queen's College, Cambridge. During the 1770s, however, he had encountered Priestley's anti-Trinitarian ideas and had moved toward the emerging Unitarian movement. During the early 1780s, he declined Anglican preferment, swiftly becoming a significant figure in the Unitarian movement as a number of its societies were established in Scotland. By 1785, Palmer was ministering a chapel in Dundee, publishing theological tracts, and was increasingly involved in reform politics, especially after a Friends of Liberty society was established there in 1792.[48]

Palmer's political radicalism, though, had developed within a praxis that prioritized moderation and working within institutions. An important early foray into political activity occurred during Palmer's years at Queen's College, where he joined the campaign against Anglican subscription.[49] Only when such efforts failed did figures such as Lindsey, John Jebb, Gilbert Wakefield, and Palmer himself move out of the Anglican Church. In contrast to the more explicitly egalitarian ethos of the LCS (chaired by Margarot between 1792 and 1794), Palmer held a pastoral and paternalist relationship to the tradesmen and artisans who largely made up the Dundee Friends of Liberty. When he was tried upon charges of seditious practices in September 1793, for arranging to print and distribute the pamphlet *Address to the People*, several witnesses testified that Palmer had sought to moderate the pamphlet's language. The weaver George Mealmaker (author of the first draft of the pamphlet) noted that Palmer wished to give the *Address* a "softer nature" and indeed was against publishing it altogether. Other witnesses spoke to the same effect: the Dundee watchmaker Thomas Ivory noted Palmer's objections to the pamphlet's "too strong" language. The weaver James Matthew said that Palmer wanted to alter it so that the society would "give offense to nobody."[50] In the editing of Mealmaker's incendiary *Address*, we see the work of a careful minister, guiding those under his paternal responsibility.[51]

Cautious and moderate as it was, Palmer's political activism clearly shows that the Unitarian movement in Scotland and England faced severe government pressure. To be a Unitarian in Scotland, in particular, made one an object of state interest.[52] But Palmer's arrest, trial, and conviction demonstrate that the beleaguered movement nonetheless offered its members a coherent support network. Palmer's chapel at Dundee was part of a developing structure of Unitarian congregations spread throughout England and Scotland that centered on the chapel at Essex Street in London and overseen by Lindsey. Upon Palmer's arrest, an array of Unitarians gave him extensive emotional and material care; he was repeatedly visited while jailed between mid-September and November 1793, and then while waiting aboard the *Surprize* before the journey to Australia.[53] Meanwhile Unitarians quickly raised funds for the Martyrs.[54] For his part, Maurice Margarot seems to have found Palmer's relative affluence difficult to stomach. When the Norwich Constitutional Society sent the prisoners £20 in April 1794, Margarot kept it for himself, justifying his decision by pointing to the disparity of wealth and resources between himself and the other prisoners, bitterly questioning why his name had not been included in parliamentary motions to rescind the sentences of the more "gentlemanly" prisoners, including Palmer.[55]

Margarot position was more vulnerable than Palmer's, for his support network generally consisted of cash-strapped corresponding societies. Moreover, he came to political radicalism from very different perspectives. What we know about Margarot's early life suggests an intriguing intersection between youth-socialization, and the ferment of popular politics. Born in 1745, Margarot was a young adult at the time that his home became a center of Wilkesite radicalism, itself hardly polite. Thomas Hardy's notes on Margarot's life (written for Margarot's obituary) emphasize Margarot's exposure to key figures associated with "Wilkes and Liberty," noting that he was "easily initiated into politicking" at a young age.[56] His father's international business interests meant that Margarot himself grew up with French connections and while in France at the time of the Revolution, he became "familiar with many founders of the French republic."[57] Hardy stresses Margarot's unmediated experience of revolution, as an "eye witness to many of the transactions that were stated by Burke and other writers to be facts – [but which] he knew to be completely false and others much exaggerated or perverted."[58] Margarot was still in Paris at the beginning of the extraordinary year 1792, before returning to London, where the LCS was just being formed. Much of Hardy's account of Margarot's background is uncorroborated – Margarot's early life remains hazy – but what is plausible seems readymade for the type of British radical that Margarot became: an advocate of secular Painite universalism, at times utterly uncompromising, and in Australia, seemingly close to insurrectionary.

Finally, there were also differences of religiosity between Palmer and Margarot. While Palmer does not seem to have shared Priestley's interest in framing French revolutionary events within biblical prophecy, the relationship between spirituality and civic life remained central for him.[59] In January 1794, Lindsey wrote fellow Unitarian Robert Millar that if Palmer was indeed sent to Botany Bay, it was no doubt a case of "God's sending him," so that Palmer could do "much good" to the colony.[60] Palmer's Dundee congregation wrote him that same month as he waited aboard the *Stanislas* prison hulk, casting their minister's exile in explicitly religious terms.[61] By contrast, it is difficult to detect any sense of spiritual presence in Margarot's extant writings. From the earliest LCS addresses to his last written works, *Thoughts on Revolution* and *Proposal for a Grand National Jubilee* (both published in 1812 after his return from Australia), Margarot's voice is almost wholly secular.[62] There is some suggestion that Margarot may have felt these differences keenly. In a letter to the LCS written while the *Surprize* was at Rio de Janeiro, Margarot alluded to "religious and political bigotry" he had experienced during the voyage.[63] He mentioned this immediately after relating that Skirving and Palmer had been confined by Campbell as a consequence of being implicated in the planned mutiny. While the specific target of Margarot's grievances cannot be fully established, the juxtaposition of his claim and the news about the mutiny are suggestive of important religious differences among the Martyrs.

With regard to the mutiny itself, the accusations and counter-accusations, the willingness to spread furtive hints about what may have happened on the ship – all were speculative and must remain so in this history. The importance of the alleged plot lay precisely in its irrecoverable nature as a nonevent. As radicals in Britain sought to know what had caused this highly public split within a group publically valorized for its unselfish sacrifice to the cause, Palmer's network of sympathizers dominated interpretations of what had occurred. Private correspondence within the Unitarian network questioned Margarot's character.[64] In late May 1796, the *Cambridge Intelligencer* published a letter claiming to be from Muir, Palmer, and Skirving, in which they announced their separation from Margarot, declaring him an "accessory to the wrongs they had suffered."[65] Such letters had an effect. Almost immediately some British reformers began dropping Margarot from membership in the heroic group of Martyrs. The Norwich reformer Richard Dinmore Jr. composed his defense of British radicalism as a series of letters to a correspondent who had asked about the "principles of the English Jacobins." One letter noted that the oppressive despotism of Scotch laws sent Gerrald, Muir, and Palmer to "mix with convicts, the very refuse of the cells of Newgate." [66] He did not mention Margarot. The following year, Palmer's friend and fellow Unitarian minister Jeremiah Joyce organized, edited, and published Palmer's account of the mutiny, *A Narrative of the Sufferings* – a large project that soon effectively controlled the sites of discourse.[67] It circulated widely within the radical and non-radical reading publics, and continues to wield force in interpretations of the mutiny.[68] While Margarot's initial letters to friends in England did not implicate Palmer in the plot, he began to offer a different version once he realized that Palmer's was becoming the dominant interpretation.[69] A generation later, Chartists drew on these letters amid efforts to commemorate the Scottish Martyrs as heroic ancestors of their own reform efforts, seeking to understand what had happened onboard the *Surprize*. Those efforts would have to return to the issue of whether Margarot had betrayed his colleagues. Moreover, Margarot's actions in Australia meant that the establishment of a constitutionalist and respectable collective memory would also have to grapple with the problem of his advocating revolution.

New South Wales: "Secret Mischief"

The conditions governing the expression of dissent in Australia were much different from those in Britain. Prior to 1795, the activities of the British radical movement centered on publicity. Popular societies such as the LCS openly advertised their meetings, printed addresses articulating the need for political reform, and sponsored mass speaking engagements. Only after the passage in November 1795 of the "Two Acts" did radicalism in Britain move to more directly conspiratorial tactics. But two factors made Australia a very different space for articulating dissent: the nature of early Australian political and legal institutions, and the phenomenon of travel, of distance. Lauren Benton has pointed to the incoherence of colonial legal regimes as a context for understanding how power was actually adjudicated among different colonial constituencies.[70] As a very young penal colony when Margarot arrived in October 1794, Australian legal and political institutions were in flux. The governor had almost complete autocratic power, and there existed almost no forums for articulating disagreement with colonial policy – no representative political institutions, and no trial-by-jury for another half-century. Nor were there any significant institutions associated with the classic Habermasian public sphere. New South Wales had no developed press of any kind, and no theater. As David Neal has shown, the absence of means for opposition to colonial policy "squeezed political action into different shapes and patterns."[71]

Margarot's actions in Australia also suggest that the very process of empire and exile, through the effects of travel upon consciousness and subjectivity, shaped colonial expression of dissent. His experiences as a political prisoner exiled to the periphery of empire would not have occurred within a cultural vacuum but rather as experienced against his recent past. Here, we might recall what Edward Said wrote almost three decades ago about exile: "For an exile, habits of life, expression, activity in the new environment inevitably occur against the memory of these things in another environment. Thus both the new and the old environments are vivid, actual, occurring together contrapuntally."[72] Memory of the old gives new places residual meaning. Anthropologists such as Mary Helms have written of the "sacred center" that travelers carry with them in order to cognitively be at home in new spaces.[73] Margarot was no exception. In Australia, the discourse of "rights of Englishmen" saturated political claims, but his own personal history as a cosmopolitan radical in contact with French republicans in 1792 and 1793, and then his experience of exile may have encouraged him to conceive of Australia as a different kind of British space, a new colony where convicts' rights should reflect Painite natural law.[74] In key ways, the sacred center from which Margarot had been exiled was not merely Britain-as-it-was but also the more utopian "radical Britain" – the unfinished project of 1793, a utopian longing projected unto empire.[75] Anticipating the spread of republican ideals, including an inevitable Australian republic, in 1802 Margarot wrote, "It has been observed that the Empire of the World has uniformly moved from East to West – in making the circuit of the globe, it must therefore after America has enjoyed it, make its way eastward once more."[76] Radical political change was an ongoing project, whether in new sites of possibility, or back "home" in a Britain envisioned to be on the brink of revolution.

This imagined country informed Margarot's tactics of dissent while in Australia, and as much as anything, sheer distance allowed rumors about revolutionary Britain to hold considerable affective force in New South Wales. The secret journal that Margarot kept demonstrates how the achievement of a British republic hovered in possibility as rumors of successful French invasion swirled through the colony during the later 1790s. Indeed, Margarot's first letter back to Britain, written to the LCS in early July 1794 from Rio de Janeiro, expressed hope that the cause had triumphed in England. It is worth remembering that his voyage left Britain before the mass arrest of Jacobins in May 1794.[77] Distance created temporal uncertainties, a vacuum of knowledge filled with longed-for outcomes. In the journal, Margarot's entry for 1 March 1801 noted "*la revolution est achevée en Angleterre.*"[78] For Margarot, these combined factors – the absence of traditional venues for dissent, the sacred center of British "Jacobin" imaginings, and condition of exile that gave power to rumor – produced a set of tactics in Australia that paralleled those practiced by many other British radicals during the 1790s. Margarot emerged as both a very public, self-appointed overseer, writing repeatedly back to the Colonial Office about instances of colonial misgovernment, and simultaneously as a conspirator in the revolutionary underground, engaging in the "deep play" of sedition and testing the edge of acceptable behaviors. While the former Margarot could be safely absorbed into later commemorative efforts, the revolutionary conspirator would have to be written out for the sake of an emerging national narrative of constitutional progress.[79]

Space permits only a brief discussion of Margarot's doubled tactics of revolutionary conspiracy and public surveillance over colonial government. With regard to the former, the most salient examples occurred with the influx of Irish political prisoners after the 1798 rising in Ireland. In early 1800, the *Minerva* brought in the first major contingent of Irish convicts, and rumors of conspiracy began to swirl about the colony. Convicts were said to be arming with pikes; the United Irishmen were reforming, and they clandestinely communicated by relaying secret songs, coded questions, or "silent Tokens" using their fingers and hands.[80] When the colonial governor John Hunter investigated the conspiracy, some suspects mentioned Margarot as a ringleader. Peter Macanna, an Irish convict sent over on the *Minerva*, said that while seeking to recruit him, the prisoner Roger Grady had mentioned Margarot and John Boston as leaders of the plot.[81] But when interrogated, Grady denied that he indicated who the leaders were; that was something to be revealed only on the last day before the rising.[82] The results of the inquiry were inconclusive, but several of those questioned, such as Grady, were given 100 lashes each as exemplary punishment. Additionally, some who seemed to be more prominent as ringleaders were given the brutal sentence of 500 lashes with the cat-o'-nine-tails.[83] Although Margarot was not formally questioned, government viewed his house as a center of political disaffection.[84] After the United Irishman Joseph Holt arrived as a prisoner in January 1800, the first invitation he received was from Margarot. Holt noted at the meeting that Margarot's conversation was troubling. In his *Memoirs*, Holt disavows himself from Margarot's "republican notions." An officer later told Holt that Margarot's was "the most seditious house in the colony."[85]

Given his original offense, it is not surprising that Margarot was suspected of conspiracy. Moreover, his journal reveals the constant presence at his house of leaders of the Irish radical community during the years after 1799. [86] After a conversation over dinner with the clerk Barnes on 1 March 1800, Margarot wrote that among the subjects at table were the rumors of a successful revolution in England. Two weeks later, Margarot noted that the United Irishman Thomas Brady, who had been sent over on the same ship as Holt, had returned to Sydney. Shortly afterward, Brady met with Margarot for dinner and related news of a decisive battle in Ireland.[87] These gestures toward a subterranean world of heated conjecture about the progress of revolution in Britain were matched in Margarot's diary by lines that pointed to plans in Australia. On 8 September 1801, the United Irishman Patrick Kennedy visited Margarot to tell him of "the fatal discovery," which seems to have been a plot for a mass escape by way of sympathetic American ships, similar to that which Muir had made back in 1796.[88] Margarot's house seems to have been a hotbed of convivial revolutionary imaginings.

Margarot once again came under suspicion after the Castle Hill rising of March 1804. The revolt was the most serious rebellion of the early penal regime and was organized mainly by Irish convicts, including a strong proportion of those transported after the 1798 rebellion in Ireland. On 3 March, convicts overpowered their guards at the Castle Hill station and then a force of 266 convicts marched south toward Parramatta, the local town, some three miles east of Sydney. The following day, about thirty soldiers of the New South Wales Corp met the insurgents in battle, and the rebel forces soon scattered. In addition to the fifteen convicts killed in the Battle of Parramatta, an additional nine were executed, and several others received a combination of floggings and sentences to hard labor. [89]

Margarot had escaped prosecution in 1800, but the investigation of the Castle Hill uprising implicated him more strongly. While no evidence of Margarot's direct involvement was found, he evidently burned some of the papers shortly before the rising.[90] In June, Governor Phillip King had Margarot's papers seized (the last entry is dated 5 June 1804), and their examination revealed Margarot's continued radical sympathies and involvement with radicalized prisoners.[91] An entry for 10 March 1804 casts the failure of the Castle Hill rising in melancholic and dramatic terms: *"deux Irlandais furent pendus à Sydney, et je suppose que cela finit la trajedie*," / "Two Irishmen are hanging in Sydney, and I believe that this will end the tragedy."[92] Moreover, several of the United Irishmen who were suspected by the government to have been active in the revolt had visited Margarot's house on numerous occasions. Margarot would barely escape being sent to hard labor, inland at Coal River. "Secret mischief" was King's term for Margarot's influence on the colony.[93] Margarot seemed central to colonial agitation and yet without direct involvement.

This strange kind of agency presented a problem for the colonial government: what to do with such a "lively, facetious, talkative," troublesome subject?[94] Here, we can turn to Margarot's other tactic of dissent. From his arrival, Margarot had cast himself as a reporter guarding the colony against misrule by repeatedly publicizing examples of poor governance.[95] As he wrote upon his arrival to the then acting governor Francis Grose, "if the Executive power can make One a Slave it may make all so."[96] Such self-representations infuriated many officers. Lieutenant Governor David Collins later wrote that "Margarot's conduct incensed me . . . . He is a dangerous scoundrel – worse – a thousand times than Stuart."[97] Governor King's letter to the undersecretary of the Colonial Office placed Margarot at the center of not only the Castle Hill rising but "every other trash of the kind that has more or less sowed such discord in this Settlement."[98] As "the Secret, and in many Instances the open, abettor and promoter of the most dangerous principles," Margarot required close watching.[99] Although King wanted to send Margarot to labor in the coalfields at the settlement of Newcastle, he decided it would be better to keep Margarot nearby, where he could be closely watched, for Margarot seemed to possess an uncanny ability to, as the previous governor John Hunter claimed, "blow up the embers of expiring sedition."[100]

From 1806 until 1810, the year of Margarot's return to England, there seem to be no surviving records of his actions.[101] But the unresolved controversy over the *Surprize* mutiny, together with Margarot's reports on the black market trade (including bitter complaints that Palmer, once a colleague in the cause of reform, was a now a well-off rum-trader) would later take new form, developing into accusations that Margarot had been a spy, informing government about radical activities in general.[102] Reincorporating Margarot into the radical pantheon of political martyrs would be a difficult work of collective remembering and forgetting, and would be achieved only through circumscribing the subversive, desirous, "Jacobin" tactics that he had adopted in Britain's distant prison outpost.

The Return "Home"

In October 1810, with three guineas to his name, and accompanied by his wife Elizabeth and a favorite cat, Margarot finally returned to

England.[103] He sought at once to restore his reputation within radical circles, a reputation heavily damaged by Palmer's *Narrative,* which had effectively dominated public discussion of the mutiny since its publication in 1797.[104] Hardy and Place also assisted, conducting a letter-writing campaign avowing Margarot's good character. Joyce was a target of special concern in the letter campaign. He had been imprisoned on charges of high treason in May 1794, along with Hardy, Thelwall, Horne Tooke, and others. Discharged on 1 December 1794 (the same morning as Thomas Holcroft's release) Joyce was one of the veterans of the repressions of 1793–94, and so held a privileged status in radical circles. Crucially, Joyce had also operated in close cooperation with his fellow Unitarian Palmer, organizing and publishing the *Narrative* for the exiled prisoner. Indeed, when Hardy and others began a subscription to assist Margarot in 1811, Joyce worried that Margarot was planning to use the funds to sue him for libel.[105]

Hardy's correspondence with Joyce reveals the delicacy with which the break between Margarot and the rest of the Scottish Martyrs had to be handled. Hoping "to set this unpleasant subject in its true light," Hardy promised Joyce that funds had been raised strictly to relieve Margarot's own poverty. Joyce should ignore the "various vague reports" that friends had sent him. Two days later, Hardy reiterated that Joyce was under no danger of prosecution from Margarot.[106] Joyce was dubious. Several persons, he wrote, had recently told him that Hardy was helping collect funds to initiate a suit against the printer and editor of Palmer's *Narrative.* If Hardy was now so adamant that this was not the case, why not produce the evidence that discredited Palmer's version of the mutiny? So the problem remained: what had been the "true light" of the affair on board the *Surprize*?

Meanwhile, Margarot was himself on the move. Traveling to Scotland in October and November 1812, he was suspected by the Home Office of encouraging the Association of Weavers to revolt.[107] Gordon Pentland has traced the republican veteran's movements at this time as Margarot met with former associates, perhaps in efforts to assist Major John Cartwright's attempts to rebuild the parliamentary reform movement. All the while, Margarot was a figure of anxious concern to the Home Office.[108] Reports from spies noted his violent language; other reports suggested that Margarot and Hardy (with the help of the revolutionary Arthur Thistlewood) were raising funds so that Margarot could return to France and convince Napoleon to invade.[109] Margarot's experiences in Australia seemed to have heightened his awareness of the link between economic and political exploitation. At this time, in quick succession, he wrote *Proposal for a Grand National Jubilee* and *Thoughts on Revolutions,* implying that the scope of change required in Britain would probably only come through revolution, though the latter work expressed wishes that this revolution could nonetheless be "loyal and constitutional."[110] He seems at this point to have been locked in dire financial circumstances.[111] He spent the summers of 1813 and 1814 in France, ostensibly seeking to restore old business connections and recover some of the family property that had been lost since his own transportation. In October 1814, Hardy and Alexander Galloway (engineer and former LCS leader) organized a fund for Margarot.[112] On 11 December 1815, at the age of 70, he died in London. Margarot was then buried among anti-revolutionary French refugees, in St. Pancras Churchyard. History has its ironies.

Margarot remained a controversial and puzzling figure, both for radicals in the years after his return to England and for historians today. Two decades after his death, Chartists sought to commemorate the transportees of 1794 as heroic ancestors of their own movement, and Margarot would continue to present problems. Was he a revolutionary, a spy, or a respectable constitutionalist reformer? His activities between 1792 and 1794 are well documented due to the relative care with which the LCS kept its own records (augmented after Francis Place began assembling his own archive of British radicalism) and then through Margarot's insertion into state judicial and disciplinary archives upon his arrest in December 1793. But transportation distanced him from the more secure domestic surveillance manifested by the British state, and placed him within a network of authority that encouraged different articulations of dissent.[113] Having become a surveilled subject of the modern state, Margarot then became a more evasive subject of empire's rule.[114] From his arrival in Sydney Cove in late October 1794 until his death in London two decades later, Margarot's activities were more shadowy. For British radicals of a later generation, the meaning of his conduct in Australia was elusive. It might as well have been written on the water the *Surprize* had sailed upon so long ago.

Commemoration: "The Real State of the Case"

Efforts to defend Margarot faded soon after his death in 1815. Although Hardy and others immediately initiated a collection for Elizabeth, the problem of Margarot's relationship to the other Martyrs diminished over the next several years.[115] But when reformers in the 1830s put forward the idea for a public monument to those transported in 1794, the ghosts of Margarot and the mutiny resumed their problematic status in radical memory. That effort began in the aftermath of the reform bill of 1832 as a cooperative project undertaken by parliamentary radicals such as Joseph Hume and the leadership of London Working Men's Association (LWMA). The LWMA was formed in 1836 by William Lovett, Place, and the radical publisher Henry Hetherington, and included both workers and middling-class reformers. As the memorial project developed, the struggles over memory reflected tensions between the LWMA

and emergent, more radical challenges to the organization, most significantly from Feargus O'Connor's Radical Association, formed in September 1835, and Julian Harney's East London Democratic Association,
formed in January 1837.[116] A key difference concerned the LWMA's
willingness to work with the Irish MP Daniel O'Connell, whose opposition to trade unionism and factory legislation, together with his support for the new poor law, engendered distrust among many English
radicals.[117] Moreover, O'Connell also stood against the valorization of
the 1798 Irish Rebellion as central to the movement for Irish justice.
Finally, the LWMA's cooperation with middle-class reformers generated
conflict over the extent of suffrage reform. By the later 1830s, Hume had
dropped support for universal male suffrage in favor of more limited
household suffrage. While the LWMA remained committed to universal
male suffrage, Hume would use the Martyrs monument project to claim
that the reformers at the British Convention of 1793 only sought household suffrage.[118] Once the project to commemorate the political Martyrs
got underway, and factions mobilized collective memory to support contemporary aims for political reform, a struggle for the ownership of the
radical tradition ensued.

Hume had been supporting a Martyrs monument since 1831, and
since 1835 had been in correspondence with Place about the project.
Place was instrumental in getting an account of the prisoners inserted
into Hetherington's *The Poor Man's Guardian*. Place had also convinced
Hume to offer Hetherington an advance order for 10,000 copies of the
relevant issue.[119] On 25 December 1836, the *London Dispatch* (also
published by Hetherington) highlighted a monument recently erected in
Bunhill Fields Cemetery honoring the veteran Hardy, who had died in
1832. During mid- to late December 1836, the *Dispatch* and several
other radical papers advertised an organizational meeting to be held on
16 January 1837 at the venerable Crown and Anchor tavern to discuss a
possible monument to the Scottish Martyrs.[120]

Given the authority that Palmer's version of the mutiny plot had
achieved by the early decades of the nineteenth century, Margarot's inclusion in such a project guaranteed controversy.[121] At the 16 January
meeting, the prospect of honoring Margarot on the monument caused
immediate division. Over cries that the mutiny episode had revealed
Margarot as a traitor to his fellow sufferers, the publisher Richard Phillips adamantly defended Margarot. He had known Margarot before the
prisoner was transported and "never was [there] a more domestic virtuous exemplary man." Moreover, Phillips had resumed his friendship
with Margarot upon the latter's return to England in 1810 and "he never
changed at all in his character."[122] Phillips's focus on Margarot's personal morality underscores the importance that middle-class reformers
and many working-class leaders, keen to distance radicalism from earlier strands of flamboyance, theatricality, and license, gave to concepts

of respectability and self-improvement.[123] Margarot's alleged betrayal of colleagues threatened to transform him from being a respected early LCS leader to a figure belonging instead to the movement's disinherited conspiratorial phase that followed the suppression of open agitation.

Place sympathized with Phillips's efforts to defend Margarot, writing of the mutiny and the fall-out between the Martyrs as an embarrassment to radicalism's heritage: he had "never liked it" and had "kept away from it until I found mischief had arisen."[124] To Place, Margarot's case seemed doubly unfair: having been unjustly transported, he was also unable to defend himself against enemies at home, such as "the Charitable Christian Beast," the liberal cleric Thomas Hobbes Scott.[125] Scott had been in radical circles in the 1790s, often attending Tooke's dinners, but in the 1820s had been the first archdeacon of New South Wales before returning to England in 1829. When Scott learned about the Martyrs project, he wrote to the Benthamite radical MP George Grote accusing Margarot ("the tool of Pitt and Dundas") of spying on fellow radicals during the early 1790s; early treachery that Scott wrote, naturally led to Margarot's "murderous attempts of 1794." [126] Scott further charged that Margarot had been in the pay of the anti-Jacobin John Reeves, and enclosed Palmer's *Narrative* as evidence of Margarot's "nefarious character." Margarot deserved "a Gibbet rather than a monument."[127] Place and Hume sought to counter these accusations by stressing Margarot's commitment to the radical cause. At a meeting of the monument committee on 8 February 1837, Galloway and Place explained "as well as we could the real state of the case," over the objections to including Margarot voiced by John Rutt, who as a leading Unitarian had been a colleague and friend of Palmer and Skirving.[128]

The "real state of the case," however, still had to be secured: Margarot's history had yet to be re-narrated in a manner that would restore a sense of collective identity among the Martyrs and allow the construction of a coherent radical past. Given the conflicting reports and relative absence of records, this would be a difficult history to write, for verifiable records were in short supply. Harriet Grote, wife of George Grote, and a key social figure associated with the middle-class radicals, warned Place shortly after the 8 February meeting, "you can scarcely establish a matter of historical detail 10 years after the fact."[129] The Margarot problem lay a generation back. Moreover, there was a risk in seeking to clear Margarot. If his political integrity was restored, what was to be made of the accusations leveled by Palmer and Skirving? As the 20 February general meeting of the LWMA approached, the memorial project's inadvertent broadcasting of discord within London radicalism caused more intense discussion. Behaviors that did not fit into a heroic and respectable narrative lurked on the peripheries of social memory, threatening public embarrassment. In frustration, Harriet Grote again warned Place that his and others' efforts to reconcile the conflicting accounts was foolish and possibly futile: "The affair of the revived martyrs is altogether untoward... You <u>have</u> cleaned things up, with a vengeance! The upshot whereof seems to be that P. and Skirving mediated a mutinous attempt....looking at the case as with the general eye of the Public, I am disposed to question the expediency of erecting a monument to them <u>as</u> martyrs."[130] Clearing Margarot threatened to disgrace Palmer and Skirving. As radical history went under sustained interrogation, it became dangerously unstable.

At the 20 February 1837 meeting, competing visions of contemporary reform dominated discussions over Margarot's inclusion in the monument project, centering on whether the reformers of the 1790s had supported universal male suffrage or a more restrictive program. Introducing the plans for the monument, Hume gave brief biographies of each of the Martyrs, and sought to preempt division about Margarot with yet another account of Margarot's "great zeal" in the cause of reform, and his difficult life upon returning to England.[131] Soon after this, however, Feargus O'Connor interrupted the meeting, moving that "the meeting recognise universal suffrage as the only basis of a free constitution."[132] By now, O'Connor had reached the point of open confrontation with the LWMA's leadership over its cooperation with middle-class reformers. Opposing Hume's efforts to pull the LWMA from its own support for universal suffrage, O'Connor gestured to the crowd and said the working classes at the meeting want "to do something greater for those martyrs than erecting cold and inanimate marble to their memory." Instead, they sought to press moderate reformers such as Hume to stand behind universal suffrage.[133] By this point, the meeting was in confusion; the *Morning Chronicle* reported much cheering, some groaning and hissing, and some laughter.[134]

With regard to the ongoing construction of a radical heritage, O'Connor's counter-claims were telling. At the previous LWMA meeting, Hume had argued that the reformers of 1794 had not supported universal suffrage, and implied instead that the Martyrs would instead have supported Hume's household-suffrage campaign. This was part of a deeper set of rhetorical moves. In February 1837, the precise demands that Chartists would make upon parliament were still being discussed. In late February, the Charter's demands would first be publicized at a meeting at the Crown and Anchor tavern. This use of the Martyrs project to claim the authority of radicalism's mythical past thus reflected the tensions within radical reform in these early years of the Chartist movement. What the heroic ancestors of the 1790s had stood for would give contemporary demands deep sanction in a political culture highly attuned to the power of historical memory.

Representations of the 20 February 1837 meeting portrayed defenses of Margarot in highly dramatic terms; the meeting became a theater of radical memory. The veteran Galloway mounted the speaker's platform, and claimed Margarot was an "excellent man both in his private and public character."[135] Galloway also sought to move beyond the power of the spoken word, announcing that he had with him a possession "that he prized beyond anything on earth." He then held aloft a stone that Margarot had sent him from Australia, upon which Margarot had written the iconic word "Reform." Evidently Galloway's use of theater made for an affecting moment, met with "Immense cheering." In a similarly dramatic instance, another supporter gestured to the spectators' gallery, where seventy-three-year-old Elizabeth Margarot watched over events. She too was a martyr, and this meeting might offer her solace for "seventeen long years in New South Wales."[136] Such talismanic survivals from the heroic 1790s held seemingly transparent meaning, powerful beyond the duplicity of words. A testimonial souvenir from the antipodean penal colony, and the ghostly presence of a long-suffering widow and martyr in her own right – both formed tokens that helped secure Margarot's reputation as an "excellent" radical predecessor.[137]

Scholars have long been aware that Place's own representations of radical history narrated a story of maturation and sober respectability gained by the laboring classes since the 1790s.[138] It may be that the boisterous and theatrical manner by which Margarot's reputation had been restored at the LWMA meeting encouraged Place to try to rehabilitate the dead martyr through a more sober, less objectionable method. Writing to Harriet Grote the following day, Place acidly complained that Hume and others had handled O'Connor's intervention badly, confirming suspicions, "carefully inculcated" among the working people, that leadership disregarded workers and instead favored moderates and an alliance with radical Whig MPs.[139] Challenges to the memorial project, such as O'Connor's, were threatening the reform alliance. O'Connor himself was "that ugly animal," from whose lips "flowed a torrent of fulsome praise, abuse and nonsense."[140] Seemingly at a loss for adequate words, at this point Place's invective moved to the graphic level, including a scribbled, racialized caricature of O'Connor.[141] Place's entire letter revealed his discomfort with the rowdiness of the crowd: O'Connor had nearly produced "a riot . . . the working people who comprised more than half the audience behaved in a way not only disgraceful but most shameful."[142] In the weeks after the meeting, Place sought to rehabilitate Margarot through an archival production of truth. Galloway sent Place copies of the minutes of depositions concerning the mutiny plot that he had obtained from Elizabeth Margarot. He also sent Place extracts of Thelwall's lectures from 1794 and 1795, which supported Margarot's good character. [143] The materials allowed Place to conduct a detailed textual interrogation of the alleged mutiny, deploying his own expanding archive of radical history.

Even as the dispute over Margarot threatened to derail the Martyrs project during 1837, official archives were becoming an important component in the institutional memory of the modern British state. The following year, the Public Record Office bill passed through parliament, establishing the PRO. If, as Patrick Joyce remarks, there has been "relatively little recognition in Britain of the archive as a political expression of the nation-state," then there has been even less attention paid to the archiving processes of subaltern or sub-cultural groups.[144] Yet Place's investigation of the mutiny plot registers the authority of archival material in the construction of collective memories.[145] He had been collecting material on British radicalism since the 1820s, partly out of interest in writing on the improvements on working-class behavior, and also as part of his desire to write a history of the LCS, a goal Place shared with Hardy and Thelwall.[146] Since the Margarots' return to England in 1810, Place had also been collecting evidence concerning the *Surprize* mutiny.[147] Certainly, Place's collection has deeply influenced interpretations of radical history; its capaciousness has revealed the modern archive's ability to shape receptions of truth-claims, seducing users through its perceived allowance of closure, "constituted as the only space that is free of context, argument, ideology – indeed history itself."[148] Yet, like the nineteenth-century British state institutions where they would eventually be housed, the Place papers sought to inscribe a particular political rationality upon the fragments of events that it catalogued.[149] Titles of the notes in some of Place's material register their ideological thrust: "Improvement of the Working Classes – Drunkenness"; "Progress of the Theatre and Popular Entertainments." Moreover, the sheer existence of Place's archive owed itself to the radical tailor's own respectable success as an artisan: few of his fellow agitators after 1795 would have had the room to collect such a massive accumulation of material. Given proper direction and reform, the respectable working classes could be both self-observing and self-governing.[150] Such a narrative, emphasizing the sober, educative aspects of British radicalism during the 1790s, helped wash out the movement's more conspiratorial or utopian politics.

For his report on the mutiny plot, Place compared key extracts from Palmer's *Narrative* with other documents from his collection of radical ephemera, seeking to correct a collective memory gone badly wrong by setting out a new version that would be articulated as a persuasive discourse of archive-based fact. His strategy was to examine in detail the *Narrative*'s logical and rhetorical framework, and suggest more plausible explanations for the breakdown of trust among the *Surprize*'s radical cohort. Place cast entirely new light on Palmer's version of the split over the combining of officers' mess with the cabin passengers. Reexamining Palmer's version of events, he highlighted Palmer's early antipathy toward Margarot, and Palmer's increasing withdrawal from the radical community well before the alleged mutiny plot was discovered.[151] Place also pointed to Palmer's broad use of unsupported hearsay evidence.

With regard to Palmer's insistence that "from the time of the pretended discovery of the plot, [Margarot] unblushingly appeared as [Campbell's] councilor, friend, and confidant," Place countered that there was "no evidence of this in any of the printed depositions" supplied by those later questioned.[152] Other interventions damaged Palmer's credibility in more troubling ways. Place noted that Palmer's account was not signed by Skirving, despite the preface to the *Narrative* claiming that it was written as a defense of both Skirving's and Palmer's reputations. Furthermore, Place determined that Joyce, who edited and printed the *Narrative*, had not obtained a journal Skirving had kept, nor had any evidence been obtained from Muir.[153] Finally, Place applied the same treatment to various affidavits and depositions he had obtained through the Margarots. For example, the surgeon on board the *Surprize*, James Thompson, had supplied a deposition in February 1795 that broadly supported some of Palmer's own account. By pointing out numerous internal inconsistencies, Place exposed much of it as simply inaccurate and sometimes dishonest.[154] Yet the point of Place's interrogations was not to incriminate Palmer, but rather to break down the authority of Palmer's version of the mutiny plot, to deconstruct the *Narrative*'s narrative. Place's authority as the archivist of radicalism allowed him to narrate a Margarot who could be celebrated by the working-class/middle-class alliance that funded the memorial project, a Margarot who could be symbolically reincorporated with the other Martyrs, all of whom could now be inscribed in stone.[155]

Martyrs Monument: "The Grandest Move against the Enemy"

Many commentators involved in the project noted that actually building a monument to the Martyrs constituted a new departure for public activism. Urban space would be used to produce counter-memory, ranged against traditional conservative built-form. An editorial published in the radical *Weekly True Sun* in the days before the 20 February 1837 organizational meeting offered a sophisticated explanation of the role of urban built-form in creating and sustaining public memory. The commentator began by setting the proposed Martyrs monument in contrast to traditional state-sponsored commemoration: "of tyrant monuments the world is full... Neroes and Caligulas, Cleopatras and Alexanders – the young tyrant, the sensualist, and the destroyer, have studded the earth with memorials which time seems incompetent to perish." The author continued, noting that contemporary empires continued to fetishize authoritarian rule: "in our own day, we still find the same infatuated admiration of merely brute qualities, leading to the erection of statues, temples, and tombs, in honour of the oppressors of the poor."[156] In contrast, a Martyrs monument would honor "improvers of the mind...who advance human happiness." The editorial thus sought to garner public support through an anti-aristocratic reading of national memory.

> We have George the Third and his pigtail in Pall-mall, and William Shakespeare put up as a kind of curiosity amongst the hippopotami in the Kentish Museum. Charles the First in Charing-cross, and John Milton, the pride of the world – *nowhere*. We have a straddling fellow of bronze in Hyde-park, to remind us of the campaigns of [Duke of Wellington] Arthur Wellesley, various human figures, taking their iron repose on pedestals in the centres of our squares, each underwrit – "This is a Duke" – so that mankind may not be blind to their merits.

There was a more immediate context to radical built-form memory. By summer 1837, two public subscriptions for additional Wellington monuments had been launched. One would eventually result in the colossal Wyatt statue at Constitution Hill, and one would help fund a smaller statue, made from cannons captured from Napoleon's army, that would be placed in front of the Royal Exchange in 1846.[157] The *Weekly True Sun*'s editorialist noted that conservative memorializing was accelerating:

> And yet, with all this, what is the case at the present moment? As though we had not Achilles and Waterloo heroes enough, or as though they thought that without another jog to the memory, we were likely to let his grace the Duke of Wellington slip into oblivious forgetfulness, the good citizens have peddled their mites, to ornament Cheapside with another statue of the great destroyer of the age.[158]

The *Weekly True Sun*'s comments register a profound sense of contested histories, revealing the Martyrs monument as a program taken on against the backdrop of a broader effort by conservatives to make city spaces produce loyalism and pride in the durability of the British state. In the aftermath of the defeat of revolutionary France, conservative readings of British history were inscribed into London's spaces, as part of a broader cultural memory crisis provoked by the disruption of the great revolution.[159] Trafalgar Square had been remodeled to honor Nelson during the late 1820s, and the Nelson Column – with its gesture to imperial Rome – was in the later stages of planning (construction would begin in 1840), even as Thompson and Place corresponded about the Martyrs monument. Projects such as the remodeling of Trafalgar Square thus constituted an important context for radical desires to offer a competing history. Monuments and place-names were chief vehicles of efforts to make the city a signifier of post-revolutionary national identity. As early as 1823, guidebooks such as *The Percy Histories or Interesting Memories of the Rise, Progress and Presentation of all the Capitals of*

Europe counted eighteen sites named after Nelson, fourteen after the Duke of Wellington, and some ten sites commemorating Waterloo.[160]

But there is also a significant local and communal context that extended centuries into the past. Prior to the eighteenth century, the area around Charing Cross repeatedly had been a site of contested encounter between the state and London's popular classes. Elizabeth I's reign saw legal battles between local parishioners, who under Henry VIII had been granted right of commoning on Charing Cross Field, and agents of the crown who wished to lease the land for state revenue. During the civil wars of the mid-1600s, Charing Cross witnessed numerous executions and after the Restoration many regicides went to their deaths there. As Rodney Mace notes, the protests that accompanied the metropolitan improvement projects of the Regency and especially the remodeling of Trafalgar Square, were part of a longer struggle over community reclamation and access to urban space carried on between Londoners and agents of the state.[161] This dynamic gave the square a lasting importance as a space of popular protest (as made evident more recently by massive reactions to the invasion of Iraq in spring 2003, and with the Women's March of mid-January 2017, held in protest at the election of US president Donald Trump). Radical claims to public space in the 1830s were a dialogic response to state conservatism, motivated in part by contemporary state use of city space to narrate a conservative history. But radical memorializing also reflected a longer-term struggle over communal use versus state use of urban spaces.[162] The radical MP Thomas Peronnet Thompson echoed this sense of contested history-making. In a letter to Place, he gleefully predicted a future scramble as conservatives and radicals built competing visions of the nation's past:

> A London monument would be the grandest move against the enemy, that God or the Devil has put into the hearts of radicals yet. There is no saying where it would stop; for after such an event, every place where any foul act of the Tories had been consummated, would be putting up its monument in imitation…. It is no business of ours to talk about it now, but we would have a monument to Peterloo in twelve months after."[163]

Thompson's note points to another divisive issue during the early days of the project: where to locate the finished monument. Many of the Scottish supporters of the project wanted to see it erected in Edinburgh.[164] After all, most of the political Martyrs had been arrested for their role in the 1793 British Convention at Edinburgh. An Edinburgh monument would not only highlight the radical cause but buttress a national myth of Scottish leadership and triumph over despotism.[165] Such plans, however, frustrated some supporters. Thompson voiced concerns that an Edinburgh monument would limit the narrative of the Martyrs to a narrow, nationalistic orientation: "the Scotchmen do not seem to be aware of how vastly more important it is to get a <u>British</u> demonstration in the shape of a monument in London, than a Scottish [one] as in Edinburgh."[166] A London monument would use the Martyrs to further a contemporary symbolic struggle in a period when conservative memorialization through built-form seemed to be all the rage. Only a London location could counter this conservative appropriation of patriotism and use London's urban topography to, as Thompson put it, "beard the monuments which the Tories are erecting every day to the objects of their worship."[167] London was symbolically central precisely because of its growing density of conservative built-form commemoration.

After continual delays, the London monument to the Scottish Martyrs eventually came to be raised – but not until 1851 – at Nunhead Cemetery in Southwark, where it stands today (Figures 7.2 and 7.3). Its history reveals the process by which radical reformers of the later 1830s sought to construct collective memories that represented their own contemporary movement as part of a longer trajectory of respectable reform, reaching back to a set of heroic ancestors from the 1790s. Such projects in part depended upon an awareness of British radicalism as a trans-imperial phenomenon whereby events "out in the empire" carried symbolic meaning "at home." Moreover, in seeking to give those events such meaning, radicals positioned their claims to public space against broader conservative efforts at collective memory-making; in the case of

MONUMENT TO " THE SCOTCH POLITICAL MARTYRS," IN NUNHEAD CEMETERY.

Figure 7.2 The Scottish Political Martyrs Memorial at Nunhead Cemetery, London, *Illustrated London News*, 26 November 1853. Image courtesy of University of Missouri Libraries.

Figure 7.3 The Scottish Political Martyrs Memorial at Nunhead Cemetery, London, 2019, inscription. Photo courtesy of James Epstein.

the Martyrs monument, radicals sought to counter a deep investment in built-form commemoration undertaken by the post-Napoleonic British state. In this sense, for radicals of the early to mid-nineteenth century, conservative memorialization opened up the city as a field-of-play for contesting narratives of the recent past. Finally, the case of the Martyrs monument reveals how the formation of moderate/radical alliances often involved a winnowing out from radicalism's heritage of its more utopian and revolutionary desires. Collective memory would not allow the recovery and articulation of British Jacobinism's seditious heart.

Acknowledgments

A shorter version of this chapter was published in David S. Karr, "'The Embers of Expiring Sedition': Maurice Margarot, the Scottish Martyrs, and the Production of Radical Memory across the British South Pacific," *Historical Research* 86 (November 2013): 638–60. Copyright © 2013 by the Institute of Historical Research. Reprinted by permission of John Wiley and Sons.

Notes

1 "Desecration of London graveyards," *Medical Times and Gazette* 1 (30 June 1866): 685–86.
2 Phil Emery, email message to author, 2 August 2008. See also Phil Emery, "End of the line," *British Archeology* 88, May/June 2006: 11–15. Elizabeth Margarot accompanied her husband as a free settler.

3 BL, Add. MS. 27816, fol. 89. On nineteenth-century popular funeral traditions, see Thomas Laqueur, "Bodies, Death, and Pauper Funerals," *Representations* 1 (1983): 109–31, and *The Work of the Dead: A Cultural; History of Mortal Remains* (Princeton, NJ: Princeton University Press, 2015), 330–32; James Stevens Curl, *The Victorian Celebration of Death* (Stroud: Sutton, 1972); Julie-Marie Strange, *Death, Grief, and Poverty in Britain, c1870 – 1914* (Cambridge: CUP, 2005); Julien Litten, *The English Way of Death: The Common Funeral since 1450* (Robert Hall, 2002, first published 1991). On relationships among space, mourning, and memory, see Thomas Laqueur "Spaces of the Dead," *Ideas from the National Humanities Center* 8 (2001): 3–16; Humayun Ansari, "'Burying the Dead': Making Muslim Space in Britain," *Historical Research* 80 (2007): 545–66.

4 The full text of the inscription can be found in Frederick Teague Cansick, *A Collection of Curious and Interesting Epitaphs, Copied from the Monuments of Distinguished and Noted Characters in the Ancient Church and Burial Grounds of St. Pancras, Middlesex* (1869), 110.

5 For later Chartist uses of commemoration as a symbolic counter-culture, see Antony Taylor, "Radical Funerals, Burial Customs, and Political Commemoration: The Death and Posthumous Life of Ernest Jones," *Humanities Research* [Australia] 10 (2) (2003): 29–39. For an excellent discussion of the complexities of British radical memory, see Steve Poole "The Politics of Protest Heritage, 1790–1850," in *Remembering Protest in Britain since 1500: Memory, Materiality and the Landscape*, ed. Carl J. Griffin and Briony McDonagh (Cham: Palgrave Macmillan, 2018): 187–209. See also Matthew Roberts, "Chartism, Commemoration and the Cult of the Radical Hero, c.1770–c.1840," *Labour History Review* 78 (2013): 3–32, and *Chartism, Commemoration, and the Cult of the Radical Hero* (Routledge, 2020).

6 From the time of his execution in 1803, Emmet's speech at the dock became a staple of radical memory; the Chartist theatrical *The Trial of Robert Emmet* was a hit play. See James Epstein, *Radical Expression Political Language, Ritual, and Symbol in England, 1790–1850* (New York: OUP, 1994), chapter 5; Marianne Elliott, *Robert Emmet: The Making of a Legend* (Profile, 2003).

7 Poole, "Politics of Protest Heritage," 189–90. The use of constitutionalist discourse did not prohibit radicals from inflecting it with republican meanings. See Epstein, *Radical Expression*, chapter 1; John Belchem, "Republicanism, Popular Constitutionalism and the Radical Platform in Early Nineteenth-Century England,' *SH* 6 (1981): 1–32.

8 See Katrina Navickas, "The 'Spirit of Loyalty': Material Culture, Space and the Construction of an English Loyalist Memory, 1790–1840," in *Loyalism and the Formation of the British World, 1775–1914*, ed. Allan Blackstock and Frank O'Gorman (Woodbridge: Boydell Press, 2014): 43–60.

9 Charles F. G. Masterman, ed., *The Heart of the Empire: Discussions of Problems of Modern City Life in England, with an Essay on Imperialism* (T.F. Unwin, 1901). See also Jonathan Schneer, *London 1900: The Imperial Metropolis* (New Haven, CT: Yale University Press, 1999), 3–11; Felix Driver and David Gilbert, "Heart of Empire? Landscape, Space and Performance in Imperial London," *Environment and Planning D: Society and Space* 16 (1998): 11–28.

10 John MacKenzie, *Imperialism and Popular Culture* (Manchester: Manchester University Press, 1998); Schneer, *London 1900*; Annie Coombes, *Reinventing Africa: Museums, Material Culture and Popular Imagination in Late Victorian and Edwardian England* (New Haven, CT: Yale University Press 1994); Anne McClintock, *Imperial Leather: Race, Gender, and Sexuality in the Colonial Contest* (Routledge, 1995), chapter 5.

11 Rodney Mace, *Trafalgar Square: Emblem of Empire* (Lawrence & Wishart, 1976), chapter 2; Marianne Czisnik, "Representations of a Hero: Monuments to Admiral Nelson," in *Reactions to Revolutions: The 1790s and their Aftermath*, ed. Ulrich Broich, et al. (Münster: Lit Verlad, 2007), 263–88.

12 Michael T. Davis, "An Evening of Pleasure rather than Business': Songs, Subversion and Radical Sub-culture in the 1790s,' *Journal for the Study of British Cultures* 12 (2005): 115–26.

13 Pierre Nora, "Between Memory and History: *le Lieux de Mémoire*," trans. Marc Roudebush, *Representations* 26 (1989): 7–24, at 7. Peter Fritzsche summarizes critiques of the concept in "The Case of Modern Memory," *JMH* 73 (2001): 87–117, at 92–95.

14 For high political culture's saturation with imperial themes, see Antoinette Burton "New Narratives of Imperial Politics in the Nineteenth-Century," in *At Home with the Empire: Metropolitan Culture and the Imperial World*, ed. Catherine Hall and Sonya O. Rose (Cambridge: CUP, 2006), 212–29. See also Mrinalini Sinha, "Britishness, Clubbability, and the Colonial Public Sphere: The Genealogy of an Imperial Institution in Colonial India," *JBS* 40 (2001): 489–521.

15 See Marianne Elliot, *Partners in Revolution: The United Irishman and France* (New Haven, CT: Yale University Press, 1982); Marcus Wood, *Slavery, Empathy and Pornography* (Oxford: OUP, 2002), 170–74; Peter Linebaugh and Marcus Rediker, *The Many-Headed Hydra: Sailors, Slaves, Commoners, and the Hidden History of the Revolutionary Atlantic* (Boston, MA: Beacon Press, 2000). On the unevenness of the relationship between empire and figurations of class, see James Epstein, "Taking Class Notes on Empire," in Hall and Rose, eds., *At Home with the Empire*, 251–74.

16 See Amanda Goodrich, *Henry Redhead Yorke, Colonial Radical: Politics and Identity in the Atlantic World, 1772–1813* (Routledge, 2019), 129–31.

17 Mrs. Basil Holmes, *The London Burial Grounds: Notes on their History from the Earliest Times to the Present Day* (New York, 1896), 163; Micheline Nilson, *Railways and the Western European Capitals: Studies of Implantation in London, Paris, Berlin, and Brussels* (New York: Palgrave McMillan, 2008), 62–4.

18 TS 11/959/3505, unsigned report, 10 February 1793.

19 Maurice Margarot, le Pêre, *Histoire, ou Relation d'un Voyage, Qui a duré Près de cinq Ans* (1780).

20 *Portugal, Baptisms, 1570–1910* (Salt Lake City, UT: FamilySearch, 2013), s.v. "Maurice Margarot" (1745–1810), www.ancestry.com, accessed 9 April 2020.

21 See Thomas Hardy, "Maurice Margarot" [biographical fragments], BL, Add. MS. 27816, fols. 214–20; E. P. Thompson, *The Making of the English Working Class* (Gollancz, 1966), 126–28; Michael Roe, "Maurice Margarot: A Radical in Two Hemispheres," *Bulletin of the Institute of Historical Research* 31 (1958): 68–78, at 69–71. See also Margarot's entry in Joseph O. Baylen and Norbert J. Gossman, eds., *Biographical Dictionary of Modern British Radicals. Volume 1: 1770–1830* (Sussex: Harvester Press, 1979), 307–10. On Gerrald, see James Epstein, "'Our Real Constitution': Trial Defense and Radical memory in the Age of Revolution," in *In Practice: Studies in the Language and Culture of Popular Politics in Modern Britain* (Stanford, CA: Stanford University Press, 2003), 59–82. On the reform movement in Scotland as internationalist, see Nigel Leask "Thomas Muir and *The Telegraph*: Radical Cosmopolitanism in 1790s Scotland," *HWJ* 63 (2007): 48–69. On Muir, see Gordan Pentland, "The Posthumous Lives of Thomas Muir," in *Liberty, Property and Popular Politics: England and Scotland 1688–1815: Essays in*

Honour of H.T. Dickinson, ed. Gordon Pentland and Michael T. Davis (Edinburgh: Edinburgh University Press, 2015), chapter 14; Christina Bewley, *Muir of Huntershill* (Oxford: OUP, 1981).

22 *Address to the Scotch Martyrs* (Sheffield, 1794), 1. Letters written on board the ship show that the prisoners conceived of themselves in similar symbolic terms. See "Petition from Messrs. Palmer and Skirving to Governor Grose," 26 October 1794, F.M. Bladen, ed., *Historical Records of New South Wales, Vol. II: Grose and Patterson, 1793–1795* (Sydney, 1893), 866.

23 With regard to the plot, the inquiry at Port Jackson in New South Wales was inconclusive: none of the Martyrs were held responsible or officially implicated in it, and Palmer and Skirving's petition for a trial was turned down by then governor Francis Grose. Grose instead warned Palmer to "avoid on all occasions a recital of those politics which have produced to you the miseries a man of your feeling and ability must at this time undergo." G. W. Rusden, "The Scotch Martyrs. Odd Notes," G. W. Rusden Mss., vol. 15, fol. 4, Leeper Library, University of Melbourne.

24 The French Committee of Public Safety may have ordered a convoy to intercept the *Surprize* and give the political prisoners asylum in France (their ships were turned away by heavy fog and weather). See Bewley, *Muir*, 108, n6. An intercepted letter from Margarot dated just before the departure from Portsmouth hints that radicals might have known of the French mission: "ten ships of war have left Spithead for the channel, and it is reported that the Brest fleet is out." See *Second Report of the Committee of Secrecy appointed by the House of Commons* (1794), 205. See also Peter MacKenzie, *The Life of Thomas Muir* (Glasgow, 1831), xxxv.

25 One of the flogged soldiers, John Draper, claimed that Skirving and Palmer had approached him about a mutiny while the *Surprize* was still at anchor in England, asking "if he knew if the Convicts... wou'd be on their side to attack the Centinel, and kill or heave him overboard, the rush the Quarterdeck; and secure the Captain, Officers, the Arms and Ammunition, and then those who did not side with the party were to be shot or hove overboard." CO 201/12, fol. 189, Campbell to Camden, 30 May 1794.

26 Ibid.

27 CO 201/12, Information of John Grant, 5 June 1794, fol. 194. Also reprinted in Bladen, ed., *Historical Records of New South Wales*, 2: 865.

28 CO 201/12, Campbell to Camden, 30 May 1794, fol. 189.

29 Ibid., fol. 190. The nineteenth-century historian G. W. Rusden later claimed that Margarot had accused Palmer and Skirving merely to ingratiate himself with Campbell. G. W. Rusden, *History of Australia*, 3 vols. (1883), 1: 216.

30 Thomas Fyshe Palmer, *A Narrative of the Sufferings of T. F. Palmer, and W. Skirving during a Voyage to New South Wales, 1794, on board the Surprise Transport* (1797).

31 See Greg Dening's *Mr Bligh's Bad Language: Passion, Power and Theatre on the Bounty* (Cambridge: CUP, 1992), 19–25.

32 Ibid, 82–83. See also Joy Damousi, *Depraved and Disorderly: Female Convicts, Sexuality and Gender in Colonial Australia* (Cambridge: CUP, 1997), 14–15.

33 Michael Flynn, *Sailors and Seditionists: The People of the Convict Ship* Surprize, *1794* (Sydney: Angela Lind, 1994), 170–71. Flynn provides biographical data for all of those who sailed on the *Surprize*, save for some twenty or so crew members who remain unidentified.

34 Hill to Wathen, 26 July, 1790, in Bladen, ed., *Historical Records of New South Wales*, 2: 367, quoted in Charles Bateson, *The Convict Ships, 1787–1868* (Glasgow: Brown, Son & Ferguson, 1959), 127.

35 Flynn, *Sailors and Seditionists*, 171.

36 Palmer, *Narrative*, 15–16. There is a helpful account of the voyage in Bewley, *Muir*, 103–18. For Palmer's *Narrative* as a synecdoche for the experience of British Jacobin exile, see Toby R. Benis, "Transportation and the Reform of Narrative," *Criticism* 45 (2003): 285–99.

37 CO 201/11, James Thomson, William Baker, and William Pattullo to Under Secretary King, 21 April 1794, fols. 154–55.

38 Ibid.

39 CO 201/11, Campbell to King, 22 April 1794, fols. 156–57. See also *Historical Records of New South Wales*, 2: 855. Palmer, *Narrative*, 15–16; Bewley, *Muir*, 106. Writing to King on 4 April 1794, Campbell complained that Margarot had been making accommodation demands over his head without his knowledge. Meanwhile, Muir and Palmer's arrival forced him "to attend to their situation as much as the crowded state of the ship and her safety will admit of." Writing again two weeks later about the problems he had experienced in securing quarters for Margarot, Campbell apologized to King for burdening him with such "trifling circumstances." CO 201/11, Campbell to Under Secretary King, 4 April, 22 April 1794, fol. 158. See also Bladen, ed., *Historical Records of New South Wales*, 2: 854–55.

40 T.G. Parsons, "Was John Boston's Pig a Political Martyr? The Reaction to Popular Radicalism in Early New South Wales," *Journal of the Royal Australian Historical Society* 71 (1986): 163–76.

41 Palmer, *Narrative*, 19.

42 Bateson, *Convict Ships*, 127. Stricter separation of men and women convicts was one of the recommendations made by the House of Commons Select Committee on Transportation in 1812, the same committee at which Margarot testified on the corrosive effects of the officers' black market profiteering. See *Report of the Select Committee on Transportation . . . and the Effects Which Have Been produced by that Mode of Punishment* (1812), Appendix.

43 Joy Damousi, "Chaos and Order: Gender, Space and Sexuality on Female Convict Ships," *Australian Historical Studies* 26 (1995): 351–72.

44 Palmer, *Narrative*, 30–31.

45 Ibid., ix–x, 21.

46 Joy Damousi, "'Depravity and Disorder': The Sexuality of Convict Women," *Labour History* [Australia] 68 (1995): 30–45.

47 For Campbell's accusation, see Bewley, *Muir*, 104. For the anonymous letter, see BL, Add MS. 27816, fol. 84. The letter is undated but was copied by Place from the original on 2 January 1815 and written as part of a campaign for a public subscription for Margarot in the months prior to his death. On the policing of homosexuality in colonial Australia, see Kim Humphrey, "'Objects of Compassion': Young Male Convicts in Van Diemen's Land, 1834–1850," *Australian Historical Studies* 25 (1992): 13–33.

48 William Turner, *The Lives of Eminent Unitarians; with a Notice of Dissenting Academies, Vol. II* (1843), 214–27; L. Baker Short, "Thomas Fyshe Palmer: From Eton to Botany Bay," *Transactions of the Unitarian Historical Society* 13 (2) (1964): 37–49.

49 Stuart Andrews, *Unitarian Radicalism: Political Rhetoric, 1770–1814* (Houndmills: Palgrave Macmillan, 2003), 24–29.

50 *The Trial of the Rev. Thomas Fyshe Palmer: Before the Circuit Court of Justiciary, Held at Perth, on the 12th and 13th September, 1793, on an Indictment for Seditious Practices, Taken in Court by Mr. Ramsey* (1793), 78, 82 (Matthew), 89 (Ivory). The defense that Palmer would have given had he not been represented by counsel was appended to William Skirving's printing of the trial, and emphasized his moderation. *Trial of the Rev. Thomas Fyshe Palmer*, 195. For a discussion of the trials of Palmer and the other

Martyrs, see Michael T. Davis, "'The Impartial Voice of Future Times Will Rejudge Your Verdict': Discourse and Drama in the Trials of the Scottish Political Martyrs of the 1790s," in *Hélio Osvaldo Alves: O Guardador de Rios*, ed. Joanne Paisana (Braga: Instituto de Letres e Ciências Humanas, 2005): 65–78.

51 Moreover, in contrast to Margarot, once in Australia Palmer seems to have moved away from political activity altogether. See Short, "Thomas Fyshe Palmer," 60–61; Michael T. Davis, "'A Register of Vexations and Persecutions': Some Letters of Thomas Fyshe Palmer from Botany Bay during the 1790s," *ED* 23 (2007): 148–66, at 151.

52 W. Hamish Fraser, *Scottish Popular Politics: From Radicalism to Labour* (Edinburgh: Polygon, 2000), 12–13.

53 Palmer had at least twenty-six visitors while jailed in Perth prior to his trial. See Val Honeyman, "'A Very Dangerous Place'?: Radicalism in Perth in the 1790s," *Scottish Historical Review* 87 (2007): 278–305, at 298.

54 See Theophilus Lindsey to Robert Millar, 16 November 1793, Lindsey to William Tayleur, 2 December 1793, and Lindsey to Joshua Toulmin, 10 January 1794, in G. M. Ditchfield, ed., *The Letters of Theophilus Lindsey (1723–1808)*, 2 vols. (Woodbridge: Boydell Press, 2012), 2: 242, 244, 247.

55 BL, Add. MS. 27816, fol. 102, Margarot to Hardy, 22 December 1795. See also *Second Report of the Committee of Secrecy Appointed by the House of Commons* (1794), appendix B. Margarot convinced Hardy (who was delivering the money on behalf of the societies) that since the others "are continually receiving private presents and are moreover supported by many noblemen and rich M.P.s," the money should go solely to himself. TS 11/953/3497, Margarot to Norwich Constitutional Society, [April 1794].

56 BL, Add. MS. 27816, Thomas Hardy, "Maurice Margarot" [biographical fragments], fol. 214. For the obituary, see *Examiner,* 17 December 1815, The British Library, British Newspaper Archive, https://www.britishnews paperarchive.co.uk/viewer/bl/0000054/18151217/008/0011#, accessed 20 December 2019.

57 BL, Add. MS. 27816, Hardy, "Maurice Margarot," fol. 215. For the British revolutionary sympathizers in Paris, see Rachel Rogers "Vectors of Revolution: The British Radical Community in Early Republican Paris, 1792–1794," (PhD diss., Université Toulouse le Mirail, 2012).

58 BL, Add. MS. 27816, Hardy, "Maurice Margarot," fol. 216.

59 See Andrews, *Unitarian Radicalism*, 31–39.

60 Lindsey to Millar, 13 January 1794, in Ditchfield, ed., *Letters of Theophilus Lindsey*, 2: 249.

61 Andrews, *Unitarian Radicalism*, 140.

62 The title of the latter work invoked the biblical concept of the restorative jubilee (popular in Spencean ultra-radicalism in the 1790s) but the pamphlet is almost completely absent of biblical rhetoric. On tensions between religious enthusiasm and enlightened reason within the radical movement, see Jon Mee, *Romanticism, Enthusiasm, and Regulation: Poetics and the Policing of Culture in the Romantic Period* (Oxford: OUP, 2003), 93–109.

63 Margarot to LCS, 16 July 1794, in Michael T. Davis, ed., *London Corresponding Society, 1792–1799,* 6 vols. (Pickering & Chatto, 2002), 2: 116.

64 See Lindsey to Russell Scott, 14 April 1794, in Ditchfield, ed., *Letters of Theophilus Lindsay*, 2: 275.

65 *Cambridge Intelligencer*, 28 May 1796, The British Library, British Newspaper Archive, https://www.britishnewspaperarchive.co.uk/viewer/BL/0002155/17960528/014/0003?browse=true, accessed 31 March 2020.

66 Richard Dinmore, Jr., *An Exposition of the Principles of the English Jaco-bins; with Strictures on the Political Conduct of Charles J. Fox, William Pitt, and Edmund Burke* (Norwich, 1796), 16–17.

67 See John Issitt, *Jeremiah Joyce, Radical, Dissenter, and Writer* (Burlington, VT: Ashgate, 2006), 107–10.

68 Michael Roe's "Maurice Margarot" is an exception. But compare David Collins, *An Account of the English Colony in New South Wales* (1798); Rusden, *History of Australia*, 1: 205–06; P. A. Brown, *The French Revolution in English History* (London: Crosby, Lockwood and Son, 1919), 124. Robert Hughes dismissed the mutiny as the product of Margarot's "nervous breakdown." See Hughes, *The Fatal Shore: The Epic of Australia's Founding* (New York: Vintage, 1986), 178.

69 BL, Add. MS. 27816, Margarot to Hardy, 22 December 1795, fol. 102.

70 See Lauren Benton, *Law and Colonial Cultures: Legal Regimes in World History* (Cambridge: CUP, 2002), chapter 1.

71 David Neal, *The Rule of Law in a Penal Colony: Law and Power in Early New South Wales* (Cambridge: CUP, 1991), 21. See also Bruce Kercher, *Debt, Seduction, & Other Disasters: The Birth of Civil Law in Convict New South Wales* (Alexandria, Australia: Federation Press, 1996), 1–22.

72 Edward Said, "Reflections on Exile," in *Convergences: Inventories of the Present* (Cambridge, MA: Harvard University Press, 2000), 173–86, at 186.

73 Mary Helms, *Ulysses' Sail: An Ethnographic Odyssey of Power, Knowledge and Geographical Distance* (Princeton, NJ: Princeton University Press, 1988), chapter 3.

74 On the discourse of "rights of Englishmen" in colonial Australia, see Neal, *Rule of Law*, chapter 1; and John McLaren, "'The Judicial Office...Bowing to No Pressure but the Supremacy of the Law': Judges and the Rule of Law in Colonial Australia and Canada, 1788–1840," *Australian Journal of the Society of Legal History* 7 (2003): 177–92. See, more generally, Isaac Land, "'Sinful Propensities': Piracy, Sodomy, and Empire in the Rhetoric of Naval Reform, 1700–1870" in *Discipline and the Other Body: Correction, Corporeality, Colonialism*, ed. Steven Pierce and Anupama Rao (Durham, NC: Duke University Press, 2006), 90–114.

75 On post-revolutionary republic utopianism, see Nigel Leask "Irish Republicans and Gothic Eleutherarchs: Pacific Utopias in the Writings of Theobald Wolfe Tone and Charles Brockden Brown," *Huntington Library Quarterly* 63 (2000): 347–67.

76 See G. W. Rusden, "Notes. Margarot's Journal," G. W. Rusden Mss. 15, fol. 15, Leeper Library, University of Melbourne. While the journal has not survived, the later nineteenth-century historian G. W. Rusden made notes from it, which can be found in his papers. Margarot's journal entries were written in French, although Rusden translated many of them in his own notes.

77 BL, Add. MS. 27816, Margarot to LCS, 16 December 1794, fol. 101. Also reprinted in Davis, *London Corresponding Society*, 2: 114–15.

78 Rusden, "Notes. Margarot's Journal," fol. 17. On 12 April 1801, Margarot noted a "great battle in Ireland—decisive." Rusden, "Notes. Margarot's Journal," fol. 21.

79 Identity and personal history in the Australian colonies were notoriously flexible. Later radical episodes such as the Tichborne case of the 1860s and 1870s would center on the malleability of personal history among immigrants. See Michael Roe's *Kenealy and the Tichborne Cause: A Study in Mid-Victorian Populism* (Melbourne: Melbourne University Press, 1974), chapter 6; and Rohan McWilliam, *The Tichborne Claimant: A Victorian Sensation* (Hambledon Continuum, 2007). For the centrality of the themes

of exile and memory, and the malleability of colonial Australian identity, see Paul Pickering, "Betrayal and Exile: A Forgotten Chartist Experience," in *Unrespectable Radicals: Popular Politics in the Age of Reform*, ed. Michael T. Davis and Paul Pickering (Aldershot: Ashgate, 2008), 201–17.

80 "Papers relating to the Irish Conspiracy," *HRA* 2: 579. See also Anne-Maree Whitaker, "Swords to Ploughshares? The 1798 Irish Rebels in New South Wales," *Labour History* [Australia] 75 (1998): 9–21.

81 "Papers relating to the Irish Conspiracy," *HRA* 2: 579.

82 Ibid., 582.

83 Ibid., 583.

84 On the desires of the leaders of the failed 1800 rising to recruit Margarot into the conspiracy, see Alan Atkinson, *The Europeans in Australia: A History. Volume One: The Beginning* (Oxford: OUP, 1997), 252.

85 Joseph Holt, *Memoirs of Joseph Holt, General of the Irish Rebels in 1798* (1838), 2: 65–73.

86 Rusden, "Notes. Margarot's Journal," fols. 22–23, 26–27.

87 Ibid., fol. 22. Diary entries were typically written in French, perhaps to discourage casual spying in a frontier culture informed not only by secret alliances but also by petty jealousies and advancement by informing. In a few areas, Rusden notes that Margarot shifted to a form of opaque code, which Rusden copied into his notes. See ibid., fol. 18.

88 Ibid., fol. 23.

89 For an overview of the Castle Hill rising, see Whitaker, "Swords to Ploughshares?"; R.W Connell, "The Convict Rebellion of 1804," *Melbourne Historical Journal* 5 (1965): 27–37.

90 *HRA* 5: 534, n156.

91 "Governor King to Under Secretary Sullivan," *HRA*, 5: 142–43; Roe, "Maurice Margarot," 73, n5. The location of Margarot's seized papers is not known.

92 Rusden, *History of Australia*, 1: 211. These would be the bodies of two ringleaders, John Brannon and Timothy Hogan, hanged in chains at Sydney and left to rot in the wind.

93 "Governor King to Under Secretary Sullivan," 21 August 1804, *HRA* 5: 142.

94 The description is by Governor John Hunter, writing to "a friend in Leith," 16 October 1795, Bladen, ed., *Historical Records of New South Wales, Vol. II,* 882. Bladen notes that it was reprinted in the *True Briton,* 20 August 1796.

95 See, for example, "Maurice Margarot to Under Secretary King," 1 October 1800, *HRA* 4: 215–17. For more on this aspect of Margarot's behavior in Australia, see Roe, "Maurice Margarot," 73–74.

96 "Margarot to Lieutenant-Governor Grose," 29 October 1794, *HRA* 5: 536–37.

97 "Lieutenant-Governor Collins to Governor King," 19 December 1805, *HRA Series 3: Despatches and Papers Relating to the Settlement of the States. Volume 1: Port Phillip, Victoria, 1803 – 1804, Tasmania, 1803 – June 1812*, ed. Frederick Watson (Sydney: Commonwealth of Australia, 1921), 345. The forger Robert Stewart had been transported to Australia in 1803 and immediately began organizing prisoners. He later led the convict takeover of the *Harrington* in Sydney Harbor in May 1808. After being caught three months later when the ship foundered on a reef in the South China Sea, Stewart was tried and hanged. See Ian Duffield, "Identity Fraud: Interrogating the Impostures of 'Robert de Bruce Keith Stewart' in Early Nineteenth-Century Penang and Calcutta," *Journal of Social History* 11 (2011): 390–415.

98 "Governor King to Under Secretary Cooke," 20 July 1805, *HRA* 5: 534.

99 Ibid.

100 Ibid., 534–35; "Governor King to Under Secretary King," 14 August 1804, *HRA* 5: 138. For Hunter's remark, see CO 201/15, Hunter to King, 15 November 1799, fol. 89.

101 Roe, "Maurice Margarot," 74.

102 Margarot's journal is filled with angry notes about corruption. Outrage against the governor's favoritism toward friends is matched by dismay that his own suggestions for expanding food resources have been ignored; anger at the official toleration of the black market operated by military officers is matched by regret that former colleagues such as Palmer have joined in the black trade. He writes: "I might have done this Colony much good had my country (not basely deserting) kept me in countenance, as it is I have kept the Junto both in fear and respect." Rusden, "Notes. Margarot's Journal," fol. 6.

103 *Kentish Gazette*, 13 November 1810. British Library Newspaper Archive, accessed 28 December 2019, https://www.britishnewspaperarchive. co.uk/search/results/1810-11-13/1810-11-13?NewspaperTitle=Kentish%2B Gazette&IssueId=BL%2F0000235%2F18101113%2F&County= Kent%2C%20England, accessed 31 March 2020.

104 HO 42/115, Freeling to Beckett, [Enclosure]: "Galloway to Hodgeson," 20 February 1811.

105 BL, Add. MS. 27816, Hardy to Joyce, 10 January 1811, fols. 80–82.

106 Ibid., fol. 97.

107 HO 102/22, reports of Colquhoun, 17 November 1812, and Connelly, 25 November 1812 fol. 511–13. See also Roe, "Maurice Margarot," 76.

108 Gordon Pentland, "Radical Returns in an Age of Revolution: Maurice Margarot, Thomas McFarlane and Andrew White," *Etudes Ecossaises* 13 (2010): 91–102, at 93–96.

109 HO 42/136, Kidder spy report, December 1812. Kidder's interpretation likely meshed subscription efforts on Margarot's behalf with Margarot's efforts to recover debts owed him in France.

110 Maurice Margarot, *Proposal for a Grand National Jubilee* (Sheffield, n.d.[1812]), and *Thoughts on Revolution* (Harlow, 1812).

111 *Examiner*, 1 December 1815.

112 BL, Add. MS. 27816, fol. 89.

113 See Alistair Davidson, *The Invisible State: The Formation of the Australian State, 1788–1901* (Cambridge: CUP, 1991).

114 Paul Gilroy, *The Black Atlantic: Modernity and Double Consciousness* (Cambridge, MA: Harvard University Press, 1993), 156–57.

115 BL, Add. MS. 27816, Unidentified newspaper clipping, 16 February 1816, fol. 228.

116 David Goodway, *London Chartism, 1838–1848* (Cambridge: CUP, 1982), 21–25, 61–63. For divisions within Chartism see Michael J. Turner, *Independent Radicalism in Early Victorian Britain* (Westport, CT: Greenwood Publishers, 2004), chapter 4.

117 James Epstein, *The Lion of Freedom: Feargus O'Connor and the Chartist Movement, 1832–1842* (Croom Helm, 1982), 39–40; Goodway, *London Chartism*, 21–25, 61–63; John Dinwiddy, *Radicalism and Reform in Britain, 1780–1850* (Hambledon Press, 1992), 406, 410.

118 Ronald K. Hutch and Paul R. Ziegler, *Joseph Hume: The People's M.P.* (Philadelphia, PA: American Philosophical Society, 1985), 112–15.

119 BL, Add. MS. 27816, Place to Hume, 13 February 1835, fol. 238.

120 *London Dispatch and People's Political & Social Reformer* 25 December 1836; *Constitutional*, 20 December, 1836. For the Crown and Anchor as a

space symbolically central to British radicals, see Christina Parolin, *Radical Spaces: Venues of Poplar Politics in London, 1790–c.1845* (Canberra: Australian National University E Press, 2010), chapters 4 and 5.

121 When the Sheffield reformer and printer James Montgomery was later asked about Margarot, his language registered the distance that many radicals sought to place between themselves and the troublesome agitator: "Margarot, the wretch! Called upon me in Sheffield, after his return from transportation, in 1811, but I would not have anything to do with him." Montgomery's friend and biographer John Holland supported that interpretation, glossing Montgomery's comment to add that Margarot "appears, while abroad, to have conducted himself with such shameless profligacy, that his fellow transports were presently compelled to separate themselves entirely from his society in New Holland." John Holland and James Everett, *Memoirs of the Life and Writings of James Montgomery,* 7 vols. (1854–56), 1: 162.

122 BL, Add. MS. 27816, Place to Harriet Grote, 16 January 1837, fol. 259.

123 See John Belchem and James Epstein, "The Gentleman Leader Revisited," *SH* 22 (1997): 174–93.

124 BL, Add. MS. 27816, Place to Harriet Grote, 16 January 1837, fol. 258.

125 Ibid., fol. 259.

126 BL, Add. MS. 27816, Thomas Hobbes Scott to George Grote, 8 February 1837, fol. 195.

127 Ibid.

128 BL, Add. MS. 27816, Place to Richard Taylor, 21 February 1837, fol. 308.

129 BL, Add. MS. 27816, Harriet Grote to Francis Place, 13 February 1837, fol. 207.

130 BL, Add. MS. 27816, Harriet Grote to Francis Place, 19 February 1837, fol. 241.

131 *Morning Chronicle*, 21 February 1837.

132 BL, Add. MS. 27816, unidentified newspaper clipping, fol. 304.

133 Ibid.

134 *Morning Chronicle*, 21 February 1837.

135 *Constitutional*, 21 February 1837. On Galloway, see Iain McCalman, *Radical Underworld, Prophets, Revolutionaries, and Pornographers in London, 1795 - 1840* (Oxford: OUP, 1993), 9–21, 108–12, 125–35.

136 *Constitutional*, 21 February 1837.

137 Ibid.

138 See D. J. Rowe, "Francis Place and the Historian," *HJ* 16 (1973): 45–63.

139 BL, Add. MS. 27816, Place to Grote, 21 February 1837, fol. 299.

140 Ibid., fol. 300.

141 Ibid.

142 Ibid., fol. 302.

143 BL, Add. MS. 27816, Galloway to Place, 7 March 1837, fol. 319; BL, Add. MS. 27816, Galloway to Place, 17 March 1837, fol. 322.

144 Patrick Joyce, "The Politics of the Liberal Archive," *History of the Human Sciences* 12 (1999): 35–49; Antoinette Burton, "Introduction: Archive Fever, Archive Stories," in *Archive Stories: Facts, Fictions and the Writing of History* (Durham, NC: Duke University Press, 2005), 1–24.

145 Rowe, "Francis Place," offers caveats to historians who use the Place Papers uncritically, but is less concerned with Place's position within a memorial radical culture.

146 Referring to Hardy a decade and a half earlier, at a meeting celebrating the thirtieth anniversary of the acquittals in the state trials of 1794, Thelwall

had said that "there was one man who would deserve to be damned if he did not write the history of the London Corresponding Society." BL, Add. MS. 27816, Place to John Thelwall, 5 November 1824, fol. 118.

147 Besides the letters mentioned above, see the depositions supplied to Place by Margarot, BL, Add. MS. 27816, "Copy of a Paper Put into My Hands by Mr Margarot, entitled 'A Conspiracy: Declaration of Joseph Draper and others'," 20 January 1815, fol. 164. Elizabeth Margarot later supplied additional depositions and affidavits to Galloway, who transcribed them for Place. See BL, Add. MS. 27816, Galloway to Place, 7 March 1837, and Galloway to Place, 17 March 1837, fols. 319, 322.

148 Nicholas B. Dirks, "Annals of the Archive: Ethnographic Notes on the Sources of History," in *From the Margins: Historical Anthropology and its Futures*, ed. Brian Keith Axel (Durham, NC: Duke University Press, 2002), 27–49, at 48.

149 Joyce, "Politics of the Liberal Archive," 37.

150 Rowe, "Francis Place," 51.

151 BL, Add. MS. 27816, Place's notes on Palmer's *Narrative*, fol. 5.

152 Ibid., fol. 6.

153 Ibid., fols. 16, 20.

154 Thompson claimed that his version was independently corroborated by other accounts that had supported Palmer's version of the event, writing that "he was never shown the depositions of the many witnesses." Place noted against this that Thompson "himself drew up the depositions taken before the [ship's] council." As Place had noticed when going through the collection of depositions by shipboard witnesses, the whole set was copied in "Thompson's hand, and by him framed." BL, Add. MS. 27816, Place's notes on the *Surprize* mutiny depositions, fols. 140–41.

155 For later nineteenth-century efforts to marginalize conspiratorial elements of radical culture, see Anthony Taylor, "Commemoration, Memorializations and Political Memory in Post-Chartist Radicalism: The 1885 Halifax Chartists Reunion in Context," in *The Chartist Legacy*, ed. Owen Ashton, Robert Fyson, and Stephen Roberts (Woodbridge: Merlin Press, 1999), 255–85.

156 *Weekly True Sun*, 17 February 1837.

157 See Philip Ward-Jackson, *Public Sculpture of the City of London* (Liverpool: Liverpool University Press, 2003), 333–34; Driver and Gilbert, "Heart of Empire?," 11–28.

158 *Weekly True Sun*, 17 February 1837.

159 Peter Fritzsche, "Specters of History: On Nostalgia, Exile, and Modernity," *AHR* 106 (2001): 1587–1618; Richard Terdiman, *Modernity and Memory Crisis* (Ithaca, NY: Cornell University Press, 1993), 3–5, 31; Reinhart Koselleck, *Futures Past: On the Semantics of Historical Time* (Cambridge: CUP, 1985), 275–76; David Lowenthal, *The Past is a Foreign Country* (Cambridge: CUP, 1985), xxi, 102, 393–94.

160 Dana Arnold, "London Bridge and its Symbolic Identity in the Regency Metropolis: The Dialectic of Civic and National Pride," in *The Metropolis and Its Image: Constructing Identities for London, c.1750 – 1950* (Oxford: Blackwell, 1999), 79–100, at 84.

161 Rodney Mace, *Trafalgar Square*, chapter 1. See also Dana Arnold, "Rationality, Safety and Power: The Street Planning of Late Georgian London," *The Georgian Group Journal* 5 (1995): 37–50; John Summerson, *Georgian London* (Harmondsworth: Penguin 1978), chapter 11.

162 Claims upon public space would continue to characterize London-based radical movements through the remainder of the century. Anthony Taylor,

"'Common-stealers,' 'Land-Grabbers,' and 'Jerry-Builders': Space, Popular Radicalism and the Politics of Public Access in London, 1848–1880," *International Review of Social History* 11 (1995): 383–407; Parolin, *Radical Spaces*; Katrina Navickas, *Protest and the Politics of Space and Place, 1789–1848* (Manchester: Manchester University Press, 2016).

163 BL, Add. MS. 27816, Thompson to Place, 28 January 1837, fol. 261.
164 Ibid.
165 For an excellent account of the memorial efforts in Edinburgh, see Alex Tyrell with Michael T. Davis, "Bearding the Tories: The Commemoration of the Scottish Political Martyrs of 1793–94," in *Contested Sites: Commemoration, Memorial, and Popular Politics in Nineteenth-Century Britain*, ed. Paul A. Pickering and Alex Tyrell (Aldershot: Ashgate, 2004), 25–56. Tyrell and Davis focus mainly on the Edinburgh efforts and only briefly mention the controversy over Margarot's inclusion.
166 BL, Add. MS. 27816, Thompson to Place, 28 January 1839, fol. 262.
167 Ibid., fol. 264.

8　Among the Romantics

E. P. Thompson and the Poetics of Disenchantment

King of my freedom here, with every prop
A poet needs – the small hours of the night,
A harvest moon above an English copse…
Oh, royal me! Unpoliced imperial man
And monarch of my incapacity
To aid my helpless comrades as they fall –
Lumumba, Nagy, Allende: alphabet
Apt to our age! In answer to your call
I rush out in this rattling harvester
And thrash you into type. But what I write
Brings down no armoured bans, No Ministers
Of the Interior interrogate.
No one bothers to break in and seize
My verses for subversion of the state.
　　　　　– E. P. Thompson, September 1973[1]

On the final page of *The Making of the English Working Class*, E. P. Thompson hails "a resistance movement in which both the Romantics and the Radical craftsmen opposed the annunciation of Acquisitive Man." He continues, "In the failure of the two traditions to come to a point of juncture, something was lost. How much we cannot be sure, for we are among the losers." According to Thompson,

> After Blake no mind was at home in both cultures, nor had the genius to interpret the two traditions to each other. It was a muddled Mr. Owen who offered to disclose the 'new moral world', while Wordsworth and Coleridge had withdrawn behind their ramparts of disenchantment.[2]

The book ends as it starts, with the figure of William Blake whose annotation from 1798, "The Beast and the Whore rule without control," is the epigraph for part one, "The Liberty Tree." The fiftieth anniversary of Thompson's classic has come and gone; at this point, one could be excused for feeling that little more needs to be said. Yet few historians have explored what might be thought an odd conclusion to a book about the "heroic" culture of working-class radicalism.[3] This chapter takes as its starting point Thompson's lament for a historical conjunction that failed to happen. To return to Thompson at the end of our book is to raise questions about when the historian's writing itself becomes part of the past, slipping across an indistinct line that demarks its terms of relevance and currency. Similarly, one might ask whether the politics that Thompson stood for, what he called "socialist humanism," retains its inspirational capacity or might be reworked to suit the cause of transformational change. In terms of his own life's work, scholarly and political, a current runs between past struggles and present conditions of possibility; the political promise, hopes, and desires of the age of revolution and the lives and literature of the Romantics were recurrent points of reference.

A number of related issues are at stake. First, this chapter explores key themes in the political and intellectual life of one of the most influential historians of the twentieth century. It argues that Thompson's history of working-class resistance and his study of romanticism should be viewed as integral to a historical project, informed by his desire to open alternatives for a socialist future. The place of the Romantics in *The Making* is neither incidental nor merely illustrative; rather, it is seen as central to the republican challenge mounted against Britain's ancien régime and to the forces opposed to the emergence of capitalist industrialization. For Thompson, the 1790s was a moment of enormous possibility ending in disillusion and "disenchantment." Indeed, the theme of disenchantment runs through much of Thompson's writing. He was concerned with how the condition of disenchantment influenced the literary and political imagination. The first section of this chapter follows the Romantics' route from political engagement to retreat and doubt, to the point at which identification with democratic principles associated with France was no longer possible.

The second section concerns the interplay between the lived present and historical past, as the disenchantment of Thompson's own era appeared to parallel both the failed aspirations of the age of revolution and the problem of political and literary reaffirmation. It underscores the importance of Communist Party priorities during the Popular Front, Second World War, and the immediate postwar period. The Popular Front not only provided a model for popular mobilization, but the goal of Marxist intellectuals to recover a "people's" literary heritage was reflected in Thompson's later efforts to merge a version of England's literary past with a "people's history." Thompson viewed the final years of the "people's" war as opening a moment of internationalist hope, a prospect soon extinguished by the rise of Cold War culture. The crisis of 1956 marked a sharp break that forced political rethinking and the founding of the New Left.

In the third section, we return to the Romantics, to their trajectory from "disenchantment" to "default" – terms Thompson initially used with reference to twentieth-century writers and intellectuals. For Thompson, Wordsworth's poetry at the moment of sustained crisis, when political hopes confront a changed reality, illustrates the complex translation of "lived experience" into poetic language. "Experience" remained a key analytical category in Thompson's writing on both history and literature, viewed as something that was lived through and articulated, and that was thus available for interpretation. No British historian of his generation, with the possible exception of Christopher Hill, contributed more than Thompson to the field of literary studies. While his work crossed disciplinary boundaries, he remained largely indifferent to the fashions of academic literary scholarship. In debates over contested questions of political theory, he assumed the historian's privileged position. Yet his work provides an opportunity for ongoing exchange between historians and literary scholars and the enhancement of cross-disciplinary awareness.

Thompson died before he was able to finish his long-planned book on the early Romantics. The chapter concludes by turning to the unfinished work. It engages with an absent text, elaborating on what Thompson left undone or what he might have done had he lived to complete his project; it seeks to offer some slight compensation for what we have lost.

"Bliss Was It in That Dawn": From Romantic Revolution to Retreat

Thompson's interest in romanticism spanned a lifetime: from his first book, *William Morris: Romantic to Revolutionary*, published in 1955 with a revised edition in 1977, to his study *Witness against the Beast*: *William Blake and the Moral Law*, published shortly after his death in 1993. He grew up within a family surrounded by poets and poetry; both his father and brother, and indeed Thompson himself, were poets.[4] Had he lived, a full-scale book on the Romantics during the age of revolution was promised.[5] We are left with the not insubstantial fragments of that book brought together by his wife, Dorothy Thompson. The signature essay, "Disenchantment or Default? A Lay Sermon," originally published in 1969, focuses on the plight of William Wordsworth and Samuel Coleridge.[6] This essay is crucial to any discussion of Thompson's interpretation of the romantic poets. It deals with the complicated relationship between literature and political commitment, with literary expression born of the shattered dream of new worlds and retreat from once-held ideologies deemed to be false. In delivering his "Lay Sermon" (a reference to Coleridge's reactionary *Lay Sermon* of 1817), Thompson returns to themes, incidents, and poetry first introduced in *The Making* concerned with the Romantics' active political engagement, their lingering disillusion, and ultimate disavowal of former beliefs. In this context, he reflects more broadly on the situation of intellectuals and artists during times of intense political struggle.

In the first instance, Thompson countered a prevailing tendency among literary critics to press Wordsworth's moment of political disenchantment earlier and earlier and to present the political break as catastrophic and total, decoupling poetic achievement from political engagement. In this way, romanticism's own ideology, whereby romantic poetry stands beyond the historical conditions of its own production, was reaffirmed.[7] In contrast, Thompson dates Wordsworth's decisive break as having come after the Peace of Amiens (1802–03), with an extended period of poetic creativity occurring before disenchantment turned to default. One cause of misunderstanding, writes Thompson, "has been an insufficiently close attention to the actual lived historical experience."[8] At this point, "experience" is set against abstraction or theory, with William Godwin as the principal culprit. When it was published in February 1793, Godwin's *Political Justice* caused a sensation among the radical intelligentsia. William Hazlitt later reflected, with a characteristic touch of irony, Godwin "blazed as a sun in the firmament of reputation; no one was more talked of... wherever liberty, truth, justice was the theme, his name was not far off."[9] Wordsworth was deeply impressed and became one of Godwin's regular visitors.[10] In 1794, Coleridge wrote Robert Southey that he had read Godwin "with the greatest attention." He sought out Godwin in London, dedicating a poem to the philosopher in which he likened the power of *Political Justice* to the aurora borealis illuminating "a sunless world forlorn" with an "[e]lectric... stream of rosy light."[11] Coleridge, ever quick to change his mind, had in fact already begun to see through Godwin's system. Wordsworth's break came somewhat later. For Thompson the falling of the scales from the poets' eyes did not mark the abandonment of republican principles but "a rejection of a mechanical psychology and an abstract enthronement of reason."[12] The break with Godwin signaled a turn toward "real man and away from abstracted man... away from the *déraciné* Godwinian intelligentsia but toward the common people." This view lines up well with Wordsworth's own version of his attraction to and subsequent rejection of the philosophy "That promised to abstract the hopes of man / Out of his feelings, to be fixed thenceforth, / For ever in a purer element" (*Prelude*, bk. 10, 806–09).[13]

Thompson captures the Romantics' release from the grip of Godwin's high rationalism; whether his hostile evaluation of Godwin is fully justified is a different question.[14] The critique of "abstract reason," the opposition of "experience" to theory, can itself be viewed as an intellectual tradition rooted in British reactions to the French Revolution.[15] The privilege according to "experience" was a key element of romanticism. There is a sense in which Thompson casts Godwin as a stock character, the philosophizing intellectual of the Left sitting out the political struggle, risk-averse, and inconstant in his politics. Versions of this figure recur in his polemics aimed at contemporaries, most notably Louis Althusser. In 1963, the year that saw the publication of *The Making*, Thompson penned a lengthy memo addressed to the editorial board of *New Left Review* (a journal he had helped to found in 1960) in which he detected among the editors "the same tendencies to deracination and intellectualization, in the name of higher socialist theory" that he disliked in Jean-Paul Sartre and "marxistentialism."[16] As for Godwin, his grand notions of "Reason" and "Benevolence" lacked roots in the soil of social reality or support among the ranks of artisan democrats. He opposed political activism; revolutions were experiments of the mind. Thompson's judgment of Godwin remained harsh. Toward the end of his life, he reiterated, "There is a sense in which the espousal of Godwinism represented an actual retreat from immediate political commitment. The very utopianism of *Political Justice* appealed in characteristic ways to the revolting intelligentsia."[17]

Opposition to what he regarded as retreat to the heights of theory formed a unifying theme in Thompson's life and writing. It is worth pausing, however, to remark on his reference to Godwin's utopianism. In his postscript to the revised edition of *William Morris: Romantic to Revolutionary* (1977), Thompson embraced Morris's "new Utopianism," an expressive mode that drew its imaginative force from romanticism. He observes that to vindicate Morris's utopianism "may at the same time be to vindicate Utopianism itself, and set it free to walk the world once more without shame and without accusations of bad faith."[18] Morris is not only freed from the critique of scientific Marxism but provides the means for reopening the Marxist tradition to the realm of human desire. The trajectory taking Morris from "romantic to revolutionary" appears less of a break than Thompson had originally proposed, reflecting his own rejection of Marxist orthodoxy and establishing continuity with *The Making* and his transition to "socialist humanism."[19]

Of course, not all utopian visions are to be commended. Tellingly, Thompson dismissed Coleridge and Southey's plans to establish a utopian community on the banks of the Susquehanna as "fantasy."[20] However, as argued in Chapter 5, "Pantisocracy" was a more serious scheme than is often supposed. Plenty of British "Jacobins" toyed with the idea of moving to America to escape the tyranny of Europe. Thompson says little about America or its revolution. In Coleridge's case, his visionary republic was linked to his attack on the institutions of private property, commercial civilization, and slavery. For the young Romantics and their partners, "Pantisocracy" represented a withdrawal, a retreat from active political struggle. Nonetheless, Coleridge's ideas on the equalization of property, which reflected Godwin's influence, arguably deserve to be considered along with the ideas of his soon-to-be friend John Thelwall and those of the communitarian socialist Thomas Spence.[21] For Thompson, the plan was obviously a nonstarter, without political significance in the real world. Yet its utopian desire reflected the uncertain horizon that momentarily seemed to separate present reality from future possibility. There was a deep radicalism at its core, as well as a deepening disappointment about the prospects for Europe once Britain entered the war against France and the French Revolution turned violence upon itself.

It is the closing of that moment of perceived possibility, the point at which hope falters and reassessments must be made, that concerns Thompson. In the first instance, retreat and the slide from disenchantment to "apostasy" was the result of the French Revolution's descent from *fraternité* to fratricide and the course of European warfare. Like most British Jacobins, the radical intelligentsia's allegiances were properly speaking Girondist; they were shocked by the spectacle of leaders such as Jacques-Pierre Brissot being led to the guillotine.[22] It is necessary to register, as Thompson does, the sustained commitment among the poets and their network of young friends to fundamental political change. Wordsworth witnessed the Revolution firsthand – chronicling a version of his experience in books nine and ten of *The Prelude*. Writing in 1794 to William Matthews, he declared himself "of that odious class of men called democrats." As an enemy of "monarchical and aristocratical governments" and "hereditary distinctions... of every species," Wordsworth commented, "I am not amongst the admirers of the British Constitution."[23] Thompson cites this correspondence to underscore Wordsworth's radicalism. This was heady stuff, written as the government was arresting over thirty leaders of London's main reform societies. Wordsworth and Matthews were looking to launch a journal, to be titled the "Philanthropist." Wordsworth kept much hidden about his activities during these crucial years, and Thompson was subsequently able to throw new light on the mystery of Wordsworth's possible involvement in a journal that appeared in 1795 under the same title, published by the Jacobin printer Daniel Isaac Eaton. Eaton was among the most intrepid radical publishers. It seems likely that Wordsworth sought out Eaton as a printer who might provide financial aid and safe cover for the young men's publishing venture. As Thompson observes, at this point "intellectual radicalism and the popular societies were bumping against each other all the time."[24]

While Wordsworth dabbled with radical publishing, Coleridge was more purposefully engaged. In 1795 he delivered his powerful series of lectures on politics and religion at Bristol. He condemned "the causeless Panic" created by the treason trials of Thomas Hardy, John Horne Tooke, and Thelwall, and concluded his diatribe "On the Present War" by asking, "shall we carry on this wild and priestly War against reason, against freedom, against human nature?" He reported to George Dyer, radical Unitarian and fellow poet, of the "furious and determined" opposition he faced at Bristol, where a mob threatened to attack the lecture hall "in which the 'damn'd Jacobine was jawing away." [25] The lecture Coleridge delivered in November 1795 against the "Two Bills" came as close to sedition as one might risk before the Seditious Meetings and Treasonable Practices Acts made such speech unlawful. [26] He moderated his tone in his short-lived journal *The Watchman* but kept pressure on Pitt's government. "A sort of little Bristol Thelwall," is how Thompson describes Coleridge at this time. [27] In an essay on Coleridge's revolutionary youth, he maintains, "the curve of Coleridge's commitment, in 1795–96, took him very close indeed to the popular societies – or towards their more intellectual component." The trajectory was one that "had [it] not been arrested by retirement to Stowey, would almost certainly have led him to prison." [28] He cites Southey's reaction to Coleridge's later denial of his political sympathies: "It is worse than folly, for if he was not a Jacobine... I wonder who the Devil was." [29] As the "Two Acts" curtailed the public presence of plebeian radicalism by restricting public meetings and enlarging the definition of treason, the Romantics felt the blast. As Hazlitt observed in *The Spirit of the Age* (1825), "It was a misfortune to any man of talent to be born in the latter end of the last century." [30] In his book on the lost literary generation of the 1790s, Kenneth Johnston argues that not only did Pitt's "reign of alarm" devastate a generation of writers but government repression affected the idiom of English letters, washing out a "republican voice" left to flourish in America. [31] Here was part of the loss to which Thompson referred.

As the current of British Jacobinism was driven underground, the Romantics also sought cover. In *The Making*, as well as in later essays, Thompson follows Wordsworth and Coleridge to the Quantock Hills, where Thelwall – Jacobin lecturer, political theorist, and poet – visited them in summer 1797, soon after the Wordsworths had established themselves at Alfoxden House. The previous spring Coleridge first wrote to Thelwall, "Pursuing the same end by the same means we ought not to be strangers to each other." This began an intense correspondence between the two men which underscored differences as well as shared sympathies. "We run on the same ground, but we drive different Horses," Coleridge soon wrote. "I am daily more and more a religionist – you, of course, more & more otherwise." [32] Thelwall, whom Thompson describes as "one of the few who tried to straddle the world of letters and that of popular agitation," was looking for a place to settle. [33] Thelwall figures as an intellectual who aligned himself with plebeian radicalism and who suffered from isolation and defeat without renouncing his former beliefs or self. As such, he becomes one of the heroes of Thompson's grand narrative and foil to Godwin. Thelwall's stubborn retreat also tracks the struggle in Thompson's life to sustain a commitment to socialist belief as conditions alter and hopes dim. Fittingly, the story of Thelwall's silencing is the subject of Thompson's final article "Hunting the Jacobin Fox," a reconnection to and expansion on his role in *The Making*.[34] It is worth noting that as Thelwall was pursued by spies and his mail was opened by government officials, MI5 kept tabs on Thompson's political activities.[35]

Thelwall's visit to Nether Stowey coincided with the collaboration between Wordsworth and Coleridge that resulted in the publication of the *Lyrical Ballads* the following year. Summer 1797 is one of the two "spots in time" that Thompson revisits in his essay "Disenchantment or Default?"[36] Not surprisingly, following the naval mutinies of the spring and with fears of a French invasion, "the patriot" Thelwall's arrival caused alarm within the local community. Thelwall was, in fact, searching for tranquility, a "sequester'd dell" where he could live "in philosophic amity" alongside his fellow poets.[37] Coleridge remembered "sitting in a beautiful recess in the Quantocks," and saying to his companion, "'Citizen John, this is a fine place to talk treason in!' – 'Nay! Citizen Samuel,' replied he, 'it is rather a place to make a man forget that there is any necessity for treason!'"[38] For Thompson, the exchange is emblematic, foreshadowing, as he writes in *The Making*, "the decline of the first Romantics into political 'apostasy.'" A nervous Coleridge was unable to find a cottage for his friend, who instead retired with his family to rural Wales. Shortly after the "Jacobin Fox's" departure, James Walsh ("Spy Nozy"), who had helped to arrest Thelwall in 1794, arrived to sniff out the seditious "nest" of poets at Stowey.[39]

Thompson carefully monitors Wordsworth and Coleridge's slow, anguished retreat from political engagement. The first spot in time illustrates how democrats were driven back into small, embattled enclaves. The second spot in time occurred in spring 1798. Thompson aligns the prosecution of Gilbert Wakefield, Unitarian divine and classical scholar, with Wordsworth and Coleridge's situation.[40] Wakefield and the bookseller Joseph Johnson were imprisoned for publishing Wakefield's *Reply to... the Bishop of Llandaff's Address to the People of Great Britain*. Wakefield, who died within four months of his release from prison, had seen fit to question the government's conduct of the war and to cast doubt on Pitt's good faith in treating for peace. He described how the ministry protected itself: "they have engendered sham plots, false alarms, and visionary assassinations, for the purposes of deluding the unwary, and to establish their own power by a military despotism in England."[41] Johnson, who up to this point had been careful to avoid prosecution, was a crucial linking figure among the radical intelligentsia. He was Wordsworth's original publisher. Mary Wollstonecraft, who reviewed for his *Analytical Review*, first met Godwin dining at Johnson's table alongside Paine. She also met Blake through Johnson.[42] Wakefield and Johnson were not the only oppositionists to find themselves in prison. Benjamin Flower, the editor of the *Cambridge Intelligencer* and publisher of

Coleridge and Southey's *The Fall of Robespierre* (1795), was also sent to prison for his attack on Richard Watson, Bishop of Llandaff. Thompson identifies Flower's journal as "the last national organ of intellectual Jacobinism."[43]

One can well imagine how Wakefield's fate might have affected Wordsworth. In 1793, Wordsworth had written his own republican response to the bishop, which he left unpublished, perhaps on Johnson's advice.[44] Interestingly, the figure of the Solitary from *The Excursion* can be linked to Wakefield. Thompson was to press the claims of Thelwall as one model for this dejected and reclusive character, a composite drawn from real persons including the poet himself.[45] It has been compellingly argued that Wordsworth also had Wakefield in mind, a double for his own predicament and for a fate he had narrowly avoided.[46] As Wakefield awaited trial, things turned dangerous for Wordsworth and Coleridge in Somerset, as "volunteers" were being recruited into service to protect the coast against an anticipated French invasion. Thompson concludes that, in departing for Germany in September 1798, they were "hopping the draft" – a contemporary nod to young American draft resisters.[47] The poets arrived at Hamburg, a neutral city teeming with spies and "suspicious persons," including Irish rebels fleeing the abortive rising of the summer. They were almost certainly on the British government's local watch-list.[48]

By this time, the final ties between "Jacobin" intellectuals and radical artisans had been severed. Here, according to Thompson, set in "that pattern of revolutionary disenchantment which foreshadows the shoddier patterns of our own century." In the narrative arc of *The Making*, the Romantics' withdrawal is linked to the earlier alienation of a reform-minded sector of the bourgeoisie that left artisans and wage-earners without allies to open the doors of revolution. While celebrating the movement's independence, Thompson recognizes the important loss of "badly needed intellectual resources" as middle-class radicals retreated from the political field.[49] With the final suppression of the Corresponding Societies, with most of their leaders either in prison or in exile, British Jacobinism turned into a small underground stream. When popular radicalism reemerged in full force at the end of the Napoleonic Wars, the movement would breed its own intellectual leaders drawn from inside as well as outside the incipient "working class."

Twentieth-Century Reversion: From the Popular Front to the New Left

As for the "shoddier patterns" of the twentieth century, Thompson had much to say; he continually brought the past to bear on the present, or as some critics would have it, his interpretations of history and literature were clouded by projections of the present onto the past. Certainly, he discerned a pattern whereby intellectuals and artists had moved through stages from political engagement to disenchantment and then to apostasy or default. The connections between the disenchantment of his own age and of the 1790s run through his writing. He was principally concerned about the role of the intellectual in movements of dissent and about what he regarded as an obligation to maintain truth to one's self even as confidence in previously held commitments and beliefs waned.

Thompson faced key moments of political doubt challenging him to revise his beliefs and to reaffirm political and moral values as historical circumstances changed. Already a committed communist, he served as a tank commander during the Second World War and, on his return home, shared a general optimism about the prospects for building a socialist Britain. He recalled the war as "an extraordinary formative moment in which it was possible to be deeply committed to the point of life itself in support of a particular political struggle which was at the same time a popular struggle… one didn't feel a sense of being isolated in any way from the peoples of Europe or the peoples of Britain."[50] This optimism did not last long as Cold War patterns set in. Thompson wrote his study of Morris in the early 1950s, while he was an active member of the Communist Party living in Halifax and teaching English literature and history as a staff tutor in the extra-mural department of the University of Leeds. [51] Morris's significance was clear; he "was the first creative artist of major stature … to take his stand, consciously and without compromise, with the revolutionary working class." Despite the book's awkward gestures to orthodoxy, as Thompson later commented, a "muffled 'revisionism'" can be discerned.[52] With the emergence of the New Left, Morris points the way to "socialist humanism"; to Thompson's call for a recognition of man's moral nature, an irreducible moral consciousness denied by Stalinist ideology, and the human agency and experience of "real" men and women.[53] The New Left was born from the "conjuncture" of 1956: the twin shocks of the Soviet suppression of the Hungarian Revolution and the British-French invasion of the Suez Canal Zone.[54] The New Left sought to build a movement for independent socialist renewal. For Thompson, leaving the Communist Party was to cross a threshold, akin to the "river of fire" across which Morris had moved; it meant abandoning ties of loyalty and comradeship. It was also liberating. Written with remarkable speed between 1959 and 1962, *The Making* reflected the loosening of ideological reins and the energy of the New Left and the Campaign for Nuclear Disarmament.[55]

The late 1950s and early 1960s were a period of reexamination. "Commitment" became a vogue word among left-wing authors, including Thompson. But it was one that he partially distrusted when connected to poetry, because "it can slide all too easily into usages which defeat its apparent intention."[56] Yet the question of how art is produced as political confidence fades recurs in his writing, along with the question of how the condition of disenchantment is negotiated in literary terms. At the point of default, Thompson contends, "Disenchantment ceases to be a recoil of the responsible in the face of difficult social experience; it becomes abdication of intellectual responsibility in the face of all social experience."[57] Thompson addressed this process at length and most directly in "Outside the Whale," his contribution to *Out of Apathy* (1960), a collection that sought to reaffirm a socialist agenda amidst the malaise of apathy. His essay is a reply of sorts to George Orwell's "Inside the Whale," and marks his first linkage of the terms "disenchantment" and "default."[58]

Published in 1940, Orwell's essay made the case for ranking Henry Miller's novel *Tropic of Cancer* among the few major works of contemporary literature. Orwell argued that Miller's acceptance of a civilization in decay gave his work an authenticity missing in so much contemporary literature. In the face of defeat in Spain, the Moscow trials, the collapse of the Popular Front, the Russo-German pact, and the outbreak of the Second World War, Miller's passivity constituted a justified reaction; his work rang true to the feelings of ordinary people.[59] Orwell concluded that on the whole the literary history of the 1930s "seems to justify the opinion that a writer does well to keep out of politics" – or at the very least, not to confuse good writing with good politics, for "the cause" and the cause of literature were separate issues.[60]

In a sense Thompson was, as Stefan Collini describes him, "a man of the 1940s."[61] Having come of age politically against the backdrop of the end of the Popular Front and the onset of war, for him to return to Orwell, W. H. Auden, and the artist's responsibility in troubled times came naturally. In "Outside the Whale," Wordsworth's Solitary arrives on cue. Whereas years of self-examination separated the romantic poet as "ardent revolutionary" from renunciation of his former political self, history now repeats itself as farce; the twentieth-century about-face took a mere decade to reenact. "To understand the first stage of this regress," Thompson turns to Auden's poem *Spain*, which was published in 1937 as a one-shilling pamphlet.[62] Whereas Orwell had expressed his scorn – he thought Auden's reference to "necessary murder" came too readily for a poet who had not shouldered a rifle in Spain – Thompson admired Auden's poem, which he thought was underappreciated. But by 1940 when he republished *Spain* in a collection of his poetry, Auden had changed his mind and revised his poem. Thompson subjects the amended version of *Spain* to close reading, detailing the omissions from and revisions to the original text (including the change of "necessary murder" to "the fact of murder"). With regard to two verses that Auden completely excised, Thompson observes that – stripped of specific reference to Madrid, "invading battalions," "Our hours of friendship" blossoming "into a people's army" – the refrain "But to-day the struggle" no longer refers to a pressing moral choice but to a universal human predicament; the poem had lost its focus and moral way. It is fair to say that Auden was ultimately unable to achieve a truthful resolution in his political poetry between private perception and public pronouncement. Thompson makes clear that it is not the "authenticity of Auden's experience" that is in dispute "but the default implicit in his response," his giving up on the problem and setting sail for America.[63]

At issue is how "authenticity of experience" is handled, how disenchantment is dealt with in verse. Thompson posits a correlation between artistic value and the complex experience of disenchantment; the tensions sustained before disenchantment succumbs to default impart an enhanced creative impulse. His treatment of Auden, the demise of the Popular Front, and the onset of the Cold War parallels his analysis of the trajectory of British Jacobinism, Pitt's regime of repression, and the fate of romanticism. Political themes from the present and near-past are transposed onto the 1790s, most centrally the relationship between disenchantment and art. In his own day, however, the final consequences of disenchantment were delayed by the Second World War. For Thompson, the socialist potential that arose during the war ended around 1948 with the capitulation to "Natopolis" and the surrender to Cold War culture, witnessing "a *trahsion des clercs* as abject as any that had gone before." Inwardly, the "insurgent, popular-front-type moment" was destroyed by Stalinism.[64] On both sides of the Cold War divide the words "romantic" and "utopian" became swearwords. The Labour government's defeat in 1951 marked the coda to this surrender.

For Thompson the narrowed vision of 1950s could be traced back to 1939 and the end of the Popular Front. Not only was the "authenticity of experience" at issue, so was the history of the 1930s. What Orwell dismissed as a "swindle" and Auden dubbed "a low dishonest decade" no more did justice to the thirties "than the self-flagellation of Wordsworth's Solitary is a true comment upon the men of the London Corresponding Society."[65] Writing in the first issue of *Universities and Left Review* in 1957, Thompson proposed that the New Left's goal should be to reopen the circuit that had been closed between intellectuals and the broader socialist movement, to reconnect the sort of lines of communication that had characterized the 1930s.[66] As cofounder and coeditor of *The New Reasoner* (1957–59), Thompson insisted on the importance of literary contributions and poetry to the journal's make-up.[67] *Left Review* (1934–38), the leading Communist literary journal of the thirties, influenced his thinking on how to produce an activist journal.[68] There were direct personal links between *The New Reasoner* and Marxist literary journals of the 1930s and 1940s, including the poet Randall Swingler, who served for a time as editor of *Left Review*.[69]

Many of the questions concerning literature and politics that Communists raised during the 1930s and 1940s stayed with Thompson.

"If poetry is to survive," wrote C. Day Lewis in 1935, "it must become necessary again to the people." In the classless society of the future, artists might realize their full potential and regain their lost relationship to the people, but in the meantime how was an authentic people's culture to be achieved? The problem of the poetry of the future was linked to recovering the poetry of England's past. Writing in *Left Review*, Swingler recommended Blake as "a good starting point for redeeming our revolutionary culture." Not only was Blake a craftsman who lacked a classical education, but "Jerusalem," the most widely known and sung of English poems, illustrated his "characteristic Englishness."[70] The writer Ralph Fox devoted the final chapter of his posthumously published book *The Novel and the People* (1937) to the nation's cultural heritage, arguing that "[a] people cannot play its part in history if it renounces its cultural past, any more than if it renounces its political past." As a case in point, Fox cites Wordsworth's pamphlet *The Convention of Cintra* (1809) as among the most sublime pieces of English prose. He finds Wordsworth's tract "revolutionary" and "heroic" in its passionate support for Portuguese and Spanish national resistance to Napoleon.[71] For a communist intellectual such as Fox soon to be killed fighting in Spain, Wordsworth's return to the cause of liberty via the uprising on the Iberian Peninsula was poignant. Thompson's older brother Frank – whom he followed into the Communist Party at age seventeen – observed in his wartime journal that the key question for the younger generation of Soviet poets was whether they could "bridge the gulf between the poet and the public" and "make poetry once more the interest and property of the people." Killed in the Bulgarian resistance in 1944, he wrote in one of his last letters of the need to build "a new communal ethic" to unite the people of postwar Europe, East and West.[72]

Following the war, as Bill Schwarz shows, the Popular Front's orientation and its construction of "the people" took hold among the Communist Party's Historians' Group with a transition taking place from the characteristically literary to the historical component of what Antonio Gramsci theorized as the "national-popular."[73] In fact, Thompson did not play a significant part in the Historians' Group, but was closely associated with the party's literary members; he contributed to *Our Time* and *Arena*, successor journals to *Left Review*.[74] One thinks of *The Making* as the fullest flowering of the Historians' Group's project, a panoramic counter-narrative of working-class struggle. But the embedding of the Romantics within the book's grand structure reflects the intersecting goals of historical and literary recovery, and a partial merging of generational priorities.[75] Significantly, Thompson relates that one of the two or three books he carried with him during the war was the *Handbook of Freedom*, "an extraordinarily rich compendium of primary sources" compiled in 1939 by Edgell Rickword, former editor of *Left Review*, and Jack Lindsay, who later contributed to *The New Reasoner*.[76] Literary sources are brought together with other documents recording twelve centuries of "English Democracy": extracts from *Piers Plowman* accompany reports of the Peasants' Revolt, Milton's poetry appears alongside Leveller debates and Digger tracts, an anonymous Luddite song joins with Bryon's "Song for the Luddities."[77] Remembered for pioneering history as seen from below, members of the Historians' Group continued to pursue literary as well as historical studies. The intellectually versatile Victor Kiernan published a long essay, symptomatically entitled "Wordsworth and the People," that prefigured aspects of Thompson's later argument.[78]

In his autobiography, *Interesting Times*, Eric Hobsbawm notes the striking number of Marxist intellectuals of his generation who moved to historical analysis from literature. He suggests that their passion for literature helps to explain "the otherwise surprising influence of the anti-Marxist F. R. Leavis," adding, "Cambridge communists who read English swore by him."[79] Thompson took a degree in history at Cambridge, with a strong emphasis on the study of literature. There were, in fact, more fundamental reasons than a passion for literature to recommend Leavis and *Scrutiny* to Cambridge Marxists. Without necessarily subscribing to a Leavisite vision of a lost organic community ruptured by industrialization, Marxists desired to reclaim a popular-national cultural tradition.[80] The appeal to a version of the opposition between the romantic and the utilitarian also struck a common chord, particularly with Thompson. Moreover, Leavis and *Scrutiny* provided a portable method of close reading as well as criteria for judging literary and cultural value.[81] The emphasis placed on the felt measure of "experience," with "lived" experience set in opposition to abstraction, had an obvious appeal for Thompson, as it did for Raymond Williams.[82] While the concept of experience may have been under-theorized, it remained central to Thompson's analysis of the first generation of romantic poets, as it did for his analysis of class. Thompson roundly rejected the idea of a shared evolutionary culture as opposed to ongoing struggle between cultures or ways of life.[83] At stake was the recovery and propagation of a national culture of opposition, with a shift in conceptual emphasis from "the people" to "the working class" – although the populist inflection persisted.

Cultural transformation was a major analytical concern of the first New Left. Yet faced with the corrosive effects of consumer capitalism and the mass media on working-class culture, Thompson insisted on the place of workers in the struggle for socialism. The "affluent worker" was not simply to be written off as captive to a materialist ethos of individualism. He took issue with younger socialist intellectuals associated with *Universities and Left Review* for viewing working people as subjects of history, pliant victims of alienation and false consciousness. Writing in 1959, he maintained, "we are lacking, chiefly, in a sense of history," a knowledge that working-class history "has always been a *way of struggle* between competing moralities" in which "the political minority has been the carrier of the aspirations of the majority."[84]

The Making was his answer to this lack of historical understanding. But by the time the book was published in 1963, the forces of the first New Left had dispersed and Thompson had entered the political wilderness. In the end, the New Left failed to inspire a broad-based socialist reawakening; the movement did not find a significant working-class following; and no lasting alliance was forged between New Left intellectuals and the labor movement.[85] *The New Reasoner* merged with *Universities and Left Review* in 1960 to form *New Left Review*, which under the editorship of Perry Anderson became a journal of Marxist theory generally detached from political activism.[86]

Thompson's lionization within the academy, where he never felt fully comfortable, coincided with his increased political isolation. In 1965, he became director of the Centre for the Study of Social History at the newly established University of Warwick; he resigned in 1970 amid protests against the university administration and its relations with corporate industry.[87] At Warwick his interests turned to the study of eighteenth-century law and society. In 1967–68, he again collaborated with Williams, Stuart Hall, and others from the first New Left to issue the *May Day Manifesto*, "a socialist alternative" to the Labour government's reformist policies.[88] Thompson delivered "Disenchantment or Default?" at New York University in 1968 as part of the Albert Schweitzer lecture series, returning to the Romantics less in the euphoric spirit of revolution sweeping Europe and America than in a state of meditation on failed political aspirations and the relationship of political disenchantment to artistic expression.

Between Disenchantment and Default: The Romantics' Response

For Thompson the recoil and ultimate "default" of intellectuals in the face of political disillusion was a phenomenon that bridged the histories of the Cold War and the 1790s. Viewed as a dishonest reckoning with former beliefs and allegiances, "apostasy" retained a strong resonance in his political lexicon. As applied to the Romantics, the characterization has been questioned by critics who discern underlying continuities as opposed to a sharp ideological break in thinking.[89] Nonetheless, much contemporary opinion, among younger poets and popular radicals alike – as discussed in Chapter 6 above – registered a sense of betrayal.[90] Thus Lord Byron's denunciation of "Bob Southey" and "the Lakers" was matched by Shelley's response on reading the *Excursion*. Shelley expressed his disappointment as Wordsworth returned the poet to the traditional path of solitude and order in a poem dedicated to his patron, the Earl of Londsdale, the most powerful landowner of Cumberland and Westmorland counties.[91] Hazlitt most forcefully brought the charge of "apostate" in his attack on Coleridge's *Lay Sermons*; his campaign "against literary apostasy" established an influential framework for distinguishing the generational conflicts and differences among the Romantics.[92] Hazlitt remained among Thompson's favorites for having battled to maintain his radical principles. As for Blake, Thompson argues that his resistance to Enlightenment reason meant that he escaped the brand of disenchantment suffered by others. The intensity of his vision, which derived from the world of the Ranters and the Diggers, made it impossible for him "to fall into the courses of apostasy," as he withdrew into antinomian quietude. Blake's own terrifying brush with the law in 1803–04, when charged for subversive speech on the information of two soldiers, drove him deeper into himself.[93]

For the Romantics, as for many radicals, the French Revolution had been a failure. A war mounted against European oppression had become a war of French conquest, and with Napoleon's appointment as First Consul in late 1799 the republic succumbed to dictatorship. The French invasion of Switzerland brought Coleridge's "recantation." His "deep worship" of the "spirit of divinest Liberty" returns from the "profitless" pursuit of freedom among governments and human society to Nature's inspiration belonging to the individual.[94] At this point, Thompson regards Coleridge as still "a man of the Left," for his continued opposition to the war, but Coleridge soon turned on former friends and disavowed his past. Like Auden, Coleridge failed to come to terms with his former political self, foregoing a sustained period to reconcile past and present beliefs, a failure culminating in the "fine fiction" found in book ten of *Biographia Literaria* (1817), where he claims always to have been an opponent of Jacobinism.[95]

"Apostasy" may seem a blunt term for evaluating the motivations and work of creative artists, even as distinguished from merely changing one's political views. For Thompson, the couplet "disenchantment" or "default" implies a question of choice as well as a trajectory. If "apostasy" marks an end point, what most concerns Thompson is the disenchanted writer's struggle to reconcile lost hopes and personal feelings with a changed reality. Unlike apostasy, disenchantment is a productive condition, a creative moment that precedes a final "imaginative failure" marked by forgetting or falsely manipulating "the authenticity of experience." Thompson defines this condition as "a Jacobinism-in-recoil or a Jacobinism-of-doubt," insisting on "both sides of this definition." He sees Wordsworth and Coleridge caught in "a vortex of contradictions" that they were unable to resolve. Aesthetic complexity arises then from "a search for a synthesis at a moment of arrested dialectic"; "it is exactly within this conflict that the great romantic impulse came to maturity."[96] "The Ruined Cottage" (1798) opens Wordsworth's extraordinary period of creativity from the

Lyrical Ballads to the 1805 *Prelude*. Margaret, the abandoned wife and mother broken on the wheel of poverty and grief, stands in "The Ruined Cottage" as a text against war. She is this, according to Thompson, and "a great deal more." For the poem "has leaped out of the rigid framework of paternalist sensibility, in which the interior life of the poor cannot be handled... It was the transposed Jacobin impulse of *égalité* which broke out of the paternalistic frame." Moreover, the impulse "is transmuted" from abstract political rights to something more local "but also more humanely engaged."[97] There is nothing overtly "Jacobin" about the poem, but Wordsworth's sensibility goes beyond romantic sympathy in his ability to get inside the life and feelings of the poor, closing the social distance between himself and his subject. Thompson confirms Hazlitt's judgment that Wordsworth's "Muse... is a levelling one."[98]

"Experience" was a key term for Thompson, as it was for the Romantics. We are more accustomed to think about Thompson's concept of "experience" in relation to his concept of class; experience mediates the relationship between material conditions of existence and consciousness.[99] Less attention has been paid to how "experience" relates to his writings on romanticism. For Thompson, Wordsworth crossed a threshold of understanding; he underwent an education in "real feeling and just sense" (Wordsworth's words) as related in book twelve of the *Prelude*:[100]

> When I began to enquire,
> To watch and question those I met, and held
> Familiar talk with them, the lonely roads
> Were schools to me in which I daily read
> With most delight the passions of mankind,
> There saw into the depths of human souls –
> Souls that appear to have no depth at all
> To vulgar eyes...
>
> (*Prelude*, bk. 12, 161–68)

Wordsworth's ultimate achievement is then to be found in the intensity of this direct engagement and the turning of the cultural table against the "vulgar eyes" of the educated elite. The moral imagination of the poet derives from experience, drawing on the sensations and utterance of "men in real life."[101] It was this sort of learning that Thompson valued in his adult classes and found largely absent from the educated culture of the university.[102]

When compared to Wordsworth, Thelwall can come off badly. Thompson cites a passage in which the Jacobin orator reports dropping in at a village ale house to refresh himself, "[sitting] down among the rough clowns, whose tattered garments were soiled with their rustic labour.... I love the labourer then in his ragged coat, as well as I love the Peer in his ermine, perhaps better." As Thompson observes, Thelwall "was far from transcending the condescending conventions of his class."[103] In contrast, Wordsworth did not lapse into pastoral idealizations; his model "Was not a Corin of the groves... / But for the purposes of kind, a man / With the most common." Quoting these lines from the *Prelude*, Thompson notes the accent placed on the word "common." Wordsworth's enduring strength was that "he aligned himself *with* the common man... The very word 'common' acquired significantly new notations: we are placed *with* the common against the [polite] culture."[104] Wordsworth's purpose and theory of poetic diction takes him from the preface to the *Lyrical Ballads* to the *Prelude*, in which subjects drawn from "Low and rustic life" provide the sources of "philosophic language." The expression of common people found in a natural setting constitutes the universal language of humanity. Here, arguably, is where Wordsworth's "experiment" in language and sensibility meets that of Paine.[105]

For a brief time, the romantic poets drew close to the fledgling republican movement that collapsed under the dual pressures of revolutionary betrayal and state repression. In Wordsworth's case, Thompson regards the poet's ability to work through and translate the experience of the disenchanted self – "the sense of philosophy as lived experience" – as a profound political, aesthetic, and moral achievement. In the *Prelude*, Wordsworth "faces the failure of utopian expectations," while "he affirms and conveys the force of utopianism." And while the transition from the *Prelude* to the *Excursion* may witness a decline in poetic energies, Thompson never judges Wordsworth an "apostate" in the same terms as Coleridge or Southey; his period of disenchantment was more protracted and complex.[106] Moreover, even as they retreated to the point of paternalism and embraced the verities of traditional authority, the early Romantics are seen to retain a measure of social radicalism. The romantic critique of industrialization, decrying the abnegation of traditional social responsibility, breakdown of family and community values, and loss of independence among small producers, shared common ground with popular radicalism. In *The Making,* Thompson warns readers against the mistake of assuming that paternalist feeling must always be detached and condescending. The passionate current of "traditionalist social radicalism" moving from Wordsworth and Southey, through Thomas Carlyle and beyond, contains "a dialectic by which it is continually prompting revolutionary conclusions."[107] This dialectic forms part of the tradition Williams mapped in *Culture and Society.*

An Unfinished Text: Patriotism, Antislavery, and the Rights of Women

Following his departure from the University of Warwick, Thompson earned his living as a writer and an independent scholar with stints at various American universities. In the late 1970s, he emerged as a vocal critic of Britain's security-state. In his defense of civil liberties, he drew on the history of the "freeborn" Briton and the long struggle to establish the independence of the jury system.[108] During the 1980s, Thompson's life was dominated by his role in the European peace movement, triggered by plans to site American cruise missiles in Britain.[109] As the moral leader of the movement for nuclear disarmament, he became a national figure, delivering impassioned speeches at public rallies and appearing regularly on television and radio. His historical and literary scholarship was put on hold. Between 1971 and 1979, he reviewed successive volumes of the collective works of Coleridge, and from the late 1980s and early 1990s, he wrote two lengthy review essays on Wordsworth and Godwin for the *London Review of Books*; his final article on Thelwall was published posthumously.

Although the main lines of argument developed over his lifetime are fairly clear, we are left to ponder how Thompson would have pulled together and fleshed out his thinking on the Romantics in the age of revolution. There are some interesting hints. The literary historian Marilyn Butler recalled a conference in 1989 on the French Revolution as a literary event at which Thompson spoke on Wordsworth's 1802 patriotic sonnets, showing what might have been encompassed by the word "patriot."[110] Thompson spoke, as he usually did, from notes, and his thoughts were left unpublished. But one can well understand Thompson's attention to the historical and literary significance of the word "patriot," and the conflicted sense of national belonging set against the background of failed hopes for an internationalist cause of human liberation. He had, of course, experienced a similar sense of isolation from the nation, defending a cause in which he increasingly lost faith. Moreover, 1989 marked not only the 200th anniversary of the fall of the Bastille, but as Butler notes, the year ended with the fall of the Berlin Wall. She might have added, that only a few years before, in 1982, the swelling of popular nationalist sentiment that accompanied the Falklands War reversed Margaret Thatcher's political fortunes. The "people" were seen as hijacked by the Right. Patriotism and constructions of national identity quickly moved onto the agenda of historians.[111] Thatcherite populism stood in stark contrast to the fusion of patriotic sentiment and socialist aspiration that Thompson had felt during and directly after the Second World War.

In the event, Thompson was out of sync with many in his audience. According to Butler, "The more sophisticated literary critics…were not after dead writers' intended meanings … but after their unconscious: their self-delusions and linguistic self-betrayals."[112] Thompson was a contextual critic whose readings aimed to establish or fix meanings; he did not read for "displacement" or slippage in the text, for how, in Jerome McGann's interpretation, romanticism suppressed its own historical context or, as Marjorie Levinson put it, how the literary work "speaks of one thing because it cannot articulate another."[113] This is merely to say that Thompson was an "old" historical rather than a "new historicist" critic.[114] He was an astute reader, alert to the measure of tone and nuance, to the sound on the page; he cast a wide textual net, from his interpretation of Methodist hymns, to his study of anonymous threatening letters, to his chapter-long reading of Blake's poem "London." He sought meanings that were available to contemporary readers, believing that such meanings could be accessed through close, contextual reading of poetry, just as he believed that by attentive "listening" archival material could speak to and eventually through the historian.[115] A parallel can perhaps be drawn with Wordsworth's view of the poet's situation as "translator" who necessarily falls short of language fitting the passion that "the real passion itself suggests."[116]

Wordsworth's return to the nation, his revived feeling for England, is a theme we might expect Thompson to have developed. While radical constructions of "patriotism" drew on England's libertarian history, among supporters of the French Revolution older chauvinistic and imperialist associations with the word "patriot" were supplanted by a cosmopolitan allegiance based on the universal principles of reason, liberty, and human benevolence. A letter to Eaton's *Politics for the People* observed that there were "few prejudices so firmly riveted in the hearts of men" as the attachments "to particular spots of earth, dignified with the founding name of patriotism," sentiments opposed to the true principle of "philanthropy."[117] By 1802 such universal values were difficult to sustain; the claim to citizenship of the world had lost its appeal. With the short-lived Peace of Amiens, Wordsworth returned to France, although he went no further than Calais.[118] The Calais sonnets record not only Wordsworth's yearnings for England but patriotic feelings in conflict. Wordsworth's alienation from France is clear, but his nationalism is qualified: "Far, far more abject is thine enemy… / Oh grief! that Earth's best hopes rest all with Thee!" Yet with the resumption of war and the threat of invasion, Wordsworth joined the Grasmere volunteers, a decisive step in resolving his ambivalent feelings toward the British nation. The same month he composed his sonnet "To the Men of Kent, October 1803," concluding, "In Britain is one breath; We are with you now from Shore to Shore: – / Ye Men of Kent, 'tis Victory or Death!"[119]

In assessing the impact of the French Revolution, Thompson stressed that whereas in France the cause of the Revolution became "entwined with that of national pride," the betrayal of its own principles had "traumatic consequences" on international Jacobinism, adding, "one thinks of Wordsworth at Calais, lamenting the imprisonment of Citizen Toussaint, the reinstatement of slavery in the French West Indies."[120] The reference is not pursued but prompts us to ask what it meant for Wordsworth to hail the black revolutionary and victim of Napoleon's treachery as liberty's lost hero, and what bearing his lament might have on shifting constructions of nationalist and humanitarian sentiment. Wordsworth's elegy

"To Toussaint L'Ouverture" is accompanied by a sonnet entitled simply "September 1st, 1802." Sailing home from Calais with his sister Dorothy, Wordsworth notices "a fellow passenger" sitting silently: "She was a Negro Woman driv'n from France, / Rejected like all others of that race." In contrast to the abstractions associated with the fallen leader – "Thy friends are exultations, agonies, / And love, and Man's unconquerable mind" – the woman of color is observed with directness and compassion for an ordinary person's dignity and sad fate : "Dejected, meek, yet pitiably tame, / She sate, from notice turning not away."[121] The two figures, Toussaint and an unnamed woman, are linked to the oppressions of slavery and race, and to the betrayed promise of universal liberty and equality.

Ten years earlier, in December 1792, Wordsworth had reluctantly returned from France, self-isolated from his native country. In *The Prelude*, he arrives to find "a whole nation crying in one voice" against "the traffickers in negro blood." The defeated effort to abolish the slave trade, "Had called back old forgotten principles" to the nation's conscience and "diffused some truths / And more of virtuous feelings through the heart / Of the English people." (*Prelude*, bk. 10, 205–07). At the time, this defeat did not trouble Wordsworth who placed his faith in the success of the French Revolution, feeling "And this most rotten branch of human shame / ... Would fall together with its parent tree"[122] (*Prelude*, bk. 10, 225–27). In 1802, things looked very different. The Wordsworths were now close friends with the abolitionist leader Thomas Clarkson, himself an early supporter of the French Revolution, and his wife, Catherine. The abolitionists scored their first victory in limiting the British slave trade with the government's decision to restrict the sale of crown lands in the newly ceded colony of Trinidad. As the French reimposed slavery in their Caribbean colonies and attempted to reconquer Saint-Domingue, Britain appeared to represent humanity's best hope. If the Revolution was to become central to French nationalism, the abolition of the slave trade and slavery became matters of British national pride.

It is difficult to work from an absent text; we cannot determine whether Thompson would have addressed the tangled relationships among slave abolition, patriotism, and the Romantics. We know popular support for the abolitionist movement does not figure in *The Making*. William Wilberforce appears only in the role of "Pitt's moral lieutenant" and arch-evangelical opponent of Jacobinism.[123] Citizen Equiano receives no mention. The book's first chapter "Members Unlimited" starts with the founding meeting of the London Corresponding Society as recalled by Thomas Hardy, its founder and first secretary. The following month, in a letter dated 2 April 1792, Hardy's wife, Lydia, writes to him from Chesham, where she is visiting her family:

> Pray let me no how you go in your society and likewise We [illegible word] as been donn in the parlement house conserning the slave

trade for the people here are as much against that as any ware and there is more people I think that drinks tea without sugar than there is drinks with.

She concludes by asking her husband to give her "best regards" to "Vasa" (Gustavus Vasa being the name Olaudah Equiano generally used in public and private) and to convey her "hope he has a good journey to Scotland" – he was on a tour to mobilize support for abolition and to hawk copies of the latest edition of his *Interesting Narrative*.[124] Equiano was a dear friend who lodged in the same building as the Hardys near Covent Garden.[125] Buried in the Treasury Solicitor's papers, Lydia Hardy's letter may well have been missed by Thompson. However, to have missed the connection between two central figures in the popular movements for democratic political rights and abolition of the slave trade, as well as the antislavery sentiments of women like Mrs. Hardy, speaks to the book's overdetermined function of class as famously defined in the preface to *The Making*.

It can be argued that, by deflecting attention and support from the cause of popular radicalism, slave abolition ultimately helped to conserve domestic authority and consolidate nationalist feeling. Nonetheless, during the 1790s, British abolitionism momentarily brought plebeian radicals together with middle-class reformers and crossed paths with the young Romantics.[126] Thus Thelwall's denunciations of the trade and support for racial equality were matched in 1795 by Coleridge's lecture at Bristol's Assembly coffeehouse, where he rebuked his audience for asking God to bless their meals, for "A part of that Food among most of you is sweetened with the Blood of the Murdered." The power of "truth-painting Imagination" is politically charged to present the horrors of slavery and turn the heart to benevolent action. "True Benevolence," Coleridge declared, "is the only possible Basis of Patriotism."[127] In conjunction with Coleridge's lecture, Southey wrote his poem, "To the Genius of Africa," calling on the forces of slave rebellion, "Avenging Power, awake – Arise!"[128]

However he might have dealt with the meanings of patriotism – and whether or how slave abolition might have figured in his study – we do know Thompson intended to include a chapter on the "woman question" in the 1790s, provisionally titled "The defeat of the rights of women." According to Dorothy Thompson, the subject was to have formed "an integral part of the proposed volume." In a short fragment from a lecture on women's rights, Thompson proposed,

Something large was happening in feminine sensibility among the middle classes in the 1790s – perhaps even beginning to happen between men and women. But scarcely had this small wave begun to rise and crest than it was overtaken by the far deeper wave of counter-revolution.[129]

Here Thompson might have told a different story to the masculine epic of class, alert to female sensibility, personal suffering, and loss.[130] Tantalizingly, Thompson suggests moving beyond the well-studied figure of Wollstonecraft and several other female writers such as Mary Hays, Anna Barbauld, and Mary Robinson to get at a wider shift in sensibility to be found through the correspondence columns of journals, letters, private diaries, poetry, and novels. He would no doubt have found evidence for an "affective revolution" among the correspondence of young women such as Amelia Alderson of Norwich and Eliza Gould of Devon.[131] Denounced locally as a "broacher of sedition" for distributing Flower's *Cambridge Intelligencer*, Gould was forced in 1795 to close her school for girls at South Molton. She went on to marry Flower with whom she had carried on an extensive correspondence; the couple first met and fell in love in 1799 at Newgate prison where the Jacobin editor was serving time for seditious libel.[132] And while Thompson more typically turned to the work of canonical (male) authors, the literary output of a "lost generation" of female writers, their reputations tainted and works buried throughout the nineteenth and much of the twentieth centuries, constitutes an archive of brilliance, disenchantment, and personal struggle.[133]

Such a study would have taken Thompson into the ranks of rational Dissent, including early female supporters of antislavery and a small group of men who endorsed women's rights.[134] With a few notable exceptions, the rights of women and the cause of sexual liberation were not taken up among artisan radicals, but were, as Thompson acknowledges, mainly championed "within a small intellectual coterie" closely associated with Wollstonecraft and Godwin.[135] As can be gleaned from his review of Linda Colley's *Britons*, rather than celebrating the activities of patriotic women as opening space for female participation in the nation, he underscores the "profoundly anti-feminist" side of loyalist culture, viewing the terms of inclusion as unfavorable to women. Thompson never let readers forget the coercive side of British patriotism and the active role that reaction and state repression played in stifling dissent and crippling individual lives. Maintaining a sharp distinction between the forces of radicalism and reaction, Hannah More remains "the well-supported anti-Jacobin and anti-feminist polemicist."[136] He might have drawn a contrast to the feminist, literary figure Helen Maria Williams; having left England, Williams related in her *Letters Written from France* (1792), how her mind "has caught the contagion of French patriotism."[137]

Thompson reported that if there were, in fact, a large number of lesser Mary Wollstonecrafts, he had not found them. But in his review of Claire Tomalin's biography, he countered the image of Wollstonecraft as an isolated thinker, and criticized biographers fascinated by her intimate life at the expense of her standing as an intellectual to be placed in the company of Paine, Godwin, Thelwall, Flower, and Coleridge: "she measured herself as an equal in the republic of the intellect." And yet "she was reminded by every fact of nature and of society that she was a woman... a human being exceptionally exposed within a feminine predicament."[138] Wollstonecraft's posthumous fate stands merely as the most symbolically charged sign of defeat. Five years after her death in 1797, her close friend and fellow feminist, Mary Hays, omitted Wollstonecraft from a list of three hundred "illustrious and celebrated" women covered in her six-volume *Female Biography*. The feminist tradition was not entirely extinguished, carried forward by Shelley, Owenite socialists, and radical Unitarians.[139] In her own lifetime, Wollstonecraft experienced the disenchantment of the age and suffered deep personal disappointment – "a female Werther" in Godwin's estimate. Had she lived, she would perhaps have persuaded Godwin to start life anew in America, despite her disillusion with the republic's growing commercialism. As Thompson concludes, she never abandoned "the resilient assent to new experience." In her *Letters Written during A Short Residence in Sweden, Norway, and Denmark* (1796), she expresses a feeling of romantic renewal akin to the pantisocratic vision of primitive independence and virtue. Deciding to press northwards from Christiana, she envisions a utopian retreat among the farmers of Norway's back-country.

> The description I received of them carried me back to the fables of the golden age; independence and virtue; affluence without vice; cultivation of mind, without depravity of heart; with 'ever smiling liberty', the nymph of the mountain. – I want faith! My imagination hurries me forward to seek an asylum in such a retreat from all the disappointments I am threatened with; but reason drags me back whispering that the world is still the world.[140]

Conclusion

Thompson was often enough drawn back by whispers "that the world is still the world." As an intellectual who experienced his fair share of disenchantment, there are various moments in Thompson's life that might be revisited – 1939, 1948–51, 1956, 1968, 1989 – points that tested left-wing beliefs and allegiances. A dialogue was maintained between past and present; a comradeship was shared with Blake and Morris, and more tentatively with Wordsworth. In 1957, he observed, "Withdrawal from the extreme left has been a central motif within our culture ever since the French Revolution left the Solitary meditating upon a creed... 'the light of false philosophy.'" And then he made clear, "I remain a Communist."[141] One is reminded of Thelwall, who in 1796 assumed the name "Jacobin" because it was "fixed upon us, as a stigma, by our enemies" and because despite the "sanguinary ferocity of the late Jacobins... yet their principles... are the most consonant with my ideas of reason, and the nature of man."[142] Under the banner of "socialist humanism," Thompson moved about as far as one could from Marxism, while maintaining an allegiance to its main goals.

In 1973, he published his prolix open letter to Leszek Kolakowski as a way to break out of the political isolation that followed the collapse of the first New Left, clarifying his allegiance to Marxism as "a tradition." He also took the occasion to rearticulate his view of the romantic tradition's centrality to a national culture of opposition. He confesses himself less alarmed than Kolakowski "to observe 'the growing romantic nostalgia for a pre-industrial society,'" discerning an "affirmative impulse" beneath seemingly "irrational" forms reacting against technocratic society, and goes on to add, "Romanticism in this country offered a more radical criticism of the values of industrial capitalism than you seem to suppose; and Wordsworth attained in *The Prelude* to an insight into the *égalité* of human worth which one would gladly see appropriated to a socialist culture."[143] His "Englishness" is on full display, a strain of nationalism that exposed Thompson to criticism on the Left. English literature, particularly the romantic tradition, provided a national frame of cultural reference, a common literary language receding in its common resonance. Yet in addressing the Polish dissident, Thompson shows his dual identification with socialist internationalism and English popular nationalism, mirroring earlier tensions in the Communist left's project of cultural appropriation.[144] Similarly, while defending history and the category of "experience" (or "the *dialogue* between social being and social consciousness") against Althusserian structuralism, he did not reject theory or structural analysis *tout court* but rather opposed a level of static abstraction divorced from political activism and "real" processes of change.[145]

The general isolation of left-wing intellectuals from larger popular movements, their inability or disinclination to engage or learn from the experience or practice of ordinary people, was a recurrent complaint of Thompson's. In the early 1980s, when Thompson reconnected with the grassroots at the head of the European movement for nuclear disarmament, it was as a peace activist and outspoken critic of Britain's security state. He became less inclined to describe himself as a "Marxist," although his experience in the Communist Party left an enduring mark. By the end of his life, he was apt to call himself a "Morrisist."[146] He was often criticized as an "idealist" prone to "voluntarism" or seen as a lone romantic figure of the Left. In a sense, he spent the better part of his life attempting to reconcile the traditions of the British Left and Romanticism, to repair the loss he felt had been suffered during the age of revolution, and to regain the capacity to imagine that which is "not yet."

Acknowledgments

An earlier version of this chapter was published in James Epstein, "Among the Romantics: E. P. Thompson and the Poetics of Disenchantment," *Journal of British Studies* 56 (April 2017): 322–50. Copyright The North American Conference on British Studies, 2017. Reprinted with the permission of Cambridge University Press.

Notes

1 "My Study," in E. P. Thompson, *Collected Poems*, ed. Fred Inglis (Newcastle: Bloodaxe Press, 1999), 80.
2 E. P. Thompson, *The Making of the English Working Class* (Gollancz, 1963), 832.
3 See, however, Michael Scrivener, "E. P. Thompson and Romantic Radicalism," *WC* 37 (2006): 52–56.
4 Bryan D. Palmer, *E. P. Thompson: Objections and Oppositions* (Verso, 1994), 25–27; Peter J. Conradi, *A Very English Hero: The Making of Frank Thompson* (Bloomsbury, 2012), 8–11, 43–48.
5 Thompson referred to a collection on the romantic poets in a number of places and over a long period. See, for instance, interview by Mike Merrill, in *Visions of History*, ed. Henry Abelove et al. (New York: Pantheon, 1976), 3–25, at 22; E. P. Thompson, *Persons and Polemics* (Merlin Press, 1994), vii–viii.
6 E. P. Thompson, "Disenchantment or Default? A Lay Sermon," in *The Romantics in a Revolutionary Age*, ed. Dorothy Thompson (Woodbridge: Merlin Press, 1997), 33–74.
7 See Jerome J. McGann, *The Romantic Ideology: A Critical Investigation* (Chicago, IL: University of Chicago Press, 1983).
8 Thompson, "Disenchantment or Default?" 34.
9 William Hazlitt, *The Spirit of the Age* (1825), in *CWH*, 11: 16.
10 Bod. Lib., GD, for Wordsworth's visits in 1795–96. For Godwin's influence, see Peter Marshall, *William Godwin* (New Haven, CT: Yale University Press, 1984), chapter 8.
11 Coleridge to Southey, 21 October 1794, in *CLC*,1: 115; "Godwin," *Morning Chronicle*, 10 January 1795, as quoted in Nicholas Roe, *The Politics of Nature: William Wordsworth and Some Contemporaries* (Houndmills: Palgrave, 2002), 25–26.
12 Thompson, "Disenchantment or Default?" 34–35.
13 William Wordsworth, *The Prelude, The Four Texts (1798, 1799, 1805, 1850)*, ed. Jonathan Wordsworth (Penguin, 1995), 446. References are to the 1805 version and appear parenthetically in the main text.
14 Compare Mark Philp, "Thompson, Godwin and the French Revolution," *HWJ* 39 (1995): 91–101, and *Reforming Ideas in Britain: Politics and Language in the Shadow of the Revolution, 1789–1815* (Cambridge: CUP, 2014), 6, and chapter 8; and Jon Mee, "'The Press and Danger of the Crowd': Godwin, Thelwall, and the Counter-Public Sphere," in *Godwinian Moments: From Enlightenment to Romanticism*, ed. Robert M. Maniquis and Victoria Meyers (Toronto: University of Toronto Press, 2011), 83–102. As Mee indicates, Wordsworth continued to share Godwin's anxieties about the uncontrolled passions of the crowd.

15 David Simpson, *Romanticism, Nationalism, and the Revolt against Theory* (Chicago, IL: University of Chicago Press, 1993).

16 E. P. Thompson, "Where Are We Now?," in *E. P. Thompson and the Making of the New Left*, ed. Cal Winslow (New York: Monthly Review Press, 2014), 215–46, at 236–37. Written in April 1963, the memo was not published. The differences between Thompson and Perry Anderson, the journal's editor, soon spilled onto the pages of *New Left Review* and *Socialist Register.* Most notably, Perry Anderson, "The Origins of the Present Crisis," *NLR*, no. 23 (January-February 1964): 26–53, and "Socialism and Pseudo-Empiricism," *NLR*, no. 35, (January and February, 1966): 2–42, both articles are reprinted in Perry Anderson, *English Questions* (Verso, 1992); E. P. Thompson, "The Peculiarities of the English" (1965), in Thompson, *The Poverty of Theory and Other Essays* (Merlin Press, 1978), 35–91. Thompson links Godwin's hyper-rationalism and Wordsworth's rejection of abstract theory to his later attack on Althusser. See E. P. Thompson, "The Poverty of Theory or an Orrery of Errors (1978)," Thompson, *Poverty of Theory*, 372–73.

17 Thompson, "Wordsworth's Crisis" (1988), in Thompson, *Romantics*, 75–95, at 88–89. See also idem, "Benevolent Mr. Godwin" (1993), Thompson, *Romantics*, 96–106.

18 E. P. Thompson, *William Morris: Romantic to Revolutionary*, rev. ed. (Merlin Press, 1977), 790–93.

19 John Goode, "E. P. Thompson and 'the Significance of Literature,'" in *E. P. Thompson, Critical Perspectives*, ed. Harvey J. Kaye and Keith McClelland (Philadelphia, PA: Temple University Press, 1990), 183–203, at 190–98.

20 Thompson, *Making*, 176, 159. See also idem, "A Compendium of Cliché: The Poet as Essayist" (1979), in Thompson, *Romantics*, 143–55, at 146.

21 For Coleridge's views on property, see John Morrow, *Coleridge's Political Thought: Property, Morality and the Limits of Traditional Discourse* (New York: St. Martin's Press, 1990), chapter 1; Nigel Leask, *The Politics of Imagination in Coleridge's Critical Thought* (New York: St. Martin's Press, 1988), chapter 3. For his assessment of Thelwall and Spence, see Thompson, *Making*, 157–63. Thelwall opposed Coleridge's views on the equalization of property.

22 For Southey's reaction to Brissot's execution, see *LCRS*, 67. For the "secret" importance of the execution of the Girondist journalist Antoine-Joseph Gorsas to Wordsworth, see Roe, *Politics of Nature,* chapter 6.

23 Wordsworth to William Matthews, 23 May and [8] June 1794, in *The Letters of William and Dorothy Wordsworth: The Early Years, 1787–1805*, ed. Ernest de Selincourt, 2nd ed., rev. Chester L. Shaver (Oxford: OUP, 1967), 119, 123–24,

24 Thompson, "Wordsworth's Crisis," 78–83. See also Nicholas Roe, *Wordsworth and Coleridge: The Radical Years* (Oxford: OUP, 1988), 175–86, 276–79; Kenneth R. Johnston, *The Hidden Wordsworth* (New York: Norton, 2002), chapter 18; Michael T. Davis, "'That Odious Class of Men Called Democrats'; Daniel Isaac Eaton and the Romantics, 1794–1795," *History* 84 (1999): 74–92.

25 Samuel Coleridge, *Conciones ad Populum, or Addresses to the People* (1795), in *CWC*, vol. 1, *Lectures 1795 on Politics and Religion*, ed. Lewis Patton and Peter Mann (1971), 61, 74; Coleridge to Dyer, [late February 1795], in *CLC*, 1: 152.

26 Coleridge reworked the lecture into the pamphlet, *The Plot Discovered: An Address to the People against Ministerial Treason* (Bristol, 1795).

27 Thompson, "Disenchantment or Default?," 46. For the political situation in Bristol, and for Coleridge's intervention, see Steve Poole and Nicholas Rogers, *Bristol from Below: Law, Authority and Protest in a Georgian City* (Woodbridge: The Boydell Press, 2017), chapter 10; Peter J. Kitson, "Coleridge's Bristol and West Country Radicalism," in *English Romantic Writers and the West Country*, ed. Nicholas Roe (Palgrave Macmillan, 2010), 115–28.

28 Thompson, "Bliss Was It in That Dawn – The Matter of Coleridge's Revolutionary Youth" (1971), in Thompson, *Romantics*, 108–32, quotation at 124–27.

29 Southey to Charles Danvers, 15 June 1809, in *NLS*, 1: 511. As Woodring noted, although Coleridge was a republican, and despite his views on private property, Coleridge was too committed to distinctions of intellectual and morality, to be considered a democrat. Carl Woodring, *Politics in the Poetry of Coleridge* (Madison: Wisconsin University Press, 1961), 19.

30 Hazlitt, *Spirit of the Age*, 11: 37.

31 Kenneth R. Johnston, *Unusual Suspects: Pitt's Reign of Alarm and the Lost Generation of the 1790s* (Oxford: OUP, 2013), xvii. See also John Bugg, *Five Long Winters: The Trials of British Romanticism* (Stanford, CA: Stanford University Press, 2014).

32 Coleridge to Thelwall, [late April 1796], and Coleridge to Thelwall, 13 November 1796, in *CLC*, 1: 204, 253.

33 Thompson, "Hunting the Jacobin Fox" (1994), in Thompson, *Romantics*, 156–217, at 163; idem, *Making*, 157–61.

34 Thelwall studies have become a crowded subfield. Thompson quipped, in a letter from 1993, "Thelwall is suddenly an O.K. subject." Nicholas Roe, "The Lives of John Thelwall: Another View of the 'Jacobin Fox,'" in *John Thelwall: Radical Romantic and Acquitted Felon*, ed. Steve Poole (Pickering & Chatto, 2009), 13–24, at 13.

35 So far five volumes of secret service files have been released covering Thompson's years in the CP and into the early 1960s. The National Archive, Secret Service Personal Files, KV2/4290-94. My thanks to Julian Harber for sending me copies of these records.

36 Thompson, "Disenchantment or Default?" 40–49.

37 Richard Holmes, *Coleridge: Early Visions, 1772–1804* (New York: Pantheon, 1989), 155–60; David Fairer, *Organising Poetry: The Coleridge Circle, 1790–1798* (Oxford: OUP, 2009), chapter 10; Damian Walford Davies, *Presences that Disturb: Models of Romantic Identity in the Literature and Culture of the 1790s* (Cardiff: University of Wales Press, 2002), chapter 5.

38 S. T. Coleridge, *The Table Talk and Omniana*, ed. T. Ashe (G. Bell and Sons, 1903), 103, 26 July 1830. Thelwall gives a somewhat different version in his 1801 novel *The Daughter of Adoption*.

39 Thompson, *Making*, 176. For "Spy Nozy," see Roe, *Wordsworth and Coleridge*, 248–62; Johnston, *Unusual Suspects*, chapter 12.

40 Thompson, "Disenchantment or Default?" 50–57.

41 Gilbert Wakefield, *A Reply to Some Parts of the Bishop of Llandaff's Address to the People of Great Britain* (1798), 23; Johnston, *Unusual Suspects*, chapter 10.

42 Gerald P. Tyson, *Joseph Johnson, A Liberal Publisher* (Iowa City: University of Iowa Press, 1979), chapter 5; Jane Worthington Smyser, "The Trial and Imprisonment of Joseph Johnson, Bookseller," *Bulletin of the New York Public Library* 77 (1974): 418–35; Helen Braithwaite, *Romanticism, Publishing and Dissent: Joseph Johnson and the Cause of Liberty* (Houndmills: Palgrave Macmillan, 2003), 127–32, 162.

43 Thompson, "Disenchantment or Default?" 5.

44 William Wordsworth, *A Letter to the Bishop of Llandaff on the Extraordinary Avowal of his Political Principles ... by a Republican*, in *The Prose Works of William Wordsworth*, ed. W. J. B. Owen and Jane Worthington Smyser, 3 vols. (Oxford: OUP, 1974), 1: 29–49.

45 Thompson, "Jacobin Fox,"178, 192–203; idem, *Making*, 176. See also Judith Thompson, *John Thelwall in the Wordsworth Circle: The Silenced Partner* (New York: Palgrave Macmillan, 2012), chapter 11.

46 Johnston, *Unusual Suspects*, 201–04, and "Wordsworth's *Excursion*: Route and Destination," *WC* 45 (2014): 106–15.

47 Thompson, "Disenchantment or Default?" 57.

48 Johnston, *Hidden Wordsworth*, 444–49.

49 Thompson, *Making*, 175–79.

50 Thompson, "Interview,"11–12.

51 Palmer, *Thompson*, 45–55; Peter Searby, John Rule, and Robert Malcolmson, "Edward Thompson as a Teacher: Yorkshire and Warwick," in *Protest and Survival: Essays for E. P. Thompson*, ed. John Rule and Robert Malcolmson (Merlin Press, 1993), 1–17; Roger Fieldhouse, "Thompson: the Adult Educator," in *E. P. Thompson and English Radicalism*, ed. Roger Fieldhouse and Richard Taylor (Manchester: Manchester University Press, 2013), 25–47.

52 E. P. Thompson, *William Morris: Romantic to Revolutionary* (Gollancz, 1955), 841; idem, *William Morris* (1977), 727, 810. For the case that Thompson remained in line with party orthodoxy, see John McIlroy, "Another Look at E. P. Thompson and British Communism, 1937–1955," *Labor History* 58 (2017): 506–39.

53 E. P. Thompson, "Socialist Humanism: An Epistle to the Philistines," *NR*, no.1 (Summer 1957): 105–43. Thompson's articles from this period are conveniently reprinted in Winslow, ed., *E. P. Thompson*. See also Kate Soper, "Socialist Humanism," in Kaye and McClelland, eds., *E. P. Thompson, Critical Perspectives*, 204–32. For the theoretical development of socialist humanism among New Left thinkers more broadly, see Madeleine Davis, "Reappraising British Socialist Humanism," *Journal of Political Ideologies* 18 (2013): 57–81.

54 Stuart Hall, "Life and Times of the First New Left," *NLR*, no. 61 (January–February 2010): 177–96; Dorothy Thompson, "On the Trail of the New Left," *NLR*, no. 215 (January–February 1996): 93–100. Earlier in the year, Nikita Khrushchev's "secret speech" had already led to internal dissent within the British Communist Party. Thompson was among those demanding an open and full account. See John Saville, "The Twentieth Congress and the British Communist Party," *Socialist Register, 1976*, ed. Ralph Miliband and John Saville (Merlin Press, 1976), 1–23. The three issues of *The Reasoner: A Journal of Discussion*, which circulated as a dissident journal within the Communist Party, are conveniently reprinted in Paul Flewers and John McIlroy, eds., *1956: John Saville, E. P. Thompson and* The Reasoner (Merlin, 2016).

55 Thompson, preface to *The Making of the English Working Class* (Harmondsworth: Penguin, 1980), 14.

56 John Mander, *The Writer and Commitment* (Secker and Warburg, 1961), 7; E. P. Thompson, "Commitment and Poetry" (1979), in Thompson, *Persons and Polemics*, 332. Compare idem, "Commitment in Politics," *ULR*, no. 6 (Spring 1959): 50–55.

57 E. P. Thompson, "Outside the Whale," in *Poverty of Theory*, 1–33, at 3–4. See also idem, "At the Point of Decay," in Thompson, ed., *Out of Apathy* (Stevens and Sons, 1960), 3–15.

58 C. Wright Mills first discussed the cultural "default" of intellectuals, in "Culture and Politics: The Fourth Epoch," *Listener*, 12 March 1959, reprinted in *Power, Politics, and People: The Collected Essays of C. Wright Mills*, ed. Irving Louis Horowitz (New York: Ballantine Books, 1963), 236–46.

59 George Orwell, "Inside the Whale," in *The Collected Essays, Journalism and Letters of George Orwell*, vol. 1, *An Age Like This, 1920–1940*, ed. Sonia Orwell and Ian Angus (Harmondsworth: Penguin, 1970), 548, 569–78.

60 Ibid., 568.

61 Stefan Collini, "Enduring Passions: E. P. Thompson's Reputation," in *Common Reading: Critics, Historians, Publics* (Oxford: OUP, 2008), 177. See also David Eastwood, "History, Politics and Reputation: E. P. Thompson Reconsidered," *History* 85 (2000): 634–54.

62 *Spain* was published by Faber & Faber with a thin red dust-jacket, stating on the inside flap that all the author's royalties were to go to medical aid for Spain.

63 Thompson, "Outside the Whale," 4–13. The revised version of *Spain* was first published in *Another Time* and republished in *The Collected Poetry of W. H. Auden* (Faber & Faber, 1945). For Auden's inner conflict and political poetry, see Edward Mendelson, *Early Auden* (New York: Viking Press, 1981), chapter 9. For an illuminating discussion of the poem see Samuel Hynes, *The Auden Generation: Literature and Politics in England in the 1930s* (Bodley Head, 1976), 251–56. Thompson's poetry reflects Auden's influence.

64 Thompson, "Outside the Whale," 20.

65 Ibid., 18–21.

66 E. P. Thompson, "Socialism and the Intellectuals," *ULR*, no. 1 (Spring 1957): 31–36. See also idem, "Socialist Humanism."

67 John Saville, *Memoirs from the Left* (Merlin Press, 2003), 114–16, and "Twentieth Congress and the British Communist Party," 18–19.

68 In the second issue of *The Reasoner*, September 1956, in Flewers and McIlroy, eds., *1956*, 187, Saville and Thompson suggested to the CP's Executive Committee turning the journal "outwards, to fight the intellectual battles for socialism among the people in the manner of the old *Left Review*," under a reconstituted editorial board. See also E. P. Thompson, "*Left Review*" (1971), in Thompson, *Persons and Polemics*, 228–35.

69 Swingler was a member of *The New Reasoner's* editorial board and a friend of Thompson's. See Andy Croft, *Comrade Heart: A Life of Randall Swingler* (Manchester: Manchester University Press, 2003), chapter 15. For the Popular Front's continued influence on Thompson's politics, see Christos Efstathiou, *E. P. Thompson: A Twentieth-Century Romantic* (Merlin Press, 2015).

70 C. Day Lewis, "Revolutionaries and Poetry," *Left Review* 1, July 1935: 395–402, at 400; R. Swingler, "The Interpretation of Madness: A Study of William Blake and Literary Tradition," *Left Review* 3, February 1937: 21–28, at 22. Left-wing contemporary writing on this issue is copious, but see, for example, C. Day Lewis, ed., *The Mind in Chains: Socialism and the Cultural Revolution* (F. Muller, 1937); and Christopher Caudwell, *Illusion and Reality* (Macmillan, 1938), particularly chapter 12, "The Future of Poetry."

71 Ralph Fox, *The Novel and the People* (New York: International Publishers, 1945), 115–16, 124–25.

72 Frank Thompson, *There is a Spirit in Europe: A Memoir of Frank Thompson*, ed. T. J. and E. P. Thompson (Gollancz, 1947), 57–58, 15; E. P. Thompson, *Beyond the Frontier: The Politics of a Failed Mission, Bulgaria, 1944* (Stanford, CA: Stanford University Press, 1997).

73 Bill Schwarz, "'The People' in History: The Communist Party Historians' Group, 1946–56," in *Making Histories: Studies in History-Writing and Politics*, ed. Richard Johnson, et al. (Hutchinson, 1982), 44–95. See also Eric Hobsbawm, "The Historians' Group of the Communist Party," in *Rebels and Their Causes: Essays in Honour of A. L. Morton*, ed. Maurice Cornforth (Lawrence and Wishart, 1978), 21–47; Raphael Samuel, "British Marxist Historians, 1880–1980: Part One," *NLR*, 120 (March–April 1980): 21–96; Wade Matthews, *The New Left, National Identity, and the Break-Up of Britain* (Chicago, IL: Haymarket Books, 2014), chapter 2.

74 See, for example, E. P. Thompson, "Comments on a People's Culture," *Our Time*, October 1947: 34–38, and "William Morris and the Moral Issues of To-day," *Arena* 2, no. 8 (June/July 1951): 25–30. The editorial boards of these journals included *Left Review* veterans.

75 See Stuart Middleton, "E. P. Thompson and the Cultural Politics of Literary Modernism," *Contemporary British History* 28, no. 4 (September 2011): 16–34.

76 Thompson, "Edgell Rickword," in *Persons and* Polemics, 241–43. See also Charles Hobday, *Edgell Rickword* (Manchester: Carcanet, 1989), particularly chapter 12; Ben Harker, "'Communism is English': Edgell Rickword, Jack Lindsay and the Cultural Politics of the Popular Front," *Literature and History* 20, no. 2 (Autumn 2011): 16–34. In fact, Lindsay's influence on the New Left was minimal, although Thompson remained an admirer. See Ben Harker,"Jack Lindsay's Alienation," *HWJ* 82 (2016), 83–102.

77 John Lindsay and Edgell Rickword, eds., *A Handbook of Freedom: A Record of English Democracy through Twelve Centuries* (Lawrence and Wishart, 1939), 20–44, 126–50, 230–33, 235–38.

78 V. G. Kiernan, "Wordsworth and the People," in *Democracy and the Labour Movement: Essays in Honour of Dona Torr*, ed. John Saville (Lawrence and Wishart, 1954), 240–70, and "Wordsworth Revisited," *NR*, no. 7 (Winter, 1958–59): 62–74.

79 Eric Hobsbawm, *Interesting Times: A Twentieth-Century Life* (Abacus, 2003), 97.

80 See Francis Mulhern, *The Moment of 'Scrutiny'* (Verso, 1979); Schwarz, "'The People,'" 64–65; Middleton, "Thompson and Cultural Politics," 423–25.

81 Mulhern, *Moment of 'Scrutiny,'* 329–30; Christopher Hilliard, *English as a Vocation: The* Scrutiny *Movement* (Oxford: OUP, 2012), 1–3, 256–57; Tim Rogan, *The Moral Economists: R. H. Tawney, Karl Polanyi, E. P. Thompson, and the Critique of Capitalism* (Princeton, NJ: Princeton University Press, 2017), 143–47, 163.

82 Lesley Hardy, "F. R. Leavis, E. P. Thompson and the New Left: Some Shared Critical Responses," *Socialist History* 30 (2007): 1–21. For the attraction of Leavis and a defense of the concept of "experience," see Raymond Williams, *Politics and Letters: Interviews with* New Left Review (Verso, 1979), 65–67, 162–68. See also Stuart Middleton, "The Concept of 'Experience' and the Making of the English Working Class, 1924–1963," *Modern Intellectual History* 13 (2016): 179–208.

83 E. P. Thompson, review of Williams's *The Long Revolution*, *NLR*, no. 9 (May-June, 1961): 24–34, and no. 10 (July–August 1961): 34–39. See also Raymond Williams, "Notes on Marxism in Britain since 1945,"*NLR*, no. 100 (November-December, 1976): 81–94, particularly 86–88, for his reflections on "populism."

84 Thompson, "Commitment in Politics," 51–53, responding to Stuart Hall, "A Sense of Classlessness," *ULR*, no. 5 (Autumn 1958): 26–32. See also Michael Newman, "Thompson and the Early New Left," in Fieldhouse and Taylor, eds., *Thompson and English Radicalism*, 158–80, at 167–73; Dennis Dworkin, *Cultural Marxism in Postwar Britain: History, the New Left, and the Origins of Cultural Studies* (Durham, NC: Duke University Press, 1997), 54–78; Sophie Scott-Brown, *The Histories of Raphael Samuel: A Portrait of a People's Historian* (Acton ACT: Australian National University Press, 2017), chapter 2.

85 For a reassessment of New Left efforts to establish links within the labor movement, see Madeleine Davis, "'Among the Ordinary People': New Left Involvement in Working-Class Political Mobilization 1956–68," *HWJ* 86 (2018): 133–59.

86 Thompson remained on the editorial board through 1961, but felt that the former editors were excluded under Anderson's editorship. For the other side of this conflict, see Perry Anderson, *Arguments within English Marxism* (Verso, 1980), 131–40.

87 E. P. Thompson, ed., *Warwick University Ltd: Industry, Management and the Universities* (Harmondsworth: Penguin, 1970); Palmer, *Thompson*, 100–13, for the Warwick years.

88 Raymond Williams, ed., *May Day Manifesto 1968* (Harmondsworth; Penguin, 1968).

89 Pamela Edwards, *The Statesman's Science: History, Nature, and Law in the Political Thought of Samuel Taylor Coleridge* (New York: Columbia University Press, 2004), particularly introduction and chapter 1; David M. Craig, *Robert Southey and Romantic Apostasy: Political Argument in Britain, 1780–1840* (Boydell and Brewer, 2007); James K. Chandler, *Wordsworth's Second Nature: A Study of the Poetry and Politics* (Chicago, IL: University of Chicago Press, 1984).

90 Marilyn Butler, *Romantics, Rebels and Reactionaries: English Literature and its Background 1760–1830* (Oxford: OUP, 1981), chapter 6.

91 Percy Bysshe Shelley, "To Wordsworth," in *Percy Bysshe Shelley: The Major Works*, ed. Zachary Leader and Michael O'Neill (Oxford: OUP, 2003), 90–91. Byron's attack comes in his "Dedication" to *Don Juan* (1819).

92 *Examiner*, 29 December 1816, in *CWH*, 7: 119; Kevin Gilmartin, *William Hazlitt: Political Essayist* (Oxford: OUP, 2015), 27, 49.

93 E. P. Thompson, *Witness against the Beast: William Blake and the Moral Law* (Cambridge: CUP, 1993), 228–29; Jon Mee and Mark Crosby, "'This Soldierlike Danger': The Trial of William Blake for Sedition," in *Resisting Napoleon: The British Response to the Threat of Invasion, 1797–1815*, ed. Mark Philp (Aldershot: Ashgate, 2006), 111–24.

94 Samuel Taylor Coleridge, "France: An Ode" (1798), *Samuel Taylor Coleridge: The Major Works*, ed. H. J. Jackson (Oxford: OUP, 2000), 89–92.

95 Thompson, "Bliss Was It in That Dawn," and "Compendium of Cliché," in *Romantics*, 114, 145–50.

96 Thompson, "Disenchantment or Default? 37–38. See also Charles Mahoney's illuminating discussion in his *Romantics and Renegades: The Poetics of Political Reaction* (Houndmills: Palgrave Macmillan, 2003), 7–9.

97 Thompson, "Disenchantment or Default?" 36–37. The poem was composed from April 1797 to March 1798. The composition history is complicated with ongoing revisions until its publication in book one of the *Excursion*.

98 Hazlitt, *Spirit of the Age*, 87.

99 His formulation has come in for significant criticism and revision. For a recent and sensitive critique, see Carolyn Steedman, *An Everyday Life of the English Working Class: Work, Self and Sociability in the Early Nineteenth Century* (Cambridge: CUP, 2013), chapter 1.
100 Wordsworth, *Prelude*, 496.
101 William Wordsworth, Preface (1802) to *Lyrical Ballads*, ed. R. L. Brett and A. R. Jones (Routledge, 1968), 255–61.
102 Thompson, "Education and Experience," (1968), in Thompson, *Romantics*, 4–32.
103 Ibid., 10, quoting *The Tribune* 2 , no. 16 (1796): 16–17; idem, "Jacobin Fox," 167.
104 Thompson, "Education and Experience," 10–13, 28, quoting *Prelude*, bk. 8, 420–25. Compare Lindsay and Rickword, eds., *Handbook of Freedom*, xi–xii, where Rickword notes "how the word 'common' and its derivations ... appear and re-appear like a theme through the centuries."
105 See Butler, *Romantics, Rebels and Reactionaries*, 58–68; Olivia Smith, *The Politics of Language, 1791–1819* (Oxford: OUP, 1984), chapter 6; John Bugg, "Revolution," in *William Wordsworth in Context*, ed. Andrew Bennett (Cambridge: CUP, 2015), 175–81.
106 Thompson, "Jacobin Fox," 199.
107 Thompson, *Making*, 342–44. See also David Eastwood, "Robert Southey and the Intellectual Origins of Romantic Conservatism," *EHR* 104 (1989): 308–31. The reciprocities of paternalism formed a central theme in E. P. Thompson, *Customs in Common: Studies in Traditional Popular Culture* (Merlin Press, 1991).
108 See the essays collected in E. P. Thompson, *Writing by Candlelight* (Merlin Press, 1980). His case for the importance of rule of law to democratic society was first articulated in E. P. Thompson, *Whigs and Hunters: The Origin of the Black Act* (New York: Pantheon, 1975), 258–69.
109 Palmer, *Thompson*, chapter 5; Michael Bess, *Realism, Utopia, and the Mushroom Cloud: Four Activist Intellectuals and Their Strategies for Peace, 1945–1989* (Chicago, IL: University of Chicago Press, 1993), 136–54; Meredith Veldman, *Fantasy, the Bomb, and the Greening of Britain: Romantic Protest, 1945–1980* (Cambridge: CUP, 1994), chapter 9; Richard Taylor, "Thompson and the Peace Movement: From CNC in the 1950s and 1960s to END in the 1980s." in Fieldhouse and Taylor, eds., *Thompson and English Radicalism*, 181–201. For his writings from this period, see E. P. Thompson, *Exterminism and the Cold War* (Verso, 1982), *The Heavy Dancers* (Merlin Press, 1985), and *Double Exposure* (Merlin Press, 1985).
110 Marilyn Butler, "Thompson's Second Front," *HWJ* 39 (1995): 71–78.
111 For the most prominent example, see Linda Colley's *Britons, Forging the Nation 1707–1837* (New Haven, CT: Yale University Press, 1992). See also Raphael Samuel, ed., *Patriotism and the Making and Unmaking of British National Identity*, 3 vols. (Routledge, 1989); Hugh Cunningham, "The Language of Patriotism, 1750–1914," *HWJ* 12 (1981): 8–33; David Eastwood, "Patriotism and the English State in the 1790s," in *The French Revolution and British Popular Politics*, ed. Mark Philp (Cambridge: CUP, 1991), 146–68.
112 Butler, "Thompson's Second Front," 71–72.
113 McGann, introduction to *Romantic Ideology*; Marjorie Levinson, *Wordsworth's Great Period Poems* (Cambridge: CUP, 1986), 9, and introduction. See also Alan Liu, *Wordsworth: The Sense of History* (Stanford, CA: Stanford University Press, 1989). Compare M. H. Abrams, "On Political

Readings of *Lyrical* Ballads," in *Doing Things with Texts: Essays in Criticism and Critical Theory*, ed. Michael Fischer (New York: W. W. Norton, 1989), 364–91.

114 Thompson aligned himself with the work of David Erdman and Carl Woodring. Of the "new historicists," he shared most in common with Butler.

115 Thompson, "Interview," 14. For Thompson as a reader of texts, see Luke Spencer, "The Uses of Literature: Thompson as Writer, Reader and Critic," in *Thompson and English Radicalism*, ed. Fieldhouse and Taylor, 96–117.

116 Wordsworth, "Preface" to *Lyrical Ballads*, 257.

117 "Plato," *Politics for the People*, vol. 2, no. 4 (1794), 49–52. In his article "Modern Patriotism," Coleridge questioned the status of the term "patriot," taking aim at followers of Godwin, an early indication of his differences with Thelwall over religion. Samuel Taylor Coleridge, *Watchman*, no. 3, 17 March 1796, in *CWC*, vol. 2, *The Watchman*, ed. Lewis Patton (1970), 98–100.

118 Wordsworth went in order to visit his former lover Annette Vallon and their daughter Caroline.

119 William Wordsworth, *William Wordsworth: The Major Works*, ed. Stephen Gill (Oxford: OUP. 2000), 275, 289. For "national defense patriotism," the feeling that best describes Wordsworth's reaction, see J. E. Cookson, *The British Armed Nation, 1793–1815* (Oxford: OUP, 1997), introduction and chapter 8. For the difference between the invasion threats of 1797–98 and 1803–05, see Mark Philp, "Introduction: The British Response to the Threat of Invasion, 1797–1815," in Philp, ed., *Resisting Napoleon*, 1–17.

120 Thompson, "Disenchantment or Default?" 70.

121 Wordsworth, *Major Works*, 282–83. A recent statute banned all persons of color from France's continental territories. My comments draw on Cora Kaplan, "Black Heroes/White Writers: Toussaint L'Overture and the Literary Imagination," *HWJ* 46 (1998): 35–62.

122 Wordsworth, *Prelude*, 410–12.

123 Thompson, *Making*, 402, 146–47.

124 TS 24/12, Lydia Hardy to Thomas Hardy, 2 April 1792. The file also includes a letter from "Gustavus Vassa the African," from Edinburgh, dated 28 May 1792.

125 For their relationship, see Peter Linebaugh and Marcus Rediker, *The Many-Headed Hydra: Sailors, Slaves, Commoners, and the Hidden History of the Revolutionary Atlantic* (Boston, MA: Beacon, 2000), 334–41; Vincent Carretta, *Equiano, the African: Biography of a Self-Made Man* (Athens: University of Georgia Press, 2007), 297, 339–40, 349–51.

126 Robin Blackburn, *The Overthrow of Colonial Slavery, 1776–1848* (Verso, 1988), chapter 4; For a typical example associating abolitionists with "Jacobins," see (anon.), *A Very New Pamphlet Indeed! ... Containing Some Strictures on the English Jacobins* (1792), 3–5.

127 Samuel Taylor Coleridge, "Lecture on the Slave-Trade," in Patton and Mann, eds., *CWC*, 1: 248–49. For Thelwall, see *The Tribune* 3 (1795), no. 35, 47–48. Thelwall reflected that at age nineteen intense discussion in debate of the slave trade opened the way to change in his political attitudes as the French Revolution began. John Thelwall, *Poems Chiefly Written in Retirement ... With a Prefatory Memoir of the Life of the Author* (Hereford, 1801), xxiv. See also Marcus Wood, *Slavery, Empathy, and Pornography* (Oxford: OUP, 2002), 169–80. Henry Redhead Yorke was another leading British "Jacobin" who combined support for democracy with calls for slave

abolition. See Amanda Goodrich, *Henry Redhead Yorke, Colonial Radical: Politics and Ideology in the Atlantic World, 1772–1813* (Routledge, 2019).

128 Robert Southey, "To the Genius of Africa," *Poems* (Bristol, 1797), 40. See also Carol Bolton, *Writing Empire: Robert Southey and Romantic Colonialism* (Pickering & Chatto, 2007), chapter 1; Timothy Morton, *The Poetics of Spice: Romantic Consumerism and the Exotic* (Cambridge: CUP, 2000), chapter 4; Chine Sonoi, "Southey's Radicalism and the Abolitionist Movement," *WC* 41 (2011): 22–26.

129 E. P. Thompson, afterword to Thompson, *Romantics*, 221–23. For a related shift in attitudes, see Kathryn Gleadle, "The Juvenile Enlightenment: British Children and Youth during the French Revolution," *P&P* 233 (2016): 143–84.

130 See Carolyn Steedman, "A Weekend with Elektra," *Literature and History* 6 (1997): 17–42, and "The Price of Experience: Women and the Making of the English Working Class," *Radical History Review* 59 (1994): 108–19.

131 For the term and argument for an "affective revolution," see Lynn Hunt and Margaret Jacob, "The Affective Revolution in 1790s Britain," *Eighteenth-Century Studies* 34 (2001): 491–521. See, more generally, Harriet Guest, *Unbounded Attachment: Sentiment and Politics in the Age of Revolution* (Oxford: OUP, 2013), and for Amelia Alderson (Mrs. Opie), chapter 4.

132 Timothy Whelan, ed., *Politics, Religion, and Romance: The Letters of Benjamin Flower and Eliza Gould Flower, 1794–1808* (Aberystwyth: National Library of Wales, 2008), and Timothy Whelan, "Politics, Religion, and Romance: Letters of Eliza Gould Flower, 1794–1802," *WC* 36. (2005): 85–109.

133 For female literary casualties, see Johnston, *Unusual Suspects*, 113–16, and chapter 7, on Helen Maria Williams. See also Gary Kelly, *Women, Writing, and Revolution, 1790–1827* (Oxford: OUP, 1993); and William Stafford, *English Feminists and Their Opponents in the 1790s: Unsex'd and Proper Females* (Manchester: Manchester University Press, 2002).

134 See Clare Midgley, *Women against Slavery: The British Campaigns, 1780–1870* (Routledge, 1992), chapter 2; Moira Ferguson, *Subject to Others: British Women Writers and Colonial Slavery, 1670–1834* (Routledge, 1992), chapters 7–11; Arianne Chernock, *Men and the Making of Modern British Feminism* (Stanford, CA: Stanford University Press, 2010).

135 Thompson, *Making*, 162–63. See also Andrew Cayton, *Love in the Time of Revolution: Transatlantic Radicalism and Historical Change, 1793–1818* (Chapel Hill: University of North Carolina Press, 2013).

136 E. P. Thompson, "Which Britons?" (1993), in Thompson, *Persons and Polemics*, 321–32; Colley, *Britons*, chapter 6. For the feminist version of More, see, for example, Anne K. Mellor, *Mothers of the Nation: Women's Political Writing in England, 1780–1830* (Bloomington: Indiana University Press, 2000), chapter 1; and Kathryn Sutherland, "Hannah More's Counter-Revolutionary Feminism," in *Revolution in Writing: British Literary Responses to the French Revolution*, ed. Kelvin Everest (Milton Keynes: Open University Press, 1991), 27–63. Feminist historians and literary scholars have continued to explore how women, particularly female writers, sought to negotiate the predominately masculine constructions of patriotism. See, in particular, Harriet Guest, *Small Change: Women, Learning, Patriotism, 1750–1810* (Chicago, IL: University of Chicago Press, 2000); Angela Keane, *Women Writers and the English Nation in the*

1790s: Romantic Belongings (Cambridge: CUP, 2000); Caroline Franklin, "Romantic Patriotism as Feminist Critique of Empire," in *Women, Gender and Enlightenment*, ed. Sarah Knott and Barbara Taylor (Houndmills: Palgrave Macmillan, 2005), 551–64.

137 Helen Maria Williams, *Letters Written From France, Containing Many New Anecdotes Relative to the French Revolution*, 3rd ed. (1796), vol. 2, 7. Her open relationship with John Hurford Stone, whose wife divorced him in 1794, was a subject of widespread rumor.

138 E. P. Thompson, "Mary Wollstonecraft" (1974), in Thompson, *Persons and Polemics*. From the large literature on Wollstonecraft, see Barbara Taylor, *Mary Wollstonecraft and the Feminist Imagination* (Cambridge: CUP, 2003), particularly chapter 6, and "Religion, Radicalism, and Fantasy," *HWJ* 39 (1995): 102–12.

139 Taylor, *Wollstonecraft*, 188, 246–55, and *Eve and the New Jerusalem: Socialism and Feminism in the Nineteenth Century* (Virago, 1983); Kathryn Gleadle, *The Early Feminists: Radical Unitarians and the Emergence of the Women's Rights Movement, 1831–51* (Houndmills: Palgrave Macmillan, 1995).

140 Mary Wollstonecraft and William Godwin, *A Short Residence in Sweden, Norway and Denmark and Memoirs of the Author of 'The Rights of Woman,'* ed. Richard Holmes (Harmondsworth: Penguin, 1987), letter 14, 148–49, and editor's introduction, 20–21.

141 Thompson, "Socialism and the Intellectuals," 31.

142 John Thelwall, *Rights of Nature, Against the Usurpations of Establishments … Part the Second* (1796), 32.

143 E. P. Thompson, "An Open Letter to Leszek Kolakowski" (1973), in Thompson, *Poverty of Theory*, 92–192, at 176, responding to Leszek Kolakowski, "Intellectuals against Intellect," *Daedalus* 101 (Summer 1972): 1–15. The passage might be compared to Marcuse, of whom Thompson was critical, discussing the reduction of "the romantic space of the imagination." Herbert Marcuse, *One Dimensional Man: Studies in the Ideology of Advanced Industrial Society* (Boston, MA: Beacon, 1964), 248.

144 See Matthews, *New Left*, chapter 3; Anderson, *Arguments*, particularly chapter 5. For a different take on Thompson's "Englishness," see Priya Satia, "Bryon, Gandhi and the Thompsons: the Making of British Social History and the Unmaking of Indian History," *HWJ* 81 (2016); 135–70.

145 E.P. Thompson, "Poverty of Theory," 196, 199–201; idem, "Interview,"17; idem, "The Politics of Theory," in *People's History and Socialist Theory*, ed. Raphael Samuel (Routledge, 1981), 396–408. Compare Stuart Hall, "In Defence of Theory," in Samuel, ed., *People's History*, 378–85. See also Rogan, *Moral Economists*, 176–83.

146 See his roundtable comments, "Agendas for Radical History," *Radical History Review* 36 (1986): 37–42. See also Michael Kenny, "Socialism and the Romantic 'Self': the Case of Edward Thompson," *Journal of Political Ideologies* 5 (2000): 105–27.

Works Cited

Primary Works

Manuscript Collections

Bodleian Library

William Godwin, Original Correspondence [1780] – 1835. MS Abinger c.511, Abinger Collection.

British Library

Francis Place Papers, BL Add. MS 27808–27817.
Francis Place Scrapbooks, set 36, 39.

National Archives

Chancery Papers: C 31/372.
Colonial Office Papers: CO 20/11–15.
Home Office Papers: HO 40/3–10; HO 42/23–36, 153–75; 43/3.
Lord Chamberlain's Department: LC 7/74.
Privy Council Papers: PC 1/- & 2/-.
Security Service Personal Files: KV2/4290–94.
Treasury Solicitor's Papers: TS 11/-; TS 24/-.

Leeper Library, University of Melbourne

G.W. Rusden MS, vol. 15, "The Scotch Martyrs. Odd Notes, Margarot's Journal."

Printed Primary Sources

Place of publication is London unless otherwise stated.

Newspapers and Journals

Analytical Review
Annual Register

Anti-Cobbett, or the Weekly Patriotic Register
Anti-Gallican Monitor
Anti-Jacobin; or, Weekly Examiner
Arena
Black Dwarf
Blanketteer (Leeds)
British Critic
Cabinet (Norwich)
Cambridge Intelligencer
Cobbett's Weekly Political Register
Constitutional
Courier
Critical Review
Daedalus
Evening Mail
Examiner
Gazette Nationale, ou Le Moniteur Universal (Paris)
Gazetteer and New Daily Advertiser
Gentleman's Magazine
Hone's Reformists' Register
Ipswich Journal
Isis
Kentish Weekly Post (Canterbury)
London Dispatch and People's Political & Social Reformer
London Gazette
Manchester Gazette
Manchester Herald
Manchester Political Register
Medical Times and Gazette
Monthly Review
Morning Chronicle
New Left Review
New Reasoner (Halifax)
Northern Star (Leeds and London)
Our Time
Patriot (Sheffield)
Politics for the People
Poor Man's Guardian
Public Advertiser
Quarterly Review
Republican
St. James Chronicle
Shamrock, Thistle and Rose
Sherwin's Weekly Political Register
Spectator
Sun
Tatler
The Times
Theatrical Recorder

Tribune
True Briton
Universities and Left Review
Weekly True Sun
World

Trials (listed chronologically)

The Genuine Trial of Thomas Paine, for a Libel, Contained in the Second Part
  of Rights of Man; at Guildhall London, Dec. 18, 1792, before Lord Kenyon,
  and a Special Jury … Taken in Short-Hand by E. Hodgson (1793).
The Trial of John Frost for Seditious Words in Hillary Term 1793. Taken in
  Shorthand (1793).
The Trial of P. W. Duffin, and Thomas Lloyd, a Citizen of the United States of
  America, and an Officer in the late American Army, For a Libel in the Fleet
  Prison (1793).
The Trial of the Rev. Thomas Fyshe Palmer: Before the Circuit Court of Justi-
  ciary, Held at Perth, on the 12th and 13th September, 1793, on an Indictment
  for Seditious Practices, Taken in Court by Mr. Ramsey (Edinburgh, 1793).
The Evidence, Cross-Examinations, Arguments of Counsel… on the Two Tri-
  als of Wm. Winterbotham (Exeter, 1794).
The Trial of Maurice Margarot, delegate from London to the British Convention, before the High Court of Justiciary at Edinburgh, on the 13th and 14th
  of January 1794, for Sedition (Edinburgh, 1794).
The Trial of Thomas Briellat for Seditious Words before Mr. Mainwaring, at
  the Sessions-House, Clerkenwell-Green, December 6, 1793, taken in Short-
  hand by Mr. Ramsay (1794).
The Trial[s] of Wm. Winterbotham … Before the Hon. Baron Perryn, and a
  Special Jury, at Exeter; on the 25th of July 1793. For Seditious Words. Taken
  in Short Hand by Mr. Wm. Bowring (1794).
State Trials for High Treason, Embellished with Portraits. Part Third, Containing
  the Trial of Mr. John Thelwall, Reported by a Student in the Temple (1795).
The Genuine Trial of Thomas Hardy, for High Treason; at the Sessions House
  in Old Bailey, from October 28 to November 5, 1794 (1795).
The Trial of Thomas Hardy for High Treason…Taken in Short-hand by Joseph
  Gurney. 4 vols. (1795).
The Trial of John Binns, Deputy of the London Corresponding Society, for Se-
  dition. Before Justice Ashurst, at the Assize held for the County of Warwick,
  on Saturday, August 12, 1797 (1797).
Report of the Whole of the Proceedings… including the Trials of Jeremiah Bran-
  dreth… William Turner, Isaac Ludlam, the Elder, and George Weightman,
  for High Treason: With the Speeches of the Counsel, and Other Interesting
  Particulars (Nottingham, 1817).
A Complete Collection of State Trials, 30 vols., ed. William Cobbett and T.B.
  Howells. Longman, et al., 1816–1822:

    "Proceedings against John Frost for Seditious Words" (1793), vol. 22.
    "Proceedings… against William Winterbotham for Seditious Words"
    (1793), vol. 22.

"The Trial of Daniel Isaac Eaton" (1793), vol. 23.
"Proceedings on the Trial of William Skirving" (1793), vol. 23.
"The Trial of Thomas Hardy for High Treason" (1794), vol. 25.
"The Trial of John Horne Tooke for High Treason" (1794), vol. 25.
"Trial of Jeremiah Brandreth" (1817), vol. 32.
"The Trial of Isaac Ludlam, the Elder" (1817), vol. 32.
"Proceedings in the Case of James Watson, the Elder" (1817), vol. 32.
"The Trial of George Weightman," (1817), vol. 32.
"Proceedings against Andrew M'Kinlay" (1817), vol. 33.

Other Printed Primary Sources

Advice to a Certain Lord High Chancellor, Twelve Judges, 600 Barristers, 700 English and 800 Irish Students of Law, 30,000 Attorneys! (1791).
Anderson, Perry, *English Questions* (Verso, 1992).
Auden, W.H., *Another Time* (Faber & Faber, 1940).
────── *The Collected Poetry of W. H. Auden* (Faber & Faber, 1945).
Bamford, Samuel, *An Account of the Arrest and Imprisonment of Samuel Bamford, Middleton, on Suspicion of High Treason* (Manchester, 1817).
────── *Passages in the Life of a Radical* (Oxford: OUP, 1984, first published 1844).
Barlow, Joel, *Advice to the Privileged Orders in the Several States of Europe,* 2nd ed. (1792).
────── *Letter to the National Convention of France, on the Defects of the Constitution of 1791* (1792).
────── *New Travels in the United States of America, Performed in 1788... Translated from the French* (1792).
Belsham, Thomas, *Memoirs of the Late Theophilius Lindsey, M. A.* (1812).
Binns, John, *Recollections of the Life of John Binns* (Philadelphia, 1854).
Bowles, John, *Postscript to Thoughts on the Late General Election, As Demonstrative of the Progress of Jacobinism* (1803).
────── *Thoughts on the Late General Election, as Demonstrative of the Progress of Jacobinism* (1802).
────── *Treason Triumphant over Law and Constitution! Addressed to both Houses of Parliament* (1795).
Brightwell, Cecilia Lucy, *Memoir of Amelia Opie* (London, 1855).
Brissot, J. P. de Warville, *New Travels in the United States of America, 1788,* ed. and intro. Durand Echeverria, trans. Mara Soceanu Vamos and Echeverria (Cambridge, MA: Harvard University Press, 1964).
Browne, Matthew Campbell, *A Leaf Out of Burke's Book, being an Epistle to that Right Honourable Gentleman, in Reply to His Letter to a Noble Lord on the Subject of His Pension* (1796).
Browning, Oscar, ed., *The Dispatches of Earl Gower, English Ambassador at Paris from June 1790 to August 1792* (Cambridge, 1855).
Burke, Edmund, *An Appeal from the New Whigs to the Old Whigs... Relative to the Reflections on the Revolution in France* (1791).
────── *Letters on a Regicide Peace* (1796).
────── *Reflections on the Revolution in France*, ed. Conor Cruise O'Brien (Harmondsworth: Penguin, 1969, first published 1790).

Byron, George Gordon, Lord, *The Major Works*, ed. Jerome J. McGann (Oxford: Oxford University Press, 2000).

Cansick, Frederick Teague, *A Collection of Curious and Interesting Epitaphs, Copied from the Monuments of Distinguished and Noted Characters in the Ancient Church and Burial Grounds of St. Pancras, Middlesex* (1869).

A Catalogue of the Larpent Plays in the Huntington Library, comp. Dougald MacMillan (San Marino, CA: Huntington Library, 1939).

Caudwell, Christopher, *Illusion and Reality* (Macmillan, 1938).

Clegg, William, *Freedom Defended, or the Practice of Despotism Deposed* (Manchester, 1798).

Cleveland, John, *The Idol of Clownes, or, Insurrection of Wat the Tyler, with His Priests Baal and Straw* (1654).

Cockburn, Lord [Henry Thomas], *An Examination of the Trials for Sedition . . . in Scotland*, 2 vols. (Edinburgh, 1888).

—— *Memorials of His Time* (Edinburgh, 1856).

Coleridge, Samuel Taylor, *Collected Letters of Samuel Taylor Coleridge*, ed. Earl Leslie Griggs, 6 vols. (Oxford: Clarendon Press, 1956–71).

—— *The Collected Works of Samuel Taylor Coleridge*, gen. ed. Kathleen Coburn, 16 vols. (London: Routledge, and Princeton, NJ: Princeton University Press, 1969–2002).

—— *A Moral and Political Lecture* (Bristol, 1795).

—— *The Plot Discovered: An Address to the People against Ministerial Treason* (Bristol, 1795).

—— *Samuel Taylor Coleridge: The Major Works*, ed. H. J. Jackson (Oxford: Oxford University Press, 2000).

—— *The Table Talk and Omniana*, ed. T. Ashe (G. Bell and Sons, 1903).

Collins, David, *An Account of the English Colony in New South Wales* (1798).

Colquhoun, Patrick, *Facts Relative to Public Houses in the City of London and Its Environs* (1794).

Commonwealth of Australia, *Historical Records of Australia, Series I: Despatches of Governors to and from England,* ed. Frederick Watson, 26 vols. (Sydney: Library Committee of the Commonwealth Parliament, 1914–25).

—— *Historical Records of Australia, Series III: Despatches and Papers Relating to the Settlement of the States*, ed. Frederick Watson, 9 vols. (Sydney: Library Committee of the Commonwealth Parliament, 1921–23).

Cooper, Thomas, *Considerations on the Slave Trade; and the Consumption of West Indian Produce* (1791).

—— *Letters on the Slave Trade* (Manchester, 1787).

—— *Political Essays*, 2nd ed. (Philadelphia, 1800).

—— *A Reply to Mr. Burke's Invective against Mr. Cooper and Mr. Watt*, 2nd ed. (1792).

—— *Some Information Respecting America* (1794).

Corfield, Penelope J. and Chris Evans, eds., *Youth and Revolution in the 1790s: Letters of William Pattison, Thomas Amyot and Henry Crabb Robinson* (Stroud: Alan Sutton, 1996).

Cottle, Joseph, *Reminiscences of Samuel Taylor Coleridge and Robert Southey*, 2nd ed. (1848).

Dent, Richard, *Revolution Anniversary or Patriotic Incantations* (1791).

Diderot, Denis, *Oeuvres Completes*, ed. J. Assézat, 20 vols. (Paris, 1875).

Dinmore Jr., Richard, *An Exposition of the Principles of the English Jacobins; with Strictures on the Political Conduct of Charles J. Fox, William Pitt, and Edmund Burke* (Norwich, 1796).

Dyer, George, *A Dissertation on the Theory and Practice of Benevolence* (1795).

Engels, Friedrich, *The Condition of the Working Class in England*, ed. Victor Kiernan (Penguin, 1987, first published 1845).

Equality, as Consistent with the British Constitution, In a Dialogue between a Master-Manufacturer and one of his Workmen (1792).

Evans, W. D., *Address of W. D. Evans, at the New Bayley Court House, Salford, On Discharging Prisoners* (Manchester, 1817).

Extraordinary, The Extraordinary Red Book... by a Commoner, 2nd ed. (1817).

Fairburn, John, *Fairburn's Account of the Meeting in Spa-Fields, November 15, 1816* (1816).

Field, William, *Memoirs of the Life, Writings, and Opinions of the Rev. Samuel Parr, LL.D*, 2 vols. (1828).

The First Report from the Committee of Secrecy appointed by the House of Commons (1794).

Flewers Paul, and John McIlroy, eds., *1956: John Saville, E. P. Thompson and The Reasoner* (Merlin, 2016). Reprints all issues of *The Reasoner*.

Flower, Benjamin and Eliza Gould Flower, *Politics, Religion, and Romance: The Letters of Benjamin Flower and Eliza Gould Flower, 1794–1808*, ed. Timothy Whelan (Aberystwyth: National Library of Wales, 2008).

Fox, Ralph, *The Novel and the People* (New York: International Publishers, 1945).

Fox, William, *On Jacobinism* (1794).

Franklin, Benjamin, *Information to Those Who Would Remove to America* (1794).

Gerrald, Joseph, *A Convention the Only Means of Saving Us from Ruin* (1793).

Godwin, William, *Cursory Strictures on the Charge delivered by Lord Chief Justice Eyre* (1794).

——— *Enquiry Concerning Political Justice and Its Influence on Modern Morals and Happiness*, ed. Isaac Kramnick (Harmondsworth: Penguin, 1976, based on 3rd ed., 1798).

——— *Political and Philosophical Writings of William Godwin*, ed. Mark Philp, 7 vols. (Pickering & Chatto, 1993).

Great Britain, *Parliamentary Debates, from the Year 1803 to the Present Time*, 1st series (1812–).

——— *The Parliamentary History of England*, ed. William Cobbett, 1st series, vols. 27–35 (1813–19).

——— *Parliamentary Papers*, 1817, iv: Report from the Committee of Secrecy, 19 February 1817; Second Report of the Committee of Secrecy, 20 June 1817; Report of the Secret Committee of the House of Lords, 23 June 1817.

Green, Thomas, *Extracts from the Diary of a Lover of Literature* (Ipswich, 1810).

Hamilton, Alexander, *The Papers of Alexander Hamilton*, ed. Harold C. Syrett, 25 vols, (New York: Columbia University Press, 1961–77).

Hardy, Thomas Hardy, *Memoirs of Thomas Hardy, Written by Himself* (1832).

Hartley, David, *Observations on Man, His Frame, His Duties and His Expectations* (1749).

Hazlitt, William, *The Complete Works of William Hazlitt*, ed. P. P. Howe, 21 vols. (J. M. Dent and Sons, 1930–34).

—— *New Writings of William Hazlitt*, ed. Duncan Wu, 2 vols. (Oxford: Oxford University Press, 2007).

Hill, John, *The Actor: Or a Treatise on the Art of Playing* (1755).

Historical Records of New South Wales, Vol. II: Grose and Patterson, 1793–1795, ed. F.M. Bladen (Sydney, 1893).

History of the Two Acts, entitled an Act for the Safety and Preservation of His Majesty's Person and Government against Treasonable and Seditious Practices and Attempts, and an Act for More Effectually Preventing Seditious Meetings and Assemblies… (1796).

The History of Wat Tyler, and Jack Straw (1730?).

[Hobhouse, Benjamin], *An Enquiry into What Constitutes the Crime of "Compassing and Imagining the King's Death," According to The Statute of Edw. III* (Gloucester, 1795).

Hobsbawm, Eric, *Interesting Times: A Twentieth-Century Life* (Abacus, 2003).

Hodgson, William, *The Case of William Hodgson, Now Confined in* Newgate (1796).

—— *The Commonwealth of Reason* (1795).

—— *Proposals for Publishing by Subscription a Treatise called the Female Citizen, or a Historical Enquiry into the Rights of Women* (1796).

Holcroft, Thomas, *A Catalogue of the Library of Books, of Mr. Thomas Holcroft, To be Sold at Auction by King & Lochee, 13 Jan. & 4 Following Days, 1807* (1806).

—— *The Deserted Daughter* (1795).

—— *Letter to the Right Honorable William Windham, On the Intemperance and Dangerous Tendency of His Public Conduct*, 2nd ed. (1795).

—— *The Life of Thomas Holcroft, Written by Himself, Continued . . . by William Hazlitt*, ed. Elbridge Colby, 2 vols. (New York: Benjamin Blom, 1968, first published 1852).

—— *A Narrative of the Facts, Relating to a Prosecution for High Treason: Including the Address to the Jury, which the Court Refused to Hear* (1795).

—— *The Road to Ruin* (1792).

Holland, John and James Everett, *Memoirs of the Life and Writings of James Montgomery*, 7 vols. (1854–6).

Holt, Daniel, *A Vindication of the Conduct and Principles of the Printer of the Newark Herald* (Newark, 1794).

Holt, Joseph, *Memoirs of Joseph Holt, General of the Irish Rebels in 1798, Edited from his Original Manuscript*, ed. T. Crofton Coker, 2 vols. (1838).

Hone, William, *Full Report of the Third Spa-Fields Meeting; With the Previous Arrests* (1817).

—— *The Meeting in Spa Fields. Hone's Authentic and Correct Account of All the Proceedings on Monday December 2nd; with Resolutions and Petition of Nov. 15 1816* (1816).

—— *Regency Radical: Selected Writings of William Hone* (Detroit, MI: Wayne State University Press, 2003).

———— *The Riots in London. Hone's Full Account of the Events in the Metropolis, on Monday 2 Dec. 1816* (1816).

———— *The Sinecurist's Creed, or Belief* (1817).

Hughson, David, *London: Being an Accurate History and Description of the British Metropolis and its Neighborhood to Thirty Miles Extent, by an Actual Perambulation* (1808).

Huish, Robert, *Memoirs of the Late Royal Highness Charlotte Augusta, Princess of Wales* (1818).

Hunt, Henry, *The Green Bag Plot* (1819).

———— *Memoirs of Henry Hunt, Esq., Written by Himself in His Majesty's Jail at Ilchester*, 3 vols. (1820–22).

Imlay, Gilbert, *A Topographical Description of the Western Territory of North America* (1792).

Jones, John Gale, *Sketch of a Speech Delivered at the Westminster Forum… on the Following Question: "Which have proved themselves the true friends of their King and country, those persons who have endeavoured to procure a constitutional reform in Parliament, or those who have opposed that measure as ill-timed and dangerous?"* (1795).

The Ladies Physiognomonical Mirror, or Lovers Portraits (1798).

Lamb, Charles, *The Letters of Charles and Mary Lamb*, ed. Edwin W. Marrs, Jr., 3 vols. (Ithaca, NY: Cornell University Press, 1975).

Lavater, Johann Caspar, *Physionomische Fragmente, zur Beförderung der Menschenkenntniss und Menschenliebe* (Leipzig, 1775–78).

[Lee, Richard], *A Summary of the Duties of Citizenship, Written Expressly for Members of the London Corresponding Societies* (1795).

Lewis, C. Day, ed., *The Mind in Chains: Socialism and the Cultural Revolution* (F. Muller, 1937).

Lillo, George, *The London Merchant; or, the History of George Barnwell*, Dedication (1731).

Lindsay, John and Edgell Rickword, eds., *A Handbook of Freedom: A Record of English Democracy through Twelve Centuries* (Lawrence and Wishart, 1939).

Lindsey, Theophilus, *The Letters of Theophilus Lindsey (1723–1808)*, ed. G. M. Ditchfield, 2 vols. (Woodbridge: Boydell Press, 2012).

Linton, W. J., *James Watson: A Memoir* (New Haven, CT, 1879).

Lloyd, Thomas, "The Diary of Thomas Lloyd kept in Newgate prison, 1794–96," in *Newgate in Revolution: An Anthology of Radical Prison Literature in the Age of Revolution*, ed. Michael T. Davis, Iain McCalman, and Christina Parolin (Continuum, 2005), 81–116.

London Corresponding Society, *Account of the Proceedings of a Meeting of the People in a Field near Copenhagen House, Thursday, Nov. 12* (1795).

———— *London Corresponding Society, 1792–1799*, ed. Michael T. Davis, 6 vols. (Pickering & Chatto, 2002).

———— *Narrative of the Proceedings at a General Meeting of the London Corresponding Society…on Monday the 29th of June, 1795* (1795).

———— *Proceedings of a General Meeting of the London Corresponding Society, Held on Monday October the 26th, 1795, in a Field Adjacent to Copenhagen House, in the County of Middlesex* (1795).

———— *Selections from the Papers of the London Corresponding Society 1792–1799*, ed. Mary Thale (Cambridge: Cambridge University Press, 1983).

—— *To the Parliament and the People of Great Britain. An Explicit Declaration of the Principles and Views of the London Corresponding Society* (1795).

Look Before You Leap: Or, a Few Hints to Such Artizans, Mechanics, Labourers, Farmers, and Husbandmen, As Are Desirous of Emigrating to America (1796).

Lovell, Robert and Robert Southey, *Poems: Containing the Retrospect, Odes, Elegies, Sonnets, &c. By Robert Lovell and Robert Southey* (1795).

MacKenzie, Peter, *The Life of Thomas Muir* (Glasgow, 1831).

Mackintosh, James, *Vindiciae Gallicae: Defence of the French Revolution, and its English Admirers, Against the Accusations of the Right Hon. Edmund Burke* (1791).

Mander, John, *The Writer and Commitment* (Secker and Warburg, 1961).

Marcuse, Herbert, *One Dimensional Man: Studies in the Ideology of Advanced Industrial Society* (Boston, MA: Beacon, 1964).

Margarot, Maurice, *Proposal for a Grand National Jubilee* (Sheffield, n.d.[1812]).

—— *Thoughts on Revolution* (Harlow, 1812).

Margarot, Maurice Margarot, le Père, *Histoire, ou Relation d'un Voyage, Qui a duré Près de cinq Ans* (1780).

Massachusetts Historical Society, *Report of the Case in the Federal Circuit Court of New York, April 4, 1798*, in *Collections of the Massachusetts Historical Society 5* (Boston, MA: 1798).

Mercier, Louis-Sébastien, *Du Théatre, ou Novel Essai sur l'Art Dramatique* (Paris, 1773).

Mills, C. Wright, "Culture and Politics: The Fourth Epoch," *Listener* (12 March 1959), reprinted in *Power, Politics, and People: The Collected Essays of C. Wright Mills*, ed. Irving Louis Horowitz (New York: Ballantine Books, 1963), 236–46.

Mitchell, Joseph, *An Address to the People* (Liverpool, 1816).

Moore, Charles, *A Full Inquiry into the Subject of Suicide. To Which Are added ... Two Treatises on Duelling and Gaming*, 2 vols. (1790).

Morse, Jedidiah, *The American Geography: Or a View of the Present Situation of the United States of America* (1794).

Musus, Johann, *Physiognomical Travels, Preceded by a Physiognomical Journal* (1800).

National Convention of the Republic of France, *A Collection of Addresses Transmitted by Certain English Clubs and Societies to the National Convention of France* (1793).

Nicholson, Henry M., *Authentic Records Relating to the Christian Churches Now Meeting in George Street and Mutley Chapels, Plymouth. 1640 to 1870* (1870).

O'Brien, J. B., *Dissertation and Elegy on Maximilian Robespierre* (1859).

—— *Life and Character of Maximilian Robespierre* (1838).

Orwell, George, "Inside the Whale," in *The Collected Essays, Journalism and Letters of George Orwell, vol. 1, An Age Like This, 1920–1940*, ed. Sonia Orwell and Ian Angus (Harmondsworth: Penguin, 1970), 540–78.

Paine, Thomas, *Letter Addressed to the Addressers of the Late Proclamation* (1792), in *The Complete Works of Thomas Paine*, ed. Phillip S. Foner, 2 vols. (New York: Citadel Press), 2: 469–510.

——— *Letter to George Washington, on the Subject of the Late Treaty* (1797).

——— *The Rights of Man* (Harmondsworth: Penguin, 1984, first published 1791–92).

Palmer, Thomas Fyshe, *A Narrative of the Sufferings of T. F. Palmer, and W. Skirving during a Voyage to New South Wales, 1794, on board the* Surprise *Transport* (1797).

Parkinson, James, *A Vindication of the London Corresponding Society* (1794).

The Patriot's Calendar, for the Year 1794, containing the Usual English Almanack, the Decree of the French National Convention for the Alteration of the Style (1794).

Pellew, George, *The Life and Correspondence of the Right Hon. Henry Addington, First Viscount Sidmouth*, 3 vols. (1847).

Pigott, Charles, *Persecution. The Case of Charles Pigott: Contained in the Defence He had Prepared and Would Have Delivered* (1793).

——— *A Political Dictionary for Guinea-less Pigs* (1795).

——— *A Political Dictionary: Explaining the True Meaning of Words* (1795).

Place, Francis, *The Autobiography of Francis Place (1771–1854)*, ed. Mary Thale (Cambridge: Cambridge University Press, 1972).

Prentice, Archibald, *Historical Sketches and Personal Recollections of Manchester* (1851).

Preston, Thomas, *The Life and Opinions of Thomas Preston, Patriot and Shoemaker* (1817).

Price, Richard, *Richard Price, Political Writings,* ed. D. O. Thomas (Cambridge: Cambridge University Press, 1991).

Priestley, Joseph, *Memoirs of Dr. Joseph Priestley to the Year 1795* (Northumberland, PA, 1806).

——— *Theological and Miscellaneous Writings of Joseph Priestley, LLD, FRS, etc.*, ed. J. T. Rutt, 25 vols. (1817–31).

Ramsey, David, *An Oration Delivered on the Anniversary of the American Independence, July 4, 1794... to the Inhabitants of South Carolina* (1795).

[Reeves, John?], *A Narrative of the Insults Offered to the King, on his way to and from the House of Lords... by an Eye-Witness* (1795).

Reform, the Watch-word for Revolution by a Civilian of Oriel Coll. Oxford (Chelmsford, 1816).

Reid, William Hamilton, *The Rise and Dissolution of the Infidel Societies in this Metropolis* (1800).

Report of the Select Committee on Transportation . . . and the Effects Which Have Been produced by that Mode of Punishment (1812).

Roach, John, *Roach's London Pocket Pilot* (1793).

Robinson, Henry Crabb, *Diary, Reminiscences, and Correspondence of Henry Crabb Robinson*, ed. Thomas Sadler, 2 vols. (Boston, 1871).

Sandford, Mrs. [Margaret] Henry Sandford, *Thomas Poole and His Friends*, 2 vols. (1888).

Saville, John, *Memoirs from the Left* (Merlin Press, 2003).

Scott, John (later Lord Eldon), *Lord Eldon's Anecdote Book*, ed. Anthony L. J. Lincoln and Robert Lindley McEwen (London: Stevens and Sons, 1960).

Scrapbook of Political Broadsides, British Library (pressmark 648.c. 26).

The Second Report of the Committee of Secrecy appointed by the House of Commons (1794).

The Second Report of the Committee of Secrecy of the House of Commons... To Which Are Added the First and Second Reports of the House of Lords (1794).

Shelley, Mary, *The Journals of Mary Shelley, 1814–1844*, ed. Paula R. Feldman and Diana Scott-Kilvert, 2 vols. (Oxford: Oxford University Press, 1987).

Shelley, Percy Bysshe, *The Letters of Percy Bysshe Shelley*, ed. F. E. Jones, 2 vols. (Oxford: Oxford University Press, 1964).

—— *Shelley's Prose in the Bodleian Manuscripts*, ed. A. H. Koszul (Frowde, 1910).

—— *Percy Bysshe Shelley: The Major Works*, ed. Zachary Leader and Michael O'Neill (Oxford: Oxford University Press, 2003).

—— *The Prose Works of Percy Bysshe Shelley, Volume 1*, ed. E. B. Murray (Oxford: Oxford University Press, 1993).

Shepherd, William, *A Selection from the Early Letters of the Late Rev. William Shepherd, LL. D.*, ed. [H. Ridyard] (Liverpool, 1855).

Société des Amis de la Constitution, séante aux Jacobins à Paris, *Discours MM. Cooper et Watt, députés de Société Constitutionelle de Manchester* (Paris, 1792).

Society for Constitutional Information [Sheffield], *Address to the Scotch Martyrs* (Sheffield, 1794).

Sotheby, William, *Poems: Consisting of a Tour through Parts of North and South Wales ... and an Epistle to a Friend on Physiognomy* (1790).

Southey, Robert, *Catalogue of the Valuable Library of the late Robert Southey, Esq., LL.D, Poet Laureate... Which Will be Sold by Auction... by Messrs. S. Leigh Sotheby & Co.* (1848).

—— *The Collected Letters of Robert Southey*, gen. ed. Lynda Pratt, Tim Fulford, and Ian Packer, *Romantic Circles*, https://romantic-circles.org/editions/southey_letters.

—— *The Contributions of Robert Southey to the* Morning Post, ed. Kenneth Curry (Tuscaloosa: University of Alabama Press, 1984).

—— *Correspondence of Robert Southey with Caroline Bowles*, ed. Edward Dowden (Dublin, 1881).

—— *A Letter to William Smith, Esq. M.P.* (1817).

—— *Life and Correspondence of Robert Southey*, ed. Charles Cuthbert Southey (New York: 1851).

—— *New Letters of Robert Southey*, ed. Kenneth Curry. 2 vols. (New York: Columbia University Press, 1965).

—— *Poems* (Bristol, 1797).

—— *Robert Southey: Later Poetic Works, 1811–1838*, gen. ed. Tim Fulford and Lynda Pratt, 4 vols. (London: Pickering & Chatto, 2012).

Spence, Thomas, *The Coin Collector's Companion. Being a Descriptive Alphabetical List of the Modern Provincial, Political, and other Copper Coins... Printed for T. Spence, Dealer in Coins* (1795).

—— *Marine Republic, or a Description of Spensonia* (1794).

—— *The Political Works of Thomas Spence*, ed. H. T. Dickinson (Newcastle: Avero, 1982), 25–33.

—— *The Rights of Infants; or, the Imprescriptable Right of Mothers to Such Share of the Elements as is Sufficient to Enable them to Suckle and Bring up their Young* (1797).

Thelwall, Cecil, *The Life of John Thelwall, By his Widow* (1837).

Thelwall, John, *The Daughter of Adoption* (1801).

————— *Poems Chiefly Written in Retirement...With a Prefatory Memoir of the Life of the Author* (Hereford, 1801).

————— *The Natural and Constitutional Right of Britons to Annual Parliaments, Universal Suffrage, and the Freedom of Popular Associations* (1795).

————— *The Politics of English Jacobinism: Writings of John Thelwall*, ed. Gregory Claeys (University Park: Pennsylvania State University Press, 1995).

————— *The Rights of Nature Against the Usurpations of Establishments... in Reply to the False Principles of Burke* (1796).

Thompson, E. P., *Collected Poems,* ed. Fred Inglis (Newcastle: Bloodaxe Press, 1999).

————— *Double Exposure* (Merlin Press, 1985).

————— *E. P. Thompson and the Making of the New Left*, ed. Cal Winslow (New York: Monthly Review Press, 2014).

————— *Exterminism and the Cold War* (Verso, 1982).

————— *The Heavy Dancers* (Merlin Press, 1985).

————— Interview by Mike Merrill, in *Visions of History*, ed. Henry Abelove, et al. (New York: Pantheon, 1976).

————— *Persons and Polemics* (Merlin Press, 1994).

————— *The Poverty of Theory and Other Essays* (Merlin Press, 1978).

————— *Writing by Candlelight* (Merlin Press, 1980).

————— ed., *Out of Apathy*, ed. E. P. Thompson (Stevens and Sons, 1960).

————— ed., *Warwick University Ltd: Industry, Management and the Universities* (Harmondsworth: Penguin, 1970).

Thompson, E. P., Perry Anderson, E. J. Hobsbawm, and Christopher Hill, "Agendas for Radical History," *Radical History Review*, 36 (1986): 26–45.

Thompson, Frank, *There Is a Spirit in Europe: A Memoir of Frank Thompson*, ed. T. J. and E. P. Thompson (Gollancz, 1947).

Thurm, Timothy, Esq. (pseud.), *The Monkeys in Red Caps, an Old Story; Newly Inscribed to the Club of Jacobins* (1797).

Turner, William, *The Lives of Eminent Unitarians; with a Notice of Dissenting Academies,* Vol. II (1843), 214–27.

Very, A Very New Pamphlet Indeed! Being the Truth ... Containing Some Strictures on the English Jacobins (1792).

Vincent, David, ed., *Testaments of Radicalism: Memoirs of Working Class Politicians 1790–1885* (Europa Publications, 1977).

[Wade, John], *The Black Book; or, Corruption Unmasked!* (1820).

Wakefield, Gilbert, *A Reply to Some Parts of the Bishop of Llandaff's Address to the People of Great Britain* (1798).

Walker, Thomas, *A Review of Some of Events which have Occurred in Manchester* (1794).

Warford, Edward, *Old and New London: The City Ancient and Modern*, 6 vols. (1881).

Wat Tyler and Jack Straw; or, the Mob Reformers. A Dramatic Entertainment as Performed... in Bartholomew Fair (1730).

Williams, Raymond, *Politics and Letters: Interviews with* New Left Review (Verso, 1979).

————— ed., *May Day Manifesto 1968* (Harmondsworth: Penguin, 1968).

Winterbotham, William, *The Commemoration of National Deliverance, and the Dawning Day: Two Sermons... Preached at How's Lane Chapel, Plymouth* (1794).

———— *An Historical, Geographical, Commercial, and Philosophical View of the American United States, and of the European Settlements in America and the West Indies*, 4 vols. (1795).

———— *An Historical, Geographical, Commercial, and Philosophical View of the American United States, and of the European Settlements in America and the West Indies*, [2nd edition] 4 vols. (1799).

———— ed., *Selection of Poems Sacred and Moral*, 2 vols. (1796–97).

———— [William Winterbotham], *AMERICA. To be Completed in Thirty-three Numbers, on January 31, 1795, Will be Published, Price 1s.* [Prospectus] (1794?).

W. J., "Memoirs of the Rev. William Winterbotham," *New Baptist Miscellany* 4 (January–March, 1830): 1–5, 45–49, 87–95.

Winterbotham, William Howard, *The Rev. William Winterbotham. A Sketch* (1893).

Wollstonecraft, Mary, *An Historical and Moral View of the Origins and Progress of the French Revolution and the Effect It Has Produced in Europe* (New York: Scholars' Facsimiles and Reprints, 1975, first published 1795).

———— *A Vindication of the Rights of Men with A Vindication of the Rights of Woman*, ed. Sylvana Tomaselli (Cambridge: CUP, 1995, first published 1790, 1792).

———— *A Vindication of the Rights of Woman*, ed. Miriam Brody (Harmondsworth: Penguin, 1992, first published 1792).

———— and William Godwin, *A Short Residence in Sweden, Norway and Denmark and Memoirs of the Author of 'The Rights of Woman,'* ed. Richard Holmes (Harmondsworth: Penguin, 1987, first published 1796, 1798).

Woodward, George, *Eccentric Excursions: Or, Literary and Pictorial Sketches of Countenance, Character and Country* (1798).

Wordsworth, William, *The Letters of William and Dorothy Wordsworth: The Early Years, 1787–1805*, ed. Ernest de Selincourt, 2nd ed., rev. Chester L. Shaver (Oxford: Oxford University Press, 1967).

———— *Lyrical Ballads*, ed. R. L. Brett and A. R. Jones (Routledge, 1968).

———— *The Prelude, The Four Texts (1798, 1799, 1805, 1850)*, ed. Jonathan Wordsworth (Penguin, 1995).

———— *The Prose Works of William Wordsworth*, ed. W. J. B. Owen and Jane Worthington Smyser, 3 vols. (Oxford: Oxford University Press, 1974).

———— *William Wordsworth: The Major Works*, ed. Stephen Gill (Oxford: Oxford University Press, 2000).

Yorke, Henry Redhead, *Letters from France: Describing the Manners and Customs of Its Inhabitants … Interspersed with Interesting Anecdotes of Celebrated Public Characters*, 2 vols. (1814 [1804]).

———— *These are the Times that Try Men's Souls! A Letter to John Frost a Prisoner in Newgate* (1793).

Secondary Works

Abrams, M. H., "On Political Readings of *Lyrical Ballads*," in *Abrams, Doing Things with Texts: Essays in Criticism and Critical Theory*, ed. Michael Fischer (New York: W. W. Norton, 1989), 364–91.

Adams, M. Ray, *Studies in the Literary Backgrounds of English Radicalism: With Special Reference to the French Revolution* (Lancaster, PA: Franklin and Marshall College, 1947).

Agnew, Jean-Christophe, *Worlds Apart: The Market and the Theater in Anglo-American Thought, 1550–1750* (Cambridge: Cambridge University Press, 1986).

Albertone, Manuela, *National Identity and the Agrarian Republic: The Transatlantic Commerce of Ideas between America and France (1750–1830)* (Farnham: Ashgate, 2014).

Algers, J. G., "The British Colony in Paris," *English Historical Review* 13 (1898): 672–94.

——— *Englishmen in the French Revolution* (Low, Marston, Searle & Rivington, 1898).

——— *Paris in 1789–94: Farewell Letters of Victims of the Guillotine* (George Allen, 1902).

Allen, Richard C., *David Hartley on Human Nature* (Albany, NY: State University of New York Press, 1999).

Anderson, Fred, *Crucible of War: The Seven Years' War and the Fate of Empire in British North America, 1754–1766* (New York: Vintage, 2000).

Anderson, Perry, *Arguments within English Marxism* (Verso, 1980).

——— *English Questions* (Verso, 1992).

Andrew, Donna. *Aristocratic Vice: The Attack on Duelling, Suicide, Adultery, and Gambling in Eighteenth-Century England* (New Haven, CT: Yale University Press, 2013).

——— "The Code of Honour and Its Critics: The Opposition to Duelling in England, 1700–1850," *Social History* 39 (1980): 409–34.

———"Popular Culture and Public Debate: London 1780," *Historical Journal* 39 (1996): 405–23.

Andrew, Donna T. and Randall McGowen, *The Perreaus and Mrs. Rudd: Forgery and Betrayal in Eighteenth-Century London* (Berkeley: University of California Press, 2001).

Andrews, Stuart, *The British Periodical Press and the French Revolution, 1789–99* (Houndmills: Palgrave, 2000).

——— "Fellow Pantisocrats: Brissot, Cooper and Imlay," *Symbiosis: A Journal of Anglo-American Literary Relations* 1 (1997): 35–47.

——— *Unitarian Radicalism: Political Rhetoric, 1770–1814* (Houndmills: Palgrave Macmillan, 2003).

Ansari, Humayun, "Burying the Dead": Making Muslim Space in Britain,' *Historical Research* 80 (2007): 545–66.

Appleby, Joyce, *Capitalism and a New Social Order: The Republican Vision of the 1790s* (New York: Columbia University Press, 1984).

——— *Liberalism and Republicanism in the Historical Imagination* (Cambridge, MA: Harvard University Press, 1993).

Armitage, David, "The New World and British Historical Thought: From Richard Hakluyt to William Robertson," in *America in European Consciousness, 1793–1750*, ed. Karen Ordahl Kupperman (Chapel Hill: University of North Carolina Press, 1995), 52–75.

Arnold, Dana, "London Bridge and its Symbolic Identity in the Regency Metropolis: The Dialectic of Civic and National Pride," in *The Metropolis and Its Image: Constructing Identities for London, c.1750–1950*, ed. Dana Arnold (Oxford: Blackwell, 1999), 79–100.

———— "Rationality, Safety and Power: The Street Planning of Late Georgian London," *The Georgian Group Journal* 5 (1995): 37–50.

Arsleff, Hans, *The Study of Language in England, 1780–1860* (Princeton, NJ: Princeton University Press, 1967).

Atkinson, Alan, *The Europeans in Australia: A History. Volume One: The Beginning* (Oxford: Oxford University Press, 1997).

Backscheider, Paula S. *Spectacular Politics: Theatrical Power and Mass Culture in Early Modern England* (Baltimore, MD: Johns Hopkins University Press 1993).

Baer, Marc, *Theatre and Disorder in Late Georgian London* (Oxford: Oxford University Press, 1992).

Barish, Jonas, *The Antitheatrical Prejudice* (Berkeley: University of California Press, 1981).

Barker-Benfield, G. J., *The Culture of Sensibility: Sex and Society in Eighteenth-Century Britain* (Chicago, IL: University of Chicago Press, 1992).

Barnett, Dene, "The Performance Practice of Acting: The Eighteenth Century. Part II: The Hands," *Theatre Research International* 3 (1977): 1–19.

Barrell, John, "'An Entire Change of Performance?' The Politicisation of Theatre and the Theatricalisation of Politics in the Mid 1790s," *Lumen* 17 1998): 11–50.

———— *Imagining the King's Death: Figurative Treason, Fantasies of Regicide, 1793–1796* (Oxford: Oxford University Press, 2000).

———— "Imagining the King's Death: The Arrest of Richard Brothers," *History Workshop Journal* 37 (1994): 1–32.

———— "Popular Political Culture in the Mid 1790s," *Anglistentag 1995 Greifswald: Proceedings*, ed. Jürgen Klein and Dirk Banderbeke (Tübingen: Max Niemeyer Verlag, 1996): 15–27.

———— "'Rus in urbe,'" in *Romanticism and Popular Culture in Britain and Ireland*, ed. Philip Connell and Nigel Leask (Cambridge: Cambridge University Press, 2009), 109–27.

———— *The Spirit of Despotism: Invasions of Privacy in the 1790s* (Oxford: Oxford University Press, 2006).

Baylen, Joseph O. and Norbert J. Gossman, eds., *Biographical Dictionary of Modern British Radicals. Volume 1: 1770–1830* (Sussex: Harvester Press, 1979).

Beattie, J. M., "Scales of Justice: Defence Counsel and English Criminal Trial in the Eighteenth and Nineteenth Century," *Law and History Review* 9 (1991): 221–67.

Behrendt, Stephen C., *Shelley and His Audiences* (Lincoln: University of Nebraska Press, 1989).

Belchem, John, *'Orator' Hunt, Henry Hunt and English Working-Class Radicalism* (Oxford: Oxford University Press, 1985).

———— "Republicanism, Popular Constitutionalism and the Radical Platform in Early Nineteenth Century England,' *Social History* 6 (1981): 1–32.

Belchem, John and James Epstein, "The Gentleman Leader Revisited,' *Social History* 22 (1997): 174–93.

Bell, Vikki, "Performativity and Belonging: An Introduction," special issue of *Theory, Culture and Society* 16 (2) (1999): 1–10.

Bend, Nathan Ashley, "The Home Office and Public Disturbance, c.1800–1832." Ph.D. thesis, University of Hertfordshire, 2018.

Bender, Courtney, "Bakhtinian Perspectives on 'Everyday Life' Sociology," *Bakhtin and the Human Sciences: No Last Words*, ed. Michael Mayerfeld Bell and Michael Gardiner (Sage, 1998), 181–95.

Bennett, Susan, *Theatre Audiences: A Theory of Production and Reception*, 2nd ed. (Routledge, 1997).

Benton, Lauren, *Law and Colonial Cultures: Legal Regimes in World History* (Cambridge: Cambridge University Press, 2002).

Bergerson, Stuart, Maureen Healy, and Pamela E. Swett, "The History of Everyday Life: A Second Chapter," *Journal of Modern History* 80 (2008): 358–78.

Bess, Michael, *Realism, Utopia, and the Mushroom Cloud: Four Activist Intellectuals and Their Strategies for Peace, 1945–1989* (Chicago, IL: University of Chicago Press. 1993).

Bewley, Christina, *Muir of Huntershill* (Oxford: Oxford University Press, 1981).

Bewley, Christina and David Bewley, *Gentleman Radical: The Life of John Horne Tooke, 1736–1812* (Tauris, 1998).

Bickham, Troy O., *Savages within the Empire: Representations of American Indians in Eighteenth-Century Britain* (Oxford: Oxford University Press, 2005).

Binhammer, Katherine, "The Political Novel and the Seduction Plot: Thomas Holcroft's *Anna St. Ives*," *Eighteenth-Century Fiction* 11 (1999), 205–22.

Blackburn, Robin, *The Overthrow of Colonial Slavery, 1776–1848* (Verso, 1988).

Bohstedt, John, *The Politics of Provision: Food Riots, Moral Economy, and Market Transition in England, c. 1550–1850* (Farnham: Ashgate, 2010).

Bolla, Peter de, *The Discourse of the Sublime: History, Aesthetics, and the Subject* (Oxford: Basil Blackwell, 1989).

Bolton, Betsy, "Theorizing Audience and Spectatorial Agency," *The Oxford Handbook of Georgian Theater*, ed. Julia Swindells and David Francis Taylor (Oxford: Oxford University Press, 2014), 31–52.

Bolton, Carol, *Writing the Empire: Robert Southey and Romantic Colonialism* (Pickering & Chatto, 2007).

Booth, Alan, "Popular Loyalism and Public Violence in the North-West of England, 1790–1800, *Social History* 8 (1983): 295–313.

——— "The United Englishmen and Radical Politics in the Industrial North-West of England, 1795–1803," *International Review of Social History* 31 (1986): 271–97.

Bonwick, Colin, *English Radicals and the American Revolution* (Chapel Hill: University of North Carolina Press, 1977).

Borsay, Peter, "'All the Town's a Stage:'" Urban Ritual and Ceremony, 1660–1800," in *The Transformation of Provincial Towns, 1600–1800*, ed. Peter Clark (Hutchinson, 1984), 228–58.

——— "Culture, Status, and the English Landscape," *History* 67 (1982): 1–12.

Boulton, James T., *The Language of Politics in the Age of Wilkes and Burke* (Routledge and K. Paul, 1963).

Bourdieu, Pierre, *Language and Symbolic Power*, trans. Gino Raymond and Matthew Adamson (Cambridge, MA: Harvard University Press, 1991).

Bowden, Ann, "William Hone's Political Journalism, 1815–1821," 2 vols. Ph.D. diss., University of Texas, 1975.

Bradley, James E., *Religion, Revolution, and English Radicalism: Nonconformity in Eighteenth-Century Politics and Society* (Cambridge: Cambridge University Press, 1990).

Braithwaite, Helen, *Romanticism, Publishing and Dissent: Joseph Johnson and the Cause of Liberty* (Houndmills: Palgrave Macmillan, 2003).

Bremmer, Jan and Herman Roodenburg, eds., *A Cultural History of Gesture* (Ithaca, NY: Cornell University Press, 1991).

Breen, T. H., "'Baubles of Britain': The American and Consumer Revolutions of the Eighteenth Century," *Past and Present* 119 (1988): 73–104.

——— *The Marketplace of Revolution: How Consumer Politics Shaped American Independence* (Oxford: Oxford University Press, 2004).

Brewer, John, "Commercialization and Politics," in *The Birth of a Consumer Society: The Commercialization of Eighteenth-Century England*, ed. Neil McKendrick, John Brewer, and J. H. Plumb (Hutchinson, 1982), 197–262.

——— *The Common People and Politics, 1750–1790s* (Cambridge: Chadwyck-Healey, 1986).

——— "This, That and the Other: Public, Social and Private in the Seventeenth and Eighteenth Centuries, in *Shifting Boundaries: Transformations of the Languages of Public and Private in the Eighteenth Century*, ed. Dario Castiglione and Lesley Sharpe (Exeter: University of Exeter Press, 1995), 1–21.

Brooke, Alan and Lesley Kipling, *Liberty or Death: Radicals, Republicans and Luddites, 1793–1823*, 2nd ed. (Huddersfield: Huddersfield Local History Society, 2012).

Brown, P. A., *The French Revolution in English History* (Crosby, Lockwood and Son, 1919).

Bryson, Scott, *The Chastised Stage: Bourgeois Drama and the Exercise of Power* (Stanford, CA: Anma Libri, 1991).

Buel, Richard Jr., *Joel Barlow: American Citizen in a Revolutionary World* (Baltimore, MD: Johns Hopkins University Press, 2011).

Bugg, John, *Five Long Winters: The Trials of British Radicalism* (Stanford, CA: Stanford University Press, 2013).

——— "Revolution," in *William Wordsworth in Context*, ed. Andrew Bennett (Cambridge: Cambridge University Press, 2015), 175–81.

Burke, Peter, "Performing History: The Importance of Occasions," *Rethinking History* (2005): 35–52.

Burton, Antoinette, "Introduction: Archive Fever, Archive Stories," in *Archive Stories: Facts, Fictions and the Writing of History* (Durham, NC: Duke University Press, 2005), 1–24.

——— "New Narratives of Imperial Politics in the Nineteenth-Century," in *At Home with the Empire: Metropolitan Culture and the Imperial World*, ed. Catherine Hall and Sonya O. Rose (Cambridge: Cambridge University Press, 2006), 212–29.

Burwick, Frederick, "Georgian Theories of the Actor," in *The Oxford Handbook of Georgian Theater*, ed. Julia Swindells and David Francis Taylor (Oxford: Oxford University Press, 2014), 177–96.

Butler, Judith, *Bodies that Matter: On the Discursive Limits of "Sex"* (New York: Routledge, 1993).

——— *Excitable Speech: A Politics of the Performative* (New York: Routledge, 1997).

———— "For a Careful Reading," in *Feminist Contentions: A Philosophical Exchange*, ed. Seyla Benhabib et al. (New York: Routledge, 1995), 119–43.

———— *Gender Trouble: Feminism and the Subversion of Identity* (New York: Routledge, 1990).

Butler, Marilyn, *Romantics, Rebels, and Reactionaries* (Oxford: Oxford University Press, 1981).

———— "Thompson's Second Front," *History Workshop Journal* 39 (1995): 71–78.

Calhoun, Craig, *The Roots of Radicalism: Tradition, the Public Sphere, and Early Nineteenth-Century Social Movements* (Chicago, IL: University of Chicago Press, 2012).

Cameron, Kenneth Neill, "Shelley vs. Southey: New Light on an Old Quarrel," *PMLA*, 57 (1942): 489–512.

Cannon, John, *Parliamentary Reform, 1640–1832* (Cambridge: Cambridge University Press, 1974).

Carlson, Marvin, *Places of Performance: The Semiotics of Theatre Architecture* (Ithaca, NY: Cornell University Press, 1989).

Carnall, Geoffrey, *Robert Southey and His Age: The Development of a Conservative Mind* (Oxford: Oxford University Press, 1960).

Carretta, Vincent, *Equiano, the African: Biography of a Self-Made Man* (Athens: University of Georgia Press, 2007).

Cayton, Andrew, *Love in the Time of Revolution: Transatlantic Radicalism and Historical Change, 1793–1818* (Chapel Hill: University of North Carolina Press, 2013).

Certeau, Michel de, *The Practice of Everday Life*, trans. Steven Rendall (Berkeley: University of California Press, 1988).

Chandler, James K., *Wordsworth's Second Nature: A Study of the Poetry and Politics* (Chicago, IL: University of Chicago Press, 1984).

Chartier, Roger, *Forms and Meanings: Texts, Performances and Audiences from Codex to Computer* (Philadelphia: University of Pennsylvania Press, 1995).

———— *On the Edge of the Cliff: History, Language, and Practices*, trans. Lydia G. Cochrane (Baltimore, MD: Johns Hopkins University Press, 1997).

Chase, Malcolm, "From Millennium to Anniversary: The Concept of the Jubilee in Late Eighteenth- and Nineteenth-Century England," *Past and Present* 129 (1990): 132–47.

———— *The People's Farm: English Radical Agrarianism, 1775–1840* (Oxford: Oxford University Press, 1988).

Chernock, Arianne, *Men and the Making of Modern British Feminism* (Stanford, CA: Stanford University Press, 2010).

Claeys, Gregory, "Four Roads from 'Genesis': Spence, Paine and Rights to Property," in *Thomas Spence: The Poor Man's Revolutionary*, ed. Alastair Bonnett and Keith Armstrong (Breviary Stuff, 2014), 27–34.

———— "The French Revolution Debate and British Political Thought," *History and Political Thought* 11 (1990): 59–80.

———— "Origins of the Rights of Labor: Republicanism, Commerce, and the Construction of Modern Social Theory in Britain, 1796–1805," *Journal of Modern History* 66 (1994): 249–90.

——— *Thomas Paine: Social and Political Thought* (Boston, MA: Unwin Hyman, 1989).

Clark, Anna, *The Struggle for the Breeches: Gender and the Making of the British Working Class* (Berkeley: University of California Press, 1995).

Clark, J. C. D., *English Society 1660–1832: Religion, Ideology and Politics during the Ancien Regime* (Cambridge: Cambridge University Press, 2000).

Clark, Peter, *The English Alehouse: A Social History, 1200–1800* (Longman, 1983).

Colby, Elbridge, *A Bibliography of Thomas Holcroft* (New York: New York Public Library, 1922).

Colley, Linda, "The Apotheosis of George III: Loyalty, Royalty and the British Nation," *Past and Present* 102 (1984): 94–129.

——— *Britons: Forging the Nation, 1707–1837* (New Haven, CT: Yale University Press, 1992).

——— "Radical Patriotism in Eighteenth-Century England," in *Patriotism: The Making and Unmaking of British Identity*, vol. 1: *History and Politics*, ed. Raphael Samuel (Routledge, 1989), 169–87.

Collini, Stefan, *Common Reading: Critics, Historians, Publics* (Oxford: Oxford University Press, 2008).

Connolly, Leonard W., *The Censorship of English Drama, 1737–1824* (San Marino, CA: Huntington Library, 1976).

Conradi, Peter J., *A Very English Hero: The Making of Frank Thompson* (Bloomsbury, 2012).

Cookson, J. E., *The British Armed Nation, 1793–1815* (Oxford: Oxford University Press, 1997).

Coombes, Annie, *Reinventing Africa: Museums, Material Culture and Popular Imagination in Late Victorian and Edwardian England* (New Haven, CT: Yale University Press 1994).

Cornell, Drucillia, "The Violence of the Masquerade: Law Dressed up as Justice," *Cardoza Law Review* 11 (1990): 1047–70.

Cotlar, Seth, "Languages of Democracy in America from the Revolution to the Election of 1800," in *Re-Imagining Democracy in the Age of Revolutions: America, France, Britain, Ireland 1750–1850*, ed. Joanna Innes and Mark Philp (Cambridge: Cambridge University Press, 2013), 101–13.

——— *Tom Paine's America: The Rise and Fall of Transatlantic Radicalism in the Early Republic* (Charlottesville: University of Virginia Press, 2011).

Cowan, Brian, *The Social Life of Coffee: The Emergence of the British Coffeehouse* (New Haven, CT: Yale University Press, 2005).

Cox, Jeffrey N., "Holcroft's Parisian Expedition," in *Literary Culture in the Napoleonic War Years* (Cambridge: Cambridge, University Press, 2014), 25–58.

——— "Ideology and Genre in the British Antirevolutionary Drama of the 1790s," *English Literary History* 58 (1991): 579–610.

Craig, David, *Robert Southey and Romantic Apostasy: Political Argument in Britain, 1780–1840* (Woodbridge: Royal Historical Society, Boydell Press, 2007).

Croft, Andy, *Comrade Heart: A Life of Randall Swingler* (Manchester: Manchester University Press, 2003).

Cunningham, Hugh, "The Language of Patriotism, 1750–1914," *History Workshop Journal* 12 (1981): 8–33.

Curl, James Stevens, *The Victorian Celebration of Death* (Stroud: Sutton, 1972).

Czisnik, Marianne, "Representations of a Hero: Monuments to Admiral Nelson," in *Reactions to Revolutions: The 1790s and their Aftermath*, ed. Ulrich Broich et al. (Münster: Lit Verlad, 2007), 263–88.

Damousi, Joy, "Chaos and Order: Gender, Space and Sexuality on Female Convict Ships," *Australian Historical Studies* 26 (1995): 351–72.

—— *Depraved and Disorderly: Female Convicts, Sexuality and Gender in Colonial Australia* (Cambridge: Cambridge University Press, 1997).

—— "'Depravity and Disorder': The Sexuality of Convict Women," *Labour History* [Australia] 68 (1995): 30–45.

Das, Veena, "Violence and the Work of Time," in *Signifying Identities: Anthropological Perspectives on Boundaries and Contested Values*, ed. Anthony P. Cohen (Routledge, 2000), 59–73.

Davidoff, Leonore and Catherine Hall, *Family Fortunes: Men and Women of the English Middle Class, 1780–1850* (Chicago, IL: University of Chicago Press, 1987).

Davidson, Alistair, *The Invisible State: The Formation of the Australian State, 1788–1901* (Cambridge: Cambridge University Press, 1991).

Davies, Damian Walford, *Presences that Disturb: Models of Romantic Identity in the Literature and Culture of the 1790s* (Cardiff: University of Wales Press, 2002).

Davis, H. W., "Lancashire Reformers, 1816–1817," *Bulletin of the John Rylands Library*, 10 (1926): 47–79.

Davis, Jim, "Spectatorship," in *The Cambridge Companion to British Theatre, 1730–1830*, ed. Jane Moody and Daniel O'Quinn (Cambridge: Cambridge, University Press, 2007), 57–70.

Davis, Madeleine, "'Among the Ordinary People': New Left Involvement in Working-Class Political Mobilization 1956–68," *History Workshop Journal* 86 (2018): 133–59.

—— "Reappraising British Socialist Humanism," *Journal of Political Ideologies* 18 (2013): 57–81.

Davis, Michael T., "The British Jacobins and the Unofficial Terror of Loyalism," in *Terror: From Tyrannicide to Terrorism*, ed. Brett Bowden and Michael T. Davis (Brisbane: University of Queensland Press, 2008), 92–113.

—— "'An Evening of Pleasure Rather Than Business': Songs, Subversion and Radical Sub Culture in the 1790s," *Journal for the Study of British Cultures* 12 (2005): 115–26.

—— "'Good for the Public Example': Daniel Isaac Eaton, Prosecution, Punishment and Recognition, 1793–1812," in *Radicalism and Revolution in Britain, 1775–1848: Essays in Honour of Malcolm I. Thomis*, ed. Michael T. Davis (Houndmills: Palgrave Macmillan, 2000), 110–32.

—— "'The Impartial Voice of Future Times Will Rejudge Your Verdict': Discourse and Drama in the Trials of the Scottish Political Martyrs of the 1790s," in *Hélio Osvaldo Alves: O Guardador de Rios*, ed. Joanne Paisana (Braga: Instituto de Letres e Ciências Humanas, 2005): 65–78.

—— "'The Mob Club?' The London Corresponding Society and the Politics of Civility in the 1790s," in *Unrespectable Radicals: Popular Politics in the*

Age of Reform, ed. Michael T. Davis and Paul Pickering (Aldershot: Ashgate, 2008), 21–40.

────── "The Noise and Emotions of Political Trials in Britain during the 1790s," in *Political Trials in an Age of Revolutions: Britain and the North Atlantic, 1793–1848*, ed. Michael T. Davis, Emma Macleod, and Gordon Pentland (Cham: Palgrave Macmillan, 2019), 137–61.

────── "'That Odious Class of Men Called Democrats': Daniel Isaac Eaton and the Romantics 1794–95," *History* 84 (1999): 74–92.

──────"Prosecution and Radical Discourses during the 1790s: The Case of the Scottish Sedition Trials," *International Journal of the Sociology of Law* 33 (2005): 148–58.

────── "'A Register of Vexations and Persecutions': Some Letters of Thomas Fyshe Palmer from Botany Bay during the 1790s," *Enlightenment and Dissent* 23 (2007): 148–66.

Davis, Michael T., Iain McCalman, and Christina Parolin, "'Patriots in Prison': Newgate Radicalism in the Age of Revolution," in *Newgate in Revolution: An Anthology of Radical Prison Literature in the Age of Revolution*, ed. Michael T. Davis, Iain McCalman, and Christina Parolin (Continuum, 2005), ix–xxv.

Dawson, P. M. S., "Shelley and Class," in *The New Shelley: Later Twentieth-Century Views*, ed. G. Kim Blank (New York: St. Martin's Press, 1991), 34–41.

────── *The Unacknowledged Legislator: Shelley and Politics* (Oxford: Oxford University Press, 1980).

Dening, Greg, *Mr. Bligh's Bad Language: Passion, Power and Theatre on the Bounty* (Cambridge: Cambridge University Press, 1992).

────── *Performances* (Chicago, IL: University of Chicago Press, 1996).

────── "Towards an Anthropology of Performance in Encounters in Place," in *Pacific History*, ed. Donald Rubenstein (Guam: University of Guam Press, 1992), 3–7.

Denney, Peter, "Clamouring for Liberty: Alehouse Noise and the Political Shoemaker," *Eighteenth-Century Life* 41 (2017): 105–21.

Derrida, Jacques, "Force of Law: The 'Mystical Foundation of Authority,'" *Cardoza Law Review* 11 (1990): 921–1039.

Dickinson, H. T., *Liberty and Property: Political Ideology in Eighteenth-Century Britain* (Weidenfeld and Nicholson, 1977).

────── "Popular Conservatism and Militant Loyalism," in *Britain and the French Revolution, 1789–1815* (New York: St. Martin's Press, 1989), 103–25.

Dinwiddy, John, "England," in *Nationalism in the Age of the French Revolution*, ed. Otto Dann and John Dinwiddy (Hambledon, 1988), 53–70.

────── *Radicalism and Reform in Britain, 1780–1850* (Hambledon Press, 1992).

Dirks, Nicholas B., "Annals of the Archive: Ethnographic Notes on the Sources of History," *From the Margins: Historical Anthropology and its Futures*, ed. Brian Keith Axel (Durham, NC: Duke University Press, 2002), 47–65.

Driver, Felix, and David Gilbert, "Heart of Empire? Landscape, Space and Performance in Imperial London," *Environment and Planning D: Society and Space* 16 (1998): 11–28.

Duff, David, *Romance and Revolution: Shelley and the Politics of a Genre* (Cambridge: Cambridge University Press, 1994).

Duffy Michael, "Pitt and the Origins of the Loyalist Association Movement of 1792," *Historical Journal* 39 (1996): 943–62.

Durey, Michael, *Transatlantic Radicals and the Early American Republic* (Lawrence: University Press of Kansas, 1997).

—— *William Wickham, Master Spy: The Secret War against the French Revolution* (Pickering & Chatto, 2009).

—— "William Winterbotham's 'Trumpet of Sedition': Religious Dissent and Political Radicalism in the 1790s," *Journal of Religious History* 19 (1995): 141–57.

Dworkin, Dennis, *Cultural Marxism in Postwar Britain: History, the New Left, and the Origins of Cultural Studies* (Durham, NC: Duke University Press, 1997).

Eagleton, Terry, *The Function of Criticism: From* The Spectator *to Post-Structuralism* (Verso, 1984).

Eastwood, David, "History, Politics and Reputation: E. P. Thompson Reconsidered," *History* 85 (2000): 634–54.

—— "Patriotism and the English State in the 1790s," in *The French Revolution and British Popular Politics*, ed. Mark Philp (Cambridge: Cambridge University Press, 1991), 146–68.

—— "Robert Southey and the Intellectual Origins of Romantic Conservatism," *English Historical Review* 104 (1989): 308–31.

Echeverria, Durand, *Mirage in the West: A History of the French Image of American Society* (Princeton, NJ: Princeton University Press, 1957).

Eckersley, Rachel, "The Drum Major of Sedition: The Political Life and Careers of John Cartwright (1740–1824)." Ph.D. thesis, Manchester University, 1999.

Edwards, Elizabeth, *English-Language Poetry from Wales, 1789–1806* (Cardiff: University of Wales Press, 2013).

Edwards, Pamela, *The Statesman's Science: History, Nature, and Law in the Political Thought of Samuel Taylor Coleridge* (New York: Columbia University Press, 2004).

Eley, Geoff, "Labor History, Social History, *Alltagsgeschichte*: Experience, Culture, and the Politics of the Everyday—a New Direction for German Social History?" *Journal of Modern History* 61 (1989): 297–343.

—— "Nations, Publics, and Political Cultures: Placing Habermas in the Nineteenth Century," in *Habermas and the Public Sphere*, ed. Craig Calhoun (Cambridge: Massachusetts Institute of Technology Press, 1992), 289–339.

Ellery, Eloise, *Brissot de Warville: A Study in the History of the French Revolution* (New York: Houghton Mifflin, 1915).

Elliott, Marianne, *Partners in Revolution: The United Irishmen and France* (New Haven, CT: Yale University Press, 1982).

—— *Robert Emmet: The Making of a Legend* (Profile, 2003).

Ellis, Frank, *Sentimental Comedy: Theory and Practice* (Cambridge: Cambridge, University, Press, 1991).

Elster, Jon, *Alchemies of the Mind: Rationality and the Emotions* (Cambridge: Cambridge University Press, 1999).

Emery, Phil, "End of the line," *British Archeology* 88, May/June 2006: 11–15.

Emsley, Clive, "An Aspect of Pitt's 'Terror': Prosecutions for Sedition during the 1790s," *Social History* 6 (1981): 155–84.

—— "The Pop-Gun Plot, 1794," in *Radicalism and Revolution in Britain, 1775–1848: Essays in Honour of Malcolm I. Thomis*, ed. Michael T. Davis (Houndmills: Palgrave Macmillan, 2000), 56–68.

—— "Repression, 'Terror' and the Rule of Law in England during the Decade of the French Revolution," *English Historical Review* 100 (1985): 801–25.

Epstein, James, *In Practice: Studies in the Language and Culture of Popular Politics in Modern Britain* (Stanford, CA: Stanford University Press, 2003).

—— *The Lion of Freedom: Feargus O'Connor and the Chartist Movement, 1832–1842* (Croom Helm, 1982).

—— *Radical Expression: Political Language, Ritual, and Symbol in England, 1790–1850* (Oxford: Oxford University Press. 1994).

—— "Sermons of Sedition: The Trials of William Winterbotham," in *Political Trials in an Age of Revolutions: Britain and the North Atlantic, 1793–1818*, ed. Michael T. Davis, Emma Macleod, and Gordon Pentland (Cham: Palgrave Macmillan, 2019), 109–35.

—— "Taking Class Notes on Empire," in *At Home with the Empire: Metropolitan Culture and the Imperial World*, ed. Catherine Hall and Sonya O. Rose (Cambridge: Cambridge University Press, 2006), 251–74.

Erdman, David V., *Commerce Des Lumières: John Oswald and the British in Paris, 1790–1793* (Columbia: University of Missouri Press, 1986).

Sister Eugenia, "Coleridge's Scheme of Pantisocracy and American Travel Accounts," *PMLA* 45 (1930): 1069–84.

Fairer, David, *Organising Poetry: The Coleridge Circle, 1790–1798* (Oxford: Oxford University Press, 2009).

Ferradou, Mathieu, "Historique d'un 'festin patriotique' à l' hôtel white (18 novembre 1792): les irlandais patriotes à paris, 1789–1795," *Annales Historiques de la Révolution française*, December 2015, no. 4: 123–43.

Fezzey, Hilary N., "Examining Jacobin Sexual Politics in *Anna St. Ives*," *Re-viewing Thomas Holcroft, 1745–1809*, ed. Miriam L. Wallace and A. A. Markley (Aldershot: Ashgate, 2012), 133–45.

Ferguson, Moira, *Subject to Others: British Women Writers and Colonial Slavery, 1670–1834* (Routledge, 1992).

Fieldhouse, Roger, "Thompson: The Adult Educator," in *E. P. Thompson and English Radicalism*, ed. Roger Fieldhouse and Richard Taylor (Manchester: Manchester University Press, 2013), 25–47.

Fischer-Lichte, Erika, *The Shadow and the Gaze of Theatre: A European Perspective* (Iowa City: University of Iowa Press, 1997).

Fish, Stanley, *Doing What Comes Naturally: Change, Rhetoric, and the Practice of Theory in Literature and Legal Studies* (Durham, NC: Duke University Press, 1989).

Flynn, Michael, *Sailors and Seditionists: The People of the Convict Ship Surprize, 1794* (Sydney: Angela Lind, 1994).

Ford, Charles Howard, "Political and Religious Responses to Royal Ritual: The Funeral of Princess Charlotte in 1817." Master's thesis, Vanderbilt University, 1988.

Foucault, Michel, *Discipline and Punish: The Birth of the Prison*, trans. Alan Sheridan (New York: Vintage, 1979).

—— "Of Other Spaces: Utopias and Heterotopias," *Diacritics* 16 (Spring 1986): 22–27.

Fraistat, Neil, "Illegitimate Shelley: Radical Piracy and the Textual Edition as Performance," *PMLA*, 109 (1994): 409–23.

Caroline Franklin, "Romantic Patriotism as Feminist Critique of Empire," in *Women, Gender, and Enlightenment*, ed. Sarah Knott and Barbara Taylor (Houndmills: Palgrave Macmillan, 205), 551–64.

Fraser, W. Hamish, *Scottish Popular Politics: From Radicalism to Labour* (Edinburgh: Polygon, 2000).

Freeman, Joanne B., "Explaining the Unexplainable: The Cultural Context of the Sedition Act," in *The Democratic Experiment: New Directions in American Political History*, ed. Meg Jacobs, William J. Novak, and Julian Zelizer (Princeton, NJ: Princeton University Press, 2003), 30–49.

Freeman, Lisa A., "The Social Life of Eighteenth-Century Comedy," in *Cambridge Companion to British Theatre, 1730–1830*, ed. Jane Moody and Daniel O'Quinn (CUP, 2007), 73–86.

Freeman, Terence M., *Dramatic Representations of British Soldiers and Sailors on the London Stage, 1660–1800: Britons Strike Home* (Lewiston, NY: Edwin Mellen, 1995).

Fritzsche, Peter, "The Case of Modern Memory," *Journal of Modern History* 73 (2001): 87–117.

Fulcher, Jonathan, "The English People and Their Constitution after Waterloo: Parliamentary Reform, 1815–1817," in *Re-Reading the Constitution: New Narratives in the Political History of England's Long Nineteenth Century*, ed. James Vernon (Cambridge: Cambridge University Press, 1996), 52–82.

Fulfold, Tim, *Romantic Indians: Native Americans, British Literature, and Transatlantic Culture, 1756–1830* (Oxford: Oxford University Press, 2006).

Furniss, Tom, *Edmund Burke's Aesthetic Ideology: Language, Gender and Political Economy in Revolution* (Cambridge: Cambridge University Press, 1993).

——— "Mary Wollstonecraft's French Revolution," in *The Cambridge Companion to Mary Wollstonecraft*, ed. Claudia L. Johnson (Cambridge: Cambridge University Press. 2002), 59–81.

Gardiner, Michael E., *Critiques of Everyday Life* (Routledge, 2000).

Garrett, Clarke, *Respectable Folly: Millenarians and the French Revolution in France and England* (Baltimore, MD: Johns Hopkins University Press, 1975).

Garnai, Amy, "'A Lock Upon my Lips': The Melodrama of Silencing and Censorship in Thomas Holcroft's *Knave, or Not?*," *Eighteenth-Century Studies* 43 (2010): 473–84.

——— "Radicalism, Caution, and Censorship in Elizabeth Inchbald's *Every One Has His Fault*," *Studies in English Literature 1500–1900* 47 (2007): 703–22.

Gatrell, V. A. C., *City of Laughter: Sex and Satire in Eighteenth-Century London* (New York: Walker and Co., 2006).

——— *The Hanging Tree: Execution and the English People, 1770–1868* (Oxford: Oxford University Press, 1996).

Gaunt, R. A., "The Pentrich Rebellion: A Nottingham Affair?" *Midland History*, 43 (2018): 208–28.

Gee, Austin, *The British Volunteer Movement, 1794–1814* (Oxford: Oxford University Press, 2003).

Geggus, David, "British Opinion and the Emergence of Haiti, 1791–1805," in *Slavery and British Society, 1776–1846*, ed. James Walvin (Baton Rouge: Louisiana State University Press, 1982), 23–49.

Gill, Stephen, *Wordsworth: A Life* (Oxford: Oxford University Press, 1990).

Gilmartin, Kevin, *Print Politics: The Press and Radical Opposition in Early Nineteenth-Century England* (Cambridge: Cambridge University Press, 1996).

—— "The 'sinking down' of Jacobinism and the Rise of the Counter-Revolutionary Man of Letters," in *Romanticism and Popular Culture in Britain and Ireland*, ed. Philip Connell and Nigel Leask (Cambridge: Cambridge University Press, 2009), 128–47.

—— *William Hazlitt: Political Essayist* (Oxford: Oxford University Press, 2015).

—— *Writing against Revolution: Literary Conservatism in Britain, 1790–1832* (Cambridge: Cambridge University Press, 2007).

—— ed., *Sociable Places: Locating Culture in Romantic-Period Britain* (Cambridge: Cambridge University Press, 2017).

Gilroy, Paul, *The Black Atlantic: Modernity and Double Consciousness* (Cambridge, MA: Harvard University Press, 1993).

—— "Specters of History: On Nostalgia, Exile, and Modernity," *American Historical Review* 106 (2001): 1587–618.

Gleadle, Kathryn, *The Early Feminists: Radical Unitarians and the Emergence of the Women's Rights Movement, 1831–51* (Houndmills: Palgrave Macmillan, 1995).

—— "The Juvenile Enlightenment: British Children and Youth during the French Revolution," *Past and Present* 233 (2016): 143–84.

Glen, Robert, *Urban Workers in the Early Industrial Revolution* (Croom Helm, 1984).

Gombrich, E. H., "The Cartoonist's Armoury," in *Meditations on a Hobby Horse and Other Essays on the Theory of Art* (Phaidon, 1963), 127–42.

Goode, John, "E. P. Thompson and 'the Significance of Literature,'" in *E. P. Thompson, Critical Perspectives*, ed. Harvey J. Kaye and Keith McClelland (Philadelphia: Temple University Press, 1990), 183–203.

Goodman, Dena, "Public Sphere and Private Life: Towards a Synthesis of Current Historiographical Approaches to the Old Regime," *History and Theory* 31 (1992): 1–20.

Goodrich, Amanda, *Henry Redhead Yorke, Colonial Radical: Politics and Identity in the Atlantic World, 1772–1813* (Routledge, 2019).

Goodway, David, *London Chartism, 1838–1848* (Cambridge: Cambridge University Press, 1982).

Goodwin, Albert, *The Friends of Liberty: The English Democrat Movement in the Age of the French Revolution* (Cambridge, MA: Harvard University Press, 1979).

Graf, Roman, "Voicing Limits: Rereading the Dramatic Theories of J. M. R. Lenz and L. S. Mercier." PhD. diss., University of North Carolina at Chapel Hill, 1992.

Graham, Jenny, *The Nation, the Law and the King: Reform Politics in England, 1789–1799*, 2 vols. (Lanham, MD: University Press of America, 2000).

——— *Revolutionary in Exile: The Emigration of Joseph Priestley to America, 1794–1804* (Philadelphia: University of Pennsylvania Press, 1995).

Graham, John, "Lavater's *Physiognomy* in England," *Journal of the History of Ideas* 22 (1961): 561–72.

——— "Lavater's *Physiognomy* in England: A Checklist," *Papers of the American Bibliographic Society* 55 (1961): 297–308.

Greater London Council, *Survey of London, vol. 35: The Theatre Royal, Drury Lane, and the Royal Opera House, Covent Garden* (Athlone Press, 1970).

Grieder, Theodore, "Annotated Checklist of the British Drama, 1789–99," *Restoration and 18th Century Theatre Research* 4 (1965): 21–47.

Griffin, Patrick, *American Leviathan: Empire, Nation, and Revolutionary Frontier* (New York: Hill and Wang, 2007).

Grimes, Kyle, "Spreading the Radical Word: The Circulation of William Hone's 1817 Liturgical Parodies," *Radicalism and Revolution in Britain, 1775–1848: Essays in Honour of Malcolm I. Thomis*, ed. Michael T. Davis (Houndmills: Palgrave Macmillan, 2000), 143–56.

Guest, Harriet, *Small Change: Women, Learning, Patriotism, 1750–1810* (Chicago: University of Chicago Press, 2000).

——— *Unbounded Attachment: Sentiment and Politics in the Age of the French Revolution* (Oxford: Oxford University Press, 2013).

Habermas, Jürgen, *The Structural Transformation of the Public Sphere: An Inquiry into a Category of Bourgeois Society*, trans. Thomas Burger (Cambridge: Massachusetts Institute of Technology Press, 1989).

Hall, Stuart, "Life and Times of the First New Left," *New Left Review*, no. 61 (January–February 2010): 177–96.

——— "In Defence of Theory," in *People's History and Socialist Theory*, ed. Raphael Samuel (Routledge, 1981), 378–85.

Hammond, J. L. and Barbara, *The Skilled Labourer* (Longmans, 1920).

Hampsher-Monk, Iain, "John Thelwall and the Eighteenth-Century Radical Response to Political Economy," *Historical Journal* 34 (1991): 1–20.

——— "On Not Inventing the English Revolution: The Radical Failure of the 1790s as Linguistic Non-Performance, in English Radicalism, 1550–1850," *English Radicalism, 1550–1850*, ed. Glenn Burgess and Matthew Festenstein (Cambridge: Cambridge University Press, 2009), 135–56.

Hardy, Lesley, "F. R. Leavis, E. P. Thompson and the New Left: Some Shared Critical Responses," *Socialist History* 30 (2007): 1–21.

Harker, Ben, "'Communism is English': Edgell Rickword, Jack Lindsay and the Cultural Politics of the Popular Front," *Literature and History* 20, no. 2 (Autumn 2011): 16–34.

——— "Jack Lindsay's Alienation," *History Workshop Journal* 82 (2016), 83–102.

Harling, Philip, "Leigh Hunt's *Examiner* and the Language of Patriotism," *English Historical Review* 111 (1996): 1159–81.

——— "Robert Southey and the Language of Social Discipline," *Albion* 30 (1999): 630–55.

——— *The Waning of 'Old Corruption': The Politics of Economical Reform in Britain, 1779–1846* (Oxford: Oxford University Press, 1996).

——— "William Hazlitt and Radical Journalism," *Romanticism* 3 (1997): 53–65.

Hartley, Lucy, *Physiognomy and the Means of Expression in Nineteenth-Century Culture* (Cambridge: Cambridge University Press, 2001).

Hay, Douglas, "Property, Authority and the Criminal Law," in *Albion's Fatal Tree: Crime and Society in Eighteenth-Century England*, ed. Douglas Hay, et al. (New York: Pantheon, 1975), 17–63.

Haywood, Ian, "'The Renovating Fury': Southey, Republicanism and Sensationalism," *Romanticism on the Net*, 32–33 (November 2003/February 2004), (https://ronjournal.org/articles/n32-33/).

—— *Romanticism and Caricature* (Cambridge: Cambridge University Press, 2013).

Haywood, Ian and John Seed, eds., *The Gordon Riots: Politics, Culture and Insurrection in late Eighteenth-Century Britain* (Cambridge: Cambridge University Press, 2012).

Helms, Mary, *Ulysses Sail: An Ethnographic Odyssey of Power, Knowledge and Geographical Distance* (Princeton, NJ: Princeton University Press, 1988).

Herzog, Don, *Poisoning the Mind of the Lower Orders* (Princeton, NJ: Princeton University Press, 1998).

Hewitt, Rachael, *A Revolution of Feeling: The Decade that Forged the Modern Mind* (Granta, 2017).

Hibbert, Christopher, *George IV: Regent and King, 1811–1830* (Allen Lane, 1973).

Higonnet, Patrice, *Goodness Beyond Virtue: Jacobins during the French Revolution* (Cambridge, MA: Harvard University Press, 1995).

Hilliard, Christopher, *English as a Vocation: The* Scrutiny *Movement* (Oxford: Oxford University Press, 2012).

Hoadley, F. T., "The Controversy over Southey's *Wat Tyler*," *Studies in Philology* 38 (1941): 81–96.

Hoagland, Terence Allan, "Romantic Drama and Historical Hermeneutics," in *British Romantic Drama: Historical and Critical Essays,* ed. Terence Allen Hoagwood and Daniel P. Watkins (Vancouver, BC: Fairleigh Dickinson University Press, 1998), 22–55.

Hobday, Charles, *Edgell Rickword* (Manchester: Carcanet, 1989).

Hobsbawm, Eric, "The Historians' Group of the Communist Party," in *Rebels and Their Causes: Essays in Honour of A. L. Morton*, ed. Maurice Cornforth (Lawrence and Wishart, 1978), 21–47.

Hoeveler, Diane Long, *Gothic Riffs: Secularizing the Uncanny in the European Imaginary, 1780–1820* (Columbus: Ohio State University Press, 2010).

—— "Illustrating Thomas Holcroft's *A Tale of Mystery* as Physiognomical Tableaux Vivant," in *Re-viewing Thomas Holcroft, 1745–1809*, ed. Miriam L. Wallace and A. A. Markley (Aldershot: Ashgate, 2012), 103–20.

Hogan, Charles Beecher, ed., *The London Stage, 1660–1800: Pt 5: 1776–1800*, 3 vols. (Carbondale: Southern Illinois University Press, 1969).

Hole, Robert, "English Sermons and Tracts as Media of Debate on the French Revolution, 1789–99," in *The French Revolution and British Popular Politics*, ed. Mark Philp (Cambridge: Cambridge University Press, 1991), 18–37.

—— *Pulpits, Politics and Public Order in England, 1760–1832* (Cambridge: Cambridge University Press, 1989).

Holmes, Mrs. Basil, *The London Burial Grounds: Notes on their History from the Earliest Times to the Present Day* (New York, 1896).

Holmes, Richard, *Coleridge: Early Visions, 1772–1804* (New York: Pantheon, 1989).

—— *Shelley: The Pursuit* (New York: New York Review of Books, 1994).

Holt, J. C., *Magna Carta* (Cambridge: Cambridge University Press, 1965).

Hone, J. Ann, *For the Cause of Truth: Radicalism in London, 1796–1821* (Oxford: Oxford University Press, 1982).

—— "William Hone (1780–1842), Publisher, and Bookseller: An Approach to Early 19th Century London Radicalism," *Historical Journal* 16 (1974): 55–70.

Honeyman, Val, "'A Very Dangerous Place'?: Radicalism in Perth in the 1790s," *Scottish Historical Review* 87 (2007): 278–305.

Hughes, Robert, *The Fatal Shore: The Epic of Australia's Founding* (New York: Vintage, 1986).

Humphrey, Kim, "'Objects of Compassion': Young Male Convicts in Van Diemen's Land, 1834–1850," *Australian Historical Studies* 25 (1992): 13–33.

Hunt, Lynn, "Freedom of Dress in the French Revolution," in *From the Royal to the Republican Body: Incorporating the Political in Seventeenth- and Eighteenth-Century France*, ed. Sara E. Melzer and Kathryn Norberg (Berkeley: University of California Press, 1998), 224–49.

—— *Inventing Human Rights, A History* (New York: Norton, 2007).

—— *Politics, Culture, and Class in the French Revolution* (Berkeley: University of California Press, 1984).

Hunt, Lynn and Margaret Jacob, "The Affective Revolution in the 1790s," *Eighteenth-Century Studies* 34 (2001): 491–521.

Hutch, Ronald K. and Paul R. Ziegler, *Joseph Hume: The People's M.P.* (Philadelphia, PA: American Philosophical Society, 1985).

Hynes, Samuel, *The Auden Generation: Literature and Politics in England in the 1930s* (Bodley Head, 1976).

Innes, Joanna, "Managing the Metropolis: London's Social Problems and their Control, c.1660–1830," in *Two Capitals: London and Dublin, 1500–1840*, ed. Peter Clark and Raymond Gillespie (Oxford: Oxford University Press, 2001), 53–80.

——"'Reform' in English Public Life: The Fortunes of a Word," in *Rethinking the Reform Age: Britain 1780–1850*, ed. Arthur Burns and Joanna Innes (Oxford: Oxford University Press, 2003), 71–97.

Israel, Jonathan, *The Expanding Blaze: How the American Revolution Ignited the World, 1775–1848* (Princeton, NJ: Princeton University Press, 2017).

Issitt, John, *Jeremiah Joyce, Radical, Dissenter, and Writer* (Burlington, VT: Ashgate, 2006).

Jager, Colin, "A Poetics of Dissent: Or, Pantisocracy in America," *Theory & Event* 10 (2007): 1–25.

Janowitz, Anne, *Lyric and Labour in the Romantic Tradition* (Cambridge: Cambridge University Press, 1998).

Johnson, Nancy, *The English Jacobin Novel on Rights, Property and the Law: Critiquing the Contract* (New York: Palgrave Macmillan, 2004).

Johnston, Kenneth R., *The Hidden Wordsworth* (New York: Norton, 2002).

—— "The Political Science of Life: From American Pantisocracy to British Romanticism," in *Samuel Taylor Coleridge and the Sciences of Life*, ed. Nicholas Roe (Oxford: Oxford University Press, 2001), 47–68.

—— *Unusual Suspects: Pitt's Reign of Alarm and the Lost Generation of the 1790s* (Oxford: Oxford University Press, 2013).

—— "Wordsworth's *Excursion*: Route and Destination," *Wordsworth Circle* 45 (2014): 106–15.

Jones, Chris, *Radical Sensibility: Literature and Ideas in the 1790s* (Routledge, 1993).

Jones, Kathleen, *A Passionate Sisterhood: The Sisters, Wives and Daughters of the Lake Poets* (Constable, 1998).

Joyce, Patrick, "The Politics of the Liberal Archive," *History of the Human Sciences* 12 (1999): 35–49.

—— *The Rule of Freedom: Liberalism and the Modern City* (Verso, 2003).

Juengel, Scott J., "About Face: Physiognomics, Revolution, and the Radical Act of Looking." Ph.D. diss., University of Iowa, 1997.

—— "Godwin, Lavater, and the Pleasures of Surface," *Studies in Romanticism* 35 (1996): 73–97.

Kapferer, Bruce, "Performance and the Structuring of Meaning and Experience," in *The Anthropology of Experience*, ed. Victor Turner and Edward M. Bruner (Urbana: University of Illinois Press, 1986), 188–203.

Kaplan, Cora, "Black Heroes/White Writers: Toussaint L'Overture and the Literary Imagination," *History Workshop Journal* 46 (1998): 35–62.

Kates, Gary, *The Cercle Social, the Girondins, and the French Revolution* (Princeton, NJ: University of Princeton Press, 1985).

Kavanaugh, Thomas, *Enlightenment and the Shadows of Chance: The Novel and the Culture of Gambling in Eighteenth-Century France* (Baltimore, MD: Johns Hopkins University Press, 1993).

Keach, William, "The Political Poet," in *Cambridge Companion to Shelley*, ed. Timothy Morton (Cambridge: Cambridge, University Press, 2006).

Keane, Angela, *Women Writers and the English Nation in the 1790s: Romantic Belongings* (Cambridge: Cambridge University Press, 2000).

Keen, Paul, *The Crisis of Literature in the 1790s: Print Culture and the Public Sphere* (Cambridge: Cambridge University Press, 1999).

Kelly, Gary, *Revolutionary Feminism: The Mind and Career of Mary Wollstonecraft* (New York: St. Martin's Press, 1992).

—— *Women, Writing, and Revolution, 1790–1827* (Oxford: Oxford University Press, 1993).

Kennedy, Michael L., *The Jacobin Clubs in the French Revolution: The First Years* (Princeton, NJ: Princeton University Press, 1982).

—— *The Jacobin Clubs in the French Revolution: The Middle Years* (Princeton, NJ: Princeton University Press, 1988).

—— *The Jacobin Clubs in the French Revolution: 1793–1795* (New York: Berghahn Books, 2000).

Kenny, Michael, "Socialism and the Romantic 'Self': The Case of Edward Thompson," *Journal of Political Ideologies* 5 (2000): 105–27.

Kercher, Bruce, *Debt, Seduction, & Other Disasters: The Birth of Civil Law in Convict New South Wales* (Alexandria, Australia: Federation Press, 1996).

Kiernan, V. G., "Wordsworth and the People," in *Democracy and the Labour Movement: Essays in Honour of Dona Torr*, ed. John Saville (Lawrence and Wishart, 1954), 240–70.

Kitson, Peter J., Coleridge's Bristol and West Country Radicalism," in *English Romantic Writers and the West Country*, ed. Nicholas Roe (Palgrave Macmillan, 2010), 115–28.

———— "Fictions of Slave Resistance and Revolt: Robert Southey's *Poems on the Slave Trade* (1797) and Charlotte Smith's 'The Story of Henrietta' (1800)," in *Race, Romanticism, and the Atlantic*, ed. Paul Youngquist (Farnham: Ashgate, 2013), 107–23.

———— "'Our Prophetic Harrington': Coleridge, Pantisocracy, and Puritan Utopia," *Wordsworth Circle* 24 (1993): 97–102.

Klancher, Jon, *The Making of English Reading Audiences, 1790–1832* (Madison: University of Wisconsin Press, 1987).

Klaus, Ian, *Forging Capitalism: Rogues, Swindlers, Frauds, and the Rise of Modern Finance* (New Haven, CT: Yale University Press, 2014).

Koselleck, Reinhart, *Futures Past: On the Semantics of Historical Time* (Cambridge: Cambridge University Press, 1985).

Knapp, Mary, *Prologues and Epilogues of the Eighteenth Century* (New Haven, CT: Yale University Press, 1961).

Knight, Frida, *The Strange Case of Thomas Walker: Ten Years in the Life of a Manchester Radical* (Lawrence and Wishart, 1958).

Knowlson, James R., "The Idea of Gesture as a Universal Language in the XVIIth and XVIIIth Centuries," *Journal of the History of Ideas* 26 (1965): 495–508.

Lamb, Robert, "Labour, Contingency, Utility: Thelwall's Theory of Property," in *John Thelwall: Radical Romantic and Acquitted Felon*, ed. Steve Poole (Pickering & Chatto, 2009), 51–60.

Land, Isaac, "'Sinful Propensities': Piracy, Sodomy, and Empire in the Rhetoric of Naval Reform, 1700–1870," in *Discipline and the Other Body: Correction, Corporeality, Colonialism*, ed. Steven Pierce and Anupama Rao (Durham, NC: Duke University Press, 2006), 90–114.

Land, Stephen K., *From Sign to Propositions: The Concept of Form in Eighteenth-Century Semantic Theory* (Longman, 1974).

Lapp, Robert Keith, *Contest for Cultural Authority: Hazlitt, Coleridge, and the Distresses of the Regency* (Detroit, MI: Wayne State University Press, 1999).

Laqueur, Thomas, "Bodies, Death, and Pauper Funerals," *Representations* 1 (1983): 109–31.

———— "Spaces of the Dead," *Ideas from the National Humanities Center* 8 (2001): 3–16.

———— *The Work of the Dead: A Cultural History of Mortal Remains* (Princeton, NJ: Princeton University Press, 2015).

Lawrence, Henry, *City Trees: A Historical Geography from the Renaissance through the Nineteenth Century* (Charlottesville: University of Virginia Press, 2006).

Leask, Nigel, "Irish Republicans and Gothic Eleutherarchs: Pacific Utopias in the Writings of Theobald Wolfe Tone and Charles Brockden Brown," *Huntington Library Quarterly* 63 (2000): 347–67.

———— "Pantisocracy and the Politics of the 'Preface' to *Lyrical Ballads*," in *Reflections of Revolution: Images of Romanticism*, ed. Alison Yarrington and Kelvin Everest (Routledge, 1993), 39–58.

———— *The Politics of Imagination in Coleridge's Critical Thought* (New York: St. Martin's Press, 1988).

——— "Southey's *Madoc*: Reimagining the Conquest of America," in *Robert Southey and the Contexts of English Romanticism*, ed. Lynda Pratt (Aldershot: Ashgate, 2006), 133–50.

——— "Thomas Muir and *The Telegraph*: Radical Cosmopolitanism in 1790s Scotland," *History Workshop Journal* 63 (2007): 48–69.

Leaver, Kristen, "Pursuing Conversations: *Caleb Williams* and the Romantic Constitution of the Reader," *Studies in Romanticism* 33 (1994): 589–610.

Lefebvre, Henri, *Everyday Life in the Modern World*, trans. Sacha Rabinovitch (New York: Harper and Row, 1971).

——— *The Production of Space*, trans. Donald Nicholson-Smith (London: Blackwell, 1991).

LeGette, Casie, *Remaking Romanticism: The Radical Politics of the Excerpt* (Cham: Palgrave Macmillan, 2017).

Levinson, Marjorie, *Wordsworth's Great Period Poems* (Cambridge: Cambridge University Press, 1986).

Lillywhite, Bryant, *London Coffee Houses* (Allen & Unwin, 1963).

Linebaugh, Peter, *Red Round Globe Hot Burning: A Tale at the Crossroads of Commons and Closure, of Love and Terror, of Race and Class, and of Kate and Ned Despard* (Oakland: University of California Press, 2019).

Linebaugh, Peter and Marcus Rediker, *The Many-Headed Hydra: Sailors, Slaves, Commoners, and the Hidden History of the Revolutionary Atlantic* (Boston, MA: Beacon Press, 2000).

Litten, Julien, *The English Way of Death: The Common Funeral since 1450* (Robert Hall, 2002).

Litto, Frederic M., "Addison's *Cato* in the Colonies," *William and Mary Quarterly* 23 (1966): 431–49.

Liu, Alan, *Wordsworth: The Sense of History* (Stanford, CA: Stanford University Press, 1989).

——— "Wordsworth and Subversion, 1793–1804: Trying Cultural Criticism," *Yale Journal of Criticism* 2 (1989): 55–100.

Lobban, Michael, "Treason, Sedition and the Radical Movement in the Age of Revolution," *Liverpool Law Review* 22 (2000): 205–34.

Loftis, John, "Political and Social Thought in the Drama," in *The London Theatre World, 1660–1800*, ed. Robert D. Hume (Carbondale: Southern Illinois University Press, 1980), 253–85.

Lottes, Günther, "Radicalism, Revolution and Political Culture: An Anglo-French Comparison," in *The French Revolution and British Popular Politics*, ed. Mark Philp (Cambridge: Cambridge University Press, 1991), 78–98.

Lovell, Terry, "Resisting with Authority: Historical Specificity, Agency and the Performative Self," *Theory, Culture and Society* 20 (2003): 1–17.

Lowenthal, David, *The Past Is a Foreign Country* (Cambridge: Cambridge University Press, 1985).

McCalman, Iain, "The Infidel as Prophet: William Hamilton Reid and Blakean Radicalism," in *Historicizing Blake*, ed. Steve Clark and David Worrall (Macmillan, 1994), 24–42.

——— "Newgate in Revolution: Radical Enthusiasm and Romantic Counterculture," *Eighteenth-Century Life* 22 (1998): 95–110.

——— "New Jerusalems: Prophecy, Dissent and Radical Culture in England, 1786–1830," in *Enlightenment and Religion: Rational Dissent in*

Eighteenth-Century Britain, ed. Knud Haakonssen (Cambridge: Cambridge University Press, 1996), 312–35.

—— *Radical Underworld: Prophets, Revolutionaries and Pornographers in London, 1793–1840* (Cambridge: Cambridge University Press, 1988).

—— "Ultra-Radicalism and Convivial Debating-Clubs in London, 1795–1838," *English Historical Review* 102 (1987): 309–33.

McCann, Andrew, *Cultural Politics in the 1790s: Literature, Radicalism and the Public Sphere* (Houndmills: Palgrave Macmillan, 1999).

McClintock, Anne, *Imperial Leather: Race, Gender, and Sexuality in the Colonial Contest* (Routledge, 1995).

Mace, Rodney. *Trafalgar Square: Emblem of Empire* (Lawrence & Wishart, 1976).

McFarland, Elaine W., "Scottish Radicalism in the later Eighteenth Century: 'The Social Thistle and Shamrock,'" in *Eighteenth Century Scotland: New Perspectives*, ed. T. M. Devine and J. R. Young (East Linton: Tuckwell Press, 1999), 275–98.

McGann, Jerome J., *The Romantic Ideology: A Critical Investigation* (Chicago, IL: University of Chicago Press, 1983).

MacGillivray, J. R., "The Pantisocracy Scheme and Its Immediate Background," in *Studies in English* (Toronto: University of Toronto, 1931), 131–69.

McIlroy, John, "Another Look at E. P. Thompson and British Communism, 1937–1955," *Labor History* 58 (2017): 506–39.

McKellar, Elizabeth, "Peripheral Visions: Alternative Aspects and Rural Presences in Mid-Eighteenth-Century London," in *The Metropolis and its Image: Constructing Identitiesfor London, c.1750–1950*, ed. Dana Arnold (Oxford: Blackwell, 1999), 29–47.

MacKenzie, John, *Imperialism and Popular Culture* (Manchester: Manchester University Press, 1998).

McKusick, James C., "'Wisely Forgetful': Coleridge and the Politics of Pantisocracy," in *Romanticism and Colonialism: Writing and Empire, 1780–1830*, ed. Tim Fulford and Peter J. Kitson (Cambridge: Cambridge University Press, 1998), 107–28.

McLaren, John, "'The Judicial Office...Bowing to No Pressure but the Supremacy of the Law': Judges and the Rule of Law in Colonial Australia and Canada, 1788–1840," *Australian Journal of the Society of Legal History* 7 (2003): 177–92.

Macleod, Emma, "British Radical Attitudes towards the United States of America in the 1790 Case of William Winterbotham," in *Liberty, Property and Popular Politics England and Scotland, 1688–1815: Essays in Honour of H. T. Dickinson*, ed. Gordon Pentland and Michael T. Davis (Edinburgh: Edinburgh University Press, 2016), 149–62.

—— *British Visions of America, 1775–1820* (Pickering & Chatto, 2013).

——"Civil Liberties and Baptists: William Winterbotham of Plymouth in Prison and Thinking of America," *Baptist Quarterly* 44 (2011): 196–222.

—— "The English and Scottish State Trials of the 1790s Compared," in *Political Trials in the Age of Revolutions: Britain and the North Atlantic, 1793–1848*, ed. Michael T. Davis, Emma Macleod, and Gordon Pentland (Cham: Palgrave Macmillan, 2019), 79–108.

McPhee, Peter, *Liberty or Death: The French Revolution* (New Haven, CT: Yale University Press, 2016).

McPherson, Heather, "Theatrical Riots and Cultural Politics in Eighteenth-Century London," *Eighteenth Century: Theory and Interpretation* 43 (2003): 236–52.

McWilliam, Rohan, *The Tichborne Claimant: A Victorian Sensation* (Hambledon Continuum, 2007).

Maertz, Gregory, "The Transmission of German Literature and Dissenting Voices in British Culture: Thomas Holcroft and the Godwin Circle," in *1650–1850: Ideas, Aesthetics, and Inquiries in the Early-Modern Era*, ed. Kevin L. Cope and Laura Morrow (New York: AMS Press, 1997), 271–300.

Mahoney, Charles, *Romantics and Renegades: The Poetics of Political Reaction* (Houndmills: Palgrave Macmillan, 2003).

Makdisi, Saree, *Making England Western: Occidentalism, Race & Imperial Culture* (Chicago, IL: University of Chicago Press, 2014).

Malone, Dumas, *The Public Life of Thomas Cooper, 1783–1839* (New Haven, CT: Yale University Press, 1926).

Manogue, Ralph A., "James Ridgway and America," *Early American Literature* 31 (1996): 264–88.

——— "The Plight of James Ridgway, London Bookseller and Publisher, and the Newgate Radicals, 1792–1797," *Wordsworth Circle* 27 (1996): 158–66.

——— "Southey and Winterbotham: New Light on an Old Quarrel," *Journal of the Charles Lamb Society*, new series, 38 (1982): 105–14.

Markley, A. A., "Aristocrats Behaving Badly: Gambling and Dueling in the 1790s Novel of Reform," *European Romantic Review* 17: 161–68.

——— "Transforming Experience into Reform in Holcroft's *Memoirs*," in *Re-viewing Thomas Holcroft, 1745–1809*, ed. Miriam L. Wallace and A. A. Markley (Aldershot: Ashgate, 2012), 181–95.

Marinis, Marco De, "The Dramaturgy of the Spectator," *The Drama Review* 31 (1986): 100–14.

Marsh, Joss, *Word Crimes: Blasphemy, Culture, and Literature in Nineteenth-Century England* (Chicago, IL: University of Chicago Press, 1998).

Marshall, David, "Adam Smith and the Theatricality of Moral Sentiments," *Critical Inquiry* 10 (1984): 592–613.

——— *The Figure of Theater: Shaftesbury, Defoe, Adam Smith, and George Eliot* (New York: Columbia University Press, 1986).

Marshall, Peter, *William Godwin* (New Haven, CT: Yale University Press, 1984).

Marshall, P. J. and Glyndwr Williams, *The Great Map of Mankind: Perceptions of New Worlds in the Age of the Enlightenment* (Cambridge, MA: Harvard University Press, 1982).

Massey, Doreen, "Politics and Space/Time," in *Place and the Politics of Identity*, ed. Michael Keith and Steve Pile (Routledge, 1993), 141–61.

Masterman, Charles F. G., ed., *The Heart of the Empire: Discussions of Problems of Modern City Life in England, with an Essay on Imperialism* (T.F. Unwin, 1901).

Matheson, Lister M., "The Peasants' Revolt through Five Centuries of Rumor and Reporting: Richard Fox, John Stow, and Their Successors," *Studies in Philology*, 95 (1998): 121–51.

Mattes, Armin, "Paine, Jefferson, and the Modern Ideas of Democracy and the Nation," in *Paine and Jefferson in the Age of Revolutions*, ed. Simon

P. Newman and Peter S. Onuf (Charlottesville: University of Virginia Press, 2013), 95–117.

Matthews,Wade, *The New Left, National Identity, and the Break-Up of Britain* (Chicago: Haymarket Books, 2014).

Mee, Jon, "'A Bold and Outspoken Man': The Strange Case of Charles Pigott II," in *Cultures of Whiggism: New Essays on English Literature and Culture in the Long Eighteenth Century*, ed. David Womersley (Newark: University of Delaware Press, 2005), 330–50.

———— *Conversable Worlds: Literature, Contention, and Community 1762 to 1830* (Oxford: Oxford University Press, 2011).

———— *Dangerous Enthusiasm: William Blake and the Culture of Radicalism in the 1790s* (Oxford: Oxford University Press, 1992).

———— "The Dungeon and the Cell: The Prison Verse of Coleridge and Thelwall," in *John Thelwall: Radical Romantic and Acquitted Felon*, ed. Steve Poole (Pickering & Chatto, 2009), 107–16.

———— "'Examples of Safe Printing': Censorship and Popular Radical Literature in the 1790s," in *Literature and Censorship*, ed. Nigel Smith (D. S. Brewer, 1993), 81–95.

———— "Libertines and Radicals in the 1790s: The Strange Case of Charles Pigott I," in *Libertine Enlightenment: Sex, Liberty and License in the Eighteenth Century*, ed. Peter Cryle and Lisa O'Connell (Houndmills: Palgrave, 2004), 183–203.

———— "Morals, Manners, and Liberty: British Radicals and Perceptions of American in the 1790s." *The American Experiment and the Idea of Democracy in British Culture, 1776–1914*, ed. Ella Dzelzainis and Ruth Livesey (Farnham: Ashgate, 2013), 31–41.

———— "The Political Showman at Home: Reflections on Popular Radicalism and Print Culture in the 1790s," in *Radicalism and Revolution in Britain, 1775–1848: Essays in Honour of Malcolm I. Thomis*, ed. Michael T. Davis (Houndmills: Palgrave Macmillan, 2000), 41–55.

———— "'The Press and Danger of the Crowd': Godwin, Thelwall, and the Counter-Public Sphere," in *Godwinian Moments: From Enlightenment to Romanticism*, ed. Robert M. Maniquis and Victoria Meyers (Toronto: University of Toronto Press, 2011), 83–102.

———— *Print, Publicity, and Popular Radicalism in the 1790s*: The Laurel of Liberty (Cambridge: Cambridge University Press, 2016).

———— *Romanticism, Enthusiasm, and Regulation: Poetics and the Policing of Culture in the Romantic Period* (Oxford: Oxford University Press, 2002).

Mee, Jon and Mark Crosby, "'This Soldierlike Danger': The Trial of William Blake for Sedition," in *Resisting Napoleon: The British Response to the Threat of Invasion, 1797–1815*, ed. Mark Philp (Aldershot: Ashgate, 2006), 111–24.

Meikle, Henry W., *Scotland and the French Revolution* (Glasgow: J. Maclehose and Son, 1912).

Mellor, Anne K., *Mothers of the Nation: Women's Political Writing in England, 1780–1830* (Bloomington: Indiana University Press, 2000).

Mendelson, Edward, *Early Auden* (New York: Viking Press, 1981).

Midgley, Clare, *Women against Slavery: The British Campaigns, 1780–1870* (Routledge, 1992).

Middleton, Stuart, "The Concept of 'Experience' and the Making of the English Working Class, 1924–1963," *Modern Intellectual History* 13 (2016): 179–208.

——— "E. P. Thompson and the Cultural Politics of Literary Modernism," *Contemporary British History* 28, no. 4 (September 2011): 16–34.

Miller, N. C., "John Cartwright and Radical Parliamentary Reform, 1808–1819," *English Historical Review* 83 (1968): 705–28.

Moody, Jane, *Illegitimate Theater in London, 1770–1840* (Cambridge: Cambridge University Press, 2000).

Mori, Jennifer, "Responses to Revolution: The November Crisis of 1792," *Historical Research* 69 (1996): 284–305.

——— *William Pitt and the French Revolution, 1785–1795* (Edinburgh: Keele University Press, 1997).

Morris, Marilyn, "Princely Debt, Public Credit, and Commercial Values in Late Georgian Britain," *Journal of British Studies* 43 (2004): 339–65.

Morrow, John, *Coleridge's Political Thought: Property, Morality and the Limits of Traditional Discourse* (New York: St. Martin's Press, 1990).

Morton, Timothy, *The Poetics of Spice: Romantic Consumerism and the Exotic* (Cambridge: Cambridge University Press, 2000).

Mulhern, Francis, *The Moment of 'Scrutiny'* (Verso, 1979).

Nachumi, Nora, "'Those Simple Signs': The Performance of Emotion in Elizabeth Inchbald's *A Simple Story*," *Eighteenth-Century Fiction* 11 (1999): 317–38.

Navickas, Katrina, *Loyalism and Radicalism in Lancashire, 1798–1815* (Oxford: Oxford University Press, 2009).

——— "Moors, Fields, and Popular Protest in South Lancashire and the West Riding of Yorkshire, 1800–1848," *Northern History* 46 (March 2009): 93–111.

——— *Protest and the Politics of Space and Place* (Manchester: Manchester University Press, 2016).

——— "'A Reformer's Wife ought to be an Heroine': Imprisoned under the Suspension of Habeas Corpus Act," *History*, (2016): 246–64.

——— "The 'Spirit of Loyalty': Material Culture, Space and the Construction of an English Loyalist Memory, 1790–1840," in *Loyalism and the Formation of the British World, 1775–1914*, ed. Allan Blackstock and Frank O'Gorman (Woodbridge: Boydell Press, 2014): 43–60.

Nead, Lynda, "Mapping the Self: Gender, Space, and Modernity in Mid-Victorian London," in *Rewriting the Self: Histories from the Renaissance to the Present*, ed. Roy Porter (Routledge, 1997), 167–85.

Neal, David, *The Rule of Law in a Penal Colony: Law and Power in Early New South Wales* (Cambridge: Cambridge University Press, 1991).

Newman, Ian, "Civilizing Taste: 'Sandman Joe,' the Bawdy Ballad, and Metropolitan Improvement," *Eighteenth-Century Studies* 48 (2015): 437–56.

Newman, Michael, "Thompson and the Early New Left," in *E. P. Thompson and English Radicalism*, ed. Roger Fieldhouse and Richard Taylor (Manchester: Manchester University Press, 2013), 158–80.

Nielsen, Caroline Louise, "The Chelsea Out-Pensioners: Image and Reality in Eighteenth-Century and Early Nineteenth-Century Social Care." PhD. thesis, Newcastle University, 2014.

———— "Continuing to Serve: Representations of the Elderly Veteran Soldier in the late Eighteenth and early Nineteenth Centuries," in *Men after War*, ed. Stephen McVeigh and Nicola Cooper (Routledge, 2013), 18–35.

Nilson, Micheline, *Railways and the Western European Capitals: Studies of Implantation in London, Paris, Berlin, and Brussels* (New York: Palgrave McMillan, 2008).

Nora, Pierre, "Between Memory and History: *le Lieux de Mémoire*," trans. Marc Roudebush, *Representations* 26 (1989): 7–24.

O'Brien, Eliza, "'The Greatest Appearance of Truth': Telling Tales with Thomas Holcroft," *Eighteenth-Century Fiction* 28 (2016): 501–26.

O'Brian, John, *Harlequin Britain: Pantomime and Entertainment, 1690–1760* (Baltimore, MD: Johns Hopkins University Press, 2004).

Ogborn, Miles, *Spaces of Modernity: London's Geographies, 1680–1780* (New York: Guilford Press, 1998).

O'Gorman, Frank, "The Paine Burnings of 1792–1793," *Past and Present* 193 (2006): 111–55.

———— "Pitt and the 'Tory' Reaction to the French Revolution and the French Wars, 1789–1815," in *Britain and the French Revolution, 1789–1815*, ed. H. T. Dickinson (New York: St. Martin's Press, 1989), 21–37.

Oldham, James, *The Mansfield Manuscripts and the Growth of English Law in the Eighteenth Century*, 2 vols. (Chapel Hill: University of North Carolina Press, 1992).

O'Neale, John C., *The Authority of Experience: Sensationist Theory in the French Enlightenment* (University Park: Penn State Press, 1996).

O'Neill, Michael, "'Pictures' and 'Signs': Creative Thinking in Shelley's Prose, 1816–21," in *Thinking through Style: Non-Fiction Prose of the Long Nineteenth Century*, ed. Michael D. Hurley and Marcus Waithe (Oxford: Oxford University Press, 2018), 70–86.

Onuf, Peter S., *Jefferson's Empire: The Language of American Nationhood* (Charlottesville: University of Virginia Press, 2000).

O'Quinn, Daniel, "Bread: The Eruption and Interruption of Politics in Elizabeth Inchbald's *Every One Has His Fault*," *European Romantic Review* 18 (2007): 149–57.

O'Shaughnessy, David, *William Godwin and the Theatre* (Pickering & Chatto, 2010).

Palmer, Bryan D., *E. P. Thompson: Objections and Oppositions* (Verso, 1994).

Park, Mary Cathryne, "Joseph Priestley and the Problem of Pantisocracy," *Proceedings of the Delaware County Institute of Science* 11 (1947): 1–60.

Parolin, Christina, *Radical Spaces: Venues of Popular Politics in London, 1790 – c. 1845* (Canberra: Australian National University E Press, 2010).

Parson, T. G., "Was John Boston's Pig a Political Martyr? The Reaction to Popular Radicalism in Early New South Wales," *Journal of the Royal Australian Historical Society* 71 (1986): 163–76.

Parssinen, T. M., "Association, Convention and Anti-Parliament in British Politics, 1771–1848," *English Historical Review* 88 (1973): 504–33.

———— "The Revolutionary Party in London, 1816–20," *Bulletin of the Institute of Historical Research* 45 (1972): 266–82.

Pauley, Benjamin, "'Far from the Consummate Lawyer': William Godwin and the Treason Trials of the 1790s," in *Reactions to Revolutions: The 1790s and Their Aftermath*, ed. Ulrich Broich, et al. (Berlin: LIT Verlag, 2007), 203–30.

Pearl, Sharonna, *About Faces: Physiognomy in Nineteenth-Century Britain* (Cambridge: Cambridge University Press, 2010).

Pentland, Gordon, "The French Revolution, Scottish Radicalism and the 'People Who were Called Jacobins,'" in *Reactions to Revolution: The 1790s and their Aftermath*, ed. Ulrich Broich, et al. (Berlin: LIT Verlag, 2007), 85–108.

——— "Militarization and Collective Action in Great Britain, 1815–20," in *Crowd Actions in Britain and France from the Middle Ages to the Modern World*, ed. Michael T. Davis (Houndmills: Palgrave Macmillan, 2015), 179–92.

——— "Patriotism, Universalism and the Scottish Conventions, 1792–1794," *History* 89 (2004): 340–60.

——— "The Posthumous Lives of Thomas Muir," in *Liberty, Property and Popular Politics: England and Scotland 1688–1815: Essays in Honour of H.T. Dickinson*, ed. Gordon Pentland and Michael T. Davis (Edinburgh: Edinburgh University Press, 2015).

——— "Radical Returns in an Age of Revolution: Maurice Margarot, Thomas McFarlane and Andrew White," *Etudes Ecossaises* 13 (2010): 91–102.

——— *The Spirit of Union: Popular Politics in Scotland, 1815–1820* (Pickering & Chatto, 2011).

Philp, Mark, "Introduction: The British Response to the Threat of Invasion, 1797–1815," in *Resisting Napoleon: The British Response to the Threat of Invasion, 1797–1815* (Aldershot: Ashgate, 2006), 1–17.

——— "Rational Religion and Political Radicalism," *Enlightenment and Dissent* 4 (1985): 35–46.

——— *Reforming Ideas in Britain: Politics and Language in the Shadow of the French Revolution, 1789–1815* (Cambridge: Cambridge University Press, 2014).

——— "Representing America: Paine and the New Democracy," in *The American Experiment and the Idea of Democracy in British Culture, 1776–1914*, ed. Ella Dzelzainis and Ruth Livesey (Farnham: Ashgate, 2013), 15–29.

——— "The Role of America in the 'Debate on France' 1791–5: Thomas Paine's Insertion," *Utilitas* 5 (1993): 221–37.

———"Talking about Democracy: Britain in the 1790s," in *Re-Imagining Democracy in the Age of Revolutions: America, France, Britain, Ireland 1750–1850*, ed. Joanna Innes and Mark Philp (Cambridge: Cambridge University Press, 2013), 101–13.

——— "Thompson, Godwin, and the French Revolution," *History Workshop Journal* 39 (1995): 91–101.

Phillipson, Nicholas, "The Scottish Enlightenment," in *The Enlightenment in National Context*, ed. Roy Porter and Mikuláš Tiech (Cambridge: Cambridge University Press, 1981), 19–40.

Pickering, Paul, "Betrayal and Exile: A Forgotten Chartist Experience," in *Unrespectable Radicals: Popular Politics in the Age of Reform*, ed. Michael T. Davis and Paul Pickering (Aldershot: Ashgate, 2008), 201–17.

——— "'Confound Their Politics': The Political Uses of 'God Save the King-Queen,'" in *Cheap Print and Popular Song in the Nineteenth Century: A Cultural History of the Songster*, ed. Paul Watt, Derek B. Scott, and Patrick Spedding (Cambridge: Cambridge University Press, 2017), 112–37.

Pincus, Steve, "'Coffee Politicians Does Create': Coffeehouses and Restoration Political Culture," *Journal of Modern History* 67 (1995): 807–34.

Plamper, Jan, *The History of the Emotions: An Introduction*, trans. Keith Tribe (Oxford: Oxford University Press, 2015).

Plummer, Alfred, *Bronterre: A Political Biography of Bronterre O'Brien, 1804–1864* (Allen and Unwin, 1971).

Poole, Robert, "French Revolution or Peasants' Revolt? Petitioners and Rebels in England from the Blanketeers to the Chartists," *Labour History Review*, 74 (2009): 6–26.

—— *Peterloo: The English Uprising* (Oxford: Oxford University Press, 2019).

—— "The Risings of 1817," Luddite Memorial Lecture, Huddersfield Local History Society, 21 April 2016, https://www.huddersfieldhistory.org.uk/events/luddite%20lecture/.

Poole, Steve, "'Not Precedents to be Followed but Examples to be Weighed': John Thelwall and the Jacobin Sense of the Past," in *John Thelwall: Radical Romantic and Acquitted Felon*, ed. Steve Poole (Pickering & Chatto, 2009), 161–73.

—— "Pitt's Terror Reconsidered: Jacobinism and the Law in Two South-Western Counties, 1791–1803," *Southern History* 17 (1995): 63–87.

—— "The Politics of Protest Heritage, 1790–1850," in *Remembering Protest in Britain since 1500: Memory, Materiality and the Landscape*, ed. Carl J. Griffin and Briony McDonagh (Cham: Palgrave Macmillan, 2018), 187–213.

—— *The Politics of Regicide in England, 1760–1850* (Manchester: Manchester University Press, 2000).

Poole, Steve and Nicholas Rogers, *Bristol from Below: Law, Authority and Protest in a Georgian City* (Woodbridge: The Boydell Press, 2017).

Pocock, J. G. A., *Virtue, Commerce, and History: Essays in Political Thought and History* (Cambridge: Cambridge University Press, 1985).

Porter, Roy, "The Enlightenment in England," in *The Enlightenment in National Context*, ed. Roy Porter and Mikuláš Tiech (Cambridge: Cambridge University Press, 1981).

Pratt, Lynda, "Patriot Politics and the Romantic National Epic: Placing and Displacing Southey's *Joan of Arc*," in *Placing and Displacing Romanticism*, ed. Peter J. Kitson (Aldershot: Ashgate, 2001), 88–105.

Priestman, Martin, "A Place to Stand: Questions of Address in Shelley's Political Pamphlets," in *The Unfamiliar Shelley*, ed. Alan M. Weinberg and Timothy Webb (Farnham: Ashgate, 2009), 221–38.

Prothero, Iorwerth, *Artisans and Politics in Early Nineteenth-Century London: John Gast and His Times* (Baton Rouge: Louisiana State University Press, 1979).

Queiroz, Juan Manuel de, "The Sociology of Everyday Life as a Perspective," *Current Sociology* 37 (Spring 1989): 31–39.

Rabin, Dana, "Drunkenness and Responsibility for Crime in the Eighteenth Century," *Journal of British Studies* 44 (2005): 457–77.

Raimond, Jean, "Southey's Early Writings and Revolution," *Yearbook of English Studies* 19 (1989): 181–95.

Raven, James, "New Reading Histories, Print Culture and the Identification of Change: The Case of Eighteenth-Century England," *Social History* 23 (1998): 268–87.

Randall, Adrian, *Riotous Assemblies: Popular Protest in Hanoverian England* (Oxford: Oxford University Press, 2006).

Reddy, William M. *The Navigation of Feeling: A Framework for the History of the Emotions* (Cambridge: Cambridge University Press, 2001).

Regis, Pamela, *Describing Early America: Bartram, Jefferson, Crèvecoeur, and the Rhetoric of Natural History* (DeKalb: Northern Illinois University Press, 1992).

Riding, Jacqueline, *Peterloo: The Story of the Manchester Massacre* (Head of Zeus Ltd., 2018).

Roach, Joseph, *Cities of the Dead: Circum-Atlantic Performance* (New York: Columbia University Press, 1996).

——— *The Players Passion: Studies in the Science of Acting* (Ann Arbor: University of Michigan Press, 1985).

Roberts, Matthew, *Chartism, Commemoration, and the Cult of the Radical Hero* (Routledge, 2020).

——— "Chartism, Commemoration and the Cult of the Radical Hero, c.1770-c.1840," *Labour History Review* 78 (2013): 3–32.

Robertson, Fiona, "British Romantic Columbiads," *Symbiosis: A Journal of Anglo-American Literary Relations* 2 (1998): 1–23.

Roe, Michael, "Maurice Margarot: A Radical in Two Hemispheres," *Bulletin of the Institute of Historical Research* 31 (1958): 68–78.

——— *Kenealy and the Tichborne Cause: A Study in Mid-Victorian Populism* (Melbourne: Melbourne University Press, 1974).

Roe, Nicholas, *Fiery Heart: The First Life of Leigh Hunt* (New York: Random House, 2005).

——— "The Lives of John Thelwall: Another View of the 'Jacobin Fox,'" in *John Thelwall: Radical Romantic and Acquitted Felon*, ed. Steve Poole (Pickering & Chatto, 2009), 13–24.

——— *The Politics of Nature: William Wordsworth and Some Contemporaries*, 2nd ed. (Houndmills: Palgrave Macmillan, 2002).

——— *Wordsworth and Coleridge: The Radical Years* (Oxford: Oxford University Press, 1988). Rogan, Tim, *The Moral Economists: R. H. Tawney, Karl Polanyi, E. P. Thompson, and the Critique of Capitalism* (Princeton, NJ: Princeton University Press, 2017).

Rogers, Nicholas, "Burning Tom Paine: Loyalism and Counter-Revolution in Britain, 1792–1793," *Histoire Sociale/Social History* 2 (1999): 139–71.

——— "Crowds and Political Festival in Georgian England," in *The Politics of the Excluded, c.1500–1850*, ed. Tim Harris (New York: Palgrave Macmillan, 2001), 233–64.

——— *Crowds, Culture, and Politics in Georgian Britain* (Oxford: Oxford University Press, 1998).

——— "Pigott's Private Eye: Radicalism and Sexual Scandal in Eighteenth-Century England," *Journal of the Canadian Historical Association/Revue de la Société Historique Canadienne* 4 (1993): 247–63.

Rogers, Rachel, "The Society of the Friends of the Rights of Man, 1792–94: British and Irish Radical Conjunctions in Republican Paris," *La Révolution française* 11 (2016), https://journals.openedition.org/lrf/1629.

——— "Vectors of Revolution: The British Radical Community in Early Republican Paris, 1792–1794." PhD. thesis, Université Toulouse le Mirail, 2013.

Rose, R. B., "The Priestley Riots of 1791," *Past and Present* 18 (1960): 66–88.

Rosenfeld, Sophia, "Citizens of Nowhere in Particular: Cosmopolitanism, Writing, and Political Engagement in Eighteenth-Century Europe," *National Identities* 4 (2002): 25–43.

—— *A Revolution in Language*: *The Problem of Signs in Late Eighteenth-Century France* (Stanford, CA: Stanford University Press, 2001).

—— "Thinking about Feeling, 1789–1799," *French Historical Studies* 32 (2009): 697–706.

Rosenwein, Barbara H., "Problems and Methods in the History of the Emotions: Passions in Context," *International Journal of History and Theory of the Emotions* 1 (2010): 1–25.

—— "Worrying about Emotions in History," *American Historical Review* 107 (2002): 821–45.

Rothschild, Emma, *Economic Sentiments: Adam Smith, Condorcet, and the Enlightenment* (Cambridge, MA: Harvard University Press, 2001).

Rousseau, G.S., "John Hill: Universal Genius *Manqué*: Remarks on His Life and Times, with a Checklist of His Works," in J.A. Leo Lemay and G. S. Rousseau *The Renaissance Man in the Eighteenth Century* (Los Angeles, CA: Clark Memorial Library, 1978), 49–95.

Rowe, D. J., "Francis Place and the Historian," *Historical Journal* 16 (1973): 45–63.

Russell, Gillian, "Burke's Dagger: Theatricality, Politics and Print Culture in the 1790s," *British Journal for Eighteenth-Century Studies* 20 (1997).

—— "'Faro's Daughters': Female Gamesters, Politics, and the Discourse of Finance in 1790s Britain," *Eighteenth-Century Studies* 33 (2000): 481–504.

—— "Spouters or Washerwomen: The Sociability of Romantic Lecturing," in *Romantic Sociability: Social Networks and Literary Culture in Britain, 1770–1840*, ed. Gillian Russell and Clara Tuite (Cambridge: Cambridge University Press, 2002), 123–44.

—— *The Theatres of War: Performance, Politics and Society, 1793–1815* (Oxford: Oxford University Press. 1995).

Russell, Gillian and Clara Tuite, eds., *Romantic Sociability: Social Networks and Literary Culture in Britain, 1770–1840* (Cambridge: Cambridge University Press, 2002).

Sack, James J., *From Jacobite to Conservative: Reaction and Orthodoxy in Britain, c. 1760–1832* (Cambridge: Cambridge University Press, 1993).

Said, Edward, *Convergences: Inventories of the Present* (Cambridge, MA: Harvard University Press, 2000).

St Clair, William, *The Godwins and the Shelleys: The Biography of a Family* (Faber and Faber, 1989).

—— *The Reading Nation in the Romantic Period* (Cambridge: Cambridge University Press, 2004).

Samuel, Raphael, "British Marxist Historians, 1880–1980: Part One," *New Left Review*, 120 (March–April 1980): 21–96.

—— ed., *Patriotism and the Making and Unmaking of British National Identity*, 3 vols. (Routledge, 1989).

Sanders, Mike, *The Poetry of Chartism: Aesthetics, Politics, History* (Cambridge: Cambridge University Press, 2009).

Satia, Priya, "Bryon, Gandhi and the Thompsons: The Making of British Social History and the Unmaking of Indian History," *History Workshop Journal* 81 (2016): 135–70.

Saville, John, "The Twentieth Congress and the British Communist Party," *Socialist Register, 1976*, ed. Ralph Miliband and John Saville (Merlin Press, 1976), 1–23.

Schor, Esther, *Bearing the Dead: The British Culture of Mourning from the Enlightenment to Victoria* (Princeton, NJ: Princeton University Press, 1994).

Schneer, Jonathan, *London 1900: The Imperial Metropolis* (New Haven, CT: Yale University Press, 1999).

Schoyen, A. R., *The Chartist Challenge: A Portrait of George Julian Harney* (Heinemann, 1958).

Schwarz, Bill, "'The People' in History: The Communist Party Historians' Group, 1946–56," in *Making Histories: Studies in History-Writing and Politics,* ed. Richard Johnson, et al. (Hutchinson, 1982), 44–95.

Scott-Brown, Sophie, *The Histories of Raphael Samuel: A Portrait of a People's Historian* (Acton, ACT: Australian National University Press, 2017).

Scrivener, Michael H., *The Cosmopolitan Ideal in the Age of Revolution and Reaction, 1776–1832* (Pickering & Chatto, 2007).

——— "E. P. Thompson and Romantic Radicalism," *Wordsworth Circle* 37 (2006): 52–56.

——— "John Thelwall's Political Ambivalence: Reform and Revolution," in *Radicalism and Revolution in Britain, 1775–1848: Essays in Honour of Malcolm I. Thomis,* ed. Michael T. Davis (Houndmills: Palgrave Macmillan, 2000), 69–83.

——— *Radical Shelley: The Philosophical Anarchism and Utopian Thought of Percy Bysshe Shelley* (Princeton, NJ: Princeton University Press, 1982).

——— *Seditious Allegories: John Thelwall and Jacobin Writing* (University Park: Pennsylvania State University Press, 2001).

Searby, Peter, John Rule, and Robert Malcolmson, "Edward Thompson as a Teacher: Yorkshire and Warwick," in *Protest and Survival: Essays for E. P. Thompson,* ed. John Rule and Robert Malcolmson (Merlin Press, 1993), 1–17.

Seed, John, "'A Set of Men Powerful Enough in Many Things': Rational Dissent and Political Opposition in England, 1770–1790," in *Enlightenment and Religion: Rational Dissent in Eighteenth-Century Britain,* ed. Knud Haakonssen (Cambridge: Cambridge University Press, 1996), 14–66.

Sennett, Richard, *The Fall of Public Man: On the Social Psychology of Capitalism* (New York: Vintage Books, 1978).

Sessler Randall A., "Print Takes the Stage: The 'Great Engine' of Literature, 'Invidious Practices,' and British Romantic Theatre," *Nineteenth-Century Contexts* 32 (2017): 105–16.

Sewell, William, Jr., "The Concept of Culture(s)," in *Beyond the Cultural Turn: New Directions in the Study of Society and Culture,* ed. Victorian E. Bonnell and Lynn Hunt (Berkeley: University of California Press, 1999), 35–61.

——— "Space in Contentious Politics," in *Silence and Voice in the Study of Contentious Politics,* ed. Ronald R. Aminzade, et al. (Cambridge: Cambridge University Press, 2001), 51–88.

——— *Work and Revolution in France: The Language of Labor from the Old Regime to 1848* (Cambridge: Cambridge University Press, 1980).

Shapin, Steven, *A Social History of the Truth: Civility and Science in Seventeenth-Century England* (Chicago, IL: University of Chicago Press, 1994).

Sheps, Arthur, "The American Revolution and the Transformation of English Radicalism," *Historical Reflections/Réflexions Historiques* 2 (1975): 3–28.

Sher, Richard B., *The Enlightenment and the Book: Scottish Authors and Their Publishers in Eighteenth-Century Britain, Ireland, and America* (Chicago: University of Chicago Press, 2006).

Shields, David S., *Civil Tongues and Polite Letters in British America* (Chapel Hill: University of North Carolina Press, 1997).

Shoemaker, Robert, *The London Mob: Violence and Disorder in Eighteenth-Century England* (Hambledon, 2004).

—— "Male Honour and the Decline of Public Violence in Eighteenth-Century London," *Social History* 26 (2001): 190–208.

Short, L. Baker, "Thomas Fyshe Palmer: From Eton to Botany Bay," *Transactions of the Unitarian Historical Society* 13 (2) (1964): 37–49.

Simpson, David, *Romanticism, Nationalism, and the Revolt against Theory* (Chicago, IL: Chicago University Press, 1993).

Sinha, Mrinalini, "Britishness, Clubbability, and the Colonial Public Sphere: The Genealogy of an Imperial Institution in Colonial India," *Journal British Studies* 40 (2001): 489–521.

Smith, Olivia, *The Politics of Language, 1791–1819* (Oxford: Oxford University Press, 1984).

Smyser, Jane Worthington, "The Trial and Imprisonment of Joseph Johnson, Bookseller," *Bulletin of the New York Public Library* 77 (1974): 418–35.

Solomonescu, Yasmin, *John Thelwall and the Materialism Imagination* (Houndmills: Palgrave Macmillan, 2014).

Somers, Margaret R., "Citizenship and the Place of the Public Sphere: Law, Community, and Political Culture in Transition to Democracy," *American Sociology Review* 58 (1993): 587–620.

—— "Rights, Rationality, and Membership: Rethinking the Making and Meaning of Citizenship," *Law and Social Inquiry* 19 (1994): 63–112.

Sonoi, Chine, "Southey's Radicalism and the Abolitionist Movement," *Wordsworth Circle* 41 (2011): 22–26.

Soper, Kate, "Socialist Humanism," in *E. P. Thompson, Critical Perspectives*, ed. Harvey J. Kaye and Keith McClelland (Philadelphia, PA: Temple University Press, 1990), 204–32.

Speck, W. A., *Robert Southey: Entire Man of Letters* (New Haven, CT: Yale University Press, 2006).

Stafford, Barbara Maria, *Body Criticism: Imaging the Unseen in Enlightenment Art and Medicine* (Cambridge: Massachusetts Institute of Technology Press, 1991).

Stallybrass, Peter, and Allon White, *The Politics and Poetics of Transgression* (Ithaca, NY: Cornell University Press, 1986).

Stedman Jones, Gareth, *An End to Poverty? A Historical Debate* (Profile Books, 2004).

Steedman, Carolyn, *An Everyday Life of the English Working Class: Work, Self and Sociability in the Early Nineteenth Century* (Cambridge: Cambridge University Press, 2013).

—— "The Price of Experience: Women and the Making of the English Working Class," *Radical History Review* 59 (1994): 108–19.

——"A Weekend with Elektra," *Literature and History* 6 (1997): 17–42.

Stemmler, Joan, "The Physiognomical Portraits of Johann Caspar Lavater," *Art Bulletin* 75 (1993): 151–68.

Stevens, John, *England's Last Revolution: Pentrich 1817* (Buxton: Moorland Publishing, 1977).

Stevenson, John, "The London 'Crimp' Riots of 1794," *International Review of Social History* 16 (1971): 40–58.

Storey, Mark, *Robert Southey: A Life* (Oxford: Oxford University Press, 1997).

Strange, Julie-Marie, *Death, Grief, and Poverty in Britain, c1870–1914* (Cambridge: Cambridge University Press, 2005).

Summerson, John, *Georgian London* (Harmondsworth: Penguin 1978).

Sutherland, Kathryn, "Hannah More's Counter-Revolutionary Feminism," in *Revolution in Writing: British Literary Responses to the French Revolution*, ed. Kelvin Everest (Milton Keynes: Open University Press, 1991), 27–63.

Tackett, Timothy, *The Coming of the Terror in the French Revolution* (Cambridge, MA: Harvard University Press, 2015).

Taylor, Anthony, "Commemoration, Memorializations and Political Memory in Post-Chartist Radicalism: The 1885 Halifax Chartists Reunion in Context," in *The Chartist Legacy*, ed. Owen Ashton, Robert Fyson, and Stephen Roberts (Woodbridge: Merlin Press, 1999), 255–85.

——— "'Commons-Stealers,' 'Land-Grabbers,' and 'Jerry-Builders': Space, Popular Radicalism and the Politics of Public Access in London, 1848–1880," *International Review of Social History* 11 (1995): 383–407.

——— "Radical Funerals, Burial Customs, and Political Commemoration: The Death and Posthumous Life of Ernest Jones," *Humanities Research* [Australia] 10 (2) (2003): 29–39.

Taylor, Barbara, *Eve and the New Jerusalem: Socialism and Feminism in the Nineteenth Century* (Virago, 1983).

——— *Mary Wollstonecraft and the Feminist Imagination* (Cambridge: Cambridge University Press, 2003).

——— "Religion, Radicalism, and Fantasy," *History Workshop Journal* 39 (1995): 102–12.

Taylor, George, *The French Revolution and the London Stage, 1789–1805* (Cambridge: Cambridge University Press, 2000).

Taylor, Richard, "Thompson and the Peace Movement: From CNC in the 1950s and 1960s to END in the 1980s." in *E. P. Thompson and English Radicalism*, ed. Roger Fieldhouse and Richard Taylor (Manchester: Manchester University Press, 2013), 181–201.

Terdiman, Richard, *Modernity and Memory Crisis* (Ithaca, NY: Cornell University Press, 1993).

Thale, Mary, "London Debating Societies in the 1790s," *Historical Journal* 32 (1989): 57–86.

Thompson, Dorothy, "On the Trail of the New Left," *New Left Review*, no. 215 (January–February 1996): 93–100.

——— *Queen Victoria: Gender and Power* (Virago, 1990).

Thompson, E. P., *Beyond the Frontier: The Politics of a Failed Mission, Bulgaria, 1944* (Stanford, CA: Stanford University Press, 1997).

———*Customs in Common: Studies in Traditional Popular Culture* (Merlin Press, 1991).

——— *The Making of the English Working Class* (Gollancz, 1963).

——— "The Politics of Theory," in *People's History and Socialist Theory*, ed. Raphael Samuel (Routledge, 1981), 396–408.

―――― *The Romantics: England in a Revolutionary Age*, ed. Dorothy Thompson (Woodbridge: Merlin Press, 1997).

―――― *Whigs and Hunters: The Origin of the Black Act* (New York: Pantheon, 1975).

―――― *William Morris: Romantic to Revolutionary* (Gollancz, 1955).

―――― *William Morris: Romantic to Revolutionary*, rev. ed. (Merlin Press, 1977).

―――― *Witness against the Beast: William Blake and the Moral Law* (Cambridge: Cambridge University Press. 1993).

Thompson, Judith, "From Forum to Repository: A Case Study in Romantic Cultural Geography," *European Romantic Review* 15 (2004): 177–91.

―――― *John Thelwall in the Wordsworth Circle: The Silenced Partner* (New York: Palgrave Macmillan, 2012).

Tinling, Marion, "Thomas Lloyd's Reports of the First Federal Congress," *William and Mary Quarterly* 18 (1961): 519–45.

Tuite, Clara, *Lord Byron and Scandalous Celebrity* (Cambridge: Cambridge University Press, 2014).

Turner, John M., "Burke, Paine, and the Nature of Language," *Yearbook of English Studies* 19 (1989): 36–53.

Turner, Michael J., *Independent Radicalism in Early Victorian Britain* (Westport, CT: Greenwood Publishers, 2004).

―――― *Radicalism and Reputation: The Career of Bronterre O'Brien* (East Lansing: Michigan State University Press, 2017).

Turner, Victor, "Liminality and the Performative Genres," in *Rite, Drama, Festival, and Spectacle: Rehearsals toward a Theory of Cultural Performance*, ed. John J. MacAloon (Philadelphia, PA: Institute for the Study of Human Issues, 1984), 19–41.

Twomey, Richard J., "Jacobins and Jeffersonians: Anglo-American Radical Ideology, 1790–1810," in *The Origins of Anglo-American Radicalism*, ed. Margaret Jacob and James Jacob (Allen & Unwin, 1984), 284–99.

Tyrell, Alex, with Michael T. Davis, "Bearding the Tories: The Commemoration of the Scottish Political Martyrs of 1793–94," in *Contested Sites: Commemoration, Memorial, and Popular Politics in Nineteenth-Century Britain,* ed. Paul A. Pickering and Alex Tyrell (Aldershot: Ashgate, 2004), 25–56.

Tyson, Gerald P., *Joseph Johnson, A Liberal Publisher* (Iowa City: University of Iowa Press, 1979).

Veldman, Meredith, *Fantasy, the Bomb, and the Greening of Britain: Romantic Protest, 1945–1980* (Cambridge: Cambridge University Press, 1994).

Verhoeven, Wil, *Americomania and the French Revolution Debate in Britain, 1789–1802* (Cambridge: Cambridge University Press, 2013).

Vickery, Amanda, *The Gentleman's Daughter: Women's Lives in Georgian England* (New Haven, CT: Yale University Press, 1998).

Vincent, Emma, "John Bowles and the Ideological War against Revolutionary France," *History* 78 (1993): 393–420.

Wahrman, Dror, *The Making of the Modern Self: Identity and Culture in Eighteenth-Century England* (New Haven, CT: Yale University Press, 2004).

―――― *"Percy*'s Prologue: From Gender Play to Gender Panic in Eighteenth-Century England," *Past and Present* 159 (1998): 113–60.

———— "Public Opinion, Violence and the Limits of Constitutional Politics," in *Re-reading the Constitution: New Narratives in the Political History of England's Long Nineteenth Century*, ed. James Vernon (Cambridge: Cambridge University Press, 1996), 83–122.

Wallace, Miriam L., "Discovering the Political Traveler in Wollstonecraft's *Letters* (1796) and Holcroft's *Travels* (1804)," *Journeys* 12 (2011): 1–21.

———— "Holcroft's Translations of the 1780s and Isabelle de Montolieu's *Caroline de Lichtfield*," in *Re-viewing Thomas Holcroft, 1745–1809*, ed. Miriam L. Wallace and A. A. Markley (Aldershot: Ashgate, 2012), 51–68.

———— *Revolutionary Subjects in the English "Jacobin" Novel, 1790–1805* (Lewisburg, PA: Bucknell University Press, 2009).

Ward-Jackson, Philip, *Public Sculpture of the City of London* (Liverpool: Liverpool University Press, 2003).

Weinstein, Benjamin, "Popular Constitutionalism and the London Corresponding Society," *Albion* 34 (2002): 35–57.

Wells, Roger, "English Society and Revolutionary Politics in the 1790s: The Case for Insurrection," in *The French Revolution and British Popular Politics*, ed. Mark Philp (Cambridge: CUP, 1991), 188–226.

———— *Insurrection: The British Experience, 1795–1803* (Gloucester: Alan Sutton, 1983).

———— *Wretched Faces: Famine in Wartime England, 1793–1801* (Gloucester: Alan Sutton, 1988).

Welsh, Alexander, *Strong Representations: Narrative and Circumstantial Evidence in England* (Baltimore, MD: Johns Hopkins University Press, 1992).

Whalley, George, "The Bristol Library Borrowings of Southey and Coleridge, 1793–8," *The Library* 4 (1949): 114–31.

Wharman, Alan, *The Treason Trials, 1794* (Leicester: Leicester University Press, 1992).

Whatmore, Richard, "'A Gigantic Manliness': Paine's Republicanism in the 1790s," in *Economy, Polity, and Society: British Intellectual History 1750–1950*, ed. Stefan Collini, Richard Whatmore, and Brian Young (Cambridge: CUP, 2000), 135–57.

Wheatley, Kim, *Romantic Feuds: Transcending the "Age of Personality"* (Farnham: Ashgate, 2013).

Whelan, Timothy, "Politics, Religion, and Romance: Letters of Eliza Gould Flower, 1794–1802," *Wordsworth Circle* 36 (2005): 85–109.

Whitaker, Anne-Maree, "Swords to Ploughshares? The 1798 Irish Rebels in New South Wales," *Labour History* [Australia] 75 (1998): 9–21.

White, R. J., *Waterloo to Peterloo* (Harmondsworth: Penguin, 1968).

Wickwar, William, *The Struggle for the Freedom of the Press, 1819–1832* (Allen and Unwin, 1928).

Williams, Gwyn A., *Artisans and Sans-Culottes: Popular Movements in France and Britain during the French Revolution* (Edward Arnold, 1968).

———— *Madoc: The Making of a Myth* (Eyre Methuen, 1979).

Williams, Raymond, "Notes on Marxism in Britain since 1945,"*New Left Review*, no. 100 (November–December, 1976): 81–94.

Wilson, Kathleen, "Inventing Revolution: 1688 and Eighteenth-Century Popular Politics," *Journal of British Studies* 28 (1989): 349–86.

────── *The Island Race: Englishness, Empire, and Gender in the Eighteenth Century* (Routledge, 2003).

────── "Pacific Modernity: Theater, Englishness, and the Arts of Discovery," in *The Age of Cultural Revolutions*, ed. Colin Jones and Dror Wahrman (Berkeley: University of California Press, 2002), 62–93.

────── *Sense of the People: Politics, Culture and Imperialism in England, 1715–1785* (Cambridge: Cambridge University Press, 1995).

Winch, Donald, *Riches and Poverty: An Intellectual History of Political Economy in Britain, 1750–1834* (Cambridge: Cambridge University Press, 1996).

Woloch, Isser, *Jacobin Legacy: The Democratic Movement under the Directory* (Princeton, NJ: Princeton University Press, 1970).

Wood, Marcus, *Blind Memory: Visual Representations of Slavery in England, 1780–1865* (Routledge, 2000).

────── *Radical Satire and Print Culture, 1790–1822* (Oxford: Oxford University Press, 1994).

────── *Slavery, Empathy and Pornography* (Oxford: Oxford University Press, 2002).

────── "Thomas Spence and Modes of Subversion," *Enlightenment and Dissent* 10 (1991): 51 77.

Woodring, Carl, *Politics in the Poetry of Coleridge* (Madison: Wisconsin University Press, 1961).

Worrall, David, "Agrarians against the Picturesque: Ultra-Radicalism and the Revolutionary Politics of the Land," in *The Politics of the Picturesque: Literature, Landscape, and Aesthetics since 1770*, ed. Stephen Copley and Peter Garside (Cambridge: Cambridge University Press, 1994), 240–60.

────── *The Politics of Romantic Theatricality, 1787–1832* (Houndmills: Palgrave Macmillan, 2007).

────── *Radical Culture: Discourse, Resistance and Surveillance, 1798–1820* (Detroit, MI: Wayne State University Press, 1992).

Wrigley, Richard, *The Politics of Appearances: Representations of Dress in the French Revolution* (Oxford: Berg, 2002).

Online Resources

Ancestry, www.ancestry.com.

Newman, Ian, *London Corresponding Society Meeting Places: Exploring the 1790s Alehouse,* http://www.1790salehouse.com/.

Diary of William Godwin, Abinger-Shelley Papers, Bodleian Library, Oxford, http://godwindiary.bodleian.ox.ac.uk.

Hitchcock, Tim, Sharon Howard, and Robert Shoemaker, *London Lives, 1690–1800: Crime, Poverty and Social Policy in the Metropolis*, www.londonlives.org.

Scottish Language Dictionaries, *Dictionary of the Scots Language/Dictionar o the Scots Leid,* https://dsl.ac.uk/.

Index

Note: page numbers in *italics* indicate figures.

Ingram Content Group UK Ltd.
Milton Keynes UK
UKHW022111040523
421267UK00006B/41